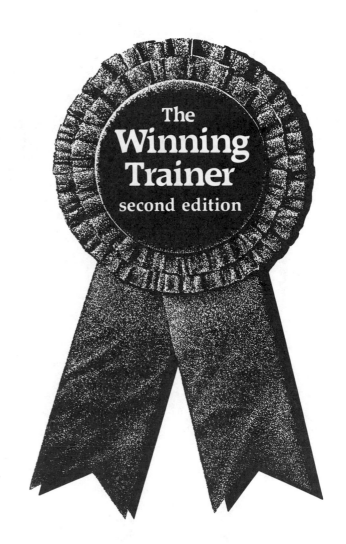

The
Winning
Trainer
second edition

Julius E. Eitington

The Winning Trainer
Second Edition

10 9 8 7 6 5

The work sheets on pages 367–489 may be freely copied and used provided proper credit is given. Please contact Gulf Publishing Company for details.

Library of Congress Cataloging-in-Publication Data

Eitington, Julius E.
  The winning trainer.

  (Building blocks of human potential)
  Includes bibliographies and index.
  1. Employees, Training of. 2. Problem solving—Study and teaching. 3. Organizational behavior.
I. Title. II. Series.
HF5549.5.T7E38   1989   658.3′124   88-21434

ISBN 0-87201-911-X

CONTENTS

Whatever you can do, or dream you can, begin it. Boldness has genius, power, and magic in it.

—Johann Wolfgang von Goethe (1749–1832), German poet and dramatist

Preface to the Second Edition viii
Introduction ix
Acknowledgments xiii

1

How to Start Things Off 1

Planning the Use of Icebreakers and Openers. Working with Icebreakers. Examples of Icebreakers. Evaluating Icebreakers. Working with Openers. Icebreakers and Openers: Classifications and Cautions. Key Points. Reference.

2

Using Small Groups Effectively 13

Small Group Composition. Seating. Assigning Tasks. Viewing-Listening Teams. The T-Column. Risk Analysis. The Spokesperson and the Recorder. Using Observers. Monitoring. Questions and Answers. Leadership in the Small Group. Coping with Problem Participants. Key Points. References. Recommended Reading.

3

Basic Techniques for Small Group Training 26

Using Dyads and Triads. Producing Definitions. Developing and Working with Lists. Sharing Personal Incidents. Prediction. Group Debates. Trial for Error (Mock Trial). Circular Whip. Learning from Field Trips. Mastering Reference Material. Saying Goodbye. Key Points. References. Recommended Reading.

4

Additional Techniques for Small Group Training 39

The Fishbowl. Working with "Mind Pictures"—Fantasy, Guided Imagery, Etc. Working with Pictures. Using Art. Using Music. The Journal or Diary. Working with Models. Key Points. References. Recommended Reading.

5

Role Playing 67

Purposes and Benefits. Role Playing Designs. Processing Role Play Data. Video Playback and Feedback. How to Write a Role Play. Special Techniques. Evaluating Results. Role Playing: Some Questions and Answers. Behavior Modeling. Key Points. References. Recommended Reading.

6

Using Games and Simulations 94

Working with Games. Why Use Games? When to Use Games. Administering the Game. Designing Your Own Games. Converting an Exercise into a Game. Working with Simulations. Advantages of Using Simulations. Implementing the Simulation. Designing a Simulation. Key Points. References. Recommended Reading.

7

Using Exercises 107

Sources of Exercise. Exercises That You Can Construct Yourself. Planning the Conduct of an Exercise. Key Points. Books Containing Exercises. Reference.

8

Using Puzzles 121

An Assortment of Puzzles. Puzzles for Fun. Experiential Learning. Objectives. Forms. Designing Experiential Learning. Skill Pointers on Processing. Key Points. References. Recommended Reading.

9

Instrumentation—A Tool for Self-Discovery Learning 139

Instrument Formats. When to Use Instruments. How to Use Instruments. Instruments You Can Make. Guidelines for Constructing Instruments. Scoring of Instruments. The Participant-Prepared Instrument. A Summary. Key Points. References. Recommended Reading.

10

Defining a Problem and Generating Data About It 151

Problem Solving—Suggested Content. Launching Problem-Solving Training. How to Define the Problem. Problem Identification—ABC Approach. How to Generate Data About the Problem. Force Field Analysis—A Tool for Problem Diagnosis. Key Points. References. Recommended Reading.

11

Generating Solutions to a Problem 165

Brainstorming. The Slip Method. Nominal Group Technique. The Delphi Technique. Ideawriting. Card Posting Techniques. The Client-Centered Approach to Problem Solving. Upside-Down Problem Solving. Devices to Unleash Idea Development. Using Analogy. The Gordon Technique. Key Points. References.

12

Selecting and Implementing a Solution 182

How to Choose Among Alternatives. How to Plan and Implement the Solution. Additional Approaches to Problem Solving. Rotational Problem Solving (PSR). Past/Present/Future Approach. Using the Journalist's Six Questions. Problem Solving for Quality Control. Quality Circles. Study Groups. Knowledge Circles. How to Maximize Idea Power at Meetings. Personal Needs Analysis. Some Problem-Solving Principles. Some Do's and Don't's. Key Points. References. Recommended Reading.

13

Team Building 197

Preliminary Work. Starting the First Session. Core Activities in the Team Building Session. Tools for Team Building. Instrumentation. Evaluation of the Team Building Effort. Giving Feedback. Key Points. References. Recommended Reading.

14

The In-Basket Exercise—How to Conduct and Design It Working with the In-Basket 211

The In-Basket Exercise—Advantages and Limitations. How to Design Your Own In-Basket. A Sample In-Basket. Comments on the In-Basket Problems. Group Processing of Completed Work. Summarizing the Experience. Summary. Key Points. Recommended Reading.

15

Other Key Group-in-Action Tools ... 234

Pre-work. Seating to Facilitate Participation. Movement. Flipcharting. Humor and Fun. Props for Empathy. Using Handouts. Using Silence. Key Points. References. Recommended Reading.

16

Involving Participants in Film/Video 258

Film Versus Video. Uses of Films. Previewing. Introducing a Film. Post-Film Activities. Pre-Film Activities. Stop-Film Technique. Other Aids and Approaches. Planning for Multiple Film Use. Participant Reactions to Film Content. Useful Scenes from Popular Movies. Key Points. References.

17

Maximizing Participation and Learning in the Case Method 271

Advantages and Disadvantages. The Case Study—A Potpourri of Formats. Program Design for Effective Transfer. Monologue. How to Develop Case Material. Learning from Cases. Techniques to Maximize Learning from Cases. Key Points. References. Recommended Reading.

18

"If You Must Lecture . . ." 297

The Lecture—A Problem-Laden Technique. When to Use the Lecture. Giving the Lecture Polish. Securing Participation at the Outset. Mid-Talk Interventions. Using the Questions-and-Answer Period Effectively. Asking Questions of Participants. Involving Individuals. Key Points. References. Recommended Reading.

19

Using Participative Methods to Evaluate Training 311

Participant Reaction Level. Learning (Changed Behavior) in the Classroom. Change in On-the-Job Behavior. Measurable Impact of Training on the Organization. Daily Pulse-Taking. The Participant Group—A Self Appraisal. Key Points. References. Recommended Reading.

20

How to Overcome the Transfer Problem 320

Making Classroom Application Activities Effective. Formats of Application Activities. Interim (Post-Session) Action Plans. Contracting at Program's End. Ensuring Skill Retention in Management Training. Additional Ways to Aid the Training Transfer. Conducting the Follow-Up Session. Key Points. References. Recommended Reading.

21

Ancillary Issues and Techniques 334

A Participative Approach to Problem Design. Determining Needs via Participative Methods. Selecting Training Methods. Climate. Augmenting Trainer Competency. How to Become a Participative Trainer. Cotraining: Some ABC's. Broadening the Trainer Base for Management Training. Vertical Training. Terminology for the Training Effort. Key Points. References. Recommended Reading.

Glossary 358

Appendices 366

Index 491

PREFACE TO THE SECOND EDITION

The first edition of this book was widely received by both new and experienced trainers in diverse organizational settings. The book proved to be a helpful source of ideas to involve the learner actively, and it prompted the trainers to suggest to me many additional participative training methods.

This second edition incorporates many of those suggestions as well as material gleaned from training and management literature, workshops and conferences, and my own experience. More specifically, the book has been expanded and enriched by the addition of a chapter on the in-basket technique; new sections on the use of music, humor and fun, small group reporting techniques, the knowledge circle, and study groups; and the expansion of practically every chapter in a variety of ways.

I am excited about this new edition and I hope it will excite you. I welcome your feedback about your experiences using the book as well as any new participative training ideas and techniques.

Julius E. Eitington

INTRODUCTION

Learning is not a spectator sport.

—Anonymous
(The author wishes
he had said it.)

Winning trainers are not only "on the ball," they get it rolling. Winning trainers get results in the form of measurable learning achievements among the individuals and groups with whom they work—greater retention, better on-the-job application, and increased learner interest. They also have this in common: They have mastered the use, and they k͟ ͟ow the importance, of *participative training methods.*

The reasons trainers* should be concerned with participative training methods are compelling:

☐ *Our understanding of the adult as a learner.* Authorities like Malcolm Knowles, Gordon Lippitt, Leonard Nadler, and many others have been telling us for years that the adult learner wants to be involved, wants to participate, wants to be treated with respect and dignity, wants to be challenged. Conversely, he or she does not want merely to sit and listen, to take notes, to struggle with exams, to be talked down to, to be bored, or to be bombarded with theory without opportunities for practical application.

☐ *Trends in society at large.* There is a significant and unwavering trend in society of people making demands for "a piece of the action." This is true of minorities, women, students, voters, consumers, parents, taxpayers, and other identifiable groups. Certainly today's higher educational levels and a stronger sense of independence among employees are triggering these demands.

Underpinning these requirements for participation, too, is an evolving humanistic philosophy, worldwide, which sees human beings as uniquely capable of personal and collective growth, self-determination, and transformation.

☐ *Trends in organizations.* Organizations of all sorts—business, industry, government, the military, volunteer organizations—have been moving gradually toward various forms of participative management. Indications of this trend include the Scanlon Plan, human relations training, management-by-objectives systems, job enrichment plans, suggestion plans, organization development programs, quality-of-worklife programs, quality circles, and the like. What these activities reflect is a recognition that employees have needs and values that relate to self-control, self-determination, self-development, meaningful work, and the like.

☐ *Training trends.* Although the use of participative methods in training was becoming noticeable in World

---

* *Trainer is used throughout the book to cover instructors, facilitators, teachers, conference leaders, etc., in all kinds of training/class/discussion room settings where participative methods are employed.*

War II and certainly existed before that time to some degree, this kind of training emphasis really reached a high point with the birth of the T-group (sensitivity training) in 1947. The T-group, of course, is dedicated *totally* to learner participation. In addition to laboratory education, many new participative training techniques were being invented in the 1940s and 1950s and thereafter, including brainstorming and other forms of group problem-solving and group decision-making techniques. Also, a whole host of training programs that involved participants to very high degrees via group-in-action methods, including The Managerial Grid®, creative thinking, transactional analysis, assertiveness training, stress management, conflict resolution, and the human potential movement, were being developed.

☐ *Brain research.* Recent research about the right and left brain has revealed that people are not only logical and rational (left-brain thinking) but also have the capacity to be spontaneous and creative (right-brain thinking). Certainly, participation provides one with the opportunity to use the right hemisphere of the brain to a significant degree.

Why This Book?

This is a book about how to make things happen in your training activity; how to make training come alive for your participants; how to involve your learners fully and actively in the *learning* process. So while the book presents many dynamic and involving methods and techniques for the trainer to use, its purpose is to help learners learn with greater depth and retention and with less pain and more fun.

Methods are what make the training activity hum (as opposed to evoking a response of "ho hum"). Methods are akin to the engine in the Mercedes, the sparkle in the champagne, the pitching in a baseball game, and the characters in a novel. But this book is not merely about participative training methods. Although it does catalog and describe many of them, it goes much farther. That is to say, it endeavors to be practical in these ways:

1. It presents numerous thought-stimulating examples of what the trainer might do in using participative training methods.
2. It shows how to *use*—and use effectively—the techniques presented, be they in-baskets, role plays, case studies, games, brainstorming, or whatever.
3. It shows how to *design* or construct various training activities such as instruments, games, role plays, diaries, and application-type exercises.

This book is a veritable "how to" in the realm of participative training methods. Books on training typically do not provide this type of aid to the trainer, since they cover the total spectrum of the training function. Methods and techniques thus tend to receive relatively short shrift, being sandwiched in with many other training topics.

A second way to use this book is to treat it as a reference work or source book. Thus, when designing a training program, the trainer might refer to it to be certain that a good range of participative methods is being employed. As trainers, we tend to develop fairly constant approaches to training design. Hence our methodologies may reflect the "tried and true" more than the exciting and the new. A certain amount of "risk-taking" obviously is entailed in this approach. But if we've never used a fishbowl, fantasy, metaphor, or whatever, these methods may merit a try. For how else can we broaden our repertoire and thus enliven our training offerings?

Those who are conducting "train the trainer" courses for instructors, discussion leaders, teachers, facilitators, trainers, curriculum designers, and others will certainly find this work useful in acquainting them with the wide variety of participative techniques available.

Our emphasis is on participative, involving, dynamic methods. That is to say, we approach methods primarily from the standpoint of experiential, interactive, discovery, or action learning. This is not to say that classroom methods of a one-way communication sort—lectures, films, slide talks, panel presentations—do not have value. In fact, imaginative ways to use lectures and films so that participation is enhanced and learning is more likely to take place are suggested in the book. But the bias of the book is that a tremendous amount of worthwhile learning can take place without reliance on traditional, one-way communication approaches. Thus, no attempt is made to provide instruction on how to give better talks or how to use the overhead projector properly, so that one becomes a better platform person. Also, since the book is group-in-action oriented, it does not concern itself with self-instruction methods such as programmed learning, interactive video (tape or disc), or computer-assisted instruction (CAI). These methods obviously have their place when very practical skill development and/or knowledge acquisition is desired.

Methods and the Training Cycle

The classic four-step model of the training cycle can help put the book into proper perspective. I have used four "D's" for mnemonic purposes, but the ideas are "standard."

Diagnose or determine need. Here we are looking for difficulties (problems), deficiencies, new developments, that point up that a training effort is in order.

Design or develop the program. Based on the identified needs, we plan and design a course or program to meet that need.

Deliver or present the training in the most effective way possible. Training methods are the most important aspect of this part of the cycle.

Discern differences or measure results of the training. Our question is this: Has the training made a difference in

☐ Knowledge
☐ Skill (behavior, performance)
☐ Attitude

Performance may relate to individual, group, intergroup, or organizational accomplishment. The term most commonly used to describe this step is "evaluation."

The book primarily covers methods that relate to the delivery of the training. However, the other three steps—diagnose, design and discern differences (evaluation)—also have been treated, but in much lesser detail, to point up that participative techniques also can and should be used in these steps.

We should also make it clear that the book deals solely with methods used in the formal training situation (classroom). Obviously, certain training needs may be met more properly with *informal* methods such as on-the-job training, performance aids, self-development (e.g., membership in a toastmaster's club), etc. This book does not treat the area of informal training methods.

How to Use This Book

The book's organization reflects my group-in-action bias—thus the more participative, experiential methods appear in the chapters at the beginning of the book, and the less involving methods (case study, film, and lecture) appear at the end. The final chapter is concerned with various participative training issues rather than techniques or methods per se.

The obvious way to profit from this book is to read it through carefully to learn of the great potential for the application of participative training methods. However, if you are already familiar with brainstorming, small group work, icebreakers or whatever, there is no reason why you should not skim those particular pages and move ahead to less familiar material.

THE TRAINING CYCLE

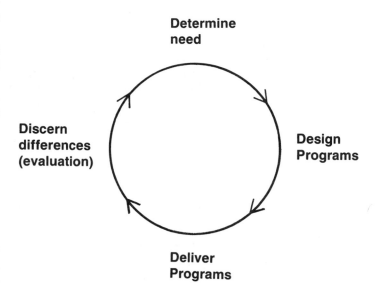

Determine need

Design Programs

Deliver Programs

Discern differences (evaluation)

Sources

The idea for this book came from my experiences as a training director in government (The National Park Service, Washington, D.C.) and private industry (BNA Communications, Inc., Rockville, Md.); as the conductor of workshops on management development for the graduate school of the U.S. Department of Agriculture; as a T-group trainer working closely with highly skilled trainers from the National Training Laboratories Institute of the Behavioral Sciences, Arlington, Va.; and as a conductor of a course on public administration for The George Washington University and a special management course for Indonesian students sponsored by Indiana University. In addition my wife, Norma Jo Eitington, a teacher, educator, and counselor with teaching and training experience at elementary, high school, college, and graduate school levels, was a major influence in this book.

The material for this volume came from various sources: conferences, workshops, meetings of professional societies, periodicals, books, colleagues, and personal experience. To the extent that it has been practicable, credit has been given to the source of particular techniques, methods, and concepts. Obviously, some material has crept into my repertoire over the years for which credit to the originator cannot be given. This I regret and can only hope that the creator of a particular technique or concept will feel pleased that his or her idea is being shared further with other training practitioners.

And Finally . . .

My goal or hope for this book is best expressed by the following Zen parable:

It seems that two Zen monks were having a heated discussion, which produced these statements:

"No, it is the *flag* that is moving."

"No, it is the *wind* that is moving."

A third monk came on to the scene and, hearing the debate, intervened with these statements:

"Brothers, listen to me. *No,* it is not the banner that is moving. *No,* it is not the wind that is moving. Yes, it is your *minds* that are moving."

So my hope for this book is that you will not merely page through the scores of techniques that are presented. Rather, that the ideas that are treated will stimulate your mind to think constantly in terms of techniques and methods. You will thereby be alerted to look for other ones and create many new ones yourself!

ACKNOWLEDGMENTS

Authors typically receive the kudos for the final version of a book. But others, behind the scenes, quietly transform a raw manuscript into the finished product. The author thus wishes to acknowledge the assistance of the following individuals who aided immeasurably in getting the manuscript into its finished form:

Dr. Leonard Nadler, Professor Emeritus, Human Resource Development and Adult Education, George Washington University, who patiently reviewed and critiqued the entire manuscript from a professional standpoint. His constant review made for a significantly better final product.

William J. Lowe, editor-in-chief, Gulf Publishing Company, Book Division, who provided invaluable advice on overall format, style, and organization.

Melissa Lewis Beck, editor, Gulf Publishing Company, Book Division, who accomplished the herculean job of sentence-by-sentence and page-by-page editing, all of which made for a tighter, more readable book.

The
Winning
Trainer

second edition

HOW TO START THINGS OFF

When we give our creative being its proper place in our lives, we have a sense of meaningfulness and purposefulness. The moment we touch upon this wellspring of life a change takes place in our personality. That is the moment of breakthrough.

—Pir Vilayat Inayat Khan, head of the Sufi Order in the West, speaker and author on science, mysticism, and holistic health

Only that day dawns to which we are awake.

—Henry David Thoreau (1817–1862), U.S. naturalist, philosopher and writer

Suppose you could, through some magical gift, have the power to tune in on the thoughts and shared conversations of the participants who are about to enter one of your training programs. Intriguing? Or frightening, perhaps?

Assuming you could tune in on their wavelengths, you might hear thoughts and statements such as these:

"I wonder if I made the right decision in coming here."

"I bet it's the same old stuff."

"It looks like I don't know any one here at all."

"I hope I can pick up all this stuff they'll probably throw at me."

"I wonder what these other people are like."

"If my boss hadn't insisted I come, I sure wouldn't be here. No way."

"I hope the lectures won't be too dull."

"I'm sure they'll tell us they want questions. I wonder if they mean it? How candid can I really be here?"

"Will I look good in this group?"

"Will the trainers be nice or just the usual smart alecs? I certainly hope they don't treat us like we're still in the fourth grade."

If these thoughts are realistic, may we, then, pose the following questions to you: How do you start your training programs? Do you begin conventionally by getting all the announcements out of the way? ("I have been asked to announce that the painters will be moving their equipment into the training room at 3:45 P.M.") Do you button down the usual "administrivia" concerning coffee breaks, starting and quitting time, the location of the rest rooms, the nature of the luncheon menu, etc.? Do you launch things with an account of the history of this program? Do you crisply list (or worse, read) the program objectives? Do you zip into session one in high gear so everyone knows you mean business? Do you introduce people to one another? Do you distinguish between "icebreakers" and "openers?" Do you use more than one icebreaker or opener? If you use one of these or another procedure, what is your training rationale for it? Have you reflected on that at all? Have you discussed it with a colleague or subordinate? Or have you merely acted out of habit?

Both icebreakers and openers are start-up activities that help participants ease into the program. Icebreakers are relatively subject-matter free whereas openers relate directly to the content (subject matter) of the session, course, or program. Thus, if everyone knows one another, icebreakers may not be necessary. But regardless of the participants' prior acquaintances with one another, an opener would seem to be quite desirable in any program.

1

Basically you can start a training program in only one of two ways:

1. By introducing the participant group to the content at the outset.
2. By easing the group into things before involving them directly in the subject matter.

Regardless of which start-up procedure you use, you should recognize that your approach to the opening of the program communicates loud and clear:

☐ Your philosophy of learning
☐ Your style of training
☐ Your attitudes toward the participants as learners
☐ Your anxiety level

In other words, your first communication effort, whether you have reflected on it or are conscious of it, is immediately creating attitudes toward you and your program. Why? Because a basic principle of communication is that all behavior with others is perceived (subject to the perception of others). Behavior does not take place in a vacuum. Rather, it is observed, sifted, weighed, interpreted, and given meaning by those who experience it. The meaning may not be the one we intend, but it registers its impact, nevertheless.

Hence the need to make certain that the opening of your program communicates what you really want it to. I think it is far more important to provide the right communication about ourselves and our program in the first hour, than it is to bombard participants immediately with the course material per se.

A well-thought-out, professional training effort should give full attention to icebreaking and/or opening activities because they:

☐ Warm up (energize) the participants and thus put them at ease; learning proceeds best when the learners are ready to learn.
☐ Set the tone for the program and indicate whether the program will be participative, "sit and listen," or some mixture of these approaches to learning.
☐ Indicate who has responsibility for learning. You want to communicate that the trainer is a facilitator and that only the participant can assume responsibility for what is learned.
☐ Communicate immediately the kind of trainer you are—relaxed or compulsive, friendly or distant, super-sober or fun to be with, subject-matter or participant oriented.
☐ May provide later linkage with a particular topic or session; e.g., an icebreaker that deals with values can serve as a bridge to such topics as motivation, career

planning, management philosophy, leadership style, and the like.

Planning the Use of Icebreakers and Openers

If you are convinced that icebreakers and openers have real merit, you undoubtedly will want to plan them properly. This means you should select ones based on such factors as:

☐ Composition of the group
☐ Expectations of the group
☐ Nature of the program
☐ Length of the program
☐ Culture of the sponsoring organization
☐ Style and personality of the trainer(s)

The nature or composition of the group will obviously influence your choice of start-up activities. For example, if your participants are mental health professionals, they probably will be comfortable with activities that stress movement, fantasy, sharing of personal data, etc. Conversely, if your learners are blue-collar foremen with strong rural roots and limited communication skills, you would be well advised to avoid novel and threatening icebreakers, which almost certainly would have boomerang effects.

Group expectations of their role in the learning process will also influence how active and involving your icebreakers or openers will be.

Program content will determine what icebreakers or openers will be used; for example, in a free-wheeling, experiential management development program in a cultural island setting, novel "warmer uppers" would be quite appropriate. But a sales program, particularly one conducted in corporate headquarters, would probably put a damper on anything that might be perceived as "too far out."

Program length should be considered, too. A program that runs a full week could easily absorb 30–60 minutes of icebreaking and/or opening activity. The three-hour program, in contrast, may only be able to spare five or ten minutes for warm-up time.

The culture of the organization is another factor influencing the choice of icebreakers and openers. Attempts at innovation, fun, and excitement have to be tempered with "what the culture will bear." As one trainer who experienced a "trust walk" (see page 4) for the first time in a workshop I conducted said, "I like this technique, but I'm not sure I could explain it to my boss's satisfaction should he happen to walk into the classroom while the activity was in progress."

The style and personality of the trainer will (and should) influence the choice of ice breakers and openers.

If you are comfortable with start-up activities that involve the group in novel, experiential ways, that may take time from the formal program, and that may reduce your "control" over the group or the subject matter, then you should explore the wide variety of such activities that are available. But if you are concerned about matters of control, getting started, "relevance," and so on, the choice of icebreakers and openers had best be limited to conventional, very brief devices.

The following pages present a range of icebreakers and openers. Regard them as one would food in a cafeteria—select only those items that make sense to you, fit into your overall program, and present no threat to those exposed to your fare.

Working with Icebreakers

Although a training group composed of participants who know one another quite well may not require ice-breaking activities, groups of strangers can certainly profit from them. Trainers, all too typically, merely warm up their groups via various introduction-type procedures. For example: "Let's go around the room and tell our name, job title, organization, and why we're here." This ritual may have some value, but all too often it becomes meaningless because the required responses are inaudible and group members do not listen or are bored by the routine involved. This is particularly true if the introductions are offered by 12–15 or more people.

Another problem is that participants may have needs more significant than merely to learn other participants' names and job titles. Since the odds are that the usual introductions won't do much for the participants, it is essential to use more dynamic, experiential activities (icebreakers) for warm up purposes. The group will benefit since:

☐ They allow participants to become acquainted with one another in a more meaningful way; that is, glimpses into attitudes, values, aspects of personality, concerns, etc., become possible.

☐ A start can be made on overcoming possible feelings of loneliness, and icebreakers certainly help to involve shy people.

☐ They help to relax the group and make people more spontaneous. By engaging in meaningful, often fun-type activities, participants' anxieties and tensions can be reduced.

☐ They set a climate, tone, and pace for the program, particularly if it is to be a participative one.

☐ They help to build momentum for the next phase of the program.

☐ They achieve the "instant involvement" of everyone.

☐ They help to build group identity and group cohesiveness.

☐ They assist in developing trust among participants and with the trainer as well.

☐ They help participants learn about the resources of the group.

☐ They help energize the group. To the extent that participants are permitted to engage early on in activities that are marked by movement, standing up, meaningful sharing, fun, novelty, and the like, they are put into an alert, stimulated, and motivated state.

☐ They help to develop the credibility of the trainer as a facilitator not a "leader" or a lecturer.

☐ They give the trainer a feel for the group—are the members open to new experiences, fun-loving, nondefensive vs. cautious, super-sober, rigid. These data can provide indicators as to how active and "freewheeling" your later exercises and games should be.

☐ Finally, icebreakers can help to reduce the anxieties of the trainer, who is is a human being, too! Since the interaction puts the participants more at ease, in a circular and contagious way it reaches the trainer as well.

Examples of Icebreakers

The following icebreakers are simply understood and easy to administer. They can be used singly, or several may be used depending upon course objectives, the nature of the group, available time, etc. Additional icebreakers are given in Chapter 14 under "Movement."

Interviews for Creative Introductions
When participants are strangers, have them:

1. Meet in pairs
2. Interview one another for five minutes or so.
3. Introduce each other, stating to the group at large: the partner's job, something interesting or different about the person, and the partner's expectations from the course. (A variation of this step is to have each pair join another pair and make introductions in and from the quartets.)

Note: If the total group is large (20–30 persons), there is little point in feeding back the data from the pairs to everyone else since it is time consuming and little will be remembered anyway. In such a case, limiting the introductions internally to the quartets is much more practicable.

My Personal Shield[1]
In a shield segmented into six boxes, have participants respond to the following list:

1. The best time I ever had
2. My greatest accomplishment
3. My most prized possession
4. What I would do if I had one year to live
5. The two descriptive words I would most want on my tombstone
6. The two descriptive words I would least want on my tombstone

Participants then stand and meet in pairs to discuss their shields for about five minutes. The procedure may be repeated with a new partner.

Trust (Blind) Walk.

In pairs, one person whose eyes are closed is led by the other. The leaders are instructed to make the trip as interesting as possible and to ensure no harm befalls the followers.

Note: I usually introduce this icebreaker by relating it to the importance of participation: "We want active participation, questioning of what is said or done, etc., but willingness to participate depends upon trust. So to symbolize the importance of trust, let's hold a trust walk." The trust walk is then explained and the participants are encouraged to participate in this activity, but their participation is totally voluntary.

For specific instructions to participants concerning the administration of the trust walk, see the section "Movement" in Chapter 14.

Values Assessment—Consensus

A good way to achieve "instant interaction" is to provide participants with a list of ten values; for example:

☐ A satisfying family life
☐ Job success
☐ Having fun, excitement, adventure
☐ Satisfying friendships
☐ Personal growth
☐ Being a good neighbor
☐ Financial achievement
☐ Community contribution
☐ Health
☐ Professional achievement

Then give the participants five minutes by themselves to drop three of the values. Participants then meet in small groups for about ten minutes to agree on the seven most significant values.

Note: It may be anticipated that some groups will have difficulty agreeing. This is not of great consequence.

What is important is that the participants have an opportunity to get to know one another on more than a surface basis.

Values Billboard

Give participants a list of values (on flipchart) that are to be prioritized by them. Participants then "mill around," find a partner, and discuss their lists. The list can be written on letter-size paper or, preferably, on newsprint (flipcharts) with felt-tip pens. Typical values include: good citizenship, financial success, a good reputation, professional recognition, new experiences, good friends.

Cardswap

In advance of the opening session, prepare numerous 3″ × 5″ slips or cards (four or five per person) with terse statements relating to a given topic such as communication, leadership, values, personality characteristics, and management philosophy. Advise each participant to pick randomly four cards and then try to exchange their cards with other participants. The idea is to end up with four cards, if possible, that one finds totally acceptable.

Note
1. Inevitably, some participants will have cards they can't trade off.
2. In preparing the cards, try to develop statements that have a range of opinions on a given topic. For example, if the topic you select relates to "personality," you may have statements such as these:

☐ I like everyone I meet.
☐ Integrity is paramount in a friend.
☐ New experiences are what I need most.
☐ I have a high tolerance for ambiguity.
☐ I am too creative to be a team member.
☐ I admire people who have self-discipline.

Know Your Sign

Post signs around the room bearing opposite personality traits, for example, adventuresome vs. cautious; theatrical vs. practical; industrious vs. fun loving. Have participants select a sign with which they can identify and then discuss with others why they chose that particular sign.

Note: If some participants select a sign without anyone else being there, they can elect to join another group with which adequate identification is possible.

Art Mart

Have each participant draw on a flipchart an illustration that describes a current problem he/she is having.

The problem may be job, career, personal (family), or community related. The drawing may be either symbolic or directly representational. Then have participants find partners to get "help" on "improving" the "art work."

Puzzle Fun

Present participants with a puzzle, which they are to solve in small groups of three to five persons. The following is an example of such a puzzle:

A farmer, on his death, left his three sons a herd of 17 cows with instructions that the oldest was to get one-half of them, the middle son one-third and the youngest one-ninth. (Solution: Since 17 is not divisible by those fractions, they decided to seek out a wise old woman on the mountain top. She quickly solved their problem by giving them one of *her* cows. They then made the division of the herd into groups of nine, six and two, respectively. They were very pleased. After the division, she then took her cow back since they no longer needed it!)

Nicknames

Have participants in small groups discuss their nicknames considering: where they were acquired, when they were acquired, when and if they were lost, and one's feelings (like or dislike) about them. If time allows, select new partners to discuss sources for nicknames. Some sources that might be considered include diminutives from regular names (Jimmy, Fran); physical appearance (Shorty, Red); personality (Smiley, Grumpy); last name influence (Mac from McDonald, Rusty—last name Irons); geography (Tex, Klondike); parental influence (Sis, Buster); occupation (Doc, Prof); and self-adopted nicknames.

Note

1. In lieu of sharing feelings about nicknames, participants may discuss their given names. Do you like it? Why or why not? Is it a family tradition? Would you like to trade it for another one? Did your name influence your choice of names for your children?
2. The sharing may take place in a pair rather than in a group.
3. After the sharing of data about nicknames/first names, participants may report back to the total group something they learned about their partner(s).

Hobby Hunt

Provide each participant with a list of 15–20 popular hobbies (e.g., gardening, movies, jogging, crocheting, golf). (See Appendix 1.) Then give participants seven minutes or so to locate other participants who have these hobbies, writing their name and organizational affiliation on the worksheet.

Early Grades

In small groups, ask each participant to think about and report on an experience they recall in grades 1 through 5. Conclude the activity by asking for volunteers to share their experiences with the group at large.

Shoe In

Ask participants to identify themselves with a shoe: "If I were a shoe I would be a _____." Possible answers are: soft shoe (a gentleperson), boot (a tough person), sneaker, gym shoe (for a highly active person), football shoe (or any shoe with cleats or spikes, symbolizing a person who may run rough-shod over others).

Note: This activity should be reserved for an experiential training program where less conventional, more personalized activities are expected.

Preferences

Pass out a worksheet listing categories that participants may have preferences in such as a favorite food, color, movie actor, sport, or world city. (See Appendix 2.) After participants have written a preference for each listing, have them share their preferences with another person or small group. The sharing may be repeated with a new person or small group.

Me: Yesterday, Today, and Tomorrow

Have participants draw a figure with three segments, such as a coat of arms or a geometric design, as in Figure 1-1. Then have them label the segments "Yesterday," "Today," and "Tommorrow" or "Past," "Present," and

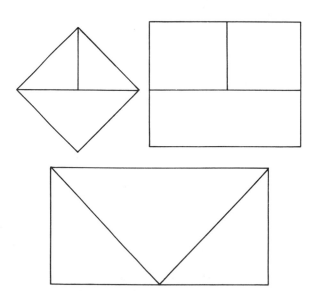

Figure 1-1. Examples of geometric designs participants might draw for use in the icebreaker *Me: Yesterday, Today, and Tomorrow.*

"Future." The participants then enter the appropriate data for each segment and process the data in pairs.

Note: To process data means to share/exchange one's completed work, to comment on or possibly critique one another's work, and to provide support/positive reinforcement to the extent possible about the other's work.

Group Creation

In small groups, participants design a worthwhile icebreaker activity. The total group then selects one approach from all the ideas and uses it as their next activity.

Note: It may be desirable to provide a warm-up activity as a prelude to this exercise to stimulate creativity, particularly for groups not oriented along these lines.

Distraction Banishment

On the assumption that participants often bring various outside concerns to the training situation, this activity may help eliminate the participants' awareness of them. Pass out the worksheet in Appendix 3, which explains to participants what they should do.

Note: Participants generally discard the envelopes when they are returned to them for they have no meaning at program's end.

Name cards

Have participants write their first name or nickname at the top of a name card. Then they should write descriptive terms beginning with each letter of their name as in Figure 1-2.

Note: A dictionary will quite readily trigger ideas if participants are having trouble.

As an icebreaking activity, have participants form pairs or triads to share their data about themselves.

Figure 1-2. An example of a name card used as an icebreaker.

Wallet Waggery

Working in a small group, have each participant take three things from his/her wallet or purse. The others then try to decide what they tell about the person.

Devilish Datum

Each person tells the others three or four things about himself/herself, one of which is not true. The others try to guess which item is the phony one.

Note: Other icebreakers appear under "Movement" (pages 241–242).

Evaluating Icebreakers

The checklist shown in Figure 1-3 may be helpful in evaluating the suitability of an icebreaker. You may want to add other elements that you find important to the checklist.

Element	Low	Moderate	High
1. Time consumption			
2. Threat potential			
3. Possible group dissatisfaction (boomerang effect)			
4. Novelty			
5. Fun, excitement			
6. Creative quality			
7. Data Producing (learn about people)			
8. Relaxes people			

Figure 1-3. A checklist for evaluating icebreakers.

Working with Openers

Openers are tools to help participants ease into the subject matter of the course. They are intended to set the stage, to avoid abrupt starts, and generally to make participants comfortable with the formal program that they are about to experience. Unlike icebreakers, they are essentially subject-matter related, work-oriented "preludes."

Openers may also provide the participants with the opportunity to express their reasons for coming and their goals and expectations about learning from the course or program.[2] If some of those objectives are quite different from yours and you procede, unaware of that circumstance, you may encounter considerable difficulty—boredom, limited cooperation, argumentation, and possibly post-session complaints from the participants' bosses. Conversely, if you learn of this variance in goals/expectations early on, you can do one of several things:

1. State candidly (and regretfully) that a particular goal is outside the purview of this course.

2. Advise the participant that his/her special interest is covered in another (later) course.
3. Adjust the program to the extent possible.
4. If someone is really in the "wrong ball park," ask if he/she wishes to leave. Why waste their time and have a disgruntled participant on your hands?

Note: At times your quest for participant expectations may unearth this added bit of useful datum: One or more participants may have been sent by their bosses and don't have any real interest in what you and the course are offering. If so, you may wish to make this type of statement to them: "I'm sorry that you were sent and you don't really want to be here. But perhaps we can make a contract that will be beneficial to all of us here. If you will try to be as patient and cooperative as you can, I will do my utmost to make this as worthwhile a training experience for you as I possibly can."

Some examples of activities that can set the stage in a substantive sense and give you ideas for creating your own openers follow:

Goal Analysis

Participants form small groups and tell the trainer their goals for the course. These goals are posted on a flipchart and the trainer categorizes them as "R" (Realistic) or "U" (Unrealistic or Unattainable). After adding the trainer's own goals, all the posted goals are discussed. This is a means of involving participants as well as trainers in planning the course and opening the communication process.

Individual Goals

In small groups, the participants declare their goals for the course or program and enter them on a flipchart. The individual goals are discussed in the small group for five to ten minutes; then the flipchart is posted on the wall. The trainer comments supportively on all goals as to relevancy, practicality, etc. The flipcharts can and should be referred to at various stages in the program.

A variation of this procedure is to have pairs discuss their goals for two minutes; the pairs merge with another pair to form quartets and buzz for four minutes; the quartets merge with another quartet (now octets) and buzz for eight minutes. The octets record their goals on flipcharts, the flipcharts are posted on the wall, and a recorder from each octet explains its goals. The trainer points out the similarities and divergencies of the stated goals.

Another variation of the goal-setting opener is to have each goal identified with its owner, e.g., in a power negotiation session we may get a T-column on a flipchart such as this:

Participant Learning Goals

Participant	My Learning Goal
Jo	Negotiate cutbacks
May	Get a raise
Hank	To learn the skill for everyday life
Edna	Get what I want from the boss
Frank	Do better in negotiations with a client
Bill	Selling change

Fears and Fantasies (Hopes and Fears)

Gather from the total group their fears of and hopes for the course and write them on the flipchart, using a T-column.

Note: This activity is particularly helpful if you sense that the participants have some concerns about the course or program.

Commitment Continuum

If you sense that several participants in your program are there reluctantly or have negative attitudes for other reasons (the boss sent them), a good way to deal directly and constructively with this circumstance is to use a ten-point continuum. Draw a horizontal line on the flipchart and number a scale on it from one to ten. Label one end "Dull, Terrible, Threatening" and label the other end "Great, Exciting." Then ask the group such questions as: Why are you here? Are you here voluntarily? Were you sent by your boss?

You can gather data for the continuum in one of two ways:

1. With your back to the participants (for anonymity) have them call out a number on the scale, which you then mark with a check.
2. Have participants enter their numbers on slips of paper, which another participant can collect and post on the scale.

If the data indicate a certain amount of disinterest, anxiety, etc., make this point: "Those of you who have doubts about or disinterest in the program because you were sent here or for other reasons, may I suggest you approach the session with this attitude: 'O.K., I'm not excited about being here; but now that I am here, what can I do to make it pay off? It just may be that by entering wholeheartedly into things I may find the course worthwhile.' I'll do what I can, as trainer, to help. But I only can be responsible for the general conduct of the program, not for your expectations or blocks. Incidentally, I'm more concerned about those 9's and 10's [assuming there are a few] than the 1's and 2's because the program may not come up to those high expectations."

Inspiring the Uninspired

If your participants are highly timid and reluctant to open up, you can change the situation pretty quickly by having *each* participant answer four pointed questions. The queries, used by trainers/consultants Lawrence Myers and Yvonne Grewe of Team Associates, Inc., Tulsa, Oklahoma, are:[3]

1. How would you estimate the degree to which your fellow participants want to be here?
2. To what degree will they be willing to be candid about their concerns and feelings in this workshop?
3. How would you describe their willingness to adopt and be committed to the proposed changes?
4. To what degree are you confident that real change will result from our sessions?

The trainers then draw up a profile of the responses and try to deal with them. They feel very strongly that it is very important to work on resistance points and barriers to change at the very outset of the workshop.

Ventilating Feelings

Again, if you sense that participants may resent attendance or be reluctant to attend, you may ask them to do the following:

"In teams of two, talk for five minutes about one, how you feel about attending this course: enthusiastic? confused? anxious? punished? resentful? neutral?, and two, why you feel this way?" (The pairs generate their data as requested.)

"Now, please introduce your fellow team member, using the data he or she provided to you."

As a final step, you should summarize the attitudes expressed and indicate how they relate to the program. For example, a feeling that "there's little to learn about supervision after twenty-two years doing of it," may be countered with: "That's certainly a lot of experience. Perhaps you can help the rest of us profit from that rich experience. I'm sure, too, that in those twenty-two years you've learned that sometimes a new idea does come along the pike unexpectedly and maybe—just maybe—there may be one here for you. So why not give it a whirl? O.K.?"

Pre-work

Assign a pertinent reading in advance of the first session. Have participants meet in groups of 4 or 5 for 15 minutes to discuss the reading. Each group then selects a spokesperson who reports back to the total group the reactions to the reading.

Hopes and Change

To elicit feelings about hopes for the program and attitudes toward personal change have participants complete a form such as the ones in Appendices 4, 5, and 6. The completed form may be shared in a dyad (pair) or simply retained in the participant's notebook for a second completion and review on an individual basis at the end of the program.

Fishbowls

Using the group-on-group observation technique (see page 32), have the group in the inner circle work on this task for 10–15 minutes: What do we hope to get out of this course (program, conference, session)? Then reverse the groups, the outer group responding to the same question and commenting on the comments of the first group. (Limit groups to six or eight participants. Two or three fishbowls can meet simultaneously, preferably in separate rooms.)

Geometrics

The following two exercises allow participants to express themselves graphically:

1. Have participants complete the worksheet in Appendix 7 in illustrative or graphic form. Then have them share the worksheet with a partner.

2. Have participants draw a box with four quadrants and have them enter data about their job concerns and career aspirations as indicated. (See Appendix 8.) The graphic data should then be processed in small groups with everyone having a chance to play both the presenter and the helper role.

The rationale for the geometric framework is that:

☐ It aids in focusing upon specific areas which should be subject to introspection. Some people have difficulty entering into or concentrating on a given task.
☐ It is a *finite* request, which gives it an aura of reasonableness and manageability. (Contrast this procedure to a totally open end set of questions about one's career.)
☐ By juxtaposing the several queries in adjacent quadrants, their relatedness is highlighted.
☐ The novelty of the structured approach heightens interest in the task.
☐ For many participants, the desire to fill or complete all the boxes is a motivational force.

Tinker Toys

Using Tinker Toys (or other construction toys or materials), have participants (in small groups) construct something which symbolizes leadership, communication, organization, time management, expectations for this program, etc. (For example, to symbolize good or effective communication, a group might decide to construct a bridge.)

Quiz

Start things off with a pertinent, thought-provoking quiz on leadership, communication, safety, selling style, customer service attitudes, etc.

Think Sheets

An effective and provocative way to kick things off is to provide participants with a think sheet, which can later be discussed in small groups. (See Appendix 9 for an example of such a sheet.)

Dyadic Analysis

This is an opener to check listening skills prior to the start of the session which treats that subject. Procedures:[4]

1. Assign participants to dyads. Provide everyone with two profound questions:
   a. The U.S. Government is preparing a time capsule for the nation's 300th birthday (2076). Which three of your personal possessions will you give them to include in it?
   b. As a child you probably had many toys. Which one is so vivid in your mind that you can describe it today?
2. Ask dyads to discuss and share the two questions (10 minutes).
3. Ask participants to examine and report to the total group who spoke first, how time was allotted, what was done when one was not speaking, and any noticeable non-verbal interaction.

Problem Census

Encourage the group to think about their problems as salespersons or managers or whatever by conducting a problem census. The worksheet found in Appendix 10 instructs participants in the procedure for conducting the census.

The values of this procedure are:

☐ You can learn of actual problems bugging your participants.
☐ You can work problems into the agenda as practicable.
☐ The census serves as a basis for program evaluation: Does the program actually provide help in resolving the participants' concerns?
☐ The census provides catharsis—a chance for the participants to get their concerns off their chest.
☐ It brings people together and they get to know one another better at the outset.

Starting with a Game

An effective way of opening is to start with a subject-matter-relevant game. The advantages are that it can in-troduce pertinent ideas and concepts or stimulate thinking about them; it initiates lively discussion, which helps set immediately the desired atmosphere of intimacy and inquiry; and it provides early on a common fund of experience for everyone. It does all this in a novel, lively, and fun way, which helps to set a relaxed, friendly, and enthusiastic atmosphere.

Note: See Chapter 6 for ideas concerning the use of games.

Garnering Goodies

To start things off on a positive note, tell the participants: "We're going to spend seven to eight hours together today. What are the 'goodies' or rewards you might get out of this course?" Then ask them to draw a T-column on a sheet of paper and list on an individual basis personal goals and organizational goals.

Note: The idea is to emphasize that there are dual benefits, including personal ones. Many courses have dual benefits. For example learning about safety, time management, communication, and problem solving can be used both on the job and off.

Have participants meet in small groups to discuss their T-columns, and then secure ideas from the small groups, posting them to a T-column on the flipchart. A long list of benefits of both types should encourage participant interest in the course.

Note: A variation is to team-up participants on a special interest group basis; e.g., in a time management course, small groups may be formed to discuss planning, delegation, telephone use, or use of secretary.

Learning Contracts

Have participants develop in writing one or more learning objectives that they pledge to work on in the course and thereafter. Process these learning contracts in small groups to add outside support for the commitment.

Introducing the Program

One way to help launch a program is to draw the diagram or model on a flipchart, as shown in Figure 1-4. Use this model to point out that

☐ The participants are a vital part of the learning process.
☐ The trainer is only one of four elements basic to goal accomplishment.
☐ The reference manuals are a tool for making learning a continuing process rather than a one-shot classroom event.

Note: After presenting this diagram, kick things off immediately with a participative opener.

Figure 1-4. A model that may be used to explain the nature of the training program.

Climate Setting

Malcolm Knowles, internationally recognized authority on training, uses this procedure to help establish a climate conducive to learning:[5]

1. Organize participants into groups of 5 or 6. (You can use tables if you have them.) And in the next 30 minutes:
2. Have them share their current work roles and how they got there.
3. Have them share one thing about themselves—a human interest story—which will set them off as unique individuals.
4. Have them indicate any relevant resources which they bring with them (from training or the job) that they are willing to share to help others learn better.
5. Have them develop a list of questions, problems, concerns, or issues they hope the workshop will cover.
6. Secure feedback on steps 2 through 5. Note:

   a. Anticipate that some of the data generated by this procedure may raise expectations which the course cannot meet. If so, candidly acknowledge that that is the case and compliment the participants for their contributions. Of course, participant suggestions which can be integrated into the course should be accepted to the degree practicable.

   b. With a small participant group of some 15 to 25 people, reports can be secured readily from all the buzz groups. With a larger group time constraints may require that you secure feedback on a "sample" basis only. You thus may wish to state at the outset of the feedback phase of the activity: "We have a large group and we will only be able to secure reports from a limited number of the teams. Who wants to start us off?" After securing several reports, you may wish to state: "O.K., that gives us a good idea of your main concerns. Does anyone in a group that has not reported have a really 'hot' item they wish to share?" Accept one or two of the added ideas, if forthcoming, and then advise the group that "We have to move on to stay with our very full program."

7. Ask for adjectives which describe the climate as they now experience it. You will probably get terms like "warm," "informal," "safe," etc. If so, tell them that these are the characteristics of a climate that facilitates learning.

Aerial Animation

I. Flying Airplanes

1. Ask each participant to respond in writing to an assigned task, e.g., "Develop a list of traits of a

leader vs. a manager." Suggest the use of a T-column to help contrast the ideas.

2. Have the participants form small groups and pool their ideas on a sheet of paper (letter or legal size). Also ask them to make a second copy since they will be exchanging their copy with another group and will need their own for reference purposes.
3. Ask each group to fold its sheet of paper into an airplane.
4. Ask all the groups to toss their airplanes across the room.
5. Ask several participants to read the statements on the newly acquired sheet of paper, comparing them to their own.

II. Flying Paper Balls

Optionally, at another point in the session or presentation, use the same procedure as above but with another topic, e.g., "What one action would you advise a manager to take to ensure effective communication?" This time, however, have them crumple their sheet of paper into a paper ball which, again, is tossed across the room for exchange purposes.

Note: Either one or both of these activities may be used in a single session. If both are used, it may be desirable to use the airplane activity first since tossing paper airplanes may be perceived as a more "conventional" task than tossing paper balls.

These paper tosses work particularly well with a fair-sized group for it produces a "wild," fun-type atmosphere—the room becomes filled with flying objects. Management consultant Geoffrey Bellman used both activities in a session on leadership at the 1987 ASTD Conference in Atlanta.

Icebreakers and Openers: Classifications and Cautions

If we can understand more fully the nature of icebreakers and openers, we can use them more properly. We thus should recognize that *icebreakers* can be divided into these two categories:[4]

☐ *The personality report*—*directly* asks participants to provide information about themselves: needs, hopes, fears, goals, details about one's background, etc. Examples: "Values Assessment" and "Art Mart" (page 4) enable participants to present data readily about themselves.
☐ *The personality clue*—provides *indicators* about one's personality. Examples: how one performs in "The

Ball Toss" (pages 10–11) and "Nicknames" (page 5) affords a few glimpses into peoples' personalities.

Similarly, *openers* can be divided into these two categories:

☐ *The attitude report*—asks participants in a *direct* way to verbalize their attitudes toward the topic or subject that they will be entering. Examples: "Ventilating Feelings" and "Fishbowls" (page 8).
☐ *The attitude clue*—provides indirect data or indicators about persons' feelings toward the subject at hand. Examples: "Goal Analysis" (page 7) and "Pre-Work" (page 8).

As was indicated in "Planning the Use of Icebreakers and Openers" (page 2) and in "Evaluating Icebreakers" (page 6), warm-up activities require care in their selection and implementation. Additionally, one trainer offers the following added cautions:[4]

☐ Don't get cute. Only use openers which relate to the learning goal.
☐ Don't use icebreakers or openers which may embarrass people or cause them to fail. Everyone should succeed and, depending on the task assigned, everyone should have fun.
☐ Don't let warm-up activities drag on. Once the point has been made, move into the program proper.

Key Points

1. Training groups typically can profit from some kind of warm-up activity.
2. Icebreakers, which usually are not course related, can help reduce tensions, anxieties, and loneliness, energize the group, set a tone for the program, and certainly involve everyone.
3. Icebreakers are particularly useful for the stranger or cousin group.
4. In choosing an icebreaker the trainer should pay attention to the organization's culture, the participant group and its tolerance for novelty, fun, and excitement, the available time, the nature of the course itself, etc.
5. If a group is well acquainted, icebreakers may not be essential. However, even such a group can profit from an opener, i.e., the use of a subject-matter-oriented device to ease into the course or program.
6. In general, icebreakers and openers are training devices that recognize the importance of establishing a proper climate for learning.

References

1. Baron, A. S., "How To Start A Seminar," *Training and Development Journal* (December 1979), p. 24.
2. Pearlstein, G., "Participant Objectives: Advice You Can Take To The Bank," *Training*, September 1983, p. 106. Also see in this same issue of *Training*: "First, Find Out What They Want," pp. 60, 64.
3. "Trainees Uninspired? Try These Tested Tips To Boost Production," *Training/HRD*, November 1982, p. 9.
4. Brue, C., "Breaking The Ice," *Training and Development Journal*, June 1985, pp. 26–28.
5. Knowles, M. S., "Some Thoughts About Environment and Learning—Educational Ecology, If You Like," *Training and Development Journal*, February 1980, pp. 34–36.

USING SMALL GROUPS EFFECTIVELY

The small group is the basic unit for participative training. By small group we mean subdivisions of a larger group that may range in size from, three to eight people. I prefer to keep such groups quite small, about three to five participants.

The small group, also known as a buzz group because of its noise production, has a number of unique advantages, including:

☐ It provides for the relatively easy and certain involvement of everyone.
☐ It permits and encourages meaningful participation in a low-risk, threat-free way. Contrast the "risk" of having to stand up in a large group to make a statement or ask a question as opposed to engaging in actual give-and-take discussion with a small number of peers.
☐ It provides for the opportunity to learn from one's peers and to test out the validity of one's own ideas.
☐ It is a flexible tool, that allows restructuring ("O.K., let's form some new groups so we can meet and work with some new people") and size expansion and contraction.
☐ Individual needs and differences can be recognized by assigning individuals to groups on the basis of interest, experience level (all new supervisors may meet together), management level (place supervisors and managers in their own small groups), job background (all sales people may be placed together), etc.
☐ It can provide the diversity of views essential for good problem solving.
☐ It can provide a sense of rapport, a source for support and recognition, and an opportunity to become acquainted with others. (The level or depth of the acquaintanceship obviously will vary, depending on the nature of the tasks, exposure time, personality differences and needs, etc.)

Just as small groups are advantageous in the previous ways, large-group situations have these disadvantages:

☐ The learning situation encourages passivity.
☐ It is much more difficult for participants to develop trust, rapport, mutual support, and intimacy—all of which are important to learning.
☐ Participants are kept out of touch with other participants and the trainer. People prefer, of course, more individualized attention.
☐ It may even become more difficult to read flipcharts or the blackboard.
☐ From a trainer standpoint, there may even be a loss of "control" of the group, indicated by such things as subgrouping, side conversations, late returns from

For learning to take place with any kind of efficiency students must be motivated. To be motivated, they must become interested. And they become interested when they are actively working on projects which they can relate to their values and goals in life.

—Gus Tuberville, president, William Penn College, Oskaloosa, Iowa (quoted in *The Washington Post,* March 7, 1981) breaks and lunch, passivity (some just sit and observe), and running behind schedule (more people produce more questions and comments; however, this additional input is usually from a minority of highly active and verbal personalities).

Note: Though small groups are the basic unit for participative training, there are obviously times when the small groups collectively function as a total group. This may be at the outset of a session before the small groups are formed or when the small groups are brought back in the total group situation to discuss their learning experience. Also, in opting for small group work we should not overlook the need to keep the *total* group relatively small and thus workable. This would be a total group of about 12 or 15 to a maximum of 20 or 25 participants.

The techniques described in the book are intended for use in the training situation. Though some of these techniques could be used in group therapy, our purpose is to give you techniques that will provide participants with the best possible learning experience. In general, our assumption is that we are dealing with normal people who function appropriately in organizations, rather than with those who have deep-seated emotional problems and require help thereon.

Throughout the book you will encounter terminology that is more or less standard in the training field. You should consider carefully whether certain terms will be accepted readily by the participants. Thus, it may be desirable to use "pair" rather than "dyad" or "trio" rather than "triad." (Interestingly, in Hong Kong the Triad is the Mafia!) Other terms that may frustrate or irritate participants are "fishbowl," "lecturette," "role playing," etc. This book, of course, suggests alternative words.

Small Group Composition

It is better to frequently change the membership in the small group because doing so:

☐ Energizes people by keeping them from getting too comfortable with the familiar.
☐ Provides for the opportunity to meet new faces, personalities, viewpoints, and talents. This is especially desirable when two or three people come from the same work unit (or the same organization in the case of a public seminar). I candidly tell cliquish participants: "We'd like to move you to another group so you can get exposed to new people, new views, etc. You won't learn anything new if you only confer with people you already know pretty well."

☐ Automatically provides you with the opportunity to restructure group membership if things are not going well in a particular group.

An easy way to gather small groups at random is simply to have people count off and have all the one's meet together, all the two's meet together, etc. Other ways are to arbitrarily restructure group formations by pointing to several somewhat adjacent people to form a group, by asking people to turn around, or by having the participants move around themselves to locate new team members.

If tables are used, set a ground rule at the outset that everyone is to seek a new table location each day. Explain the reason for this procedure, of course.

When considering the formation of groups, take into account that at times it may be desirable to balance the small groups, e.g., headquarters and field, line and staff, newcomers and seniors, men and women, functional combinations (such as sales and production).

Seating

Use flexible seating (light, comfortable chairs) so that participants can readily rearrange themselves for dyads, triads, buzz groups, role playing teams, etc. Try to avoid the use of tables and desks—much too classroom like—unless there is a real need for them, e.g., considerable writing or note taking. I prefer a "free-flowing" room that allows for informality, ready movement into new small group configurations, and easy circulation.

The initial configuration can be lecture hall fashion or even a circle (with a total group of about ten participants). However, the starting arrangement doesn't really matter too much. For if you use group-in-action methods, as I advocate, the furniture will soon be in friendly disarray.

Note: Participants new to small group techniques often are reluctant to form an actual circle with their chairs. The trainer should establish clearly, the first time around, that a buzz group is a truly circular arrangement; and that for the best communication and rapport to take place, they need full eye-to-eye contact.

Assigning Tasks

The key to effective group action is the nature of the task given to the small groups. Groups thrive on assignments that entail challenge, novelty, some element of controversy, and certainly relevance to their job situation. Cited in Figure 2-1 are some typical thought questions to which most groups should be able to respond

---

Thought Questions

1. If I were the head of the organization I would _____ .
2. How could this situation have been prevented?
3. Now that this incident has taken place, what should _____ do?
4. If I had unlimited funds (or staff) I would _____ .
5. If we were organized along these lines (centralization, or decentralization, or flat organization, etc.), we would be able to _____ .
6. Would you work for (this company, this boss, etc.)? Why or why not?
7. Would you invest in this company? Why or why not?
8. At this stage in the organization's history, it should _____ .
9. Assume it is the year 2025. What should our program for _____ be?
10. Assume that the life span of the average American is 110 in the year 2025 (or that unlimited energy is available, etc.). What implications would this have for our products (or our recruitment program, etc.)?
11. Pareto's Law tells us that 80% of the results are a result of 20% of the activity; e.g., 80% of the revenue comes from 20% of the product line or 20% of the sales force; or 80% of the accidents comes from 20% of the work force; etc. How does this "principle" apply to our results (in marketing, research, management of time, etc.)? _____ .
12. What would make this work team effective is (are) _____ .
13. The current (or future) trends affecting our activity in a significant way are (or will be) _____ .
14. Based upon what you have read in the case (or seen in the film or in the role play), what assumptions have you made about the boss (or the subordinate or the colleague, etc.)?
15. Has our organization experienced any major environmental or internal changes that affect careers (marketing strategies, product lines, personnel policies, etc.)?
16. Look back 10 years (or 20 years). What changes have occurred in government policy (technology, overseas marketing, etc.)?
17. Is this act (behavior, policy, program) a broad-gauged or narrow one? If it is narrow what would it take to make it broad-gauged?
18. Is this behavior (plan, program) a short or long-range view?
19. What criteria would you use to decide whether the organization has a "good" marketing program (communications program, pay plan, safety program)?
20. If you could be "Dutch Uncle" to the comptroller (personnel director, production manager, sales manager), what advice would you give?
21. If we were only to select people who could _____ (or had certain qualifications), would that solve these kinds of problems?
22. Suppose you were asked to resolve a problem like that. What would you do? How would you go about doing it?
23. What values seem to underly his (the organization's, work team's) decision?
24. What does the situation tell us about creativity (delegation, career development, motivation, sales success)?
25. If we could come up with a machine to _____ , what effect would it have on _____ ?
26. How can we tell that the plan (project, program, policy) has succeeded?
27. Is _____ in touch with reality? Explain your answer.

Figure 2-1. Examples of questions designed to stimulate discussion in groups.

with vigor. You may not care to use these questions; but they merit study as to their general thrust or tenor.

Assignments to small groups in the form of questions may be given orally, written on the flipchart, or presented in handout fashion. Questions which are relatively easy to understand may be assigned orally. However, it is probably wise to repeat the question and then check for understanding by everyone. People absorb (listen, understand) at different rates of speed and with different degrees of comprehension.

If a question (or set of questions) is of some complexity and likely to be misunderstood, it's a good idea to present it in handout fashion. This procedure will ensure that everyone can digest it at an individual pace and have the chance to reread it if necessary. Questions reduced to writing also force the trainer to think through more carefully what he/she actually has in mind and can serve as a

permanent record for future use (or revision, if necessary).

In making assignments to small groups, set a definite time limit for completing the task. Use a timer or a digital watch as a monitoring aid for this. Provide the groups with a warning when their time is about up. If time is not a big factor, just tell participants: "Take a few minutes to discuss _____ ."

Consider giving assignments to the groups that have some element of controversy, and advise them that they must agree in ten minutes on a particular point. The need for a group decision coupled with time constraints provides an up-beat tempo for motivated, energized performance.

To ensure clarity in giving task instructions to small groups, trainer/consultants Chip R. Bell and Fredrick H. Margolis, have developed a helpful four-step guide:[1]

1. State the *rationale* for the assignment from the *learner's* view. People are entitled to know not only what they will do, but *why* they are to do it. As the learner might well phrase it: "What's in it for me?"
2. Explain the *nature* of the task. Step 1 responds to the *why* question. This step answers the *what* question, i.e., what is to be done. It describes a *product* to be produced: develop a list, answer a question, solve a problem, take a position on an issue, etc. The quality or quantity of the product should also be spelled out.
3. Specify the *context* or setting of the task, i.e., *how* the task is to be done. This instruction specifies: (a) whether the task is individual, small group, or both, (b) group composition (homogeneous or heterogeneous), and (c) time allotted.
4. Describe the feedback report to be provided. This request for reporting is also known as "processing" or "sharing." Participants must know precisely what they are going to have to communicate to the total group about their learning.

Viewing-Listening Teams

Consider using listening-viewing teams when your program calls for inputs of a one-way communication nature, that is, talks, lectures, films, slide shows, panel presentations, etc. These teams are small groups that have been given an assignment to look/listen for something in particular while the talk or film is in progress.

Note: If the input is a film, the small group is a *viewing-listening team;* if the input is a talk the small group is a *listening team.*

The rationale for this procedure is that it gives the participants something specific to do while the one-way input is in process. This encourages tune in, commitment, and responsibility as opposed to a possible tune-out or drift effect.

Procedurally, the trainer gives a listening and/or viewing assignment to each small group in advance of the presentation. After the presentation, the small groups meet to discuss their assignments and then report back on them to the group at large.

The assignments to the teams may be specific or more general. An example of specific assignments in the case of a talk on communication might be the following:

"Group 1, pay attention to and be prepared to report back on the role of feedback in the communication process.

"Group 2, pay attention to the relationship of communication and decision making.

"Group 3, you will be asked to respond to this question: What are the relative merits of two-way versus one-way communication?"

The more general assignments can be treated in this manner:

"Group 1, you are _the questioners._ Listen (or look) for anything which triggers a question in your mind.

"Group 2, you are _the clarifiers._ Listen for anything that comes across in a muddy or obscure way.

"Group 3, you are _the agreers._ Listen for anything that you can most readily accept or 'buy.'

"Group 4, you are _the disagreers_ (not the 'disagreeables'). Listen for anything that doesn't make sense and which you can't 'buy' or accept.

"Group 5, you are _the implementors_ or _the appliers._ Listen for something so practical that you can pick it up and run with it starting Monday morning."

The T-Column

Groups can be helped to see dichotomized or polarized issues in better perspective if you:

1. Assign the two different sides of an issue to different groups.
2. Elicit data from the groups and post the data in a T-column:

Reporting Requirements As Seen By

Headquarters	Field
Basic to policy development	Too many reports
Needed for control and supervision	Too short deadlines
Frequently late.	Instructions not clear
Data often obscure or missing	Looks like data is collected for data's sake
	Not staffed to do reports right

In general, the T-column is useful in highlighting comparisons and contrasts, pros and cons, risks versus ways of overcoming them, our views-their views, past-present, benefits-losses, headquarters-field, reports on a single issue from two groups (Group A-Group B), hopes and fears (as an anxiety-reducing program opener), etc.

Risk Analysis

Issues often arise in groups that relate to the taking of risks; e.g., the risks supervisors run if they delegate, hire minorities, allow subordinates to rate their effectiveness as a coach, let work teams make group decisions.

A good way to resolve the "risk-laden" issue is to

1. Ask the small groups to enumerate all the risks they can think of. This helps participants reveal their concerns so that they can be analyzed and it allows the participants to vent their feelings.
2. Rank the lists in priority order (the most serious is number one). This shows that not all risks are equal in gravity.
3. Develop procedures to overcome the risks. This encourages a great deal of positive thinking about what often are only presumed or minor fears.

A T-column can be used to help sharpen the issue:

Risk Analysis: Letting Work Groups Make Their Own Decisions

Risks	Overcoming the Risk
1. Decisions made without all the facts	Provide written background Encourage group members to visit units that have pertinent data Only allow them to work on problems where they readily have the facts Meet with the group, but only at the outset
2. Decisions made that ignore cost factors	
3. Loss of management authority	
4. Too much time spent away from the job	

Risk Zapping

Risk taking concerns also arise in training programs concerned with assertiveness, career planning, and other personal growth areas. Educator Merrill Harmin, Southern Illinois University, suggests posing these two questions to low risk takers:[2]

1. Are there steps ahead that I *know* would be good for me and that would serve me *now*, but which I feel are too risky to take?
2. What can I do to "zap" that risk so I *can* take those steps, to get myself moving the way I want to move?

If these questions are recognized as realistic means to reach personal goals, participants can be presented with these options:

☐ *Worst scenario.* What's the worst that could happen? *Note:* Asking this question, identifying the most frightful situation or event and talking about it, often helps one to decide that "the worst" is not all that bad—nothing to really run from.

☐ *Comfort-zone action plan.* Assume a participant has expressed a fear of some sort—embarking on a new career, transferring to another location, confronting the boss about a vexing issue, etc. Use this procedure:

Procedures:

    a. Ask him/her to auto-brainstorm a long list of things (6 to 12 items) he/she could do to resolve the problem, to overcome the fear or reluctance. The list should include both easy, small steps and large, frightening ones.

    b. Mark the items on the list A, B, or C—A for frightening steps, actions that are "impossible" to take; B for in-between acts, neither easy nor frightening; C for easy actions.

    c. Then ask the participant to begin with a step within his/her "comfort zone," no matter how tiny or insignificant. Once started with C steps, one's comfort zone can be expanded to include B steps.

☐ *Taking the fear and going anyhow.* Assume that someone is generally afraid to give a talk to a group or ask the boss for a raise. We know that king-sized butterflies will invade the tummy. But self-talk can help: "O.K., it's scary, I've got the butterflies, but I have to do it. And once I start, my fears will dissolve in the energy of the action." In effect, we accept the existence and scary reality of the fear, but stride ahead nevertheless. We can also be comforted by the memories of other past actions where we rose above a big fear.

☐ *Living a purpose.* Another good way to dissolve a fear is to have participants get in touch with their "larger purposes." What are my goals? What are my values? What is really best or right? Am I living my life as fully as I should? Once we can act on our persisting inner wisdom, as opposed to transient superficial impulses, we can become satisfied and powerful. Fears will fade when we recognize that we are using our life in ways that it was meant to be used.

Note:

1. The options just listed are for possible integration into an established program in the areas suggested, such as assertiveness training. They are intended to serve as an adjunct to such programs.
2. Procedurally, one or more of these four options may be assigned by the trainer to the participants in the small groups. Your decision as to which one to assign would be based on how well participants seem to be progressing, residual needs, and the like. Also, any one of the options may be presented to an individual participant in a group-at-large discussion for his/her processing and further general discussion.
3. Also consider securing feedback from the small groups as to how helpful any one option may have been: "Group 1, can you share with us your experience with the 'Worst Scenario' technique? Was it easy or hard to use? How was it helpful? Would anyone care to share their experience with the technique?"

The Spokesperson and the Recorder

If a spokesperson is necessary for reporting back on small-group-generated data, have the group designate one person using objective selection critera. (See discussion on "Leadership in the Small Group.")

If a recorder is needed, you should advise the group of that, too. As to selection, the group often gives the task to a "low-status" person. Conversely, someone may simply grab the ball and run with it. Again, see the discussion on "Leadership In The Small Group" for ways to make this appointment more objective and thus less "traumatic" to participants.

Using Observers

Observers are a helpful adjunct to small group work. Using them is valuable technique for reporting what went on in the group, in a role play, in an exercise, etc. This may relate to leadership, to such processes as communication, goal setting, and decision making, to group morale (via giving support, encouragement, recognition, etc.), to planning, to creativity, and to participation.

The observer also learns by seeing group activities from a detached perspective, an opportunity that one does not ordinarily have in organizational life.

To ensure that the observation process produces meaningful results:

1. Provide guide sheets to the observers, so that they will know precisely what to look for. The alternative: floundering and frustration.
2. Provide enough time for the observers to familiarize themselves with the guide sheets.
3. Meet with the observers (perhaps while the role players are reading their instructions) to be sure that they understand their responsibilities. Sometimes it helps to tell the observer that: "You have the most important job. If you don't pick up the needed data, the whole exercise will fall flat on its face and no one will learn a thing from it." The reassurance about job importance is often necessary since the observers may feel left out or that they are just unnecessary extras.
4. Consider using a team of two observers if the data to be garnered is adequately complex. A pair of observers may also have greater credibility with the observed.

One valuable and well-established form of observation is the use of a "sociogram," which reports on the nature (who speaks to whom) and frequency of group member contribution. For example, let's assume we have six participants in a group. We give each person a number, as in Figure 2-2.

The observer is instructed to make two kinds of diagrammed entries:

1. Hook up appropriate numbers with lines when one participant speaks to another participant; e.g., 3 to 5, 2 to 4. Use arrows to indicate recipients of the communication.

2. When a participant speaks to the group at large direct the line to the center (designated by a square).

An example of a completed sociogram is given in Figure 2-3. In this diagram person 2 has received most of the communication and person 5 is the heaviest contributor in the group.

The data should be processed fully by the group.

In connection with the observer role, we might mention that sometimes visitors come to the training room and take an observational role. They may be members of management, invited colleagues of the trainer, etc. Naturally group members are curious about these "interlopers." Why are they here? Who are they? What is their role? Are they spying? The best procedure is to nip in the bud any suspicions and anxieties by promptly introducing the observers to the group.

Monitoring

While the small groups are working on their tasks, it may be desirable to look in or listen in on their discussions so that you can

☐ Answer possible questions about the assignment. By circulating around the room, as opposed to standing aloofly up front, you are more likely to get questions and various requests for help.
☐ Ascertain progress on the assigned task. Teams that finish too soon are suspect—check to see if they were on track.
☐ Pick up at first hand some ideas that may be useful in the general or summary session following the small group work ("I heard group two make the point that . . .").
☐ Show that you are interested in their work.

These listening visits should be accomplished as unobtrusively as possible and be conducted only long enough

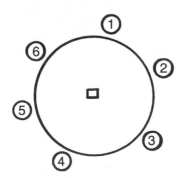

Figure 2-2. Diagram showing how members of a small group are assigned numbers for the purposes of a sociometric analysis.

Figure 2-3. Example of a completed sociogram.

to get an idea of where the discussions are trending. Visits should be made to all or most of the teams so that there is no feeling that only one group is being "picked on."

In more specific terms, the roles of the trainer in these visits are:

☐ *Sensing:* interest-disinterest, anxiety, frustration, teamness, conflict, incompatibility, participation, etc.
☐ *Listening:* for methods of attack, attitudes, reactions, learnings, "being with it," key ideas expressed, progress, creativity, winding down, etc.
   Note: Sensing relates to the affective or emotional side of the group's work; listening relates to the subject matter or task aspects of the work.
☐ *Intervening:* this should be done only if the group is floundering or because instructions were poorly delivered or simply misunderstood. If a group asks for help, you should respond enthusiastically to the request, of course.

Note: See "Using the Question-and-Answer Period Effectively," pages 304–306, for more detail on the use of the question and answer technique. The "Thought Questions," Figure 2-1, on page 15, may also be helpful.

Questions and Answers

Small groups function as a total group for such purposes as processing (discussing) the data they have generated and listening to a lecturette. In the course of such total group activity you may, at times, pose questions to the participants. What if no one responds? Here are some suggestions for coping with this problem:

☐ Wait a little longer. Place the pressure on the group. The odds are that someone will break the hard-to-bear silence and respond to your query.
☐ Rephrase the question: "I guess I didn't state that very well. Let me restate the question. What if . . . ."
☐ Introduce a bit of humor into the situation: "Gee, I didn't realize I came up with such a profound question."
☐ You may wish to call on someone. "Mary, could you help us on that one?" Or, "George, could you give us the benefit of your experience?" Consider this as an opportunity to involve the hesitant contributor.

As to questions from the group, try to be the "good facilitator" and let other group members answer as many of them as possible. Remember, this is *their* program and *their* opportunity for growth. One workable response technique for this is: "I could answer this, but I think we ought to get some input from a few other people."

Reporting

The final and most important opportunity to learn from small group work takes place when each team reports back its conclusions—essentially, *what was learned.* This phase of small group work is also termed "processing," "debriefing," and "sharing." For added guidance in this area, see "Skill Pointers On Processing," Chapter 8, pages 135–136.

Small groups may present their reports via a single spokesperson, a pair of reporters or even the whole group on a division-of-labor basis. Observers may also provide reports, either totally or as supplements, to the key team reporters.

As to methods of communication, it may be done verbally, non-verbally, via flipchart, or with the aid of overhead transparency slides. If the reports are delivered orally for recording on the flipchart, you must be certain that you are capturing their ideas faithfully. Recognize that since you are trying to pick up key words and phrases from possibly windy speeches, you must tune in very carefully. And even if you don't like or agree with what you hear, record it as presented, nevertheless. You can discuss the "disturbing" point later. It is a good idea to check with the reporter from time to time to see whether you have extracted the essence of what was said. Participants will appreciate your concern for careful recording of their ideas. (See Chapter 15, "Flipcharting," pages 248–250, for pointers on this process.)

Note: Although the reporting process is essentially designed for learning from the ideas of others, it also serves another vital function. Namely, it gives each team, through its spokesperson, a chance to "strut its stuff." It is a form of "show and tell" wherein the teams have a chance to say to everyone else: "We have a good group. We're proud of it. And here's what *we* came up with!" Anticipate reactions such as "Hey, we already said that," or "Group B always has the best list."

Regarding actual reporting procedures, Margolis and Bell suggest that reports from the small groups be secured in one of the following ways:[3]

1. *Cream off the top.* This procedure entails securing *key* data from all group reporters on a rotational basis. It is used when all groups have had the *same* assignment. In this way, all groups have the chance to contribute equitably, as opposed to one team sharing all the items on their list and thereby leaving the others with little more to add. A typical query to the reporters is "What is your *best* reason for your decision?" or "Give us the *one* approach of which your group is particularly proud."
2. *Report plus add-ons.* Use this procedure when all the teams have been given totally *different* assign-

ments. (See examples under "Viewing-Listening Teams," in the preceding.) Elicit information from Group 1, then Group 2, and so on. Each group learns by doing its own work and from the contributions of the other small groups as well.

3. *Formal presentations.* When all small groups have been working on a total problem/issue/question, they may be asked to report back on *one* aspect of it. Again, people learn from their own work and that of others.

4. *Polling.* This entails securing a quick response (answer/solution) to a problem. Example: "How would you deal with Manager Pat White?" (*Note:* This procedure is akin to the "Circular Whip" described on page 36.)

Leadership In The Small Group

When a small group works on an assigned task, from a leadership standpoint it can proceed in one of three ways:

1. Operate without a designated leader.
2. Operate with a leader of its own choice, using its own criteria as a basis for selection.
3. Operate with a leader of its own choice, using criteria for selection provided by the trainer.

Let's examine the learning implications of each of these three approaches.

☐ *A leader is not designated.* In most cases a formal leader need not be designated. This is particularly true if the task is not too complex and is to be accomplished in relatively short order, say, 5–30 minutes. The leaderless group may learn from this situation that:

a. In problem solving brainpower and insight are more important then the status of leadership.
b. Leadership roles (e.g. summarizing, supporting) can be assumed by any and all group members.
c. A single leader, if really necessary, will emerge in an informal way. Sometimes, of course, the leader who emerges does so simply by taking over. The learning, then, for most participants, is that no one appreciates a "power-hungry" autocrat.

☐ *The group chooses its own leader based on its own criteria.* This procedure often is not too effective since no one (or most participants) wants to be perceived as pushy. Hence, someone may say: "George, why don't you be the leader?" And since ordinarily no one will contest this quick act of coronation, the "winner" is ac-

tually the one who made the uncontested designation of leadership. In reality, the leadership role is merely that of recorder, spokesperson, or a combination of the two roles. Consequently, no one really objects too much to the railroading procedure used to select the leader. Group members may learn that some people are dominators (like the one who selected the leader), others may have strong power needs and thus may be very willing to be designated as leader, and most participants have the insight to avoid involvement in any power making or receiving ploys. They may also observe that the one selected may be a "high-status" person and that the sponsor or king-maker was deferring to that fact.

☐ *The group chooses its own leader based on trainer-supplied criteria.* If you sense that a high-status or dominant person is likely to be "given" the leadership job, or you have seen it occur previously in a small group, you may provide selection criteria that will ensure more rotation of the leadership role. Thus, the small groups can be instructed to select a leader using very arbitrary, but impartial and fun-type criteria; e.g., the person with the least seniority, the youngest person in the group, the one with the brightest or lightest colors (this may produce a female leader), the one who had to travel the farthest to this session, the one who was born farthest from this locale, the one whose birthdate is closest to today, etc. Fun-type instructions of this sort will prevent power ploys, deflate the importance of the formal leadership role, and help to spread the leadership job around. The learnings for the group may be that leadership may well merit rotation as opposed to having it doled out on the basis of such traditional factors as status, seniority, power needs, and bartering and that the leadership function, in the absence of a strong or autocratic leader, can be shared with no adverse (and possibly salutary) effects on productivity.

Coping with Problem Participants

While most participants are cooperative and quite manageable, at times you will encounter a few problem-types. Some of the more common ones are The Hesitant One, The Monopolizer, The Voice of Experience, The Arguer, The Clown, The Show Off, and The Tangent Taker.

While there are no easy answers for dealing with these difficult personalities, here are a few pointers that may be of help, at least some of the time.

The Hesitant One

This kind of person—shy, reluctant, silent much of the time—is found in almost every group. Hesitant Hanna is easy to overlook since she melts into the background so successfully and certainly is not annoying anyone. In fact, some might say: "Why worry? Hanna will participate when ready." However, if we look at a training program as a vehicle to help people grow, and if growth is dependent on one's opportunity to contribute (analyze ideas, present ideas, defend them, etc.), then we must figure out ways to "draw out" and thus to draw in Hesitant Hanna. Some suggestions: Use a lot of dyads and triads, for participation is certain in the very small group. Also, call on the silent one politely from time to time ("I don't think we've heard from Hanna yet on this issue.") Ask the shy person "easy" questions, particularly those that relate to everyday or back-home experiences. Some trainers make it a point to socialize with the shy participant at the break. It gives such a person an ego boost and often has an encouraging impact thereafter.

Other techniques are to smile at Hanna and offer encouraging statements like: "You look like you were about to add something to that" or "You've had a lot of work with . . . May we have the benefit of your experience?" (Hanna is probably saying to herself: "I was afraid you wouldn't ask.") Also, you can use the "chained" or "relay" technique, i.e., ask the same question in sequence of several participants, which would automatically include Hanna. The latter device avoids putting Hanna on the spot since others are being asked to contribute. And if she is a bit slow to assemble her ideas, she won't be called on first.

You also can assign participants to work in pairs. Specify that their report to the total group is to be in two parts, each partner to give one portion of it. Finally, be sure to give Hesitant Hanna a lot of praise for her contributions. Positive reinforcement will encourage added responses.

The Monopolizer

This participant is the "big talker" and will gobble up all the available air time if permitted. In a polite but firm way, ask Monopolizing Mike: "Would you mind if we got another opinion on this one? Several haven't had a chance to respond yet." Or: "Could we talk about that at the break?" The message to Monopolizing Mike is that "we play fair here, so let's please share the available air time." However, as with any of the other "difficult" participants, we can't afford to put Mike down. Why? Because, as a participant, the group may well rally to *his* side. In sum, we want Mike to know we appreciate his help, but on a more selective basis.

At times, peer pressure may also be relied on, viz., "What, you again?" or "Hey, knock it off Mike. Give someone else a chance."

The Voice of Experience

Like the Monopolizer, Victor, the Voice of Experience, seems to have a tremendous need to be heard. Victor probably is not getting adequate job satisfaction currently, hence the need to bring in incidents and anecdotes from more halcyon days. Treatment of The Voice's malady is not easy since the inputs are not necessarily offensive, just somewhat tedious and unnecessary. The best advice is to treat Victor politely, but endeavor at times to communicate that: "This is very interesting, but we do have to move on." Or, better still: "We do have to get to our main issue, which is . . . ."

The Arguer

Arguing Arthur is a "tough kind" with which to deal. He constantly looks for opportunities to disagree, to show up the other participants and the trainer. While healthy disagreement is great, incessant quibbling is annoying and disruptive. One approach to coping with Arthur is to let the group deal with him: "Anyone want to respond to that?" Also, avoid getting trapped or baited into a debate with him. If, after an exchange of views, Arthur persists, simply say: "I understand your position. You believe that . . . Can we agree to disagree on this one?" Or: "We've given this issue considerable attention. We really should move on to something else. See me at the break and we'll talk some more about it."

Another technique is to look for a chance to defuse Arthur's disagreements by stating promptly whenever you can: "I agree with you and I think the group does, too. Any comment, anyone?"

The cardinal rule to remember: No trainer ever won an argument with a participant. For as we said before, participants are quite likely to identify with problem participants for they are one of their group. They also expect finesse and patience from the trainer.

The Nonlistener

Nonlistening Norma presents a unique challenge to the group and its leader. Norma tends to interrupt, cuts others off, and leaps into the fray before others have had their say. Her eagerness to get in keeps her from listening. On the one hand Norma's nonlistening simply may be due to a desire to be heard, to "best" others in the discussion. But it may also be due to her keen interest in the subject; hence her strong desire to advance her ideas. But regardless of Norma's motivation, her harrassing behavior hardly facilitates group satisfaction and progress. Hence the need to cope with Norma's listening peccadillos. Some tactics to deal with Norma are these:

☐ Insist on sharing the available air time: "I know you have a worthwhile observation, but we haven't let Hank have his full say yet, have we?"

☐ Ask for a restatement: "Norma, just to be sure we're all in the same ballpark, could you restate for us what Tom just said?" If Norma has not heard Tom properly, ask Tom to repeat his statement and then go back to Norma: "OK, Norma. You heard Tom. Can you tell us what he said before you give us your view?"

☐ Ask for a comparative analysis: "How does your idea/viewpoint stack up with Ann's?"

Tactics such as these will help Norma to see that she must try to incorporate other's views—which requires listening—before she unleashes her own opinions.

The Idea Zapper

Idea Zapping Ida is a past master at putting down other people's ideas. She predictably offers an endless barrage of suggestion squelchers to anything new or different: "It'll never work." "We've tried that before." "Too early." "Too late." "Top management will never go for that." "Good theory, but not useable in the real world." Often her negatives come forth with a "Yes, but . . ." If we could crawl into Ida's head, we would probably find that her motivation is envy of the ability of others to ideate. So she uses what creativity she has to deflate everyone else.

Ida is particularly dangerous because her tendency to toss buckets of cold water on new approaches may inhibit creative suggestions from others.

Some possible ways of coping with Idea Zapping Ida are these:

☐ Rescue the idea promptly from Ida's trash bin by asking the group: "How do the rest of you see this? Is there another side to it?"

☐ Ask Ida if she can use her creativity to come up with an idea of her own, in lieu of the one she just zapped. If she doesn't, you may wish to say: "Well, if we don't have a better idea than Kim's, maybe we ought to look at that one a little bit."

☐ If you happen to like the idea that was zapped on arrival, don't hesitate to agree with it and say to the group: "I think there may be some possibilities here. Can anyone provide any arguments for it?"

The Complainer

Complaining Chester is a specialist in blaming, fault-finding, griping, and sharing his endless pet peeves. Chester not only finds life and the world "unfair," but he insists on foisting his jaundiced view of things on any au-

dience he can get. His ploys are easy to spot for he is likely to begin his gloomy observations with such statements as: "Ain't it awful that . . ." or "If it weren't for . . ." He tends to sprinkle his laments with the all-encompassing "never" and "always." Chester is not a problem solver, but a problem magnifier. He's unhappy with top management, other departments ("those clods in shipping . . ."), his boss, his staff, the suppliers, the union, the local sports team, the press, etc.

To cope with Complaining Chester try these approaches:

☐ Ask him: "Do you have any ideas to cope with Department X?" or "Would you want the group to suggest some ways of dealing with. . . .?" or "Have you leveled with . . . and told . . . how you feel about it?" The approach is to force Chester into a problem solving mode, something he typically shies away from.

☐ Encourage a search for the other side of things: "O.K., you've told us how terrible they are in Department X. But you're a fair person. Can you think of anything good about them at all? Just one thing?" If he begrudgingly admits to that one thing, ask "Anything else?" If you can squeeze two or three admissions out of him about another or opposite point of view, and possibly a few positives from the rest of the group, you may elevate Chester to a more positive level for a little while. A T-column, to show contrasting views, should help him put things in balance.

☐ Switch him to the high ground by stating early on: "Yes, there may be a problem with Department X. And the reason we're here is to find some answers (or better ways of cooperating). So if you and I and all the rest of us can keep thinking about ways to cope with this kind of issue, we'll have a truly profitable experience this morning (or this week). How can we accomplish that?"

The Rigid One

Rigid Roberta is a tough cookie, indeed. Roberta is not obnoxious in the sense that she argues, disagrees, pontificates, quibbles, etc., but in that she staunchly takes a position on an issue and will rarely, if at all, move from it. Since Rigid Roberta is so unyielding and positive that she has a monopoly on *The Truth,* she makes it difficult for the group to make any progress. One way to deal with Roberta is to try to get her to admit that there *is* another side to the issue. Thus, the trainer might say: "Roberta, we're pretty clear about your position since you have stated it so well. But there is some other thinking on it. Can you cite any evidence at all, as an objective person, that would indicate that the problem can be seen in different terms?"

If Roberta does supply some data or opinion contrary to her own, follow this up by saying: "Yes, that is an argument on the other side. Can you cite one more view (or piece of data) that the other side considers important?" If Roberta supplies two opposing arguments, they should be put on the flipchart and the other participants asked for added evidence which is contrary to Roberta's position. In effect, Roberta is being asked to verbalize some opposing views, kickoff the development of a "laundry list" of such views, and inspect visually the posted opposition views. No guarantees here to reduce Roberta's rigidities, but at least it forces her to recognize more directly that other views *do* exist.

The Hostile One

Hostile Harry is even more annoying than Arguing Arthur. Harry has a need to zero in on a defenseless target, and the trainer, as he sees it, is as good a victim as any. He thus presents highly hostile questions designed to embarrass or inflame. The best response to Harry's hostility is to keep your cool and simply rephrase the question in milder, more objective terms. Or, you may respond in this fashion: "I see that you have some strong feelings on this issue. Would you care for my opinion? (Or the group's opinion?)" It may also help if the answer is given to the group at large rather than to Harry. These procedures should "defang" Harry a bit at least for the time being.

The Angry One

While Hostile Harry is antagonistic, aggressive, and unfriendly, Angry Arnie is a much more complex personality. His behavior may range intermittently from total silence and withdrawal to constant complaining—hard seats, lousy coffee, cold room—and the posing of harassing, negative questions. His forte is to find loopholes in your ideas and/or presenting impossible "what if" scenarios. The interesting thing about Arnie is that he is not mad at you, the trainer. Rather, he is mad at the world, including his boss, who had the gall to send him off to training.

Obviously, few trainers have the therapeutic skills to deal with an intimidating, somewhat paranoid trainee who is probably having serious problems at home, on the job, or both. Dr. Sandra Weintraub,[4] a management trainer and psychotherapist, suggests that when you encounter Angry Arnie, deal with him by asking yourself these questions:

☐ Am I regarding the situation as a professional challenge and acting accordingly?

☐ Have I done everything I can to eliminate possible threats from the training?
☐ Have I created a climate/atmosphere where all participants can freely share possible frustrations about all aspects of the training?
☐ Have I considered the use of activities (exercises, role plays) to allow venting of frustration in a positive manner? Feedback to Arnie resulting from a role play may be a helpful "shock" to him.
☐ Have I considered addressing the problem openly with the group? It may be helpful to Arnie to find out how people feel about his behavior. Arnie may not be aware that his behavior is affecting others, making them feel uncomfortable, until he receives some candid feedback from them.
☐ As a last resort, should I approach his organization about his possible need for outside professional help?

The Negative One

Negative Nellie can be counted on to find the gloomy side of things: nothing will work, people are impossible, the world has long gone to the dogs. Nellie is a specialist in dredging up gripes, past grievances, cantankerous complaints. She is a tough cookie to deal with, indeed. The best approaches with Negative Nellie are to ask her if she can find anything positive in the situation (also ask the group the same question) and suggest that she may have a point, but that we're all here to find constructive answers to these difficulties. Sometimes it helps to respond merely by saying: "I understand" or "Uh, huh."

The Clown

"Clowns" come in all shapes and sizes, but their main characteristic is an abundance of ill-fitting, sometimes irritating humor. Some trainers may say: "I'd rather have a little humor than no participation at all." Possibly. But the effective discussion leader's job is to keep things moving in an orderly, productive way. And if Charlie the Clown is hindering group progress or annoying participants, he certainly should be dealt with. Some suggestions: Call on Charlie on occasion for "serious" dialogue. Show him that he can be heard (his real objective, of course), but at a more sophisticated and adult level. Compliment him (positive reinforcement) when he makes a worthwhile, serious contribution. Conversely, don't reward his attempts at humor. In some cases you may ask Charlie for a restatement of the joke: "I guess I missed the point of your quip. Could you give me your idea straight?"

Sometimes the problem is compounded by Charlie's clique who continually reinforces his behavior by exchanging banter and assorted put downs. It is not an easy problem, of course. Again, the best strategy is to try to tap and reward his serious side.

The Show Off

Show-off Sandra likes to parade her knowledge before everyone—big words, fancy phrases, lots of statistics, name dropping, describing her long-time or "unique" experiences, etc. If Show-off Sandra contributes with the frequency of Monopolizing Mike, she can be treated in somewhat the same way. If the contributions are not as frequent, but merely pompous, the problem, although annoying, probably is one the group can live with. The odds are that some group members will "kid" her quite clearly about the big words and her other ploys. In effect, let the group deal with this type of problem participant.

The Tangent Taker

Tangent Tanya is the kind of person who has interesting inputs, but they typically belong in some other "ball park." One suggestion is to state politely to her: "This is an interesting experience, but could we try to bring it in a bit closer to home? You see our issue is . . ." Or: "Anyone want to comment on Tanya's experience as it relates to our concern here?" Group silence may reduce her meandering inputs. Some of Tanya's tangents may, of course, have to be lived with. But it's still worth a try or two to plead for relevance from her.

Summary

Problem participants are a fact of training work. We have tried to suggest some ways of coping with them. Basically, you will be ahead of the game if you regard the problem-participant as a challenge rather than as a headache. This means that you must show patience and avoid arguments and put downs. Endeavor to deal politely with the problem-participant's peccadillos, using some of the suggestions made above. Also, wherever possible, let the group try to deal with such participants. They will probably do it more effectively than you can, most likely in a kidding way. For example, I recall one participant who employed "two-dollar" words and thus was soon referred to by several group members as "Parameters," a favorite word of his. Needless to say, "Old Parameters" began to get the message before too long.

Of course, in extreme situations you can exercise other options such as:

☐ *Group critique.* Take time to process group behavior. "Zero in" on the trouble maker, if no one else does.

☐ *Confrontation.* At the break, you might speak candidly to the obstructionist: "I think we have a good group and it has a potential for a lot of progress. It would be helpful to the group and myself if you tried to involve others in the discussions and soft-pedaled some of your own inputs. Can I secure your help on this?"

☐ *Expulsion.* "May I be open with you? You have disrupted several sessions and no one here knows what to do about it. I don't either, but I do not intend to have you interfere with group accomplishment. If you cannot avoid arguing, disagreeing, and monopolizing our limited time, I shall have to ask you to leave."

Another possibility is to endeavor to spot the obstreperous ones before the session begins. Armed with this knowledge, you can develop your strategy accordingly.

One approach that is *not* recommended is that of manipulation, e.g., special seating for purposes of better control, asking the difficult person to serve as an observer, ignoring the person by devices such as turning your back to him/her, etc. Being up front about the problem will retain the respect of the group and possibly the irritating one, too.

Key Points

1. Small-group work is a basic tool for high participant involvement and learning. It entails limited "risk" for the participant and provides significant opportunities for peer learning, support, recognition, and comraderie.

2. Effective use of small-group techniques requires attention to such issues as getting started (icebreakers/openers), group composition, seating arrangements, task assignments, leadership, monitoring group work, using spokespersons, recorders, and observers, and dealing with problem participants.

3. When participants work in small groups for considerable time periods their composition should be changed. This will energize them and allow them to work with and learn from new people.

4. Participant seating should be so planned and organized that movement into small group configurations is quick and painless. Desks and tables, which add to formality, should only be used when considerable writing takes place.

5. Effective small group task assignment procedures entail concern with clarity of instruction, thought-provocation, time limits, and as appropriate, requiring group decision or agreement on the task. The use of viewing-listening team assignments can enrich the discussion process.

6. The effective trainer endeavors to stay on top of things via monitoring small group proceedings. Key skills are sensing, listening, and intervening if necessary.
7. Leaders, recorders, and spokespersons ordinarily should be permitted to emerge naturally. If the small groups are having problems in deciding on who executes such roles, the trainer may introduce random methods of selection.
8. Problem participants should be looked at as a challenge rather than a headache. While many strategies are available to deal with such people, quite often the group itself can best decide how to deal with them.

References

1. Margolis, Frederick H., and Bell, Chip R., *Managing The Learning Process,* Lakewood Publications, Minneapolis, 1984, pp. 53–63.
2. Harmin, Merrill, "Zap The Risks From The Steps Ahead," *AHP Perspective,* Newsletter of the Association for Humanistic Psychology, November 1987, p. 17.
3. Margolis, Frederick H., and Bell, Chip R., *Managing The Learning Process,* Lakewood Publications, Minneapolis, 1984, pp. 69–79.
4. Weintraub, Sandra, "Defusing Anger in the Training Room," *Training News,* July 1986, pp. 13–14.

Recommended Reading

Hultman, Kenneth E. "The Trainer as 'Scapegoat'," *Training and Development Journal,* July 1982, pp. 44–53.

Participants who attend workshops may engage in "dysfunctional" behaviors such as arriving late, arguing, dominating, withdrawing, embarrassing others including the trainer, etc. The article presents causes for and strategies to deal with disruptive behavior.

Jones, John E. "Dealing With Disruptive Individuals in Meetings," in *The 1980 Annual Handbook for Group Facilitators,* San Diego, University Associates, 1980, pp. 161–165.

This provides a repertoire of responses to deal more effectively with difficult participants including pre-session and in-session approaches.

Pickhardt, Carl E. "Participant Hostility: Why It Comes With The Territory," *Training/HRD,* September 1980, pp. 16, 18, 19, 20.

This offers a psychological explanation for trainer-directed hostility as well as five strategies to cope with difficult individuals.

Suessmuth, Patrick. "Handling Classroom Problems," *Canadian Training Methods,* October 1975, pp. 26–27.

Based on his personal experience, the article provides suggestions to deal with the big talker, the silent person/group, the person who starts to cry, the late comers, the excessively polite group, undesired conflict in the group, an attack on one person, etc.

Zander, Alvin, *Making Groups Effective,* Jossey-Bass Publishers, San Francisco, California, 1982.

This presents practical advice on making groups stronger and more cohesive; on setting realistic goals and standards; on overcoming obstacles to group decision making; on improving member communication; on coping with conflict and power.

BASIC TECHNIQUES FOR SMALL GROUP TRAINING

Many ideas grow better when transplanted into another mind than in the one where they sprang up.

—Oliver Wendell Holmes Jr.
(1841–1935), Associate Justice,
U.S. Supreme Court

In the prior chapter we discussed in a general way the use of small groups to enhance participant learning. In this chapter we shall present a number of specific small group training techniques that are considered "basic," or relatively easy for the trainer to use. In the following chapter we shall present additional small group techniques, which require more skill and experience on the part of the trainer.

Using Dyads and Triads

The Dyad

The dyad, or pair, is a "sure-fire" participative technique. Every trainer or discussion leader can readily use it to involve the total group—and with remarkable quickness and efficiency. For example, all the trainer need do is to tell the group: "Turn to the person on your right (or your left, or your neighbor behind you) and discuss for five minutes the implications of _____." And presto! The training room is filled with the enthusiastic sound of all the participants partaking of a piece of the action. A skill point: The "turn around" procedure is a good way to meet a new person as opposed to conversing with a pal from the shop or office with whom one is buddied up.

Why does the dyad work practically all the time? Because it places two persons in a no-threat, eyeball-to-eyeball, head-to-head relationship where rapport is easy to achieve (just like starting a conversation with a passenger on a plane) and neither party can readily "escape" from it. Rare, indeed, is the participant who can block out the intimacy that the dyadic encounter provides.

The dyad can be employed in many ways such as to:

☐ Serve as an icebreaker: "Find someone you don't know (at all or very well), introduce yourself and talk about why you are here and what you hope to accomplish in this program."
☐ Encourage thought and discussion about a topic *prior* to its presentation.
☐ Discuss an assigned topic and have a spokesperson report back on it. "What do you think should be done about this issue (or problem, event, situation, development, influence, difficulty, shortcoming, result, conflict)?"
☐ Serve as a team of two observers who are to give feedback about an on-going training activity (e.g., an exercise, a role play).
☐ Give feedback on an exchange basis concerning one's behavior (participation, etc.) in a fishbowl activity. This "private" approach to feedback would be in lieu of the more usual "public" feedback. A procedure of

this sort would be followed when it is evident that fishbowl participants are not ready for public feedback. (Of course, private feedback, since it is not subject to public scrutiny, may be watered down or not given at all.)

☐ Give support (encouragement, ego building) to another group member.

☐ Serve as a two-person training team, where the task is facilitated by working in pairs (e.g., how to lift properly, how to listen).

☐ Orient and/or break in a new employee (the buddy system).

☐ Critique one another's plans or targets (contracting) for back-home improvement.

☐ Resolve a conflict between two group members. For example, in an experiential training program such as team building, the trainer may use "role negotiation" to resolve the interpersonal block; that is, the trainer may start a rational dialogue by asking each party to the conflict to respond to this question: "What do I (John) want (or expect) from Mary (the other party to the conflict)?" And, in reverse: "What do I (Mary) expect from John?"

☐ Confer with another participant concerning the nature of an assignment to ensure full understanding of the ramifications of the assigned task.

☐ Share information about oneself (e.g., regarding management style: whether one feels it is important to be close to subordinates, and if it is, how one goes about it).

☐ Serve as the basis for the formation of a larger group; e.g., a dyad, after discussion of a topic, may be asked to merge with another pair and continue to discuss the topic. Another pair may be added a bit later until six participants are discussing the topic. The added participants should serve to provide more "windows" on the topic and to energize the group.

☐ Use in first aid training, especially in such activities as patient examination; find the pulse in one another's neck and wrist; executing the Heimlich maneuver (when food is stuck in the windpipe); bleeding control; and treating the injured for shock.

In some training programs dyads have been used in more intensive fashion:

☐ In a Consolidated Edison Co. of New York, Inc., "Communication Flow" seminar, 234 first- and second-level supervisors were brought together from all over the company. The objective was to improve horizontal communications in this large organization. Since this very large group was "intimidating," the trainer had the managers pair off, after an icebreaker task, with a person they didn't know. The members of the dyads then interviewed one another to learn about work location, area of specialization, length of service, career history, and job performance areas most praised and criticized. Other small group activities followed the dyadic work. The training program, overall, was intended to establish a "horizontal peer network" across functional areas. Communication and social support were deemed to be more attainable in this fashion than by relying on those above or below the level of the program participants.[1]

☐ In a leadership or human relations program, which runs a week or more, two participants can be assigned to meet each day for 30 minutes. They can discuss topics such as learnings from the course, relationships back on the job or career objectives.

Note
1. If the dyads are scheduled for 30 minutes before lunch, the pair can then go on to lunch together.
2. In a nonurban setting, a dyadic walk and talk through the countryside will provide an added dimension to the experience.

☐ Participants in a management training program can be assigned a different (or possibly the same) luncheon partner each day. At lunch they can build on the discussion that the formal program has initiated.

☐ In a leadership laboratory (sensitivity training or the T-group) pairs can be formed the first morning for an in-depth (one hour) get acquainted session. Weather and other conditions permitting, this can, again, be a "walk and talk" activity.

☐ *Personality perceptions*. In a training program where participants are adequately well-acquainted and it is desirable to provide feedback to one another as to how they are peceived, e.g., in training programs concerned with leadership, team building, assertiveness, or other personal growth areas, the following procedures may be used:

1. Team-up participants in pairs.
2. Provide them with a list of personality characteristics, such as the one below.
3. Have each person in the dyad write his/her partner's first name (use initial only) after the 5 or 6 characteristics which are most descriptive of him/her. Characteristics not on the list may be added in the blank spaces.
4. Repeat step 3, this time each partner selects characteristics most applicable to himself/herself.
5. Ask dyad members to share perceptions of other and self, noting areas of agreement/disagreement. Explanations are to be provided as to why a particular trait was assigned to one's partner. (Total time: 15–20 minutes.)

6. If time allows, repeat the activity with a new partner.
7. Wind up the exercise by securing comments from the pairs. Some questions: Any learning about self? Was there a lot of agreement? Disagreement? Was there candor? Any surprises? How do you feel about your partner?

Note: If the program is designed for "confidence building," instruct the participants to select *positive* traits only.

Figure 3-1 lists some personality characteristics that participants might attribute to one another.

Personality Characteristics				
Flexible	Aggressive	Earnest	Feminine	Stubborn
Playful	Docile	Cheerful	Masculine	Suspicious
Lively	Thoughtful	Self-confident	Calm	Hostile
Social	Receptive	Energetic	Sexy	Angry
Creative	Kind	Practical	Stable	Negative
Optimistic	Cooperative	Conforming	Persuasive	Impatient
Cautious	Pleasant	Submissive	Assertive	Pessimistic
Reserved	Dominating	Organized	Impulsive	Opinionated
Enthusiastic	Timid	Warm	Vigorous	Argumentative
Affable	Humorous	Determined	Open	Competitive

Figure 3-1. A list of personality characteristics participants in "Personality Perceptions" might draw ideas from.

These more intensive dyads provide an opportunity to build a deeper relationship with one or more participants, something that the formal program generally does not provide. (I remember one participant, who when asked how her 11:00 a.m. dyad was working out after two attempts at it, replied facetiously: "I'm not sure, but it does give me someone to go to lunch with every day!")

As to possible limitations of the dyad, it obviously can generate only a lesser amount of data about or insight into an assignment, compared to a larger group (triads or quartets). Also, on rare occasions the dyad may not work out too well because of "bad chemistry" between the two participants (e.g., one person may be timid, hostile, uninformed, extremely nonverbal, not into the program, physically ill).

Note: If you have an odd number of participants and thus need an extra person to form a pair, you, as trainer, can join in and fill that gap.

The Triad

Triads or trios are an important configuration in small group work. They are small enough to provide privacy and intimacy, and at the same time they are large enough to bring a "multiple" viewpoint to bear on a problem or training assignment. They also provide for variety in small group work.

They are particularly useful in certain training situations, such as:

☐ In forming three-person role playing teams—two role players and an observer. For example, the three roles—boss, subordinate, and observer—may be rotated, allowing one triad to participate in all three roles.

☐ In providing help on the completion of an in-depth training assignment, e.g., in working on a project for "back-home" application, the trio operates in this fashion: one person presents his/her project and the other two participants react to it in the form of feedback, critique, help, reality testing. Each person has an opportunity to present his/her project for analysis by the other two members of the trio.

☐ In a stress management workshop, one person presents a stress-laden situation (the participant's or the trainer's) to the other two, e.g., a strong belief that he/she should have gotten a promotion awarded to someone else. One team member presents the irrational or emotional beliefs and attitudes that might be adopted by the non-promotee ("The best qualified person should always be promoted" or "Hard work should be rewarded.") The other team member presents the rational or logical position for the non-promotion action ("In the real world many factors other than merit are at work.") Both team members, in essence, are trying to point out that in any stress situation the irrational factors in our heads—our perceptions—may be as significant to that stress as the external event itself.[2]

☐ Trios may be used as project teams or small task forces to work on an assigned problem. For example, if the program calls for field trips, plant visits, and the like, triads could be formed for such purposes.

☐ To improve communication, interaction, and relationships among key operating officials in an organization, a team of three managers may be sent to an outside facility for special training. For example, the prestigious Center for Creative Leadership, Greensboro, North Carolina, conducts a workshop designed to encourage and facilitate the management of innovation in an organization. Participants attend in triads, teams representing three pertinent functions, e.g., manufacturing, R&D, and marketing. The course works to develop each triad's ability to communicate and coordinate across organizational lines. Through such cross-functional team building, and with an awareness of the organization as a whole, the team will return prepared to help their organization put innovation into practice.

Note: Selection of those to attend the external facility on a joint basis would be based on *need*, e.g., a possible history of less-than-cooperative relationships, mission changes which now require a very high need of cooperation, the impact each manager's function has on the other, and so on. The training experience would not in itself be a substitute for a true team building effort. However, it may lead to better working relationships, greater coordination and communication, and possibly a start toward a more profound effort at team building.

☐ Triads may be formed early in the program to work intermittently (small group work) and to serve as a support system. If a participant group has not worked previously in triads, you may wish to point out that the best position for the triad is one that ensures that participants are "connected" via a very tight circular arrangement. Figure 3-2 illustrates seating arrangements that diminish productivity because eye contact is very difficult. (Since people are not fishes, they don't have eyes on the sides of their head.) Figure 3-3 shows the most effective arrangement.

Note: In most training situations participants are sitting on standard rather than swivel chairs. Hence, unless the chairs are positioned properly by the participants, the furniture may get in the way of their learning.

Figure 3-2. Examples of ineffective seating of triad members.

Figure 3-3. Examples of effective seating of triad members.

The communication dynamics among a triad are quite different from a dyad.[3] In a conversation among a trio, any exchange between two of the parties is automatically subject to observation of the third person. Since the pair in communication is aware that there is an "observer," they become more self-conscious, more aware of their own behavior, and thus tend to behave with greater reasonableness and courtesy. This subtle social control serves to make the threesome more relaxed than a duo.

Other advantages of a triad: If a conflict arises or seems to erupt, the third person may serve as a "mediator" (voice of reason) between the two disagreeing parties. In addition, unlike in the dyad, one member can intermittently reduce his/her involvement/interaction and can take a "breather," i.e., become a listener, only offering a comment now and then. Finally, it is easy for a party to disengage totally. He/she simply picks an opportune time to leave, e.g., when the pair is so engrossed in conversation, one can leave with the clear implication that his/her presence is no longer needed. The departure may be accomplished without an oral comment since the conversing dyad recognizes that the third person is out of the conversation.

You should also be aware that the dynamics of a triad can make for a certain amount of conflict. Why? Because one member may team up with another, producing an "odd person out" situation. This phenomenon of rejection is particularly likely to occur if the triad is composed of two men and one woman. One man may "hit it off" with the woman leaving the other man in a rejected state. Of course, the "pairing off" problem can also occur in a triad of two women and one man in which one woman is left out. An answer to the possible pairing-off/rejection problem is to have the three participants collectively and candidly explore their feelings about their interpersonal relationships.

Skill pointer: If a dyad is "struggling" because of differences in personality, capability, interest, or enthusiasm level, consider adding a third party to alter the interaction/communication pattern. Also, replacing a member of a struggling triad may "revitalize" the unit.

Producing Definitions

At one or more points in a training program, terms must be defined: motivation, time, discipline, coaching, counseling, manager, sexual harassment, women's liberation, etc. Although the trainer readily can provide a definition, it frequently is more thought-provoking to participants if they, individually and/or in small groups, create one of their own. You can anticipate, of course, that different individuals and small groups will produce different definitions. Thus, the learning, at a minimum, is that you cannot take for granted essentially complex terms—there are varying perceptions about them.

Sometimes a certain definition of a term or the term itself may not be acceptable to participants; e.g., discipline may be considered too "harsh" a concept. Thus, you may ask the group for other more acceptable terms. You might use a flipchart for this procedure.

DISCIPLINE (put an X through it and ask for more acceptable terms)
CORRECTING (more acceptable)
TRAINING (more acceptable)

If a term or concept is quite complex and defies ready agreement as to its definition, you can use this divergence of opinion to construct an exercise or activity along the following lines:

□ Ask each person in a mixed group (men and women) to define first a woman and then a man. A T-Column on a flipchart or a previously prepared sheet of paper can be used as a guide by the participants as shown:

Adjectives and Roles that Describe or Define

A Man	A Woman

Have participants meet in small groups (quartets or quintets) to compare definitions. Instruct them to look for stereotypes as to role (e.g., the woman must take care of the children) and traits (e.g., men are more creative or more artistic or more athletic). Then secure feedback from the small groups as to principal learnings from the exercise.

Note: A variation is to put all the completed T-columns in a box and have participants select on a random basis new sheets for analysis.

□ Assign a definition to several small groups. Tell them that their definition will be judged by an impartial panel which will select a winner. The criteria for the decision will be based on:
   a. Quality (maximum 15 points)
   b. Creativity (maximum 10 points)
   c. Language or phraseology (maximum 10 points)
Select the judges either from outside the class, if practicable, or from the group at large. You may wish to provide a small prize to the winning team.

□ In the selling area, it may be essential to introduce (or reacquaint) sales personnel with the "feature-benefit" concept. A good way to do this is to begin with a definition of the product or service concerned. To illustrate, let's assume our product is a toaster.

Definition: A toaster is an electrically powered appliance used primarily in the kitchen to produce dry bread quickly. Since everyone knows that much about a toaster,

Product: Toaster

Features	Benefits
1. Electronic sensor	No need to adjust control for dryness for it is done automatically and thus can never burn the bread. It also saves energy.
2. Expandable receptacle	Permits toasting thick slices of bread, muffins, rolls, biscuits, etc. and even handles irregular shapes and sizes.
3. Plastic cover, insulated	It doesn't heat up like metal so there is no danger of hand burns.
4. Push-button tray removal	Simplifies removal of tray which captures crumbs.
5. Extended warranty (10-year period) because of its advanced precision engineering	High quality all-around permits you to buy it and forget about replacements or annoying minor repairs.

Figure 3-4. Example of using a T-column to distinguish between features and benefits.

it is hardly a reason why a customer should be interested in our product as opposed to the dozen or more that our competitors make. Hence we need to provide additional information about our product that will make the prospect take real notice. We do this by moving from definition to features and benefits: This toaster has an electronic sensor, an expandable receptacle or well, an insulated plastic cover, push-button tray removal, and extended warranty. But your customer wants to know: "What's in it for me?" A T-column can help here as in Figure 3-4.

Developing and Working with Lists

A thought-provoking and easy-to-administer task for small groups is to have the participants develop a list and then have them process it in some fashion. The simplest format is for the trainer to state: "Come up with a list on _____ (problems, goals, challenges, reinforcers, characteristics of something, concerns, satisfactions, worries, strengths, needs, causes, etc.)."

Other formats follow:

Priority Development
The task is to develop a list and then prioritize all the items on it. The criterion for prioritizing may be on the basis of creative value, criticalness or urgency, cost, feasibility, etc. Two possible lists are a list of stressors on the job and a list of needs retirees will have in the post-retirement period.

Weight and Rank
Another form of prioritizing is to have participants develop a list—each item on the list subject to a weight of ten votes (maximum). All members of the group vote (1–10) on each item, thereby producing a ranked preferences list. For example, members of the ORI (Organiza-

ORI NETWORK MEETING
April 9, 1980
"WHAT ARE WE PLEASED TO SEE IN THE FIELD OF HRD IN 1982"?

	Number of Votes	Element
1.	17	Career and life planning systems are installed within the new educational system, organizations and corporations
2.	15	The public school system is organized for the benefit of each individual child
3.	12	We have standards of certification for trainers and consultants.
4.	12	The American Management Association and National Institutes of Health have declared a requirement for meditation and reflection periods to improve quality of work life.
5.	11	More follow through on recommendations has been developed with the help of consultants
6.	10	We have a free and functioning clearing house for consultants and trainers.
7.	10	There is greater concern with values and purpose (organizational and individual)
8.	9	Organizations realize the value of and support training at all levels.
9.	9	Many members of the Third World emerging governments are involved in our training workshops and are inviting us to theirs.
10.	7	There are more academic training courses on consulting.
11.	7	There are better systems for predicting and producing future outcomes.
12.	7	There are closer links to organization goals and the activities of trainers.
13.	7	There is more EEO development and involvement.
14.	6	There is an increased commitment to stress management.
15.	6	Greater line involvement in HRD.
16.	5	There is greater emphasis on development of in-house staff competencies.
17.	5	There is more scientific rigor in consulting.
18.	5	There are more in-house consultants and trainers.

Figure 3-5. Example of a ranked preference list. (Reproduced by permission of Organization Renewal, Inc., Washington, D.C.)

tion Renewal, Inc., Washington, D.C.), a sophisticated, highly professional trainer-consultant network, produced a weighted list (in April 1980) on "What Are We Pleased to See in the Field of Resource Development in 1982?" (See Figure 3-5.)

Enrich the List

Give the participants a "starter" list of three to four items and ask them to expand on it.

Complementary Pairs

The task is to develop data in list form on "complementary pairs" such as parent-child, teacher-student, doctor-patient, husband-wife, male-female, boss-employee, consultant-client, coach-trainee, performer-audience.

Opposing Pairs

A list is developed on contrasting elements such as cause-effect, cost-benefit, most-least, newest-oldest, the practical-the impractical, etc. (Data on the complementary and opposing pairs can be collected via a T-column or posted on separate flipcharts.)

We Need to Know

Ask participants to provide "must have" type of data. For example, in a time management course the task may be as follows: "We need to know what time it is to _____ (keep appointments, eat our meals, watch our favorite TV program)."

Question List

Participants are asked to develop a list of questions rather than statements, such as: What questions would you use to interview properly a prospective secretary (or director of marketing, or personnel manager, etc.)? What questions should a manager use to conduct a good career development interview?

Making Decisions

Ask participants to come up with as many options or courses of action as they can regarding a possible decision on a problem (e.g., handling a marginal employee, conducting supervisory training). Then for each option have participants list its pros and cons, thereby ensuring a carefully thought-out decision.

Causes/Reasons

Have participants individually develop a list of ten reasons or causes for problem areas such as failure to sell successfully, failure to delegate properly, failure to communicate properly, high accident rates, and lack of cooperation in an organization.

Ask a participant to read aloud the most important reason from his/her list, and then ask the group for solutions to the reason given. Then have another participant offer his/her most significant reason and, again, secure group solutions. Continue the process until everyone has had a chance to present a cause or reason for resolution by the group.

Criteria Development

Ask participants to develop a list of criteria for such matters as: evaluating communication effectiveness in an organization; resolving conflicts between offices; giving feedback; conducting a coaching (or any other kind of) interview; making a sound decision; and administering an effective safety program. (One way to introduce this assignment is to say: "If you had to measure or assess the effectiveness of your promotion plan, what would you look at?").

After the participants have developed their lists, they may be asked to prioritize them, share them in small groups, develop a "master" list for each group on a flipchart, and post the flipcharts on the wall for total group review and discussion.

Bug List

Ask participants to develop a list of the things which are "bugging" the operation, the team, the organization, etc.

Wish List

Have participants imagine or brainstorm as many "wishes" as they can concerning something. This is done without concern for their feasibility since the idea is to trigger insights.

Advice Giving

Have participants describe the advice they would give to another on a particular concern (e.g., "My advice to the manager who wishes to manage his boss properly is to _____ ").

Expanding the List

At times it may be desirable to have participants develop a list that can be expanded upon or added to continuously *after* the training. For example, in an assertiveness training program participants may be asked to develop a list of needs they feel they have a right to have met, such as to return an item to a store or to ask one's boss for feedback about one's performance. Group members are then told to keep this list and add to it frequently as their personal growth continues.

Quantity Considerations

From a quantity standpoint, you can present the task of developing a list as:

Unlimited. Ask for as many items as possible. This is the old "laundry list" idea. (In fact, the task can be introduced as follows: "Come up with a 'laundry list' regarding the skills the effective supervisor must have.") The aim of this approach is to stimulate broad thinking on a given topic.

Limited. Here we are seeking a well-screened list pertaining to something. For example: "Agree upon the three most significant characteristics of an effective leader?" Note that we are asking the small groups to *agree* upon something which gives them an added challenge to perform well.

In both the limited and the unlimited requests, we can build competition (added motivation to perform) into the task if we wish. An example is: "We have four small groups. Let's see which group can come up with the most suggestions or ideas on how to use secretaries effectively. You have fifteen minutes to do this." In some instances a prize may be offered to augment interest.

Task Assignment Considerations

From a task assignment standpoint, the request to develop a list can also be presented differently:

□ *Oral vs. written.* You have the option of giving your instructions verbally, putting them on the chalkboard or flipchart, or providing them on an instruction sheet. The written instructions are preferred if you need to ensure clarity of the assigned task or if you desire to operate more formally, e.g., in respect to a course or program which is to be presented uniformly by different trainers.

□ *Structured vs. unstructured.* When using a worksheet we can do this in a relatively unstructured fashion by simply stating the task on the top of the paper. The remaining white space is the area to be filled in. Conversely, we can add motivation by giving participants a structured worksheet which in effect sets up numerical targets for them. An example of a structured worksheet is given in Appendix 11.

□ *Public vs. anonymous.* Although lists ordinarily are developed for publicly posting the items, there may be instances when participants may wish to treat their data more privately. For example, in an in-house stress management workshop public listing of one's sources of stress may be perceived by some participants as too threatening. In such circumstances, each participant may develop a separate or private list. The trainer would then collect the lists and randomly post the stressors on the flipchart for further action or discussion.

□ *Individual vs. group.* Assignments can be made directly to individuals, directly to groups or to both individuals and then to groups. In the latter instance, we use a two-stage process:

1. Individual work for ideation.
2. Small group work to consolidate (combine, screen) the individual lists.

The final steps in list development, regardless of our approach to generating quantity or quality, are to:

1. Post them (preferably on flipcharts) for public display.
2. Hold a group-at-large discussion about them.
3. Process the data in other ways; for example, a list of problems on employee discipline (violation of safety rules, lateness, insubordination, etc.) may form the basis for role plays wherein the supervisor has to coach, counsel, or reprimand the offender in some way.

Trainer-Developed Lists

The previous paragraphs have been devoted to the development of lists by participants. It is also possible for the trainer to provide participants with lists which they can work from. For example, in a stress management program participants may be given the two lists in Figure 3-6 and asked to circle those items in each list which relate to their current circumstances. The selected items are then shared and discussed in pairs or triads.

Note: The same format used in Figure 3-6 could be used for other topics. Some examples: What I would like my work to be/What I would not like my work to be; What I would like my career to be/What I would not like my career to be; What I would like my work group to be like/What I would not like my work group to be like.

Sharing Personal Incidents

Group members can be quickly and significantly involved by asking them to draw on their past experience for incidents or events which relate to or exemplify course concepts. Some examples of tasks which might be assigned:

Payoff Discussion
Where did careful listening (or planning, or customer relations, or reinforcing desirable behavior) pay off? Have participants discuss their incidents in small groups and then secure reports from the small groups on the importance of these events.

Helped-Hindered Approach
Divide the total group into buzz groups with one set of groups to come up with personal experiences wherein their boss failed to (or was reluctant to) delegate or hin-

dered delegation. The other set of groups reports on the opposite—where delegation was accomplished and how it affected them favorably.

An alternate topic relates to incidents when the supervisor was a coach who encouraged personal growth/versus instances where the supervisor's poor coaching was detrimental to growth.

Note: A T-column on a flipchart to collect small group data can help sharpen the issue.

A variation on these procedures is to have the participants respond to the assignment on an individual basis before the small group work. The individual work can be facilitated via a worksheet as given in Appendix 12. By reducing the incidents to writing, participants are aided to think through the ramifications of the event in more precise and meaningful detail.

Influence vs. Authority
Have participants in small groups share instances where they, as supervisors, got something important done with subordinates because of the influence they had as opposed to the authority they had and could have used. Then show a film (or give a lecturette) on informal authority or leadership. Discuss the film (or talk) in relation to the previously discussed personal experiences with influence.

New Worker Orientation
To start a supervisory training session on the orientation of the new worker, assign participants to small groups. One set of groups is to cite personal experiences they recall when their orientation was very effective; the other set of groups produces examples of orientations they experienced which were not effective. Post examples to a flipchart, using the T-column again, compare the two sets of examples and develop from them principles of orientation.

Card Draw
Using a set of topics on cards that you have previously developed, have each participant draw a card and cite a personal experience pertinent to the card. For example, in a supervisory (or sales) training course the cards might read as follows:

☐ The best boss I ever had_____.
☐ As a supervisor (or salesperson) the most important thing I've learned is_____.
☐ An employee I almost gave up on but didn't was
_____.
☐ My most successful case of delegation (or selling) was_____.
☐ The most important thing I ever did for my self-development was_____.

I see work as	I see my life style/situation as
a challenge	adventuresome
opportunity	confining
pleasure	draining
a chore	exhilarating
tedious	buoyant
travel/field trips	affluent
new experiences	neutral
repetitious	care-free
wearing	over-extended
all pay	balanced
new contacts	harried
reports	worrisome
in-basket	successful
growth-oriented	pleasing
a hassle	growth-inducing
endless	oppressive
energizing	rapid-paced
professional	relaxed
tops	fulfilling
enervating	anxiety-laden
dull	joyful
stimulating	questionable
rewarding	superficial
stifling	casual
delightful	meaningless
treadmill	zestful

Figure 3-6. Example of a trainer-provided list for participant response.

☐ An experience I had which really made me feel good as a supervisor (or salesperson) was_____ .

Note
1. The cards should be written so that practically everyone can come up with a personal incident relating to it. If not, have the participant put the card back in the deck and allow the drawing of another card.
2. This activity should make for a good opener in a supervisory (or sales) training course.

Goal Setting

In an MBO (Management by Objectives) or goal setting training program, have participants:

1. Individually select a key task (major responsibility) in one's job and come up with the "indicators" or control data governing it. (For example, indicators concerning the success or failure of an executive recruitment program, in the case of a personnel director's job, would be: the number recruited, the quality of the recruits as measured by annual performance data, meeting of deadlines, adherance to budget.)
2. Meet in pairs or trios to discuss the validity of their selected indicators.
3. Hold a general discussion regarding the value of indicators, the difficulty if any in identifying them, problems of validity (are they measuring what they are supposed to?), etc.

Best-Worst Approach

Ask participants to think of incidents in best-worst terms, e.g.:

☐ The best boss I ever had did_____ .
☐ The worst boss I ever had did_____ .
☐ The best communicator I ever knew did_____ .
☐ The worst communicator I ever knew did_____ .
☐ My most successful sales experience occurred when
_____ .
☐ My least successful sales experience occurred when
_____ .

Note: The individually developed data can be processed either in small groups or the total group.

Near-Miss Analysis

In a safety program ask participants to recall "near-miss" accidents they have seen or experienced personally. Then record them on a flipchart. Use a tri-column, to aid the group to understand better the causative factors involved and how to minimize or remove them:

Near-Miss Analysis Chart

Near-miss Incidents	Causes	Preventive Measures

To conclude the near-miss analysis activity, give participants a blank copy of the preceeding worksheet. Encourage them to use it wherever accidents may occur—on the job, at home, on vacations, on the highway, etc. Point out, too, that near-miss accidents cannot be dismissed lightly, for they are indicators, or even warning signs, of hazards to guard against.

Prediction

A means of introducing a topic in an interest-generating and involving way is to use the technique of "prediction." For example, assume you are introducing brainstorming to a group that is not familiar with it in the full sense of the term. You thus might start out in this fashion: "We're going to have some skill practice in working with the technique of brainstorming. But before we have our brainstorming session let's go around the room and get some words, phrases, characteristics, or qualities that describe brainstorming as you understand it."

The elicited ideas or adjectives then are posted to the flipchart. You then say: "O.K. this describes brainstorming as you see it. Let's run this set of slides and see what they tell us about brainstorming. We'll then compare our ideas—essentially a prediction—with those on the slides."

After the slide presentation the ideas presented by the group can be compared and checked off as to their appropriateness. *Note:* Be complimentary concerning the predicted items which were on target. (For the use of prediction in working with films, see Chapter 15.)

Group Debates

Debates are a helpful way of exploring opposing sides of an issue. If done on a team basis rather than via the more typical individual basis, everyone can "play." Suggested procedures are:

Formal Debate
The following is a step-by-step procedure for organizing a debate:

1. Assume the total group size is 19. Set up four debating teams of four each, two teams taking the pro side of the issue and two the negative side. Advise the teams that their positions can be presented by one or more members.

2. Appoint as judges the remaining three members. Give them criteria to judge the debate: force (logic, powerfulness) of argument (10 points maximum); creative ideas produced (20 points maximum); etc.
3. Provide for adequate preparation time (20–30 minutes).
4. Set time limits for the presentations (5–7 minutes).
5. Have one quartet present the affirmative position and another the negative.
6. Have another quartet present a rebuttal to the negative view and have the last team of four rebut the affirmative position.
7. Have the judges retreat for their deliberations.
8. Conduct a group-at-large discussion as a "wrap-up" to the debate.
9. Have the judges announce the results of the debate. *Note:* It is desirable to have the judges' decision come after all discussion has been completed. This procedure will avoid an over-emphasis on who "won" and who "lost."

Informal Debate

A less formal way of debating is as follows:

1. Announce a topic that has a potential for differences of view.
2. Ask participants to select the pro or con side of the issue.
3. Ask the "pros" to move to one side of the room, the "cons" to the other. (Try to have the two sides be roughly equal in number.)
4. Ask each group to muster all the arguments it can for its position.
5. With the groups in their different locations, informally secure affirmative and negative arguments. Continue the debate until the topic is adequately discussed.

Note: This highly participative procedure is particularly useful to introduce a session or a topic. It may also be used on an *ad hoc* basis when opinions differ in the course of a discussion.

Facing Chairs

Another way to deal with a controversial issue is to place the chairs in two lines so that participants can face one another. Then use these procedures:

1. Seat everyone, e.g., seven participants (the pros) in one row and seven participants (the cons) in the other.
2. Let the pros state their arguments to the cons.
3. Now let the cons state their arguments to the pros.
4. Shift participants to the opposite chairs so that the pros are now the cons and vice versa.

5. Have all the "new" pros state arguments for the pro side.
6. Have the "new" cons state the arguments for the con side.
7. Hold a general discussion, noting if there is a shift away from the earlier polarized views.

Note: In contrast to the fishbowl (see Chapter 4) where one group is active and the other is silent, in this technique *both* groups are interacting with each other.

Seeking Consensus

A variation on the typical "win-lose" debating procedure, such as the ones just described, is to have the teams strive for consensus. Here are the procedures:

1. Divide the full group into two teams, one taking the positive view and the other the negative side of a controversial issue.
2. Have each team discuss its position "in private" (20–30 minutes).
3. Have each team appoint a spokesperson to articulate its position. Allow five minutes for each presentation.
4. Have each team present a rebuttal to the initially stated position of the opposing team (three minutes). Have the teams select another spokesperson for the rebuttal.
5. Now ask each team member to contribute $1.00 (or more) to "a kitty." Tell them it will go to "a worthy cause," which will be explained shortly.
6. Tell the participants that they are now to start a second phase of the debate. This phase requires the *total* group to reach a consensus on the issue. (Allow 30–45 minutes for this). Advise participants that if they reach a consensus, you will add 50% of the amount already contributed to the kitty, to be spent by the group in any way it wishes. But if they do *not* agree in the time allotted, you will pocket all the money.
7. After the time is elapsed, discuss with the total group such issues as the ease or difficulty of achieving consensus on a controversial issue, the importance of money as a motivator, how they felt about the trainer arbitrarily setting ground rules involving money, the application of this debating procedure to the back home situation, etc.

Research on Controversy

How well do participants learn from debates, controversy, etc.? An experiment involving 84 sixth graders in a Minnesota school indicated that controversy may be a valuable learning device.[4] Three student groups were set up along these lines:

☐ *Controversy group.* Half the group were told to defend strip mining, the other half to oppose it. But the group as a whole had to reach a consensus on the issue.

☐ *Concurrence seeking group.* Their instructions were to decide whether to strip mine coal, but to avoid arguments, stress agreement, and compromise quickly.

☐ *Individual work.* Each student in this group worked on the issue without talking to others about it.

The results were these:

Those in the *controversy group* saw the others reach an opposite conclusion and thus felt their own new point challenged. Since no one could be sure that he/she was right, additional information had to be secured. This meant everyone was forced to articulate their positions and try to understand that of the others, too. After arguing one's views, a joint conclusion was reached and, per the study, this group had a better grasp of the material.

Those in the *concurrence seeking* group suppressed differences to achieve a compromise, became fixed in their positions, were reluctant to explore options, and failed to see validity in different perspectives. They later expressed dislike of the other students and the subject matter!

Those *working alone* did not need to elaborate their position. Since they were unaware of other alternatives, they closed their options prematurely.

The conclusions of the study: Openness to alternative views means better communication and problem solving; clearer thinking results in better management of conflict and ethical reasoning.

Trial for Error (Mock Trial)

This group-in-action technique is an old standby, entailing a "trial by a jury" for some "egregious" behavior. Examples of "crimes" for which its perpetrators could be "prosecuted" are

☐ A lost sale
☐ A lost customer
☐ Failure to delegate
☐ Failure to develop an able subordinate who, as a consequence, leaves the organization
☐ Failure to conduct an appraisal interview
☐ Failure to level in the appraisal interview
☐ Failure to face up to widespread bad morale caused by an overbearing key assistant who reports to you
☐ Reluctance to develop a needed policy
☐ Toleration of unsafe work practices or conditions

Unless the group is unusually large, the jury trial provides the opportunity to establish roles for everyone:

☐ The Defendant
☐ Attorney for the defense (this may be a single participant or a team of two or three)
☐ Witnesses for the defense (optional; useful if more roles are needed to involve everyone)
☐ The Prosecuting Attorney
☐ Witnesses for the prosecution (optional)
☐ Judge
☐ Jury (12 participants including a foreperson)
☐ Bailiff (very optional for this is only a nonsubstantive role)

To give the "courtroom" adequate atmosphere, try to have the judge seated at a higher level complete with black robe and gavel.

Remember, the "secrets" to a good jury trial are:

☐ Careful casting of the key characters.
☐ Adequate preparation by the key participants—attorneys, witnesses, defendant.
☐ Allowing enough time for the case to be developed in the court.
☐ Allowing enough time for the jury to weigh the evidence before it reaches a decision. Have these deliberations take place publicly so everyone in the group can listen to the issues again and in another, possibly more "objective," setting.

Circular Whip

With everyone (maximum of 10–15) seated in a circle, "whip" around it and allow everyone to make a *single,* brief contribution on an assigned topic. As illustrations, this may be on:

☐ My major goal in this program
☐ The most important trait of an effective leader
☐ What really counts in customer relations
☐ As I see motivation
☐ A key to accident prevention
☐ My most important learning in this program

The whip, as a round robin device, adds elements of novelty, energy, and involvement to a session or program.

The Circular Whip is effective only in a relatively small total group. This follows since it would be extremely awkward, for example, to seat 30–50 participants in a circle and then solicit their opinions. In a large participant group, two or more such whips may be conducted simultaneously.

Learning from Field Trips

Visits to points of interest away from the training room, wherever practicable, are advantageous because they:

☐ Are a means of enriching the training experience.
☐ Are particularly essential if much of the training is theoretical and conceptual.
☐ Provide a desirable change of pace.
☐ Provide an opportunity for participants to get to know one another in a more in-depth way.
☐ May provide fun, excitement, novelty, new motivation to learn, and so on.
☐ Provide a chance to develop oral and/or written communication skills in respect to the reporting phase of the trip.

To maximize results from field trips, these guidelines should be considered:

1. Be certain that the objectives of the trip are well defined and related to the central purposes of a given training unit and/or the total training program. Literally ask yourself: Is this trip really necessary?
2. Plan logistics properly: who to contact, how to reach the visitation point, when to arrive, when to depart.
3. Provide written instructions to the participants concerning what to look for at the point of visitation. Also provide appropriate background materials.
4. Indicate whether the work is done individually, in pairs, in small groups, etc.
5. Indicate what kind of tasks participants are responsible for upon return to class: a report (written or oral), a case study, a completed survey, summaries of interviews, certain documentation such as photographs, collection of materials, etc.
6. Schedule enough time for the processing of the learnings from the field trip.
7. Secure feedback (evaluation) from the group concerning the trip. This will enable you to strengthen your programming for future trips.

Field trips obviously may be organized as a total group activity, with each member being *individually* responsible for observing and reporting on his/her experience. However, our concern is with the use of small groups or teams of two to five who engage in the field trip.

Mastering Reference Material

At times it is desirable to have participants become familiar with various resources or reference material. This may be textual material in a notebook, a set of handouts, policies/procedures in a manual, etc. One way to do this is to:

1. Establish teams of two to four participants.
2. Assign several problems to the teams which can be answered by checking the reference work. This is essentially the "open book" method used frequently in college courses.
3. Secure reports from the teams concerning their findings.

Note: The "research" may be done in class or treated as a homework assignment.

Saying Goodbye

Typically, courses or programs end with the trainer and the participants saying goodbye to one another. And for all practical purposes all meaningful contacts are ended. Of course, on occasion a participant may drop the trainer a note of appreciation or even telephone to ask for some help. Formal follow-ups by the trainer, either in the form of post-course sessions or some type of contracting (action plans), may also prolong the contact for a month or two.

One way you can continue the relationship is to offer continuing assistance to the departing participants. A sample form for participants to use in seeking post-program assistance is found in Appendix 13. Thus, you may say: "Now that we've met and worked together, I would like very much to be in touch with you even though the program has ended. So when you turn in your evaluation form, please pick-up two or three of those forms on the table. I have also provided envelopes addressed to me. The envelopes will make it easy for you to contact me for any help you may think I can offer."

Note: While techniques for saying goodbye may also apply to large training groups, the request to "keep in touch" takes on special and significant meaning with a relatively small total group (10–20). Why? Because the trainer has been in a position to establish rapport with all or nearly all group members, something which cannot happen with a larger total group.

In an experiential training program one way to close things out is to have participants stand and form a tight circle, arms firmly around one another's shoulders. Then ask for a volunteer to say something positive or complimentary about the person on one's immediate right and then indicate one's primary learning from the program. Repeat the process until everyone has participated. As a final (optional) step, participants may say goodbye via a hug with the person next to him/her.

Key Points

1. Small group work, by definition, includes dyads and triads as well as buzz groups. Dyads provide intimacy and thus instant interaction. Triads have the advantage of offering multiple views on the problem being discussed.
2. Assignments to small groups typically assume the form of a question or problem. Other ways to challenge small groups are to ask them to produce a definition, develop a list, share personal incidents, and make a prediction.
3. Producing a definition requires group members to engage in focused rather than generalized thinking. The "pressure" of agreeing on a definition intensifies the learning experience.
4. Producing a "laundry list" on a subject challenges participants to tap fully the resources of the group.
5. Sharing of personal incidents has the merit of introducing "live" data into the discussion. Realism is thus substituted for someone else's experience and problems.
6. Additional ways to involve participants are via group debate, field trips, "trial by jury," the circular whip, and mastering reference material.
7. In closing out a training program, attention should be given to procedures for saying goodbye.

References

1. *Training/HRD* (December 1981), pp. 16–17.
2. This example is adapted from "A Cognitive Approach to Stress Management," *Behavior Today* (March 2, 1981), p. 7.
3. "Conversation In Two's or Three's?," *The Pryor Report*, September 1987, p. 5 (from the book by Emile Pin, *The Pleasure of Your Company: A Socio-Psychological Analysis of Modern Society*, Praeger, New York, 1985).
4. "Minnesota Experiment Shows Controversy May Be Teaching Aid," *Leading Edge Bulletin* (February 1, 1982), pp. 1, 3.

Recommended Reading

Davis, Larry N. and McCallon, E., *Planning, Conducting and Evaluating Workshops,* Learning Concepts, Austin, Texas, 1974.

This presents an overview of workshop planning and management from the standpoint of adult education. A section on methods is included.

McLagan, Patricia A., *Helping Others Learn: Designing Programs for Adults,* Addison-Wesley Publishing Company, Reading, Massachusetts, 1978.

This approaches the training function from the standpoint of the learner, and focuses on these components of the learning process: motivation, information processing (using appropriate methods and strategies to facilitate learning), learning results, and learning application and transfer.

ADDITIONAL TECHNIQUES FOR SMALL GROUP TRAINING

The only kind of learning which significantly influences behavior is self-discovered or self-appropriated learning—truth that has been assimilated in experience.

—Carl R. Rogers, U.S. humanistic psychologist, founder of client-centered or nondirective counseling/therapy

The prior chapter discussed a number of basic training techniques for small group work. In this chapter we will present a number of added small group training techniques, all of which require more skill and experience on the part of the trainer. They are:

☐ The fishbowl
☐ Working with "mind pictures"—fantasy, guided imagery, etc.
☐ Working with pictures
☐ Using art
☐ Using music
☐ The journal or diary
☐ Working with models

Other chapters will deal with additional methods wherein groups are put to work very actively, particularly via role playing (Chapter 5), games and simulations (Chapter 6), exercises (Chapter 7), puzzles (Chapter 8), and instrument-data analysis (Chapter 9). The chapters on problem solving (Chapters 10, 11, and 12) treat other group-in-action methods such as brainstorming, working with metaphor and analogy, etc.

The Fishbowl

Also known as clusters or the group-on-group technique, the fishbowl is a highly worthwhile tool for the trainer who is interested in dynamic group involvement methods.

The fishbowl can assume several configurations. Its most common form is simply an inner ring (Group A), which is the discussion group, surrounded by an outer ring (Group B), which is the observation group, as shown in Figure 4-1.

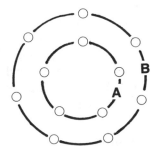

Figure 4-1. Diagram of a typical fishbowl.

The inner group can be given an assignment based on content, processing, or content and processing. If the assignment is one of content you ask the inner circle (Group A) to address itself for 10–30 minutes to a given subject such as production problems, scouting the competition, the sales program, how to improve communications (or safety, or employee morale, or field relations, or supplier relations). The outer group (Group B) observes silently.

After the inner circle's time is up, the outer circle can be asked to respond to the same assignment as Group A had, or comment on Group A's deliberations, or do both. It is also practicable at times to repeat the same process a second time. Each group thus engages in discussion and observation twice.

If anxiety exists in the inner circle because of the presence of the observers in the outer cluster, it (the anxiety) should be processed. By talking about it, the imagined fear can be readily allayed. Conversely, until the anxiety has been acknowledged orally, the inner group is likely to be inhibited in its discussion.

In discussing process as opposed to content, the inner group focuses on the behavior of the other group as a functioning unit. In effect, one small group is giving the other small group feedback about its performance or behavior. The feedback may relate to individual or group functioning, or both.

Note: An alternative to public discussion of individual behavior is to process such data privately in dyads (pairs). This more private procedure may be essential if one senses that participants are not ready for the more usual public feedback. But a possible shortcoming of this procedure is that in the absence of group surveillance the feedback may be toned down or not given at all.

Guide sheets for observation of both group behavior and individual functioning are given in Appendices 14 and 15.

Fishbowls work best when the inner and outer groups are small in number—not more than ten persons. The smaller group ensures more "air time" for everyone and encourages greater willingness to contribute.

If the total training group is fairly large, e.g., 20–30 participants, there is no reason why 2 to 4 fishbowls cannot operate simultaneously. A good-sized room or separate rooms will facilitate this operation. You should try to monitor all fishbowls a bit to get a feel for what is being said. Data that is picked up in this way can be used as feedback in the summary session.

Additional Configurations

Fishbowl configurations other than the basic type just described are these:

☐ Place an empty chair in the center of the discussion group or in the ring itself as in Figure 4-2. Then allow anyone from the outer circle to take the empty chair at anytime for one minute and use it as a springboard to interject his/her comment or viewpoint.

Figure 4-2. Diagram showing two options for placing the empty chair in a fishbowl configuration.

Another way for a member of the outer circle to get into the act is to allow someone in the outer circle to tap the shoulder of someone in the inner circle every three minutes and take the inner member's place. The new fishbowl member may then amplify, clarify, disagree, call attention to silent participants, etc.

Each of the two empty chair techniques has a specific purpose. If the participant sits on the empty chair inside the circle, the purpose is to engage in an interaction with everyone in the inner ring. If the participant sits on the empty chair within the ring, he/she is merely trying to enter the discussion as an added fishbowl participant.

Added involvement of the observers is possible via this procedure:

1. Let the inner circle (Group A) discuss the assigned topic or problem (15–20 minutes).
2. Then have those in Group A turn around and secure feedback from those in the outer circle (Group B), on a one-on-one basis, recalling what was heard and the related feelings.
3. Group A returns to its prior discussion mode, integrating into the new round of discussion the comments of Group B (10–15 minutes).
4. Groups A and B switch places and Group B is now the discussion group (15–25 minutes).

☐ Assume you have three or four fishbowls going simultaneously. Upon completion of these data-generating discussions, have one or two representatives from each cluster join with their colleagues to form a new fishbowl. In effect, we have in action a new set of A and B groups of four to eight members each. The objective is to augment or enrich total input on a given problem but one drawback is that not everyone can participate, for the rest of the groups' participants are only observers. To overcome this problem, allow the observers to interject at five or ten minute intervals.

☐ A variation of the preceding procedure is to have several clusters work on a problem and then have each small group select a representative to present its views in the center cluster.[1] The four representatives would discuss the problem for 10–20 minutes and then return to their respective small groups for further discussion. Again, a representative (preferably another person) from each small group would join the cluster. You might elicit specific proposals for action and post them on a flipchart. This procedure is particularly useful in conflict management.

☐ A novel way to improve interaction and possibly understanding of the view of others is to "mix up" the groups after one or two usual rounds of fishbowl activity. Thus, if you began with six participants from sales and six from production, you might set up a fishbowl with a new mix: two clusters, each having three members from sales and three members from production.

☐ It is also possible to use the same cluster groups but to have them switch their positions or arguments. Thus, in your Sales—Production fishbowl situation, after one or two usual fishbowl encounters, you might ask each side to argue the other's position. This would force verbalization of the other viewpoint and thus promote understanding of the position taken by the other group.

Fishbowl Uses and Limitations

To put the fishbowl in proper perspective, you can say that the fishbowl has a number of highly worthwhile, dynamic uses. These are:

As a problem solving tool. By having one cluster listen to and critique the other, and vice versa, a great deal of interaction and stimulation is engendered. In essence, this is putting "sparks" into the communication and problem-solving process.

As a tool to generate divergent views. The fishbowl can be particularly helpful when it is essential to learn of perceptions from groups having divergent viewpoints, such as headquarters and field, line and staff, sales and production, "old line" people and minorities, parents and teenagers, men and women, etc.

For team building. The fishbowl is a long-time tool of many trainers who work in the area of team building. It is used so widely because it is a powerful tool to get people to open up, to generate divergent views, and to hold these views up for analysis.

For improvement of intergroup communication and relations. By bringing divergent groups together, conflict can be worked through. The dynamics involved are these: possibly for the first time, "warring" groups are given the opportunity to listen seriously to one another. In time, both groups learn that neither group is totally "on the side of the angels."

As an icebreaker. In experiential training programs, the fishbowl is very useful to get people into action quickly. This approach is not recommended for more conventional, didactic training programs, particularly those having very cautious participants.

To learn of group behavior. As has already been indicated, this is a good way to study the dynamics of groups—leadership, membership, decision making, communication processes—and to give feedback on them.

As an agenda setting device. Some groups can work well with the fishbowl to establish an agenda for a conference, use as a problem solving device, etc.

To identify objectives. In either training or problem-solving situations, it may be necessary, at times, to clarify objectives: Why are we here? What are our goals? What does headquarters (or the chief executive) expect? The fishbowl can aid immeasurably in clarifying possible confusion and misconceptions about program purposes.

To resolve conflict. If there is conflict or controversy concerning a substantive issue, the trainer may introduce the fishbowl as an *ad hoc* device to help resolve it. "Talking it through," as opposed to letting the controversy smolder, is certainly preferred.

To resolve a training issue. On occasion, participants may be in conflict with some aspect of the training endeavor. For example, participants may resent being "forced" to attend the program. Or participation may be inhibited because bosses are in attendance with their subordinates. In such circumstances, the trainer may suggest that the participants "fishbowl" the difficulty.

For mid-program assessment. One way to find out how well the training is going is to use the fishbowl. To the extent practicable, mid-program corrections thus may be accomplished early on rather than waiting until program's end, at which time it may be too late. Typical issues that may emerge are clarity of objectives, the degree to which objectives are being met, pace (too fast or too slow), possible problems in applying the new learning, etc.

For evaluation of training. The fishbowl can be used to assess how well a training effort went. In fact, this is one use that all kinds of training groups—technical, professional, management, sales, safety—can use to equal advantage. The evaluation may take place at one or more points in the on-going program or, more typically, at program's end.

As a tool to engender fun and novelty. Too many training programs suffer from a surplus of the conventional, the expected, the tried and true. The fishbowl reverses this deadly process by injecting, instead, a great deal of spark, excitement, novelty, fun, change of pace, and the like. Participants are thus energized instead of bored.

As to the limitations of the fishbowl, it is not likely to be productive in technical or skills training where the overall training format is heavily didactic as opposed to experiential. However, even in these situations, it can be used:

1. To have participants talk about applications of their new learning to the back-home situation—will it be easy? Difficult? What are the problems (concerns, anxieties) in application or implementation?
2. To evaluate the training effort—what went well? What went less than well? What do we recommend for program improvement?

The fishbowl also may present problems if participants are highly self-conscious, not open to new experiences, not too verbal, not accustomed to the give and take of a vigorous problem solving encounter, etc. A word to the wise: Trainer, know thy participant group.

Working With "Mind Pictures"—Fantasy, Guided Imagery, Etc.

To imagine is everything.

—Albert Einstein, physicist
(1879–1955)

When I train the biceps, I picture huge mountains. You do something to the mind. The mind is the limit. It's all mind over matter.

—Arnold Schwarzenegger, body
building authority, actor, and
TV personality

The ability to fantasize is the ability to survive.

—Ray Bradbury, science fiction
writer

Participants often can be involved and reached with "mind pictures," which they create and use when other more conventional training approaches may not be productive. These techniques bear such diverse names as fantasy, guided fantasy, group fantasy, mental imagery, guided imagery, visual imagery, visualization, symbolic visualization, and so on. Regardless of the terminology, however, we are talking about processes that use and develop the intuitive, creative part of our brain (right brain thinking). These processes relate to our ability to think in *images* as well as verbally.

In respect to the terminology just cited, we should point out that in the area of fantasy the nomenclature is not used by writers in any consistent way. However, for our purposes we will group these devices into several rather precise categories, using titles and definitions which seem to be most descriptive and helpful. Here, then, are several key definitions:

Fantasy entails the creation of a mind picture by the participant in response to a *general* idea or topic provided by the trainer. (The terms "imagining," "imaging," or "imagistic thinking" are adequately synonymous with fantasy.) For example: "Imagine that you are on a flight in outer space . . ." or "Project yourself into the year 2100. You are alive and well. You see the world as . . ." or "Fantasize that you are the president of this company . . . ."

Guided fantasy entails the joint development of a scenario by the facilitator and a participant as fantasizer. The former guides the latter via such techniques as questioning, channeling, overcoming obstacles, encouraging, and supporting. Used primarily in human potential development programs, it may entail entering one's own body, becoming someone else, etc.[2]

Group fantasy entails the development of a story via contributions of the total group. After one member kicks things off ("We are on a large ship at sea. The waves are very tall . . . "), the other participants may build on the fantasy in sequence or on an *ad hoc* or random basis. This device may be used in highly experiential, personal growth programs rather than in more conventional training activities.

Mental imagery involves the creation of images or mind pictures via one's own command, such as when a tired jogger might create an image of a cold beer in an over-sized, icy glass which is available at the end of the run and thus is revitalizing. Other examples of self-imaging are given later. However, our concern is with the creation of images guided by the trainer, hence our use of the term "guided imagery." (See definition which follows.)

Guided imagery entails the provision of a *specific or detailed picture or image* by the trainer, which participants react to and build on with their own mind pictures.

Visualization, as we will use it, entails the recall and interpretation of images of actual situations, events, persons, relationships, etc., both past and present.

In general, these approaches to the augmentation of our intuitive capability are a recognition that most of us use no more than ten percent of our creative potential. Hence the need to tap the wisdom buried below our normal level of awareness.

Using Fantasy

Fantasy is an "auto-process" of creating mind pictures on demand. A general suggestion by the trainer triggers the image. It is used in various training situations to stimulate creativity, tap potential, improve problem solving capability, make participants more aware of their feelings, aid in overcoming ungrounded fears, reduce stress, introduce an element of fun or play, energize the group, and generally aid in personal growth. It is a process of tapping and developing the intuitive, creative, and spontaneous part of the brain. In current psychological language, it is a form of "right brain" (or creative) thinking.

Its rationale is that by engaging in "creative day dreaming," we can imagine the impossible, which can provide us with insights into the possible. Several uses follow:

Management training. In management training fantasy can be helpful in expanding the imagination of managers and thus opening up new, unthought of possibilities of accomplishment. Too often managers limit their capabilities for dynamic action by an over-concern with barriers—actual and presumed. Some examples of the use of fantasy in management training are as follows:

What If (Let's Pretend) Technique

Ask the group to fantasize various management issues such as:

☐ What if I had all the time in the world? What would I do that is worth doing that I'm not doing now?

☐ If I were to delegate to my staff as much as I wanted to, my operation would _____.

☐ If we had the perfect management team we would _____.

☐ If I could design the truly effective performance appraisal system (or pay plan, or marketing plans, or product line, etc.), it would _____.

☐ If I could build the ideal organization it would be able to _____.

In-House Prophet Technique

"Fantasize that you get a call at home at 9:30 p.m. on Saturday night. It is the big boss. This person wants very much your advice on _____. You are elated. This is your big chance! What do you say?"

Worst Case Scenario Technique

"What are the worst results that could happen if you asked for a raise (or quit, or transferred, or disagreed with your boss, or expressed your feelings about an issue candidly.)?" The objective is to get all the fears, anxieties, and negatives out and hold them up to the light of day for reality testing. Verbalized fears, as opposed to unexpressed ones, tend to lose their intensity.

Worst Case Scenario Follow-up

Ask the participants to fantasize: "What are the benefits that might accrue if you did A rather than B?" (With the fears out in the open and discussed, the gains will look more attractive.)

Top Dog Technique

"Fantasize that you are the plant manager (or district manager, or company president) for the month. What would your goals or methods be to improve productivity (union relations, quality of worklife, employee enthusiasm, etc.)?"

The Magic Wand Technique

"Plop! A magic wand has been dropped in front of you. Oh, how it sparkles. You hear a voice somewhere above which tells you encouragingly: 'You can change anything you like with the wand. Just hold it with both of your hands and decide to change that which needs to be changed.' How would you change yourself (your job, your priorities, your boss, your staff, your organization)?"

Sudden Enrichment

It is the day before Christmas. Your boss has been chatting with you at your desk. As he gets up to leave, he says: "Oh, by the way, here's $250,000 you can use to help your unit in any way you deem best." How would you use this windfall?

Note: The above devices, such as "What If," "The Magic Wand," and "Sudden Enrichment" can be used in other areas as well, e.g., career planning, personal growth, stress management, etc.

Career development. In career development workshops there are numerous opportunities to use fantasy. Some examples follow:

As a confidence-building vehicle: "You are about to enter an office for a job interview. You stride in alertly and energetically, displaying a big smile of pleasure and confidence. You are asked to be seated. You explain with enthusiasm why you are interested in the job . . . . " (The participant, in fantasy, begins a monologue.)

In an in-house career development workshop participants were asked to describe the "images" that career development brings to mind in this organization. Some responses were: "A farce." "A P.R. gimmick." The participants were then asked to fantasize what a real or ideal career development program would be like (ideal images). Some responses were: "Learn about all vacancies so we can apply for self-development interests and efforts." "Establishment of career ladders." "Accomplishment rather than seniority as a criteria for advancement."

The data were then forwarded to management for their consideration.

In another in-house career development workshop participants were asked to fantasize a real (ideal) career development program if they were first, management; second, employees; third, the personnel office; fourth, the training department. By using fantasy, specific goals were developed expending a minimum amount of energy and time.

Personal growth. Fantasy is extremely well-suited to training activities that encourage personal growth—building greater self-confidence, increasing assertive behavior, reducing weight, being more friendly at meetings, getting rid of anger, facing up to unpleasant tasks such as making tough decisions affecting people, etc. As the trainer, you can direct fantasy experiences (guided fantasy) about some of these problems in a "two-stage scenario" fashion:

Trainer: Think of a problem you have with yourself or with others. (Pause for a minute or two.) O.K., who has a problem that they will share with us, one that we can use as a "demo?"

Participant: I would like to be more friendly, more congenial, more supportive at meetings.

Trainer: That's a good one; very much worth working on. O.K., close your eyes; lean back in your chair; relax; relax some more; make yourself comfortable, very, very comfortable; very loose. (Pause.) Now visualize yourself at a recent meeting. Can you do this?

Participant: (Nods head.)

Trainer (Starts Scenario I): O.K., visualize your behavior. (Pause.) Can you tell us what you are doing, how are you "coming on?"

Participant: I am glum, unsmiling; at times I make negative comments.

Trainer: O.K., visualize the people at the meeting. Can you do that? (Pause.)

Participant: (Nods head.)

Trainer: How are people reacting to you? (Pause.)

Participant: Several are throwing unfriendly glances at me. Others don't pay any attention to me at all.

Trainer: And how do you feel about that?

Participant: Not too good.

Trainer (Starts Scenario II): O.K., let's see if you can change things a bit. Fantasize, imagine, that you come on as a very warm and friendly person. You are really smiling; you have a big, easy smile and your eyes sparkle; you give people encouragement, praise for their ideas. You are enjoying yourself. (Pause.) Can you do this?

Participant: I think so; yes.

Trainer: Good. Can you see the others at the meeting? (Pause.)

Participant: Yes, I can.

Trainer: And how are they reacting to you?

Participant: It's different; very different. They seem to like me. Yes, they like me. They're smiling back at me.

Trainer: How do you feel as a member of this group?

Participant: I feel as if I'm now part of the group. Yes, I'm really part of the group.

Similar fantasies can be encouraged on other problems such as being overweight. The participant can be asked to fantasize a significant weight loss (pause after each question for a response): What if you were to lose 40 pounds? What would you look like? How would people you know react to you? Your spouse? Your boss? Your associates at work? Your children? Your neighbors?

Or take a situation where a participant would like to be more confident or more assertive. Again, the first, "unsatisfactory" scenario is reproduced visually by the participant. Then the second, more satisfying scenario is fantasized. The aim is to give the participant opportunities (in fantasy) to be successful in situations that normally are not very satisfying or successful.

Other fantasy-type situations to encourage introspection for personal growth purposes are:

☐ Imagine that you have been given all the resources and skills to make a movie of yourself. What would be its major theme? What major areas would you try to cover? What would you call it? Why? Who would you cast as you?

☐ Pretend that you can live anywhere in the world that you wished. Where would you go? What would it be like? How would you feel?

☐ You have been given a magic wand. See how is sparkles. You can tell instantly that it has great powers. Suddenly a voice tells you that you can use it to choose the kind of work that you always wanted to engage in. What would you decide to do? What satisfaction would it bring?

☐ Imagine that you have befriended an older person a good number of times. That person passes on and to your great surprise and satisfaction leaves you with $500,000. What would you do with this sudden enrichment?

Note: After fantasizing wishes such as in the examples of relocation and job change, the trainer would then ask the fantasizer to visualize the plans that should be taken to reach those desirable ends.

It should be stressed that fantasy is only one technique to aid participants to resolve personal growth-type problems and would not necessarily be used in isolation from other devices. For example, in a workshop concerned with career burnout, you might utilize talks along with small group discussion, group or individual tasks, role plays, and fantasy.

Stress management. You can encourage your participants to use fantasy to deal with everyday stressful situations. Eleanor Rowe, a physical and mental fitness philosopher and professor of comparative literature at The George Washington University, offers these examples:[3]

☐ You are in a bad traffic jam. You transport yourself to a far-off mountain top, observing the tangled mess from on-high. Simultaneously, you imagine a pleasant rain pouring over you, washing away the stock market, irritated customers, and all your problems at home.

☐ You are very tense, filled with negative thoughts. Imagine that you are walking in a large field filled with spring flowers. You encounter a wooden stand which has attached to it balloons in gay colors. Each one has one of your problems/worries written on it. Slowly, you release the balloons, one by one, and watch your cares gently float far away. You lie down on the spring grass, close your eyes, relax, and smile.

☐ You have a lot of concerns and negative thoughts. Fortunately, you have an extra-large garbage bag. You recap all your gloomy thoughts, load the bag with them, and you watch yourself dropping them off at the local garbage dump (or throw the bag off a high cliff or let it float out to sea).

Similarly, group members might be asked to fantasize ways of discharging anger. Some responses to this fantasy are: Pour several tons of concrete on X's front lawn, which spell out a four-letter word. Hit a baseball (really a head) on top of Y's shoulders. Beat Z's new car with a heavy six-foot chain. Stick an 18-inch pin into A's bottom. Treat B's charcoal with a skunk potion so that when the barbecue fire starts it promptly breaks up the party and enrages the neighbors. The idea, of course, is to get the hostility out in a harmless, make-believe way, as opposed to acting it out in a confrontation-type situation. After the fantasizing, group members can be asked to brainstorm other ways of dealing with anger, such as writing (and then discarding) a nasty letter; talking to a friend about it; yelling out the negative feeling through the car window when going to or returning from work; jogging or other strenuous exercise; beating on a mattress with a canoe paddle; adopting a "resolution" that I—and only I—will decide when to become angry, i.e., I won't let anyone else determine (influence or produce) my anger.

Retirement planning. In a preretirement seminar it may be desirable to stimulate participant thinking about such key postretirement concerns as retirement location, possible job activity, investment planning (possibly reshuffling one's portfolio of assets), etc. Thus, you may say: "Let's pretend that you could live anywhere" or "You could work at what you always wanted to do" or "Someone gave you $500,000 to invest."

Fantasy as play. Fantasy can be used as a "fun thing." One can exhilarate and enliven the group by giving them a play-type task. For example, in a session on motivation you may ask the group to fantasize doing their jobs in a fun way, free from the usual restraints, protocol, decorum, etc., of the organization. A group of radio newscasters was asked to engage in this fantasy: How would you deliver the news if you could really be yourself? Some responses were:

☐ Do it in a hot tub.
☐ Sing it instead of speak it.
☐ In shorts and my running shoes.
☐ In the nude (!).
☐ With a swinging musical band.
☐ Like a sports announcer I know with a lot of "You know's," "Hey man's," etc.
☐ Spoof the commercials.

Using Guided Imagery

This is designed to tap a person's inner world. It entails using and developing the intuitive, creative hemisphere of the brain (right brain). It can be used for career planning, life planning, creative writing, exam preparation, stress reduction, building the confidence of public speakers, general problem solving, improving interpersonal relations and communication, etc.

Procedurally, it is generally begun by introducing a relaxation exercise. ("Remove your shoes, loosen your tie and belt, lie down, close your eyes, be real loose and comfortable . . . breathe in slowly . . . slowly, exhale slowly . . . slowly, etc.") The idea is to inhibit somatic muscle activity and verbal thoughts, thereby permitting mental images to come alive and supersede conventional brain action. In effect, by quieting the left hemisphere of the brain (the logical, rational side), the right brain can take over with all its potential for spontaneity, creativity, imagination, etc.

When participants are relaxed, provide an image for everyone to visualize and build upon:

"You are walking on the bottom of the sea . . . you come to a coral-coated cave . . . you enter it . . . "

"You are walking down a winding road . . . now there's a fork in it . . . which do you take? You follow it and you see . . . "

"You go into a cave . . . it is dark . . . you walk along the wall, feeling your way . . . Now there's a light . . . on a ledge is a large treasure box . . . you open it up . . . there is a book in it . . . you look at the title . . . "

"You are on a desert island . . . it is sunny and warm . . . "

Note: The creation of an image by participants need not only be a visual one. Participants thus may be asked to feel the wind on their faces, imagine the smells and sounds on the beach, the texture of objects at hand, etc.

After participants have developed images in their minds, ask the participants to share them with the small group. The group helps individual participants to interpret the image, gives support about them, etc. A further sharing may entail the presentation of experiences from participants to the total group.

You may also present an image with enough detail so that it stimulates a specific form of problem solving. For example, after a brief relaxing exercise, including closing of the eyes, you may say:

"Imagine you are near a waterfall . . . experience it . . . what do you see . . . what do you feel . . . what do you smell . . .

"You now see two people standing near the waterfall. They are observing you enjoying yourself. One person is someone you relate to very well. The other person is someone you don't relate to well at all. Think about both relationships. Now open your eyes.

"Share in your small group your feelings about the two persons, indicating who they are and why you feel about them as you do."

Sharing takes place in the small group for 10–20 minutes. Then continue the imagery.

"You are near a stream. The person with whom you have the conflict is on the other side. The stream can be a slow moving stream or a raging river. You decide that. What do you do? What does the other person do? Do either of you communicate with the other person? If so, what do you say?" (Deciding upon a roaring river obviously will prevent or impede communication.)

"Open your eyes. Share your experience along the side of the river with the members of your group."

After the small group work, you may ask: "How many improved relationships? How many did not? Any comments, observations?"

Another way of using guided imagery is to ask participants to tap their Inner Advisor. The Inner Advisor is part of one's own "deeper" wisdom, that is, below the level of our usual awareness.

1. Explain the Inner Advisor concept.
2. Assign a topic about which participants are to seek wisdom or advice, e.g., health, careers, relationships.
3. Provide the usual instructions for a relaxation activity.
4. Provide an image to facilitate the use of the Inner Advisor, e.g., "Imagine a lake and an animal comes out and talks to you. You decide on the animal, one that you like."
5. The experience is shared in the small group, both as to the advice received and the animal selected.

One way to close a session concerned with personal growth, communication, interpersonal relations, etc., is to conduct this nonverbal exercise: Have participants get comfortable again, take a deep breath, etc., then tell them:

"Imagine you're at a remote beach. There is no one there. It is very quiet. Take in the sights, smells, sounds. Now, you are to cast something away: an undesirable attitude, behavior, habit, something you have wanted to rid yourself of for a long time. Cast it far out on the water—the tide will carry it away.

"Now move to a new spot on the beach. You are still very relaxed. The tide is now coming in. Try to take something in: a new attitude, behavior, etc."[4]

One organization development (OD) consultant used the following guided imagery in an MBO workshop:[5]

"Imagine that this company is a very old and beautiful Victorian house and that each department in the company is a room in the house. How would your room look? What would be in it? To illustrate, as the OD consultant, I really don't see myself right now as a permanent part of the house. I feel more like a temporary addition that was recently built. So, I'm the newest part of the house, and I'm on the second floor, over the garage. My decor is mixed, because everyone else has donated some of their own furniture to the addition. I have a water bed, a lovely old oak bureau with a mirror, a large closet, an oriental rug, a small bathroom with a cast-iron tub, a nineteenth-century roll-top desk and lots of green plants. I'd like to hear what the rest of the house looks like."

He then asked participants to share their fantasy or imagery by describing their own "rooms." He then asked if this would be a desirable place to reside, who else would be living there, etc. The objective was to help participants to gain insight into the nature of the organization—

perceived hierarchy, authority structure, communication patterns, climate, etc. The concept of the organization as an interdependent system is more easily understood when everyone sees everyone else as "residents" of the same "house."

Another practical use of guided imagery is to help people imagine desired changes in their workplace. By picturing such changes in their minds, they can more readily believe that they can overcome the status quo and commit themselves to taking appropriate steps. Example: A managerial group wishes to streamline/improve operations. After the usual breathing and relaxing procedures, ask them to paint a word picture of the hoped for changes. Knowing these specifics, you can then ask general questions that will help them to picture the hoped for changes: "The time is 30 days from today—July 1. How does the office look? What things look differently? Who is in the office? Where are they? What are they doing? What are the signs/indicators that the change has really worked?" These images of change can be captured on paper, e.g., who will do what after the change has taken place.[6]

Using Mental Imagery For Learning

One way to enhance learning is to have participants form "mind pictures" or mental images related to the task to be mastered. For example, elementary school students (fifth and sixth grade) who formed pictures in their mind concerning complex textbook material they had read—about fictitious people living on a remote Pacific island—performed better on both immediate and delayed recall tests than control group students.[7]

Similarly, mental imagery aided flight attendant trainees at one airline. They had had to memorize for an FAA examination the location of some 50 pieces of emergency equipment (masks, flashlights, fire extinguisher, etc.) on five different planes, but they were flunking out at a 30% rate—obviously an expensive cost to the airline. However, with the aid of relaxation and visualization techniques, the trainees enjoyed a 100% pass rate. The specific procedures used were these:

1. Test anxiety was reduced via relaxation techniques.
2. A tour was made of the five planes to see the location of the equipment. Equipment was also touched, lifted, etc. which stimulated the other senses.
3. After leaving the plane they filled in equipment locations on cabin diagrams.
4. The next day they were again relaxed and taken on a guided imagery journey through the five aircraft.
5. Again, the cabin diagrams were completed.

6. The above procedure was repeated for five days before the exam.
7. On the morning of the exam the trainees were told to use the relaxation-mental image walk before and during the exam, as needed.[8] As indicated above, the exam was a tremendous success experience.

Some added uses follow:[9] Memory can be aided if connections are made by developing a mind picture with the items to be remembered such as peoples' names, a grocery list, new vocabulary, new spelling words, and lists of numbers. Weight control can be aided through imagery ("imagine your slim self"). Stress can be reduced by developing "mini-vacations" in one's head. Sales personnel can overcome "phono-phobia" (call reluctance) by creating success images. High school students improved their free-throw shooting ability by practicing this skill in their heads; they actually out-performed a conventional practice group as well as another group that didn't practice at all. Confidence in public speaking and being more assertive can also be aided in this manner.

One writer suggests using mental imagery to improve trainee study skills, particularly insulating oneself against irrelevant thoughts and problems and thus improving needed concentration. His procedure is to teach trainees to begin a study session by picturing themselves studying and learning successfully while resisting distractions. The mental imaging gets them psyched-up for study/learning; that is, it creates a proper study mood and centers all thoughts to relevant issues. He also encourages trainees to form mental images or to draw diagrams or flow charts about the study material. In this way, what is real is reinforced by a picture, doubling the chance of recall.[10]

Gerry Reid, an authority on "accelerated learning," states that many mnemonics (memory devices) depend on using imagery. For example, learners can use their imaginations to create far-out, silly, humorous, out-of-proportion, illegal, immoral, or impossible images to provide an interesting diversion to the assigned task. The diversions themselves provide the mechanism to associate the new information, thereby accelerating the learning process.

Reid also points out that the learners' imagination allows them to experience situations and events not in the training room. They can go anywhere, anytime, and observe anything under any condition. Learners can see, hear, feel, smell, taste, and experience any subject via their imagination. They can watch themselves perform numerous tasks or skills related to their learning, everything from organizing their approach and using reference materials to seeing the success of proper application of the information being learned. Once a task has been performed in the mind, the learner need only recall what was imagined to perform it.

As Reid phrases it, "The physical performance becomes a repeat performance rather than an attempt to do the unknown. The brain, of course, can't distinguish between the real and the imagined since it undergoes the same electro-chemical processes when something is done in actuality or is imagined."[11]

The challenge for the trainer, obviously, is to encourage participants to seek out situations where learning and performance can be improved via the creation of mind pictures or images by them.

Using Visualization

As is apparent from the previous paragraphs, when using fantasy, guided imagery, and mental imagery, we are *imagining, creating,* or *manufacturing* an event or situation. In visualization, however, we draw upon or recall an actual experience, particularly one where strong feelings were involved or emerged. The recalled event is then subject to one or more forms of analysis. Here are the examples.

☐ In a session on interpersonal relations, you may wish to have your group experience the following:

"Think of an experience you had some years ago with another person. This was a hurtful experience: You were embarrassed, humiliated, put down, pained in some way.

"Close your eyes. Bring to mind the details of the experience. How old were you? Why did it take place? Where? What was said to you? What did you say, if anything, in reply? What were your feelings at the time?

"Open your eyes. How do you feel about that experience now?

"Close your eyes again. Restructure the incident in light of all the experience you have had, and everything you have learned since that event. Give yourself a second chance. What would you say to the other person now? (Most should approach the problem now more constructively. But some participants may say: "No change; I was trapped:" or "I really told her off this time.")

"Close your eyes again. Now visualize the incident from the other person's point of view. (Possible responses might be: "It throws a new light on it." "Maybe I took it too hard.")

This visualization activity is useful in helping participants get in touch with their feelings, to become more sensitive to the feelings of others, etc.

☐ In a sales training situation have the participants visualize a success experience such as the best sale they ever made. Ask them questions such as these: What made it successful? What did you do? How did you feel? Was it a learning experience, that is, have you been able to apply the learnings to other sales situations? Have you ever shared this experience with anyone else? Why or why not? If you did share it, to whom and how often? How did the other person react to your experience? Ask several participants to share their visualizations.

☐ In an assertiveness training situation have participants visualize an actual unsatisfying experience (e.g., an attempt to return a dress to a store in which one was "browbeaten" by the salesperson). Then have participants fantasize how they might have handled the same situation with greater effectiveness.

Using Fantasy Outside the Classroom

Our discussion so far has related to invigorating and liberating the participant group via fantasy and related techniques *in the training room.* It also may be desirable to give them added pointers regarding the continuing use of fantasy, imagery, etc., in their everyday situations: at work, at play, in the home, etc. Some examples of opportunities to use fantasy and mental imagery on one's own follow:

Imagined behavior or action. The idea is to develop a picture in one's mind about the accomplishment of a difficult event or activity, for example: "I am jogging and am feeling tired. But do I have to feel tired? No! I imagine a giant hand lifting me up and propelling me forward and I easily move with it, the tiredness having vanished."

That positive mind pictures, at least in athletics, are more than a pipe dream is illustrated by research on "imaging" of free throw shooting. In one controlled study, three groups of students practiced throwing basketball free throws. Group 1 practiced for 20 days. Group 2 didn't practice at all. Group 3 spent 20 minutes each day imaging or visualizing the taking of free throws. The results: Group 1 improved 24%; Group 2 showed zero improvement; Group 3 improved by 23%.[12]

There are many opportunities for imaging or imagining success in on- and off-the-job situations; e.g., confronting successfully a "hard-to-reach" peer or subordinate; delivering a speech with confidence before a large group; asking the boss for a raise; securing "one's rights" on a warranty problem; discharging anger by fantasizing the causing of "discomfort" to someone (far better than acting it out!); preparing for a tough exam.

Industrial psychologist Dr. Harry Levinson advises enlisting the aid of fantasy and imagination when major life changes are coming—the death of a parent, the birth of the first child, marriage, divorce, promotion, retirement, etc. In respect to personal acceptance of and planning for retirement, he suggests: "It takes time to get past the glib characterizations ('Oh boy, I'll never get out of bed!' or 'My husband and I will drive each other nuts!') and start imagining how you'll really feel. This sort of mental rehearsing is very important. Of course things won't be exactly as you imagined them, but you'd be surprised what insights will come if you let your imagination go. One of the reasons widows do better than widowers is that they rehearse this way for the probable loss of their husbands. Men rarely do. The more different situations you daydream yourself into, and the more different reactions you can imagine having, the more complete a picture will emerge of what retirement will mean to you. And the meaning *will* be complex, with conflicting aspects and alternating feelings."[13]

Self-reinforcement of one's behavior. The procedure is to create an image of an event with highly favorable consequences. These consequences obviously will be reinforcing for the desired behavior, for example: "I give the boss a new proposal on the restructuring of the marketing organization. He really eats it up and tells me so repeatedly! Wow! Since my boss is so receptive and complimentary, I intend to submit the proposal immediately. And I *know* I'll pull it off and feel great about it!"

Fantasy—Using It Wisely

To maximize results from the use of fantasy in its various forms, the following skill pointers should be considered:

☐ Have a specific learning objective in mind. Is it to "loosen" people up? To encourage creativity? To build confidence? To have fun? etc.

☐ Know your group. Will they enter into the spirit of the thing with enthusiasm or will they hold back?

☐ Watch your timing. Use fantasy, guided fantasy, etc. when it "fits" best into the training program. For example, you probably wouldn't start most programs with a fantasy experience. Also, fantasy works best when the group is free and easy with one another, something that is not likely to develop until later in the program.

☐ Consider both structured (planned) and unstructured (*ad hoc*) fantasy. The latter may be more effective if it meets a real need, e.g., at a point when the group is "stuck" on an issue or needs a "lift." To illustrate: I recall a situation in a management training course, which I was conducting, wherein the group was polarized over the issue of leveling with subordinates about an instruction or policy from the boss with which one didn't agree. Some felt vigorously that one must be "a

good soldier" and support the boss regardless of one's own feeling's about the issue. Others felt strongly that it was dishonest not to say how one feels about the policy or instruction and, besides, the subordinates would probably sense the lie anyhow. I resolved the impasse by asking the group to fantasize the "worst"—what if you were to actually level with the staff about one's own true attitude toward the policy? What might happen to you? Then, what would be the "best" payoffs if one leveled?

☐ Introduce the fantasy in an exhilarating, challenging way: "Close your eyes. Let's fantasize that _____. Let your imaginations soar! Be creative! Pull out all the stops! You have the power to do this!"

☐ A good way to process the fantasy is by having participants share their images/ideas in small groups. Then hold a general group-at-large discussion about the results/effects of the fantasizing.

☐ Don't expect everyone to enter into the process with the same degree of enthusiasm, spontaneity or success. One or more may not wish to "play" at all. Individual differences are certainly to be expected and respected.

☐ Obviously, this kind of activity is best done in an experiential training program by a trained facilitator.

Working with Pictures

Pictures (photos, drawings, advertisements) can be used to involve participants in meaningful and novel ways. Some examples are given below.

Quiz

Give participants a 10–20 item safety quiz. Working from photographs showing hazardous situations (some obvious, others less so) in the shop, plant, laboratory, etc., have participants identify as many unsafe working conditions as they can in each photograph. Then have the participants meet in small groups to compare and discuss their responses to the quiz. At the end of the small-group discussion period, pass out the answer sheet for self-checking purposes. Wind things up with a general discussion about hazards in the workplace.

Developing Nonverbal Communication Skills

Show participants various photos, drawings, etc., and have them describe the nonverbal communication that is taking place. Some examples are: a group is sitting lethargically around a conference table looking pained or bored; a prospect is showing signs of impatience as the salesperson makes a presentation; a subordinate has just had an idea turned down by the boss. Then, in small groups, have participants discuss ways of dealing with the exhibited behavior.

Photographs that require interpretation of emotional states, relationships (boss-subordinate, married-unmarried, etc.), group behavior, etc., can also be subject to a multiple choice or true and false quiz and subsequent group discussion.

Icebreaker

Working in triads, instruct each participant to come up with five or more interesting things about the other two members. The data is written on 3″ × 5″ cards which are then hooked up vertically with tape. Photos (self-developing) are taken of each participant and attached appropriately to the card chains, and the completed displays are posted to the wall for "permanent" exhibit.[14]

Adding Captions

Provide participants with cartoons, novel photos, etc., and ask them to supply the caption. The captions can be analyzed in various ways; e.g., in relation to basic Transactional Analysis concepts of parent, adult and child; in respect to motivations or needs people may have.

Using Projective Techniques

Participants can be involved in a meaningful way by the use of pictures, drawings, ads, etc. from magazines or newspapers. The idea is to ask participants to select those subjects (people, situations, objects) with which they can identify or accept. Two examples are:

☐ Working from a folder containing many (one hundred or more) photos culled from magazines, a participant (particularly one who is shy or reluctant to communicate for various reasons) is asked to group the pictures into three piles: those that elicit positive feelings, those that elicit negative feelings and those that elicit only neutral affect (emotion). The sorting out process will "smoke out" feelings or attitudes that the participant may not be able to present verbally. I have used this device in leadership laboratories to help participants indicate who they really are, where they are coming from, what their preferences and prejudices are, etc. The group may then query the participant about the overall patterns produced by the selections, why a particular photo was preferred or rejected, etc.

☐ Participants may be given a group of old magazines and asked to cut out quickly those items which point up the career or lifestyle they favor. These may be put in a folder or mounted on the wall or on a poster board in collage fashion. Again, the pictorial selections are subject to group questioning and analysis and serve as a form of feedback to aid participants to "reality test"

better their career decisions. A good training design is to have the participants share their data about the selected pictures in trios or quartets.

A variation of this technique is to have participants identify both their current career or life style and the preferred career or life style, assuming they see a need for a change.

☐ Show participants a picture (ad, photo, drawing) and have them write a short story or account of its significance for them. Possible subjects are: an intensely involved group at a meeting; a harried executive with an over-flowing in-box reaching for the phone; a foreman with an angry look on his face pointing with his finger as a worker looks on; two people conversing at the water cooler. Then have participants discuss their stories in pairs or trios. Complete the activity by a group-at-large sharing of what was learned.

☐ Show participants a somewhat ambiguous photo of a boss-subordinate interaction; e.g., going over a workplan, an interview situation, a discussion in an office or on the shop floor, etc. Then ask them to rate the subordinate on various aspects of personality, performance, and attitude, using the rating scale as shown in Figure 4-3. Have participants discuss their ratings in small groups and then discuss the results with the group at large.

Subordinate's Traits	Low	Moderate	High	Don't Know
Cooperativeness				
Enthusiasm				
Creativity				
Initiative				
Dependability				
Listening skills				
Other				

Figure 4-3. Example of a rating sheet used by participants to evaluate an ambiguous photo.

The objective is to ascertain to what extent we project our feelings about subordinates (and others) in general to an essentially neutral situation. Halo effects or hypercriticalness are cues to lack of objectivity in judging others.

☐ In training managers to hire and work with handicapped workers, pictures may be used to reveal hidden attitudes about such persons. Two examples are:

1. Pictures are distributed of people observing handicapped individuals in a variety of situations. The trainer then asks the participants how they would react to seeing a disabled person. This activity generally reveals a whole gamut of attitudes and feelings: guilt feelings that they themselves aren't handicapped, a belief that the disability is "contagious" (!), that the disabled are bitter or feel sorry for themselves, etc.

2. Similarly, when asked to choose a prospective employee from four handicapped applicants, a subjective decision typically results—the one chosen is usually one disabled in later life or one who is least threatening to them personally. The "rationale" for picking the one disabled later in life is that people can identify more readily with one recently disabled. The latter exercise shows managers that people may *think* they can make objective decisions in such cases, but in actuality they don't.[15]

Note: The first example of projective techniques would be best used on an *ad hoc* basis with only two or three group members. Otherwise, its novelty and thus its effectiveness would be lost. Conversely, the other activities could be used readily by and with the *total* group. The second, fourth, and fifth examples are essentially "projective devices" for they ask the participants to project themselves as individuals into the picture to the degree they are able to, thereby revealing or explaining a certain aspect of their personality, value system, attitudinal system, etc.

Using Participant Photos

In the previous examples, the photos used for analysis were not related personally to the participants. However, it may be desirable in highly experiential training programs to use photographic material which relates directly to the participants. Some examples include:[16]

☐ In weight-reduction groups photograph the participants intermittently, e.g., monthly. Paste the photos on large sheets of paper and have participants describe themselves below the photos. The objective of these self-image descriptions, according to Dr. David Krauss, a visual therapist, is to give participants "reinforcing feedback about their weight and looks which is generalized into other areas, such as grooming, attitudes and self-esteem."

☐ In leadership laboratories (the T-Group), encounter group, stress management courses, etc., it may be desirable to have participants bring in to the program photos of themselves. The instructions about the types of photos to be selected should be quite general:

"Bring in photos of yourself, as many as you wish, in any period of your life, alone or with others, in any situations you prefer, etc." Obviously, the photos will serve as a rich personal resource for the exploration of one's feelings, attitudes, values, about self, family, early history, career, etc. One of the specific ways Dr. Krauss uses these kinds of photos is to have participants project themselves into the photo. For example, a photo may show a person, a car, a tree, or a house. Dr. Krauss then asks the participant to speak about these objects in the present tense: " . . . tell me what it is like to be the person, house, tree, car, driveway and so forth." The metaphoric content of the discourse, as disclosed by the participant, serves as a rich source of data about the participant and may provide him/her with self-insight as well.

☐ Take photos of group members, then discuss their degrees of relaxation, attentiveness, etc. The photographic data could be used by the participants to attempt to change their behavior, as appropriate.

☐ You may also photograph one or more participants and use the photos as a basis for their reaction to and critique of themselves. Thus, Dr. Krauss may ask participants questions such as: Who is this person? What do you like about this photograph? Is there a part you dislike? If we take another photo of you in six months, what do you think we will see that may be different? How would you title this picture?

Note: These examples reported by Dr. David Krauss are used by him in therapeutic situations. Obviously, the trainer's skill and the type of training involved would determine whether similar photographic approaches would be appropriate in nontherapeutic training situations.

Using Art

The arts are a way to bring order out of chaos—the chaotic feelings and impulses within and the bewildering mass of impressions from without. The arts are a means to discover both the self and the world—and to establish a relationship between the two.

—Dr. Elinor Ulman, authority on
art therapy, The George
Washington University

Participants can be involved dynamically in the learning process via tasks that require some form of artistic expression. The art forms may be representational, symbolic, abstract, or some combination of these forms. The emphasis, of course, is not on perfected productions, but on free expression of feelings: "Try to draw the emotions you're now feeling. Just let yourself go!"

Why would we want our participants to engage in an activity which requires them to respond in a graphic, pictorial, illustrative or artistic way? The best response might be: "Why not?" But some specific reasons are:

☐ It taps our creativity. If you will recall the findings of recent brain research, our brain has two hemispheres, known as the left brain and the right brain. The left brain's functions control our thought processes, the cognitive-analytical realm. Its proper functioning assures that we engage in logic, reason, caution, rationality, analysis, evaluation (seek and weigh the evidence), assessment of consequences, sequential thinking, etc. Conversely, the right brain governs our intuitive-feeling processes, i.e., the side of ourselves that is curious, impetuous, emotional, speculative, creative, open to new experiences, playful, etc. In other words, the two hemispheres produce control and spontaneity, respectively.

Now most of our work and our training activities, too, ask (or insist) that we think and be logical. Only infrequently are we challenged to tune in to our feelings and emotions that can unleash our playful, intuitive, and creative self. Art is a medium to encourage spontaneity and creativity. Since it can help us to think in images as well as words, it can capture the potential of the total brain.

☐ Since art expression reaches the affective or emotional side of ourselves, it can generate and communicate data about feelings, values, attitudes, etc., something that conventional written or verbal approaches may not be able to do. In other words, art can get at thoughts and feelings more readily since it works in a less direct way.

☐ It can lower defenses—both psychological and perceptual—of our participants since they are "approaching themselves" through a new perspective and an unfamiliar medium.[17] (*Note:* Psychological defenses relate to such mechanisms as denial, repression and projection; perceptual defense relates to our tendencies to select data with which we are comfortable and reject data with which we are not.)

☐ It can improve communication among participants. To the extent that our participants are encouraged to express what they really think and feel, understanding of one another is simplified and accelerated.

☐ It can help to reduce status differences. When participants engage in activities which create a relaxed, playful atmosphere, one's job title, rank, and grade are of much lesser significance. Camaraderie and openness are thus more easily developed.

☐ It can highlight individual differences of the participants—values, emotions, life goals, stresses, coping strategies, and the like.

☐ The images which our participants create tell us a lot about themselves. In fact, the bit of art work may tell us more about the "artist" than the item being imagined or described. In essence, the artistic renderings about a person, problem, event, or interaction expresses the participants' own method/style of seeing reality. So we are getting an authentic piece of information about each of the participants.[18]

☐ It can help to discover and develop hidden resources in the participants; e.g., the imaging/visualizing technique—important components of drawing—is a device for understanding and remembering complex information; the use of art allows adding intuition to one's usual rational mode of problem solving; art is a means of seeing various phenomena from different perspectives.

☐ It gives participants an opportunity to achieve a special focus, to perceive from a different standpoint, often from a deeper part of the mind and uncluttered from the details of day-to-day living and working.[19]

☐ It is interest-arousing because of its novelty and lesser structure. Typical participant expectations are that their training will be patterned, structured, predictable, uneventful, and generally pretty dull.

☐ It is fun to do. Engaging in the creation of art forms provokes the child in us, i.e., those aspects of our personality that are curious, spontaneous, intuitive, alive, bold, carefree, imaginative, idealistic, etc. In other words, it "loosens us up."

☐ To the extent that we are encouraged to be playful and imaginative, we are more likely to be motivated to learn. It gives us a mindset that seeks out the new rather than the tried and true.

☐ Finally, our artistic constructions let us take pride in our accomplishment, let us feel good about ourselves. As one participant said: "It's not Rembrandt, but *I* made this."

Some examples of the use of art in the training situation follow.

☐ In a career-planning activity, participants can be asked to draw their career progress to date. The career "lifeline" should depict successes, plateaus, setbacks, etc., using illustrations, symbols, and graphics.

☐ In a personal growth program, participants can be asked to draw their *personal* lifeline, complete with such symbols as mountain peaks, valleys, plateaus, clouds, sun, and other appropriate drawings to highlight major events.

☐ In a management development seminar, have participants draw a segmented geometrical form on a flip-

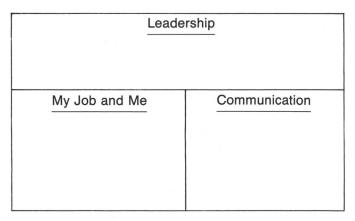

Figure 4-4. Example of a geometrical figure labeled and ready for completion artistically.

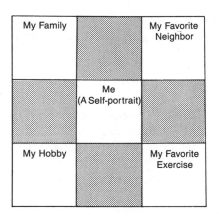

Figure 4-5. Getting Acquainted—A Patchwork Quilt.

chart or sheet of paper. Then have them label each segment (usually three or four) to encourage reflection on particular issues, e.g., leadership, communication, my career, my job, the organization, my staff. See Figure 4-4 for an example. Finally, each labelled segment is to be responded to in an artistic, graphic, or symbolic way.

☐ As an opener, have participants describe a current problem they are facing, using artistic, graphic, or symbolic expression. The problem may be work-related, career-related, personal (e.g., stress), in the community, etc., depending on the nature of the course.

☐ Have participants draw their "support system." Our support system enables us to cope with vexations, frustrations, disappointments, etc., and may include people (friends, carpool, colleagues, the boss, mentors, relatives, family); resources (our bank account, home, car, pension plan, other assets); off-the-job activities (hobbies, vacations); our ego strength or resources within ourselves; organizations (church, professional associations, social and fraternal groups), etc.[20]

☐ In a supervisory training course have participants draw a symbol(s) which represent a strong or attractive attribute of a boss or a characteristic which depicts the negative or undesirable side. Examples: an ear might symbolize that the boss listens; a group of people in a circle might indicate that a team has been developed and that the boss operates as a team manager; an open door would show good communications and interpersonal relationships; dull meetings conducted by the boss might be depicted by an assembled group with "Z's" over their heads; a boss who does not delegate might be shown at a desk overflowing with paper or overloaded in-baskets.

Note
1. A variation of the preceding activity is to divide the flipchart sheet in half, one side showing negative sources of support and the other side positive sources of support. Bosses, colleagues, subordinates, family may be either a negative or a positive source. Some negatives are debts, travel, long hours. Some positives are praise, recognition, successes.
2. This activity can be used in many training situations: leadership, human relations, sales, assertiveness, sensitivity and encounter groups, stress management, etc.

☐ As a getting-acquainted activity, participants can be asked to complete the diagram entitled "Getting Acquainted—A Patchwork Quilt" (Figure 4-5)[21] and then share the data.

☐ In a course on strategic or corporate planning, participants may be asked to: "Take a metaphorical leap. Imagine your company as a vehicle. Any kind of vehicle. Now draw it on a piece of paper and describe it in a few words." This was the assignment given in a seminar on strategic management to a group of senior executives at the Wharton Applied Research Center, University of Pennsylvania. The seminar director says that the exercise forces the executives to think of their company as a whole, where the company is and where it is going (or not going). Some examples of the art work: one participant portrayed his company as a bike with *two* sets of handlebars—one in front and one in the rear—to show movement in opposite directions. Another executive drew a car which was ancient in its front half and super-modern in the other section. The idea was to show that the company was struggling to get into another field, but the old phase of the business was a drag on the new side. A third executive drew a solid, fully-tracked vehicle, the idea being that the firm was hard-charging and steady, but certainly not built for speed.[22]

In another Wharton seminar, which tackled problems of family-owned companies, one drawing showed a car with three people in it—all driving. A father who had grave doubts about his children's ability to run the business drew a truck speeding into a brick wall. Other drawings revealed generational conflict, sibling rivalry for control of the firm, and resentment toward nonworking relatives living off the business.[23]

☐ A problem with another unit can be worked on by drawing the roles of the various individuals involved and then using the pictures as references in an actual meeting with the other group.[24]

☐ In a session or program concerned with confidence building, ask the participants to draw their most positive attribute of self and then to discuss it in pairs or trios.

☐ Cited previously under "Icebreakers" in Chapter 1 as a paper and pencil or flipchart task, the six items in *My Personal Shield* also could be presented in a graphic or illustrative way in a highly experiential program.

After the individual completion of the art work in each of the above activities, participants can be placed in dyads or triads to share the significance of their work. The intimate nature of these small groups should encourage full communication about the meaning of their graphic work. It should also provide added insight about it.

☐ In a public speaking training course, participants may be given colored felt tip pens and flipchart sheets and asked to draw "ideographs" (symbolic pictures) to pictorialize the points of a speech. The ideographs are used in lieu of notes or outlines. The rationale for this is that the bulk (85%) of what we retain is learned visually. So if speakers can translate an idea into an easy-to-comprehend picture, they can clarify their own thinking and imbed the idea better in the minds of their listeners.

Participants were advised to have their ideographs follow the usual speech outline: (a) statement of the problem; (b) solution; (c) positive results from the solution; (d) evidence for the solution—a personal incident, an analogy, the judgment of an expert, an example, and statistics/facts; (e) summary (restatement of a, b, and c). This added up to nine ideographs.

An example of a convincing but simple presentation: a personnel administrator drew a large table, with a missing leg, about to fall. This symbolized a warning to the branch personnel directors—that if in-

formation was missing from their budget presentations, their budgets could not be approved.[25]

Group Art Activities

Group Identity

To aid in the development of group identity, ask each group to draw a picture on a flipchart that describes the group. *Note:* It may be anticipated that less cohesive groups will draw something about *individual* group members. Conversely, a more cohesive group will produce something that symbolizes the nature of the total group.

Group-at-Large Mural

☐ In an experiential training activity post five or more flipchart sheets (or brown wrapping paper) on a wall. Advise participants that they can enter each day reactions to or feelings about any aspect of the course in artistic form. The art work will give the group a "running account" of course progress, movement, impact, learnings, feelings about the course, etc.

☐ A group of participants may be given an assignment of drawing a mural with the objective of studying their interaction while at work. The observers, one or two participants, or the group-at-large, may focus on decision making, communication patterns including possible breakdowns, formation of alliances, willingness to assume responsibility, planning approaches and skills, and so on. Start the assignment by giving each participant a different color marker and ask them to draw a picture of themselves at work or assign any other task which is of group concern. The purpose of the differently colored pens is to track clearly the nature and amount of each person's participation.[25]

Small Group Mural

Participants, in small groups, may construct a group mural in response to an assigned subject. For example, in an intercultural training program women from particular developing countries could be asked to depict (draw) the status of women—past, present, and future in their country.

Group-at-Large Collage

You may wish to ask your total group to construct a "collage" which represents their image, spirit, mission, nature of their learning, feelings about the course, communication prowess, etc. Provide colored construction paper, old magazines which have photos and ads in them, 5″ × 8″ cards, felt-tipped marking pens and/or crayons, tape, cord, paper clips, stapler, paste or glue. Depending on course objectives, this activity, using observers, could be processed or critiqued upon completion in terms of leadership, decision making, participation, co-operation, planning, intimacy and rapport, member satisfaction, and the like.[26]

Problem Perception

A group of 5–10 participants collectively describe (in art form), on three adjacent flipchart sheets, how they (1) see the nature of a given problem (problem definition or description), (2) how they feel about it, and (3) what should be done about it.

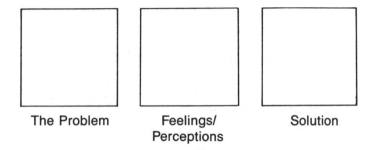

The Problem   Feelings/   Solution
               Perceptions

Geometrical Forms

Most of the examples of art assignments we have presented are drawn without any prescribed "boundaries." However, at times it may be advantageous to provide such structure. The rationale for the use of "geometrics"—squares, triangles, rectangles, a segmented shield—is given fully on page 8. (We have provided such art assignments on pages 5, 8, 53, 313.)

Another thought-provoking geometric form is the circle. Participants can draw several circles to provide highly significant meaning about self and/or various interpersonal relationships. It is to be noted that the circle is the easiest form to draw. Examples:

☐ Organization development specialists Fordyce and Weil[26] have their participants draw circles in team building sessions to describe influence and communication relationships. More specifically, participants draw a circle for each team member including the boss and his/her boss. Team member names are entered in the circles. The circles are drawn "to scale"—larger circles for those who have greater influence over the way the group operates. The circles are placed near or far apart from one another to show how closely team members must work together for proper results. Blue lines are then drawn to connect those who are personally close to one another. Red lines are drawn to depict relationships in difficulty—either little communication or the existence of friction. The highly revealing data are then processed.

☐ A three-circle "test" can be used to communicate attitudes toward life, per Tulane University social psychologist Frederick Koenig.[27] The test is quickly done and its nature is such that it always works. Try it yourself now by simply drawing three circles, one representing the past, one for the present, and the third signifying the future. Then label the circles. The circles may be of any size, and arranged in any way.

The psychological principles at work are circle *size* and their *relationship* (distance) to one another. If things are in close relationship we tend to draw our circles close together and somewhat apart if they are not.

Circles which are drawn separately indicate that one's life periods (past, present, future) are perceived as being separate and unrelated. Overlapping circles show life as being continuous and related. This means that past and present actions impact on what we will do in the future. People who view life as a continuous process typically are those who have control over their destiny.

A large circle about the past indicates that family and background are very important. A large present circle indicates the leading of a very busy life, a lot of living for today. A large future circle equates with optimism, a good future is ahead.

In Dr. Koenig's tests, very few people are past oriented.

Possible uses: In workshops concerned with personal growth, stress management, assertiveness training, career planning, management development, etc.

Note: As in any other art assignment, it is desirable to ask the participant to verbalize why he/she drew his/her circles as he/she did. The trainer may draw on the above analysis to help explain individual drawings; however, the trainer's attempts at processing past actions and insights should be governed by the limits of his/her psychological background.

Combining Guided Imagery and Art

Present a guided image to the group in sufficient detail so that they are led to the point where it is possible for them to: complete the imagery; develop a *symbol* of their experience, thoughts, feelings; and draw the symbol on paper. The symbol may be very simple or quite complex, just so it interprets what was experienced.

Typical scenes or situations for the guided imagery: at the bottom of the sea, in a shaded wood, on a space ship, etc. Present imaginative imagery by building sound, smell, color, flowers, animals, etc., into it. Develop the imagery to a point where the participants can take it over: "You enter the farm house. There is a long, circular mahogany staircase in it. Sunlight is shining on the staircase. You mount the staircase. You have the feeling that . . . . ''

Be certain to have the participants close their eyes when the activity begins.

Allow several minutes to reflect on the experience. Instruct participants to select a symbol that summarizes it. Then have them draw their symbols as described below.

Individual Approach. Provide each participant with several crayons and a sheet of sketching paper which has a large circle on it, lightly drawn in pencil. The circle is a focusing element. Have them enter their symbolic representation in or outside the circle. Then have each participant share the drawing with a partner.

Small group approach. Divide the total group into two or three sub-groups. Place a large (six to eight feet in diameter) circle, constructed out of brown wrapping paper, on the floor, one paper circle for each small group. Provide each participant with a box of pastel-colored chalk. Have participants sit on the floor around the paper circle and enter their symbol on it. If participants wish, they may merge their drawing with the work of others. Have the participants share their drawing with the small group.

Note: As an optional feature of this activity, you may wish to point out that the circle has special significance in early cultures. The late Swiss psychologist Carl A. Jung used the Hindu word *mandala* (or magic circle) as a symbolic representation of the "nuclear atom" of the human psyche, the essence of which we don't know. In Eastern cultures the mandala is contemplated to bring about an inner peace, a feeling that life has again found its meaning and order.[28] The circle is, of course, found in nature in the form of the sun, moon, certain flowers and fruits, etc.

Skill Pointers

To ensure that your use of art in the training situation is accomplished in an effective and professional way, these guidelines should prove helpful:

1. Have a clear-cut training objective, e.g., as an ice-breaker, as a means of generating more profound and/or personal data, to develop intimacy and rapport, to get the creative juices flowing, etc.
2. Limit the subject matter of a drawing to avoid confusion and possibly resistance to the total assignment.
3. Introduce the assignment in an up-beat way, as a fun thing. For example, say, "We're going to do something a bit different this afternoon and have some fun doing it. Any great artists here? None? Good. Then we're all on an equal footing, skill-wise. Now here's the task. I'm going to ask you to do something in a graphic, illustrative, or artistic way."
4. Present clear instructions. Remember, drawing something in a training situation is a new experience for most adults. You thus may wish to present the assignment in writing as well as orally. (See Figure 4-6 for a sample task assignment sheet.)
5. Anticipate that some participants may have difficulty expressing themselves in art fashion. Actually, *everyone* can draw. The "I can't draw anything" complaint is essentially a fear of expressing one's self in a new manner. Ask the "reluctant dragon" to "give it a whirl and do the best you can."
6. Monitor (walk around) the group and offer suggestions as may be indicated, e.g., suggest use of stick figures, symbols, simple graphics, etc. Also, don't be too concerned if someone does only partial work or "goofs up" the task totally.

Task Assignment Sheet: Visualizing Your Work Team

Procedures:

1. Think a moment about your back home situation. Now identify the work team of which you are a member; e.g., if you are a trainer in a training department, that is your work team; if you are the trainer in the personnel office, that is your work team. If you are a manager, you are part of two work teams: your own and that of your supervisor.

2. Reflect on *your* work team in terms of these two dimensions:

   a. What is it like?
   b. What *should* it be like?

3. Now draw a picture of your work team, both *present* and *ideal*, in a graphic or illustrative way. Use as your artistic concept a vehicle, animal, bird, fish, plant, or whatever else comes to mind.

4. Use the reverse side of this paper for your work. Turn the sheet horizontally; segment it into two parts by drawing a vertical line down the middle. Label the left segment "My team—what it's like." Label the right segment "My team—what it should be like."

5. Now let yourself go! Be as creative and imaginative as you can in depicting your team. You have 10 minutes for this task.

6. Share your drawings in a trio (10 minutes).

7. Processing—group-at-large discussion (15 minutes).

Figure 4-6. Example of a Task Assignment Sheet entailing the use of art in a team-building session.

7. As in any experiential activity (exercise, game, role play), processing or debriefing is a must. Dyadic and small group work should be supplemented by total group discussion.
8. The group-at-large phase of the work typically entails a sharing of the meaning of the drawings. As facilitator, set the right tone by encouraging the group to ask clarifying questions and providing praise for creative work. ("I particularly liked the motorcycle you drew to show your need to go into the country after work to get away from it all.") Discourage negative comments, argumentation, psychoanalyzing of drawn objects and persons, etc.
9. In vertically structured training, such as in team building, let the boss present (explain) his/her drawing last to avoid possible influence on the other presentations.

Added Skill Points

It is a good idea to post completed art work to the walls for purposes of later reference, to help create an atmosphere, for recognition of accomplishment, etc.

A word about the use of art materials. Flipcharts are preferred to the usual 8½″ × 11″ writing paper. Because of their large size, flipcharts permit greater freedom of expression. As to drawing implements, large felt tip pens are easier to use than crayons, charcoal, pens, etc.

The previous examples, as has been indicated, relate to activities in the training situation. If these activities produce insight and learning in the classroom, that in itself is worthwhile. However, with proper emphasis by the trainer concerning the potential (transfer) of these activities for on-the-job use, there is no reason why at least some participants should not use art in their work. For example, at Weyerhaeuser Company, Tacoma, Washington (manufacturers of wood, paper products), members of three departments—information systems, engineering, and research and development—hold weekly problem-solving meetings. In groups of 15, in three-hour sessions, the reps set up a problem to solve. They then share free-flowing images about the problem on a large drawing board. The process at work is this: As the symbols and their possible meanings emerge, new solutions often arise.

Participants in these sessions also learn:

☐ To be more flexible, more open to change and risk.
☐ New ways of looking at work—reps find that the group problem-solving effort is fun as well as productive.
☐ Intuition is strengthened via the freer imagery; it serves as a complement to traditional left-brain thinking about problems.[29]

Using Music

Music can enhance many types of learning experiences. Trainer/consultant Gregory J. Trulson (President, Training Solutions, Boca Raton, Florida) believes that: "Music has magic. You can't see it or taste it, but it can arouse emotions, create moods."[30] Gerry Reid, consultant and engineer with IT Services, Kasson, Minnesota, and a proponent of "accelerated learning," sees music as a tremendous way of accelerating and intensifying the learning experience. He points up these worthwhile benefits:[31]

☐ Reduces anxiety in the classroom and builds a team feeling.
☐ Builds a "whistle while you work" environment.
☐ Challenges and inspires participants.
☐ Provides an atmosphere of relaxation and achievement.

Specific Uses

Music may be used to advantage in these situations:

☐ *Prior to the start of a session.* Typically, people are sitting around awkwardly and uncomfortably, possibly in silence, waiting for things to start. Why not turn those painful moments into a pleasant and relaxing experience? Canadian trainer/consultant John Spencer (President, Universal Training, Inc., St. Catherine, Ontario)[32] suggests filling the void via a good quality table-top radio. Locate a tasteful radio station and you should be able to provide music which most people will find pleasant, easy-to-take, and enjoyable and should help to put them into a relaxed mood. (*Note:* If you prefer to play your own tapes on your cassette player, that's O.K., too.)
☐ *During breaks.* The break can begin with music. The cessation of music can serve as a signal to return to work. Upbeat music is appropriate.
☐ *At close out.* The musical selection should relate to the nature of the course, the nature of the group, overall program accomplishment/success, etc. An upbeat, inspiring piece should work in many situations.
☐ *For motivational purposes.* Gerry Reid favors motivational theme music and popular light classics for it implies that: "This is a challenge, but you can do it and enjoy it."
☐ *For background/atmosphere while people work.* Gerry Reid uses very soft baroque music, environmental sounds/relaxation compositions during formal sessions—lecture and individual and small group activities—to keep the atmosphere of relaxing and achieving alive.

☐ *For guided imagery, meditation, and fantasy.* Use soft, gentle music to serve as a soothing, relaxing background. Music which suggests outdoor sounds as wind, streams, brooks, birds, etc., is appropriate.

☐ *For training in nonverbal communication.* Varying, contrasting styles of music may be played—romantic, hard rock, folk, etc.—with the participants (in a personal growth program) acting out their feelings in dance.[33]

Gregory J. Trulson suggests the use of music in these varied situations:

☐ *To represent a decade:* The Vietnam era, the era of the Big Depression, World War II, the Eighties. The Vietnam era had numerous anti-war pieces; the Thirties had "Brother Can You Spare a Dime?" and so on.

☐ *Women's workshops:* For example, points about the mores and folkways of days gone by can be made with such pieces as "The Girl That I'll Marry" vs. "Anything You Can Do I Can Do Better."

☐ *Personal growth workshops:* Uplifting music such as "The Impossible Dream," particularly at program's end, can be impacting. Theme music from such films as *Rocky* and *Chariots of Fire* may be appropriate.

☐ *Creativity enhancement:* The goal is to evoke innovative imagery, facilitate self-expression, and dislodge surface material which impedes creative flow. Thoughtful, relaxing, and impressive symphonic music should help.

☐ *Marriage retreats ("couples labs"):* Members of each sex group may be given the opportunity to pick a musical piece from a large collection of cassette tapes. After listening to several, they select one which they want to play to their partner to communicate how they feel. Some people can't express their feelings verbally and the music can serve as a helpful substitute. Each partner plays his/her tape to the other. (*Note:* With the popularity and ready availability of cassette players, the logistical problems involved, if any, are insignificant.)

☐ *Stress management workshops:* Music which helps people to relax, to improve their state of mind, to create pleasant and positive images, etc., is helpful. Music can be played in the workshop while conducting relaxation exercises. Also, you can pass along these pointers to your participants for their post-workshop use:

1. Since all of us give our own meaning to music, select pieces that you like and find peaceful, restful, and soothing.
2. Make a 30-minute tape of that music.

3. Play it each day in a period that you have set aside for relaxation. *Note:* Repeated use of music that has helped relaxation in the past provides a positive association that is likely to be beneficial thereafter.
4. While the music plays, assume a comfortable position and close your eyes. Concentrate on the music and your relaxed state. Check your body mentally. Are there areas of pain, tension, or relaxation? What is your mood? If unrelated thoughts invade your relaxed state, discard them, and focus on the music and relaxing.
5. When the music ends, scan your body again. How does it feel? Any difference now compared to the start of your relaxation period? Any change in your mood?

☐ *Career development workshops:* Consider a courage-building tune like "Take This Job And Shove It" for those who are enmeshed in no-win job situations. The "Rocky" and similar inspirational musical pieces may be helpful, too, at appropriate points in the program.

Career planning workshops lend themselves well to the use of music. Training Specialist Mitch Mitchell of Hewlett-Packard, San Diego, recommends the following musical pieces (presented at the Annual Conference of the National Society for Performance and Instruction, April 8, 1988, Washington, D.C.):

Keep On Working, Peter Townsend
Working Man, Creedance Clearwater Revival
Work To Do, Average White Band
Working 9 To 5, Dolly Parton
New Attitude, Patty LaBelle
Theme from *Rocky*
Theme from *Chariots of Fire*
It's My Job, Jimmy Buffett

Song

When considering music, we should not overlook song. Singing is a dynamic way to accelerate learning. Why? Because tunes and lyrics are stored and processed in the right hemisphere of the brain, areas which relate to imagination, spontaneity, and emotion. Song can aid learning and recall tremendously since it utilizes powerful mental circuitry.

Old, well-recognized tunes can be given new lyrics. This makes recall of the new information easy and fun. Or the trainees, in small groups, can write their own subject-related lyrics to a tune you select. Pride in creation and ownership can further aid the long-time storing of the new material.

Songs which lend themselves to new lyric development are "Three Blind Mice" and "The Mexican Hat Dance."[34]

Skill Pointers

Gregory J. Trulson offers these suggestions and cautions regarding the use of music:

1. If you have not used music before, ease into it. Use it initially as a pre-session relaxer and at breaks. As you get more comfortable with it, expand your use to serve as adjuncts to specific subject matter areas.
2. Don't force your musical preferences (biases) on people. It has been said "that one person's tune is another person's tomb." Try to hit "a common denominator" and use musical pieces most people will relate to. Take into account a possible "generation gap" factor if you have a mixed participant age group.
3. Try to provide music with simple equipment. Hauling expensive, bulky stereo equipment to the training room is overkill.
4. If you are conducting training programs commercially, i.e., receiving some sort of fee or honorarium, be aware of copyright laws. You may be able to get permission from the publisher for only occasional and minor use. Some publishers may appreciate that you wish to "tout" their music.

The Journal or Diary

. . . no feeling fully experienced is inappropriate; that its expression, whether within the privacy of the journal or among trusted intimates, may well be a matter of mental health, an important tool of adjustment or a creative solution to the difficulties of any life. To restrain or deny feelings limits our depth of perception, loses empathy for other people and leads to an inner disunity. And for us men, especially, to become a man of more conscious feeling is to become more fully human.

—Michael Rubin in *Men Without Masks*, Addison-Wesley, Reading, Mass., 1980.

More and more, the personal journal or diary, as a supplement to the group experience, is becoming recognized as an invaluable tool to help participants acquire insight about their behavior, motivations, values, attitudes, and feelings. The twin acts of introspection and recording one's thoughts and feelings help considerably to produce something none of us can get enough of—self-awareness. Some recent and varied examples of where and how journals have been used follow:

☐ In the CBS, Inc. five-day Professional Management Program, students are asked to keep daily diaries and to discuss their experiences at the end of the week.[35]
☐ Trainer-consultant Patricia McLagen, president of McLagen & Associates, St. Paul, instituted two different training activities at NASA on the premise that people, as learners, learn in different ways. One was group-oriented: group discussion; the other was solitary for "stop-and-think" purposes: the activity journal. McLagen recommended the journal as a tool to bridge (apply) the classroom learning to the on-the-job environment.[36]
☐ In an experimental New York City program for the elderly, 300 recruits from the welfare and unemployment rolls attended an Intensive Journal Workshop. This was a part of their on-the-job training for such jobs as nurse's aids, housekeepers, dietary workers, guards, maintenance men, etc. Surprisingly, 90% of them kept their journals over a six-month period (they met weekly), finished their training and stuck with these low-status hospital jobs. After a year, 80% were still on the job or had moved on to better ones. Also, one in three secured better housing, and one in four started night school or community college. The journal method was credited with much of the program's success by program officials. Ira Progoff, founder of the Intensive Journal Method, said this of the trainees and their initially impoverished condition: "Poverty is not simply the lack of money. Ultimately, it is a person's lack of feeling for the reality of his own inner being."[37]
☐ In a stress management program participants identify sources of stress they encounter on the job; they then select a target problem that they wish to manage; and, as a third step, they keep a record for a week about what happens when the problem occurs. The rationale for the diary approach is that a basic step in changing behavior patterns is the observation and recording of cues that trigger a particular behavior. The recording of the behavior helps participants to learn how their thoughts and actions, as well as the influences (actions or stimuli) of others, may be inducing the stress. In effect, the recorded data is feedback basic to managing the unwanted stress.

As an aid to keeping their week-long record, participants are given these kinds of questions to respond to when the problem arises: What precipitated the problem? What were you doing at the time? What were you thinking about? What was the nature of the tension that was experienced? What was your response to the stressor?[38]

☐ Roger W. Axford of the Department of Higher and Adult Education, Arizona State University, Tempe, asks participants in his management seminars to keep a weekly journal to record learnings of the week. He finds that the insight it provides managers tends, among other things, to reduce stress on the job. He also reports that having a week's record of insights and ideas provides "a sourcebook for program planning, administrative revisions, and possible career changes or development."[39]

☐ In the area of creativity, writer and teacher of writing Nancy Kuriloff advises her clients to keep a "process log" as a way of unleashing one's creativity. She recommends these steps:

1. When the ideas won't come, write down all your feelings and frustrations.
2. Focus on your creative periods. What circumstances seem to help the ideas flow?
3. Jot down, brainstorming style, whatever comes to mind. Polish the material later.[40]

Industrial psychologist Harry Levinson, commenting on Kuriloff's journal technique, points out that the creative process is the same whether it's writing or engineering design.[41]

Eugene Raudsepp, a psychologist and president of Princeton Creative Research, a consulting firm that specializes in creative problem solving for industry, states that diary-keeping is the best way to check whether one has genuine "intuitive hunches" or mainly "wishful projections." He suggests that if your record shows that your hunches are mostly inaccurate, make a serious self-appraisal to ascertain how personal interests or anxieties might be distorting your perceptions. Committing your insights to writing as they arise, also aids in retaining ideas that all too readily evaporate due to an interruption or distraction.[42]

☐ Charles M. Vance, Syracuse University, recommends that you, as a trainer in human relations or management, mention the journal idea as the program starts. Point out to participants that it is a good tool to record insights about themselves and their relationships with others that they reach during the training. Then distribute a "mini-journal" for recording these insights in relation to the back-home situation. Schedule time at the end of each day to share one's personal journal with a fellow participant. At program's end allow enough time for each participant to prepare and leave with you a summary of the insights gained during the week. Also advise participants to keep their journals alive by constantly recording successes, failures, and insights relative thereto. Finally, tell them you will follow up in six months to assess their progress with the insights recorded in their journals.[43]

☐ Management trainers Michael J. Kruger and Kay H. Smith used the journal approach as a means of a post-training "reminder" following a two-week management training course. Specifically, they secured agreement from the managers to take their journals home, review and revise them, and return them to the course coordinator within 30 days. The latter then forwarded a complete set of *one* manager's weekly journal entries to all 24 course attendees for 24 consecutive weeks. This procedure provided each manager with the opportunity to "relive" the learning experience via peer writings and insights for a six-month period after course's end.[44]

Reference was made earlier to the need to transfer classroom learning to the job. Although contracting (self-contracts for action plans) is one way to do this, we know from experience that not everyone is willing or able to develop easily an action plan. The diary is a good way to help participants develop the "mind set" basic to the preparation of their action plans. A tool for this purpose is a journal-type worksheet given in Appendix 16. It starts the proper thought processes at the program's outset so that participants can ease into the preparation of their contracts and action plans at program's end. Advise participants on Day 1 that they should complete their diary as the program goes along and review it regularly to update, revise, complete, and refine their statements. Completion of the last column—Possible Action Plan— may be deferred until the end of the program. The important thing is that a lot of the thinking basic to the action plan will already have been completed on a regular and continuing basis.

Another example of a structured form of the journal or diary is given in Figure 4-7. It is an aid to resolving a problem in interpersonal relations, communication, etc. A separate page, such as in a notebook, should be used to record the daily reactions to one's new behavior.

Sharing Data Developed by Journaling

A final step in the journaling process is sharing what one has recorded. Of course, not all recorded data need be shared. In fact, if it is very personal, it may not be desirable to do so. In such a circumstance, the task of the journal keepers may be to share what was learned from the experience, as opposed to sharing the details of the journal.

In general, whether participants share data from their journals will depend on such factors as:

Resolving a Problem with Another Person

Here's where I am now:

I'm a negative person

People react to me in this way:

They avoid me; they seem to be startled by some of the things I say.

I will try the following new behavior:

I will say nice things; give praise; be patient.

Reactions from others on Day 1:

I haven't noted any changes by others toward me yet; I'll keep trying tomorrow, however.

Figure 4-7. Example of a structured form of journaling.

☐ *Nature of data.* If the recorded material relates to, say, delegation problems, this would probably be easy to share. Conversely, if the data relates to personal stressors, there may be an understandable reluctance to share them.

☐ *Nature of program.* In a management development seminar with limited experiential activities in it, sharing may seem inappropriate and threatening. Conversely, in a highly experiential leadership laboratory, full sharing may be a very natural thing to do.

☐ *Recording time.* If the journaling has proceeded for a very short time, sharing may be premature.

☐ *Nature of participant group.* A group of blue-collar foremen, law enforcement supervisors, or upper level business executives may be less likely to share their journal data than mental health workers at a "burnout" conference, or participants at a career planning workshop.

Keeping a journal of events, thoughts, perceptions, etc., enables us to capture them before they become hazy or disappear entirely. By reducing them to writing, they also serve as building blocks for the development of new (future) observations/perceptions. The more complete and candid the journal becomes, the greater the self-insight one can garner from it.

Post-Training Use

Attention should be given in the classroom to the use of the journal *after* the training experience. The operative concept is that journaling is both a form of personal stress management and personal growth. It thus should not die at training's end.

When should a diarist do his/her recording? One long-time diarist suggests doing it "when the spirit moves rather than to force it. It might be easier to find things to write about in the evening, when the chaos of the day can be sorted." Since we are creatures of habit, some journal writers will ritualize the time, place, chair, lighting, beverage. All of which is O.K. if it establishes the mood for writing. And if one can't evoke a thought, reference can be entered in the journal to the effect that "didn't feel like writing."[45]

Working with Models

A model is a conceptualization. It gives us a way of looking at a lot of information quickly and with greater overall understanding, too. In short, it gives us something we all want and need—the big picture.

Typically (but not universally), the model is presented in a diagrammatic or graphic form.

In the training situation, models provide a framework against which individuals and/or groups can test the validity of their attitudes, values, assumptions, and behavior.

Several examples of ways trainers can work with models follow.

Working with the Hierarchy of Needs

The late Abraham H. Maslow, a creative clinical psychologist and the founder of humanistic psychology, postulated the most widely quoted theory of motivation called "The Hierarchy of Needs." His theory or model identified the five different levels of human motivation. It also asserted that one could move up to a higher level only if the prior level was satisfied. The model is often presented diagramatically as in Figure 4-8.

Figure 4-8. Diagrammatic presentation of Maslow's "The Hierarchy of Needs."

Four ways of involving participants with the Maslowian model are given below:

1. Have participants complete the form given in Appendix 17 and then share it in small groups.

    Note: The objective of this activity is to encourage introspection or soul-searching in respect to one's job satisfaction, or values, or career aspirations, etc.

2. In a time management course, draw the Hierarchy of Needs on a flipchart, explain it briefly, and then pose this question for general discussion or small group work: Assuming that managers often are reluctant to manage their time better, can the Hierarchy explain their possible motivations for such behavior?

    Example answers include:

    Safety/Security: The workaholic can be explained, in part, by anxieties and insecurities which drive him/her to constant effort.

    Social: If a need to socialize (to be loved) with others is very strong, socializing will be done even if it results in wasted time. Thus, time-consuming interruptions by phone, drop-ins, etc., will be tolerated.

    Ego: The dirty or cluttered desk syndrome, a real time-waster, may be explained by the desire to look busy and important. (Any rational observer would assert that a dirty desk, often accompanied by one or two other cluttered tables, hardly makes for efficiency.)

    Self-actualization: If one has a strong need for self-fulfillment, to be creative, to plan ahead, one will seek ways to find the time to so function. Conversely, if one is "stuck" at a lower level of motivation, there is no real need to move up to the apex of the Hierarchy.

3. Working with five small groups (or five sets of small groups if there is a large participant group), have each come up with practical motivators in relation to one level of the Hierarchy. (This means assigning one of the five levels to each small group.)

    Note: This assignment can be varied by letting each group decide for itself which level it wants to treat.

    Some examples of what may be produced by the groups:

    Physiological level: pay, fringes, good working conditions.

    Security level: share information to reduce anxieties about what is going on; manage consistently (don't upset people via sudden changes); don't shake people up by "big bear" behavior; provide a safe place to work.

    Social level: encourage recreational activities, car pools, picnics, Christmas parties, informal groups, etc.

    Ego level: provide opportunity to do one's job well, delegate, use job enrichment approaches, give praise and recognition, use participative methods such as the Quality Circle.

4. A Maslowian concept, at the self-fulfillment or self-actualization level, is that of the "peak experience." It is a "high" from an event or accomplishment where one goes beyond the normal or everyday expectation. It is a state of becoming, not just being (the Ego level). Examples include: climbing a mountain, natural childbirth (or any birth), being elected to an office one prizes, writing a book, conducting a unique piece of research, overhauling an engine for the first time, a hole in one, etc. Have individuals reflect on and share such experiences in small groups.

    Note: This exercise might be used in a course on career development, in a session on self-development, in a session on motivation, in self-assertiveness training. (What are you doing to move up the Hierarchy? Are you letting others keep you down? What is keeping you from being a self-actualizing person?)

Choosing a Leadership Pattern

Robert Tannenbaum and Warren H. Schmidt, in the now-classic "How to Choose a Leadership Pattern," *Harvard Business Review,* March-April 1958, presented an array or continuum of leadership styles ranging from "boss-centered" to "subordinate-centered." The styles in their leadership model are these:

☐ The manager decides alone and simply announces it.
☐ The manager makes the decision alone, but tries to *sell* it to subordinates.
☐ The manager presents an idea (or decision) and *tests* subordinates by asking them: "What do you think?"
☐ The manager presents a decision tentatively, subject to possible change after the discussion. (There is no commitment, of course, to accept the advice, no matter how sound.)
☐ The manager presents *the problem* and consults with subordinates who are asked for suggestions *before* the decision is given to them.
☐ The manager asks the *group to make the decision* subject to the manager's boundaries or limits.

☐ The manager *joins* with the group in problem identification, diagnosis, consideration of alternatives and making of the decision (team management)

The model avoids value judgments concerning the wisdom or the correctness of decision-making along any point on the continuum. Rather, such a decision may be made depending on the situation, i.e., the need for telling, selling, testing, consulting, or joining. In addition to the forces in the situation, the manager also considers the forces in himself/herself and in the subordinates.

Have participants draw the continuum, as just described, then have them locate the point at which they, as managers, typically operate. Assign participants to small groups, and have them address themselves to these questions:

☐ Does my leadership style vary at all? If so, when? Why? Do I choose or merely use a style?
☐ Does my style match by boss' style? If it varies, why does it? Is it desirable or undesirable for the styles to match?
☐ What about my style in relation to my subordinates? What do they prefer? If I vary it, do they understand why I do so? (This is a consistency-logic-perception issue.) Or do the changes, if any, confuse them?
☐ Have I always had the same style? Do I anticipate any change in the future? Why or why not?
☐ How does one's personality affect or influence the style one employs?

Note: Since there are many profound questions here, allow enough time (30–45 minutes) to deal with them.

Secure reports from the small groups regarding learnings from the exercise.

A Model of Personal Power and Influence

To understand the "influence process" Roger Harrison and Jim Konzes[46] have presented a model comprising four ways we use our psychological energy to bring about change.

☐ *Pushing:* Here we direct our energy toward others in an aggressive way to bring about what we consider to be a desired change. When we are pushing we engage in direct attempts to move; to induce; to teach; and to control through orders, information, arguments, criticism, pressure, and threats.
☐ *Attracting:* We behave in ways that draw others to us based on our attractiveness, magnetism, excitement, and the like. We may also appeal to common values,

ideals, goals. This, obviously, is more of an inspirational approach than a frontal attack.
☐ *Joining:* The change effort entails adding our energy to theirs, thereby increasing it. We do this by encouraging, empathizing, summarizing, reflecting feelings, and seeking cooperation. Trust, support, and concern are key elements in this mode.
☐ *Disengaging:* We avoid or deflect the other's energy. This entails withdrawal, failing to respond, changing the subject, postponing, reducing (needed) conflict and interchange.

Using a 10-point scale, rank each mode of influence as to the frequency that you use it in your work (home, community, etc.). Then discuss your rankings with a partner.

A Model Regarding Burnout

Dr. Paul O. Radde, president and founder of Thrival Systems, has presented a model regarding the Burnout Syndrome.[47] Participants were given this definition of burnout (by R. Kundel): "a progressive cycle which depletes one's energy, results in loss of vitality, and progresses to more serious stages that affect the body, emotions, and spirit. The end result of burnout is dysfunctional behavior and low productivity." Dr. Radde then asked the participants, in small groups, to check their own experience of burnout against a five-stage progression of the syndrome: physiological, social, intellectual, psycho-emotional, and spiritual. The groups then developed strategies, both organizational and individual, to counter burnout.

Working with Transactional Analysis

The TA model covers three "ego states"—Parent, Adult, and Child. The model may take the following diagrammatical form when two people are in communication:

To chart the nature of a given transaction or communication event between two persons, draw an arrow from one circle to another as shown. The charting process is done for all transactions.

Two examples of the use of the TA model in the training situation follow:

☐ To help participants understand better their organization's culture, ask them to think of the organization as a person. A good way to do this, per TA authority Dorothy Jongeward, is to have participants draw the organization's three "ego states," a basic TA concept. The idea is to see how large its Parent (both nurturing and critical sides), Adult (rational side) and Child (both creative and rebellious sides) would be. In effect, the TA model is used to help analyze and explain organizational culture.[48]

☐ Explain this problem to participants: "Allied Widgets is facing severe financial problems. Management appeals to employees for help have been ineffective thus far. The reason: A total reliance on Parent to Child appeals. Thus, people feel that they are being talked down to. Can you provide examples of such appeals?"

"One example of a Parent to Child appeal is: 'Everyone will have to watch their arrival and quitting times and the length of their coffee breaks. Five minutes here and there multiplied by the total work force can add up to many lost dollars.' Can you provide examples of more *effective* appeals, that is Adult to Adult? An example of this kind of appeal is 'We need your ideas to help turn things around. Exercise your creativity. Every idea for improvement, big or small, is wanted and may well prove helpful.'"

Key Points

1. A variety of more "specialized" techniques may be used to secure high involvement. These include fishbowls, fantasy, guided imagery, mental imagery, working with pictures, using art, keeping journals, and using models.
2. Fishbowls can provide added means of increasing interaction and "ideation" as well as novelty. The technique is useful for analysis of a given problem and/or group functioning.
3. Fantasy, guided imagery, and mental imagery are tools to augment creativity by having participants produce "mind pictures." The stimuli may be provided by the trainer (in fantasy and guided imagery), by the participant (in mental imagery and visualization), or by both parties (in guided fantasy).
4. Pictures can provide added opportunities for participant involvement and learning. Their use may range from the conventional (e.g., to identify parts of a piece of equipment) to the more advanced (e.g., as a "projective" technique in an experiential training program).
5. Art is another way to tap participant emotions, creativity, and the "child" within us. Art activities may be individual, small group, or total group.

6. As part of your overall training design, consider the use of music for fun, mood-setting, invigoration, inspiration, etc.
7. Keeping a journal is a relatively new training tool designed to help participants develop insight into their needs, motivations, emotions, attitudes, and behaviors.
8. Models are a useful tool to help participants visualize better major ideas, concepts, theories. By working with them in the training situation, the abstract model can come alive and provide participants with insight into the model's ideas and possibly into themselves.
9. Regardless of the kind of technique in which small groups engage, the activity must close with a complete analysis (processing) of it. If adequate time is not allowed for such closure, learning will be minimal and participants may experience a sense of frustration.

References

1. Based on a format presented in Hart, L. B., *Learning from Conflict: A Handbook for Trainers and Group Leaders,* Addison-Wesley Publishing Company, Reading, Massachusetts (1981), pp. 189–90.
2. Banet, A. G., Jr., and Jones, J. E., "Fantasy: Theory and Technique," in *The 1978 Annual Handbook for Group Facilitators,* University Associates, San Diego, California (1978), p. 198.
3. Smart, William, "Diversions: The Waiting Game," *The Washington Post,* December 9, 1983, p. D5, which draws on the book by Eleanor Rowe, *Waiting Games: How To Get Rich, Powerful, Sexy, and Healthy While You're Killing Time,* Facts On File, New York, 1983, 126 pages.
4. The examples of training exercises in guided imagery are based on a presentation by Dr. Marilyn Saunders, a specialist in guided imagery, to the Washington, D.C., Chapter of the Association for Humanistic Psychology, January 10, 1982.
5. Larquit, L., "Work In The Fast Lane," *Northeast Training News* (June 1980), p. 18.
6. Pearlstein, Gloria, "Guided Visualization Fact Sheet," *Performance and Instruction Journal,* September 1987, p. 22.
7. *Training/HRD* (July 1976), p. 7.
8. "Right-Brain Training Helps Flight Attendants Pass FAA Exams," *Training/HRD* (June 1981), pp. 17–18.
9. Zemke, R., "Picture This: Using Mental Imagery to Enhance Learning," *Training/HRD* (January 1981), pp. 79–81.

10. Diekhoff, G. M., "How to Teach How to Learn," *Training/HRD* (September 1982), pp. 36–40.
11. Reid, Gerry, "Accelerated Learning: Technical Training Can Be Fun," *Training and Development Journal* (September 1985), pp. 24–27.
12. *Newsletter,* Association for Humanistic Psychology (December 1979), p. 27.
13. *The Levinson Letter* (October 15, 1981), p. 2.
14. Per Lee Beckner, Sales Training Manager, Coca Cola Foods Division, reported in *Meeting News* (May 1980), p. 98.
15. "Seminar Enlightens Managers On Best Ways To Hire and Handle Disabled Employees," *Wall Street Journal* (May 27, 1981).
16. "Phototherapy Enhances Therapeutic Process—Start to Termination," *Behavior Today* (February 15, 1982), pp. 4–5.
17. Culbert, Samuel A., and Fisher, Jerry, "The Medium of Art As An Adjunct To Learning In Sensitivity Training," *The Journal of Creative Behavior* (Winter 1969), pp. 26–40.
18. Garanzini, Michael J., "What We Learn Through Children's Art," *Today's Catholic Teacher* (March 1984), pp. 53–55.
19. Goldstein, Marilyn; Scholthauer, David; and Kleiner, Brian H., "Management On The Right Side of The Brain," *Personnel Journal* (November 1985), pp. 40–45.
20. Connelly, S., *Participant's Manual to Accompany Self-Motivation in Selling—A Sales Training Program,* BNA Communications Inc., Rockville, Maryland, 1979.
21. Javernick, Ellen, "Off To An Art Start," *Today's Catholic Teacher* (September 1984), pp. 50–51.
22. Jacobs, Sanford L., "Wharton Course Teaches Planning Using Managers' Drawings of Firms," *Wall Street Journal* (October 31, 1984), second section, first page.
23. Jacobs, Sanford S., "Problems Of Family Companies Tackled At Wharton Seminar," *Wall Street Journal* (July 9, 1984), second section, first page.
24. Ault, Robert E., "Draw On New Lines of Communication," *Personnel Journal* (September 1986), pp. 72–77.
25. Haight, G. G., "Fear of Speaking," *Across The Board* (March 1980), pp. 44–45.
26. Fordyce, Jack K., and Weil, Raymond, *Managing With People: A Manager's Handbook Of Organization Development Methods,* Addison-Wesley, Reading, Massachusetts, 1971, pp. 152–155.
27. Dworken, Art, "The Three Circle Test," *The Washington Post,* Health Section (February 6, 1985).
28. Jung, C. G., *Man And His Symbols,* Doubleday and Company, New York (1964), p. 213. Also see "How to Use the Mandala," *Newsletter,* Association for Humanistic Psychology, Washington, D.C. Chapter, July 1983, reprinted from *Expansion Magazine,* undated.
29. "Weyerhaeuser Groups Tune Intuition, Imagination," *Leading Edge Bulletin* (October 19, 1981), p. 2.
30. Trulson, Gregory J., "The Sounds of Music," presentation at the National Conference of the American Society for Training and Development, June 22, 1987, Atlanta, Georgia.
31. Reid, Gerry, "Accelerated Learning: Technical Training Can Be Fun," *Training and Development Journal* (September 1985), pp. 24–27.
32. Spencer, John D., "How To Provide A Sensational Environment," *CTM (Canadian Training Methods): The Human Element* (December 1982), pp. 16–17.
33. Pfeiffer, William J. and Jones, John E., *A Handbook Of Structured Experiences For Human Relations Training,* Vol. 1, activity #22, Nonverbal Communication, item 19, University Associates, Inc., San Diego, 1970.
34. Reid, Gerry, "Accelerated Learning: Technical Training Can Be Fun," *Training and Development Journal* (September 1985), pp. 24–27.
35. *Business Week* (October 20, 1980), p. 125.
36. *Training World* (September–October, 1979), p. 29.
37. Kaider, R. B., "The Way of the Journal," *Psychology Today* (March 1981), p. 67.
38. Weigel, R., and Pinsky, S., "Managing Stress: A Model for the Human Resource Staff," *The Personnel Administrator* (February 1982), p. 57.
39. Axford, R. W., "A Journal: Management and Development Tool," *Training and Development Journal* (September 1980), p. 8.
40. *Time* (July 14, 1980). Cited in *The Levinson Letter* (September 15, 1980), p. 2.
41. *The Levinson Letter* (September 15, 1980), p. 2.
42. Raudsepp, E., "You Can Trust Your Hunches," *Inc.* (July 1981), p. 89.
43. Vance, C. M., "Personal Journals in Training: Get More Mileage Out of Your Training Programs," *Training and Development Journal* (August 1979), pp. 54–55.
44. Kruger, Michael J., and Smith, Kay H., "Evaluating Management Training," *Performance and Instruction* (November and December 1987), p. 23.
45. O'Neil, L. Peat, "For Write-Minded People: The Journal," *The Washington Post* (April 3, 1987), p. B5.
46. Harrison, R., and Konzes, J., "The Power Potential of Organization Development," *Training and Development Journal* (April 1980), pp. 44–47.

47. The presentation was made to the Washington, D.C. Chapter of the American Society for Training and Development (April 1980).
48. Caplin, D., "Corporate Culture: Training Problems and Prospects," *Northeast Training News* (August 1981), p. 10.

Recommended Reading

Barnet, Anthony G., Jr., and Jones, John E. "Fantasy: Theory and Technique," in *The 1976 Annual Handbook for Group Facilitators*. University Associates, Inc., San Diego, 1976, pp. 191–201.

This provides a discussion of psychological underpinnings for fantasy and describes its types, techniques for structuring it, training considerations, and precautions.

Casewit, Curtis W. *The Diary: A Complete Guide to Journal Writing*, Argus Communications, Allen, Texas, 1982.

This contains advice to the diaryist including benefits, how to get started, how to keep it going, diary style, and formats.

Galyean, Beverly-Colleene "Guided Imagery in Education," *Journal of Humanistic Psychology*, Fall 1981, Vol. 21, No. 4, pp. 57–72.

This describes how educators use imagery processes for higher consciousness, relaxation, receptivity to learning, and increased mastery of information.

Jaffee, Dennis T., and Bresler, David E. "The Use of Guided Imagery As An Adjunct to Medical Diagnosis and Treatment," *Journal of Humanistic Psychology*, Fall 1980, Vol. 20, No. 4, pp. 45–59.

This offers examples of the use of imagery to obtain diagnostic information, for relaxation, to make positive suggestions to alter physical processes, and in the discovery of "an inner adviser."

Pfeiffer, J. William, and Jones, John E. "Fantasies," in *A Handbook of Structured Experiences for Human Relations Training* Vol. 1., University Associates, Inc., San Diego, 1969, pp. 77–80.

This presents fantasy exercises including 15 individual fantasies, 5 guided fantasies, and 3 group fantasies. It cites professional standards for their use.

ROLE PLAYING

You cannot teach a man anything. You can only help him discover it within himself.

—Galileo Galilei (1564–1642),
Italian astronomer and physicist

Role playing is one of the trainer's primary techniques to provide participation, involvement, and action learning. It allows the acting out (experiencing) of real-life situations in a protected or risk-free locale. That is to say, it is far safer and wiser to make mistakes as a role player in the training situation than in the work or other social environments.

Role playing in the training situation makes possible the receiving of adequately objective feedback about one's performance so that one can learn from what others (peers, the trainer) see, hear, and feel. Conversely, in the actual life situation we perform and behave, but rarely does anyone share their reactions about what we've done and how we can improve upon it.

We should also note that in role-playing activities participants are learning "full time." This accrues because they are either experiencing (acting out the role play), introspecting, engaging in self-critique, or critiquing others.

Purposes and Benefits

In a more specific sense, role playing has these purposes and benefits:

☐ *To present information* to participants; for example, a top management official and the personnel manager assume the roles of a manager and an accountant, the latter "learning" that there now are legal taboos on sexual harrassment.

☐ *To learn certain principles* of coaching, counseling, customer relations, conflict management, interviewing for fair employment, etc.

☐ *To change attitudes,* for example, to become less prejudiced toward another department, a minority group, the opposite sex, foreign persons or those of another culture, handicapped persons. (In respect to the latter group, student attitudes toward the disabled were altered in a positive direction after students sat in a wheelchair for an hour.)

☐ *To develop practical skills,* such as how to close a sale, how to handle customer objections, how to handle a disciplinary interview or a grievance, how to apply for a job, how to "upgrade" a sale.

☐ *To "reality" test* or check out the effectiveness of one's approaches or techniques; e.g., in sales training one can try out one's ability to anticipate problems, to make timing more effective, or to employ sound reasoning. *Note:* Role playing provides for practice without penalty.

☐ *To disclose one's attitudes* towards others, a given subject, a problem, etc., so that one may receive related feedback.

☐ *To provide a "mirror"* (via feedback) so that participants can see themselves as others do, a basic step toward fostering insight (about self) and sensitivity (toward others).

☐ *To identify with others;* by acting out the role of another person one can understand better "where the other is coming from." For example, a student having problems in school can achieve new insights into his/her behavior by assuming the roles of parent, teacher, and principal.

☐ *To learn how others think and feel* (empathy), such as customers, prospects, subordinates, members of the opposite sex, minority group members, persons of other ages, employees of other departments, persons of another organizational level (e.g. headquarters vs. staff, line vs. staff).

☐ *To change behavior,* such as to become more assertive, to become more spontaneous, to learn how to listen actively, to learn how to counsel nondirectively, to learn how to coach subordinates so they feel rewarded (psychologically) when the interview is over.

☐ *To prepare employees realistically* for some of the "discouraging" experiences they may encounter on the job. Thus, several major real estate firms have used role-playing courses to prepare their rookie sales personnel for encounters with difficult customers. For example, in one scenario a trainee vendor was constantly interrupted by the seller's mother. Finally, he told the old woman: "Why don't you take a walk in the garden?" and literally threw her out, obviously a "no, no" in conducting proper customer relations. Other specialists have to learn how to deal with a lot of unpleasantness; e.g., police officers who have to mediate nasty family disputes, park rangers who have to calm would-be campers who are squabbling over the last space in a campground, foreign service officers who have to deal with troubled Americans and anxious foreigners.[1]

Role Playing Designs

The following sections will show the considerable variety role-playing formats may take, and will give you, as a trainer, practical role-playing models, all of which have been tested in the training situation. These explanations will also challenge you to use your own ingenuity to create new formats or to adapt the ones provided based on your study of them.

Informal Role Playing

Informal role playing[2] develops from the needs and special circumstances in the training situation. It thus is unplanned, unstructured, unwritten, and unrehearsed

(compared to the structured or more formal role play where the role players are given a fairly good set of role instructions plus time to think about them).

It may arise in one of two ways:

☐ *From a participant problem.* A participant may say: "I have this problem at home (in the office, in the community) . . . ."

Trainer: O.K., Doris, tell us a little bit more about your subordinate—name, age, personality, skill level, etc.

Doris: (provides added detail)

Trainer: O.K., let's see if we can develop any strategies to deal with Mary and her tendency to deliver put downs, sarcastic and negative comments, etc. Fran, would you like to be Mary? (Fran agrees.) You (Mary) and your boss, Doris, have just completed reviewing a project of yours. Doris has complimented you on it and now she's about to bring up some other business—the put down problem.

(The role play is conducted)

Trainer: That was quite good. But let's see if you can deal with this problem in any other way. Let's try this with another role playing team. Who wants to be Doris? Good. Who wants to be Mary? Great. O.K., here's the office. Doris is seated and Mary walks in . . .

☐ *From the need to sharpen issues.* In the discussion of a case or problem, a participant might say: "If I were the field rep, I would tell the inspector . . ."

Trainer: O.K., Pat, you be the field rep; Kim, you be the inspector. Here's your office, Pat. The inspector has just brought up the matter of _____ which you are quite irritated about.

The rationale for this procedure is that it is one thing to *say:* "If I were the boss . . . " It may be something entirely different to have to actually handle that situation. Hence the need to reality test what can or can't be done in a given interpersonal situation as well as the more effective ways of accomplishing it.

In some cases you may decide to assume one of the two roles should you feel that the desired behavior or skill can be better portrayed by the trainer. Or the person who brought up the problem with another person may be asked to assume the role of the other person (role reversal) to develop insight concerning how the other person feels.

In general, the alert trainer will be on the lookout for situations where role play opportunities arise in discussion naturally. They give the training effort an extra, vivid dimension, something which participants will appreciate and learn from.

Spontaneous Role Playing

Spontaneous role playing,[3] also known as "live" or "hot" role playing, deals with real people (the participants) and their actual problems with others—on the job, at home, in the community, elsewhere in the everyday world.

Typically, the trainer asks the participants to cite the problems they have on a given subject. For example, in a course on interviewing techniques you may say: "What are your most perplexing or difficult problems in your interviews?" You then post them on the flipchart and the group prioritizes them. The top problems (e.g., how to conduct a firing interview or how to listen more effectively) on the list are selected for the role play.

Then ask for volunteers to do the first role play. You may advise the group: "Here's a great opportunity to try out some things, to take some risks, for that's how we'll learn and grow. Also, it's not too serious if we come up with a mistake or two here. The idea is to get rid of the mistakes in the training situation so we won't make them where they really count—back on the job."

The first role play is subject to group critique and may be conducted again if it is inconclusive or if another approach is desired. Principles and skill pointers are developed by the group for the conduct of a particular type of interview, such as coaching. The group then moves on to another problem in interviewing.

Using live cases has real appeal to participants. In fact, it would be hard to imagine a course in, say, assertiveness training, where the participants were not allowed to work through some of their own problems; e.g., communicating directly to the boss that one cannot work overtime due to other commitments, returning a dress to a small specialty shop, complaining about a bad steak in a first class restaurant, or being given a hard time at work by another department.

In processing (critiquing) the action, you may explore the role players' feelings—tensions, frustrations, satisfactions, dissatisfactions, inhibitions, etc. The group should be encouraged to engage in the same kind of exploration of emotion plus an analysis of what was learned, what behavior was predominant, what behavior was lacking or in need of improvement, etc.

In general, spontaneous role play works well because participants are utilizing their own experiences rather than trainer-assigned roles. This tends to heighten their emotional involvement in the training being provided, which in turn, augments learning and facilitates on-the-job application.

The Demonstration-Type Role Play

Demonstration-type role plays are acted out before the rest of the participant group. Typically, they are of two types: the dramatic skit and the personal growth enactment.

The dramatic skit. A skit is presented to the total group by two or more role players. The objective is to illustrate a problem or skill approach and to generate total group discussion about it. The enactment is based on instructions about the roles provided by the trainer. The instructions may be given orally in either a general or specific manner. Sometimes a written script may be given to the role players to ensure that they present the problem accurately or that a particular point is made. The script may also help "to speed things up." For some role players, reliance on the script may be "tension reducing," too. Since the role players are only *presenting* a problem, their behavior per se is not subject to critique. In consequence, there is no expectation that greater "personal growth" will accrue for the role players, as opposed to the group-at-large, from the enactment of the skit per se.

A variation of the dramatic skit format is for the role players to engage in the "Wrong-Way, Right-Way" technique. The enactment follows the trainer's general instructions. Participants observe the "improper" procedure demonstrated by the role players (e.g., how to orient a new worker, how to close a sale) and critique it. Then the second role play follows, which depicts the "proper" way to carry out the orientation, or closing of the sale, etc. Another discussion ensues.

An added variation entails the use of small group planning for the enactment before it is given to the total group. This procedure helps to involve all participants more fully than in the typical dramatic skit. The procedures are as follows:

1. Disseminate general background data about the role playing case, if any, to all participants.
2. Divide the group at large into two smaller groups (A and B). Give all the A's one set of role playing instructions and the B's the other.
3. Ask each group (A and B) to discuss and agree on the purposes (goals, end results) of the interview and, as appropriate, the specific strategy to be followed in the role play.
4. Ask for a volunteer from the A and B groups to role play the case. Give them enough "prep time" to internalize their respective roles.
5. Simultaneous with step 4, brief the rest of the group, who are to be observers, concerning what to

look for in the role plays. (It's a good idea to give the observers a written question or guide sheet.)
6. Run the role play (about 20–25 minutes).
7. Hold a general discussion after the role play. Start things off by comparing each group's planned strategy and expectations as to results with what actually transpired. If there was a difference, try to learn why. Use the observer's question sheet to guide the discussion.
8. Summarize learnings from the role play.

Still another variation of the dramatic skit is for one role player (e.g., an employee in a disciplinary interview) to choose at random a role from an envelope or box having five or six different role playing instructions. Neither the other role player (the boss), the observer group or the trainer knows which role has been selected. They, therefore, do not know the attitudes, values, emotional state, etc., of the employee. Their task is to be sensitive to the employee, to pick up or read the cues and clues which the employee communicates. In effect, this is an exercise designed to test and develop awareness to feedback. The participant playing the role of the supervisor has the task of assessing the employee's current attitudinal state and makes adjustments in strategy as it comes into focus.

Note: Since there are a half-dozen or so different employee roles available, the enactment, using different role players, can be repeated several times, if desired.

The personal growth enactment. In this type of demonstration role play any number of role players enact an interpersonal situation of some complexity. The role players are challenged to deal with a situation that has no single or "best" solution. In the course of their enactment they exhibit or demonstrate their actual feelings, attitudes, and skill approaches. In effect, they play the role as they see it. The learning for the role players ensues from the opportunity for skill practice, self-critique, and the critique of the total group. The learning for the group is presumed to come from observing, analyzing, and giving feedback rather than from doing.

Note: The personal growth enactment is discussed as a demonstration-type role play because it is demonstrated or appears before the total group. The other types described hereafter are accomplished on a more private basis.

Advantages and Limitations. The advantages of the two demonstration-type enactments are several:

☐ Since the total group observes the same role play, and thus acquires the same data (at least in a general sense,

for obviously perceptions will vary), they can analyze and critique it collectively.
☐ The group can bring multiple judgment or perceptions to bear on the role play.
☐ As a limited participation device—few do the role playing—it gets reluctant or anxious players "off the hook." They observe and engage in critique rather than act out a given situation before their colleagues. (Of course, the program may call for everyone in the group to "have their turn in the barrel." In fact, some participants may welcome it.)

On the other hand, the demonstration-type role play has certain serious disadvantages:

☐ Since the bulk of the group merely observes, most participants do not have the opportunity to engage in the actual development of appropriate skills, empathy, sensitivity, etc.
☐ In fact, some (or even many) may not be very active observers and may engage in a rather mild and passive critique.
☐ The role players may feel anxious or embarrassed because they are acting out the problem before the total group.
☐ The trainer can control the enactments to highlight certain principles, skills, or problem areas for the group. This may be done via explicit instructions to the role players or by structuring the situation so that certain desired behaviors are quite likely to ensue. Of course, while the control is quite certain to produce the desired results if the dramatic skit is used, if the personal growth enactment is employed the outcomes are less predictable or not predictable at all.

Reducing role player anxiety To overcome feelings of anxiety about role playing before the full group you can:

☐ Conduct such an activity late in the program when people feel comfortable with one another and are more willing to take some risks.
☐ Utilize volunteers only.
☐ Provide a full orientation as to purposes, values, methods, how feedback will be given, if all participants will, in time, appear before the group in role-playing situations, etc. The fact that "we're all doing it" should reduce some of the anxiety.
☐ Start off with volunteers, if all are "to play" in time.
☐ Set a model for the group by playing in the first role play with a volunteer.
☐ Ensure that feedback to the role players is gentle, with heavy emphasis on positive reinforcement for the things done well in the role play(s).

□ Use role plays judiciously, even sparingly.
□ Select role play situations that have little or no "threat potential." Or, putting it in the positive, select role plays which participants will readily recognize as having worthwhile learning benefits.
□ Select role plays which are easy enough to produce a success experience, particularly in the first try.
□ Select role players who are strongly extroverted rather than shy.
□ Let the participants develop or present their own cases for enactment and the criteria for critique as well.
□ Avoid role plays in vertically structured training, i.e., where the participant and his/her boss are being trained together. No one wants to risk looking silly in front of the boss!
□ Explain to the participant group that here's a chance to get some worthwhile skill practice in a risk-free atmosphere, that is, it's far wiser to make a mistake or two here than in real life.
□ Introduce structure into the role plays in the form of pre-role-play planning sheets and post-role-play self-critique sheets. (See "Using Structure.")
□ If practicable, select, in advance, the role players who are to engage in the demonstration role play. Rehearse it once or twice so the acting is appropriate and natural.

Low-and high-threat role plays. Descriptions of several demonstration-type role plays follow. They are given in the order of their threat potential, (the first ones are low-threat, the latter ones are more "threatening").

Low-threat situations

□ A single participant, as a near graduate of a training program, gives a three minute talk before a group "back home," describing what was learned, endeavoring to "sell" them on the desirability of their attending the program, or attempting to persuade management that the total organization should adopt such training (e.g., time management, team building)

Note: This is a low-threat role-playing assignment since (a) it is one-way communication and thus is "interaction free," (b) depending on group size, either all of the group or at least a significant number of them would ordinarily make this presentation, (c) participants are presenting their own material to the group, and (d) the situation is not one involving working with feelings, attitudes, conflict, sensitivity, etc. Of course, not everyone is comfortable in giving a talk to a group, even a very short one; in fact, one or two participants may even decline the opportunity.
□ Four to seven participants engage in a "group role play," acting out situations such as a work group holding a staff meeting, a new committee or task force holding its opening session, a problem-solving group having to deal with an obstreperous group member, etc. The low-threat, obviously, results from being in a small group rather than in the usual "one-on-one" role play.
□ A history professor, seated in his office, receives three visitors in succession: a student who lost his book and wants to borrow one in preparation for an exam; a fellow instructor who wishes to borrow a book; the university president who wishes help in the preparation of a talk before a community group. The group at large has the task of observing how status influences the communication process in the three situations. This is a low-threat situation since the enactments are typically very short; the role assignments are clear-cut and thus easy to execute; and the role players' performances are not subject to critique.
□ Two role players present a situation of an interpersonal sort. The presentation, however, only entails reading an assigned script. There is no interaction between the participants, the role play setting the stage analysis by the participant group.

Moderate-threat situations

□ An employee has violated a clear-cut disciplinary standard such as a no-smoking rule, a parking violation, a failure to safeguard classified documents, etc. Cases of this type are relatively easy to handle because the rules are clear. Thus, the threat in role playing a case of this sort is reduced considerably.
□ In a role play concerned with listening, one role player is instructed to communicate nonverbally that he/she is not tuned in (by yawning, looking away, fidgeting). Or both role players may be instructed to utilize nonverbal behavior to demonstrate "active listening" (engaging in restatement, nodding one's head actively, maintaining eye contact, smiling). Since the assigned tasks are clear-cut, the threat potential is not too great.

High-threat situations

□ In a two-person role play, a young manager has the task of bringing about a change in attitude/behavior on the part of a 55-year old supervisor with 30 years of supervisory experience and a top-notch production record. It seems that the "old timer" harasses new hires, especially college graduates, as part of the breaking-in process. The young manager is concerned about possible turnover, community image, etc. This is a tough case to resolve. Why? Because the old timer is hard to reach—not motivated by threats of firing, or denial of advancement (the old timer isn't going anywhere, anymore, anyhow). The protagonist may well anticipate resistance, too, from the long-tenured manager.

☐ A salesperson has the task of closing a sale with a tough, somewhat combative prospect.

☐ The role players are concerned with other tough human relations situations such as counseling an employee who is depressed, alcoholic, highly suspicious, or in someway troubled; conducting an appraisal interview; counseling a male subordinate accused of sexual harassment; informing the boss that a favorite program simply isn't working; etc.

While there are ways to reduce the possible threat inherent in the demonstration-type role plays, to the extent possible you should utilize *mass role playing* —either multiple role playing or multiple group role playing— where the role players perform more privately in small groups such as in triads or quartets. And, of course, in such a situation everyone gets to play and can learn from doing rather than from observing.

One way to make the personal growth enactment or interview less threatening, and thus more effective, is to use the Advisory Role Play (ARP) advocated by William Cooper, Queen's University, Ontario, Canada.[4] In the ARP the trainer capitalizes on the possible "sensitization" participants may have already developed after experience with a standard role play. The idea is to have fellow participants (possibly managers) give advice to the interviewer about to conduct an interview (possibly a performance appraisal). The procedures are these:

1. Everyone is given background on the case to read.
2. Both parties to the interview read their role instructions.
3. The interviewee is sent out of the training room.
4. The group advises the interviewer how to conduct the interview. Typically, the initial advice is general, but soon gets into more helpful particulars.
5. The interviewee is called back into the training room and the interview begins.
6. The interviewer then evaluates his/her own performance.
7. The interviewee evaluates the interview.
8. The group critiques the interview.

According to Dr. Cooper, the interview works well when the interviewer is able to apply at least some of the group's advice, thus giving the coaching/observer group a chance to assess the effect of their advice-giving. The ARP obviously has the merit of involving the nonrole players to a greater degree than is the case with the more standard personal-growth role play.

A final note on reluctance to role play before others: The greatest reluctance to participate in a demonstration-type role play comes from those who may not have experienced it before, those who are not too verbal, those who are shy, etc. On the other hand, those who are highly motivated to improve their interpersonal skills, such as management trainees, graduate students majoring in counseling, disadvantaged persons who are very much in need of a job, are quite likely to welcome it. In fact, in one training group[5] the trainers gave the participants (cosmetic sales clerks) a choice of role playing fairly privately in a triad (cosmetician, customer, and observer, with a chance to rotate in all three roles) or appearing before and receiving feedback from the total group. The choice was given to ten different classes. The result: All classes chose to do the role plays "up front" rather than in the small groups. Because the cases and resulting roleplays were seen as real, i.e., job related, and there was a desire to learn how to do the job well, they realized group feedback was superior to that of a single observer.

Multiple Role Playing

Multiple role playing entails formats that allow all participants "to play" simultaneously. The advantages of this type of design are:

☐ It is a low-threat procedure since no one is asked to appear on center stage. Rather, the action takes place privately in small role-playing teams. Also, "since everyone is doing it, it can't be too bad."

☐ It embodies the principle of learning by doing as opposed to merely observing. The opportunity to try out a particular behavior is essential for skill development and personal growth.

☐ Since a number of teams experience the role play, more ideas can be generated for comparative analysis as to how to tackle a given interpersonal situation.

Two forms of the multiple role play are the triad and the quartet.

The triad. The procedures for forming triads and using them in role playing follow:

1. Divide the participants into groups of three. You can have them count off with the "ones" being the salespersons or bosses, the "twos" the prospects or subordinates and the "threes" the observers. Extra participants can be paired and work without an observer or they can be added observers in other groups.

2. Give the observers their guide sheets, and give the role players their respective role assignment sheets. Copies may also be given to the observers for background purposes. Advise the role players to read only their own sheet and not to discuss it with anyone, since in a real-life interview they would only know their side of the issue. A major purpose of the interview, obviously, is to exchange views about the problem or difficulty as the first step in resolving it.

   Note: Every role play requires instructions, either oral or written, for the role players. Trainers tend to write complex instructions out to ensure full understanding of the assigned roles.

3. Give the role players their guide sheets as explained in the section "Using Structure," to prepare properly for the interview. (The observers may also be given the guide sheets for general background purposes.) Allow 10–15 minutes for Steps 2 and 3.

4. Privately explain to the observers their observational role and its importance and answer any questions they may have. Also explain briefly the nature of the problem the role players will be tackling. Advise the observers to observe and take notes, but not to interfere in any way.

   Note: While the observers are being briefed, the role players are reading their role-play instruction sheets silently and privately.

5. Assign the role-playing teams to different corners of the room and/or other break-out rooms. This will enable the role plays to proceed without distracting noise from other role players. Instruct them to role play for about 20–30 minutes. This should allow enough time to reach an "agreement" of some sort.

   Note: Role plays will end at different times despite set maximum time limits. In fact, some of the role-playing teams may finish prematurely and some may not finish in the alloted time. (Keep the finished role players in their respective locations so that they do not disturb the others who may still be at work.) Of course, different data may emerge because of varying use of the available time. But that is to be expected. Actually, we should expect different data from the various role players due to a host of factors, namely, the time invested by them, energy invested, prerole play preparation including development of a strategy for the role play, personality factors and the resultant compatability/incompatability mix. In sum, we can only set the same time for all (a goal, in effect), but we can hardly expect that time to be used up equally by all or used in the same way.

6. While the role players are interacting, "monitor" each team briefly and unobtrusively to get a sense of how the role plays are trending.

7. Tell them when time is up.

8. Pass out post-interview self-critique guide sheets to the role players. (Again, a copy may be given to the observers.) Allow about 10–15 minutes for the self-appraisal aspect of the role plays. Ask the trios to stay together since in the feedback session there will be a "cross-checking" of observer data with the role players and between role players as well.

9. Secure observer reports (see "Processing Role Play Data"), discuss results of the role play, and extrapolate general principals from the data.

To secure maximum benefits from this design, it is desirable to:

☐ Conduct *three* role plays so that all members of the triad can perform in all three roles (e.g., salesperson, customer and observer, or boss, subordinate and observer). This rotational procedure will provide maximum insight into the problem involved since it will be experienced and thus viewed from more than one perspective.

☐ Start the first role play, if three cases are used, with an easy-to-resolve case. This will give the role players a "success experience" and confidence and encouragement for the next two role plays.

☐ Allow enough time for each role play experience. Preparation time, the enactment, and the feedback phase should take about an hour, possibly a bit more. Don't give the processing time short shrift, for this is where the "pay offs" from the role plays will come. If at all possible, keep the schedule loose so that a lively discussion about the role plays doesn't have to be cut off. A possible *minimum* time schedule for a single role play is as follows:

Instructions by trainer	5 minutes
Preparation time by role players	10 minutes
Role play	20 minutes
Self-critique (Post role play)	5 minutes
Feedback/discussion phase	20 minutes
Total	60 minutes

In general, if three role plays are conducted, as recommended, allow about three to three and one half hours. (The extra 30 minutes will allow for longer feedback periods.)

☐ If the group is new to role playing and there is reason to believe that several or even more group members may be reluctant, it may be desirable to begin with a demonstration-type role play. The role playing pair may comprise the trainer and another participant or two volunteers from the participant group.

The quartet. Sales trainer William H. Cover[6] has developed a role playing procedure to improve the coaching skill of sales managers. Teams of four are set up, with each customer rotationally taking the roles of salesperson, customer, coach, and observer. The coach leads the critique for the group using these steps:

1. Observes the role play, noting things done well and those needing priority improvement.
2. Asks "customer" for reactions to the interview, considering commitment to agreements reached, feelings, what helped and hindered progress, what could have been done differently, etc.
3. Asks sales representative for a self-critique—what helped, what hindered; what could have been done differently.
4. Checks for similar data with observer.
5. Secures reaction of sales representative to the feedback and checks for understanding and agreement of added or alternative skills proposed by the others.
6. Summarizes, pointing up things that went well and possible desired improvements; checks for group agreement.

To wrap things up, each team reports back to the total group the things that helped or hindered the coaching process, such as concentrating on only a few important points; enhancing the representative's self-esteem and confidence; involving the rep in problem solving; being specific about behaviors requiring improvement, and not playing "parent" with a lot of lecturing, quizzing, etc.

The multiple role play can be used with small or very large participant groups. For example, I attended a session on "The Changing Roles of Men and Women in the '80's" at the 1980 conference of the American Society for Training and Development. The presenters had a large audience role play a manager interviewing a secretarial job applicant. Information sheets were provided for both role players. I played the role of the secretary (a form of "role reversal" indeed!) and acquired some extremely worthwhile insight into that particular role. An observer helped each team to process the action. A role-play-process questions sheet was also given to each team. It contained questions such as:

☐ What is there about the manager/secretary position that implies power or powerlessness?
☐ What factors seem to influence the amount of power an individual has within your organization?

☐ What are the implications for male or female training professionals?

Using Structure

Informal and spontaneous role plays are invaluable means to enrich the participant learning experience. But if we are planning a training program and have specific learning goals, we can't rely on the *ad hoc*, serendipitous event; we must instead depend upon planning and considerable structure. Structure, as used in role playing, may range from brief instruction sheets for the role players to complete scripts which are to be read before the group with pre- and post-role play guide sheets for the participants and detailed check sheets for the observers.

Structure obviously directs or channels the learning experience so that participants are given the opportunity to assimilate what they are supposed to. Structure can also ensure that the role play experience is a meaningful, easy-to-take learning activity rather than a source of frustration, anxiety, or embarassment.

One of the main causes for role-play failure is that participants are rushed into the role play without being given a chance to internalize their roles and reflect on the possible course of action they will take in the role play. Thus, when the trainer says: "O.K., read your role play sheets for a couple of minutes and we'll begin our role plays," visualize the confusion and anxiety the participant is certain to experience.

To overcome this shortcoming, I advocate using a role-play planning work sheet. Certainly, one of the learnings from the training experience should be that an effective interview, whether it be for selling, counseling, performance appraisal, employment, termination, etc., takes adequate planning time. A suggested "Guide Sheet to Plan for the Interview" is given in Appendix 18.

If the guide sheet is completed with adequate thought by the role players (allow 10–15 minutes for this), we can expect a role play that is:

☐ Well-conceived rather than hastily contrived
☐ Calmly executed rather than anxiety-laden
☐ A pleasurable and natural experience and thus more likely to be replicated on the job

The observer, too, needs a guide sheet in order to know precisely what to look for in the role play and thus have specific data to provide feedback about it. The observer sheet may be general or specific. Samples of both types are given in Appendices 19, 20, and 21.

Using Observers

A highly participative role playing design is to set up teams for three participants—two role players plus an observer. Rotating roles will ensure that all members of the triad will function in the observer role one time.

The observer is a vital adjunct to full learning from the role play. Since the observers are a "neutral," detached party, they are in a postition to see and hear things that the engrossed role players may not; e.g., whether and how rapport is established, whether a role player interrupts, whether there is two-way communication, etc. The presence of the observer will also help the role players to take their roles more seriously.

You should communicate to the observers that they have a very important function to perform lest they assume that observing is a secondary chore. I assemble all observers outside the training room, while the role players are studying and internalizing their roles, and explain to them their tasks and how important they are. At this time the observer sheets are reviewed to ensure full understanding of them. The observers are also told in specific terms what feedback they will be asked to report on to the total group.

Note that we said to "the total group." This public procedure, rather than giving feedback privately to the role players, is recommended for these reasons:

1. A more formal report will ensure that the job is done more thoroughly, both in collecting data and in reporting back on it
2. It establishes the norm that "we're here to learn and feedback is a vital way to do this"
3. Greater learning is made possible when one hears the reports of all the observers

There is no reason why the observers should not be given the total set of materials—role playing instruction sheets, role players' guide sheets (pre-role and post-role play, etc.). It will help to give them a better overview of the total case.

Although we indicated that our structured role plays included previously prepared guide sheets for the observers, it may be desirable, at times, to have the group develop its own criteria for the observers to use as they observe the role plays. This procedure should give the observational criteria greater understanding, credibility, and thus acceptance. You can, of course, add items that you feel the group overlooked.

Although we stated that all observers receive the same guide sheets, you may want to vary the observational role; e.g., one set of observers may be instructed to observe specifically nonverbal communication, another set to observe how a decision was reached, another set to look for dependency needs and relationships, etc. These special assignments would be in addition to their regular one.

Incidentally, if the total group does not break down neatly into triads, assign the extra person to another triad

as a second observer. Or if there are two extras, they may role play the situation without an observer. In the latter instance, the trainer may assume the observer role.

In advance of the interview it should be pointed that the observer role is a critical one. For it is their feedback that will provide the basis for a significant portion of the participant learning from the interview. Obviously, few of us can see ourselves as well as a neutral observer. Point out, too, that the "Guide Sheet for the Observer" encourages a search for strong points in the interview so that at least some feedback can be supportive (positive reinforcement). Also, the guide sheet asks for behaviors in the interview which could be strengthened, not for those which are poor, ineffective, weak, or "lousy." The final item asks for a forecast as to the relationships that will exist now that the interview is over. The rationale for this item is that an effective interview should result in improved relationships. In fact, everyone embarking on an interview should ask themselves: "What impact will my behavior have on the relationship?"

A guide sheet that helps the role players assess their own behavior in the interview is useful because:

☐ Introspection is basic to meaningful learning. Behaviors or skills in need of strengthening, which are self-perceived, are easier to internalize than those which are pointed out by others.
☐ Since the role players are encouraged to engage in self-critique, they are more likely to be receptive to observer feedback. In other words, we wish to establish an atmosphere wherein critique becomes an understandable and welcome norm rather than an extraneous and threatening element that might produce defensiveness.

The "Guide Sheet for Self-Critique of the Interview" is given in Appendix 22.

A good use of observers to critique the action takes place in the State Department's training program which readies its foreign service officers for overseas work. A mock consulate office is set up in "Land Z," a nation "a bit west of the continent of South America," discovered in 1508 by Zenry the navigator and famous for the Zramp Mountains and the cities of Zruch, Ziff, Zeel, Zorrest, and Zug. Much of the role playing involves handling troublesome issues, with the trainees impersonating people who pop in with demands for help from their government. The consulate officers in Z have to deal with haughty opera stars, the student arrested for drugs, a psychotic, etc. After every session students critique each other on why they "approved" or "denied" requests for aid. They learn pretty quickly from their role play work that there usually are no "right" or "wrong" answers, as will be the case on the job.[7]

Group Role Playing

As mentioned before, a role play need not be limited to two participants. An example of a group role play follows:

A group of six managers are listening and responding to a proposal from the personnel officer for a dynamic supervisory training program. The role players have been given different instruction sheets, including favorable, neutral, and negative positions. Two observers note and record the interaction, one being concerned with "task" roles (initiator, summarizer, etc.) and the other with "group maintenance" roles (morale, support, encouragement, etc.). After the observer reports are given, the total group discusses the interaction and its implications for group problem solving.

Multiple Group Role Playing

In this design the total participant group is broken down into role playing groups or teams. So everyone "gets to play." The procedure can be followed with a small or large (several hundred participants) group.

Another advantage of MGRP is that to the extent that "all play," no one feels singled out or embarrassed. Also, it enriches the feedback process—data can be collected from a number of role playing teams and compared critically.

In the case of the large group, feedback is elicited from the role playing teams only on a sample basis.

An example of a role play enacted by several groups is one role played in the week-long "family awareness" workshops held by General Motors's Hydra-Matic Division. The objective of the role plays is to learn consensus decision making. Procedurally, eight hourly and salaried workers are randomly assigned headbands with various labels, e.g., "boss" or "expert." Their task is to plan a picnic. Typically, things go wrong. The meetings degenerate into a scrapping match. They are then asked to doff their headbands and try again for agreement. Success comes easier on the second try. People learn, in the words of one union official, "that if we all take off our headbands, we can work together to get the job done."[8]

For a now-classic book containing numerous multiple group role playing situations and detailed instructions for the trainer to conduct such activities properly, see N. R. F. Maier, A. R. Solem, and A. A. Maier, *The Role Play Technique: A Handbook for Management and Leadership Practice,* University Associates, Inc., San Diego, 1975.[9] This volume contains the well-known "New Truck Dilemma" wherein each group has to decide how to distribute a new truck among six members of a telephone repair crew. Since the various groups generally come up with different solutions based on the varying values of the groups, the learning is that the foreman is better off opting for a decision made by the group that satisfies them. The alternative is for the foreman to impose his values on the group with the very likely risk of producing dissatisfaction with the decision.

Total Group Role Playing

It is also possible to design and conduct a role play that involves the total group simultaneously. As an example, let's take a situation involving "conflict management." The activity may be planned in advance or it may be used as a "live experience" when the group is divided on an issue. Here are the procedures:

1. Select a topic which divides the group. This may be an in-house issue or an external one such as gun control, legalizing marijuana, outlawing abortion, etc.
2. Divide the total group (14–20) into two smaller groups (7–10), each of which takes a pro or con position on the issue in question. (Try to form groups of equal size.)
3. Send one small group to another room for their discussion, the other group remaining in the training room. By separating the two groups physically, we are polarizing the two groups further. We are establishing a strong "we vs. them" and a "win-lose" outlook.
4. Give both groups the following instructions. (This may be in writing if this is a planned rather than an extemporaneous activity.)
   a. Develop as strong a case as you can for your position.
   b. What arguments do you believe the other group will use? List them. (Allow 30 minutes for Steps a and b.)
   c. Select a representative or spokesperson who will best present your group's position to the other group.
5. After the 30 minutes is up, give both groups a short attitude questionnaire to measure their strength or intensity of feeling about the issue. Keep separately the forms for the two groups.
6. Seat both representatives at opposite ends of a *long* table. (Two or three tables may be used for length.) This will further emphasize the strong cleavage between the two groups.
   Note: You may wish to label the groups "Pro" or "Con" or simply "A" and "B."
7. Let both representatives alternately present their group's position to the other group for five minutes.

8. Let a cross-dialogue ensue between the two representatives for about five minutes.
9. As a form of "role reversal," select a member of Group A to join Group B to help the Group B representative strengthen their case.
10. Continuing the role reversal procedure, select a member from Group B to help the Group A representative.
11. About five minutes later, send two members of Group A to help group B and two members of Group B to help Group A. Continue the discussion for another five to seven minutes.
12. Repeat Step 11 at about five minute intervals until there has been a complete turnover in both groups' memberships.
13. As a final switch, have the two leaders change places. We now have the A group arguing for B's position and vice versa. Continue this discussion for seven to ten minutes.
14. Administer the attitude questionnaire again to both groups, keeping their forms separately. Tally results to check whether the role reversal procedure tended to reduce the intensity with which attitudes were held.
15. Hold a general discussion about attitude rigidity and its implications for intergroup conflict. Point up the need to shift groups from "we vs. them" and "win-lose" positions to a more open dialogue and "win-win" possibilities. This role-play procedure is one way to start the dialogue.

Note: In both MGRP and TGRP everyone is involved. However, in MGRP the action takes place in small groups or teams. This procedure permits comparative analysis of data generated by the teams. Conversely, in TGRP the learning comes essentially from what is experienced without the opportunity—or possibly the need—to learn from such comparative analysis. For example, see the role play "Trial For Error" described in Chapter 3.

Write Your Own Role Play

Participants in role play situations often feel a lack of realism in their assigned roles. Why? Because they have to work with (enact) a contrived scenario based entirely on trainer-supplied information. One way to give "canned" role plays a real-world flavor is to allow role players to modify the role play. They do this by supplementing the trainer-furnished information with their own. They thus may be given questions which ask for details relevant to their own work situations and then adapt the conduct of the role play accordingly.

For example, assume the participants have to make a persuasive presentation. They could be asked to enact it as if they were making it to a particular official in their organization whom they know. They would be asked to take into account prior contacts with that manager, his/her personality, major organizational issues, and preferences for how the material is to be presented to the decision maker. For greater authenticity, also encourage participants to brief the other role players on how to personalize the enactment before conducting it.

If you decide to take this modified real world approach to role playing, you may have to contact your participants in advance (a pre-work assignment) to develop requisite information pertaining to the forthcoming enactment in class.[10]

Processing Role Play Data

Participants learn from a role play they have enacted in either one of the following ways, or in some combination of them by:

☐ Reflecting upon and talking about one's assigned role, one may develop insight into the concerns, problems, outlooks, etc., of the role portrayed.
☐ Practicing new interpersonal behavior (e.g., being more assertive, exhibiting more concern for the customer or subordinates, listening actively), one may acquire new, worthwhile behavioral skills.
☐ Receiving feedback from the observers after the role enactment, one may be helped still further to improve one's skill or behavior.
☐ Observing others one may improve one's skill or acquire self-insight.
☐ Discussing in depth all that we have seen and done, we can round out and button down our pertinent learnings.

In short, in role playing one learns by doing, by introspecting, by observing, by giving feedback, by receiving feedback, and by engaging in an overall analysis of the total activity. And since changing attitudes and behavior are not easy things to accomplish for most of us, being involved in all of these operations is the way we are most likely to really learn.

So for more complete learning, to ensure that it actually "glues in" and will be carried over to the real-life situation, the trainer must give ample time to processing the data generated by the role plays. Processing means giving and receiving feedback about the behavior exhibited in the role plays and critiquing (discussing, extrapolating general principles) the enactments.

Trainer-consultants John E. Jones and J. William Pfeiffer[11] of University Associates distinguish between "processing" and "generalizing" as follows: Processing is "sharing one's reactions . . . The dynamics that emerged in the activity are explored, discussed, and evaluated (processed) with other participants." Generalizing, the next logical step, "is the need to develop principles or extract generalizations from the experience. Stating learnings in this way can help participants further define, clarify, and elaborate them."

Feedback, as a device to help us see ourselves as others do, can be given to the role players in several ways:

☐ If the enactment takes place publicly before the total group, the feedback necessarily is given to the role players on a public basis by the group and the trainer.

☐ It can be given quite privately after the role play by the observers and/or the coaches in three- or four-person role playing teams. In a team of four there are the two role players, an observer, and a coach who coordinates the feedback and analysis of the role play.

☐ It can be given publicly by the observers after the role playing teams have completed privately their enactments. In this circumstance you control the feedback with these objectives in mind:

1. To ensure that feedback by the observers is balanced rather than one-sided; minimal or moderate rather than overwhelming (the instruction to the observers might be to report on two things they liked in the interview and one thing that could have been improved upon); easy rather than hard to take (internalize); cross-checked with participants for reality testing.

2. To extrapolate from the feedback general principles applicable to all of the group.

Two procedures, the T-column and the spread sheet may be used to give feedback publicly after private role playing. These procedures may be used singly or in combination.

The T-Column

This can be used in various ways to elicit from the observers, subject to a cross-check with the participants, data about the role play. For example, if the behavior of both parties to the role play is to be critiqued, a double T-column may be used. See Figure 5-1.

Team	Pat		Kim	
	Did well	**Could be strengthened**	**Did well**	**Could be strengthened**
1.	Used active listening	Lacked specifics re nature of problem	Tried to define problem	Tendency to sit back
2.	Opened in a friendly manner	Never got to closing the sale		

Figure 5-1. Example of a double T-column.

If only one role play is to be subject to critique a single T-column will suffice.

The Spread Sheet

In various role plays both parties often are in a conflict situation. Hence their meeting or interview is intended to bring about some reconciliation, some plan of action to reduce their interpersonal differences. Typically, then, we wish data from the various observers which tell the group at large the following things: the strategy of the protagonist (i.e., the one who is initiating the action such as a supervisor or a salesperson); was the strategy followed? (good intentions often go awry); was the strategy successful?; if so, what was the motivator that "reached" the other party?; what agreement, if any, was reached?; will their future relations be stronger, weaker, or unchanged?

A sample spread sheet covering these points, designed to secure data on a flipchart from the role playing activity in all the teams, is given in Figure 5-2.

In respect to the timing of feedback, it's a good idea to let the role players engage in self-critique before the group prior to their receiving feedback from the observers. This will help to defuse possible defensiveness from observer feedback since the idea of critique—from self and others—is introduced on a gradual basis.

Video Playback and Feedback

Participant learning from a role play experience ordinarily depends upon one's recollection and impression of what one did in the role play and feedback from the observer, the other role player, and possibly the trainer. These multiple sources, although certainly helpful, have limitations; for example, recollection is obviously dependent on memory, one's impressions may be marked by self-deception, the observer may not have captured pertinent behaviors or may be reluctant to state them, and the other role player may be limited by individual biases.

Videotaping can overcome the problems cited above. It can capture accurately what was said and done and present it for analysis by the role players, the observing participants, and the trainer. Videotape, then, makes possible the rendering of multiple-source feedback based on objective data the total group can observe and critique simultaneously.

Videotaping role plays has another advantage—it can capture the highly significant nonverbal behavior that ensues between two parties in an interview. We have reference to facial expressions of all sorts; hand gestures; body positions; the distance between the role players;

Team No.	Planned strategy of boss	Was it followed?	If strategy was used, was it effective?	What "motivator" was used?	Nature of Agreement Reached	Future Relations (+, −, 0)
1	Persuasion	Became hard sell	No, produced resistance	Pressure	None	− (weaker)
2	Mutual problem solving	Yes	Yes	Chance for larger travel budget	Expanded program	+ (stronger)
3	etc.					

Figure 5-2. Example of a spreadsheet.

touch, if any; eye contact; movement; etc. By studying nonverbal behavior (their own and that of others), participants can be made aware of the nonverbal behavior they exhibit and its importance on others. They can also learn to assess how effective they are in transmitting and receiving nonverbal cues.[12]

Several examples of the use of videotape with role plays, in vastly different settings, follow.

Counseling the Disadvantaged

In a program designed to teach disadvantaged youths and adults how to find a job, these videotape procedures (along with other training techniques) are used:

☐ *Stimulus:* A five-minute videotaped vignette presents a problem, e.g., a job applicant flounders in an employment interview.

☐ *Evocation:* A small group (15 or less) analyzes the problem presented.

☐ *Objective inquiry.* The trainer introduces the group to new information, concepts and behavioral models; e.g., how employment agencies work or where to find training programs.

☐ *Application:* Each member of the group tries out the new learning, e.g., how to be effective in a job interview. A videotape is made of the interview subject to group critique.

The ten-week Employability Skills Series was developed by the Research and Development Center for Life Skills and Human Resource Development, Teachers College, Columbia University and is used nationwide.[13]

Teaching Counseling Skills

Dr. Diana Teta, a clinical psychologist at the Capital District Psychiatric Center, Albany, N.Y., uses video-

tape and role playing to teach counseling. She uses video 90% of the time in her counseling classes for it enables the student to go beyond textbook knowledge and theory.

Some of her skill pointers in working with video are these:

☐ Many criticisms don't even require mention; e.g., video clearly shows excesses in hand movement or head nodding or deficits such as lack of eye contact with the client.

☐ The students who operate the camera are instructed to zero in on significant nonverbal behavior, thereby stressing the importance of body language; e.g., the counselor can give support through body posture as well as verbally, hand movement should be congruent with verbal messages, leaning forward or looking attentive can show an understanding.

☐ Verbal interventions can be reinforced or critiqued; e.g., reflecting back (restatement) feelings or clarifying a client's statement. Dr. Teta believes that the correct intervention at the right time enhances client progress.

☐ The before and after method is used by Dr. Teta in teaching assertiveness training via videotape. The class comes up with a problem such as a dissatisfied customer who seeks redress from a service manager at a department store. A video enactment then takes place subject to critique by Dr. Teta and the class. The aim is to try to "shape in" a better performance for the role player. The same role players then act out the problem again and the two tapes are compared. Says Dr. Teta: "There's really a big difference between the two videotapes and since the improvements are so apparent, the playback is intrinsically rewarding."[14]

Communication Skills For Judges

Many judges communicate poorly. They may mumble, murder grammar, talk in a monotone, cover their mouths while talking, ramble on in legal jargon, and maintain poor eye contact. Dr. Jack Barwind, head of the Syracuse University's speech department, was therefore hired by New York State to train 600 judges in a mock courtroom where they can be taped, say, imposing a sentence, and then critiqued.

The need for better communication skills by judges arises from the fact that they are really "on stage." They are communicating non-verbally as well as verbally. The way a judge addresses a defendant may influence whether the latter complies with probation or a conditional discharge. Also, judges, once they assume a power position, tend to accept less responsibility for their message getting through. All in all, the judges readily provide much grist for the videotape mill.[15]

Developing Skills in Conflict Resolution

Jerome Barrett, formerly Associate Director, Office of Mediation Services, Federal Mediation and Conciliation Service, Wash., D. C., teaches specialized skills essential to settling disputes. He uses short and long role-play scenarios that simulate conflict resolution situations. The short ones are for warm-up purposes. The longer ones require study and consultation with team members. The trainees, in a group of six to ten participants, play a lead role in a short scenario and participate in the long one. All sessions are videotaped for playback and feedback by trainer. Barrett's suggestions for best results are:

☐ Advise trainees that the tapes will be erased and reused; this reduces a lot of unnecessary anxiety.
☐ The critique made of the trainees playing the lead roles includes trainer comments and group discussion.
☐ Very sensitive feedback such as on personal mannerisms is given privately.
☐ Tapes may be reviewed alone during the breaks.
☐ Feedback should cover all the skills treated in prior sessions. The aim is to encourage reflection on one's skill inventory and to develop action plans for further skill development.[16]

Question-Asking Role Playing For Sales Managers

At a brokerage firm sales managers are taught how to question salespersons after a sales call so as to secure valid, informative answers for managerial decision making. The procedures involve the use of a videotaped sales call. The manager watches the tape and is asked to assume he/she is accompanying the salesperson. As the tape is watched, the manager should be thinking about the questions to be presented when they're both "back in the car." The questions are then posed live to the same salesperson who appeared in the tape.

Three managers are selected for the questioning process. They do their role plays one at a time, the second and third role players do not get to observe the ones who proceded them. Having three role players assures two things: a presentation of different ways of conducting the questioning and an assurance that at least one of the role plays will "work."

The training is designed to learn how to ask "open-end" rather than directive, manipulative or answer-laden questions; to listen; to learn to focus on the concerns and feelings of subordinates; to deal with salespersons who may exhibit frustration and candor; to avoid backing off from a problem; to respond to body language (e.g., signs of frustration, boredom, or astonishment).

In general, the technique is designed to help the managers to see themselves as they interact with sales personnel and to learn new ways of managing and working with subordinates.[17]

Sales Training

In a well-thought-out training program for sales persons of the American Poclain Corporation,[18] sales personnel learn both people skills and product information. The course's procedures are these:

1. The selling skills required for an effective sales call are shown on videotape.
2. The salesperson prepares for a series of sales calls, each dealing with a specific selling problem.
3. A group discussion is held about the calls.
4. Three salespersons are selected to show their selling skills in a simulated customer's office. While the sales calls are taped, the other sales personnel work on other selling situations. The role plays on the various skill areas are done in separate rooms. To ensure that no one is influenced by the others' actions, one salesperson role plays the problem and the other two wait their turn outside the "customer's" office.
5. The full group reassembles to critique all videotaped role plays. Typically, they learn about personality effects, the impact of suggestions and persuasion, the value of structuring ideas for clarity, the role of nonverbal communication, the gap between self-perception (deception?) and what is shown on the monitor about one's performance.

The playback points up weaknesses in both selling skills and product knowledge. From this may develop new ideas to improve the next role plays. The role plays, as might be expected, increase in difficulty. This tends to encourage a pooling of techniques and approaches.

The distinguishing feature of this course, compared to others that use videotape, is that each role play is preceded by a taped presentation illustrating different selling techniques and also updating product knowledge.

The participants receive a broad perspective of their selling roles by being first, observer, then role player, and then self-appraiser.

It is apparent from the previous discussion that a vital key to learning from videotaped role playing is the quality of the feedback the roleplayers receive after the enactment. Recognizing that feedback often may be either hard-hitting (punitive and threatening) criticism or vacuous statements of support rather than helpful critiques, two trainers[19] report on their model for feedback that overcomes such shortcomings. Briefly, their procedures are these:

1. In a supervisor-employee role play before the total group, feedback is given only to the "boss." Why? To prevent those who volunteered for the subordinate role from feeling that their material will be subject to analysis by the group. In other words, the "employee" only serves in a data-generating or facilitating capacity so that the supervisor can receive the feedback about his/her performance.
2. Feedback must be phrased only in terms of what was observed. Thus, participant-observer statements assume these forms: "I saw . . . ," or "I heard . . . ," or "I felt that . . ," The objective is to reduce defensiveness. For if one is busy defending oneself, the feedback most likely will proceed unheard.
3. Feedback is received silently. The role player thus can accept or reject whatever is presented without having to justify or defend such a posture.
4. The camera person also provides comments about the role play
5. The trainer is the last to give feedback. The objective is to tie up loose ends, bring up unexplored issues, etc. Feedback, again, is based on observable behavior.
6. The videotape is then reviewed, the principal role player critiquing his/her own role play. The tape can be stopped for analysis only by the trainer and the principal role player, although others may make comments or ask questions once the tape is stopped.
7. In the feedback process, it is the trainer's job to allow all who wish to be heard to comment and at the same time to prevent the role player from being overwhelmed by data overload.

Another issue of concern is video-based role playing is how to process "image shock" for participants new to the process. Dorothy Bolton,[20] Ridge Consultants, Rochester, N.Y., has pointed out that viewing oneself on video can be a "painful" experience because of the gap between a long-standing self-perception and what is seen on the screen. The specific elements of concern are body image, voice image, and personal/social image. One way to deal with the concerns empathically is for the trainer to relate to the group his/her personal experience (reactions) when viewing a videotape of self for the first time.

Note: Dorothy Bolton advises how to intervene in an on-going role play without disrupting the training:

☐ Don't let a poorly performed role play continue; stop it immediately and correct it.
☐ Set key phrases such as "reflect" ahead of time in the minds of the role players.
☐ Whisper the word "reflect" as the role play progresses to keep the role players on track.

How to Write a Role Play

While published role plays ordinarily may be quite satisfactory, at times you may need to develop your own role plays for a particular subject. To do so decide on the problem to be presented, write the role play, and then field test it.

Deciding on the Problem

The best way to select a problem for the role play is to draw on your own experience or that of others. For example:

☐ If you wished to develop a role play for sales personnel dealing with overcoming customer objections, you might jot down typical objections you know about such as price, color, certain convenience features not available, delivery date, warranty, and so on.
☐ If you wished to develop a role pay on discipline for supervisory training you might consider topics such as tardiness, absenteeism, insubordination, safety rule violation, drinking on the job, gambling on premises, and failure to secure classified documents.
☐ If your concern is with delegation problems, you might brainstorm alone or with others problems such as the subordinate who won't take on added responsibility, the boss who doesn't really "let go," or the boss who abdicates rather than delegates.

Once you have your problems identified, all you need do is select those that seem most relevant, practical, and credible. If time will allow and several problems will be used, try to develop role plays that vary in difficulty and complexity. In this way the group can begin with an "easy" situation and move up to more involved ones.

Writing the Role Play

In our second stage we take the topic and make it "come alive" by

1. Looking for a point of conflict or difference, an area where both parties view the problem or situation from different perspective, such as
   - ☐ The employee who feels she was denied a promotion unfairly.
   - ☐ The colleague who won't cooperate with his peers.
   - ☐ The employee who sees little point in observing certain safety rules
   - ☐ The executive who "nitpicks to death" everyone's letters.
   - ☐ The young supervisor who is hurting his career by antagonizing others.

2. Decide on the characters to be involved in the role play. If they are a customer prospect and a salesperson or a manager and a subordinate, give the characters a set of characteristics that define them clearly: age, sex, status, reputation, personality, job title and responsibilities, strengths, weaknesses, family ties, job history, seniority. These characteristics along with the view of the problem give the role player the basis for the enactment of the role.

3. Give the characters names. We suggest using sexually neutral names to avoid the problem of a female participant trying to assume the role of the supervisor John Hanks. Some common across-gender names are given in Table 5-1. You could also use nicknames, initials, or last names. Sometimes "fun" names like R. U. Eager, O. Gurr, Kerr Les or T. D. Umm may be used.

4. Use these guidelines in writing the role play:
   - ☐ Keep it short—the role players have only a limited time to read and think about their roles.
   - ☐ Keep it readable—use short sentences, simple words, very short paragraphs, and job-related vocabulary.
   - ☐ Keep it credible and realistic.
   - ☐ Keep it adequately flexible. While each character has to be defined to give it clarity, strength (or weakness), credibility, identifiability, etc., it should not be so overdrawn that the role player has no discretion whatsoever to depart from the prescribed role. In other words, the "best" role play occurs where the role player recognizes weaknesses in the assigned role prescription and given a chance or reason "to change" will do so.
   - ☐ Keep it general enough to avoid possible nitpicking. Avoid inclusion of data in the role prescriptions which may be "attacked" as out of date, inapplicable or rarely occuring.

Table 5-1
Examples of Sexually Neutral Names

Sexually Neutral Names	Derived from the Name of	
	Male	Female
Jerry	Gerald	Geraldine
Bobby	Robert	Roberta
Les	Lester	Leslie
Robin	Robin	Robin
Sal	Sal	Sally
Sam	Samuel	Samantha
Joyce	Joyce	Joyce
Sandy	Sander	Sandra
Win	Winston	Winifred
Kim	Kim	Kimberly
Lee	Leland	Leona
Fran	Francis	Frances
Ross	Ross	Ross
Val	Val	Valerie
Shirley	Shirley	Shirley
Kyle	Kyle	Kyle
Gene	Eugene	Jean
Marion	Marion	Marian
Carol	Carrol	Carol
Pat	Patrick	Patricia
Charlie	Charles	Charlotte
Terry	Terrance	Theresa
Chris	Christopher	Christine
Alex	Alexander	Alexandra
Sherry	Sheridan	Sharon
Vern	Vernon	Verna

Complete your write-up by giving the case a title that will excite interest in it, such as:

☐ The Case of the "Retired" Supervisor
☐ Role Play: Allen and Gibbs in Conflict
☐ The Reluctant Prospect
☐ The Case of the Oversupervised Employee
☐ Chris Confronts the Boss—A Role Play
☐ Application Session: Morale and Motivation at the Maintenance Shop

Field Testing the Role Play

If possible, try out the role play in a "mini" situation, rather than a full-blown one. As a minimum, check it out with colleagues, line officials, one's boss, or subordinates for readability and realism.

Revise the role play, as indicated, after the session is over. Participant feedback should indicate possible ambiguities, inaccuracies, omissions, etc.

Special Techniques

While role players can acquire considerable skill, self-insight, and sensitivity to others in the usual two-person role enactments, greater impact is possible by experiencing a number of special role-playing techniques,

Note: Most of these techniques depend upon a high degree of trainer intervention. They thus would be more applicable to single rather than multiple role playing. Also, they would be used in more in-depth, spontaneous, and highly experiential training programs.

Role Reversal

This is the most commonly used device as an adjunct to the conventional role play. By taking the role of the other person, one can now see the world from that person's perspective, though in real life we are too preoccupied with self (our own problems, needs, anxieties), to do so. Via the magic of role reversal, we can look through a new set of lenses and learn of the other's values, attitudes, concerns, and needs. Some examples are:

Police officer ⟶ Citizen
Sales rep ⟶ Prospect or customer
Teacher ⟶ Student
Nurse ⟶ Patient
Boss ⟶ Employee

The role reversal can be accomplished by:

☐ *The training design.* For example, working in teams of three, each person can experience rotationally the roles of supervisor, subordinate, and observer. Three role plays are necessary, of course, to accomplish this.

☐ *The situation.* For example, a role play before the group may result in a block or conflict between the two role players. No one is willing to give. The trainer may intervene as follows: "Jan, why don't we switch roles here. You take Ann's role as the employee. Pick up your line where your boss, Jan, says . . . "

The trainer may ask both participants to switch roles more than once in an attempt to give greater insight into the other's feelings and world view and thus "loosen up" one's rigidities.

Empty Chair Technique

In this role-playing procedure one talks to the (imaginary) person in the other chair. One says everything to the other person that one would like to if that person were really there. The emotionality can be heightened and insight augmented by switching chairs (roles) and attempting to say the things the other would be very likely to say. The chair switches should be repeated as many times as may be necessary to complete a meaningful dialogue between the two parties in question. Some examples of where this technique might be used are: a hus-

band and wife in a dual-career conflict; an employee asking the boss for a raise; a mixed performance appraisal by the boss; or a lost sale.

A variation of this technique is to have another participant sit in the empty chair to help explore and develop the role relationships more fully.

The Soliloquy

In this technique the role player talks alone before the audience. Some uses are

☐ To define and explain one's role before the total group as an introduction to the actual enactment. For example: "I'm Pat. I've been around 30 years. I'm a good producer and I know the ropes. No one shoves me around because I'm pretty good at shoving right back. Now, lately . . . ."

☐ To heighten one's awareness of who one really is and how one sees the world—others, the situation, a given problem, one's concerns, needs. The trainer may intervene and ask a role player to describe his/her feelings, perceptions, etc. at this point in the role play. By talking aloud about these circumstances, one can develop greater insight into what one really feels and believes. It may also serve to elicit feedback from others about that view of self and the world.

The Double

While the enactment is taking place, the trainer may assign a participant to verbalize one of the role player's unstated feelings and thoughts. Physically, the double (also known as the "auxiliary ego") sits behind the role player and as "the inner voice" or conscience expresses feelings whenever it seems the role player is unable or unwilling to do so.

One way to introduce this technique to the group is for the trainer to model the double before asking anyone else to do it. The modeling not only shows how it's done but, in addition, "legitimatizes" it. Of course, the trainer may assume the role of the double at any stage of the role play where a role player's blocked feelings or thoughts need to come out.

The doubling process, it should be noted, is a form of soliloquizing for in it one is expressing feeling out loud. The double, of course, is expressing a role player's feelings rather than his own.

Mirror Technique

At times a group member may have a block or impasse and cannot achieve the necessary involvement to share meaningfully an element in his/her experience. In this circumstance, the trainer may ask another participant to assume the reticent role player's entire role. This is done by "mirroring" the feelings that the participant is having difficulty expressing. In effect, the other participant is saying: "This is the way I feel you coming across. This is what I see." The trainer encourages the inhibited person to correct or amplify upon the mirrored statements. With successful mirroring, the reticent role player may be able to return to the role and continue the role play.

Some typical mirroring dialogue:

Mirror: (attempting to express strongly the other's feelings) I *resent* the way she conducts our staff meetings. It *really* upsets me.

Role player: (playing the statement down) I guess it does make me a bit irritated. But not always.

Mirror: (still with feeling) It *really* ticks me off, makes me feel *very, very* angry.

Role Player: (hitchhiking on the mirroring) Yes, angry.

Mirror: (developing the problem further) It makes me *so* angry I tune out the *whole* thing.

Role player: (agreeing) I just retreat. It's too much.

Mirror: So I don't contribute. I clam up.

Role player: (now more fully in the role) Sometimes the boss asks if I have anything to offer. I just sit there and shake my head.

Mirror: (developing the role further) I wish I had the guts to tell the boss what I really think.

Role player: Yes, I would really like to speak up. I *really* would. In fact, I came close two meetings ago . . . "

Multiple Role Taking

Two or more persons can perform a given role, e.g., two supervisors and three subordinates may each enact a given two-person role play. The objective is to explore more facets of the role relationships. The generation of more data helps to produce a richer postenactment critique and thus greater insight into the roles for the role player.

An example of how the multiple role-playing process takes place may be illustrated by the following diagram.

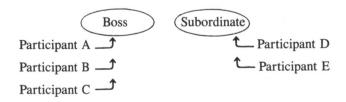

The trainer may also put a number of participants through a given role, each of whom makes a short statement about how he/she sees an aspect of the role or role relationship. For example, in a session concerned with

male-female relationships, several women may move quickly through one of the roles to express their feelings about a particular attitude or relationship.

Behind the Back Technique

With an inhibited group, the trainer may ask the role player to turn his back to the group while they discuss his performance in the role play. This procedure makes it easier for the group to discuss the role play since they do not have to look directly at the "absent" role player nor interact with him. Similarly, the one receiving the feedback can listen more objectively since he is not in a face-to-face situation with the group.

After receiving the feedback, the role player may turn his chair around, in effect "rejoining" the group, and give his own feelings about the role play and comment on the group's feedback.

Evaluating Results

Role playing is a dynamic means of developing skill and changing attitudes and behavior. Role playing works because it gives participants "real life" skill practice; it provides a rare opportunity to experience the roles others assume but which one ordinarily does not in real life because of one's "superior" position; and it affords opportunities to critique one's performance and to receive feedback from others as to how one did.

Some examples of payoffs from role playing follow:

☐ One study analyzed short- and long-term effects of six methods used to get English workers to use safety gear: a poster campaign, films, fear techniques, discussion groups, role playing, and discipline. Most of these approaches produced an immediate effect, but only role playing resulted in a long-term increase in the use of helmets, shoes, glasses, and gloves. The training procedure involved was to have employees play the roles of managerial personnel, safety officials, and people who failed to get compensation due to their own negligence. Assuming these new roles produced these impressive results: In the experimental group, the wearing of hard hats went up from 27% to 68% immediately and only dropped to 62% four months later. Those not wearing hard hats dropped from 32% to 5% in the long run.[21]

☐ In a two-day sales training course, using role plays and videotape, the American Poclain Corp., Fredricksburg, Va., produced very satisfactory results. One distributor who attended the course marvelled at how hard the sales personnel worked at improving their techniques. He thus decided to send his 30 sales people to the course, even though their product line was broader than that of Poclain's. One of his salesmen reported after the training: "Thanks to the new insights I got concerning the customer/salesman relationship, I feel I now have better tools to solve these problems I have been avoiding in the past."

A Poclain salesman stated: "I sold two $200,000 machines only one week after I attended the course. During the final negotiations with the customer, I had to handle the same objections I had been faced with in the video role play. Since I had a better insight into the customer's problems, I was able to handle the situation easily and made a sale I did not really expect to make."[13]

☐ New York City police officers learned how to negotiate with a hostage taker. "Through simulations and role playing, police officers were taught to depersonalize situations, to withdraw their own egos, to make it possible for concessions to be made to a hostage taker without a cop fearing a loss of his own status. Officers were instructed in the interpretation—and communication—of body language nuances, as well as verbal strategies that might reinforce or stabilize a gunman's mood."[22]

Role Playing: Some Questions and Answers

☐ *What is the best response to the participants question "How do I play this role?"?* As a trainer I usually say: "I guess you have three choices; One, you can play the role literally per the instruction sheet; two, you can be yourself and just do what comes naturally, so if you're a nice guy, be a nice guy; if you're an s.o.b., be that; or three, you can strive for the execution of an 'ideal' set of behaviors."

While offering choices may confuse or overwhelm some participants, it's still a better procedure than to tell people how to behave.

The simplest procedure, of course, is to say: "Just be yourself; act it out as you see it."

☐ *Is it desirable to use the term "role playing" if participants might react negatively to it?* If you have concerns about the language, exercise caution. Talk about an "application session," "skill practice," "skill building session," "try-out phase of our work," "practical work," "problem solving session," "we'll act out some situations," etc.

☐ *What is the best physical set-up for role playing?* Any size room will do if the enactments take place on a one-at-a-time basis. If multiple role playing is used and everyone plays, a good-sized room is essential so that the role plays can take place without too much competitive noise. Some buzzing from the other role-playing teams is helpful—it literally sets the tone for the work, communi-

cating that "we're all involved in this." Adjacent breakout rooms may be used, too, of course. If plants, partitions, or a large blackboard are available, use them for added privacy.

☐ *What are the relative merits of written versus oral instructions to the role players?* Written instructions about roles eliminate fuzziness and aid absorption (people do receive at different rates). They are particularly helpful if the roles have some element of complexity to them. They also avoid arguments with the trainer about your poor communicating ability: "I thought you told us that . . . . " On the other hand, a short role instruction may be given orally. Its merit lies in its spontaneity. Example: "Georgie, you be the secretary. Alice you be the salesperson. You've tried to see Mr. Frank, Georgie's boss, three times. This time you're determined to see him and not let Georgie sweet talk you out of it."

☐ *To what extent are role players permitted to add their own facts to the situation?* No set of instructions is intended to button-down every detail for the role players. A certain amount of improvisation is almost inevitable. The role players then can introduce added facts, just so they're in "sync" with the basic thrust of the role.

☐ *How many role-playing enactments should be used in a single multiple role playing session?* It all depends on course objectives, available time, etc. The trainer can assume that the first one is an "opener" and that at least two or three added situations of greater complexity are essential for adequate skill practice.

☐ *What is the best use of volunteers in role playing?* In enactments before the total group, volunteers can help break the ice and set a norm that role playing is worth doing and not too scary. Of course, by using multiple role playing, where everyone plays, volunteers are unnecessary.

☐ *Should the trainer intervene in a role play that is proceedingly poorly?* If the role plays are being conducted privately (in pairs, trios, quartets), the answer is no. The odds are that the trainer does not have enough data about what took place to correct things. The observers and/or the role players probably will report back to the total group on their less-than-successful experience. If such a role play is subject to group analysis and discussion, learning from it should take place. On the other hand, if a role play *before the total group* is developing poorly, it should be stopped and corrected at once. Obviously, no learning for anyone—the role player or observer—will accrue if appropriate skill elements are not being applied.

☐ *Is it desirable to have the role players engage in public self-critique before the observers give their feedback?* Very much so. This approach encourages introspection—a basic tool for learning in role playing—and also defuses a possible negative reaction (defensiveness)

Table 5-2
Sources of Critique—Advantages and Limitations

Source	Advantages	Limitations
Self-critique	Basic to development of insight; also, aids to defuse negative feedback	No one can see themselves as others can; hence the need for other sources of feedback
Critique from one's partner	Provides another desirable perspective	But this is only one person's opinion, and it may not be objective because of involvement in the role play or may be cautious to avoid hurting other's feelings
Single observer	An added worthwhile source due to the detachment of the observer role	One person's opinion; may be reluctant to level; may lack skill and be too hard-hitting in giving feedback
Two or several observers	Multiple judgment is desirable	Ineffective only if observers are inexperienced, biased or reluctant to level
Trainer	Can provide his/her experienced view including being supportive (positive reinforcement)	One person's view; not too helpful in multiple role plays
Coach (used in multiple role plays in addition to observer)	Adds an element of experience to the critique; objective, since not involved in the role plays; assumes worthwhile roles of coordinator and summarizer	Depends on high skill and personal qualities (patient, empathic, candid, supportive, enthusiastic, etc., all of which establishes good rapport with role players)

to observer feedback. Self-critique is a good way to help the role players save face, should that be necessary.

□ *What is the best type of feedback for the role player?* Keep it low key and supportive, and stress the positive reinforcement approach. Negatives may be introduced, but in a gentle way—not "This was lousy," but "The interview could have been strengthened by . . . . " Also, don't "clobber" anyone with a "ton" of negative feedback.

□ *What is the best source of critique for the role players?* There is no single best source; rather, multiple-source critique is more effective. The pros and cons of each source are included in Table 5-2.

□ *What are the skill factors in making role playing succeed?* It takes quite a few, actually. Adherence to some or more of the major ones, listed below, should help.

1. Have clear cut learning objectives lest the role playing be perceived as an add-on. So be sure to provide participants with a clear understanding of what they are to do any why.
2. Try to involve everyone. Do this via paired enactments before the total group for everyone, on a one-at-a-time basis; or, better still, via multiple role playing.
3. Use group-developed situations or members' problems.

4. Consider using group-developed criteria for the observers.
5. Make certain the observers know what to look for and understand the importance of their job.
6. "Field test" your cases especially the instructions to role players and observers.
7. Allow the role players enough time to internalize their assigned roles (in structured role playing) and to develop a strategy for dealing with the other person.
8. Provide enough try-out experiences so real learning is possible. Since role playing is designed to teach skills, the concept of "repractice" is basic.
9. If the cases are yours rather that those of the participants, make certain they are marked by a high degree of realism; for example, in sales training the problems and type of customers obviously should be those that the participants will actually encounter.
10. Allow enough time for the processing (critiquing) of the action. This is where the pay-offs will come from.
11. Include a summary of group learnings at session's end. Let the group tell you what they learned or, possibly, what they still need to learn.

Behavior Modeling

The latest innovation in role playing is known as "behavior modeling."[23] It is a reaction to some of the weaknesses or limitations of role playing as it is typically used to develop interpersonal skills. Specifically, critics of role playing assert that role play exercises only provide general guides for the trying out of new behavior, thus allowing the role players latitude to improvise within that framework. Also, on repeating a role play the same role players may do it differently and fail to button-down the skill to be learned.[24]

Role playing authority Malcolm E. Shaw[25] cites these flaws in role playing used to teach selling skills:

□ Participants are allowed to do the wrong things, a trial-and-error learning approach.
□ Participants are often "set up" to receive negative reinforcement.

Workshop Phases

To overcome these deficiencies, behavior-modeling workshops proceed along these six very specific phases:[26]

□ *A conceptual presentation is made.* This entails an explanation of the concepts basic to the skill to be mastered. Each step in the skill is described in detail along with the uses of it.

□ *A modeled videotaped demonstration of the skill is provided.* A company supervisor (not an outsider), with whom the group can identify, shows the right way to apply the skill. (The skill can relate to performance appraisal, a disciplinary interview, a selling skill, etc.) Key actions are performed on the videotape on a step-by-step basis. Participants are required to identify each action step, record them in their notebooks, and then discuss them.

The modeled behavior takes place within the company (not in a "foreign" location) and is introduced by an executive of the firm the supervisor would know. This shows that management supports the program. By using an "in-house" model, the participants could identify with the company person and thus perceive that person and the program as credible. They also gain confidence that the behavior modeled was one that they, too, could do.

Another view on the "customizing" of models is held by Donald T. Tosti. He states that customizing "to produce effective skill learning has not been supported. In fact, there is some evidence that model demonstrations that match the work environment too closely, or use familiar settings and co-workers as actors, may be distracting."[27]

□ *A rehearsal period is provided to practice the behaviors.* Following the viewing of the videotape, the demonstrated skill is rehearsed, one pair at a time. The trainer guides the role-playing supervisor's attempts at skill replication, one step at a time. The rehearsal is videotaped for feedback and reinforcement, stage four in the process.

Note: The videotape is not used as a "trigger film" to provoke discussion. Thus, the trainer would never say to the observer group: "What did you like, what did you not like?" Instead, a skill-oriented question such as this would be posed: "How did the sales manager use active listening with the subordinate?"

Active listening entails acceptance of what is said without engaging in value judgments; also, clarification of expressed feelings and restatement (reflecting back) what is said.

Note, too, that the enactment is not an open end role play—"do it as you see (or feel) it"—which often produces a lot of anxiety. Also, the approach is trainer intensive.

□ *Feedback and reinforcement are provided to fine-tune the behavior.* Using the action steps shown in the videotape as their criteria, the observers provide the role player with supportive feedback. Successes rather than miscues are stressed. Action steps improperly performed

or skipped are reenacted, at the request of the trainer, until properly executed. So every role play becomes a success story.

Besides trainer and observer feedback, the role players also engage in self-critique.

The most significant skill for the trainer is to emulate what is taught; e.g., the trainer can't teach the value of self-esteem and then erode it.

□ *Commitments are made by participants to apply the learned skills to their on-the-job problems.* Written contracts are secured from the trainees to use the new learning.

□ *Follow-up discussions are provided.* Each session begins with a review of the contracts developed in the prior session—what worked well on the job and what didn't. If a problem or block is encountered, the trainer calls for another rehearsal to ensure that the pertinent skills are learned.

Several features of the program design, which ensure a "glueing in" of the classroom learning, are these:

□ The training is spaced out over a six-week period. This allows for on-the-job practice after each full day's session.
□ The trainees' supervisors, who have had the training, provide added reinforcement upon their return to the job.
□ Line managers, who have been properly trained, are used as trainers in the workshops.
□ A "reinforcement day" is provided every four or six months. This prevents "erosion" of the classroom learning.

The supervisors who have been trained via behavior modeling are expected to use several general principles of motivation:[28]

□ It is essential to maintain and enhance the employee's self-esteem along with a concern for productivity. Candor rather than manipulation is to be employed.
□ The focus is on behavior, performance, results (e.g., errors, absenteeism) not on changing anyone's personality. This approach avoids defensive reactions.
□ Individual differences of subordinates are to be recognized.
□ Positive reinforcement is the key to shaping behavior. This procedure avoids possible negative side effects from other kinds of reinforcement.
□ Active listening is to be used to demonstrate understanding of the other's feelings, attitudes, etc.
□ Reasonable goals and follow-up dates therefore are the "contracts" to get the specified changes in behavior.

Starting a Program

If you or your organization are considering embarking on a behavior-modeling training program, you should ask these key questions:[29]

☐ Is the performance deficiency due to a clear-cut lack of skill and knowledge or are there other factors at work (e.g., lack of motivation)?

☐ Is it a skill or a knowledge deficiency? Actually, most skill training also requires attention to an accompanying cognitive component so both elements typically have to be attended to. However, one must be able to distinguish between the two deficiencies to be able to provide the proper training for them.

☐ Are the behaviors needed to overcome the deficiency identifiable? Often, one set of learned behavior is inadequate since different situations, requiring different behaviors, may be encountered.

☐ Will there be an opportunity for *all* learners to practice the desired skills? A small group (about 8–12) makes for a manageable training operation.

☐ Will there be adequate reinforcement for the new skills that are learned? This should take place in class *and* on the job. Sources of reinforcement: peers, workers, managers, and the total organization.

☐ Is the training cost effective? Quantitative data must be gathered before (an estimate) and after the training (evaluation) to demonstrate actual payoffs.

Uses and Results

Behavior modeling has been used to train supervisors in skills relating to performance review, to improve poor work habits and/or performance, to discipline effectively, to reduce conflict between two subordinates, to introduce a new procedure or policy, to reduce turnover of new hires, and to maintain a supportive and open climate. It has also been used in sales training; in training newly promoted scientists in people-handling skills; in training inner-city minority youth in interpersonal skills to avoid possible failure on the job.

A growing number of research studies have reported favorable outcomes as a result of training in behavior modeling. One sophisticated study, using before and after measures plus comparison or control groups, merits citation. The study took place in a manufacturing operation (700 unionized employees) of a major forest products company. The key findings were as follows:[30]

☐ Supervisors who received training in supervisory skills via behavior modeling were perceived by their employees to be using these skills at levels significantly superior to supervisors in the control groups (untrained supervisors).

☐ Over a 6-month period, the running average of total monthly production per direct worker-hour improved 17% compared to a control (or untrained) plant.

☐ Average daily production, again compared to the control group, was up 25% in the fifth month.

☐ Significant waste reduction, over a six-month period, was also accomplished compared to the controls. Raw material converted to end product increased at a rate equal to a reduction in cost from $40,000–$50,000 monthly. This meant a $250,000 cumulative saving for the 6-month research period.

In another evaluation study, employees of supervisors who had undergone behavior-modeling training completed anonymously a "Supervisor Interaction Behavior Profile" to rate their bosses on their progress in resolving work problems. The ratings took place six months after the training was completed. Sixty-five supervisors had been trained and 19 volunteered to receive the feedback from their subordinates. The results: Each profile served to motivate and maintain job use of learned interaction skills. Action plans were developed by the supervisors to overcome highlighted deficiencies. Also, the assessments improved communications and awareness among all concerned.[31]

Overcoming Shortcomings

Despite the wide use of behavior modeling and its numerous successes, many users have encountered shortcomings with it. For example, Scott Parry and Leah R. Reich, president and vice president, respectively, of Training House, Inc., Princeton, New Jersey, see these kinds of lingering issues:[32]

☐ *Simplistic models.* Trainees typically learn to handle all situations in a given way—"one size fits all." In reality, a single model cannot accommodate all situations in varying work environments. *The solution:* Regard the model as a starting point, not the end-all. The trainees should be taught to discriminate between situations where the model is and is not appropriate. Trainers (and the programs) must be flexible enough to accept alternatives and to apply some models (and modules) and reject others which don't fit the organization's norms and culture.

☐ *Absence of theory.* Employees today want to know the "why" as well as the "how." As has been said, "There is nothing as practical as good theory." *The solution:* Trainers should know and share behavioral science concepts and data underlying each model before participants are given the model and asked to enact it. Other responses (behavioral options) which derive from these theories should be elicited and enacted.

□ *Boredom.* The above two problems create boredom, as does the fact that all classes follow the same format. Also, all participants reenact the same basic role play. Finally, behavior modeling puts the trainer in a parental role, i.e., total reliance on the "show-and-tell" *inductive* method. Trainees' experiences are not tapped. They learn to do as instructed without opportunity to contribute or question despite their job experience. *The solution:* Use more *deductive* methods, i.e., draw from the participants their experience to vitalize and enrich concepts and skills.

Note: Another view on the inductive vs. deductive issue is held by Kenneth E. Hultman, a director of ministerial counseling services.[33] He does not believe that inductive learning has to be parent-child in nature. He asserts that an effective trainer can make most points in a module by asking the learners questions and allowing opportunities to discover the answers for themselves. He would have them respond to questions and draw on their experience in the module introduction, following the video model, prior to skill practice exercises, and after those exercises.

□ *Wrong examples are not used.* Trainees are given only "perfect" models to study. But other experts in this field believe that people also learn by seeing negatives, non-ideals, and learning to distinguish between effective and ineffective behavior patterns. *The solution:* Expose the learners to weak/ineffective models, too. When they understand the difference between the desirable and the less so, they should then practice in their role plays the appropriate concepts and skills.

Note: In respect to the issue of positive vs. negative models, Darlene Russ-Eft and Linda Zucchelli, of Zenger Miller, Inc., Cupertino, California, a firm with extensive experience in behavior modeling, has researched this area. Their study provides these implications for training:[34]

□ Showing two *positive* models (positive/positive) results in improved learning. But using a negative model with a positive one produces similar effective results.

□ When employing a negative model, use the "negative/positive ordering." This format is most effective if you are training people in subtle, ambiguous behaviors. Why? Because it provides more contrast, improved retention and heightened trainee satisfaction.

□ Using more than one model improves learning, probably due to repetition and generalization. One of these models must be positive.

□ Two negative models produce ineffective learning. People learn best from a correct model. So if you only use one model, be certain it is a positive one.

□ *Weak transfer to the job.* Actual application on the job may not occur for these reasons:

1. Learners are not motivated by the satisfaction of measuring their own improved performance. Why not? Because on entry into class they did not assess their own strong points and weak points. Consequently, they can't share with their bosses and/or subordinates any real basis for change or improvement.

2. Since the program is essentially a "canned" rather than a tailor-made one, the training may not be seen as relevant.

3. Positive reinforcement to support the new behavior may be absent.

The solution: Participants' bosses should be trained in coaching and mentoring to support the new learning. Also, action plans should be prepared and reviewed with the boss after the training has been tried to review successes and failures in applying the new behaviors.

Another criticism of behavior modeling as it is taught, comes from Dr. Melvin Sorcher,[35] who developed it in 1969–70 when he was Manager of Personnel Research at General Electric. (He co-authored *Changing Supervisory Behavior* with A. P. Goldstein, Pergamon Press Inc., New York, 1974, the pioneering work in this field. He is currently Director of Management Development at Richardson-Vicks Inc.) He states that he got better results than current practitioners because he carefully trained *employees* how to react to these kinds of situations: how to react to constructive criticism, how to ask for help or information, how to ask for performance feedback, how to cooperate with change, and so on. In his training classes at GE he used different behavior modeling video tapes for supervisors and employees and trained them separately. He found that training both parties on how to interact with one another made for effective responding.

Key Points

1. Role playing is a technique basic to every trainer's repertoire. It is a skill-oriented form of experiential training.

2. It is a versatile training tool, taking such forms as the informal (*ad hoc,* unplanned); the spontaneous (using participants' live cases); the demonstration type (includes dramatic skits and personal growth enactments); multiple role playing (teams of three or four, including observers); group role playing (a group assumes roles and works on a problem subject to total group critique); multiple

group role playing (several or more groups or teams work on the same problem producing comparative data); total group role playing (e.g., in a simulation).

3. The trainer must be aware that role playing and the feedback received from it may produce anxiety and should take appropriate steps to reduce the threat involved.

4. Structure (using worksheets, instruments) is a tool to direct learning and reduce possible anxiety or embarassment.

5. Observers are useful for collecting data for feedback purposes. They should be oriented fully as to the nature and importance of their task.

6. "Processing" the role play properly is basic to participant learning from it.

7. Video feedback is a means of capturing the full dimensions of a role play in an objective way.

8. Trainers should acquire skill in developing their own role playing situations. A good role play is short, easy to understand, has believable characters, contains enough conflict to be realistic, and relates directly to learning goals.

9. The role playing experience can be enhanced via special or "advanced" techniques such as role reversal, empty chair, the soliloquy, the mirror technique, multiple role taking, and the "behind the back" technique.

10. Behavior modeling is a powerful tool—and a system—to ensure that role playing produces real learning and is transferred to the job.

References

1. "Role Playing Polishes New Sales People," *Wall Street Journal* (September 30, 1987).

2. Broadwell, M. M., "Rediscover Role Playing," *Training, The Magazine of Human Resources Development* (July 1977), p. 19.

3. Wohlking, W., and Weiner, H., "Structured and Spontaneous Role Playing: Contrast and Comparison," *Training and Development Journal* (January 1971), pp. 8–14.

4. Cooper, W. H., "Play Well Thy Part," *Training and Development Journal* (August 1980), pp. 64–68.

5. Bub, J. and Suessmuth, P., "Lesson Design: Predicting Student Choice," *Canadian Training Methods— The Human Element* (June 1980), pp. 35–36, 38.

6. Cover, W. H., "Curbstone Coaching," *Training and Development Journal* (November 1980), pp. 33–37.

7. McAlister, Bill, "Service In A Foreign Fantasy Land," *The Washington Post* (March 6, 1987), p. 21.

8. Schlesinger, Jacob M., "Auto Firms and UAW Find That Cooperation Can Get Complicated," *Wall Street Journal* (August 25, 1987), p. 20.

9. Maier, N. R. F., Solem, A. R., and Maier, A. A., *The Role Play Technique: A Handbook for Management and Leadership Practice,* University Associates, Inc., San Diego (1975).

10. "Training Away Work Place Problems," *Training and Development Journal* (Nov. 1987), pp. 18–19, which provides suggestions by Michael Shahnasarian, ISFA Corporation, Tampa, Florida.

11. Jones, J. E., and Pfeiffer, J. W., "Role Playing," *The 1979 Annual Handbook for Group Facilitators,* University Associates, Inc., San Diego (1979), pp. 182–193.

12. Millington, W. G., and Gross, L. S., "Video for Teaching the Non-Verbal Language," *Educational and Industrial Television* (August 1976), pp. 20–22.

13. *TC Today, The Newsletter of Teachers College/Columbia University* (Spring 1981), p. 4.

14. Goldfaden, B., and Teta, D., "Video for Psychology Instruction and Practice," *Educational and Instructional TV* (December 1980), pp. 43–45.

15. Power, William, "With Any Luck Soon All Judges Will Be Like Joseph Wapner," *Wall Street Journal* (August 12, 1984).

16. Barrett, J., "Skilled Are the Peacemakers," *Northeast Training News* (June 1980), p. 19.

17. Whyte, R., "How to Role-Play Your Way to Better Management/Salesman Communications," *Sales Management* (May 1, 1972), pp. 29, 31, 86, 88.

18. Gschwandtner, G., "A New Approach to Videotaped Role Plays," *Educational and Industrial Television* (March 1978), pp. 66–69.

19. Klein, R., and Smith, F., "Supervisory Feedback in Training," *Training and Development Journal* (September 1981), 106–110.

20. At the September 1981 ASTD Region II Conference in Rochester, N.Y.

21. *Personnel Journal* (June 1976), p. 270.

22. Horne, J., "Cops to the Rescue," *Quest* (July–August 1981), pp. 32–36, 85, 88–89.

23. Goldstein, A. P., and Sorcher, M., *Changing Supervisory Behavior,* Pergamon Press, New York (1974). (The technique was originated at General Electric in 1970.)

24. Porras, J. I., and Anderson, B., "Improving Managerial Effectiveness Through Modeling-Based Training," *Organizational Dynamics* (Spring 1981), p. 66.

25. Shaw, M. E., "Sales Training in Transition," *Training and Development Journal* (February 1981), p. 81.

26. Porras, J. I., and Anderson, B., "Improving Managerial Effectiveness Through Modeling-Based Training," *Organizational Dynamics* (Spring 1981), pp. 64–67.

27. Tosti, D. T., "Behavior Modeling: A Process," *Training and Development Journal* (August 1980), p. 73.

28. Rosenbaum, B. L., "Common Misconceptions About Behavior Modeling and Supervisory Skill Training (SST)," *Training and Development Journal* (August 1979), pp. 40–44.

29. Robinson, J. C., and Gaines, D. L., "Seven Questions to Ask Yourself Before Using Behavior Modeling," *Training, The Magazine of Human Resources Development* (December 1980), pp. 60–69.

30. Porras, J. I., and Anderson, B., "Improving Managerial Effectiveness Through Modeling-Based Training," *Organizational Dynamics* (Spring 1981), pp. 70–76.

31. "Low-Threat Truth-Telling Aids Supervisor Assessment," *Training* (August 1983), pp. 69–70.

32. Parry, Scott B., and Reich, Leah R., "An Uneasy Look At Behavior Modeling," *Training and Development Journal* (March 1984), pp. 57–62.

33. Hultman, Kenneth E., "Behavior Modeling For Results," *Training and Development Journal* (December 1986), pp. 60–63.

34. Russ-Eft, Darlene, and Zuchelli, Linda, "When Wrong Is Alright," *Training and Development Journal* (November 1987), pp. 78–79.

35. Sorcher, Melvin, "Developer of Behavior Modeling Shows How To Make It More Effective," *BNAC Communicator,* BNAC Communications Inc., Rockville, Maryland (Summer 1987), p. 2.

Recommended Reading

General

"Bosses, Cops, G-Men Prepare for Crises by Acting Them Out," *Wall Street Journal,* November 25, 1981.

This is an account for the lay person concerning current uses of role playing in business and government.

Callahan, Madelyn R., "Art Imitates Work Life: The World According To PACT," *Training and Development Journal,* December 1986, pp. 56–59.

This article describes the work of the Manhattan-based Performing Arts For Crisis Training (PACT), an actor-trainer group that recreates actual scenes of crisis used to teach handling situations "in reality": rape victims, angry customers, problem employees, hijackers, alcoholics, abused wives, suicidal teenagers, etc. PACT calls its work "structured improvisations," presenting the realities of office, plant, school, police precinct, emergency room, and the like.

Harmon, Paul, and Evans, Kay, "When To Use Cognitive Modeling," *Training and Development Journal,* March 1984, pp. 67–68.

Behavior modeling works for overt, observable activities. But to teach covert cognitive skills, e.g., teaching a loan officer to make correct loans, a sequential cognitive procedure must be identified. Job aids are used for this such as a worksheet, decision chart, checklist, flow chart.

Jones, John E., and Pfeiffer, J. William. "Role Playing," in *The 1979 Annual Handbook for Group Facilitators,* University Associates Inc., San Diego, California, 1979, pp. 182–193.

Topics covered include the context of role playing, its use in human relations training, advantages and disadvantages, designing role plays, role playing in the experiential learning cycle, conducting role plays.

Maier, Norman R. F., Solem, Allen R., and Maier, Ayesha. *The Role-Play Technique: A Handbook for Management and Leadership Practice,* University Associates Inc., San Diego, California, 1975.

This is a unique role playing case book containing role plays for both multiple-group and single-group situations. Instructions for the trainer are provided for each case so that the activities can be conducted successfully.

Shaw, Malcolm E., Corsini, Raymond J., Blake, Robert and Mouton, Jane S. *Role Playing: A Practical Manual for Group Facilitators,* University Associates Inc., San Diego, California, 1980.

This is an updated version of a classic work on the role play method. It describes why and how it is useful and how it can be applied to meet problems of information dissemination, individual assessment, and training.

Behavior Modeling

"Behavior Modeling Trains Underprivileged Youths for Jobs," *Behavior Today,* November 17, 1980.

Learning interpersonal skills through observing role models on videotape, role playing and group feedback helped underprivileged youths prepare for retail sales jobs in Philadelphia.

O'Connor, Terence, "How to Set Up, Run and Evaluate a Training Program Based on Behavior Modeling Principles, *Training/HRD,* January 1979, pp. 64–67.

At St. Luke's Hospital, New York City, supervisors learn through behavior "rehearsal" these seven skills: greeting the new employee, introducing a new policy or procedure, improving poor work habits, improving poor performance, the discipline interview, performance appraisal, and reducing conflict between two subordinates.

Validation studies indicate that problems are solved by the program.

Porras, Jerry I., and Anderson, Brad, "Improving Managerial Effectiveness Through Modeling-Based Training," *Organizational Dynamics,* Spring 1981, pp. 60–67.

Tangible payoffs from a behavior-modeling program in a major forest products company are reported. An outside team of investigators conducted the research.

"Retailers Discover An Old Tool: Sales Training," *Business Week,* December 22, 1980, pp. 81–82.

Using behavior modeling principles and techniques, a training/consulting firm teaches retail clerks these selling points: greeting, ascertaining what the customer wants, benefit to the customer, overcoming objections, closing the sale, selling extra items, and enhancing buyer self-esteem.

Robinson, James C. and Linda E., "How to Make Sure Your Supervisors Do On-The-Job What You Taught Them In The Classroom," *Training/HRD,* September 1979, pp. 21–22, 24–25.

This asserts that for actual transfer of the new behavior to the job, two conditions must be met: determination of needs of supervisors who are to be trained and management support of the new skills that are learned.

Robinson, James C., and Gaines, Dana L., "Seven Questions To Ask Yourself Before Using Behavior Modeling," *Training/HRD,* December 1980, pp. 60–65, 67–69.

Behavior modeling training, to be successful, requires decisions in respect to these seven questions: (1) Could he/she do it if his/her life depended on it? (2) Is it a skill deficiency? (3) Can you identify behavior needed to overcome the skills deficiency? (4) Can a positive, credible model be demonstrated? (5) Can each learner practice the skill? (6) Will the new skills be reinforced? (7) Is it cost beneficial?

These principles were applied to a training program for the Homespun Insurance Company with financial benefits to the Company.

Robinson, James C. and Linda E., "Modeling Techniques Applied to Performance Feedback and Appraisal," *Training and Development Journal,* January 1978, pp. 48–53.

Describes a system wherein supervisors can deal more effectively with employee performance in today's work environment. The system overcomes these shortcomings in supervision: (1) lack of specific goals/standards; (2) lack of immediate feedback; (3) lack of planning for discussions about performance; (4) lack of future orientation; (5) lack of supervisory skills; (6) lack of management support.

Rosenbaum, Bernard L., "Common Misconceptions About Behavior Modeling and Supervisory Skill Training," *Training and Development Journal,* August 1979, pp. 40–44.

If behavior modeling training for supervisors is to be successful, these principles must be followed by them: (1) maintain and enhance self-esteem of the employee; (2) focus on behavior not personality; (3) use reinforcement techniques to shape desired behavior; (4) use active listening to show understanding; (5) set goals, follow-up dates and maintain communications.

Rosenbaum, Bernard, "New Uses For Behavior Modeling," *The Personnel Administrator,* July 1978, pp. 27–28.

Besides training of supervisors, behavior modeling can be applied to blue-collar workers to improve peer relations; to reduce conflict among professionals and managers; to improve security guards' skills in dealing with executives and employees; etc.

Shaw, Malcolm E., "Sales Training in Transition," *Training and Development Journal,* February 1981, pp. 74–76, 78–83.

Answers these two related questions: (1) What are the desirable sales behaviors which should be supported and enhanced in sales training? and (2) what are the methodologies, structures, and design elements that will develop and sustain those desired behaviors?

Tosti, Donald T., "Behavior Modeling: A Process," *Training and Development Journal,* August 1980, pp. 70–71, 73–74.

This points up shortcomings in application of behavior modeling training such as use of poor models, ineffective practice situations, ineffective feedback. ("Poor" models relate to a confusing or distracting situation, unconvincing actors, demonstration of inappropriate verbal and nonverbal behavior along with appropriate actions. Ineffective feedback entails more criticism than encouragement, failure to focus on critical behaviors, poor timing, or sequence.)

Wehrenberg, Stephen, and Kuhnie, Robert, "How Training Through Behavior Modeling Works," *Personnel Journal,* July 1980, pp. 576–80, 593.

This is a well-rounded treatment of the subject, including the motivational/learning theories at work, history, steps in a model program, and a summary of several evaluation studies.

Zemke, Ronald. "Building Behavior Models That Work—The Way You Want Them To," *Training/HRD,* January 1982, pp. 22–27.

This discusses various issues in behavior modeling that may facilitate or inhibit identification with the model by the trainees: the "dressiness" of the set; perfect vs. coping performance; real company problems or neutral issues; negative vs. positive examples.

USING GAMES AND SIMULATIONS

Games, simulations, exercises, and puzzles, also known as structured experiences, provide participants with significant opportunities to experience learning. By "experience" we mean to learn from one's personal involvement with the structured event or incident as opposed to being told by the trainer what should be learned from it. Thus, in the classic "NASA (Lost On The Moon)" exercise,[1] participants learn *experientially* of the power and value of group decision making. Or participants may be assigned the task of constructing a tower out of construction paper, cardboard, newspapers, magazines, and tape, and learn from this the importance of and approaches to planning, organizing, leadership, utilization of member skills, participation, communication creativity, teamwork, decision making, and pride in accomplishment.

Note that although the trainer provides the vehicle for the learning—the exercise—the learning comes about by actually undergoing the experience. The point we are making, then, is that although the structured event itself is not reality, the learning from it, coming as it does from one's experience, is very real indeed.

To put this type of learning into proper perspective, we should recognize that other—and possibly more powerful—learning ensues when you learn primarily or even totally from your experience. Such experience-based activities include laboratory learning (the T-Group, or sensitivity training, encounter groups, the Managerial Grid®); team building; keeping a diary or journal or completing various instruments as tools for introspection; participating in a simulation; and role playing a live or real job-oriented case. An overview and summary of experiential learning is provided in Chapter 8. Several brief definitions of games and simulations, etc. as forms of experiential learning follow:

Simulation—Any training activity designed to reflect reality. This may, then, include a role play, an in-basket exercise, or any other learning experience that has real-life aspects integrated into it. The learning comes from the participant's own experience in the activity.

Game—A learning activity governed by rules, entailing a competitive situation, having winners and losers. Although games do *not* reflect reality, there is (and must be) learning. The learning typically comes from experiencing the game, including the interaction of the participants, but not from the subject matter or content of the game per se.

Simulation-game—A reality-based game wherein the participants experience what people do in the real world. The learning comes from the real-life content of the game. The game is played competitively and, of course, has outcomes (including scores, winners, losers).

Exercise—A structured experiential activity. The learning comes from participant input, participant interaction, and participant analysis of the attitudes and/or behaviors generated by the activity. Competition is *not* an element of the exercise.

The common denominators of all of these learning tools are:

☐ Concrete learning objectives
☐ Structure provided by the trainer
☐ High participant involvement
☐ Generation of data
☐ Participant/trainer analysis of completed results (data)

Note that competition and reality are *not* the distinguishing features of *all* of these experiential forms of learning.

In this chapter we shall discuss games and simulations. In Chapter 7 we shall introduce the reader to exercises. In Chapter 8 we will show how puzzles can be used in the training situation. To integrate the key ideas of Chapters 6, 7, and 8, we shall provide some key concepts about experiential learning at the close of Chapter 8.

Working with Games

A simulation game is like a kiss, interesting to read about but much more interesting to participate in. And those that do tend to repeat the experience.

—From a promotional brochure of
the Institute of Higher
Education Research and
Services, The University of
Alabama.

Games set up a "free space" which participants can use to experiment with new roles or variations of their present roles . . . . It is a space where norms of validity are suspended and totally new approaches to the real world can be formulated.

—Burkhart Holzner,
Department of
Sociology,
University of
Pittsburgh

A good game will drive itself. In some exercises, the facilitator is constantly saying, "Now this is the next step." But a good game takes on a life of its own.
—Barbara Steinwachs, training
consultant and authority on
games.

What is a game, insofar as the training situation is concerned? One group of trainers[2] endeavored to respond to

this question by brainstorming the characteristics of a game. Here's what they came up with:

Rules	Action learning
Competition	Processing of data
Skill	Imagination
Win/lose aspect	Fantasy
Threatening	Discipline
Beginning/end	Options
Focus	Strategy
Self/others	Luck
Brings out child	Problem solving
Fun	Motivational
Noisy	Team spirit
Scoring	Applications (cognitive/
Chance/skill	affective/psychomotor)
Roles	Communication
Goal	Skills
Betting (sometimes)	Chance to try out new
Spectators	ideas, roles, skills
Rewards	behaviors, simulation
Risk (low/high)	of real`world
Experimental	

This list is interesting in that it shows the multifaceted character of a game. However, it does not provide us with a clear-cut definition of a game; rather it combines purposes, major and minor attributes, and end results. Actually, a game is marked by the presence of these principal elements:

☐ Learning goals
☐ Rules (which are clearly defined)
☐ Competition
☐ Player interaction/participation
☐ Termination point or closure (time, points, most money earned, etc.)
☐ Outcomes (winners and losers are determined)

Current language used to describe many games is "simulation-game." The term "simulation" is intended to point up that there is also present a representation of reality, a "slice of life." The simulation-game could be diagrammed as in Figure 6-1. The simulation-game then is a combination of the game and the simulation.

Of course, not all games are a slice of life. For example, several groups may compete in placing 30 pegs in a peg board. This is what might be termed a "pure game." The learning comes from analyzing participant behavior exhibited in the course of the game—leadership, communication, planning, organizing—rather than the components of the game per se.

Other games may involve competition in constructing a bridge out of Tinker Toys or a tower out of newspaper,

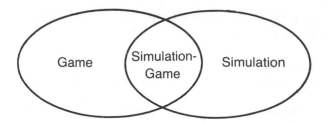

Figure 6-1. Diagram illustrating the concept of a simulation game.

magazines, and construction paper. Again, the learning typically comes from the interaction of the participants and the data generated by them rather than from the subject matter or content of the game.

Sometimes games are referred to by trainers as exercises, learning exercises, activities, application sessions, etc., to "defuse" a possible negative reaction by some participants to "playing a game."

Simulation-games, including war games and business games, have been used for many purposes: decision making, negotiation, sales, communication, planning, problem solving, delegation, time management, equal employment, urban affairs, transactional analysis, goal setting, career planning, safety, performance appraisal, communication, and so on.

In the balance of this section we will use the term "game" to include games and simulation-games as well.

Why Use Games?

A game has these purposes and advantages:

It is an experiential form of learning. Participants learn from what they do, as opposed to what the trainer tells them they should know. It is active rather than passive learning.

It may provide a degree of reality that other learning devices may not be able to. For example, compare learning about how a decision was made in a case study situation versus reaching a decision required by the game.

It has high motivational value. Learners respond to a game because they are actively involved, and it is a fun way to learn. Competition—beating the other teams—is also an incentive to "dig in."

It provides participation for everyone. All learners—fast, medium, slow, or ostentatious—have the same opportunities for involvement. (Of course, prior familiarity with the subject, possession of certain skills, etc., may determine the nature and degree of the involvement.)

It emphasizes the role of the participants. The participants are the active ones and the role of the trainer is de-emphasized. The trainer is removed from the usual roles of knowledge-disseminater, expert, authority figure, and evaluator. Typically, the trainer need only help participants to get started and to assess learning progress and outcomes.

It emphasizes peer learning. Participants learn from their interaction with one another. It recognizes that the participant group is a splendid learning resource. To the extent that this is true, it reduces the usual dependency on the trainer.

Learning is rapid. Since a game compresses considerable experience into a short time frame, learning is accelerated.

The game only produces winners. A game produces winners and losers insofar as the rules of the game are concerned. But, in fact, everyone is a "winner" since everyone learns (or at least has the opportunity to learn) from the experience.

It allows for risk-taking in a safe atmosphere. It is far better to err in the training situation than in real life. Games reward (learning or experience is the reward) rather than penalize the learner.

It serve as a projective device. To the extent that participants are caught up in the spirit of the game and become themselves, their behavior is displayed for the others to see. The behavior can be critiqued and thus becomes the basis for learning about one's own behavior in relation to others within the rules of the game.

It can aid skill development. Since the game requires active participation, there typically are opportunities to develop such skills as planning, conferring, negotiating, analyzing, prioritizing, decision making, giving and receiving feedback.

It helps to "glue in" the training. Participants are much more likely to remember the game experience than something they were told by the trainer. It is not unusual for a trainer to encounter a participant who experienced a game several or more years back who says: "Remember when we played the game of . . . ."

It reinforces principles, concepts and techniques previously taught.

It taps the right brain, thereby stimulating the intuitive, creative, emotional, spontaneous side of the participants.

It permits learning the costs, benefits and effects (results, impacts) of decisions sans risking the costly resources (money, material, manpower, machinery, minutes) of the real world. People can learn safely the trade-offs and pros and cons of different strategies and alternatives.

Despite their many advantages, games may not work well if the game is not "in sync" with learning objectives, if participants have difficulty getting caught up in the spirit of the game (a rare event), if the trainer is not familiar with the game or is not prepared to administer it, or if time runs out before the game is fully processed (discussed and analyzed).

One writer suggests other limitations: some participants get "hooked" on winning and may thus overlook training goals, others may not take the game seriously enough to garner any learning, and learnings may dissipate at game's end unless there is reinforcement back on the job. (I would point out that reinforcement is always a problem regardless of the training technique employed.)[3]

When to Use Games

From the standpoint of course design games are indeed versatile learning tools that can be used in several ways.

☐ Games may be used to open an activity or program. It is an effective way to secure participant attention, heighten interest, set the tone of the program (high participation, an atmosphere of inquiry), and set the stage for the next activity. It can also get participants to interact with one another very quickly, and it gives everyone a common experience at the outset.

☐ Games may be used at many points in the on-going course or program. It is particularly helpful to provide a change of pace and/or to introduce variety into the learning experience. Should interest begin to lag in the middle of a course, a game can help rekindle interest. Of course, the trainer should have prepared an appropriate game for that part of the course.

☐ Games may be used to conclude (possibly summarize) a session or program. The impact of the game should serve to provide participants with an enthusiastic close and durable reminder of course learnings.

Administering the Game

Good "game management" requires concern with issues and procedures such as the following:

☐ Is the game being played at the most appropriate time in the session or program?

☐ Have I familiarized myself with the game—objectives, procedures, materials—so I can introduce it, conduct it, and process it properly?

☐ Have I allowed enough time for the game, particularly for processing it? (With good planning, you can avoid participant reactions such as this one: "Imagine, we worked two and one-half hours on the game and now the trainer tells us we only have 11 minutes left to 'summarize learning.'")

☐ Have I planned for all pre-game preliminaries such as game materials; instruction sheets; instructor's manual; seating arrangements; flipcharts and pens? Do I

have extra items likely to get lost, such as dice, chips, markers, and cards.

☐ How will I introduce the game? What should I say? Will I be sure to keep the introduction brief?

☐ Are my written instructions, if any, clear?

☐ Will I allow enough time to let participants "ease into" the game before they start, or will I rush them into it? Will I remember to ask for questions before the signal to start is given? ("Does this make sense?" "Are we on the same wavelength?" "Have I rushed the explanation?")

☐ Will I remember that a game is a form of experiential learning and that one must avoid taking away the participants' experiences by over-communicating about it before the game starts or while it is underway?

☐ How do I form groups? On the basis of propinquity of participants? Randomly (count-off method)? Self-selection? Does it matter?

☐ Will I remember to advise participants of time limits? Should I warn of the approaching deadline (five or ten minutes) before it arrives?

☐ When I give participants the time warning ("Three more minutes, please"), do I adhere to that time limit strictly or do I use it just as a reminder that things have to be wrapped up very soon?

☐ Will I remember to instruct observers and/or judges, if any, about their roles?

☐ Will I need a co-trainer? Is the role of the co-trainer or assistant clear?

☐ Will I strive to keep the atmosphere informal, fun-filled, remembering that this *is* a game?

☐ What is my role during the game? Do I move around to clarify procedures and rules? Do I "tune-in" a bit to get a sense of participants being with it, questions or issues arising, team feeling, etc.? Do I avoid intervening, remembering that this is *their* game?

☐ Do I know quite well what is to be accomplished in the processing or debriefing period and how it is to be done?

☐ Do I recognize that debriefing should proceed at two levels: game analysis *and* its application to the real world?

☐ In the processing, do I recognize that although everyone has had the same experience that they may still perceive it differently?

Designing Your Own Games

Although a great number and variety of games are available from publishers, at times it may be desirable to design your own game. This may be to meet better the needs of the course or program; for economy or cost reduction; to exercise or test one's creativity; to ensure that participants have a fun as well as a learning experience.

Keep in mind the following suggestions when designing a game:

1. Develop a good feel for games in general. Do this by participating in or administering a number of them. Try to experience a variety of games: pure games, paper and pencil games, board games, card games, construction-type games, and so on.
2. Work with one or more colleagues on the project. A well-thought-out game has many nuances to it, and two or three heads can zero in on them more readily than one.
3. Use the check list in Figure 6-2 as a guide to meaningful game design.

Checklist For Design of a Game

	NO	YES	NOT SURE
1. Terminal objectives (attitudes, skills, behavior) are fully thought out and reduced to writing.	□	□	□
2. There is a high probability that the game will actually provide the desired learning outcomes.	□	□	□
3. There is a logical relationship between the length of the game session and participant learning (cost effectiveness).	□	□	□
4. The game is the best training method to achieve the terminal objectives.	□	□	□
5. The game has been constructed so that winners and losers will learn equally.	□	□	□
6. Observers have been included to facilitate the post-game analysis.	□	□	□
7. Provisions have been made, either orally or in writing, to instruct the observers properly in their roles.	□	□	□
8. Judges have been included since the end-result requires an "objective" appraisal (such as in the construction of a tower).	□	□	□
9. A prize will be awarded to stimulate interest.	□	□	□
10. If a prize is awarded, money will be collected from all participants.	□	□	□
11. If a prize is awarded, it will be awarded by the trainer or an impartial judge or referee.	□	□	□
12. Total time of the game has been carefully measured.	□	□	□
13. Time for processing (analysis) of the game is planned for.	□	□	□
14. The game has been subject to a "dry run" before it is used in class.	□	□	□

If any of these critical questions do not have a clear-cut response, one is well-advised to "go back to the drawing board." Remember, a game should produce an "ah ha" rather than a "ho hum" response.

Figure 6-2. A guide for designing a game.

Descriptions of games you probably can design follow:

Board Game

This is fairly easy to create. As in board games such as Monopoly, the players have money ("funny bucks" or poker chips will do), roll dice, and move their counters around the board. The play objective is to win the most money or points possible. This is done by answering questions, typed on cards. The questions could relate to any subject desired: product knowledge, customer service, safety, management topics such as communication, effective supervision, etc.

Let's say you wanted to create a game dealing with delegation. You would first brainstorm data for the cards such as the advantages of delegation, problems in delegation, techniques to make delegation work (the control side of delegation), why managers may be reluctant to delegate, why employees may be reluctant to assume greater responsibility, etc. This data could be used to form questions, which if answered correctly, earn points.

You also could introduce positive (rewarding) and negative (punishing) experiences as a result of delegation practices, for example:

"You have been recognized as 'The Delegator of the Year.' Go to the next green square and collect two hundred fifty dollars."

"One of your more promising employees has resigned because she felt she was not growing in the job. Pay three hundred fifty dollars to the United Community Fund and fifty dollars to each player."

"You introduce a weekly meeting with the Manager of Task Force Z-Four to ensure that the project is on target. Add thirty points to your total."

The end result should be the acquisition of new insights about delegation. And unlike with the lecture method, they would be acquired in a fun way.

If you are interested in constructing your own board games, you will want to review the many helpful details provided by trainer Stephen E. Sugar.[4]

Frame Game[5]

The idea is to give you, the game designer, a structure (the frame) and you then "plug in" the content you wish. For example, let's say you want to create a game on leadership. You follow these procedures:

1. Prepare in advance of the game five cards ($3'' \times 5''$ or $5'' \times 8''$) for each participant. Each card should have typed on it statements about leadership. Include statements that participants will be likely to accept ("I want to employ Theory Y management techniques"), statements participants will readily reject ("Leadership is keeping everyone happy"), and statements participants may feel ambiguous about ("Group decision is a useful technique for developing standards").
2. Prepare a similar batch of cards (the same number) for the table, mixing the positive, negative, and ambiguous cards.
3. Give each participant five cards.
4. Tell participants to read their cards and group them into two piles: likes (agrees with) and dislikes (disagrees with).
5. Have participants find a partner and endeavor to trade off their worst cards and garner better ones from one another. Tell them an explanation must be

offered for surrendering or taking a particular card.

6. Participants are free to secure a "fresh" card from those on the table after every two or more exchanges, but may only take the top card, putting discards on the bottom of the stack.
7. Allow 30 minutes for the exchanges or until the "decibel count" seems to be receding.
8. Ask participants to form trios or quartets and to agree on the five "best" cards. The discards are to be put on the table.
9. Secure reports from several groups concerning the cards they retained. Secure comments from the other groups concerning the cards that were not retained.

Note: A variation on Step 1 is to have the participants rather than the trainer prepare the cards. This step will add more time to the game, but it will produce added involvement. You, as trainer, may have to edit the cards a bit, too, for clarity.

Tic-Tac-Toe

Remember Tic-Tac-Toe, which has nine boxes that are to be completed with X's and O's? Well, the Tic-Tac-Toe frame can serve as the basis for another frame game, letting you provide whatever content you wish. As an example, in a management development/career development workshop for trainers we might have the participants label the vertical cells "first line supervision," "middle management," and "top management" and the horizontal boxes "early-career," "mid-career," and "late-career," as in Figure 6-3. Procedurally, we might then do the following:

1. Split the group into two smaller groups, "A" and "B."
2. Toss a coin for the first play. The starting team picks any cell it wishes and tries to fill it in (answer it). The trainer should be prepared with answers on all cells to approve or disapprove the participants' answers. Since opinion is involved in these career-oriented decisions, the trainer should be liberal in approving subgroup data. Each subgroup may challenge the other group's answers, the trainer, again, arbitrating the decision.
3. Play continues until one subgroup completes a line of three cells in a row in any direction.

Note: A variation of the game is to let each team fill up all nine boxes, with the winner being decided on the basis of who completes the whole matrix first. Factual data will be less controversial and will thus allow the game to proceed more smoothly. For example in a game involving determining accidents the vertical axis could be labeled "day shift," "evening shift," and "night shift."

	Early-Career	Mid-Career	Late-Career
Top Management			
Middle Management			
First Line Supervision			

Figure 6-3. The Tic-Tac-Toe format or frame as used in management training.

The horizontal axis could be labeled "plant," "warehouse," and "loading docks." Then the accident type could be inserted in appropriate boxes.[6]

Construction Games

Groups can be given materials, such as blocks, Tinker Toys, newspapers and magazines, to produce a physical structure such as a tower. The purpose of the construction activity is to allow the small groups to generate behavior for analysis, e.g., planning, leadership, communication, cooperation, participation, decision making, manpower utilization, and teamness. Observers can report on the data generated by the participants as they performed their tasks. Judges may be used to evaluate the completed work; e.g., construction of a free-standing tower may be awarded points on the basis of height, stability, aesthetic design, creativity, etc.

Production Games

Instead of constructing physical objects, as above, participants in teams may produce greeting card verses, political or advertising slogans, management sayings, laws or proverbs (such as Murphy's laws). Again, the behavior generated in team production is subject to observation, feedback, and analysis.

Maximum Numbers Games

A "sure-fire" way to produce competition between or among small groups is to assign them a task wherein they are required to produce a maximum number of something. Two examples of such games, using this approach, follow.

Archeological Game

The objective is to point up how our screening mechanism filters out unwanted data, detail, minutiae. This is important to us so that we can get through the day, and get our tasks accomplished without being sidetracked by trivia bombardment.

Note: This objective is *not* given to participants since this perceptual phenomenon is what they will learn from the game

Give participants the following instructions:

1. "You are to function as archeologists. This means that you are interested in reconstructing a given culture based on artifacts you discover."
2. "The culture you are concerned with is the United States in the year 7000—5,000 years or so past today."
3. "You are in a 'dig' and come up with a small, flat, round object. It has a man's face on it; the man has

a beard. The object is a U.S. penny and has this year's date on it."
4. *"Without* reaching for a penny from your pocket or purse, come up with as many characteristics of U.S. culture at that time as you can. This is what archeologists do all the time. You will have to rely on your memory to recall the data on the penny. You are in competition with the other teams. You have five minutes for the task."

At the five-minute mark, call time and ask participants to total their cultural characteristics. (The totals typically run in the "teens.")

Secure a verbal report from the highest team and list its data on a flipchart. Anticipate items such as these:

Bi-lingual (English and Latin)	System of writing
Architecture (if Lincoln Memorial in on rear)	Appearance conscious (Lincoln's beard)
Metallurgy	Liberty-loving (liberty)
Calendar	Sewing skills or tailoring (Lincoln's
Coinage system	shirt and coat)
Hero worship (Lincoln)	Cloth production
A federal government ("E Pluribus Unum")	Dress conscious (coat, tie)
Religion ("In God We Trust")	System of numbers
Mining	Agriculture (if a "wheat" penny)
	Patriarchal society

Also anticipate friendly rivalry—the losing team will deny the validity of certain cultural traits listed by the winning team. Secure added (new) items from the other teams.

To process the game ask participants what was learned. Some possible responses from the groups, which are put on a flipchart, are: Importance of team work (several heads are better than one); a leader in group is not necessary; importance of background or perception (i.e., different groups see different things). At this point add: "I'd like to pick up on the perception aspect. Was the task difficult to do, relying solely on memory?" (Participants respond affirmatively.) "Why was it difficult to remember what is on an object that you handle *daily?"* (Pause at this point for this is *the* profound question of the game.) Some possible participant answers are: "We don't pay attention to it." "It's not important information." "We take it for granted."

At this point say: "Yes, we overlook the detail, the trivia because we have a mechanism in our heads (phenomenon of perceptual choice or selective attention) that screens out the unimportant. This is a tremendously helpful device because it allows us to get through the day without getting bogged down by the innumerable stimuli that bombard us constantly—trees, signs, houses, stores, cars, ladies' dresses, colors. But at the same time our screening mechanism may work the other way. It may screen out data we *should be cognizant of,* for example, to call old Harry to our meeting. We forget him and he gets mad at us. So our screening device works for good and for less than good. So we must be aware of this perceptual process and try to keep it from overlooking the important stimuli, which also are out there."

25 Object Game

The objective is to demonstrate that creativity is more likely to flourish under unstructured as opposed to structured supervision. (But don't tell the group this in introducing the game.) Before introducing the game assemble 25 objects and place them in a $8\frac{1}{2}'' \times 11''$ envelope, one envelope per team. Each envelope should contain the identical 25 objects. The objects should cover a wide variety of materials and may include:

Commemorative postage stamp	Key
	Piece of wire
Plastic spoon	Screw or nail
Highway map	Hair pin
Ketchup (in small plastic bag)	Pencil
	Telephone memo slip
Sugar packet	Needles or pins
Coin	Button
Stone	Piece of cloth
Small pine cone	Matches
Aspirin	Beer can opener
Candle	Coping saw blade
Piece of plastic (apparently functionless)	

To play the game:

1. Divide the group into teams of five to nine persons.
2. Appoint a leader for each group. The leaders are to function differently, some will be relaxed, encouraging, "unstructured" leaders (Supervisors A); the others will be more "structured" (Supervisors B). Each leader receives only his/her instructions in writing and does not see the other instructions.

The instructions to be given to the unstructured leader, Supervisor A, follow:

Instructions for Supervisor A

Your group has the task of grouping (classifying) a number of miscellaneous objects. Your group's creativity will be measured by its ability to come up with as many groupings as it can in the *ten minutes* available.

Your job is to unleash the creativity that resides in the group. Since the task is clear-cut, just start them off with an encouraging sentence or two.

Then give them their instruction sheets, dump the 25 objects on the table and begin to work for the ten minutes.

The instructions for the structured supervisor are:

Instructions for Supervisor B

Your group has the task of grouping (classifying) a number of miscellaneous objects. Your group's creativity will be measured by its ability to come up with as many groupings as it can in the *ten minutes* available.

Prior experience with this game indicates that your group will perform well if it receives a helpful "pep talk" preliminary to their actual work on the task. It is thus essential that you talk to them for four or five minutes on the importance of putting things into groups or categories. Use examples from:

☐ Everyday experience, for example, a supermarket couldn't function if it didn't group its products properly such as apples, oranges, cookies, cereals, meats, frozen foods, etc.; the auto industry couldn't serve its clients if it didn't group its replacement parts carefully using various lists and catalogs; or imagine a library without a system of classifying its books; or stamp collectors who didn't group their stamps by country; or zoologists and botanists who failed to classify fauna and flora.

☐ Company experience, for example, the personnel office groups jobs in classes for recruitment and pay purposes; secretaries maintain groupings of letters (files) for easy reference; etc.

After your introduction, *don't* pause for questions. Just pass out the instruction sheets, dump the 25 objects on the table and begin to work for the 10 minutes.

---

3. The best physical arrangement for the game is to have each group work in a separate room. A large room may also allow for privacy and noninterference from the other group(s). If a private room is not available, let the teams work one at a time, with the nonplayers staying outside the game room. Instruct each group to stay together and not to talk to each other, or it will spoil the game.
4. Each team should have a table to work on, a flip-chart sheet or two to record their categories, and a felt-tip pen.

5. Have the team leaders hand out the following instructions to each member of their team when the task begins, but not before that time:

Group Instructions

This game is designed to ascertain the creative power of your group. Your task is to:

- ☐ Come up with as many different groupings (categories or classifications) as you can of the 25 objects that you have been given; for example, your ball point pen can be put into such groupings as plastic, metal, etc.
- ☐ List the groupings on the newsprint sheet.
- ☐ Perform the task in 10 minutes.

---

6. If manpower allows, appoint observers, one for each team. Instruct them to look for factors which influence—help or hinder—creativity. Also pay particular attention to items in their instruction sheet, which follows:

Instructions for Observer

As observer you observe the action silently. Do not intervene except to call time after 10 minutes of work.

Note: The team leader begins the assigned task after he/she has made his/her introductory remarks. He/she is not to allow for a question period since the participants have instruction sheets.

Pay particular attention to:

- ☐ Factors or influences which encourage group creativity.
- ☐ Factors or influences which inhibit creativity.
- ☐ The role of the leader: Is he/she encouraging, friendly, supportive, dominating, discouraging, argumentative; neutral or passive; or what?
- ☐ Climate: What is the group atmosphere and is it conducive to creativity?
- ☐ Participation: Is it widespread or do one or two people take over? Does this help or hurt creativity?
- ☐ If there were any real breakthroughs, what were they and what produced them?

---

7. Divide the total group into sub-groups and position them at different points in the room.

Introduce the game as follows: "We are about to engage in a game which will test the creative power of your group. I will now appoint team leaders and give them

their instructions. Will the team leaders please step forward and read your instructions privately." After they have read their instructions, give them each the big envelope of objects and a group of participant instruction sheets.

Call *each* group of leaders (A vs. B) aside separately to check if they have questions. Tell them that their sequence of operations is as follows:

1. "Have everyone find a seat around the table."
2. "Deliver your introductory remarks and get going. Do *not* pause for questions since the participants are being given an instruction sheet."
3. "Pass out the participant instruction sheets and 'dump' the 25 objects on the table. This is the signal to begin work."
4. "Conduct the task for 10 minutes."

After all teams have done their work, either simultaneously or in sequence as privacy conditions may allow, have the team leaders post their flipcharts to the wall and count the number of categories their groups produced.

Note: Every entry is a category since the instructions said nothing about general categories, subcategories, etc. Anticipate some argument on this point, but hold firm to your position.

Experience with this game indicates that these results typically will ensue:

1. The structured team(s) will perform less well than the unstructured ones. Why? Because structure inhibits creativity: "If you give Johnny a paint brush and ask him to paint a horse, you'll only get a horse. But if you say: 'Johnny, draw whatever you like,' you may get the Mona Lisa."
2. Sometimes both kinds of teams have a tie, or nearly so. If so, the question is: "If lectures don't make a difference, why give them? Why run the risk of smothering creativity with a lot of patter? If you over-communicate, the group has *two* problems: The assigned task *and* how to cope with the leader's input about the task."
3. If, as a less likely possibility, the structured team wins by a large margin, ask the observer what produced the creativity. Also, tell them that this result is unusual, for typically the added structure tends to confuse people, slow down the group, and inhibit its creativity.

Conclude the discussion by asking participants to draw on their own experience concerning the impact of high/unnecessary structure on creativity.

Converting an Exercise into a Game

Some exercises can be converted into a game by introducing a competitive element into it. For example, take an exercise that is concerned with getting participants to become more aware of feelings or emotions. The participants act out an emotion, such as disgust, affection, fear, anxiety, embarrassment, anger, determination, and the total group tries to guess what the emotion is. To convert this exercise into a game, follow these procedures:

1. Divide the group into two teams.
2. Place a packet of cards on a table (or put them in a box), each of which has a particular emotion typed on it.
3. Have a participant from Group A take the top card from the table and act out (pantomime) the emotion for his/her group. This is to be done in a fixed time limit (such as a minute or two).
4. If the emotion is guessed correctly by Group A, they receive ten points.
5. Now have a participant from Group B act out an emotion and award points as appropriate.
6. Rotate the acting opportunities between the two groups.
7. After 20–30 minutes, call time and announce the winning team based on its point total.

Note: A prize will heighten the competition.

Working with Simulations

Simulation is a training device designed to give the participants an experience comparable to what they will encounter in real life. Some examples include:

☐ Company officials participate in mock disasters to provide experience in dealing with corporate crises such as possible product tampering, the burning or explosion of a plant, a power outage in a utility, the kidnapping of the company president, etc. Part of the simulation may include "confrontational training" wherein some managers play the role of "tough" reporters who vigorously try to obtain information about the crisis from the company president or a designated spokesperson.[7]
☐ Commercial pilots receive special training, on the ground, to simulate the take off and landing of planes under severe winter conditions.
☐ Office workers undergo a "dry run" evacuation due to fire in a high-rise building (or a bomb threat or an approaching tornado).
☐ Hotel workers receive training in how to calm concerned guests in case of a fire alarm and how the fire

detection and alarm system operates in case of emergency.
☐ A group of public sector managers experience the operation of a hypothetical federal field agency, the simulation running for two full days.
☐ New fast-food store managers operate a "mock" restaurant. The many problems of dealing with young workers, a wide range of customers, food preparation, cash control, contingencies are experienced.
☐ A community undertakes an elaborate civil defense exercise, simulating evacuation, rescue work, medical treatment of the injured, etc.
☐ New auditors are given a full range of financial statements to "audit" a fictitious company. Interviews with operating officials are also conducted to ferret out discrepancies in data.
☐ New meter readers read residential, commercial, and industrial meters in a simulated urban area. Special problems such as discrepancies in meter figures and tampering with meters are included in the training.
☐ A special U.S. military helicopter unit rehearses a rescue of Americans in the Iranian Embassy. The embassy and its grounds have been re-created in complete detail to facilitate the operation.
☐ An electric power company trains its nuclear power plant operators how to react to a variety of emergency situations. A replica of a plant's control room is used to help the operators think through accidents and perform the proper functions to resolve the simulated crises.
☐ A bank instructs its new clerical hires in a simulated banking center, including a staged drive-in window, to learn prescribed procedures to open accounts and process the full range of daily transactions.
☐ A local fire department burns an abandoned house to provide paid and volunteer firefighters with a live fire-fighting experience. A blaze is set on the contents of the rear bedroom. The participants learn to locate a fire they can't see by feeling for a hot spot, such as a door, or by sound. Team coordination is part of the training. Other fires are also experienced in the attic and another bedroom.[8]

Advantages of Using Simulations

Simulation is beneficial for many of the following reasons:

☐ Participants are involved in a real-life rather than a theoretical situation. This training facilitates entry on the job or readiness for "the real thing."
☐ Learning is active rather than passive; everyone "plays."

☐ The learning process relies on the best approaches to adult learning, namely, experiential or discovery learning.

☐ Mistakes can be made in a risk-free atmosphere. The boss is not there to grimace, raise eyebrows, "chew out," or to punish in other ways for a miscue. Also, mistakes can be made without cost—not always the case in real-life decisions.

☐ Time spans can be compressed; e.g., key problems likely to be encountered in the next two months or more may be presented in the simulation in a few days.

☐ The learning situation provides the opportunity for immediate feedback concerning proper and improper actions or decisions. Thus, participants can correct their behavior promptly rather than continuing to err, and they can be rewarded psychologically for proper performance.

☐ The trainer's role can shift from a didactic one to that of learning facilitator.

Possible drawbacks of the simulation include:

☐ A simulation, while very real, may still not be able to replicate all situations or complexities that may arise. (For example, a new hotel, which was just about to open, operated a mock registration desk to provide experience with the myriad of expected problems. But a power failure, which was not expected, caused havoc on opening day.)

☐ Participants may tend to generalize (or over-generalize) from what is only "a slice of life," but not life itself. They may also develop a false sense of confidence concerning their ability to cope with reality on the job.

☐ A simulation must be carefully constructed to ensure that the desired learning outcomes are certain to be reached.

Implementing the Simulation

Attention to these skill pointers will help participants to maximize their learning from the simulation:

1. Introduce the simulation to the participants so that objectives, roles, rules, procedures, time frames, are clear.
2. Monitor the simulation in a facilitating way. That is to say, recognize it is *the participants'* learning opportunity so don't intervene unnecessarily. Provide help as requested or as seems indicated by events. "Tune in" to group work to get a feel for progress, possible resistance points, team cohesion, etc.

3. Assess performance in the simulation: What have Helen and George mastered or assimilated which they were previously deficient in? How do we find out what Helen and George have learned?
4. Allow for enough processing time so that "loose ends" in the form of principles and key skill points, are firmly "buttoned down."
5. Provide for other kinds of training activities that may be needed in support of the simulation. Relate those activities to the simulation ("You will recall that in the simulation we . . .").

Designing a Simulation

The best way for the trainer to design a simulation based on the organization's activities is to work with a group of operating officials on the project. First, explain the nature of simulation and provide them with several examples. Then have them draw on their practical experience to develop situations and problems they want the participants to experience.

Hindy Lauer Schachter of the New Jersey Institute of Technology, Newark, provides these ten guidelines to construct a meaningful simulation, using a "pilot run" approach.[9]

1. Determine its purpose, listing each ability you wish to develop.
2. Design activities that develop the stated abilities; e.g., if the group is to learn how to negotiate with an outside group, create such a learning situation.
3. Outline the "scenario," deciding on the purpose and name of the organization involved, nature and number of roles, and so on.
4. Use a plotline and props (e.g., manuals and contracts if a union negotiation is involved) that are logical, believable, consistent.
5. Assign participants appropriate roles; realism, in relation to objectives, is essential, of course.
6. As the simulation develops, ask participants to generate alternatives and to choose a solution or course of action there from.
7. Make certain all activities have been assigned enough time for their completion.
8. Provide opportunities for the giving of oral feedback to participants with particular emphasis on the giving of praise for good performance. (Positive strokes will encourage greater participation.)
9. Conduct a dry run to "debug" the simulation.
10. Arrange for participants to critique the simulation; use the data to make it more realistic, relevant, and exciting. The feedback may also improve the clarity of participant instructions and eliminate unnecessary detail and dull spots.

Key Points

1. Structured experiences, in the form of games, simulations, simulation-games, exercises, and puzzles, are ways for participants to learn experientially; that is, they learn from what they do rather than what they are told, observe, or read.
2. All of these training devices are marked by flexibility and may be used at various stages in a course or program.
3. Games, simulations, and exercises may be designed by the trainer. This may be accomplished by studying such activities developed by others and paying attention to certain design principles.
4. Although games, simulations, and exercises have specific learning goals, it is not always practicable to share such information with the participants at the start. The reason for this is that the learning comes only from experiencing the activity; stating the goal in specific terms may "spill the beans" unnecessarily.
5. Since a key characteristic of a game is competition, an exercise often may be converted into a game by introducing a competitive element into it.
6. Games provide learning by doing, realism, motivation, peer learning, intense learning in short time frames, a participant rather than a trainer-centered learning experience, fun, and novelty.
7. Design of a game requires general familiarity with games as training tools, setting specific learning objectives, selecting a game format, developing written instructions for participants and observers, deciding upon time frames, developing a scoring system, and planning for a debriefing or processing session at game's end.
8. Simulations, which can provide experiences resembling real life, should be designed in conjunction with operating officials. This will ensure that the fullest possible realism will be cranked into them.

References

1. Pfeiffer, J. W., and Jones, J. E., *A Handbook of Structured Experiences for Human Relations Training,* Vol. 1, University Associates Inc., San Diego, 1969, p. 52.
2. At the monthly meeting of the American Society for Performance Improvement, Potomac (Washington, D.C.) Chapter, October 14, 1981.
3. Broadwell, Laura, "Business Games: They're More Than Child's Play," *Successful Meetings* (June 1987), pp. 36–39.
4. Sugar, Stephen, "Training's The Name Of The Game," *Training and Development Journal* (December 1987), pp. 67–73.
5. Hutson, H., and Dormant, D., "The Name of the Game Is Frame," *Training/HRD* (April 1981), pp. 54–56.
6. Stolovich, H. D., "Frame Games," *National Society for Performance Improvement (NSPI) Journal* (December 1978), pp. 8–10.
7. Jeffrey, Nancy, "Preparing For The Worst: Firms Set Up Plans To Help Deal With Corporate Crises," *Wall Street Journal* (December 7, 1987).
8. Hall, Charles, "Training With Fire," *The Washington Post* (May 21, 1987).
9. Schachter, H. L., "Role Plays: 10 Rules for Development," *Training and Development Journal* (February 1982), pp. 9–10.

Recommended Reading

Games

Ellington, Henry, Addinall, Eric, and Percival, Fred, *A Handbook of Game Design,* Nichols Publishing Company, New York, 1982.

This is a practical introduction to designing games, including manual, card, board, and computer games.

Ellington, Henry, Addinall, Eric, and Percival, Fred, *Case Studies in Game Design,* Nichols Publishing Company, New York, 1983.

This is a companion volume to the preceding *A Handbook of Game Design.* In 12 case studies, it examines in depth the detailed design of the many types of games.

Hitchcock, Darcy E., "Building Instructional Games," *Training,* March 1988, pp. 33–39.

The author presents a step-by-step process to aid in developing your games.

Olivas, Louis, and Newstrom, John W., "Learning Through the Use of Simulation Games," *Training and Development Journal,* September 1981, pp. 64–66.

The article presents a rationale for games, guidelines for their use, and an explanation of how learning is facilitated by their use.

Perry, Scott B., "The Name of the Game Is Simulation," *Training and Development Journal,* February 1971, pp. 28–32.

This discusses why games and simulations should be used; distinguishes between those that aid application of prior learning and those that aid discovery of one's behavior and that of others; and describes several games and how participants learn from them.

Rausch, Erwin, "30,000 Ways to Invent Your Own Group Games," *Successful Meetings,* March 1976, pp. 50–51, 178–179

By using the author's matrix, literally thousands of different types of games may be constructed. (Note: The article does not advise how to construct a game, but indicates what one's choices are.)

Stolovich, Harold D., "Technology of Simulation Gaming for Education and Training," *National Society for Performance Improvement Journal,* December 1981, pp. 24–28.

This is an overview, providing definitions, uses, and examples.

"Game-Playing to Help Managers Communicate," *Business Week,* April 9, 1979, pp. 76–78.

The article describes the use of games in the business world.

Simulations

Mallory, W. J., "Simulation for Task Practice in Technical Training," *Training and Development Journal,* September 1981, pp. 13–20.

Although we ordinarily think of games as part of management or other "higher-level" training, they also can be used at the skilled trades level.

Waddell, Geneva, "Simulation: Balancing the Pros and Cons," *Training and Development Journal,* January 1982, pp. 80–83.

This cites key concepts and the advantages and limitations of simulations.

Games and Simulations

Chartier, Myron R., "Facilitating Simulation Games," in Jones, John E. and Pfeiffer, J. William, editors, *The*

1981 Annual Handbook for Group Facilitators, University Associates, Inc., San Diego, 1981, pp. 247–257.

This is a comprehensive presentation of simulation games, covering games as simulated social systems, designing games and facilitating games.

Gray, Lynton, and Waitt, Ian, *Perspectives on Academic Gaming and Simulation 7—Simulation in Management and Business Education,* Nichols Publishing Company, New York, 1982.

The book contains proceedings of the 1981 Conference of the Society for Academic Gaming and Simulation in Education and Training, covering experience-based and theoretical material.

Sugar, Stephen E., "The Teaching Game—Curing The Night Student Blahs," *Training News,* May 1984, pp. 15–16.

The author advocates the use of games to provoke student interest. The article covers the essential features of a simulation game (flexibility, adaptability, cost, playability, proper instructions), how to use it (introduction, briefing, actual playing, debriefing) and costs and payoffs.

Sussman, Vic, "What's In A Game? Often Not Enough," *The Washington Post Magazine,* November 8, 1987, pp. 39–41.

Discusses the role of the computer in games and simulations, particularly its ability to provide interaction and thus "intellectually stimulating and substantial experience." Also states that the interaction between people is more important than the game per se.

"A Shopping Guide to Training Games and Simulations," *Training/HRD,* February 1982, p. 31.

The article lists the major categories (25) in which games may be found commercially (e.g., time management, values clarification, productivity improvement) and the suppliers (some 55) of them.

USING
EXERCISES

I never teach my pupils; I only attempt to provide the conditions in which they can learn.

—Albert Einstein (1879–1955),
German/U.S. physicist

In the prior chapter we were introduced to two forms of experiential learning: games and simulations. In this chapter we will treat the exercise as another form of experiential learning.

Exercises are easier to describe than they are to define. This is so because they come in such a great variety of shapes and sizes. Exercises may be:

☐ Simple or multifaceted
☐ Short or long in duration, ranging from a few minutes to one or more hours or even all day
☐ Job-related or nonjob-related
☐ Personal-learning based or with a more general learning outcome
☐ Physically active (e.g., the trust walk or trust fall) or fairly passive (e.g., a paper and pencil activity plus discussion)
☐ Accomplished with or without observers
☐ Trainer guided, totally group conducted, or some mix of the two
☐ Individual participant or group oriented
☐ Accomplished in small groups, in the total group or on an intergroup basis
☐ Group member input only or including inputs of participants' bosses
☐ Instrument or noninstrument oriented
☐ "Homemade"or publisher supplied

Because of the great diversity in formats and purposes, some trainers prefer to use more general terminology in describing exercises: namely, "experiential learning," "structured experiences," or simply "activities" or "application activities." In any case, an exercise may be distinguished by these characteristics:

☐ Directed toward specific learning goals
☐ Structure, i.e., guidelines/instructions as to procedures, individual/group roles, time limits
☐ High participant involvement
☐ Generation of data for participant analysis
☐ Debriefing: Processing or analysis of data by participants/observers/trainers to make the experience meaningful. The learning from the exercise may be general, consisting of the acquisition of principles and concepts; it may be personal resulting in the acquisition of new skills, attitudes, insights, etc.; or it may be *both*.

Note: If an activity involves competition between individuals or groups, it becomes a game rather than an exercise.

Sources of Exercises

Exercises may be obtained from publishers, (see the listing of several books at the end of the chapter); from colleagues; from participation in training programs, professional conferences and institutes, and occasionally in university courses; and from professional training/personnel journals. However, professional trainers would agree that the best trainers are those who can create their own exercises. This is an essential trainer skill, since quite often an outside source may not be able to meet your need for an exercise. Of course, not all exercises need be as "profound" as, say, Jay Hall's NASA Exercise ("Lost on the Moon"). The important thing is that they meet participant needs, have predictable outcomes (meet learning goals), and have high learner involvement.

In the pages that follow a number of easy-to-use exercises are given. These "models" may be administered "as is" or adapted to varying degrees to meet better the needs of your participant group. By studying them carefully, they should help to give you a good "feel" for ways to put your groups into action productively.

Exercises That You Can Construct Yourself

Laundry Lists

Have participants develop individually, in pairs or in small groups, a "laundry list" on a given subject; e.g., principles of good listening, how to give feedback, principles/techniques of delegation, customer objections we encounter, hazards in our unit, etc. Then post data and discuss.

Checklists

Have participants develop a check list for back-home use; e.g., procedures to develop a follow-up call on a prospect who responded to some advertising; how to orient a new worker; how to check a work area for unsafe situations; how to plan an effective meeting; how to investigate an accident.

Sharing a Personal Experience

Have participants describe and share a personal experience concerning, e.g., a boss who showed interest in one and encouraged growth, delegation to a secretary to make a boss-secretary team, enriching a routine job, saving time at a meeting.

Brainstorming and Solution Selection

Have participants brainstorm the solution to a problem and then select the top three solutions via a simple voting procedure, such as a show of hands.

Feedbacking

Design activities which provide for giving and/or receiving feedback based on data developed from instruments. Use dyads or triads for sharing data. For example, in an experiential training program participants may rate the effectiveness of their own listening skill and that of their colleagues on a ten-point scale and share these ratings.

Sharing a Contract

Participants may be asked to develop and then share a personal contract concerning the performance of a new behavior, e.g., greater delegation to staff. A form may be designed for this purpose: the far left vertical column should list one's responsibilities; several other columns list staff members' names, which are to be checked off wherever delegation is deemed possible; and a final column (far right side of sheet) should have room for comments such as whether the delegation can proceed fully or whether some training may be required. (See Appendix 23.)

Developing a "Behavior Mod" Plan

After indoctrinating participants in behavior modification principles and procedures, have them develop a behavior modification plan to control absenteeism, to reduce accidents, to increase production, to reduce customer's complaints, etc.

Group Instrument Design

Have participants design an instrument, such as a quiz on leadership, communication, coaching, etc., complete the instrument individually and discuss their answers in small groups.

Situational Problem Solving

Provide participants with concepts pertaining to situational problem solving, and then give them one or more problems to resolve using that approach. (Situational problem solving refers to bringing about a change in behavior by "working on" or changing the situation as opposed to working on the employee via lectures, counseling, discipline, threats, training, or transfer. An everyday example: We influence driver behavior via the placement of a white line down the middle of the road as opposed to the use of signs which say "Keep to the right." Similarly, we can reduce complaints about slow elevator service by placing large mirrors on the wall near the elevator; or we can reduce complaints about waiting in line by having two parallel lines so that people can talk to one another while they wait. The latter approach—encouraging conversation—can also be used to reduce boredom in routine assembly-type jobs.) Some possible problems for resolution: floors are messy (use more wastebaskets in the area); theft of materials at night from outdoor storage area (use lights); people are tripping over a pipe protruding above ground (cover it with a wooden ramp).

Dynamic Use of Films
Use films dynamically via pre-film, stop-film and post-film assignments; also use other devices such as question lists, nonverbal or silent (no sound) viewing, and predictions.

Using a Model
Develop an activity around a model; e.g., after having explained a particular model, have participants develop data to support it. Or have small groups discuss the model: Is it valid in all respects? What are its limitations or weaknesses? Would you amend it in any way? Does it have relevance to your work situation?

Group Self-Evaluation
Provide opportunities for the group to assess its own functioning. Give them criteria to do this or let them develop their own. You can provide guides such as task and maintenance roles used as observation/check sheets and a sociometric diagram plotted by an observer to note who speaks to whom and the frequency of contributions by participants.

Dealing with Risk
1. Use *ad hoc* exercises such as a risk analysis if there is reluctance to "buy" a concept because of its "risk." Participants in small groups use a T-column to identify risks and to list solutions—ways of overcoming the risks.
2. Another way to deal with risk or fear of dire consequences is to have participants use mental imagery or fantasy to build positive images of accomplishment; e.g., making that tough sale or asking the boss for a raise and succeeding at it.

For details on this exercise, see "Risk Analysis," pages 16–17.

Using Fantasy
Don't hesitate to use fantasy to solve other problems, too: "What if we were to . . . . " (See Chapter 4.)

3-C Analysis
Have participants use a 3-C Analysis Chart to solve problems they have identified, as shown in Figure 7-1.

Group Construction
Provide acitivities involving the physical construction of an object such as a bridge or tower, via construction paper, newspaper, magazines, blocks, etc. Use observers to study and report back on group planning, interaction, creativity, communication, participation, decision making, leadership, etc.

Tapping Group Creativity
Provide activities that involve group creation of greeting card verses, pithy management sayings, "Confucius Says" (He who delegate in depth/Will surely have little to regret), limericks, etc. Process the work as in the group construction exercise.

Best-Worst Assignment
Assign a "best-worst" task; e.g., the attributes of the best/worst boss I ever had; the characteristics of the best/worst communicator; the qualities of the best/worst salesperson; the nature of the best/worst delegator.

Resolving a Perplexing Situation
Present a perplexing situation, for example, sexual harassment in the job, denial of a promotion, or multiple (and ambiguous) responsibilities for an accident. Pose these questions to small groups: How would you handle this situation? How would your boss handle it? How could this problem have been prevented from occurring?

Designing a Plan
Have participants in small groups design a model performance appraisal plan, a fool-proof promotion posting plan, a policy on sexual harassment, etc.

Preparing Concrete Goals
Present the group with vague, overgeneralized goals or objectives. Request them to convert these statements into specific targets, preferably quantitative ones so that they are measurable.

Developing Terminal Objectives
Present the group with general statements concerning training to be accomplished. Have them convert these fuzzy statements to behavioral objectives (specific end results or terminal behaviors).

Ego Bombardment
Have group members form a circle, standing up. On a rotational basis, have group members give each other positive feedback. A variation is to form two lines, so

Resolving Problems		
Concern (Problem, Difficulty)	Cause (Source)	Cure (Solution)

Figure 7-1. Example of a 3-C Analysis Chart.

that each person has a partner. Have participants in Line A give those in Line B positive feedback on dress, appearance, performance in this class, etc., for three minutes. Those in Line B only listen and do not respond. Then process the action via discussion of such issues as: Is it easy or hard to give praise? How does it feel to receive praise? Do we tend to discount praise?

Value System Origins

To demonstrate the importance (possible influence) of one's family on one's value system, provide the group with one or more of these activities:

1. Have group members recall and report on family sayings, e.g., "If you always do the right thing, you won't have to worry about explaining why you did it." "What will the neighbors think?" "It's important to save for a rainy day."
2. Have group members report on "shoulds" which were emphasized at home; e.g., "You should always be on time for work." "You should get good grades in school." "You should dress so you make a nice impression." "You should lock the door at night." "You should introduce your date to the family."
3. Have participants develop a "values list" which represents family influences; e.g., party affiliation, role of government, sexual attitudes, charity, school attitudes, work attitudes.

Each activity may be conducted in sequence. An alternate design is to assign all three tasks to three separate small groups and secure reports from each for total group discussion. A worksheet as in Figure 7-2 may be prepared, incorporating these ideas.

Family Influences

Family Sayings	Family "Shoulds"	Family "Should Nots"	Family Values

Figure 7-2. Example of a worksheet to help participants recall and record family influences and values.

Sharing "Peak Experiences"

In a session devoted to Maslow and his "Hierarchy of Needs," have participants share "peak experiences." (This could be a great personal or professional achievement, marriage, birth of a child, an athletic accomplishment, a super vacation or trip.) Have participants describe how they felt at the time.

Strength Billboard

Have each person draw a T-column as follows and provide the data as requested.

Strengths

As a Man/Woman	As a Manager (or Teacher, Engineer, Salesperson)

Then have participants find partners and present and discuss their billboards.

Note: The "billboard" display idea can also be used to share values as an icebreaker, to share objectives or goals in an experiential course, or to present and share a personal or job problem in a graphic or illustrative way.

Enriching a Job

Ask participants to select a subordinate's job, preferably a routine one, and then come up with several ways it could be enriched (not just enlarged). Process the data in dyads. You may want to provide a worksheet with a T-column for this activity, including a column for subordinates' names and a column for enrichment suggestions.

Tips from the Expert

Ask participants to assume the role of expert and list on a worksheet their tips on a particular subject, such as how to deal with the angry customer; how to deal with an upset employee; or how to provide motivation to people in dead-end jobs. Entitle the worksheet "My Tips on _____ Are." The sheet may be completed on a pre-work or in-class basis. The ideas may be collected and fed back to the other participants by posting them on flipcharts and discussing them or producing a member-prepared handout.

Achieving Consensus

1. To give small groups practice in achieving consensus, give them five or ten problems of an interpersonal sort. Advise them that they must agree on the answer or solution to the problems. Observers may be used to analyze how the groups made their decisions or what hindered the making of such decisions. Sample problems:

   □ A colleague engages in hard-hitting humor (putdowns) at other people's expense, including yours.
   □ A very able computer specialist who reports to you is frequently late to work
   □ Your boss' staff meetings are boring, drawn out, and generally nonproductive.
   □ Petty stealing has reached a noticeable point in the office—staplers, scissors, cellophane tape—

disappear; also several employees have reported losses of coins and postage stamps from their desks.

Note: The problems may be presented on an open-end, answer-free basis, or you may offer several solutions (in writing) from which the participants choose one. For example, the person who over-does the "put down bit," may be dealt with in these ways:

☐ Ignore the comments; just live with them. Look at it as *her* problem.
☐ Confront her about her behavior by telling the put down artist how the put downs make you feel. ("When you talk to me in this way, I feel less good about myself.")
☐ Respond in kind; "fight fire with fire," which should cause her "to cool it."
☐ Combine with other colleagues to deal with the put-down giver on a "team basis."
☐ Ask your boss for help on this problem.
☐ Assume an "educator" role. Suggest to the person who engages in put-downs to consider using a new and more effective behavior. Thus, she should ask herself this question: How many times today have I made those with whom I have interacted feel better about themselves? By consistently posing this question to oneself one will look for ways to be supportive, considerate, encouraging, and praise-giving rather than cutting.

2. Another way to give small groups practice in achieving consensus is to give them a list of ten statements on a given subject. Give them about five minutes to indicate individually whether they agree or disagree with the statements. They then meet in small groups for about fifteen minutes to seek agreement or consensus.

Finding Problems and Solutions
Provide participants with a worksheet such as in Figure 7-3, and have them add to it. The example worksheet lists two common problems in performance review, but any problem area could be used. Participants should add three more problems and then meet in small groups to agree on solutions to all the problems identified.

Analysis
Have participants select a problem they are currently facing and enumerate in force-field-analysis fashion (see Chapter 10) the favorable and unfavorable forces that exist in the situation. A T-column a can help the diagnosis, and the data can be processed in dyads or triads.

Identifying Motivators
To set the scene for a presentation on motivation, ask participants to approach motivation from a retrospective, current, and prospective viewpoint. A tricolumn as shown may be given to participants for them to complete.

My Motivators

As a Teenager	Today	At Retirement

Another way of focusing attention on motivators is to encourage reflection on them throughout one's career or to have participants think about them from the three different standpoints shown in the following tricolumn.

My Career Motivators

Early Period	Mid-Career	Late Career

Another way of differentiating motivators is to encourage reflection from the standpoints of my boss, my subordinates, and myself. Provide a worksheet with a tricolumn as in the preceding examples. The data can be shared in small groups. Learnings from the exercise should be reported to the full group.

Problems in Performance Appraisal

Problem	Solution
1. Manager tries to avoid conducting annual performance review sessions.	1. Appropriate modeling by his/her superior, i.e., the manager's boss conducts an in-depth apraisal 2. The reward system should be changed to recognize the importance of the annual performance review system. 3. Institute an MBO system. 4. Training
2. Manager conducts an annual review session that deal with traits rather than accomplishments	1. Change the system, e.g., introduce an MBO system. 2. Training
3.	

Figure 7-3. Example of a worksheet that focuses on problems and solutions.

Tapping the Motivation of Others
Another motivational exercise is to have participants list the names of their employees in one column of a tricolumn, and the employees' principal motivators in the next column. After participants have discussed their data in small groups, have them complete the third column—"How to Tap the Motivation." Share Column 3 results in the same small group, then hold a general discussion about what was learned in this exercise.

Using an Opener
As an opener, to reduce anxieties and to get participants into the swing of things, have participants form a double line, everyone standing and facing another person. In the paired situation, have them discuss for ten minutes questions such as: "Why am I here? How can I best help others in this program? How can others best help me?" A variation is to have the participants present data about their partner to the total group based on the preceding questions.

Converting Negatives to Positives
As a fun-type, small group activity have participants come up with as many negative approaches as they can to such problem areas as giving feedback, orienting a new worker, developing employees, and conducting an annual performance review. Then in the discussion convert the negatives to positives.

Evaluation Activities
In the evaluation phase of the course, use "novel" approaches such as the fishbowl, the human continuum, the whip, etc. (See Chapter 19.)

Working with Principles
Have participants in small groups come up with ten principles concerning a given topic, and then have them cite an example to illustrate each principle. Figure 7-4 gives an example list on the topic of conflict. The small

Conflict—Some Principles

Principle	Example
1. Conflict provides a test of power	1. A strike
2. When a group is subject to conflict with an external force or source, cohesion is likely to increase	1. Attack by another nation 2. A disaster, either natural or man-made
3.	
4.	

Figure 7-4. Example of a T-column that elicits principles and examples of those principles.

groups' ideas should be written on flipcharts, posted, compared, and discussed.

Working with Theory X and Y
Participants can work through Theory X and Y concepts via activities such as the following.

1. To determine leadership styles, have participants complete and process in small groups a forced-choice instrument on Theory X and Y. Appendix 24 presents such an instrument.
2. Present a problem for discussion, such as the following: One of your subordinates expects guidance all along the way on a given project, is reluctant to make decisions on her own and seems content with low-risk or even no-risk approaches. You decide to use Theory Y principles to meet this problem head-on. How would you do this? What specific actions would you take?
3. *Have small groups discuss the following question:* Which leadership styles—Theory X or Theory Y— would you apply in these situations:

   □ A city police force
   □ A correctional institution
   □ An R & D laboratory
   □ A steel mill
   □ A national chain of fast-food restaurants
   □ Harvard University
   □ A major state university system

Career Counseling
Have participants, in small groups, come up with solutions to these typical career counseling situations:
□ The young and able engineer who has a great future except for his tendency to irritate those with whom he interacts.
□ A senior, very capable professional has reached a plateau career-wise, and should be "kept alive" via imaginative motivation techniques.
□ A middle-aged manager has grown roots in the community and has turned down two cross-country promotions.
□ Your secretary, aged 29, has been making "noises" about getting out of the "dead end" job in which secretaries often find themselves. Your practice of "raises and roses" no longer seems to be working. There is no evidence of any serious self-development activities on your secretary's part.
Note: 1. In addition to the small group work, role plays may be used to "reality test" proposed solutions.
   2. "The wrap-up" discussion should include an identification of "career divergencies" and

"career commonalities" pointed up by the several situations.

Planning for Goal Accomplishment

Have participants develop two allied lists: one for goals, the other for specific action plans or steps for goal accomplishment.

The Boss as a Communicator

Provide participants with several boss-subordinate communication (or other type) problems and have them exchange solutions in trios or quartets. Typical problems might be:

☐ Your boss communicates in three ways: face-to-face; via notes and memos (or notes on your memos); through someone else.

You find that the face-to-face contacts are relatively pleasant. The memos are often negative, even nasty, sort of "hit and run." The communication with others at times relates to you and may be negative in character. In effect, he talks "behind your back."

Some questions to answer are: What is going on? Is it a problem? Do you do anything about it? If so, what action(s) do you take?

☐ Your boss frequently closes the door of his office, which bothers some employees. Why should it bother them? Should you take any action about this?

☐ Your boss' staff meetings are not too productive. No one really "levels" on important subjects.

☐ At times you receive instructions, policy statements, etc., from your boss with which you do not agree. You would like to be "loyal" and support your boss by stating to your subordinates that you agree with these policies. On the other hand, you hate to be dishonest with your staff, and besides, they will probably know you're being less than truthful when you say you support poor policies.

Studying Nonverbal Behavior

To study nonverbal behavior in a group at work, use the following procedures:

Select a problem of enough complexity and controversy for a group to tackle. This may be an in-house issue or a social issue such as prayer in the public schools, abortion, or gun control. Or a management problem may be used with roles assigned to the discussion group (in writing). The roles should be designed to engender a fair degree of conflict.

Select a discussion group of about eight participants. The balance of the group is to function as observers. Assign an observer to a designated discussant.

While the discussion group is thinking about the assigned topic or problem, or reading its instructions as to role, instruct the role players to observe nonverbal behavior exhibited by the discussants. Give them a list of such behaviors as eye contact or the reverse, winks, smiles, scowls, hair twirling, nail biting, yawning, chair moving, shrugs, tenseness, hand use, leaning forward or the reverse, fidgeting, head nods, head shakes, ear pulling or scratching, and doodling.

Hold the discussion for 20–30 minutes, then secure reports from observers. Hold a general discussion of the significance of nonverbal behavior in the communication process.

Success Analysis

One way to augment participant understanding, insight, skill, etc., is to have them analyze experiences which have been marked by success (meaning a real "pay off" occurred) and something less than success (note that we avoid the negative term "failure"). The topic may relate to introducing a change, enriching a job, motivating, delegating, selling, listening, communicating, confronting a peer on an undesirable behavior, etc.

Break the total group into two or more small groups. Give the first subgroup's members a worksheet entitled "Describing a Less-Than-Successful Experience" (see Figure 7-5). Give the other subgroup a similar worksheet entitled "Describing a Success Experience," with the column headings changed accordingly. Have participants complete the worksheets on an individual basis and then share their experiences described in the worksheet in small groups.

Describing a Less-Than-Successful Experience

Incident or Experience	Factors Which Made for Non-Success
	1.
	2.
	3.
	4.
	5.
	6.

Figure 7-5. Example of a worksheet used in the Success Analysis Exercise.

Secure reports from the small groups and post on flip-charts factors contributing to successful and unsuccessful experiences. Ask the group at large to note differences and commonalities between the positive and negative lists.

Constructing an Attitude Survey Form

Have the group construct an attitude or "climate" questionnaire for possible use in their departments.

Explain to participants the purpose of the climate survey, then pass out sample questionnaire items which allow for either a "Yes-No-Not Sure" response; or for ratings on, say, a 7-point scale.

Once the format is understood and agreed upon, divide the item construction task among the several small groups; e.g., one group might develop survey items on working conditions, another on adequacy of communication, another on team feeling, another on motivation/job interest, etc.

Have participants read aloud completed survey items for review by the total group. This checks for adequate coverage of the topic, clarity of survey items, possible overlappings or duplications, etc.

Coping with "Sticky" Situations

Divide the total group into small groups, each of which addresses itself to and reports back on how a supervisor should cope with such "sticky" situations such as:

☐ Delegating deeply but not losing control of the situation.
☐ Intervening when a delegation is not working out, yet not nullifying the delegation per se.
☐ How to draw the line between desired intimacy with subordinates and undesired fraternization.
☐ Deciding when a group decision is and is not proper.
☐ Deciding when to share and when to withhold information from subordinates.
☐ Deciding how to communicate to subordinates a decision of one's boss with which one does not agree.

Criteria Development

1. Give the group a problem or organizational concern such as
   ☐ Is communication in our organization good or bad?
   ☐ Is our work team effective?
   ☐ Is our office work force productive?
2. Ask the group to develop criteria as to what to look for in assessing the problem area. For example, if we are trying to determine whether our work team is effective we would look at the nature of our

goals, the communication process, the decision-making process, member satisfaction, leadership, etc.

Note: Once we know which areas to investigate, then the group might go further and actually develop specific standards for analysis. For example, if we are studying communication in the team, we might examine how open people are, how effective staff meetings are, how willing people are to share information. But as far as this activity is concerned, we are only asking the group to work on Step 2, not any added steps.

How People Make Meaning

Recent thinking (neurolinguistics) about communication, particularly how you and I transmit and receive messages, indicates that we may be classified as one of the following types of communicators:

☐ Kinesthetic (touch)
☐ Visualizing
☐ Auditory

That is to say, we tend to *use* to a greater degree—and *receive* better—words which fall into one of the above three groupings. An exercise on this concept may take this format: Explain the preceding three-style communications concept to participants. Then ask them to offer words or phrases which fall into each category. Anticipate responses such as the following which are to be posted on the flipchart:

Kinesthetic	Visualizing	Auditory
I'm beaten	like a fish	noisy type
latch on to	see	hear this
get a feel of	perceive	rings a bell
handle	imagine	listen
grasp	focus	sounds good
grab	clarity	tuned in
I can't budge	the big picture	bend an ear
him	open door	roar of the
break bread	in a nut shell	crowd
pushing 40	hazy	windy
butt in	crystal clear	buzz group
hot stuff		makes a big
		splash

Assign participants to pairs. Have both members of the dyad talk for five minutes to the partner on any subject desired. While one person is talking, the other listens silently and takes notes about the type of words or phrases which are used, i.e., kinesthetic, visual, or auditory. The note taking should produce a pattern to identify the speaker's communication style.

Summarize by pointing out that if we know another person's style we can reach that person better by using words or phrases more likely to bring response. The same approach may also apply to communicating with a group.

Dice Toss

You can easily design an activity using a pair of dice. One helpful use: for review and reinforcement of prior learnings. Procedures:[1]

1. Develop a group of questions on your topic of interest. Prepare as many questions as you have participants.
2. Write each question on individual cards and give each a number (2 through 12).
3. When starting the game, explain the ground rules (see the following).
4. Let each player roll the dice. The number on the dice determines the question to be answered. If a number has been rolled, have the player roll the dice for a new number.
5. Participants should be encouraged to add to the responses of the one responding initially to the question.

Variations of the above activity are:

1. Use a roulette wheel or playing cards to select questions.
2. Prepare a circular board, having alternating colors, with numbers on the colored spaces. Add a needle or indicator which can be spun to select a number.
3. With group members in a circle, spin a beer or soft drink bottle (on the floor or on a table) to select participants to respond to prepared questions which are on cards.

Headliners

Have participants describe who they are in "headline" style, i.e., using only two or three highly descriptive words. Examples: Support Giver, Big Talker, Computer Memory, Constant Debater, Most Friendly Fellow, Dedicated Dieter, Free Spirit, Constant Worrier.

Note:

1. The exercise may be used both early and late in a course to note if there is any change in participants' self-perceptions.
2. The headliners may also be used as a form of feedback, participants giving the descriptors to one another.

3. More authentic descriptors are likely to be forthcoming later in the course when participants are more relaxed and candid with one another. Hence, consider using this device at course's end if it is only done once.

Planning the Conduct of an Exercise

To ensure that a given exercise works, that is, provides participants with a high-quality learning experience, the following questions can serve as a guide to the trainer:

☐ Why am I doing this? Is this the best vehicle to achieve the learning outcome?
☐ Is the exercise realistic and relevant? Or is it too theoretical?
☐ Are the procedures fully developed and likely to be clear to the participants? Should the instructions be reduced to writing to ensure participant understanding?
☐ Will the trainer's role in the exercise be clearly understood?
☐ Should a lecturette or talk be used to set the stage for the exercise?
☐ Are the time frames for each phase of the exercise realistic? Have I allowed enough time, in particular for the all-important processing (analysis) phase?
☐ Is the exercise being introduced at the proper stage of the program? Might learning be aided by programming it at an alternate time?
☐ Have I planned for necessary supplies, materials, equipment?
☐ Have I considered the use of observers? If observers are being used, have they been properly briefed?
☐ Have I considered the use of a summary sheet (handout) at exercise's end to help participants "button down" learnings?
☐ When the exercise is completed, how will I know that participants have learned what they were supposed to? What are my procedures for assessing results?

Books Containing Exercises

Exercises are available from publishers in several formats:

1. Books devoted exclusively to exercises and covering a variety of topics on management and human relations.
2. Books that have textual material for the trainer, but also contain exercises on a variety of management and interpersonal subjects. The exercises are presented independently of the text.
3. Books on a single subject containing many exercises and a minimum of text.

4. Books that treat a single subject (e.g., assertiveness, time management, supervision) in traditional textual fashion but also contain exercises throughout the books. These exercises are an integral part of the books, intended to aid in "glueing in" key ideas. These skill practice or application materials may be used individually (self-instruction) or on a group basis.

Books Devoted Exclusively to Exercises

Forbes-Greene, Sue, *Encyclopedia of Icebreakers,* University Associates, Inc., San Diego, 1983, 417 pages, looseleaf.

Broader than the title implies, the book is a compilation of 155 structured activities covering these areas: energizers and tension reducers, feedback and disclosure, games and brain-teasers, getting acquainted, openers and warm-ups, professional development topics.

Mill, Cyril R., *Activities for Trainers: 50 Useful Designs,* University Associates, San Diego, 1980.

The book's "resources" are divided into eight categories: group dynamics and laboratory training, the training of trainers, cross-cultural training, stress training, women's issues, supervisory training, the training of consultants, management and O.D. *Note:* Materials may be reproduced freely for educational/training purposes.

Newstrom, John W., and Scannell, Edward E., *Games Trainers Play: Experiential Learning Exercises.* Mc-Graw-Hill, New York, 1980.

This exercise book is divided into 13 categories: conference leadership, climate setting and icebreakers, presentation, methods (for problem solving), motivation, self-concept, learning, communication, listening, perception, problem solving and creativity, evaluation, transfer of training.

Pfeiffer, J. William, and Jones, John E., *A Handbook of Structured Experiences for Human Relations Training,* Vols. 1–10, University Associates, San Diego; Vol. 1 appeared in 1969; Vol. 10 was published in 1985. *Note:* The editors for this series have been: Vols. 1–8, J. William Pfeiffer and John E. Jones; Vols. 9–10, J. William Pfeiffer.

Each volume contains some 24 activities on such topics as group work, team building, communication, icebreakers, stress, delegation, feedback, conflict, interviewing, self-awareness, cooperation, etc. All activities

may be freely reproduced for educational/training activities.

Each volume carries a consolidated listing, by category, of all structured experiences published to date in *The Handbooks* and *The Annuals* (see reference which follows).

Pfeiffer, J. William, and Jones, John E., *The Annual Handbook for Group Facilitators,* University Associates, San Diego, 1972–1988.

Note: These volumes have had different titles and editors:

Volumes 1972–1981: *The Annual Handbook for Group Facilitators,* J. William Pfeiffer & James E. Jones (Eds.).

Volumes 1982–1983: *The Annual for Facilitators, Trainers and Consultants,* J. William Pfeiffer & Leonard E. Goodstein (Eds.).

Volumes 1984–1986: *The Annual: Developing Human Resources,* J. William Pfeiffer & Leonard E. Goodstein (Eds.).

Volumes 1987–1988: *The Annual: Developing Human Resources,* J. William Pfeiffer (Ed.).

Each volume contains 12–14 structured experiences similar to those which appear in *Handbooks of Structured Experiences,* cited previously. The book also contains several instruments, various lecturettes, theory and practice articles, and a resources section.

The Annuals contain up-dated listings of all structured experiences, arranged by subject, which have appeared to date in both *The Handbooks* and *The Annuals.* Materials may be reproduced for training/educational use.

Note: The Handbooks and *The Annuals* are the most comprehensive and varied collection of all exercise books. They also are the most useful.

Pfeiffer, J. William, *Reference Guide to Handbooks and Annuals (revised),* University Associates, San Diego, 1985.

This classifies all material that has appeared in *The Handbooks* and *The Annuals* through 1985.

Books Having Text for the Trainer Plus Independent Exercises

Engel, Herbert M., *Handbook of Creative Learning Exercises,* Gulf Publishing Co., 1973.

This contains chapters on how to use case study and write your own cases; 19 cases for supervisory and management training in basic concepts of role playing; how to convert case study materials into role playing situations; writing role plays (several role playing exercises are included); an in-depth discussion of the in-basket (including two complete in-baskets).

It contains an index of the 50 learning exercises (cases, role plays, in-baskets, etc.) used in the book, arranged by subject, e.g., communication, competition, leadership, planning.

Malamud, Daniel I., and Machover, Solomon, *Toward Self-Understanding: Group Techniques in Self-Confrontation,* Charles C. Thomas, Springfield, Ill., 1965.

Chapter 6, "A Repertoire of Group Experiments" (53 pages), contains exercises useful in an interpersonal experiential workshop.

Nylen, Donald; Mitchell, J. Robert, and Stout, Anthony; *Handbook of Staff Development and Human Relations Training: Materials Developed for Use in Africa,* National Training Laboratories Institute for Applied Behavioral Science, Rossalyn, Va., 1967.

The book combines text (117 pages) and exercises (some 250 pages). The latter portion is divided into the topics exercises, intergroup activities, exercises for intercultural conflict resolution, skill practice, the trainer and his work.

Suessmuth, Patrick, *Ideas for Training Managers and Supervisors: Useful Suggestions, Activities, and Instruments,* University Associates, San Diego, 1978.

This contains 16 activities (118 pages) for group work plus text covering: setting up courses, learner-centered teaching, classroom interaction, a-v aids and resources, evaluation and costs.

Woodstock, Mike, and Francis, Dave, *Unblocking Your Organization,* University Associates, San Diego, 1978.

The text covers 12 common "blockages" in organizations such as low creativity, poor teamwork, and unclear aims. To work on clearing these blockages, 63 activities are provided.

Books Containing Exercises on a Single Subject

Conflict

Hart, Lois B., *Learning From Conflict: A Handbook for Trainers and Group Leaders,* Addison-Wesley, Reading, Mass., 1981.

This is an exercise book, with a minimum of text, to aid trainers in conducting training in the area of conflict; contains over 50 exercises plus suggested programs for these designs: three-hour, one-day, three-day, five-day.

Creativity

Parnes, Sidney J.; Noller, Ruth B.; and Biondi, Angelo M.; *Guide to Creative Action,* Charles Scribner's Sons, New York, 1977.

Part I has several articles on the development of creative behavior. Part II is a 15-unit instructional program for cultivating creative behavior. Each unit states objectives and has application exercises. Part III contains 22 readings on the cultivation of creative behavior.

Parnes, Sidney J.; Noller, Ruth B.; and Biondi, Angelo M.; *Creative Action Book,* Charles Scribner's Sons, New York, 1976.

Accompanies the *Guide to Creative Action,* previously cited, and is organized into 15 units. It is totally devoted to exercises on creativity.

Books on a Given Subject, Supported by Exercises That Are Integrated into the Text.

Assertiveness Training

Adler, Ronald B., *Talking Straight: Assertion without Aggression,* New York, Holt, Rinehart & Winston, 1977.

A course in assertive behavior, this is useful for both self-help and group work.

Burley-Allen, Madelyn, *Managing Assertively: How to Improve Your People Skills,* John Wiley and Sons, Inc., New York, 1983.

This is an aid for the supervisor who wishes to become more assertive, to learn to say "no," to take more risks, to listen better, to give constructive feedback, to handle criticism, to give and receive positive feedback. It contains 55 exercises, suitable for individual or group work.

Kelly, Colleen, *Assertion Training: A Facilitator's Guide,* University Associates, San Diego, 1979.

This contains numerous exercises, role plays, etc., to aid the trainer in conducting assertiveness training.

Management by Consequences (Behavior Modification)

Brown, Paul L., *Managing Behavior on the Job,* Addison-Wesley, Reading, Mass., 1982.

This uses self-teaching exercises to ensure understanding of text. The book provides a systematic way to understand and modify job behavior, which the author calls the ABC approach. Specifically, antecedents or events preceding the behavior (rules, schedules, signs) or consequences or events following the behavior (feedback, results, money, praise, criticism) determine performance.

Career Planning: Life Planning

Hagberg, Janet, and Leider, Richard, *The Inventurers: Excursions in Life and Career Renewal,* Addison-Wesley, Reading, Mass., 1978.

This contains numerous imaginative activities and worksheets, along with text, designed to release one's potential via self-assessment.

Miller, Donald B., *Personal Vitality,* Addison-Wesley, Reading, Mass., 1977.

A highly humanistic book, it can aid one in life and career planning.

Morrisey, George, *Getting Your Act Together: Goal Setting for Fun, Health and Profit,* John Wiley and Sons, Inc., New York, 1980.

This uses a goal-setting approach to "ordering" one's life; numerous exercises are provided.

Roseman, Edward, *Confronting Non-Promotability: How to Manage a Stalled Career,* AMACOM, New York, 1977.

This book uses check sheets and question lists along with the text to assess one's career possibilities and difficulties. The worksheets are readily useable in group training situations.

Weiler, Nicholas W., *Reality and Career Planning: A Guide for Personal Growth,* Addison-Wesley, Reading, Mass., 1977.

Using TA concepts, the author provides a guide for helping individuals achieve personal fulfillment in career planning. Exercises are interspersed throughout the text.

Conference Leadership

Hon, David, *Meetings That Matter: A Self-Teaching Guide,* John Wiley and Sons, Inc., New York, 1980.

This discusses types of meetings, how to *lead* meetings with subordinates, *conduct* meetings with peers, and *guide* meetings with superiors.

Listening

Burley-Allen, Madelyn, *Listening: The Forgotten Skill,* John Wiley and Sons, New York, 1982.

Aided by examples, numerous exercises, and lively drawings, this book presents a 12-point program to project active interest, overcome language barriers, and change listening habits.

Management by Objectives

Giegold, William C., *Management by Objectives,* McGraw Hill, New York, 1978.

This is a boxed, four volume set of MBO materials, with exercises, designed for self-instruction but readily adaptable to group work.
   Vol. 1: *Strategic Planning and the MBO Process*
   Vol. 2: *Objective Setting and the MBO Process*
   Vol. 3. *Performance Appraisal and the MBO Process*
   Vol. 4: *Leader's Manual to the MBO Series*

Power

Cuming, Pamela, *The Power Handbook: A Strategic Guide to Organizational and Personal Effectiveness,* CBI Publishing Company, Boston, 1981.

This contains many checklists, questionnaires, rating scales, quizzes and exercises and is useful for both self-assessment and group work.

Productivity

Harrison, Jared F., *Improving Performance and Productivity (Why Won't They Do What I Want Them To Do?),* Addison-Wesley, Reading, Mass., 1978.

This is a text and exercise book designed to give the manager/supervisor insight and skill practice in augmenting employee performance.

Quality Circles

Ingle, Sud, and Eitington, Julius E., *Implementing Quality Circles: Trainer's Manual and Leader's Handbook,* BNA Communications Inc., Rockville, Maryland, 1985, looseleaf, 179 pages.

Designed for those in both manufacturing and service organizations who need to lead quality circles and to manage the process, it covers basic concepts, leadership roles and skills, Q.C. training guidelines, and detailed instructions to train members (in 10 sessions).

Ingle, Sud, and Eitington, Julius E., *Implementing Quality Circles Member's Workbook,* BNA Communications Inc., Rockville, Maryland, 1985, spiral bound, 105 pages.

Provides the text and exercise material for 10 training sessions needed for new Q.C. members to learn Q.C. problem solving techniques. Each session's materials has questions for discussion, exercises, a quiz to check understanding, and key points.

Stress Management

Davis, Martha; McKay, Mathew; and Eshelman, Elizabeth, *The Relaxation and Stress Reduction Workbook,* 2nd edition, Harbinger Publications, Oakland, California, 1982, 207 pages.

The book covers reactions to stress, body awareness, progressive relaxation, breathing, meditation, autogenics, thought stopping, coping skills, assertiveness training, time management, biofeedback, nutrition, and exercise.

Gmelch, Walter H., *Beyond Stress to Effective Management,* John Wiley and Sons, Inc., New York, 1982.

An interactive guide to managing stress, this book contains text plus self-assessment devices and exercises.

Tubesing, Nancy L., and Donald, A., *Structured Exercises in Stress Management,* Vol. 1, 1983; Vol. 2, 1984; Vol. 3, 1986; Vol. 4, 1988; Whole Person Press, Duluth, Minnesota, spiral bound.

Each handbook contains 36 group learning experiences: icebreakers, stress assessments, management strategies, skill builders, action planning, group energizers.

Tubesing, Nancy L., and Donald, A., *Structured Exercises in Wellness Promotion,* Vol. 1, 1983; Vol. 2, 1984; Vol. 3, 1986; Vol. 4, 1988; Whole Person Press, Duluth, Minnesota, spiral bound.

Each handbook contains 36 exercises which focus on whole person health: icebreakers, wellness, self-care, action planning, group energizers.

Time Management

Kerner, Jack, D., *Successful Time Management: A Self-Teaching Guide,* John Wiley and Sons, Inc., New York, 1980.

This covers basic time management concepts; the time log; daily planning; work team time problems; self-assessment; setting goals and priorities; delegation; meetings; controlling interruptions, crises, paperwork, the in-basket, procrastination.

Stokes, Stewart L., Jr., *It's About Time: A Practical Guide to Managing Your Most Important Resource,* CBI Publishing Company, Boston, Mass., 1982.

This contains numerous practical exercises to improve one's time management; it is useful for both classroom and self-help work.

Transactional Analysis

Bradford, J. Allyn, and Guberman, Reuben, *Transactional Awareness: Now I've Got You . . . In Business,* Addison-Wesley, Reading, Mass., 1978.

This provides text and dialogue of "crossed transactions" to explain TA concepts in the business setting. The reader is then asked to revise the script, which may be compared with the authors' improved dialogue.

Values

Bargo, Michael, Jr., *Choices and Decisions: A Guidebook for Constructing Values,* University Associates, San Diego, 1980.

This combines test and self-help exercises to aid in developing an integrated system of values. The activities are readily adaptable to group work (see following reference).

Bargo, Michael, Jr., *A Facilitator's Manual for Choices and Decisions: A Guidebook for Constructing Values,* University Associates, San Diego, 1980.

This provides guides to work with participants on the activities in the book cited in the prior reference. Discussion questions have been added.

Key Points

1. Exercises take many forms. They may be borrowed from printed sources and from colleagues, adapted from games, or created anew by the trainer.
2. The exercise will produce a worthwhile learning experience if the trainer pays attention to such skill elements as setting learning objectives, developing and/or providing clear-cut procedures and instructions for participants and observers, setting realistic time frames for the elements of the exercise, conducting it at an appropriate stage in the training program, and planning and conducting the vital processing (debriefing) session to wrap-up the exercise.
3. The exercises suggested in this chapter may be used "as is" or adapted to meet participant needs better. A study of these exercises, plus those in the cited exercise books, should help the reader to develop a "mind set" or orientation toward exercises. Of course, the best way to learn about exercises is to use them in the training situation and constantly critique such experiences (what went well, what did not).

Reference

1. McLaughlin, Ian, "Why Not Play Games?" *Successful Meetings* (March 1983), pp. 51–53.

USING PUZZLES

People who have learned to organize their ideas into sequences or chains of logic can usually reason their way effectively through confused or complicated situations in the business of living.

—*IFTDO NEWS,* newsletter of the International Federation of Training and Development Organizations, July 1983.

In Chapter 6 we learned how to work with games and simulations. In Chapter 7 we studied the exercise and how to work with it. In this chapter we shall explore puzzles and how to work with them in the training situation. We shall conclude our chapter with a general discussion of experiential learning, thus integrating the skill-oriented material contained in Chapters 6, 7, and 8.

Puzzles, another useful tool for the trainer, may be used for various purposes, such as to:

☐ Stimulate curiosity and creativity
☐ Encourage a broad-gauged, free-flowing approach to problem solving (right-brain thinking)
☐ Encourage a logical approach to problem solving (left-brain thinking), whenever appropriate
☐ Serve as an icebreaker, i.e., to "loosen up" participants
☐ Serve as an opener, i.e., to introduce subjects such as career planning, assertiveness, risk-taking, perception, and following instructions properly.
☐ Provide fun, excitement, a change of pace, new experiences
☐ Point up that learning need not be dull, dreary, totally didactic
☐ Provide for participant involvement (with puzzles everyone "plays")

We will first present a number of puzzles, indicate how to introduce them to a group, and point up the purposes of each of them in the training situation.

Secondly, we will take a global view of puzzles, relating them to current ideas about left/right brain thinking.

An Assortment of Puzzles

These puzzles serve various substantive purposes, and they come in various formats, i.e., they may be presented visually (via a handout or a flipchart or a blackboard), orally, or physically (via toothpicks, matchsticks, coins).

Nine-Dot Puzzle
This is probably the oldest and most widely used puzzle in training.

Presentation format: The figure may be posted on flipchart/blackboard with oral instructions or it may be given to participants as a handout, complete with written instructions, as in Figure 8-1. Since it is an "old" puzzle, ask those who have seen it before to "disqualify" themselves. Quite often, however, even those who have experienced the puzzle previously have since forgotten its solution.

Instructions: Place the pencil on one of the dots and draw *four* straight lines through all of the remaining dots, without lifting the pencil from the paper or retracing any of the lines you have drawn.

Figure 8-1. The classic Nine-Dot Puzzle as presented to participants.

Figure 8-2. Solution to the Nine-Dot Puzzle.

Figure 8-3A. Fold the bottom part of the paper so that the bottom line of dots half-covers the middle line of dots.

Figure 8-3B. One solution to the Nine-Dot Puzzle using three lines.

Figure 8-4. One way to solve the Nine-Dot Puzzle with three lines: The lines meet "in infinity."

After several minutes, ask if anyone has the solution. If someone has it, have that person come forward and provide the answer to the group. (A large "display" copy of the puzzle should have been drawn on the flip-chart/blackboard by the trainer as the group worked on the puzzle.) If no one has the answer, provide it yourself. The correct answer is given in Figure 8-2.

Processing: Now ask: "What does this solution tell us?" Some answers are that it teaches us the need to go beyond the boundaries when solving a problem; the need to overcome tunnel vision; and the need to take some new approaches or risks.

Now ask: "Can anyone do it with *three* lines?" This is a request for a still more novel solution and few, if anyone, will figure it out. In any case, here are *two* three-line solutions.

1. Fold the bottom part of the paper so that the bottom line of dots half-covers the middle line of dots. The *overlap* will produce the result shown in Figure 8-3A. Now connect the dots or circles with the three lines as shown in Figure 8-3B.
2. Draw the lines vertically so they slant a bit. Somewhere "out in infinity" they should meet and (hypothetically) permit the three-line result shown in Figure 8-4.

Now ask: "Can anyone do it with *one* line?" Here we are encouraging the group to use its creativity which we hope has been stimulated by the prior challenges. At this point the group may come up with solutions such as the following (if necessary provide one or two possibilities yourself to stimulate their thinking):

1. Just use a paint roller or wide paint brush and make a single, fast downward sweep. (Whoosh!)
2. Connect the lines as in Figure 8-5. (No one said the line had to be straight!)

Figure 8-5. A one-line solution to the Nine-Dot Puzzle: The dots are connected with a curved line.

Figure 8-6. A second one-line solution to the Nine-Dot Puzzle: The dots are moved close together so they can be covered by one stroke of a felt-tip pen.

Figure 8-7. Another one-line solution to the Nine-Dot Puzzle: The dots are stacked vertically and one line is drawn through them.

Figure 8-8. A one-line solution to the Nine-Dot Puzzle: If the paper is folded *twice*, the nine dots overlap and one line can be drawn through them with a felt-tip pen.

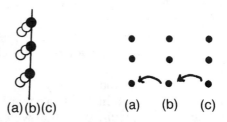

(a)(b)(c)   (a)   (b)   (c)

Figure 8-9. By moving the dots in vertical line C to line B, and by moving lines B and C to A, we can then cover the nine dots with a single line drawn vertically.

Figure 8-10. A one-line solution to the Nine-Dot Puzzle: A line is drawn through one row of dots and the other two rows are moved onto the line.

one line	one line	one line
one line	one line	one line
one line	one line	one line

Figure 8-11. The word "one line" is superimposed on each of the nine dots.

3. Move the nine dots very close together as in Figure 8-6 so that they can be covered in one downward sweep with a felt tip pen. (No one said the dots were stationary and could not be moved.)
4. Stack the nine dots, one on top of the other, and draw a line through them as in Figure 8-7 (!).
5. Make a *double* fold of the paper, and then draw a line through the overlapping lines of dots with a felt tip pen as in Figure 8-8.
6. Move the last line of dots into the middle line and move both of those lines into the first line. Then draw a line through the nine dots, as in Figure 8-9.
7. Draw a line through three dots and then move the other two rows of dots *onto* the drawn line as in Figure 8-10.
8. Write "one line" through each dot as in Figure 8-11. (The question was "Can you do it with one line?")

6. Move the last line of dots into the middle line and move both of those lines into the first line. Then draw a line through the nine dots, as in figure 8-9.

There are several practical applications of the nine-dot puzzle, such as to:

☐ Point up the need for taking a broad, "free-form" approach to problem solving. Don't hem yourself in by imagined restrictions, regulations, "can't do's," "should not's," etc.

☐ Unleash one's creativity by stretching the imagination.

☐ Overcome tendencies to lock oneself in career planning: "I'll never pass the math test." "I'll never pass the graduate school entrance exam." "They'll never take a woman (or a black person or a 50-year-old person) for the job."

☐ Overcome prejudices and stereotyping: Just as we screen out other possibilities in problem solving by making faulty assumptions (i.e., that we can't go beyond the boundaries), so, too, in assessing people we may prejudge/misjudge them. In other words, let's not limit our potential to understand what they are really like and what they might do.

☐ To demonstrate in assertiveness training that there are often other options besides the usual timid, nonproductive approach of "backing off."

☐ To encourage risk-taking: "Why stick with the tried and true?" "Why not break out?" "Who is the loser if I always do the conventional thing?"

Cake Cutting Puzzle

Presentation format: Draw an aerial view of a cake on the flipchart as shown in Figure 8-12. Tell the group: "A woman had baked a cake for her party to be attended by eight guests. Her (and your) task is to produce eight pieces of cake with only three cuts of the knife."

Figure 8-12. Can you produce eight pieces of cake with only three cuts of the knife?

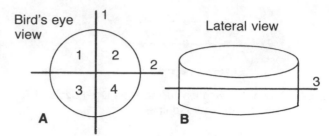

Figure 8-13. The Cake Cutting Puzzle lateral cut solution: (A) Right angle intersecting cuts produce four pieces; (B) a lateral cut produces eight pieces.

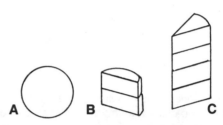

Figure 8-14. The Cake Cutting Puzzle stacking method solution: (A) a vertical cut down the middle produces two pieces; (B) stacking the two pieces and cutting them vertically produces four pieces; (C) a final stacking and cutting of the pieces produces eight pieces.

Figure 8-15. The Cake Cutting Puzzle circular cut solution: Two vertical cuts and then a center circular cut are made to produce eight pieces.

Possible Solutions:

1. The Lateral Cut Method: First make two cuts as in Figure 8-13A, which will produce four pieces. Now cut the cake laterally as in Figure 8-13B to give eight pieces, all of equal size.

2. The Stacking Method: Start with one cut across the center and stack the two pieces. Make a vertical cut, producing four pieces, and stack them. Make a final vertical cut, and you have eight pieces, all equal at that. (See Figure 8-14).

3. Center Cut Method: Make two vertical cuts at perpendicular angles, and then a circular cut as in Figure 8-15.

   Note: No one said the pieces had to be equal or the cuts made via a straight line. Remember this is *her* party with *her* guests, and she can cut the cake any way she wishes!

Figure 8-16. A solution to the Cake Cutting Puzzle that uses two curved lines and a center straight cut to produce eight, albeit unequal, pieces.

4. The Disgustingly Sneaky Method: Make one straight cut and two curved ones as shown in Figure 8-16 to produce eight unequal pieces.

Processing: Ask: "What does the puzzle tell us?" Some answers are: "There may be more options than we think; let's stretch our imaginations and we can produce solutions that are varied and unique."

The puzzle may be used to stimulate thinking about problem solving, creative approaches, alternative seeking, etc.

The Garage Window Puzzle

Presentation format: Instructions are given orally since the group has to visualize a garage window. Tell them: "A homeowner had a single garage window which let in only a limited amount of light. He decided to double the amount of light which came in and to do this without changing the height or width of the window. So he measured the window, up and across, as a good carpenter should. It measured 15 inches by 15 inches. He now made four cuts around the window. He had succeeded—twice as much light now came in. He took new measurements and the window was still 15 inches high and 15 inches wide! How come?"

Solution: The window took the form shown in Figure 8-17.

Processing: Ask: "What does this tell us about communication/perception?" Then provide this answer: "You had a picture in your head of a conventional square window; the picture I had was the same square window, but 'tilted' to stand on one point. We had different pictures of windows because our experiences, our worlds, are different. Hence our perceptions are different. So if we try to communicate without 'matching up' or exchanging perceptions, we'll be in deep trouble. Remember, meanings are in people and people are different, so

meanings must be shared to ensure understanding of one another's meanings."

The Dollar Bill Quiz

Presentation format: Ask orally: "Can you tell me how many 'one's' there are printed on a dollar bill? No, *not* counting the serial number. This should be easy since all of us use it every day."

Solution: There are 8 "ones" in numbered fashion and 8 more spelled out for a *total* of 16.

Processing: Ask: "Why should it be hard to know the answer when we use and glance at a one dollar bill almost daily?" Answer: "We have a screening mechanism in our heads (selective attention or perceptual choice) that helps us screen out the unnecessary, the unimportant, the details, the trivia. This allows us to get our jobs done properly. If we had to pay attention to all the stimuli that comes at us all of the time, we'd never get through the day. Imagine driving to work and noting precisely each tree, each person and his/her clothing, each house, each store, etc. Of course, this screening device can work the other way, too. It may cause us to overlook pertinent, vital details. For example, we may forget to call George and Mary to our meeting, and they may get pretty mad at us. So we have to be on guard to avoid screening out necessary detail. We can do this via checklists, memos or notes to self, calendar notations, reminders from one's secretary, and so on."

Geometric Figures

Various puzzles challenge us to design geometrical figures such as squares or triangles by using toothpicks or matches.

Presentation format: Pass out a bundle of 24 toothpicks (matches or nails would do, too). Draw on the flip-

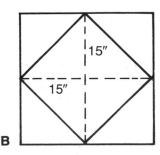

Figure 8-17. The Garage Window Puzzle solution: (A) The window before the cuts are made; (B) the window after the cuts are made.

Figure 8-18. A diagram of the figure made of 24 toothpicks used in a geometric puzzle.

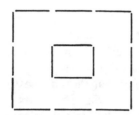

Figure 8-19. Eight toothpicks are removed from the figure, leaving two squares. The solution to the geometric puzzle.

chart the figure illustrated in Figure 8-18; it represents 12 toothpicks down and 12 toothpicks across. The toothpicks are touching each other. Assign this task orally: "Can you make two squares by removing (not moving) eight toothpicks?"

The answer is shown in Figure 8-19.

Presentation format: Pass out a bundle of nine toothpicks. Draw the three triangles on a flipchart as shown in Figure 8-20. Now ask participants to move three toothpicks and come up with five triangles.

Solution:
1. The right triangle is broken up and the three toothpicks are placed as shown by the dotted lines in Figure 8-21.
2. In the second solution (Figure 8-22) the right triangle is moved to the top of the other two triangles as shown. The fifth triangle is the entire configuration.

Processing: Both of these toothpick problems are typical of many puzzles. We know there is a solution, generally simple, but yet it is elusive. Why? Some might say because it takes a kind of imaginative approach, which is hard to achieve in a "strange" field. After all, how much time do we ordinarily spend moving matchsticks or toothpicks around? But there still is a principle for us which applies to our own fields: To be creative or at least to create new applications does not mean we have to be

Figure 8-20. A diagram of the arrangement of the three triangles for the geometric puzzle.

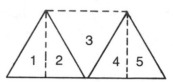

Figure 8-21. A solution to the geometric puzzle involving the three triangles: Five triangles are created by placing the toothpicks from the right triangle in the positions shown.

Figure 8-22. A second solution to the triangle puzzle: The right triangle is placed on top of the other two triangles.

an Edison, a Kittering, or a Bill Lear. But it does mean that we have to reassess and reprogram our modes of attack, back off and start again, search for another alternative, explore many possible avenues, be patient, and, most important, we must ask ourselves: "Are we going at this conventionally or are we rising above our conventional approach? Are we settling for a conventional, 'tried and true' solution when what we may really need is a bold, new one ('right brain' thinking)?"

Solution:
1. The right triangle is broken up and the three toothpicks are placed as shown by the dotted lines in Figure 8-21.

How Many Squares?

Presentation format: Make reference to your subject matter (typically a problem of some sort) and say: "Here's a fun task related to it. Total the number of squares that you see and we'll compare scores." Pass out the sheets with the squares, as shown in Figure 8-23. Allow several minutes for the task and then post scores to the flipchart as you receive them. Sample:

No. of Squares	Frequency
16	I I I I
17	I I I
18	⊦⊦⊦ I
20	I I I I
24	I I

Solution: The "correct" answer is 35 squares. See Figure 8-24.

Uses of the puzzle: This puzzle has several uses or learnings. (You may think of some others than those we provide.) They are:

1. *Be tolerant of different opinions.* Every answer is O.K. No one is really wrong for one's answer is what one happens to see. So if in the course of everyday events people come up with different answers, it's not because they're ignorant, malicious, or stubborn. Rather, they see what they are able (programmed) to see.

2. *Creativity.* In problem solving we should not be content with the "obvious" answer. Typically, we need to keep digging and probing lest we only come up with minimum possibilities.

3. *Planning and problem solving.* Any problem is a puzzle with overlapping pieces. Some parts (squares) are portions of other parts which makes for difficulties in sorting out the pieces. Planning is problem solving in that it is a matter of recognizing how all the (apparently unrelated) parts fit together.

Everyday Things

Presentation format: Pass out the sheet "Everyday Things," shown in Figure 8-25. Ask your participants to "decode" these abbreviations of very familiar things. Allow about 5 minutes for the task.

Uses of the puzzle: It can be used as a "fun thing" to start any session or, possibly, to provide some fun and stimulation if people seem to be showing signs of fatigue. It can also be used in a more profound way. Point out that in problem solving/creative thinking we may get "hemmed in" by overlooking the obvious or commonplace when it appears in another form. *Question:* Are we

How many squares do you see?

Figure 8-23. Multiple square puzzle.

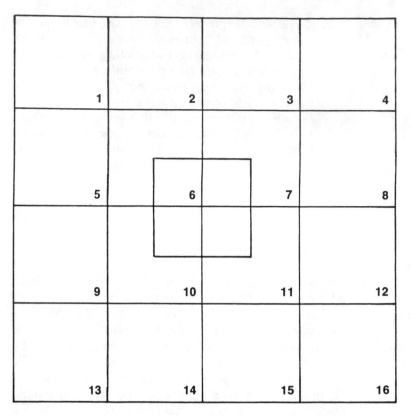

16—All the 1-in. squares.
1—The entire figure is a square.
4—The 4 small squares in the center of the figure.
1—The 4 small squares combined make a single square.
4—There are 4 easy-to-spot groups of 1-in. squares which form 4-in. squares: top left (1, 2, 5, 6); top right (3, 4, 7, 8); lower left (9, 10, 13, 14); lower right (11, 12, 15, 16).
5—There are 5 other groupings of 4-in. squares: (5, 6, 9, 10); (2, 3, 6, 7); (6, 7, 10, 11); (10, 11, 14, 15); (7, 8, 11, 12).
4—There are 4 groups of 9 squares which form 3-in. squares:
(1, 2, 3; 5, 6, 7; 9, 10, 11);
(5, 6, 7; 9, 10, 11; 13, 14, 15);
(2, 3, 4; 6, 7, 8; 10, 11, 12);
(6, 7, 8; 10, 11, 12; 14, 15, 16).
___
35—Total no. of squares

Figure 8-24. Thirty-five squares answer sheet.

Everyday Things—What are they?
7 = D. in the W.
32 = D.F. at which W.F.
26 = L. of the A.
54 = P.C. in a D. plus J.
11 = P. on a F.T.
8 = H. in a W.D.
3 = B.M.—S.H.T.R.
64 = S. on a C.B.
3 = L. on a T.L.
100 = S. in the U.S.S.
8 = S. on a S.S.
6 = N. on a D.
7 = C. in the S.
16 = P. in a C.G.
18 = H. on a G.C.
4 = B. on a B.D.
76 = T. led the B.P.
110 = C. close B.
Source: Unknown

Figure 8-25. Abbreviations for *Everyday Things*.

Everyday Things—Answer Sheet
7 = days in the week
32 = degrees Fahrenheit at which water freezes
26 = letters of the alphabet
54 = playing cards in a deck plus Joker
11 = players on a football team
8 = hours in a work day
3 = blind mice—see how they run
64 = squares on a chess board
3 = lights (or lamps) on a traffic light
100 = senators in the U.S. Senate
8 = sides on a stop sign
6 = numbers on a die (as in dice)
7 = colors in the spectrum
16 = pawns in a chess game
18 = holes on a golf course
4 = bases on a ball diamond
76 = trombones led the big parade
110 = clarinets close behind
Source: Unknown

Figure 8-26. Answer sheet for *Everyday Things—What Are They?*

"overprogrammed" with the "tried and true" so that we can't strike out in a new direction? *Note:* In football the mark of an effective quarterback is his ability to "read" new defensive formations and adjust his lines of attack accordingly. Similarly, say in product development or marketing, if conditions have changed, adjustments and new approaches are necessary. A principle worth remembering is this: If you're not getting what you want, quit doing what you're doing! The answers to the puzzle are given in Figure 8-26.

Pun Fun

Presentation format: Pass out the sheet "Check Your I.Q. (Imagination Quotient)" found in Appendix 25. Read off each item on the sheet and secure group responses. Pass out the answer sheet after completing the 22 items.

Use of the puzzle: To "warm up" a participant group about to begin a brainstorming or other problem solving activity, i.e., to get them in a play-oriented, creative mood.

THE ENCYCLOPEDIA ATTACK

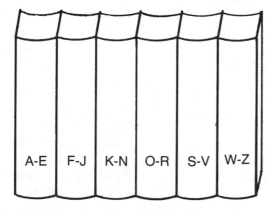

A six-volume encyclopedia set, which belonged to entymologist Gwen Brown, was attacked by a voracious beetle. The beetle's trip/feast began on page 1 of the first book (A-E) and continued through the last page of the last volume (W-Z).

When Gwen discovered the damage the beetle (bookworm?) had accomplished, she was dismayed. At the same time she, as a scientist, was curious to know how many inches the bug had traversed from the starting to the finishing point. She made her measurements quickly since all six volumes were of the same dimensions:

Thickness of total pages in each book—$2^1/2$ inches
Thickness of each cover—$^1/10$ inch

Question: What was the length of the journey of our book-biting bug, measured in inches?

Figure 8-27. Instruction sheet for The Encyclopedia Attack puzzle.

The Encyclopedia Attack

Presentation format: Pass out an instruction sheet with the data and drawing, as shown in Figure 8-27.

Solution: Eleven inches. Note that the beetle began his journey on page 1 of the *first* book which is on the *right* side of the book as it rests on the shelf. He finished eating on the last page of the last book which is on the left side of the book. So he ate through *all* of the pages of the *middle four* books, which totals ten inches ($4'' \times 2^1/2'' = 10''$). The beetle also ate through *all* the covers of the *middle four* books (eight covers), the *right* cover of the *first* book (one cover), and the *left* cover of the *last* book (one cover); or a total of ten covers, equal to ten tenths or one inch. Ten inches of pages plus one inch of covers equals eleven inches in all.

Processing: Ask: "What is significant about this puzzle? What can we learn from it?" Some answers are: It points up the need for carefulness in interpreting instructions; sometimes one has to look at the instruction from more than one angle to really understand it; also, one must avoid "traps" such as oversimplification in assuming all that there is to the problem is to add a few figures together.

I have told groups who worked on this puzzle that it is a hard puzzle for today's culture; no one reads books anymore because of T.V., so how should one know where page 1 of a book is?

The Farmer's Will

Presentation format: Give the group the following problem, either orally or in writing:

A farmer, who had three sons died. His will stipulated that his 17 cows be divided as follows: one-half to the oldest son, one-third to the middle son and one-ninth to the youngest. Since the sons knew enough about arithmetic to recognize that the 17 cows could not be divided as stipulated, they discussed the problem and finally hit on the idea of seeking help from The Wise Old Man On The Mountain.

So they presented the old man with their dilemma. He listened carefully, was silent a long time, and then said, "Come back in 17 days and I will have a solution for you." They returned at the designated time and The Wise Old Man On The Mountain gave them this solution: "I will lend you one of my cows. Now make your division of your cows." They did, and they found that 18 broke down readily into 9 (one half), 6 (one third), and 2 (one ninth), as the will had required.

The Wise Old Man asked, "Are you satisfied?"
They replied, "Oh, yes. You are very wise."
So the Wise Old Man said: "Since you are satisfied, you don't need my cow any more. I, therefore, will take it back. Please note that nine plus six plus two equals seventeen." They left pleased, but a little perplexed as to the arcane arithmetic the Wise Old Man had employed.

Processing: Ask: "What is going on here? What does the story tell us?" Answer: The three sons thought they had an insoluble problem. Using their conventional problem-solving approaches, they were correct in that assessment. But what was needed was an *unconventional* approach. This was provided by The Wise Old Man who stepped back, looked at the problem in new, more creative and more global terms, and gave it a new framework (the eighteenth cow). So there's nothing really arcane about the arithmetic. Just good right-brain (creative) thinking. Could it be that the farmer expected his sons to do some right-brain thinking?

The Hotel Refund

Presentation format: Present the following data orally or in writing:

Three itinerant farmers bedded down for the night in a motel in a small town, all three in the same room. The desk clerk, a part-time worker, asked for $30.00 which they paid without question. Later that evening, the regular desk clerk discovered that the three farmers had been overcharged. He called his teen-age son over and said, "Our day clerk made a mistake on the rate for Room 42. He overcharged them five bucks. Here's five singles. Split it among those three travelers."

This, understandably, was a tough arithmetic problem for the teenager. But being a sharp kid, he simply gave them each a dollar and pocketed the other two dollar bills. As the boy walked back to the motel office he thought about the new rate the men had received. It was now $9.00 each ($30 divided by 3 = $10, and $10 − $1 = $9). But, he thought to himself: "Three times nine dollars equals twenty-seven dollars, and I've got two bucks, which only totals twenty-nine dollars. Where is the other buck?"

Processing: Ask: "What's going on here?" Answer: The teenager is simply trying to resolve too much at once. He is simultaneously (and unnecessarily) looking at the problem from *two* standpoints: i.e., what the farmers paid for their motel room and what monies are circulating outside their room. What our teenager should do is to engage in very logical left-brain thinking; that is, just deal with three clear-cut realities: The three farmers paid

$27, the hotel collected or netted $25 ($30 less the returned 5 singles), and the teenager now has two unexpected bucks in his pocket. In these terms, there is no problem at all for the boy. But if he persists on focusing on and intermingling two unrelated issues, one of which is really irrelevant, he will be eternally confused. Moral: Try to define a problem in its simplest, most coherent, and uncluttered terms; don't use right-brain thinking (creative approaches) on a left-brain (logical) problem.

Bookkeepers, who necessarily engage in a lot of left brain thinking, would immediately see that there is no missing dollar. They would simply look at the *expenditures* involved: the $27 ($25 in the hotel till and $2 in the boy's pocket). And the initial outlay—$30—of the lodgers now looks like this: the hotel racked up $25, the farmers had the rebate of $3 and the teenager had a self-administered tip of $2. Why the confusion? Our bookkeepers would point out that the trouble arose because the lad added an *asset* ($2) to an *expense* ($27) instead of the other asset ($25)!

Both of these problems, i.e., the division of the 17 cows and the $5 refund, have appeared in many formats and in many places. They are classic cases of "good" puzzles. In fact, they are so good that in one sense they can't be answered: Where is the missing dollar? Were the 17 cows divided fairly?

One writer, Robert H. Long, director, Advanced Studies, Bank Administration Institute, Park Ridge, Illinois, has analyzed these two stories in terms of problem-solving principles and left-brain, right-brain thinking.[1] He asserts that poor problem solving is often a result of "one-sided" thinking, whereas coordinated, two-hemisphere (left and right brain) thinking could easily resolve things. He sees both puzzles as illustrations of how problem formulation, language and logic can cause problems rather than generate solutions. Long's analysis of the puzzles is this: "Combining these parts of different situational viewpoints creates a verbal illusion—and an unresolvable problem—as long as these two viewpoints remain in the same problem statement."

Here is a final personal incident to illustrate the power of creative, right-brain thinking in a simple problem in the office. I asked the typist to provide "bullets" to a manuscript. Bullets are black dots placed before key words or sentences to highlight them; e.g.,

● Communication
● Motivation
● Innovation

The typist said this was difficult to do with her word processor. She asked if "dashes" would do. I said O.K.
Several days later a manuscript appeared in the office, from an outside author, with nice big, round, black bul-

lets. They were used in several places. I happened to notice, however, that one set of bullets had not been "filled in" and were just o's:

o Communication
o Motivation
o Innovation

The author had come up with a creative solution to the bullet typing problem: regular o's were typed and then filled in with a thick-pointed black-ink pen!

I then asked several other expert typists if they could make nice, large bullets if they had to. None could. (They could, of course use periods to form small bul-

lets.) In each case I showed them the manuscript with the black o's and then the "plain" o's. Their jaws dropped.

Question: Are we doing enough to train people to use right-brain thinking?

Summary Chart. Table 8-1 sums up the significance and uses of the previously presented puzzles.

Puzzles for Fun

The previous paragraphs have discussed the use of puzzles in relation to the subject matter being treated. It may also be desirable, at times, to introduce puzzles as a

Table 8-1
A Summary of Puzzle Uses

Puzzle	Uses in the Training Situation
Nine dots Cutting the Cake	Learnings: In problem solving • Go outside the boundaries • Take some risks • Take new approaches • Avoid "tunnel vision" • Avoid setting artificial limits In creative thinking • Stretch the imagination • Use the right brain In career planning • Overcome tendencies to set up unrealistic limits, restraints, barriers In dealing with prejudice • Overcome tendencies to stereotype, limit, or narrowly define others In assertiveness training • Look for new options as opposed to staying "frozen" in a given nonproductive position
The Garage Window	Perception: When we are not "on the same wavelength" with others, we make assumptions that are not likely to be valid, hence the need to share perceptions for effective communication
Dollar Bill Quiz	Perception: The screening mechanism in our heads can eliminate unnecessary detail; it may also screen out important information
Geometric Puzzles (using toothpicks or matches)	Learnings: • Look for new approaches • Use the right brain to solve problems creatively rather than conventionally

Puzzle	Uses in the Training Situation
How Many Squares?	Learnings: • Respect the opinions of others • Planning entails understanding many overlapping parts • Problem solving requires persistence, looking beyond the obvious
Pun Fun ("Check Your I.Q.")	Uses: • To warm up the group • To provoke curiosity
The Encyclopedia Attack	Learnings: • Follow instructions carefully • Avoid making faulty assumptions or oversimplifying
The Farmer's Will	Learning: Creative, right-brain approaches to a problem are important
The Hotel Refund	Learnings: • There are times when logical, left-brain thinking is appropriate • Define a problem clearly and simply, and avoid extraneous considerations
Everyday Things	Learnings: • Shows need to overcome tendencies to be limited by our "programming" • Demonstrates the need to adjust to new conditions

change of pace, a relaxer, attention stimulator, etc., without any direct integration with a topic at all. Thus the puzzles need not be learning tools, but rather "fun things." Some puzzles of the fun type follow.

Bowling Pin Puzzle

Tell participants: "Ten bowling pins are set up in conventional bowling array." (Post the configuration shown in Figure 8-28A on the flipchart.) "Your task is to move three pins and thereby produce a totally reverse effect; that is, the first pin should be on top and the four pins on the bottom."

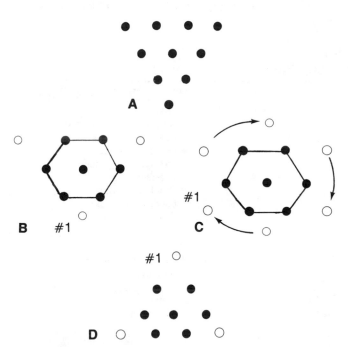

Figure 8-28. The Bowling Pin Puzzle: (A) This diagram of the configuration is drawn for the participants; (B) a line enclosing or linking seven of the pins is drawn; (C) the three pins are rearranged; (D) the final solution—the configuration is reversed.

The answer may be given out later in the day if no one comes up with the solution immediately.

Solution: Draw a ring hooking up or enclosing the seven pins as shown in Figure 8-28B. Then move pin number one to the line immediately above and place it on the left; move another pin from the top line to form a new row of four as shown in 8-28C. Finally move the far-left pin in the original row of four to the number one position as shown in 8-28C. (The line of three pins was not touched.)

This is a very straightforward puzzle that only requires the use of logical thinking and spatial visualization to achieve the correct solution.

Six Figure Puzzle

If you wish to provide a more "sneaky" puzzle, draw the following figure and tell participants: "Make this figure into a six by adding one line."

IX

Solution:
1. Add an "S" as shown:

SIX

Note: No one said the line had to be a straight one or that only Roman numerals were involved. (Why limit yourself by setting up a particular frame of reference?)
2. In this approach add the line as shown:

IXI

Then count all the lines and *segments* thereof. The left line equals one line; the X, counting its segments equals four lines (!); and the line on the right is one line, again. So we have made the figure "IX" into six.

Experiential Learning

When your training activities provide participants with the opportunity to *experience* their learning rather than to be told what they are to learn, you are providing experiential learning. Helpful synonyms for such learning are "discovery learning," "experience-based learning," "action learning" and "interactive learning."

The significant differences between experiential and traditional classroom learning can be summarized with the aid of Table 8-2.

We can understand experiential learning better if we look at adult learners and the things that they don't need or want and which, thus, are quite likely to turn them off:

☐ Sitting and listening (one-way communication)
☐ Note taking
☐ High formality
☐ Isolation from peers (They want interaction)
☐ Tests, grades
☐ Overload of theory
☐ Homework (unless it contributes to learning goals and could not be structured in any other way)
☐ Evening sessions (unless there is a reason for them, e.g., as in the T-group or the Managerial Grid® or

Table 8-2

Traditional Versus Experiential Learning

Element	Traditional Learning	Experiential Learning
Learning unit	The Individual	The Group and the individual
Learning emphasis	Content	Content and process
Nature of learner involvement	Cognitive (intellectual)	Cognitive and affective (self-knowledge)
Role of participant	Listening, memorizing, passing exams, passive rather than active	Involvement, participation, interaction—highly active
Role of course conductor	Teacher/instructor/ lecturer/presenter/ evaluator	Resource person/ facilitator/trainer; at times a participant too
Responsibility of course conductor	Primarily to provide one-way communication devices (lectures, films, slide talks, panel discussions)	To create conditions for participant experiences from which learning will result
Climate for learning	Formal, inhibiting, status-emphasizing	Informal, relaxed, encouraging, status-reducing
A major concern of course conductor	To come up with "better" questions to ask the class	To find ways to stimulate group members to think of deeper questions and better approaches to finding answers
Responsibility for learning outcome	Instructor/presenter ("If the student hasn't learned, the teacher hasn't taught.")	Participants are responsible for their own learning, for their own behavior
Person whose needs are satisfied most	The Presenter	The Participant
Possibility of transfer of learning to job	Typically low or uncertain	Moderate to high degree for most participants

there is a "trade-off" for recreation time in the afternoon)
☐ A lot of reading
☐ Being talked down to
☐ Gimmicks (they can very easily sort out the "cutesy" from the vital)

In short, they want a learning experience, not a classroom experience.

Objectives

In more specific terms, experiential learning has these objectives:[2]

Affective objectives—Creating changes in one's feelings, attitudes, values from an intense or profound training situation/experience/event is a typical goal.

Empathic objectives—Learning how it feels to be in another's shoes is another goal. For example, being pushed in a wheelchair in a crowded shopping center can help one to realize the unconscious cruelty, patronizing attitudes, and even revulsion with which society treats the handicapped.

Interactive objectives—Learning can also take place at cognitive levels to learn cognitive skills such as interviewing, listening, counseling, debriefing, etc. And with proper structuring by the trainer, participants may experience/perceive the interactions from the view of both parties, e.g., listener-speaker, coach-subordinate, salesperson-customer. *Note:* These cognitive skills typically require affective learning, too, in support of the cognitive.

Higher-level cognitive skills—Evaluation and synthesis skills can also be practiced and learned; feedback to the learner can make certain that the skill will be effective in the real world.

Unlearning objectives—Since many of us carry around such psychological impediments as prejudices, stereotypes, phobias, and the like, it is all to the good if we have the opportunity to "unlearn" them. For example, a good simulation game can help males to divest themselves of male chauvinism; or meek persons can have their confidence built via a series of role-playing opportunities involving returning a damaged article to a store and, in time, doing it in a real store.

Forms

Experiential learning assumes a number of forms, but can be divided into two major types:

1. Learning primarily from one's experience:
   ☐ T-group
   ☐ Managerial grid®

☐ Team building
☐ Encounter groups
☐ Instruments
☐ Simulations and simulation games
☐ Diary or Journal keeping
☐ Transactional analysis programs
☐ Stress management programs
☐ Career planning programs
☐ Values clarification programs
☐ Assertiveness training programs
☐ Time management programs (not the lecture-type course)
☐ Conflict management programs
☐ Role Plays (Live, real, or current cases)

2. Learning from structured or trainer-prepared experiences:
☐ Icebreakers
☐ Puzzles
☐ Games
☐ Exercises
☐ Role plays ("canned" or trainer-provided cases)

Obviously, the learning experiences in the first list are likely to be more profound than those in the second. On the other hand, not all trainers may have the skill, inclination, or management support to conduct such training activities and would probably utilize those in the second list.

Although this discussion relates to training events of a formal or planned sort, we know, of course, that participants also may learn from informal or unplanned events, too. This requires the trainer to be alert for the introduction or highlighting of significant "live data" should it arise. For example, in a training session I was conducting where several participants knew one another, a group member complimented another participant on her ability to operate her office (a real estate office) on a team basis with high communication, high cooperation, etc. I asked the recipient of the praise how she felt about the compliment. Her enthusiastic response: "It makes me feel good, real good. I'll communicate this feedback to my staff and we'll all work hard to keep things (the team-type operation) that way."

Designing Experiential Learning

To design such activities (programs, courses) properly, the trainer must pay attention to: the key parameters, basic principles, and various "do's and don't's" of such design. The paragraphs that follow develop these points in detail and reflect the perceptive ideas of Dr. John Jones,[3] a leading exponent and practitioner of experiential learning and co-editor of the many books on structured experiences for experiential learning published by University Associates Publishers, San Diego.

Major parameters in designing experiential learning. Nine parameters or guidepoints, per Dr. Jones, are paramount and can be used as a checklist in planning an experiential training program.

The psychological contract. What degree of involvement do the participants expect? Ideally, their expectations and those of the trainer should be mutual.

The length and timing of the event. Is there enough time to work with the group so that the necessary trust will develop?

The location and physical facilities. Are facilities flexible enough for the program? Is the trainer flexible enough for the program? Is the trainer flexible enough to adjust to "problem-type" facilities? Will there be interruptions, spectators, etc., and how are they to be dealt with?

Familiarity of participants with one another. Should initial tension be expected? Will their past interpersonal history bear on the design or its execution?

Participants' training experience. Have they engaged in prior interactive learning?

Staff size. How much interaction do I need in the design and is the availability of staff a limiting factor?

Size of participant group. Do I recognize that the larger the group the more structure I will have to provide? What if a smaller-size group than expected shows up? What logistical contingencies should I anticipate?

Access to materials and other aids. What A/V and reproduction support do I have?

Follow-through opportunity. Can participants be brought back? If they are brought back, how will this influence the design?

Basic principles in designing experiential learning. In addition to understanding and utilizing the parameters basic to experiential learning, the trainer also must engage in a variety of mental processes, per Dr. John Jones, to design his/her programs. He provides us with ten principles:

Investment/involvement. Since in a sense all learning is experiential, it follows that participants should be occupied and challenged all the time.

Sequencing. Build from prior activities and toward ensuing ones.

Content. Keep all activities related to the job situation. Participants expect activities marked by realism, credibility, practicality, etc.

Processing Don't generate more data than can be analyzed by the group. Remember, the big pay off is from "the talk through." So plan carefully for the discussion period.

Pacing. Keep things lively and moving, but be sensitive to possible fatigue effects. (The afternoon recreation period with an evening session is one way to deal with this concern.) Going too fast will jeopardize learning.

Goals. Keep things goal-directed throughout the program.

Voluntariness. Since experiential learning is intended to encourage introspection, it inevitably requires disclosure of one's feelings, attitudes, perceptions, values, etc. Giving and receiving feedback may also be entailed. Yet participation must be voluntary in nature. The trainer's zeal to "help" should not permit this principle to be abandoned.

Norms (or expectations). Although it is the trainer's job to encourage sensitivity, participation, experimentation, openness, it must be done only as the participants' "comfort level" allows.

Data. Something is always going on, so data is always present. In fact, there may be more there than one can deal with. So we don't need a lot of gimmicks to manufacture data. Dr. Jones' advice is to publish and focus what is being left unsaid.

Flexibility. Be prepared to change the basic design as the program evolves.

Points to include. Some "do's" in experiential design according to Dr. John Jones are:

☐ Find out what you have to work with (people, norms, expectations, facilities).

☐ Explore what design elements are and are not "negotiable." (The major source or motivator for negotiation about design change is participants' anxiety, says Jones. This includes fear of what could happen or fear of confronting what actually did.) In general, changes in design should be made only if there is group consensus to do so, for different individuals inevitably will hold different views on what should or did take place.

☐ Set clear objectives (and "weld them onto your eyeballs").

☐ Plan for contingencies. (Murphy's Law has not been repealed.)

☐ Build in "maintenance" for the group and for individual participants—people need to talk about what's going on or anxiety builds up.

☐ Establish a "home base." (People need a space to go back to, to talk to someone else about what they learned.)

☐ Stress application throughout. (Fun and games are great, but only as they direct learning to the back-home situation.)

☐ Walk a colleague through your design—if you can't pass this test, you're in trouble.

☐ Provide a general road map; e.g., tell people the coverage extends to 4 rather than 40 topics.

☐ Plan to participate yourself. (In fact, the best trainer is one who can become accepted as a member of the group. This phenomenon will occur if the trainer's behavior indicates that the trainer is there to learn, too.)

Actions to avoid. Some "don't's" in experiential design, per Dr. John Jones, are these:

☐ Expect the group to be able to design as a group. (So don't let them plan Wednesday night's work if they have never planned before. *Realism* is the operative word.)

☐ Overstructure things (e.g., providing excessive detail or procedures).

☐ Cover more than people can absorb.

☐ Establish participant-trainer distance (e.g., via eating separately, conferring with other trainers so frequently that one sets oneself apart from the group).

☐ Take care of people. (You should let people stand up for themselves, exercise their rights, etc.)

☐ Use the same design twice. (You should learn from the prior one and revise it accordingly.)

☐ Overuse favorite techniques. (Don't be "Johnny One Note.")

☐ Use noncumulative units. (Models should correlate with each other.)

☐ Include material you don't like (e.g., don't select non-preferred models which you then are certain to shoot down.)

☐ Short-change time for the vital discussion/integration phase.

Skill Pointers On Processing

It has been pointed out that processing is the pay-off aspect of experiential learning. Basic skill pointers relative to this are the need for planning, alloting enough time, and keeping things job-related. Added key elements for effective processing are:

☐ To decide whether activities will be processed by individuals, small groups, the total group, or some combination of these.

☐ Tell participants what to zero in on.

☐ Decide who collects the data: the trainer, the participants, observers from the group, outside observers, or some combination of these sources.

☐ Decide on formats such as video tape; instruments; oral reports, with or without flipcharts, by individuals, small groups, or the total group.

☐ Decide on the role of the trainer(s) in the process.

☐ Process at appropriate points during an activity as well as at the end.

Typically, we think of our processing/debriefing of the training experience in terms of reporting back solutions, conclusions, learnings, and so on. But other approaches/aids to processing may also be appropriate, per trainer/consultant Sivasailam Thiagarajan:[4]

☐ *Emotional ventilation.* Allow people to let off steam about their experience in the exercise, role play, game, etc. By getting the emotions out, more objective analysis is possible.

☐ *Role dropping.* If participants were in particular roles in an exercise or role play, allow time to have them discuss their roles fully as a prelude to the return to the "real world."

☐ *Insight sharing.* Have participants exchange perceptions of the experience to serve as the basis for a set of generalizations for discussion.

☐ *Hypothesis generating.* Ask participants to focus on cause-effect relationships to provide principles for extended exploration of the topic under review.

☐ *Reality check.* Provide a focus as to how closely attuned the experience was to the real world.

☐ *Real-world transfer.* To ensure a maximum return from the experience, zero in on how it can be transferred or applied to the work place.

☐ *Second thoughts.* After the experiential activity, ask: Would you do things the same way, given another opportunity?

☐ *What-ifs.* Ask: If we were to change X, Y, or Z, how would that affect your application of the principles involved?

☐ *Formative suggestions.* Secure suggestions to modify (change, improve, expand, reduce) one or more aspects of the training experience. *Note:* a cornerstone of experiential learning is that the "lesson plan" is in no way engraved in stone. Rather, it should be perceived as a dynamic, flexible, versatile learning device which constantly seeks amendment.

Good questions to ask in processing are these, according to Paul Gustavson, manager, organization development, Zilog Inc.:[3]

☐ What was the purpose?
☐ How did we do against the objectives?
☐ What did we learn from the activity?
☐ What did we learn about the learning process?
☐ What did we learn about our group process?
☐ What did we learn about others?
☐ What did we do well?
☐ What were our areas for improvement?
☐ What can we apply to the job?
☐ How is this similar to the back-home setting?
☐ How is this different from the back-home setting?
☐ What changes would you suggest as a result of this?
☐ What is your action plan (e.g. objectives, specific steps, time frame, social support, plan for evaluation)?
☐ Is this something we can work on? If so, how?
☐ Is this something others can work on? If so, how?

☐ Why did we do what we did?
☐ Why do things seem the way they do?

Ordinarily, we think of the debriefing/processing as something we should do *after* the training experience ends. But as Sivasailam Thiagarajan suggests, it can occur helpfully at other points, too:

☐ *Before the experiential activity.* Ask participants to think back on their prior experience(s) related to what is about to take place. This affords an opportunity for comparative insight, using the earlier experience as a "baseline."

☐ *During the experience.* With a lengthy activity, it may be helpful to secure mid-point or other interim "readings" or reactions as to what is occurring.

☐ *Emergency debriefing.* If things have gone haywire for one reason or another, stop the action. This may be necessary because instructions were not clear, teams may be getting too hostile, people may feel uncomfortable with the thrust of the action, and so on. By providing a debriefing to learn of the cause for the difficulty, tensions can be reduced and "play" resumed.

☐ *Delayed briefings.* At times it may be wise to avoid the usual post-activity debriefing. If people need to "cool down" and return to the real world, a coffee break or lunch preceding the processing may be highly appropriate. Or, in some cases, it may even be desirable to carry it over to the next day to get a more "detached" view of the experience.

A final point. If you don't provide formally for the processing of the experience, the participants will do it on their own. And the obvious likelihood is that it will be done in ways, speaking psychologically, which are not what you, as trainer, would hope for.

Key Points

1. Puzzles can provide interest, novelty, and fun; encourage a mind-set oriented toward problem solving and creativity; and involve all participants to a high degree.

2. Experiential learning, which includes learning from unstructured as well as structured experiences, involves the group as well as the individual, stresses process as well as content, reaches both cognitive and affective domains, is active rather than passive, and emphasizes participant rather than instructor responsibility for outcomes.

3. In designing an experiential learning activity, the trainer should consider participant expectations about involvement; length and timing of the experience; adequacy of facilities; participants' prior

training experience as well as their familiarity with one another; size of the group and training staff; and use of aids/materials.

4. Design principles for experiential learning include continual participant involvement; keeping things moving; logical sequencing of activities, concern with realism; avoidance of over-generating data; processing what is generated; voluntary participation; and being prepared to redesign things, if indicated.

5. It is a good idea to subject planned experiential learning activities to a discussion with colleagues and a "dry run," too, if practicable.

6. Processing, the pay off phase of experiential learning, requires concern with such issues as deciding what will be processed and who collects the data, formats for data collection, the trainer's role in the process, and relating the data to actual back-home concerns.

References

1. Long, R. H., "Avoiding One-Sided Thinking through the Other Brain Hemisphere," *The Magazine of Bank Administration* (August 1980), pp. 8, 10.
2. Thiagarajan, S., "Experiential Learning Packages," *National Society for Performance Improvement Journal* (September 1979), p. 14.
3. Presented at the 1980 Annual Conference of the American Society for Training and Development, Anaheim, California.
4. Thiagarajan, Sivasailam, "Debriefing," *Performance and Instruction* (June/July 1986), p. 45.

Recommended Reading

Cooper, Cary L., and Harrison, Kenneth, "Designing and Facilitating Experiential Group Activities: Variables and Issues," in *The 1976 Annual Handbook for Group Facilitators,* Pfeiffer, J. William, and Jones, John E. (Eds.), University Associates Inc., San Diego, 1976, pp. 157–168.

To design and implement experiential training, these variables need to be considered: *initial* variables (learning objectives, learning environment, group structure, training staff); *emergent* variables (management of differences, depth of intervention); and *evaluative* variables (presentation of self, feedback, supportive climate, goal clarity, structure and procedure).

Gibb, Peter, "The Facilitative Trainer," *Training and Development Journal,* July 1982, pp. 14–19.

This presents a tripartite model for program responsibility: (1) leader (traditional trainer) has authority and responsibility; (2) leader and group share responsibility (facilitative trainer); (3) group has authority and responsibility (facilitator). Shows how the facilitative trainer, combining the styles of the other two, functions. The facilitative trainer utilizes participant expectations, secures participant feedback, uses active listening techniques, and communicates in a congruent way.

Marks, Stephen E., and Davis, William L., "The Experiential Learning Model and Its Application to Large Groups," in *The 1975 Annual Handbook for Group Facilitators,* Jones, John E., and Pfeiffer, J. William (Eds.), University Associates, Inc., San Diego, 1975, pp. 161–166.

This compares the experiential with the didactic and therapeutic models, and presents hazards to be avoided when using the experiential model, advantages, rationale for use, and role of facilitator.

Middleman, Ruth R., "The Concept of Structure in Experiential Learning," in *The 1972 Annual Handbook for Group Facilitators,* Pfeiffer, J. William, and Jones, John E. (Eds.), University Associates Publishers, La Jolla, California, pp. 203–210

This discusses the role and importance of structure, e.g., certain experiential learning may use very little (the T-Group) whereas other forms may have quite a bit (such as The NASA Exercise); cites advantages of the structured training experience, e.g., deemphasis on personality of trainer, "psychological safety."

Pfeiffer, J. William, and Jones, John E., "Design Considerations In Laboratory Education," in *The 1973 Annual Handbook For Group Facilitators,* University Associates Publishers, LaJolla, California, 1973, pp. 177–194.

This treats major design parameters to be considered (length of event, number of participants, familiarity of participants with one another); use of particular methods; major considerations in design (sequencing, content, processing); sequencing in personal growth and leadership development programs; acquiring the requisite professional skills to design laboratories.

Pfeiffer, J. William, and Jones, John E., "Introduction To The Structured Experiences Section" in *The 1979 Annual Handbook For Group Facilitators,* University Associates Inc., San Diego, 1979, pp. 3–6.

THE WINNING TRAINER

138   *THE WINNING TRAINER*

This presents a list of do's and don't's pertinent to the conduct of structured experiences. Some do's: prepare, plan for contingencies, facilitate the process, facilitate learning. Some don't's: overinstruct, overload, end without closure.

Pfeiffer, J. William, and Jones, John E., "Introduction To The Structured Experiences Section" in *The 1980 Annual Handbook for Group Facilitators,* University Associates Inc., San Diego, 1981, pp. 3–8.

This presents their five-step experiential learning cycle that includes experiencing, publishing, processing, generalizing, and applying.

Sternberg, Robert J., and Davidson, Janet E., "The Mind of the Puzzler," *Psychology Today,* June 1982, pp. 37–44.

Based on research, the authors suggest that insight alone is not enough to solve problems. Rather, a composite of elements is essential: prior knowledge related to the problem; certain "executive processes" such as how one plans or approaches the problem, how one monitors one's solution process, tendencies to switch strategies; motivation/perserverance; style—a combination of impulsive and reflective styles work best.

Walker, Gordon A., and Marks, Stephen E., *Experiential Learning and Change: Theory, Design and Practice,* John Wiley and Sons, New York, 1981.

The authors' purpose is to provide unity to a field that is currently fragmented. Part one examines the foundations of experiential learning. Part two emphasizes applications, examining 16 common methods of instruction.

INSTRUMENTATION—A TOOL FOR SELF-DISCOVERY LEARNING

In the outskirts of Dubuque, on the farm, when I was growing up—back there, back then—I learned, with all the pigs and chickens and the endless sameness everywhere you looked, or thought, back there I learned—though I doubt I knew I was learning it—that all of the values were relative save one . . . "Who am I?" All the rest is semantics— liberty, dignity, possession. There's only one that matters: "Who am I?"
—Elizabeth, in *The Lady from Dubuque,* a play by Edward Albee, American Playwright.

To know one's self is, above all, to know what one lacks. It is to measure one's self against truth, and not the other way around.
—Flannery O'Connor (1925–1964), American novelist and short story writer

I have to live with myself and so I want to be fit for myself to know.
—a couplet taught to Dan Rather, CBS newsman, by his mother (quoted in *The Wall Street Journal,* November 19, 1981).

Instrumentation is a technique to facilitate learning via the gathering of data in a systematic or structured way. The learning may relate to individuals, groups, or the total organization (organization development). The data may come from oneself or from others.

Robert R. Blake and Jane S. Mouton of Managerial Grid® fame and pioneers in the field of instrumentation state that a learning instrument "may be the most important discovery in education since programmed learning or even the podium. Certainly, it differs fundamentally from either."[1]

As every trainer who has worked with instruments knows, they are dynamic tools for live, action learning. Their key characteristics are:

Involvement: When instruments are used in the training situation, everyone "plays." There are no passive bystanders. Participants are either giving data to others (feedback) or generating data about themselves, or both. If high (or full) participation is desired, instruments are indeed one of the best ways to go.

Realism. Since the data generated by instrumentation comes from and about live people in the on-going training situation, there is nothing remote, second-hand, contrived, or artificial about it. The data is "here and now," live, personal, pertinent, (often) observable, and thus highly believable.

Introspection. Instrumented data are designed to make one think about oneself—one's values, attitudes, practices, behavior. In the real world most of us are too busy to "stop the clock," as it were, and say: "Hey, am I doing this the best way?" But in the training situation the rules are reversed. The norm becomes one of stopping the action for the express purpose of learning about oneself. This situation is akin to the athletic world—in the heat of the game one cannot stop to "process" the action. But in practice (the training situation) stepping back and looking at one's performance is what it's all about.

Attitude and behavior change. The purpose of instruments is to bring about a change in attitude and/or behavior. One's outlooks, habits, and performance are the grist for the mill. Since the data is our own (a credible source!) and/or from peers with no special ax to grind, why shouldn't we take the data to heart? At least the data is believable enough so that we have the basis for making appropriate changes.

In this connection, I recall conducting a management seminar that used a "coaching practices survey." This entailed securing live data from the subordinates of those attending the program and feeding it back to the participants in the session on "the manager as a coach." Several participants, months later, told me this was the most meaningful part of the (two-week) program for them.

Are there any disadvantages to instrumention? Pfeiffer and Jones[2] cite several. Some participants may feel threatened by the information it reveals. (One predictable reaction is nitpicking the instrument.) Others may be overly impressed by the "numbers" involved. Still others may feel that they are back in school, conjuring up unpleasant memories of test taking, grading, and the like. Data overload may also be a problem. However, in my experience (and that of many other trainers as well) if the instruments are related to worthwhile learning objectives, administered in a professional, low-key way, used sparingly, and the group climate is supportive rather than threatening, there really is no problem.

A final general point about instruments: In the training situation they typically are *not*—and need not be—validated psychological instruments complete with norms or validity/reliability data. Rather, they are stimuli for:

☐ Self-assessment of one's behavior and thus self help
☐ Assessment of others' behavior—individual or group—so that those assessed may use the data (feedback) for examination (introspection, discussion, analysis) and possibly a change in behavior.

Instrument Formats

Behavioral scientists use many types of instruments. Undoubtedly, you have heard of such devices as the semantic-differential rating instrument, the Likert scale for attitude measurement, the forced-choice technique, sociometric ratings, plus many other inventories, questionnaires (sometimes called opinionnaires), opinion-rating scales, reaction forms, surveys, tests, quizzes, and checklists. But regardless of the precise nomenclature of a particular instrument, our interest in them, as trainers, is simply to generate data for assessment (diagnosis) of individual, group, or organizational attitudes or behavior.

In a more specific sense the instruments—let's call them *learning instruments*—most helpful to trainers fall into two categories: feedback devices and self-report inventories.

Feedback devices are tools which are used by participants to collect data about the attitudes or behavior of other participants. The data collectors typically are called observers. Their job is to report back to the "learners" information which can help them to identify strong points (positive feedback) or shortcomings (negative feedback). The learners, armed with data that they ordinarily would not be aware of, are now in a position to alter their attitudes or behavior. Any such modification assumes, of course, that (1) the data is acceptable ("makes sense") to the learner and (2) the data is something that is under the learner's control so that change *is*

possible. For example, if the learner is a rather serious person, there is little point in feedback which suggests the greater use of humor in group work. Conversely, the person who monopolizes the available air time at group sessions or who regularly "holds back" (the low participator) may find observer data about such behavior quite helpful.

Feedback devices are discussed in more detail in Chapter 13, which is about team building.

Self-report inventories (also called self-description and self-assessment inventories) are tools that produce data in a structured way about an individual's on-the-job behavior and attitudes, values, traits, perceptions, and the like. Typical inventories used in the training situation relate to how one sees one's leadership style or one's skill as a delegator, time manager, communicator, motivator, coach, planner, risk-taker or salesperson; or if one sees oneself as a safety-oriented person; or as a customer service person; etc.

Although these self-report devices obviously may be used to measure and evaluate results of training on a "before and after" basis, we are concerned with these devices primarily as tools during the training situation. In short, they are designed to encourage introspection about one's attitudes and/or behavior in the work environment so that one can bring about such changes as seem appropriate.

When to Use Instruments

Instruments can be used at various points in the training situation. For example, they can be used as:

Pre-work. Instruments are a good way to involve participants very early in the training process. To the degree that group members work on a task before they even come to class, they are clearly involved in the course or program. Additionally, they are motivated by it, made aware that they are in an active program, and alerted to the fact that the trainer is trying to maximize everyone's return from the training experience.

An icebreaker. An instrument may be used to warm up the group. A simple, fun-type one to use is the sentence-completion instrument in Appendix 26.

A session opener. A formal session, such as one that ordinarily opens with a formal presentation—a talk, panel discussion, or film—can be made participative and thought-stimulating by starting things off with an instrument. In some cases data may be collected from the group and used as "live" input to make certain points.

A mid-session stimulator. The instrument may be used strategically at various stages in the on-going program. In some cases it can be used as part of a group exercise.

A program wrap-up. The instrument can also be used as a practical way to end a session or a total program. Assuming the participants have been exposed to a certain amount of theory and practice, the instrument can be used as a means of applying what was learned to one's personal situation.

Note: The best use of instruments takes place when the data is processed thoroughly by the group. So be certain to allow enough time—30 to 60 minutes—for working it through.

A back-home thought-stimulator. Training programs dealing with leadership, human relations, assertiveness, personal growth, team building, time management, communications, etc. often are concerned with the encouragement of introspection after participants return to their job. One or more instruments may be given to participants for such a purpose.

Note: Most instruments may be used at various points in the program, as suggested, but certain instruments, because of their possible frustration or stress potential for some participants, should be used late in the course or program. This thought is developed in more detail in the chapter summary.

How to Use Instruments

These guides should help to maximize the use of instruments.

1. Before using an instrument in the training situation, you should ask yourself: Why am I doing this? Will it fit into and further the overall training design? Am I relating it to a specific theory, a model, a film, an exercise, or what? How does the quiz relate to participant expectations? Am I allowing enough time for processing by participants? Will the instrument create anxiety for the participants?

2. The first step in the use of an instrument is for the trainer to explain to the participants that it is not a test in the traditional classroom sense; no one is going to be graded on it. Say that rather, it is a tool to encourage an inward look (introspection) about one's practices (or beliefs) about the subject under discussion and that the forms will be discussed in small groups after they are completed.

3. When everyone has completed the questionnaires, have them score the forms if a scoring key is provided. Alternatively, it may be desirable to score the instruments *after* the small group work. The latter procedure will avoid a focus on the scores.

4. Assign participants to small groups for discussion of the quiz. Trios work out well for this since they permit diverse thought plus intimacy for candid sharing of results. Typical questions for the groups

to discuss are: "Which items gave us the most trouble? Was there a pattern in our responses and, if there was, do we agree with it? Was the quiz helpful, overall? What was our major learning? Give the groups 30 or 40 minutes for discussion.

5. Wrap-up the activity by holding a group-at-large discussion of the learnings in the small groups. A "sure-fire" starter for this is: "Who would like to share what went on in their trio?" Be prepared for one or two participants to challenge the clarity or even the validity of certain quiz items. A good way to avoid unnecessary confrontation is to turn the (possibly hostile) question back to the group and ask: "Does anyone else also feel that way? Yes, two or three others do. You may have a point." In some instances it may be desirable to respond to a persistent challenger in this fashion: "Do you feel that those two questionable items destroy the overall value of the quiz?" A "no" response to this question will be an admission that the experience, overall, was helpful.

Action Planning

A good way to maximize results from the individual, small group, and group-at-large work is to take an additional 10–15 minutes for Action Planning (self-contracting for change). A sample form for this purpose is given in Appendix 92.

To reinforce the pledges for change made on the form, you may wish to have your participants meet in pairs or trios to discuss their self-contracts. Advise the participants that the purpose of the small group work is to give and receive feedback about the realism of the self-contracts, to secure any other help about the contracts that may be indicated and generally to give help, support and encouragement to one another.

As a final step to minimize slippage, the action plans could be discussed again—a progress check—in a follow-up session (see pages 329–331).

Instruments You Can Make

Instruments can be obtained, ready-made, from certain publishers of training materials, management and training books, articles in periodicals, consulting firms, training programs you attend, colleagues, and so on. The following is a list of publishers who supply instruments for training.

Dr. Jay Hall, President
Teleometrics Int'l.
P. O. Box 314
The Woodlands, Texas
77380

Omnisystems
631 Mayfair Road
Milwaukee, Wisconsin
53226

Dr. Donald L. Kirkpatrick
4380 Continental Drive
Brookfield, Wisconsin
53005

Dr. Gordon L. Lippitt
Development Publications
5605 Lamar Road
Washington, D.C. 20016

Organization Design and
Development
101 Bryn Mawr Ave.,
Suite 310
Bryn Mawr, PA 19010

Dr. W. J. Reddin
Organizational Tests
P. O. Box 324
Fredericton, N.B. Canada
E3B 4Y9

University Associates, Inc.
8517 Production Avenue
P. O. Box 26240
San Diego, California
92126

However, if you cannot readily locate an instrument on a particular subject or if you feel purchasing them in quantity is too costly, there is no reason why you can't design many of them yourself. If you have any doubts about your capability to do so, let me assure you that you don't need to have a Ph.D. in tests and measurements to design worthwhile instruments for training purposes. We say for *training* purposes because we are not talking about tests that have to be marked by a high degree of validity and reliability. Rather, we are talking about instruments or quizzes whose aim is essentially to irritate, provoke, unsettle, stimulate, excite, and challenge rather than to measure in the psychometric sense. In short, we are talking about training tools to encourage introspection.

To appreciate how this might be done, let's take a look at five commonly used instruments:

☐ The yes-no type
☐ The sentence-completion type
☐ The rating scale
☐ The forced-choice technique
☐ The multiple-choice type

The Yes-No Type

Several forms of the yes-no type are given in Appendices 27–30. It is suggested you take these quizzes yourself to get a good "feel" for them. After you have done this, you will note these patterns in them:

1. The quiz quite clearly tries to elicit all "yes" answers ("Selling an Idea to the Boss," Appendix 27).
2. The quiz clearly tries to elicit all "no" answers ("Giving Employees Feedback," Appendix 28).
3. The desired responses in the quiz may be both "yes" and "no" with the first half of the questions calling for one response and the last half calling for the other response. ("My Time Management Practices," Appendix 29).

4. The preferred responses to the quiz do not fit a predictable pattern.
5. The quiz is designed to elicit a "yes," "no," or "sometimes" response to give the participant more leeway than he is given in the yes-no format.

It really doesn't matter what form the quizzes take, because the instruments are designed to encourage introspection, much of which comes from the discussion of the quizzes in small groups. Of course, some instrument designers would argue that the mixed or nonpatterned yes-no type forces more careful concentration by the respondent.

Further variations in the format of the yes-no-type instrument include:

1. The quiz items themselves can be presented either as statements ("My Time Management Practices") or questions ("Giving Employees Feedback"). Some instrument designers would argue that the question style is more challenging, more stimulating, and more encouraging. This is possible, but I feel that the real learning takes place when the data are processed via small group work.
2. Responses may be placed in a box or on a short horizontal line, or the boxes and lines may be completely omitted. This is a minor matter and only reflects designer preference. (I like the "professional" look of the boxes as in the instrument "Selling an Idea to the Boss.")
3. Questions may be phrased in one of two ways: "Do *you* believe . . ." ("Giving Employees Feedback," Appendix 28) or "Do *I* favor . . ." ("My Capabilities as a Delegator," Appendix 30). The latter is certainly more personal, possibly more inviting. But whether one style encourages more introspection, and thus more learning than the other, is doubtful.

All of these variations are of minor importance. The content of the quiz items and the opportunites to process one's answers are the major keys to learning from instruments.

The Rating Scale

As we saw in the yes-no-type instrument, the respondent is asked to reply to questions or statements that only require a positive or negative answer. In other circumstances it may be more realistic to ask the participants to indicate the degree to which they hold a certain attitude or the frequency with which they behave or perform in a certain way. Hence the need for a rating scale.

Examples of two rating scales are given in Appendices 31 and 32. Note that they differ both as to format and as to scoring:

1. "My Skill As a Listener" uses the words *Never, Seldom, Occasionally, Frequently,* and *Always* rather than numerical weights to express degree. It also uses questions rather than statements to present the 15 elements to be rated. The data are summed up by the participant in the form of a profile as in Figure 9-1.

Figure 9-1. Example of a rating worksheet that uses a rating scale with a sample profile drawn in.

2. "My C.S.Q.," conversely, uses a four-factor numerical scale to express degree. It employs statements rather than questions in presenting the 15 elements, and the data is summed up via a single score.

In respect to the five words we used in "My Skill As a Listener," we could have retained the basic format and made these variations in that rating scheme: We could have replaced the words with a simple numerical rating scheme, which also would express degree, or we could have combined the word and numerical rating scales as in the following:

My Skill As a Listener

Element	Never	Seldom	Sometimes	Frequently	Always
	1	2	3	4	5

We could also have reversed the sequence of the words, putting *Always* first and *Never* last.

Note: I do not ordinarily favor the reversed format because I want the respondent to read all the words carefully before considering checking one of higher frequency.

We also could have altered the format along this line:

Do I listen for feelings, attitudes, perceptions, values as well as for facts?
Never (1) .... Always (10)

Another way to score the quiz "My Skill As a Listener" besides using a profile is to assign points to each rating such as:

Never	2 points
Seldom	4 points
Sometimes	6 points
Frequently	8 points
Always	10 points

On this scale a large score is best. The points could also be assigned conversely so that a low score would be desirable. However, a profile seems to be more helpful to the participant than this scoring procedure. The point of all this is that there are many ways to present rating scales. We have presented some of the more common variations.

Another way to use the profile is to have the participants complete the form twice—at the outset of the program and at its end. They would use separate forms for each rating and enter the second set of data on the first form. This would give two profiles on one form for comparison.

The profile technique as just described is designed for self-evaluation. It may also be used to allow participants to evaluate each other. For example, in a program concerned with learning counseling skills, participants could compare their actual performance as perceived by their peers with their original self-evaluation. The two profiles would show dramatically the difference in self and peer perceptions.

Another form of the rating scale follows:

1	2	3	4	5	6	7	8	9
(LO)								(HI)

It is essentially a continuum with a high and low range. It could be used, for example, to rate oneself, one's boss,

Trust Exercise

Many authorities on leadership, communication, and management assert that a trusting relationship is basic to leadership effectiveness. On the scale below enter data at three points on it to indicate the degree to which:

1. You trust your subordinates (S)
2. You trust your boss (B)
3. You believe your subordinates trust you (S-I)

Here is a sample of a complete rating on the scale:

Here is the scale *you* are to use:

After you have made your entries on the scale, you will meet with two fellow participants to discuss your ratings. We will conclude this exercise by a general discussion of (1) the importance of trust as a factor in successful leadership and (2) how it can be developed further if we are so inclined.

Figure 9-2. Example of an exercise containing a continuum-type rating scale.

one's subordinates, peers, and other group members in the training situation. A specific example of its use is given in Figure 9-2.

In respect to the continuum approach, such rating procedures could be used to assess assertiveness, intimacy (getting close to others for more authentic communication), one's delegation prowess, skill and/or interest in developing subordinates, one's creativity, etc.

Another way to use the continuum is on an *ad hoc* or informal basis—that is, when a situation arises when it is desirable to help an individual or the total group better think through a problem, concept, feeling, or decision by applying a measurement ("quantitative thinking") to it.

For example, here is a dialogue between a participant and the trainer.

Participant: I'm not sure I could succeed in that kind of job situation.
Trainer: Not sure?
Participant: No, not really sure.
Trainer: Let's see if you can be more specific about your feeling. Here's a 10-point scale (Draws scale on flipchart.), Could you express your feeling for us on this scale?

Another participant-trainer exchange that could precipitate using a continuum follows:

Participant: I just can't count on my staff.
Trainer: They're not a dependable group?
Participant: Overall, I'd say not really.
Trainer: Let's see if we can make this more specific. Here's a scale of 1–100. If you had to rate them on "dependability," where would you put them on this scale?
Participant: OK, about a 20. (Trainer enters 20 on scale.)
Trainer: That's pretty low.
Participant: Right.
Trainer: And how would you rate them on creativity, risk taking and cost conciousness?

Or, in a race-relations-improvement program, the trainer may begin a discussion:

Trainer: Minorities often make references to a "lack of concern" by the majority of society at large. Betty, where would you see yourself on this concern continuum?"
Betty: I'd say about 85.
Trainer: (Enters Betty's score on continuum) Emma, do you agree with Betty's self-rating?
Emma: Definitely not. I'd say she's at about 30. (Trainer enters score.)

Or, the trainer may present a scale dealing with confronting conflict—the willingness to face up to and work through differences candidly and constructively. The trainer would then ask each person to rate themselves, entering each rating on the continuum.

The Sentence-Completion Type

One of the easiest instruments to develop, assuming one has the content well in hand, is that which asks participants to complete a group of open-ended statements. The objective is to have the participant react to the incomplete sentence and thereby disclose something about attitudes and perceptions about self, job, career, working with and supervising others. The rationale for this procedure is that the best way to achieve personal growth is to hold up to the light of day one's attitudes, values, and practices. In the absence of such self-disclosure and subsequent self-examination, growth or change is not very likely.

Parenthetically, it may be observed that other instruments, for example, the yes-no type, could do a good job of encouraging disclosure and introspection about self. But the point is that the sentence-completion type is particularly well-suited for this purpose. Why? Because it necessitates deeper *reflection* and actual *verbalization* about the data being elicited, as opposed to requiring a response to a complete statement someone else previously prepared.

In any case, we can readily identify four typical uses to which we can apply the sentence-completion instrument:

As an icebreaker. One simple use of this type of instrument is for social or fun purposes—more specifically, to loosen up and acquaint group members with one another. It merely asks participants to disclose everyday favorites or preferences among a variety of things. See Appendix 26 for an example of this type of instrument.

A more profound form of this instrument, "As I See Myself" in Appendix 33, may also be used as an icebreaker. However, because of its personal character, it would be used only in a training program that is highly experiential and personal-growth oriented.

As a program opener. Another type of sentence-completion instrument takes a different tack. For example, at the very outset of the program it may ask for disclosure concerning one's career, leadership beliefs, job satisfaction, and relations with bosses, subordinates, peers, and the organization. Aside from the usual objective of instruments—to encourage introspection—an added value is that it alerts the participant at the outset that the program is for deeper, personal development, not merely for teaching abstractly "about management." For an illustration of this type of instrument, see "Management Development—Openers," in Appendix 34.

For mid-program use. Completion-type instruments, like other instruments, can be used at various points in the program. The instrument "As I See The Coaching Process" in Appendix 35, would be useful before, during, or after a session concerned with "the manager as a coach." It might be used early in the program to help set the stage for things to come or at the close of the program as a "wrap-up" activity. Although our sample instrument would stimulate the participant's thinking to a fair degree, it would not be as challenging as "Management Development—Openers" since it is less personal.

As a personal awareness stimulator. In an experiential training program, that is, where one learns primarily from one's experience, the encouragement of introspection is very much the norm, such as in assertiveness training, T-Groups, encounter groups, and race-relations-improvement programs. The sentence-completion instrument might be used as an opener (see "As I See Myself," Appendix 33) or at other stages in the program (see "As I See You," Appendix 36).

A question might be raised whether the statements presented in "As I See Myself" and "As I See You" ask participants to engage in considerable self-disclosure and thus might be "stressful" to some people. It should be remembered that in the context of the goals and norms of the aforementioned experiential training programs (assertiveness training, etc.), few, if any, participants would be subject to undue anxiety by completing the statements as requested.

The processing of the data generated by the sentence-completion instruments is typically shared in pairs or trios. The small-group procedure allows for intimacy, privacy, and support, as may be needed. In less experiential (more conventional or intellectual) programs, the instrument can be processed, instead, on a "solo" basis. More specifically, the participant could:

1. Complete privately the instrument at the start of the program. (See "Management Development—Openers, Appendix 34.)
2. File it in a notebook as opposed to discussing it with anyone.
3. Complete it again, using a second copy, at program's end. Different responses on any of the items represent the "net gain" of the program.
4. Optionally, the participants could (at program's end) meet in pairs to share their reactions to both forms, discussing their before and after responses.

Here are a few sample open-end statements in areas where sentence-completion-type instruments could be used.

☐ *Communication*
   I am at my communication best when I _____.
   I am at my communication worst when I _____.
   In communicating with peers or colleagues I find that _____.

☐ *Group functioning*
   I see this group as _____.
   What bothers me about this group is _____.
   What I like about this group is _____.

☐ *Development of intimacy*
   My pet peeve is _____.
   I see money as _____.
   My hobby is _____.
   If I were to change my name (first, last or both) I would _____.

☐ *Giving feedback*
   My feeling about giving praise is _____.
   My feeling about giving criticism is _____.

☐ *Careers*

Five years from now I hope to _____.
The biggest obstacle to attaining my career goals
is _____.
As I see my boss in relation to my career _____.

Remember, the "trick" in developing open-end statements simply is to "auto-brainstorm" ideas and concepts in relation to a given theme or topic, select the best ones, and write them out, as in the preceding examples.

The Forced-Choice Technique

In the forced-choice technique participants are given an inventory form (see "My Style As a Manager" in Appendix 24) that asks them to choose between two items or statements. The preferred item may be hard to decide upon since both statements may be ones that the respondent can readily "buy." However, by being constantly forced to choose between the two more or less acceptable statements, the participant creates a pattern of responses.

As is explained under "Scoring of Instruments," a numerical score on the forced-choice quiz is useful primarily as an indicator of a tendency toward a point of view or set of behaviors. It is *not* intended to measure the general "correctness" of one's responses.

Note: Anticipate complaints about the difficulty of making a hard choice. You can only agree with the complainants and simply advise them to do the best they can under the circumstances. (Life frequently offers us difficult choices!)

The Multiple-Choice Type

The multiple-choice technique is particularly useful when you want to help participants see their pattern or style when a number of patterns or styles may exist; for example, a style of leadership, a communication pattern, a consulting style, a training style, a selling style, a style in "managing" one's boss, or a problem-solving style. An example of a problem-solving style quiz, in multiple choice format, is given in Appendix 37, "My Approach to Problem Solving."

As you have probably surmised, this type of quiz is more difficult to construct than the yes-no type, the rating scale or the forced-choice type. This follows since several well-thought-out and well-stated choices have to be developed for each quiz item. And all quiz items have to be consistent and logical with one another. In respect to the quiz on problem solving, we built seven problem solving styles into it. This was the most complex to construct of all the sample instruments we have provided.

Guidelines for Constructing Instruments

If you should find it necessary to develop your own instruments, here are some suggestions that should help you accomplish this task.

1. Build a reference file of instruments of *varying formats*. Don't worry too much about the content. And as we indicated above, they can be found in books, magazines, even newspapers, or purchased from instrument publishers.
2. Study the formats which have been used by others—yes-no, multiple choice, rating scales, etc.
3. As you analyze them, try to acquire a feel for their rhythm, style, tone. Note the way the authors of particular instruments have chosen word patterns to stimulate thought. Also note the length and variety of the quiz items.
4. Collect data about the content of the area you wish to instrumentalize. For example, if you decide to construct an instrument on delegation check out five or ten meaty articles on that subject. Extract the key points from those articles and add them to what you already know about the subject. You are now ready to go to work!
5. Put each major idea on a separate note card. Then rank (arrange) them in order of importance. The odds are that you'll have more ideas than you need.
6. Select the most important ideas to constitute the quiz. You may have as many as twenty, possibly a few more. Remember that a "fancy" questionnaire that seeks opinions on trivial or irrelevant questions is really no instrument at all.
7. Arrange your quiz ideas in the sequence that makes the most sense. For example, in a quiz on one's skill as a communicator, you probably would group together all ideas that pertain to listening, all that pertain to perception, all that pertain to feedback, etc.
8. Decide on the format you wish to use. The yes-no, the sentence-completion, and the rating-scale formats are the easiest to construct.
9. Develop your instrument by writing the necessary quiz items. Review them several times for clarity, logic, coverage, etc.
10. Decide whether you wish to provide a scoring system. If you do decide to have one, select a simple one.
11. Check out your handiwork further on one or more colleagues. They may note some things you missed—ambiguities, inconsistencies, or even omissions.

12. "De-bug" the instrument further by trying it out on a small group of participants informally. Try to ascertain which items, if any, "bothered" them. Correct or drop such items.
13. After your first use of the instrument in the training situation, revise it and keep revising it, as indicated, based on feedback from the participants.

Scoring of Instruments

If you have taken the quizzes cited in this chapter, or at least studied them, you will have noticed that the scoring procedures vary quite a bit. In fact, if you begin to "collect" instruments, as we suggest you do, you will find a great variety of such procedures. But regardless of the variations, we can say that in the training situation an instrument may be scored in either one of two ways: generally or precisely.

If the scoring is intended to call attention to "tendencies," only general scores are necessary. For example, the forced-choice instrument "My Style As a Manager" in Appendix 24 only asks participants to identify and tally their Theory X and Y items. It does not ask them to compute percentages or to total points to ascertain "how much" of a Theory X or Y leader one is. Such a precise computation would not be too meaningful.

Conversely, a number of our sample instruments provide scoring instructions so that participants can assess quite precisely *the degree* to which they are effective delegators, effective givers of feedback, effective introducers of change, effective "sellers" of an idea to one's boss, etc. For some participants "numbers" can have worthwhile catalytic value.

How general or how precise you decide the scoring of your quizzes should be will depend, of course, on such factors as the composition of your group, your course objectives and your own pedagogical philosophy. In fact, you may wish to try out different procedures from time to time. But regardless of the approach you take to scoring, here are some suggestions regarding the use of scoring systems:

Keep them simple and logical. Avoid complex scoring systems which are likely to produce confusion, frustration, or defensiveness. For example, a scoring system that gives a 3 for the desirable responses and a 1 for the undesirable ones or one that *subtracts* points for undesirable responses may be questioned vigorously by at least some participants.

Emphasize to participants that the scores are hardly final, iron-clad, scientific judgments. Rather, they are merely general guides as to patterns or tendencies.

Stress to the group that discussion of the quiz items is what it's all about. The quiz is intended to encourage one to focus on one's behavior, attitudes, values, and perceptions, not on the "numbers" which acompany it. *Introspection* is the name of the game.

The Participant-Prepared Instrument

Participants may be utilized to construct their own instrument. This makes for a novel, fun-type activity. It is also a good way to defuse hostility toward or questioning about an instrument inasmuch as the participants have developed it themselves. This follows since all of us are more likely to accept what we create, even though someone else's product may be superior in certain ways.

A procedure for developing the participant-prepared instrument is as follows:

1. Have the total group develop a list of the points to be covered. This may relate to the qualities of an effective leader, or an effective team, or an effective communicator, etc. This may be done via brainstorming, the slip method, small-group work, or contributions by the group at large. I prefer for this work to be done on a small-group basis to ensure maximum participation.
2. If it is done by small groups, have them put their data on flipcharts. Then post the completed charts on the wall for a brief discussion about them.
3. Have the participants return to their small groups to prepare a master list, selecting the best ideas from all the flipcharts. Have the small groups limit their lists to a certain number of items, possibly 15 or 20.
4. Post the lists again, noting similarities and differences. Then working from one flipchart, have the total group agree on the best 10 to 20 items. This can be done by a voice vote or a show of hands: "How many want to include this item? Sixteen. This one? Ten." Then go to the other flipcharts and repeat the process. The items which have the most votes become the quiz items.
5. Let the group add a numerical rating scale to the quiz items such as 1-5, 1-7, or 1-10.
6. The instrument, in final form, can be typed and reproduced (assuming clerical help and equipment are available) for all participants or it can be written on flipcharts.
7. Have the participants complete the new form and then discuss their self-ratings in trios, as described in the prior section.

Table 9-1
Evaluation of the Five Types of Instruments

Evaluation Factor	TYPE				
	Yes-No	Rating Scale	Sentence Completion	Forced Choice	Multiple Choice
Ease of construction	Easy	Easy	Very easy	Very difficult	Fairly complex
Degree of structure in format	High	High	Low	Very high	Very high
Ease of responding	Easy	Easy	May be difficult, depending on quiz	Often difficult	Not too difficult
Possible stress on respondent	Little	Little	May be high, depending on quiz	A fair degree	Moderate
Discussion stimulator	High	High	High	High	High
Introspection stimulator	Good	Good	Good (or better)	Good (or better)	Good
Data collector and organizer	Very effective	Very effective	Poor	Very effective	Very effective
Time required by group to process data	Variable, depending on number and complexity of items, group motivation	Variable	Variable	Variable	Variable
Effectiveness in relation to nature of group	No special problem	No special problem	Group should be verbal and "loose"	No special problem	No special problem
Best use in relation to stage of program	No special problem	No special problem	With an "uptight" group, use later or not at all	With an "uptight" group, use later on	No special problem
Face validity	Fairly high	Excellent	Low	Fair to good	Fairly high

A Summary

The following paragraphs and Table 9-1 summarize the nature and use of the five types of instruments previously presented.

Ease of construction. The sentence-completion type is the easiest instrument to construct (just come up with pertinent ideas you want participants to "spell out") and the forced-choice type is the hardest. Forced choice is difficult because *two* statements have to be created for a given concept, both of which are plausible and acceptable enough so that they present the respondent with a dilemma as to choice. But despite the apparent plausibility of the two statements, they must be, in fact, different enough to consistently help set off one set of beliefs or behaviors from another.

The multiple-choice type of instrument is also fairly complex to construct since it entails working with a large amount of data essential to differentiating a variety of patterns and styles (e.g., of leadership, communication, assertiveness). Our example, "My Approach to Problem Solving," is "very complex" since this instrument delineates *seven* problem solving styles.

Structure. By "structure" we mean a set of completed statements or questions, a scoring procedure, etc. All but the sentence-completion type of instrument are high in structure. The sentence-completion type is "free form" and permits no scoring.

Ease of responding. The sentence-completion type, if it probes fairly deeply into feelings, attitudes, beliefs, may be the most difficult instrument to respond to. This follows since the participant is "forced" to use his/her own thoughts and words to complete the sentence. Obviously some participants may find this hard to do. The forced-choice type, while not a "strain" on one's verbal ability, as in sentence completion, often presents a problem to the participant because of the *apparent* acceptability of the paired statements. Not everyone enjoys wrestling with alternatives.

To put the "ease of responding" issue into proper perspective, we should recognize that *any* instrument which encourages introspection about one's style, attitudes, beliefs, values, practices, etc. may be difficult for participants who are not comfortable with self-disclosure, that is, talking freely about themselves. Fortunately, this is not a problem, for most adults, in training programs that match participants and course content properly.

Stress. In light of the previous considerations, "stress" on certain respondents may be highest for the sentence-completion and forced-choice types of instruments. The best training procedure, therefore, is to know one's group well, and if a negative reaction is expected either use the more challenging instrument late in the program or possibly not at all. Stress may also be related to participant expectations of the program. For example, participants may expect somewhat "stressful" activities at an experiential learning program but not at all at an "intellectual" management development program relying primarily on case study, films, and lectures. Feelings of stress may be based, too, on whether attendance in the program is voluntary or required.

Discussion stimulator. All instruments, given the right content and training environment, are good discussion stimulators. Experience with instrumentation indicates that it is highly "natural" for participants to respond to statements or questions that either inquire about or challenge their beliefs and practices.

Introspection stimulator. Again, all instruments, if properly constructed, possessed of the right content, and in the "right" training situation, will encourage participants to look inward.

Data collection. As to the feasibility of collecting data for individual or group scoring, all but the sentence-completion type work well. The latter type obviously cannot be scored or tallied.

Processing time. All instrumented work in the training situation takes time. There are no shortcuts to a (desired) profound discussion. Depending on the number and complexity of the items in a quiz, 30–45 minutes is a minimum time period; 60 to 90 minutes may be more desirable. Processing the data in pairs or trios, rather than in larger groups, does help to move the discussion along. The two- or three-person teams also provide the desired privacy and intimacy.

Group factors. What about effectiveness in relation to the nature of the group? As mentioned before, the only possibility of a negative reaction is from a group that has several "up tight" members who are asked to deal with a highly *unstructured* instrument such as the sentence-completion type. (Of course, some respondents may be uncomfortable with any instrument that they perceive as too personal in its probing.) The resistance may come because of the requirement of verbalizing and declaring

oneself on issues that may be regarded as too close to home. On the other hand, most participants should respond favorably to sentence completion, given the psychological need for closure, that is, to complete the sentences on the form.

Stage of program. Most instruments may be used at any point in the program. Some groups, however, may not be ready for the sentence-completion and forced-choice types until later on in the program. Of course, *any* instrument that asks for considerable self-disclosure of attitudes and feelings has to be employed judiciously.

Face validity. Finally, all instruments by virtue of their formal structure, except possibly for the sentence-completion type, should be well received by participants. The scoring, development of one or more profiles, etc., all help in this regard. Actually, since the material generated by the quizzes relates to oneself (as opposed to, say, a case or an abstract game) acceptance is typically high. Most participants find instruments to be a "fun thing," even fascinating. Learning about oneself, even if somewhat discomforting, is ordinarily perceived as being very much worthwhile.

Note: The intent of the evaluative comment "no special problem" in Table 9-1 is to encourage the trainer to use all the types of instruments since most groups, if they are "with the program" and if properly indoctrinated, should not resist the assignment. Certainly any instrument may provoke a negative reaction from *some* participants, at times. But basically the instruments work, with the caution that the sentence-completion type requires a bit more sophisticated (and verbal) group.

Key Points

1. Instruments are basic tools for experiential learning.
2. Instruments are useful for generating data that individuals, groups, and the total organization can look at to augment their effectiveness.
3. In the training situation instruments are a tool for introspection and discussion. Accordingly, it is not essential that they be subject to validation, norming, etc., as are instruments used in psychological assessment, counseling, therapy, and attitude measurement.
4. Instrument data is generated via self-report and/or feedback from others. Although self-assessment is not necessarily an objective source of data, it, nevertheless, serves as a basis for discussion with others.
5. Instruments may be used at various stages in a training program—as pre-work, as icebreakers and/or openers, in mid-session, to close things out, or as a back-home follow-up.

6. Instruments may be purchased, found in professional journals and books, or be designed by the trainer.
7. Instruments that are fairly easy to make are the yes-no, sentence-completion and rating-scale types. Of greater complexity are the forced-choice and multiple-choice types.
8. Rating scales can assume many formats. Certain ones lend themselves readily to the construction of *profiles*. Profiles may also be used for self-comparison and comparison with scores given by others.
9. To construct an instrument one should collect data on the subject it is to treat, select a format and scoring system; develop 10–20 statements/ideas; prioritize the ideas; check out the instrument with colleagues for logic, readability, and the like; and "field test" it if possible.
10. Instruments also may be developed by participants. It is a "fun thing" to do and gives the device ready acceptance by participants.
11. A key factor for maximizing results from instrumentation is to allow adequate time for processing.

References

1. Blake, R. R., and Mouton, J. S., "Instruments to Create Involvement," *Sales Meetings* (October 1971), p. 62.
2. Pfeiffer, J. W., and Jones, J. E. (Eds.), *The 1976 Annual Handbook for Group Facilitators,* University Associates, San Diego, California (1976), p. 65.

Recommended Reading

Blake, R. R., and Mouton, J. S., "Instruments to Create Involvement," *Sales Meetings,* October 1971, pp. 62–68.

This discusses theory and advantages of instrumented learning. Also describes various types of instruments including ratings, forced-choice, and multiple choice.

Bumstead, R., "Delicate Measures," *Northeast Training News,* July 1980, pp. 10, 12.

This article treats various issues in instrumentation such as overcoming resistance by participants, keeping data private, do's and don't's in instrument use.

Buzzota, V. R., Lefton, R. E., and Sherberg, M., "Instruments," *Sales Meetings,* October 1971, pp. 77–87.

This describes various instruments which can be used in training including feedback instruments, questionnaires and surveys, tests, and problem solving instruments.

Lomac, J., "On Tests and Behavior Change: Individualizing Feedback," *Northeast Training News,* December 1981, pp. 19–20.

This describes how to individualize the feedback that develops from a well-constructed diagnostic assessment instrument.

Pfeiffer, W. J., and Hestin, R., *Instrumentation in Human Relations Training: A Guide to 75 Instruments with Wide Application to the Behavioral Sciences,* University Associates, San Diego, California, 1973.

The book is designed to introduce group facilitators from a variety of orientations to the use of instruments in human relations training.

Pfeiffer, J. and Jones, J. E., *Annual Handbook for Group Facilitators,* University Associates, Pubishers and Consultants, San Diego, California, 1972 and in each following year.

Each *Annual* contains a section on instruments, comprising (1) summary statements about instrument theory and use as well as (2) a number of actual instruments authored by various trainers.

Zemke, R., "Using Testing Instruments In Your Training Effort," *Training/HRD,* November 1982, pp. 30–32, 36–38, 40–44.

An overview of instrumentation in training, including its impact on the training function, how to use instruments properly, vendors, and a survey of its intended usage (e.g., in communication, personal growth).

DEFINING A PROBLEM AND GENERATING DATA ABOUT IT

No problem is so large or complex that it can't be run away from.

—Charlie Brown, character in
Peanuts cartoon strip.

Creative thinking may mean simply the realization that there's no particular virtue in doing things the way they have always been done.

—Rudolph Flesch, U.S. author
and popularizer of
communication skills

To an ever increasing degree, organizations are insisting on pay offs from all training activities. As a consequence, more and more training programs are becoming job oriented, either in whole or in part. This is true whether we are talking about management development, supervisory training, team building, quality circles, sales and customer service training, or whatever.

Trainers, then, are expected to utilize their skills to help participants generate new ideas rather than just to have them listen to old ones. The concern is to increase productivity/quality by helping people to work smarter, rather than just harder.[1]

One way to ensure that training is organization and job related is to introduce into the training endeavor opportunities for identifying and solving real problems. Consequently, the lines between what is ordinarily termed a conference or a sales or management meeting and a training program are often quite blurred.

The value of working on live problems is well stated by one writer: "When participants use the training session to solve their own problems, they do not experience 'training shock' from returning to their jobs and not knowing how to apply their newfound knowledge and skills. The reason: they brought chunks of their jobs into the classroom."[2]

On the assumption, then, that organizational personnel should be encouraged to solve their own problems effectively, the trainer must be well-equipped to provide such guidance as may be necessary. This means providing instruction to participants in problem solving for:

☐ Use in the training situation
☐ Use back home on a continuing basis after the training is over.

Problem Solving—Suggested Content

What kind of problem solving skills should the trainer be able to develop among those who solve problems? The skills, which relate to the classic model of problem solving and decision making, are how to:

☐ Define the problem
☐ Generate data about the problem
☐ Generate ideas or alternate courses of action for problem resolution
☐ Choose among the alternative solutions
☐ Implement the solution or decision

The pages that follow develop these skill areas in more detail. This chapter will treat the first two steps in the problem solving process: "How to define the problem" and "How to generate data about the problem."

Chapter 11 will treat the third step: "How to generate ideas (solutions) about the problem for its resolution."

Chapter 12 will discuss our final two steps (or skill areas) in the problem solving process: "How to choose among alternatives" and "How to plan and implement the solution." The chapter will also discuss a number of additional approaches to problem solving.

The whole thrust of this and the following two chapters is this: problem solvers and decision makers should be equipped with a *broad* repertoire of techniques/approaches to augment their potential to develop strategies to resolve difficulties and capitalize on opportunities. As the late, great humanistic psychologist Dr. Abraham Maslow stated it: "If the only tool you have is a hammer, you tend to see every problem as a nail."

Launching Problem–Solving Training

Before beginning a problem solving session, consider these warm-up activities:

☐ Help participants to get into a problem solving mood by "walking them through" the exercise sheet entitled "Check Your I.Q. (Imagination Quotient)," in Appendix 25. This is a fun-type activity and will make the point experientially that problem solving requires nonconventional, even bizarre thinking.

☐ Puzzles may also be used for this purpose.

☐ Conduct a dry run of the particular technique to be used. For example, if the group is new to brainstorming, conduct a mini-brainstorming session to give them the feel for the process.

How To Define the Problem

Said management authority Peter Drucker: "The most common source of mistakes in management decisions is the emphasis on finding the right answer rather than the right question." Scientist Albert Einstein put it this way: "The formulation of a problem is far more often essential than its solution, which may be merely a matter of mathematical or experimental skill."

Unquestionably, groups (and individuals) often handicap themselves by failing to define a problem properly. For example, a school superintendent was advised he had two choices to resolve a temporary classroom shortage. They were to either add more mobile classrooms to the playground already crowded or to bus students to other schools, further crowding them. Instead of choosing either of those two solutions, however, he redefined the problem. This approach indicated that more space was needed, not just more units or busing. He thus recommended the purchase of an adjacent vacant lot which the school district agreed to buy and construct a building on. It was later sold off as commercial property.[3]

In a similar vein, a languishing firm producing audio-visual materials for the industrial market had difficulty solving its problem as long as it saw it simply as a "poor selling effort." It was not until it defined the problem as vending dull and dated materials ("yesterday's bread winners" as Peter Drucker calls them) was it able to make any real headway in resolving its difficulties.

Clinical psychologists have long observed that people often formulate their problems in ways which actually prevent them from solving them. Some examples, both organizational and individual, are these: "Our problem is that the field is too competitive." "Our problem is that the market is too fluid." "Our problem is that we just don't understand *that* market." "Our problem is that we just don't have the trained personnel." "My problem is that I can never get the boss to listen to any of my ideas." "My problem is that I don't have the . . . (time, energy, connections, education, track record, "smarts") to pull it off." In other words, problems which are defined in terms of resignation, blame of others, self-blame, insurmountable barriers, and the like, are certain routes to non-resolution.

This concept is illustrated by the incident involving the boy who showed his dad a book containing only blank pages. This brief dialogue ensued:

Dad (discarding book in dismay): "This book says nothing."
Son (retrieving book respectfully): "This book says anything!"
Moral: You can't find new ways of doing things if you insist on looking at them harder in the usual way.

Besides working on a wrong problem, problem solvers may be grappling with one that suffers from vagueness. The symptoms of a vague problem, per David Murphy, are these:[4]

Buzz words. Reliance on generalized buzz words such as "communication," "morale," "marketing," "productivity," etc., terms which no one really understands.
Many versions/answers. Due to the vagueness of the problem, people are certain to define it differently and come up with many different answers. Guideline: When there were many answers, all dissimilar, look for a vaguely stated problem.

Murphy's answer to the vague problem is to ask people what the buzz words means *to them.* Also ask them to assume they have a magic wand. If the wand is waved, what will people stop doing or begin doing? And third, ask people to assume that they are a movie director, directing George C. Scott or Jane Fonda. "How would you tell them to act?" "What would you have them say or do?"

As a final solution to the vagueness problem, develop a model which explains it as you see it. If it's wrong, people will tell you about it pretty fast.

The trainer or moderator can help a group to look at its problem more realistically by posting the following criteria on a flipchart and asking them to respond "yes" or "no" to each of the five items in response to the question:[5] Is the problem as now stated . . .

☐ Clear?
☐ Concise?
☐ Realistic?
☐ Achievable?
☐ Measurable (as practicable)?

If there are one or more "no" responses to these criteria, the problem must be restated or rephrased.

Another way to zero in on the real problem is to use techniques such as Pareto's analysis, brainstorming, statistical procedures, the check sheet, check list, and problem identification—ABC approach. Descriptions of these techniques follow.

Pareto's Analysis

Vilfredo Pareto (1848–1923), an Italian mathematician and economist, is famous for his "Law of Disproportionate Distribution." His "law" was based on an economic finding: 80% of Italy's wealth was subject to control by 20% of the total population. This finding has been applied by management writers to a variety of management circumstances, e.g.,

☐ 80% of a budget may be allotted to 20% of the budgeted items.
☐ On the average, 80% of a firm's sales may be accomplished by 20% of the sales staff.
☐ 80% of sales may come from 20% of the customers.
☐ 80% of the company's gross profit may be produced by 20% of the product line.
☐ 80% of a productivity effort may come from 20% of the total input or effort.
☐ 80% of the complaints may come from 20% of the customers.
☐ 80% of the grievances may arise from 20% of the work force.
☐ 80% of the down time may derive from 20% of the equipment or machines.

☐ A political candidate, who analyzed his schedule, found that 80% of his exposure came from 20% of his speeches.
☐ Time management authority Alan Lakein advises that 80% of one's success comes from 20% of one's activities. Hence the need to avoid getting bogged down on low-value activities.

Extrapolating Pareto's rule to the safety area, it is not unusual to find that the largest preponderance of accidents are caused by relatively few personnel, or occur in a few specialized situations.

In general, the "maldistribution rule" or the "law of 20/80," while hardly an accurate predictor of results in all organizational situations, is useful as a way of getting managers (and others)

☐ To think in terms of inputs and outputs
☐ To recognize that there is *not* an automatic relationship—one to one—between input (effort) and output (results)
☐ Most likely there are inefficiencies aplenty because of failure to concentrate on the results-producing inputs, be it financial controls, personnel, products, daily activities, or training courses. (In respect to the latter item, you might assess carefully your training program offerings lest a mere 20% of them are producing 80% of the benefits to the organization!)

Pareto's analysis, then, is a useful tool for looking at problems and what seems to affect them. It tells us that although many factors may be present or at work in a problem situation, quite often only a vital few may have pay-off possibilities. The technique could be used to advantage in team building sessions, quality circles, management and sales training courses, etc.

As an illustration of how we can apply Pareto's analysis to a specific problem, let's assume we operate a lawn mower plant. Our franchised dealers have given us data concerning customer complaints for the past one-year warranty period. Their defect data are shown in Table 10-1. We then group and tally all the defects, which gives us the data shown in Table 10-2.

The data are then put in a bar chart—the Pareto diagram—which takes the form shown in Figure 10-1.

Note that the chart shows each category of defect on *both* a numerical and percentage basis. The 100% figure relates to the numerical total of defects (400) and by segmenting or scaling the percentage line downward (from 100 to 0) we can see at a glance how the percentages relate to the numerical data. That is, we can readily identify the percentage of each category of defects. Note, too, that the line going from 0% to 100% is a cumulative line (also known as the "cum line") and shows us the ac-

Table 10-1
Customer Complaints Concerning Lawn Mowers

Defect	Number of Complaints
Handle assembly fell apart (at welds)	120
Bolts on handle snapped	53
Controls defective	32
Tire fell off wheels	26
Tire fell apart	5
Height adjusters inoperative (when new)	9
Height adjusters snapped	15
Wheel bolts snapped	14
Wobbly wheels	36
Oil leak	14
Air filter fell apart	6
Engine block cracked	4
Carburetor not functioning (when new)	7
Idling screw could not be turned	19
Tear in grass catching bag (when new)	11
Zipper in grass catching bag inoperative (when new)	19
Blade fell off chassis	7
Safety device in rear fell off	3

Table 10-2
Grouping of Customer Complaints

Defect	Number
Handle and controls	205
Tires, wheels, height adjusters	105
Engine problems	50
Bag problems	30
Miscellaneous problems	10
Total	400

cumulated numerical total of defects as we go from the far left bar to those on the right.

In our chart, then, we can see that the first two bars represent the bulk of our problem—310 defects or over 75% of the cases. This sets our priorities for us.

Brainstorming

Problems can also be identified via brainstorming. This technique may be used in such areas as:

☐ Team building sessions
☐ Quality circles
☐ Meetings with employees such as "gripe" sessions
☐ Determining training needs
☐ Determining hazards in the work place
☐ Generating topics for conference agendas

Figure 10-1. A Pareto diagram that shows the number and corresponding percentage of defects in each category of for each component of the lawnmower.

Since brainstorming typically generates a long list of ideas, the list, obviously, must be whittled down to a workable number. This can be done quite easily by having the group vote on the importance of the identified problems. Those problems with the most votes become the ones that will receive priority attention.

Brainstorming, a multipurpose technique, also can be used to generate (1) data about a problem, such as causes and defects (Step 2 in our five-step problem solving model) and (2) solutions to resolve the problem (Step 3). Details concerning the conduct of a brainstorming session are included in Chapter 11 about generating ideas about the problem for its resolution.

Statistical Procedures

Various statistical procedures can help us to "zero in" on the problem. They entail collecting data so that we are operating from fact rather than conjecture. Two simple examples follow:

Scatter diagram. This procedure is designed to ferret out and show graphically a relationship between two sets of data presumed to be related. Some examples are relationships between test scores and I.Q., grades and I.Q., salary and college major, salary and sex, weight and age, heart disease and smoking. In the workplace some examples are absenteeism and seniority (or absenteeism and age, sex, or type of work), accidents and seniority, age, sex, or type of work, and factory defects and day of the week. An example of a scatter diagram is given in Figure 10-2. It plots the relationship between accidents and time of day. In this hypothetical instance, the relationship is a very strong one.

Ordinarily we use the horizontal axis for the variable impacting on the other one and the vertical axis for the variable subject to or influenced by that change. Thus, in our diagram we have placed time of day on the horizontal axis and number of accidents on the vertical axis.

A check sheet. This is a device to aid in collecting data about a problem. After data is fully collected, a pattern emerges that highlights the problem or difficulty. For example, a supervisor may keep records for a month of all employees' arrival times; a shop foreman may keep a daily record of defects of particular parts for a five-day period; a customer relations supervisor may keep a weekly record of orders and inquiries processed by the staff to analyze workload. The latter checksheet is given in Figure 10-3.

Note that by glancing across the columns from left to right, the supervisor can quickly learn that Jo and Chris are the weakest producers and Fred and Ed the strongest. Also, Will seems to have "tapered off" during the last four weeks. Note, too, that we could add three more vertical columns: one to sum up individual production for the eight weeks and two others for average individual *and* group weekly production.

Check List

A check list has two functions:

Preventive—To ensure that a mistake does not occur or that quality is maintained; for example, a supervisor may develop and use a check list in orienting a new worker to the job.

Diagnostic—To locate a trouble spot, error, malfunction, etc.; for example, auditors may examine the internal operations of an office with a check list; an engineer may try to isolate a mechanical or electrical problem on an automotive engine.

Check lists provide system, particularly if a sequence of events is involved. By using a check list as opposed to relying on memory, you ensure that all items are checked out or covered. Check lists thus save time in locating the shortcoming or problem.

Problem Identification—ABC Approach

On the assumption that if we sincerely want to identify problems it's "as easy as A B C," a comprehensive question list that should aid groups in locating their problems is given in Figure 10-4.

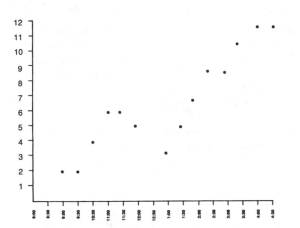

Figure 10-2. A scatter diagram showing the number of accidents in January by time of day.

Weekly Orders and Inquiries Processed

Name	Week 1	2	3	4	5	6	7	8
Fred	26	25	28	30	29	30	28	31
Alma	22	25	24	26	30	28	26	27
Jo	12	14	12	14	15	ON LEAVE	12	11
Jean	29	26	28	36	28	34	30	33
John	32	24	32	26	22	26	33	32
Will	24	20	34	26	14	20	14	19
Chris	15	26	13	14	22	12	12	15
Ed	35	31	30	35	34	30	37	33
Total	195	191	203	207	194	180	192	201

Figure 10-3. Example of a checksheet.

A —Attitudes? Antagonisms? Apathy? Adaptability? Aesthetics? Automation?
B —Behaviors? Bottlenecks? Bargaining? Bureaucracy? Budgets?
C —Communication? Climate? Change? Crises? Complaints? Careers? Conflict?
D —Delegation? Decentralization? Defects? Danger? Difficulties? Deviations? Durability? Deadlines?
E —Environment (situation)? Economy? Errors? Ethics (morality)? Experimentation?
F —Frustration? Fear? Fantasies? Fun? Failure? Forecasting?
G —Garbage (as in computer inputs-outputs)? Goals? Group (processes)?
H —Hazards? Half-measures? Hierarchy?
I —Indecision? Interaction (inadequate, inappropriate)? Intentions? Insensitivities? Ideas? Ideals?
J —Job (design, enrichment, cycle, rotation, security)?
K —Knowledge?
L —Listening? Loyalty? Leadership? Lemons? Laziness?
M —Motivation? Money? Manpower? Material? Methods? Mixups? Meetings?
N —Negativism? Nitpicking? Negotiation? Needs?
O —Organization? Objectives? Operations? Opportunities? Obstructions?
P —Pressures? Performance? Policies? Plans? Personnel? Procedures? Pay? Pessimism? Production?
Q —Quality? Quantity?
R —Resistance (to change)? Rejects? Reward System? Relationships? Responsibility?
S —Safety? Standards? Seasonal set-ups? Scheduling? Sales? Secretaries? Staff?
T —Training? Turnover? Time Management? Timing? Team (building, management)?
U —Utilization? Urban (aspects)? Union? Unity? Unification?
V —Vendettas? Venom? Variables? Visibility?
W —Waste? Workweek? Workday? Warehousing?
X —eXpense?
Y —Yesterday's breadwinners? You-I?
Z —Zero defects? Zig zags?

Figure 10-4. An alphabetically arranged question list to aid in problem identification.

Groups working with this list have several options:
1. They can define or redefine any item in the list.
2. They can add new items, the one's provided triggering other more pertinent ones.
3. They can respond directly to what they see: "Yes, our problem is the 'half-measures' we take."

How to Generate Data About The Problem

Once we have properly defined our problem, we are ready to collect data (causes, effects) about it. Several methods are described below, including:

☐ Force field analysis
☐ Value analysis
☐ Structured analysis
  • 5-M analysis
  • 7-S analysis
  • T-column
☐ Analogy
☐ Working with metaphors
☐ Analogies vs. metaphors
☐ Imaging
☐ Brainstorming
☐ Other idea-producing techniques

Force Field Analysis—A Tool For Problem Diagnosis

According to the late Kurt Lewin, a renowned social psychologist and father of the group dynamics movement, any problem situation can be understood better if we use this metaphor: "a sea of forces in motion." Some of these forces, as we may perceive them, are favorable (positive) and some are unfavorable (negative or undesirable). Although these forces are in constant motion, their pressures and counter pressures produce a situation of stability at any one point in time. In other words, we have movement, but yet stability. Lewin described this situation as one of "quasi-stationary equilibrium."

As problem solvers then, we can look at (diagnose) any problem situation and understand it more properly by identifying the forces at work and their relative influence on the situation. This is true whether our problem is the current level of production, the sales picture, the accident rate, the state of employee morale, the amount of participation in the classroom, the degree of support for a public policy, etc.

Force field analysis is an extremely useful concept and technique since it says to us: "Hey, don't try to come up with a solution to the problem or change a situation before you know what forces at work underlie it. Be an expert diagnostician first, and then you'll be a much better problem solver or change agent. So discern carefully the forces that are favorable to your desired goal (the driving

forces) and those which are unfavorable (the restraining forces)."

We can diagram a typical problem situation as shown in Figure 10-5. Note that while each force may have a different intensity, in concert they exert an impact of a particular degree. As an example, take the number of cigarettes consumed by young people in the United States per year. There may be forces such as holidays, exams, parties, etc., which increase consumption at certain times of the year. But basically, despite ups and downs in consumption, we can plot a trend line (our point of stability or equilibrium) that reflects the interaction of the driving and restraining forces.

Thus, if we wish to change the status of a current phenomenon (problem, difficulty, area of concern,) we have to diagnose the forces at work and then change (influence) certain of those forces. To illustrate, let's take the state of participation in our classroom. Let's assume it is at a particular level (low) and we would like to raise that level. Our diagnosis of the forces at work gives us the following data as displayed in a T-column.

Present Level of Participation

Driving Forces	Restraining Forces
Student complaints about dull classes	Too much lecture
New progressive Director of Training Center	Non-verbal participants
Training Department at corporate level concerned	Formal classroom atmosphere (desks, lectern, etc.)
Many new participative techniques are now available	Instructors not trained in participative methods
Etc.	Tradition, inertia
	Indifference
	Etc.

How might we alter this situation? Our change strategy can consist of (1) adding to or strengthening the driving forces, or (2) removing or weakening the restraining forces, or (3) doing both (1) and (2) in some combination.

Note: While increasing or strengthening the driving forces may work, one runs a big risk—that is, by applying pressure the response may be a natural one of resistance to that pressure. Hence, a more effective (less chancy) strategy is to eliminate or weaken the restraining forces and let the driving forces "take over." Thus, in our participation in the classroom example, we might remove a restraining force—too much lecture—via instruction in participative (group-in-action) training methods. This would be preferable to adding more driv-

Figure 10-5. An example of a force field analysis showing the forces at work that increase or reduce cigarette smoking by college students.

ing forces such as pep talks, memos and more (negative) participant feedback data.

To allow your participants to try diagnosing an existing force field of their own, a set of instructions and a diagram are provided in Appendix 38. It may be used on problems of the participants' choice (this is the recommended option) or one provided by the trainer.

Value Analysis

Value analysis (or value engineering) applies principles of group problem solving to reduce costs or to increase value. Its basic assumption is that any product or service can be refined, reengineered, or replanned to cut the costs of producing it.

Credit for the term is given to H. A. Winne, vice-president of engineering, General Electric Company. Under his direction GE began an intensive effort (in 1947) to identify the essential functions of consumer products as a means of lowering component costs. In the 1950s the Navy Department's Bureau of Ships launched a major value engineering program.[6]

The procedure for working on a value engineering problem is:

1. Analyzes the item in question as to function and cost. As an example, let's take a power lawnmower and describe its functions and costs (hypothetical):

Function	Cost
Power	$50.00
Cut	7.00
Control	10.00
Movement	10.00
Safety	25.00
Total	$100.00

Each of the above functions is then broken down further; e.g.,

Movement Function	Cost
Wheels	$ 5.00
Tires	3.00
Bearings	1.50
Bolts	.50
Total	$10.00

2. Ask cost improvement questions such as these:

☐ Can a smaller part be used?
☐ Can another (less expensive) type of material be used?
☐ Can a weight reduction in any part be accomplished?
☐ Can a part be bought more cheaply "on the outside?"
☐ Can any part be eliminated?
☐ Are all features necessary?

Another approach to value management/engineering is the "FAST" method, for Function Analysis System Technique. Here are its six-step procedures:[7]

1. *Information.* A function is reduced to a two-word definition, e.g., "kill mice," "remove staple," or "ripen melon." The value management task force team (people from different departments) gather all the data on the item: specs, cost, etc. These questions are used:
☐ What is the item?
☐ What does it do?
☐ What must it do?
☐ What must it cost?
☐ What else will do the job?
☐ What does that cost?

2. *Speculation.* Alternatives are brainstormed that fulfill or exceed the basic function of the service or product. Outside vendors may also be contacted for ideas. Negative thinking which serves as roadblocks to creativity is to be avoided. In the "kill mice" problem alternatives to the standard mouse trap might be a cat or a poison.

3. *Planning.* Ideas are ranked in terms of effectiveness and the "how" (ways and means) of implementation is developed. The major focus is on ideas which have greatest cost-benefit potential. In the kill mice problem it develops that an improved mouse trap, using lighter weight wood, was No. 1 and poison the alternative.

4. *Execution.* Unit and volume costs are figured along with a discussion of alternatives. Plans with proofs and models are forwarded to management. In our kill-mouse mission, proposals for both methods of eliminating mice are drawn up. Costs of mouse trap materials (spring and wood) and alternatives are calculated. Measurements of effectiveness for both alternatives are presented, too.

5. *Reporting.* Oral and written reports are presented to sell management on the proposal. The task force uses sketches, outlines alternatives, and highlights cost and performance gains.

6. *Implementation.* If management accepts the proposal, people are assigned specific implementation tasks, information is provided to all those who are involved/concerned, schedules are set, follow-up reports to management are prepared, etc. A responsible value engineer is assigned to monitor the project and to answer questions from plant personnel.

Similar approaches can be taken in respect to office activities, programs or projects. Again, the functions of each operation must be identified, cost factors assigned, and an analysis undertaken to reduce costs.

Note that in conventional cost-reduction programs the goal is to produce the same item at reduced cost; whereas in value analysis, which approaches the problem from a *functional* standpoint, a totally fresh, global, and open-ended attack is undertaken.

Also, while in the fullest sense of the term value engineering is a technical and professional function (e.g., its practitioners may belong to The Society of American Value Engineers, founded in 1959), the principles nevertheless can be used by non-professional personnel on many in-house projects where cost should (and can) be reduced.

Structured Analysis

Groups can be aided in working on their problems via "structure" provided by the trainer—worksheets, guidesheets, T-columns, etc. Structure serves these purposes:

☐ It provides a framework so participants know with certainty how to attack the problem. In the absence of such structure, feelings of "wheel spinning" and frustration are likely to develop.

☐ It provides a basis for self-checking: "Have we covered all bases?"

☐ It serves as a motivator by meeting the needs participants may have for completion. In effect, people are saying to themselves: "Hey, we have to fill up those empty columns."

Several examples of structured formats follow:

5-M Analysis. The traditional "M's" or resources of management—manpower, machinery, methods, materials, and money—can be used as a guide to diagnose what affects (hinders) a given operation or causes a problem. A sample worksheet for this purpose appears in Appendix 39.

Note:

1. Some groups may wish to add a sixth "M": *minutes,* reflecting a recognition that time is also a resource and may be poorly managed. Other groups, such as quality circles, typically drop "money" since it is not a factor in determining causes for defects in a product or the malfunctioning of a system or a procedure.

2. Causative data about the "M's" can be collected via individual ideation such as the slip method, group methods such as brainstorming and buzz groups, and/or general discussion by the group-at-large.

3. Structured analysis can also be used to learn why an operation, activity or project has been successful as well as why it has been problem laden.

7-S Analysis. A more "up-to-date" way of management problem solving is the 7-S approach developed by two business school professors—Richard Pascale of Stanford and Anthony Athos of Harvard. In their book *The Art of Japanese Management* (Simon and Schuster, 1981), they contrast Japanese and Western approaches to management. They refer to the three "hard S's" of Western management—structure, strategy, and systems—and the four "soft S's" of the Japanese—*superordinate goals, skills, style,* and *staff.* The latter "S's" relate to people: their values, uniqueness, talents, and process. Shared values are considered to be most central and the "secret weapon" of the Japanese.

The "7 S's," in combination, could be used by groups at various levels in the organization to assess their functioning. A chart, such as used in the 5-M Analysis, could be employed for this purpose.

T-column analysis. Problems facing groups can be put into better focus by framing (highlighting) them via the T-column. Dichotomizing and thus sharpening the issue challenges the group to a greater degree. The T-columns might address the advantages of an in-house program vs. using an outside consultant or the concerns of employees vs. management or short term gains vs. long term gains.

Analogy

An analogy is a direct comparison of things, concepts, etc. which have a similarity, for example, both a heart and a pump have similar actions. It is useful both as a data-generating device (Step 2 in the problem solving process) and as a tool to produce ideas or solutions about a problem (Step 3). The latter use is developed in more detail in Chapter 11.

Experiential training programs, having a heavy concern with personal growth, team building, etc., typically utilize such involving techniques as introspection, self-disclosure, feedback, and the like. However, at times, depending on the participant group, disclosure and feedback may not provide the hoped for involvement and learning. Consequently, other less direct techniques such an analogy may be more appropriate. Examples of the use of analogy as a data-generating tool are cited by two experiential trainers:[8]

☐ A personnel unit in a team building session would not acknowledge its problems. The trainers, therefore, introduced an exercise based on a fictitious company that required the participants to create an ideal personnel system. The result was that in the simulation the personnel managers gradually began to focus on (rather than deny) their own problems!

☐ A professional group was reluctant to be candid about its needs for professional growth so another analogy-type exercise was employed. The trainers gave each of the participants a hypothetical budget for their professional development. It consisted of the usual budgetary items such as an allotment of days, travel costs, tuition charges. The ground rule was that one's budget could be expended as one saw fit. As might be expected, the exercise "smoked out" honest disclosure about growth needs and real development opportunities.

In essence, the same learning goal may be achieved via alternate and sometimes less direct methods as in the preceding instances. Hence the need for analogy.

Working with Metaphors

A metaphor is "a figure of speech in which a word or phrase literally denoting one kind of object or idea is used in place of another to suggest a likeness or analogy between them" (per Webster's *New Collegiate Dictionary)*. In effect, it is a reference to one thing to suggest a resemblance to something else. When used in everyday speech or writing, metaphors help us to view a situation, concept, or behavior in ways which may be new, more concrete, or more vivid. In short, they create images. Some everyday examples:

"Gofers"	Voodoo	High and dry
Stonewalling	economics	Wallflower
Horseplay	Pig-in-a-poke	No shrinking
Brainstorming	Trojan horse	violet
Cogs in a wheel	Montezuma's	A real prima
(or in a	revenge	donna
machine)	Sacred cows	Gone
Bearhug	Saturday Night	Hollywood
Ivory tower	Special	Grapevine
Basket case	Paint yourself	Protecting one's
Star gazing	into a corner	turf
The ship of	Cold turkey	Paper shuffler
state	Trickle-down	Wool gathering
	theory	

Note that these metaphors are brief, using only a single word or a phrase. Metaphors may also be more lengthy and involved, their impact depending on the way the metaphor is developed in its many facets. In effect, the metaphor user, having stated the metaphor, then talks about the subject in metaphorical terms. Several examples of such metaphors follow.

The Boston Globe, in discussing roles of female entrepreneurs, said "the metaphor of bearing a child and watching it grow was repeated constantly by the women entrepreneurs to describe their feelings about their ventures. One of the great joys, they say, is creating something where there had been nothing."[9]

Industrial psychologist Harry Levinson uses the metaphor of the spider's web to help us understand better the importance of interpersonal communication.[10] He asks us to visualize the spider positioned at the web's center, listening for vibrations to alert it to other life at the web's periphery—its mate, possible prey, and/or enemies. In other words, the spider is constantly sensing, seeking out information which is basic to its survival.

We, too, says Levinson, occupy a central point in relation to others. Some people are close at hand, other farther off. But the closeness-distance dimension is *not* only a physical concept. It also has emotional significance. That is to say, some people are close to us emotionally, some are distant; some send strong and clear signals to us, regardless of their physical distance; some can only send weak or unclear signals. Of course, some of us may be more tuned in to these signals, whether strong or weak, than are others.

But regardless of our perception or awareness of these signals, they represent "connections" with others, hookups which all of us require to the fullest extent. Why? Because they can provide affection and support as well sheer information. They keep us from being isolated and from having to sort out these signals without the aid of others. Man, as a social being, can hardly function without full interchange with others. Sometimes isolation can, of course, produce creativity; more typically it produces distress. In sum, the images, thoughts, fantasies that we constantly create in our heads can only be understood and thus managed by interaction with others.

Dr. Levinson asks us, then, to study the vibes in our own web. How strong and clear are the signals? Who sends them to us? From what (emotional) distance? What is the content of the signals? Do they give us information, support, approval, intimacy? What happens if a signal fades due to death or other separations? Do we lose support? Do we replace the signal? With whom? Some people only give us information; others a lot of emotional richness. Levinson concludes his metaphor by saying: "But perhaps the most important thing is the knowledge that the web exists—that we will pick up whatever vibrations are sent out, because we are connected."

A metaphor to point up man's tendencies to resist change is the "Wallenda complex." It relates to the late Karl Wallenda of the famous Wallenda family of high-wire circus performers. Karl Wallenda, a performer until his death in his seventies, had learned early in his childhood to use his 16-foot pole for balance. He was told repeatedly he would always be safe and balanced if he used his pole.

Wallenda accepted a challenge of walking a high wire between two buildings, ten stories above ground level. It was a windy day and Wallenda nearly lost his balance, but regained it with the aid of his pole. As he continued across the wire, a sudden strong gust hit him hard and he began to fall. He could have caught hold of the wire as he went down, but he did not. Why not? Because he did what he had been taught to do—to hold tightly to the pole. The unfortunate result: Wallenda hit a taxi on the city street below, still holding on to his pole.

Rick Thyne, an international peace advocate, used the tragic Wallenda experience as a metaphor to describe the current arms race. He said: "We, too, are on a high wire . . . we're determined to hold on to our pole—our weapons—as we have been taught. We think that in them lies our only safety. And we may die believing that.

"We can let go of our old learning. We can still try to catch the wire. That doesn't mean we'll be safe, but at least we'll have a chance to struggle back to the window." [11]

Trainers will be interested in a metaphor used to describe "quiet leadership" of the training department, i.e., doing the job but giving the line departments credit for effective training results. The metaphor is not leaving any fingerprints which permit the tracking of a project to the training department. It was cited at the 1980 A.S.T.D. conference in an awards presentation to a corporate trainer at Ford Motor Co.: "When Duke Schmidt left corporate training at Ford . . . his staff gave him a framed picture with five fingerprints in it, because Duke's management philosophy was that the training department never took credit for anything—never left its fingerprints on any project. They put out a brochure at the end of the year and all the brochure contained were examples of the divisions in Ford solving performance problems." [12]

Examples in the training situation. In the training situation, too, we can help participants to generate data about problems and to see problems, concepts, behaviors, etc., in new lights or more concretely, by having them work with or construct metaphors. Several examples follow.

☐ In a leadership session or course, give participants the worksheet in Appendix 40 to complete individually, and then have them discuss it in small groups. Conclude the activity by securing comments from each small group.

☐ Have participants individually analyze their leadership or management style by drawing on an analysis and description of the three major U.S. sports. How coordination is achieved by the manager or coach is the major differentiating factor among the three games.

1. *Baseball:* Highly independent player action, with the necessary coordination of a highly general sort being achieved by the manager; e.g., the latter can hardly predict a double play or direct its execution should the opportunity arise. At the most, he can advise his players to try to make one, if possible, because there are less than two outs and there are one or more players on base. Of course, this is hardly unexpected advice to his professional infielders who have handled double plays innumerable times in their careers. Baseball is essentially a game of *autonomy*.

2. *Football:* Coordination comes from above, top-down direction from the head coach. Visualize him constantly signaling in each play from the sidelines. He even has observers in the stands to provide him with intelligence to sharpen his many de-

cisions. His assistant coaches on defense, offense, and special teams constantly provide further inputs to ensure that everyone stays with the game plan. The result: each player has a minute piece of the action. Football represents *control*.

3. *Basketball:* The coach is the catalyst who provides coordination to the spontaneous interaction of the players themselves. The game is so fast paced and interdependent that the coach can hardly orchestrate in detail the many moves and plays the players make on a minute-to-minute basis. Basketball represents *voluntary cooperation*, free-form team work.[13]

After everyone has decided on his/her current managerial style, have participants meet in small groups to discuss (1) the adequacy of one's current style to meet the unit's needs; (2) the nature of the boss' style; (3) if one wishes to change one's style, which one would be most appropriate, given one's personality, management philosophy, the nature of the work itself, and the nature of the group being supervised; and (4) if a change is to be accomplished, how would one go about it?

☐ In a supervisory or management training program you may want the participants to reflect on how employees really see their organization. You thus might ask them to:

1. Take a sheet of paper and jot down some answers to the following question: "If we were to ask our employees to imagine our company *as a person*, what kind of person might they describe?" (Some possible answers: An energetic youth; an old man with a pot belly; an erect, sturdy middle-aged person; a happy giant; a relaxed, care-free person; a cold, insensitive miser. Allow five minutes or so for this.)
2. Meet in small groups (three to five persons) and discuss their metaphors. "See if you can agree on the kind of person that best describes our organization, as our employees are likely to see it. You have 15 minutes for this."
3. Share their metaphors with the group at large.

☐ In a session concerned with problem solving, creativity, imagineering, etc., give the participants the following task to point up how our possible rigid attitudes and conventional thinking may hinder our creativity or originality.

1. "In small groups have participants come up with as many metaphors—descriptive words or phrases—

they use regularly to connote such concepts as "flight from reality," "ignoring the real world," "narrow mindedness." To start them off say: "'Head in the sand' would be an example of flight from reality; 'tunnel vision' would be an example of narrowmindedness. You have 20 minutes for this."
2. Tell them: "O.K., let's get some data from each group." Process the data with a T-column, as in the following example.

Metaphors Indicating

Flight From Reality	Narrowmindedness
Living in a cocoon	Wearing blinders
Ostrich mentality	Blind side
Head in the clouds	Can't see beyond one's nose
Blue sky thinking	Going by the book
No man is an island	Throwing out the baby with the bath water
Maginot Line psychology	
Dream world	Penny wise and pound foolish
Ivory tower	

☐ In a leadership program or management retreat, it may be desirable to encourage participants to think about the nature (character) of organizations in general and possibly their organization in particular. If so, the task[14] in the worksheet in Appendix 41 may stimulate such thinking.

Complete the exercise by securing group reports, posting their data on flipcharts, and discussing the implications of the data for organizations (or your organization).

☐ In a human relations/communications program, metaphor as a data-generating device may be used to develop closer relationships among participants. For example, participants in a dyad may be assigned this task: "Write a metaphor to describe your partner."

The metaphors are written as instructed, then shared with one's partner, and on a volunteer basis, several may be read to the total group. Two examples of metaphors developed by dyadic partners in response to the preceding task follow. Note that the first one deals quite directly with the person and her work, whereas the second one is written as a fairy tale. (The latter metaphor was based on the fact that Kim had indicated earlier to Joyce that he engaged in vegetable gardening as a hobby.)

1. "My partner, Joyce, is the prototype of the good baseball coach. She is concerned about uncovering developmental needs, has patience to work on

those needs, and uses empathy plus her professional skills to bring about the needed change. She is on the lookout for new techniques, recognizes individual differences, is content to settle for small changes in difficult cases. She relates well to the trainees/pupils/students/clients and has a knack of gaining their confidence so they will trust her. Her skills and attitudes should make for a lot of home runs and a winning team."

2. "Kim was the best gardener in the village of 'Plenty.' No one in the kingdom grew bigger, better, or more squash.

"One day he said: 'Oh, if only these squash would turn to gold how rich I would be.'

"Lo and behold the next morning he found several squash had turned to gold! He was astonished and wondered why *this* wish had been granted, when so many others had never been answered.

"What he didn't realize was that it happened because his heart had also 'turned to gold.' He now had the ability to turn all he touched to gold if he desired."

Analogies Vs. Metaphors

An analogy is a direct comparison with a similar thing, object, idea. For example, we may compare the manager to the nurturing parent, for both are concerned with the growth of those for whom he/she has responsibility.

In contrast to the analogy, a metaphor is a reference to one thing, object, idea, person, etc., to suggest a reference to something else, e.g., "The Ship of State" in relation to government or the batter drove a *clothesline* to right field.

Although metaphors are more potent than analogies because they encourage (demand) a greater change of perspective, both help participants to see new principles, relationships, possibilities, and the like.[15] As figurative tools, they are useful to both Steps 2 and 3 of the problem solving process; that is, to generate data and to produce ideas or solutions about a problem.

Imaging

According to management psychologist Dr. Warren H. Schmidt of U.C.L.A., groups can improve their problem-solving capacity significantly by assuming or thinking of a problem as already solved! The first procedure involved, then, is to visualize or imagine (engage in "imaging") what the situation would be like with a solution in effect.

Second, have participants imagine the conditions that existed just *before* the solution was produced; also, visu-alize the changes that might have influenced that final increment of improvement. Now have the group work backward, step by step, until it reaches the current (unsolved) status.

In general, the idea is that we can understand much better the first steps—identified last in the imaging process—because we have shifted from "the fetters" of our usual and ordinary forward-looking ways of attacking a problem to our novel, idea-provoking, rear-ended approach. The imaging process lets us create our own panoramic view of the situation, with the helpful option of tracing causes/events backward and thus understanding more objectively the forces and factors at work.[16]

Another form of imaging or visualizing is to have the group reduce to writing the conditions that will exist once the problem or difficulty is resolved. The next step is to have participants think positively and creatively about how to ensure that those conditions can be made to reach fruition.

Brainstorming

Brainstorming is a versatile problem solving tool. It is extremely useful in the first three stages of the problem solving process; that is, to:

☐ Identify problems for resolution
☐ Generate ideas (about causes, about the problem)
☐ Generate solutions to resolve an identified problem

Brainstorming is described in detail in Chapter 11 under Step 3—How to generate ideas (solutions) about the problem for its resolution.

Some common examples of the use of brainstorming to generate data about a problem (causes, effects, etc.) are these:

☐ A group of factory workers in a quality circle identify the causes for a high reject rate on products produced in their department.
☐ A sales/marketing group identifies the reasons why a new product is not moving.
☐ A personnel office group develops a "bug list" concerning the ineffective operation of the company's suggestion plan.

Other Idea-Producing Techniques

Another technique to help generate data about a problem is "the journalist's six questions"—who? what? when? where? why? and how? This technique is described in more detail in Chapter 12 dealing with additional approaches to problem solving.

Various techniques are useful for *both* Steps 2 and 3 in the problem solving process. These techniques—brainstorming, the slip method, card posting techniques, etc.—are discussed in detail in Chapter 11 under Step 3.

Key Points

1. Training programs that teach managers and others to solve their problems are being demanded more and more by organizations.
2. Training in problem solving should begin with a workable model. A five-step model for this is one that involves defining the problem, generating data (causes, effects) about it, generating various courses of action (solutions), choosing (deciding) among the alternatives, and implementing the decision.
3. Problem definition (Step 1 in the model) may be accomplished via Pareto's analysis, brainstorming, statistical approaches, checklists, and problem identification—ABC approach.
4. Brainstorming may be used to identify (define) the problem, determine its causes, and produce solutions about it. Key principles in brainstorming are quantity in ideation and deferred judgment.
5. To generate data about a problem (Step 2 in the model), including cause and effect factors, these techniques are useful: force field analysis, value analysis, structured analysis, analogy, metaphor, imaging, brainstorming, the journalist's six questions, the slip method and card posting techniques.

References

1. Stredl, Henry J., and Rothwell, William J., *The ASTD Reference Guide To Professional Training Roles and Competencies,* ASTD Press and HRD Press, 1987.
2. Yates, L., "Wrestling the Alligators," *Northeast Training News* (September 1980), p. 12.
3. "Creativity: Looking for the Right Questions," *Leading Edge Bulletin* (September 28, 1981), pp. 1–2.
4. Murphy, D., "When a Problem Is Not a Problem," *Northeast Training News* (December 1979), p. 12.
5. *Bulletin on Training* (November–December 1978), p. 7.
6. Tocco, A. R., "Value Engineering (Value Analysis)," *The Encyclopedia of Management,* 3rd edition, Van Nostrand Reinhold Company, New York, 1982, pp. 1,277–1,283.
7. "Value Management—What Comes After Quality," *Productivity* (December 1983), pp. 8–11.
8. Margolis, F., and Bell, C., "Making Organization Development Work at the Department Level," *Training/HRD* (September 1981), pp. 116–119.
9. Quoted in *The Levinson Letter* (October 1, 1981), p. 3.
10. *The Levinson Letter* (December 1981), p. 2.
11. *Leading Edge Bulletin* (November 30, 1981), p. 2.
12. Cited by McCampbell, J. F., "Six Guiding Images to Measure Training Results," *Training/HRD* (September 1981), p. 38.
13. "Game Plans and Sports Strategies," *Training News* (January 1986), p. 4 (based on an interview of Robert Keidel of the Wharton Applied Research Center, University of Pennsylvania, as reported initially in *Inc.,* November 1985).
14. The entire task, slightly modified, is borrowed liberally from a presentation made by Dr. Warren H. Schmidt, a leading trainer and educator at U.C.L.A., at the 1980 Annual Conference of the American Society for Training and Development, Anaheim, California.
15. Yates, L., "Wrestling the Alligators," *Northeast Training News* (September 1980), pp. 12–13, 19.
16. Giegold, W. C., *Objective Setting and the MBO Process,* Vol. II, McGraw Hill Publishing Company, New York (1978), p. 183.

Recommended Reading

Bial, Boris, "Eight Steps To Successful Problem Solving," *Supervisory Management,* January 1986, pp. 7–9.

The author presents an eight-step problem-solving model, the last step being one not found in most models: know what alternative action can be taken if the original decision fails.

Goddard, Robert W., "The Vital Few and the Trivial Many," *Personnel Journal,* July 1987, pp. 30–34.

The article presents a solid overview of Pareto's Law and provides guidelines to apply it to one's own job. The bottom line: spend most of your effort on the critically few but vital tasks.

Phillips, Steven R., and Bergquist, William H., "Focusing Problem Management," *Training and Development Journal,* March 1987, pp. 87–89.

The writer advocates a three-step problem-solving model called "STP" for *situation* (what is the current state?), *target* (what is the desired state or goal?) and *proposal* (identifies the path from situation to target and defines the strategy/plan to make the change).

"Involve Your People In Organizational Problem Solving," *Training and Development Journal,* July 1987, pp. 73–74.

A three-step problem solving model is presented: *data gathering,* which includes problem definition, *problem solving* which encompasses finding alternatives and choosing among them, and *action planning.* Stress is placed on the need for consensus at all stages of the process to secure *commitment*.

GENERATING SOLUTIONS TO A PROBLEM

If you continue to think the way
You always thought
You will continue to get
What you always got
Is it enough?

—Anon.

There is always an easy solution to every human
problem—neat, plausible and wrong.

—H. L. Mencken (1880–1956),
American journalist, essayist,
critic, and lexicographer

In the prior chapter we learned about the first two steps (skill areas) in the problem-solving process: "How to define the problem" and "How to generate data about the problem." We are now ready to learn about Step 3: "How to generate solutions or ideas for resolving the problem."

Devices for generating ideas or solutions to a problem are abundant. Described below are a number of these techniques, including:

☐ Brainstorming
☐ The slip method
☐ Nominal group technique
☐ The Delphi technique
☐ Ideawriting
☐ Card posting techniques
☐ Client-centered approach to problem solving
☐ Upside down problem solving
☐ Check lists, attribute listing, morphological analysis, and forced relationships
☐ Using analogy
☐ PCT approach and analogy
☐ The Gordon technique

Brainstorming

One of the oldest forms of systematic group problem solving (introduced in the 1950s) is brainstorming. Originally developed in the U.S. advertising industry, it has been used in all kinds of organizations, worldwide. Its basic tenet is to separate idea creation from idea evaluation. Why? Because if the two processes are combined, ideation is likely to suffer. Visualize these typical reactions anyone of us might have to a new idea:

"Good theory, but it'll never work."
"We've tried that one before."
"It conflicts with current policies."
"The boss (or headquarters, or the field) won't go for it."
"Sounds expensive."
"It might set a precedent."
"Not in the budget."
"Is this the time for it?"
"Let's not rush into *that.*"
"But our people (or customers) are different."
"What about the extra people to implement it?"

Many more of these "killer phrases" could be added. The point is that if you or I come up with an idea and someone reacts negatively to it, it isn't very likely to encourage further ideation on our part. Conversely, if all of our ideas are accepted (recorded) without evaluation, we'll keep contributing.

Brainstorming works best with a group of 6–12 people, a recorder, and a moderater who encourages ideation: "We've produced twenty-eight ideas in four minutes; let's see if we can get another dozen more." The moderator may ring a bell (a cow bell would work well) if someone expresses a negative reaction to an idea in the idea-generating phase.

Brainstorming in the training situation may be programmed or it may be used informally, that is, as the need arises. By programming, we mean including it in the training design on a planned basis. For example, in a customer relations course participants may be asked to brainstorm the benefits or characteristics of a particular product, or in a supervisory training course, participants may be asked to brainstorm key points for developing a check list to ensure that new employee orientation is conducted properly.

Informal or *ad hoc* brainstorming may occur in a variety of ways; e.g., the trainer may hit a dull or dead spot in a session and thus may ask the group to brainstorm ways to teach this topic more creatively or imaginatively; in a management development seminar, should a discussion arise about the ineffective nature of staff meetings, the trainer may suggest the use of brainstorming to come up with ways to pep up such meetings. In general, the trainer should be alert for opportunities to say: "Why don't we brainstorm it?"

Encourage participants to use brainstorming back on the job by showing its versatility in different settings and situations. Typical examples of brainstorming topics in different locales are the following:

☐ In advertising: How to sell a video recorder to all households.
☐ In the community: How to improve the local transportation system. How to make our home town more beautiful. How to collect taxes more effectively.
☐ At home: How to cut down on expenditures. How to improve the garden. What shall we take along on a motor trip to Canada? What do we give Aunt Nellie for Christmas?
☐ On the job: How do we deal with litterbugging in this park? What shall we do with employees who are passed over for promotion? How can we reduce motor vehicle accidents by our drivers? How do we make this year's Christmas party different or more successful?

The rules for brainstorming are these:

No critical remarks are allowed. If the bell rings while you're speaking, it means you're breaking this rule. Remember, the basic principle of brainstorming is *deferred judgment.*

"Hitchhiking" is O.K. If you can improve on someone else's idea, or combine two or more fragments of ideas that others have offered, so much the better!

"Free wheeling" is welcomed. The "wilder" the ideas the better; it's easier to tame them down than pump them up. Free-wheeling also helps to keep the group pepped up.

Quantity is wanted. The percentage of usable ideas that comes out of the average brainstorming session typically is quite small. Obviously, the more ideas, the more winners! Out of quantity will come quality.

Evaluation comes later. Hold a screening and evaluation session *after* the idea generating session.

To conduct a brainstorming session properly, these procedures *will* help:

1. Narrow or limit the problem. People need a finite problem they can tackle.
2. Limit the group to 6–12 persons.
3. Work in a circle.
4. Keep it informal; refreshments may help.
5. Each person gives only *one* idea at a time.
6. A chairperson (moderator, trainer) is necessary to lead and encourage "ideation," especially when it lags.
7. A recorder (two are even better) is necessary to record ideas. This is best done on a flipchart because visibility of the ideas is a stimulus to added ideation.
8. Keep the tempo quick-paced to keep everyone alert and the ideas flowing.
9. Use praise concerning volume, not individual ideas, to keep the ideas flowing: "That's great, group; let's see if we can get another dozen." We avoid saying a *particular* idea is "great" or "terrific" for it may imply the others are not.
10. If the group is new to brainstorming, use a "warm-up" topic before the real effort; e.g., "What uses can we make of a ball of cord (or a brick)?"

Newer Approaches

To update brainstorming, a number of variations developed in recent years merit citation.

Reverse Approach

In our usual brainstorming sessions we want positive thinking—new ideas, new solutions, new procedures, new uses. Using the reverse procedure, we approach our problem or concern in a *negative* way; that is, we assume that the way to make things "right" is to identify first the things that are "wrong." So we list all the deficiencies we can of a policy, procedure, product, etc. and then brainstorm ways to overcome these short-comings. For example, assume our problem is to reduce crime in our city. We can stimulate new thinking about this concern by asking: How can we *increase* crime in city X? Some possible answers are to give guns away, leave doors unlocked, reduce lights on the street, reduce the size of police force, disarm the police, increase heroin usage, reduce punishment, increase the time it takes to get the accused to court.

Rotational Ideation

Ideas can be presented in the brainstorming circle in sequence on a one person-at-a-time basis. The trainer or moderator obviously has to exercise more "control" over member contributions than in conventional, free-flowing, contagion-oriented brainstorming. The advantage of this orderly procedure is that it encourages everyone to get into the act. The disadvantage is that the spontaneity, the stimulating "disorder" of everyone shouting out ideas, almost at once, is lost.

Note: This technique is similar to "the whip," wherein the trainer whips around the circle in a rotational way to elicit ideas from everyone.

If one does not have an idea to offer, "pass" is stated. The procedure continues until *everyone* says "pass."

SIL Method

SIL, a German acronym for "Successive Integration of Problem Elements," entails these procedures:[1]

1. Ideas about a problem are generated in writing on an individual basis.
2. The written ideas are read aloud by two group participants.
3. The other group members try to integrate those two ideas into *one* solution.
4. A third participant reads his/her idea.
5. The group integrates the third idea with the solution obtained in step 3.
6. The integration process proceeds until all ideas are tapped.

Note: Not all ideas may be used, but all are heard and given a try in the integration process.

Developing Creative Alternatives

Trainer/consultant Harold Scharlatt builds on the brainstorming technique to enhance creativity in this manner:[2]

1. Present the usual objections/misgivings managers (and others) may have about creative thinking approaches, e.g., "I'm not the creative type," "That's impossible," "They'll never go for it," "I

might appear foolish," "It's not logical (or practical)," "We're making assumptions," etc.

2. For each of these objections, doubts or fears, ask for ways to overcome them. For example: "It's not logical" can be countered with "No, it's *creative*," or "It's not exactly right" can be responded to with: "We don't want perfection—yet."

   Note: Steps 1 and 2 are designed to confront gently people's doubts and fears and thus break down some of their self-imposed barriers to their creativity.

3. *Clarify the mission/goal/problem.* What decision on our part requires fresh, new possibilities?
4. *To secure alternatives,* brainstorm the problem or concern in two or more sub-groups: How can we accomplish our goals?
5. Have each buzz group expand its list based on a review of the other list(s).
6. *Choose the most outlandish ideas.* Have each participant write down three of the most preposterous/weird/impractical ideas which are in this (or another) list: Which ones look crazy?
7. Record all the wild ideas on a flipchart.
8. As a group, list all the *positive attributes* of each wild idea. Search for the positive attributes, the good points, in each.
9. Divide participants into small groups. Their task is to *combine* two or more of the ideas to create a new alternative: How can we merge two or more ideas into one so that it maximizes the positive characteristics of the original components?
10. Secure participants' *concerns* (lack of practicality) about each alternative.
11. In small groups or as a total group discuss this concern: Why is the idea not perfect?
12. In the same group configuration, discuss *ways to overcome* these concerns: What can we do to overcome these anxieties or fears?
13. *Identify acceptable attributes:* Which of these ideas have enough positive attributes, balanced with manageable concerns, to be considered an alternate for evaluation?

The theory behind these sequential procedures it that it neither disrupts the logic behind sound decision making nor people's needs to move ahead comfortably in developing and selecting unique, creative alternatives.

Rolestorming

In traditional brainstorming some participants may be reluctant or even afraid to offer their wildest ideas, something which brainstorming typically seeks. One way to secure wacky ideas is to allow participants to attribute them to someone else, e.g., the boss, a peer, or a subordinate. Procedurally, after each brainstormer has given his/her ideas, have them adopt a new identity and then toss out ideas as they believe the absent person would conceive them. Sample statement: "The person I've identified would favor a *daily* newspaper to all employees" (as a response to improvement of organizational communication).

According to Richard E. Griggs of Management Fitness Systems, Inc., Mountain View, California, the added process of rolestorming—so named because it combines features of role playing and brainstorming—can increase a group's idea production by 60%–70% and up their quality significantly, too.[3]

Pause That Refreshes

As has been indicated, brainstorming typically involves a rapid-fire burst of ideation, a count of the quantity of ideas produced, praise by the trainer for the idea generation, and a return to ideation with encouragement to produce more ideas. A variation of this basic procedure is to begin with ideation, follow this with a silent period for "renewal" of group energy and creativity and return to the ideation phase again. Ideation and pauses may be "programmed," too, for example, a three-to-four-minute burst of ideas is encouraged, an equal period of silence is introduced, and then ideation proceeds again for three to four minutes. The pause may be longer, too—a few hours or a day or two.

Overcoming Boredom, Frustration, Etc.

Even highly imaginative groups may find that, on occasion, "the well has run dry." When that occurs, creative thinking authority T. Rickards recommends these measures to get the group back into its creative mode:[4]

Trigger sessions. Ideas are first generated independently and silently and then read aloud to the group. Members then are encouraged to hitchhike or build on those ideas.

Recorded round robin. Everyone is given a card bearing the problem with instructions to add a new idea thereon. The card then is passed on to a fellow participant who adds an idea, which has been triggered by the prior idea. Cards are passed around several times.

Wildest idea. Each participant is asked for the most "far-out" ideas imaginable. The others use this stimulus to produce as many new ideas as possible.

Creativity via Environmental Changes

To increase ideation after an initial start, try changing the environment, e.g., close (or open) the blinds; open (or close) the door; turn on the lights; replace the re-

corder and/or the moderator with another person; switch to a new color of felt tip pens; move the flipchart easel to a new position in the room; rearrange participants so they are in different chairs; have everyone stand up and stretch or yell aloud, "Creativity;" execute the task standing up in a circle.

Experimental Approach

To prove the efficacy of brainstorming, give a trained group (i.e., one familiar with or instructed in brainstorming) and an untrained group the same problem in the same time frame (about five minutes). The problem should be one that is likely to generate a lot of ideas; e.g., how to manage time or how to use a secretary most effectively. Appoint an observer to note what helped/hindered the group's ideation.

Let the two groups brainstorm in separate rooms. Then compare their results. Ordinarily, the trained group should be much more effective (i.e., having a greater pool of ideas) than the untrained one. If not, the observer may shed some light on the atypical difference in results.

Evaluation Aid

A power of brainstorming lies in *deferred judgment.* Thus, ideation always proceeds independently from the possible "onslaught" of evaluation. One way to make the evaluation process more challenging and objective is to have the group select two ideas from the total list: the most bizarre and the most appealing. Then ask the group: What conditions would have to be met to make each idea—the bizzare one and the appealing one—work?

The rationale for this procedure: Something that looks ludicrous on the surface may not be that at all when the group gives it a fair trial.

Disadvantages of Brainstorming

Generation of many ideas in a short time frame and in a fun way are the main reasons for the popularity of brainstorming. However, it also has several limitations:[5]

☐ It is not useful as a problem solving tool where trial and error as opposed to judgment is vital.
☐ It often produces only superficial (low-quality) ideas.
☐ It works best when the problem is simple, specific, or limited.
☐ Recognition for one's ideas is not possible (all ideas go on the flipchart anonymously); on the other hand, most people seem to respond favorably to the procedure of having their ideas posted publicly.

Hence the need for other techniques to help solve problems. A number of these are given in the following paragraphs.

The Slip Method

A productive, rapid, and highly participative means of identifying problems and solving them is to use "the slip method."[6] This entails writing ideas on slips of paper on an individual basis. The completed slips are grouped into logical categories and then analyzed. Procedurally, the method requires these steps:

1. State the problem or difficulty being faced, using "how to" language, since people respond well to a challenge. That is to say, such language encourages them to think in action terms. Some examples are: How can we reduce litterbugging in this park? How can we improve relations with our customers? How can we save energy in this plant? How can we ensure a safe working environment? How can we raise morale?

   Note: These questions are designed to elicit solutions to known problems. A prior step may be to identify problems, for example: What are the things which keep us from being fully effective (or more competitive or more profitable)? What needs changing in our organization?

2. Pass out a large quantity of 3″ × 5″ slips to each participant. Slips should be purchased (preferred procedure) or cut up from full-size sheets of bond paper in advance of the problem-solving session. Don't use cards since they look "expensive" and may inhibit some people from writing on many of them. The whole idea, as in brainstorming, is that many ideas are wanted. Basically, this is a "brain-picking" process. Instruct participants to put only one idea, tersely stated, on a slip. Tell them not to worry about economizing on paper, that they should use a lot of slips.

   Visualize a small group of ten people engaged in this process. If each participant averaged only 10 ideas, we would have 100 of them in short order. With 15 participants, possibly 150 ideas could be generated.

3. Provide participants with these specific instructions:

   a. Organizing the slips will be easier if everyone writes the same way on the slips, so turn the slips so that the long sides are on the top and bottom.
   b. Write at the *top* of the slip. (This will help you, as trainer, to arrange the slips, one under the other.)
   c. Write only one idea per slip.

   Note: It is a good idea to collect a handful of slips from a few writers to ensure that your instructions are being followed.

4. Keep the writers at work, since the first few ideas may be the more common or obvious ones. More ideation, "going deeper in the well," should produce more novelty and quality.
5. After the group has been "drained dry," collect the slips and group them into appropriate categories. Discard duplicates, ambiguous and illegible items, etc.
6. If the first round of activity entails identification of problems or difficulties, use the second round to garner solutions. Each problem, stated in "how to" fashion, is treated procedurally as in step 3. Each participant is given another batch of slips to produce solutions to the problems that were identified. If problems are specialized in character, subgrouping with "specialists" may be in order.

The slip method is particularly useful to:

☐ Ensure full participation
☐ Generate a large number of ideas quickly
☐ Guarantee privacy or anonymity to contributors
☐ Aid those who are more skilled via the written rather than the oral medium
☐ Generate ideas on an individual rather than on a group (interactive) basis

The major shortcoming of this method is that the contagion of the group, as in brainstorming and other group methods, is not utilized. Some trainers or discussion leaders may also feel that the procurement and handling of slips is a burdensome procedure.

If it is desired to make the method more "groupy," a procedure such as the one in Appendix 10 may be used.

Another important use of the slip method, in addition to problem solving as discussed, is to create a manual, guidebook, or text. The procedures are:

1. Round up a group of experts on the subject of concern.
2. Give them a batch of slips and instruct them on slip-method procedures.
3. Have them list on slips the major chapters for the book (in "how to" fashion) and collect them.
4. Have a panel review the slips and decide on the chapter headings.
5. Working with one chapter at a time, have participants list subheads (subtopics) for the chapter. Collect slips.
6. Have the panel screen slips to decide on the subtopics.
7. Have the group develop answers or solutions, on slips, to each subtopic.

The end-result is a detailed outline, complete with answers to topical areas. The text per se can be developed in relation to the material garnered on the slips.

Nominal Group Technique

The NGT, developed by Andre Delbecq and Andrew Van de Ven at the University of Wisconsin in 1968, is a relatively new technique.[7] It brings people together for problem solving, but limits their interaction so that ideation will not suffer due to premature evaluation, social pressures, etc. The term "nominal" is used because true or full verbal communications of the group is not employed.

NGT employs the following procedures:

1. A group of five to nine problem solvers are assembled at a table. They are given a written question and asked to "ideate" *individually* and *silently* on that sheet of paper for five to ten minutes. (A more complex problem may take more time.)
2. Going around the table, each participant presents *one* idea at a time from his/her list.
3. The moderator records these ideas on a flipchart.
4. After posting all ideas, the group discusses them, providing clarification, support, or nonsupport for the posted ideas. Hitchhiking on others' ideas is encouraged.
5. Participants vote individually (rank-ordering) on the ideas. This statistical procedure produces a group decision, either on the first or a later ballot.

Note that unlike other group problem-solving techniques, consensus through discussion is subordinated to simple mathematical pooling of individual judgments. Whether this is a plus or a minus will depend upon how one feels about the importance of "working through" (full and open group discussion) a problem for a group decision.

As to its advantages, NGT does separate the fact-finding and ideating activities from the evaluation phase of the problem-solving process. It also balances participation, avoiding the not-unusual problem of the eager beavers taking things over. Good results can be produced in a short 60–90 minutes, and it is easily learned by participants.

The nature of the NGT is such that it does have some limitations: A very able and objective trainer is needed, i.e., one who enforces the rules (especially the nonverbal aspects) and refrains from amplifying the stated question or endeavoring to influence group thinking; the question to the group must be very precisely stated or the results will be less than expected; since group interaction is limited, it may not produce a true consensus.

NGT Rating Procedures

In step 5, the participants ranked the ideas in their small groups. A sample rating procedure follows.

1. Assume there are five or six groups of five participants each (part of a larger group of 25–30 people). The small groups are asked to come up with one powerful solution to a problem presented to them.
2. In each small group the participants present their ideas to the group. The individual ideas are *not* evaluated, although they may be discussed to ensure understanding.
3. Each idea in the small group is rated by the other participants on a five-point scale. This produces a set of scores for a given group as given in Figure 11-1.

Participant	Idea A	Idea B	Idea C	Idea D	Idea E
A	X	3	2	3	1
B	4	X	3	3	3
C	2	2	X	4	4
D	2	1	3	X	4
E	2	1	2	5	X
Total Points	10	7	10	15	12

Note: *Participants only rate their colleagues' ideas, not their own.*

Figure 11-1. A record of NGT scores for a hypothetical group.

The best idea from each small group might be subject to another round of ratings, as in the preceeding step 3, or a panel of judges might do the rating. In either case, the best idea will receive the highest point score.

Note: The NGT, like brainstorming, is useful for identifying problems (Step 1 of the problem-solving process) and determining causes (Step 2) as well as generating ideas for solutions to the identified problem (Step 3).

The Delphi Technique

The Delphi technique (named after the "Delphic Oracle") is a consensus-seeking device wherein anonymous ideas are generated and then run through a filter, but without any group interaction and discussion. (The technique has been referred to as "absentee brainstorming.") Initially developed to elicit individual ideas solely "through the mail," it has been adapted more recently to group use. Both formats are described below to ensure full understanding of their procedures and potentialities. Trainers can use the Delphi to forecast training needs.

Original Format

The Delphi technique was originally developed as a forecasting tool by the RAND Corporation (credited to Norman Dalkey and colleagues) in the early 1950s. It is now used for problem solving as well as forecasting. Its key tenet is to seek consensus from experts and avoid confrontation. Procedurally, it operates as follows:

1. Experts are selected to work on a given problem, policy, or issue by a decision-making team.
2. Questionnaires are developed by a staff unit and mailed to the participants in the study.
3. The respondents complete the questionnaire individually and mail it back to the staff unit.
4. The staff unit summarizes all responses from the experts, develops a second questionnaire, and mails it back to the respondents with a request to reconsider their ideas in light of the new or composite opinions.
5. The experts vote on or rank ideas as to priority and return their responses to the staff team.
6. The staff team prepares a final summary and feedback report, which is sent to both the respondent and decision-making groups.

Three to five rounds of questionnaires and rankings may be necessary to secure consensus. The decision makers then take it from there.[8]

Advantages

The Delphi technique works best under these conditions:

☐ Participants can't be brought together for group discussion purposes because of geographical or scheduling problems.
☐ Participants are strong individual thinkers, working better without group interaction.
☐ Since the experts involved engage in what is essentially an anonymous debate with opinions being exchanged through a removed neutral party, problems of over-protecting one's ideas, domination of group discussions by high-status or highly verbal types, and acquiescence to group think need not arise.
☐ Since there is no cost entailed in convening the experts, large numbers of respondents may be used, if desired. (Of course, too large a group may have other cost implications. A minimum of 7 experts and a maximum of 100 is a general guideline.)

Other advantages are:[9]

☐ Generation of ideas in isolation produces high quality ideas.

☐ The writing process forces a careful thinking through of the complexity of the problem.
☐ The respondents' behavior is proactive since they can't react to anyone else's ideas.
☐ Since all ideas submitted are pooled, the Delphi participants are treated on an equal basis.
☐ The process concludes with a moderate perceived sense of closure and accomplishment.

Limitations

The method also has several drawbacks. They are:

☐ The considerable time involved in the process—sending opinions back and forth several times and awaiting responses—hardly creates a rapid sequence of events.
☐ The lack of personal interaction and healthy conflict resulting therefrom may limit the quality of ideas or solutions garnered.
☐ Participants must be highly motivated to spend the required time on the series of questionnaires forwarded to them.

The Delphi Technique—Group Approach

Although the original Delphi technique operated solely on a "mail order" basis, it has since been modified to permit use with a group. Its procedures are these:

1. Participants are given a problem and are asked to generate on an individual basis as many ideas as they can about the problem. They are to record their ideas on a sheet of paper. (If the participant group numbers 10 and each member produces 10 ideas, 100 ideas may be collected.)
2. The moderator consolidates the batch of ideas, eliminating duplicates. Let's assume this procedure produces a total of 75 ideas.
3. The new list of 75 ideas is given to group members, and each is requested to select and circle the 5 most important ideas. This step should produce some 50 "screened" ideas.
4. Working from the list of 50 ideas, everyone is asked to pick 3 of the most important ideas. The moderator now has 30 ideas, some 70 having been dropped or consolidated.
5. The 30 ideas go back to the participants with a request to pick 1 or 2 of the "best" ones. This procedure produces 10–20 ideas.

In essence, this filtering process produces, say, five to seven worthwhile solutions or ideas. It does not, of course, rank or prioritize them.

Note, too, that while the assembled group is polled for ideas, *all* the ideation is actually individual and discussion free. The whole idea is to avoid discussion on the assumption that "the strong" will attempt to beat "the weak."[10]

Ideawriting

With a participant group that can easily express themselves in writing, worthwhile ideas to solve problems can be generated quite simply and rapidly. Idea writing—also known as "brainwriting"—entails individual ideation, which is reduced to writing and followed by written comments about those ideas by colleagues or fellow participants. More specifically, here's how it works:[11]

1. Break the total group into small groups (four to six persons). Seat them at tables.
2. Provide all participants with full-size writing pads.
3. Assign a task for idea production. This may be a single topic (problem, question, issue) to all groups, or the small groups may select a topic from several provided.
   Note: If groups select their own topics, duplication may occur; but the "trade off" is high topic interest.
4. Have all groups count off one through six, the "ones" becoming the leaders. The leader's role is to keep operations on track.
5. Ask participants to write their names on the top sheet of their pads (upper right corner) and the assigned "trigger" question at the top. The top sheet is *not* to be removed from the pad.
6. Participants respond in writing to the question in any form they wish (20–30 minutes).
7. Pads are then exchanged, each small group member commenting on the ideas of *all* other colleagues.
8. Pads are returned to their owners. Each now has his/her original comments plus four or five added comments on those ideas.
   Note: Steps 1–8 have been accomplished silently.
9. Each participant summarizes the ideas on his/her pad orally for the small group. (An alternative is to turn the pads in to a monitoring team for a later reporting). A discussion is held on the ideas generated within the small group.
10. The ideas of each small group are summarized on a flipchart sheet and reported back by the group leader to the total group.
11. The session concludes with a group-at-large discussion of all ideas or solutions recorded on the flipchart.

Brainwriting works best when there is a large group, limited time, and minimal participant need for the give-and-take of group interaction. It can also be used to avoid the possibility of the influence of status smothering creativity.

Card Posting Techniques

A useful way to generate ideas is via the "pin cards" technique developed by the Battele Institute, Frankfurt, Germany. Its procedures are these:[12]

1. Inform participants that the initial ideation phase of the problem-solving activity is done individually and nonverbally.
2. Present the group with a problem.
3. Provide participants with a stack of cards.
4. Instruct participants to enter only one idea on each card (as in the slip method).
5. Instruct participants to pass on their completed cards (on a one-at-a-time basis) to the person on their right.
6. Ask each person to quickly study the card he/she has received and to utilize it as a stimulus to create new ideas.

The cards are moved on to the other participants for about 20–30 minutes. Upon completion of the written work, the cards are collected by the trainer, screened for overlaps or repeats, grouped into major subjects, and pinned to a pinboard. A title card heads up each group of cards.

The group peruses all pinned or posted cards. Participants may ask for clarifications and add new ideas as well.

Another ideation approach, using card posting procedures, is as follows:

1. Provide participants with a stack of $5'' \times 8''$ cards.
2. Instruct them to enter only one idea on a single card. Ideas are to be printed in large letters, using a felt-tip pen.
3. Advise group members that they can post their cards to the wall (via masking tape) as soon as they have completed several of them. (The movement of people to the wall for posting encourages the others to keep producing ideas.)
4. When the individual ideation phase is over, have participants collectively group (categorize) the cards. (*Note:* The large print facilitates this procedure.) Possible categories in a team building session are people problems, policies, procedures, equipment needs.
5. On the basis of the card array, encourage another round of individual ideation.

What function do the posted cards serve? Several, as a matter of fact:

☐ Everyone's ideas are considered. As in a good brainstorming session, no one's idea is criticized, argued with, or minimized. Instead, all ideas are accorded equal recognition via the posting procedure.
☐ It forces people to give the essence of an idea sans unnecessary elaboration, exemplification, justification, and pontification.
☐ It encourages added ideation.
☐ It permits the easy "patterning" of concepts (or problems) as previously described.
☐ It also facilitates the prioritizing of ideas (or problems).
☐ It provides a written record for later use.

Both card posting techniques produce the same result: a set of posted cards, which are then rearranged into logical groupings for further ideation, discussion, etc. The first technique emphasizes moving the cards to fellow participants to stimulate added ideas. The second procedure uses the visual display and movement of people to stimulate ideas. This procedure is more group-oriented since the group rather than the trainer (or leader) does the grouping.

The Client-Centered Approach to Problem Solving

A unique problem-solving firm, Synectics, Inc., Cambridge, Massachusetts, has been researching the process of innovation, creative problem solving and meeting effectiveness since 1960. (*Synectics* is a Greek word that means joining together different and apparently irrelevant elements.) It finds that although the quality of the thinking of groups—*content*—is generally O.K., groups run into difficulty in the *process*. Content relates to the *what* of the problem-solving process; process relates to the *how*. In other words, how groups go about their business of problem solving is the core source of their problems. Process problems include unclear problem definition, groups too large to function, status, nitpicking, judgmental attitudes, hidden agendas, information being hoarded rather than shared, negativism and put downs, sloppy time management, and poor listening.

Synectics' solution to the process difficulty is to recognize that one person—usually designated as chairperson—cannot effectively monitor both the content and process roles. Synectics splits the chairperson role into two parts or two chairs: one for content and one for process. The former is designated the "client," i.e., the one who has the problem. The latter is designated "traffic cop" or facilitator.

The client, the problem owner, has these responsibilities: calling the meeting, directing the discussion to be sure people stay on track, making decisions, and evaluating. The facilitator assumes the responsibilities of scribe (records ideas on flipchart), time keeper, protector of idea presenters from attack or criticism, and idea catalyst (peps up group when they go flat).

Both the client and the facilitator respect the other's responsibilities and avoid crossing over. (In rare instances a highly sensitive and participation-oriented manager can assume both roles.)

In the Synectics approach, then, we have three roles:

☐ Client
☐ Facilitator
☐ Resources (participant group of five or six)

In planning for the most effective functioning of those who perform in those roles, the journalist's six questions merit consideration as follows:

☐ Who—The client plus a divergent group including a "novice."
☐ What—What is the objective?
☐ Where—Away from phones, interruptions.
☐ When—Ask: are you an a.m. or a p.m. person?
☐ Why—Why is it a problem? Why am I calling this meeting? Do I need a group?
☐ How—The process issue.

The Synectics approach also stresses the importance of the "mental dynamics" of problem solving. It hypothecates two selves: the "safe keeping" self and the "experimental" self. The former evaluates, reassures, supports, is realistic and logical, avoids surprises and risks, punishes mistakes. The latter takes risks, breaks rules, is intuitive, speculates, sees fun in change, takes chances. Ideally, participants in problem-solving activities need to work on expanding their experimental selves, something which has been inhibited in many of us as we left childhood and became adults.[13]

Upside-Down Problem Solving

Typically, when we are confronted with a problem we tend to think of the approaches we've used before or have heard about, all of which are based on common sense and logical thinking. But what if we were to tackle the problem by approaching it in less conventional terms—more particularly, in opposite terms—and forgot about "common sense"? For example, assume we have the classic supervisory problem of the habitually tardy employee. What have we done before about this kind of problem? We give the usual lectures and warnings, circulate memos to *everyone* concerning the need to report to work promptly, possibly count the lateness as time to be reduced from annual leave, etc. But what if we were to turn things around and consider strategies which would make it *easier* rather than harder for the employee? If so, we might conceive of new strategies (bizarre ones are O.K.) such as these: changing (delaying) the starting time, putting the employee on another shift, introducing flextime, ignoring the problem for several weeks, asking the employee when he/she would *like* to start (!), having everyone wait until the employee arrives before beginning the day's work, starting the employee's work yourself or assigning someone else to do it, giving the late employee the key to open the door in the morning for everyone, putting the employee on a committee that is to develop a new lateness policy.[14]

This approach, known as "second order" thinking, is a means of achieving some new breakthroughs on our problem. This is not to say that the preceding ideas are necessarily worthy of adoption, but they do encourage participants to think in nonconventional terms. The alternative is to continue to treat the ailment with the same "tried and true" remedies.

Devices to Unleash Idea Development

Although many of us have considerable potential to produce new and different ideas for purposes of problem solving, all too often that capacity remains untapped. Hence the need for trainers to utilize devices that stimulate idea production.

Sidney J. Parnes, president of the Creative Education Foundation, State University College at Buffalo, New York, distinguishes between techniques that encourage the free flow of ideas, like brainstorming, and devices that *initiate idea development,* such as checklists, forced relationships, attribute listing, and morphological analysis.[15]

Using Checklists

A checklist is a tool to aid participants to focus on a list of categories to which the problem under review might relate. The checklist, consisting of a series of verbs (also known as "trigger words"), is used to change one's conventional approach or mind set to a problem. Three potent verbs for this purpose, per Alex F. Osborn, brainstorming inventor and author of the now classic work *Applied Imagination,* are:

☐ Magnify
☐ Minify
☐ Rearrange

As a simple illustration of the way these verbs might be used to stimulate ideas, take the problem of space utilization in a shop, lab, office, or store. We can take the three verbs and expand them into questions relating to our problem.

Question 1: How can we increase (magnify) our space? Some answers are: knock down unnecessary walls and partitions; eliminate minimally used storage areas, closets; negotiate for more space with Divisions X and Y; rehabilitate the attic and the basement; close in the porch; since we have high ceilings, make two-story levels out of one level wherever practical.

Question 2: How can we shrink (minify) our need for space? We could eliminate bulky furniture and unneeded file cabinets; use microfilm for files; reduce staff; drop unnecessary activities and operations.

Question 3: How can we rearrange our space more effectively? Some answers are: start with a floor plan; use wall space more imaginatively; reduce size of reception area; use modular furniture; stack file cabinets from floor to ceiling; use an open plan instead of partitions, and use potted palms for privacy; put all typists in one section of our large room behind noise-proof walls.

Note: These three verbs represent only a partial list of those used by Alex F. Osborn. Others are modify, manipulate, substitute, combine, adapt, and reverse, with each category having several subquestions under it.

Two other types of checklists are *area thinking* and *work stimulation.*[16] Area thinking is the opposite of attribute listing. With this procedure we start with several major aspects of a problem and then work toward details and specifics. In word stimulation we use word lists to trigger creative ideas and solutions.

Note that these checklists, as well as attribute listing discussed later, are designed to unleash creativity. They are not to be confused with checklists that auditors, managers, and others might use to be certain that the right procedures are being followed in a given situation, such as in responding to a bomb threat in an office building, inspecting the effectiveness of a decentralized operation, or orienting a new worker.

Attribute Listing

This technique is intended to generate ideas about a product, service, or situation. After the list is developed, the various attributes, traits or characteristics listed are analyzed for means of improving the product, service, or situation. Thus, each item may be subject to a special focus using the techniques of checklists (described previously) and forced relationships (described later).

Example: We may wish to improve the landscaping around our plant or office. We thus develop a list of its features or attributes such as the following:

Lawn
Beds, flower
Beds, nonflowering (e.g., ivy)
Fences
Flowering trees
Other shade trees
Shrubs
Hedges
Walks
Stone walls
Picnic/luncheon areas
Signing
Hazards

Internal Management Activities	Promotional Methods	Employee Incentives
Notices on bulletin boards	TV spots, radio spots	Contests with prizes ("Dog Mover of the Week")
Memos to employees with tips on selling the "dogs"	Newspaper ads	Special commissions
Boxed items in company news letter	School newspaper ads	Supervisory praise
Encouragement of brainstorming sessions with employees	Suburban newspaper ads	Letters of commendation from top management
Pep talks at supervisors' meetings	Leaflets with customers' bills	Special time off
Review of pricing practices	Small catalog featuring "dogs"	Extra employee discounts on these items
Study of competitors' practices	Mail flyers to homes	Give some items away as prizes for perfect attendance
Special campaigns as "Discard Sale," "Overstock Sale," "Three-for-Two" pricing, etc.	Leaflets on individual items at various points in store	Suggest these items for early Christmas gift buying (get your shopping done early!)
	Ads on store delivery trucks	

Figure 11-2. Example of a morphological matrix.

We may then develop checklists concerning these items; for example, in considering the picnic/luncheon areas, we may highlight benches, tables, trash cans, shade, shrubbery, flagstone, etc.

Morphological Analysis

This is a problem-generating and problem-solving approach that relates (or interrelates) all elements (independent variables) of a problem to aid in discovering fresh solutions. As will be apparent from the following discussion, it entails combining attribute listing with forced relationship in a matrix approach. The steps for conducting the analysis include:

1. Identifying the major elements (variables, parameters) of a problem.
2. Further identifying the subelements or factors that relate to the major variables.
3. Establishing a matrix to highlight the several variables and its subelements.
4. Choosing, generally on a random basis, the subelements in the matrix. One subelement from each of the major variables is selected and combined with the others.
5. Analyzing the feasibility of combining the elements.
6. Selecting and analyzing the practicality of added combinations of elements.

In general, the whole process is designed to generate ideas. The combining and recombining of subelements provides numerous opportunities to look at a problem and come up with fresh, novel solutions, and our natural tendencies to ideate along habitual lines are upset.

To illustrate the process, let's assume we have developed a morphological matrix such as the one in Figure 11-2 relating to slow-moving products in a retail department store. Our objective is to design a program or campaign to help move these ten "slow-movers": men's

hats, toasters, suede jackets, half-inch garden hoses, portable first-aid kits, small electric fans, ladies' garter belts, porch paint, roll top desks, and classical records. Our three key variables to accomplish this are internal management activities or programs, promotional approaches, and employee incentives.

Going to our three-columned matrix,[17] we might consider as our program the use of special sales or campaigns (column 1), via radio (column 2), coupled with special time off to employees who are the best performers (column 3). This tri-partite program, along with others selected similarly, would be evaluated as to possible pay-offs.

Forced Relationships Technique

To develop new combinations of ideas, participants may be given a new word, concept, phrase, or object and asked to relate it to the problem being studied. All senses may be tapped, attention being called to a sound or odor as well as items in view. Or the group may be asked to take an imaginary trip somewhere. In general, the idea is to find new stimuli to force creativity.

Example: Assume the group is working on a problem of tardiness. The moderator or supervisor introduces a bag of lemons (!) and asks participants to use it to help solve the problem. Some possible solutions: Using behavior modification principles, give the latecomer a glass of lemonade whenever arrival is prompt; add oranges to the lemons and set up a "data" display (visual feedback) for two weeks: give a lemon for tardiness, an orange for promptness; promise a cake (a lemon cake) and coffee party for the whole group if arrival time has improved materially at week's end; put a lemon on the employee's desk whenever he/she is late; add to the lemons a case of cokes as a reward for improved arrival time.

Using Analogy

One effective way to augment problem-solving capacity is to work with the principle of "making the strange familiar." This is an approach developed by William Gordon of Synectics, Inc., Cambridge, Massachusetts.[18] It is a recognition that people, as problem solvers, are basically conservative. New concepts or ideas thus are perceived as threatening. Hence, there is the need for many of us to dredge up or draw upon the familiar to accommodate the new or strange idea.

To facilitate the familiarity process, Gordon encourages the use of *analogy* or model or comparison seeking. he has his problem solvers use these three types of analogies:

☐ Direct analogy
☐ Personal analogy
☐ Symbolic analogy

Direct Analogy

Also called example seeking, this entails the comparison of one thing with another. Two historical examples are: The telephone is based on the human ear; Darwin's theory of evolution resulted from comparing the natural state with controlled breeding on stock farms.[15]

Even those fields unrelated to the field one is working on can give the problem solver a viable analogy. An engineer, for example, might study human systems to give insight about a mechanical problem. In general, the process calls for drawing upon one's experience and knowledge to locate examples similar (analogous) to the subject being studied.

To "tease out" an analogy, it helps to use this sentence: "This situation (or thing) is comparable to _____" or "This situation reminds me of _____."

An example of the use of *direct* analogy in the training situation relates to the training by the airlines of flight attendants to smile continually, despite various job pressures and irritations from customers. (One West Coast airline's jingle is "On PSA our smiles are not just painted on, so smile your way from L.A. to San Francisco.") A Delta Airlines trainer advised a group of trainees to: "Think of the airplane cabin as your own living room. Now, if you invited some people into your own home, wouldn't you want them to think you had gone to some trouble for them? Wouldn't you want to put them at ease? It's exactly the same thing in the cabin. These people are your guests."

Further, the flight attendants are told to think of demanding passengers "as if" (analogy again) they were your own children seeking your attention. One trainer advised the use of this "as if" principle: "It can help to think of rude passengers as having had some terrible tragedy in the past."

In general, by using these analogies in flight, the attendant is better equipped to handle stressful situations as well as to maintain a continuing appearance of pleasantness.[19]

Personal Analogy

This is a form of creative problem solving wherein one takes on the identity of something else or somebody else. In respect to the "something else," the idea is to look at an object subject to change or improvement from "the inside." By being in and part of it, one can better understand the thing and its "feelings," and thus be in a superior position to improve on it.[20] For example, small groups may be asked to brainstorm improvements in a toaster, a woman's purse, a man's shirt, or a power drill, using the personal analogy approach to unleash their creativity.

In human potential programs, where group members are trying to achieve greater sensory awareness, a greater ability to express feelings, and greater personal insight, the participants may be asked to take on the identity of a flower, a cloud, the sun, a brook, etc. The data (feelings) produced individually may then be subject to pairing and sharing plus later general discussion with the total group.[21]

People problems as well as technical and marketing problems also can be subject to personal analogy. This is essentially a form of role playing (minus the enactment): "If I were the sales manager. . . ." In this process one hypothecates or imagines how the other person would think, feel, behave, react.

Obviously, the identification with an object rather than a person is much more difficult to do. Why? Because in everyday life we (at least some of us) do, at times, try to empathize with another person; viz., "I know what she is going through" "I know how he feels." But how many of us have had an experience trying to think and feel like, say, a kitchen sink?

Symbolic Analogy

Also called compressed conflict, this analogy uses a "close-coupled" phrase where the words engage in "combat" with one another. For example, Pasteur's antitoxin research was based on the expression "safe attack;" Nobel Prize winning Spanish neurologist Ramon Y. Cajal was stimulated in his accomplishment by the phrase "protoplasmic kiss."[22]

Creating symbolic analogies can aid materially in creative problem solving. Procedurally, we do the following:[23]

1. Select a key word or ask participants to select a key word from the problem statement.
1. Ask participants for its meaning to *them,* empathizing or feeling for its most important significance.
3. Ask participants to put the feeling into one or two words to form a symbolic analogy.

Some examples:

Key Word	Symbolic Analogy
Ratchet	Dependable intermittency
Solidity	Enforced togetherness
Mixture	Balanced confusion
Receptivity	Involuntary willingness

Productivity Teams Aided by Analogy

To appreciate more fully how analogy works in problem solving, the experience of a consulting firm concerned with productivity improvement merits citation.[24]

A Pittsburgh-based consulting firm, The Advanced Manufacturing Cost Reduction and Productivity Service Group, PROFITCO, forms two-day productivity improvement teams in manufacturing plants to work on problems that:

☐ Have been studied extensively by staff experts without success
☐ Have *not* been attacked at all because everyone "knows" they are "impossible" to solve
☐ Persist due to lack of time to work on them or because necessary technical personnel resources are limited

In sum, the teams work on the kinds of problems that typically tend to remain untackled in manufacturing plants.

The teams are formed from internal supervisory and managerial personnel drawn from various units of the plant. The team members' main qualification is an ability to approach a "strange" problem in a fresh, inventive, and creative way. They are successful because they avoid thinking like "experts." These teams help one "key man," the supervisor who has been living with the problem. The latter explains the problem, answers questions of team members and converts the team's "semiuseful" ideas into practical reality.

The teams are successful on one out of every four problems tackled. Savings typically range from $100,000 to $1,000,000 or more.

The "targets of opportunity," as the problems are called, are subject to "invention-thinking." This means defining the problem differently and looking at the problem differently than the technical experts such as those in quality control, R & D, value engineering, and human resources. The techniques the productivity teams use are direct analogy, projection (or personal analogy), and fantasy (described elsewhere).

Let's take a look, then, to see how a productivity team employed direct analogy to solve a perplexing productivity problem. The problem was as follows: There were delays in completing metallurgical test reports, which prevented the timely release of ore shipments via railroad cars. The team defined the problem as "overcoming delays" and "speeding up" testing. Accordingly, comparisons (analogies in other contexts such as sports or music) were utilized. Some examples:

☐ How runners manage to have a speed up kick left for the finish
☐ How harmonica players manage to play the melody at the same time they produce a rhythmic accompaniment
☐ How traffic moves at a complex intersection with and without a police officer
☐ How pass receivers in football speed up and vary their running patterns to outwit the defense
☐ How power failures are circumvented in electrical distribution systems
☐ How leap-frogging and flanking are used in military operations
☐ How credit collection agencies speed up collections on seriously delinquent accounts
☐ How artillery units get on target faster via bracketing versus creeping fire
☐ How flywheels continue to operate long after being speeded up
☐ How hang gliders can accelerate upward
☐ How sailboats accelerate going into the wind at an angle
☐ How the old Western stage coach managed to race across great distances in just a few days

The productivity team studied these analogies to resolve the railroad car delay problem. The key man saw the stage coach practice (last item in the list of analogies) as being pertinent, i.e., it entailed replacing fatigued horses with fresh ones at regular intervals. Also, not all horses ran simultaneously. The logical solution, then, was this: Transfer a staffer of the metallurgical test lab to a special one-person late shift (3 p.m. to 11 p.m) to continue conducting critical tests on steel specimens on loaded railroad cars awaiting release. The shift in thinking from "not running all horses at the same time" allowed test reports to be accomplished and forwarded to the production departments in time to release the railroad cars before the 7 a.m. deadline the next morning. (The lab, of course, was closed from 5 p.m. to 8 a.m. daily.)

Net savings for a half-day of this team study was a whopping $181,000!

The PROFITCO consultants point out that analogy-type thinking works because it puts the problem in a remote and strange context. This allows for the discovery of a much-needed, productive, new viewpoint.

Another steel manufacturing problem, one of quality control, was solved via *projection* or *personal analogy,* i.e., the team becomes part of the problem. This solution produced an annual cost reduction of $540,000. The problem was the following: Unwanted black streaks (snakes) formed on the surfaces of steel strips rolled into coils. These snakes came from strip surface oil not completely removed by the internal environment of the box annealing heat treatment furnaces. Not all coils were bad, but some were. Though some of the bad coils could be cleaned up, some could not and had to be junked. The oil treatment was required in making the strip and in preventing rusting during storage before heat treating.

The team examined the defective coils carefully and noted their thickness (they were thinner than the good ones) and their length (usually longer when uncoiled). Size and weight were the same for both good and bad coils.

After the study of the defective coils, the team projected themselves momentarily as oil drops. From this they concluded that they had all started to move toward the edges and out of the coils while in the heat treating furnace, but had stopped short for some reason.

The team then made a further projection (personal analogy): they became the steel strip, all coiled up, with a need to shed the oil completely "like good coils should." In this projection or personal analogy mode, these preferences (personal analogies) were stated by the various team members:

☐ It would be nice to be a bit more slippery so I could shed the oil and not feel gunky

☐ I'd like to stay longer in this nice hot furnace because it feels so good.

☐ I feel superior to all the "good" coils because I'm so much longer and I have these pretty black lace decorations that they don't!

☐ I hate this greasy stuff on me—I wish I had a million tiny blow torches to burn each drop away.

☐ I'm so skinny and weak that I get exhausted pushing the entire oil film to my edges.

☐ I detest crowds and there's so many oil drops on me that I feel like I'm at Times Square on New Year's Eve.

☐ I'm suffocating, wrapped up so tight in this coil; I'm drowning in oil; and it tastes, ugh, awful.

☐ I'm disgusted, getting bad-mouthed because I can't shed five times as much oil from my surfaces as the "good" coils have to unload. Why can't I get credit for trying?

The productivity team studied these personal analogies and saw the problem as "too-much-oil-on-too-much-surface" of these coils coming out of the furnace with "snakes." (This was inspired by the last-cited personal analogy.) But how to reduce the amount of oil film remaining on the strip surfaces, and yet leave enough to prevent unwanted rust formation while being stored before the heat treatment?

Quick agreement was reached that the oil film on the steel strip coming into the final series of roll stands could be reduced. An oil (or other substance) that would self-destruct under high temperature also would be helpful. Other ideas included the realization that nearly all the oil on either the top or bottom of the strip at the end of the rolling sequence could be removed via steam blast or air knife; oil remaining on the other side should spread out on the "dry" side as the strip was coiled and compacted—this could cut to one-half the total volume of oil on the coils sent to storage awaiting heat treating.

Why does this approach to problem solving work so well on such tough problems? PROFITCO provides these skillpoints:

☐ Total top management support, including tolerance for "nonsuccesses."

☐ A team approach to problem solving, members being drawn from different parts of the plant.

☐ Use of the key man (the one having the problem) as part of the team. He helps the team by explaining the problem and answering questions about it. He zeroes in on and adapts the pertinent idea and follows up on it or gets authorization to act on it.

☐ The teams define the problem differently than the staff experts and often find it to be something other than as stated. Their thinking about the value of negative information—where and when the problem is and is not occurring—is often more important to this kind of problem-solving group than to more conventional groups.

☐ The team assumes any problem can be solved; that the experts are wedded to obsolete approaches.

☐ Team members are results-oriented. Their only interest is to see the creation of low-cost solutions that get tried out and implemented when effective.

☐ The team thinks laterally, not vertically; e.g., a chemical problem might be solved via a mechanical or biological approach.

☐ The teams define the problem differently than the staff experts and often find it to be something other than as stated. Their thinking abou the value of negative information—where and when the problem is and is not occurring—is often more important to this kind of problem-solving group than to more conventional groups.

☐ The teams carefully separate idea generating from idea evaluating (as in brainstorming).

☐ The two-day work period is long enough to sustain interest and short enough to avoid "burnout."

☐ The use of the highly imaginative techniques of analogy (direct and personal) and fantasy are basic to the way the teams go about their business of problem solving.

PCT Approach and Analogy

"Purposeful Creative Thinking" (PCT) is another way to solve problems via analogy or comparison. It encourages us to tap or draw upon the vast storehouse of information all of us have. It entails a six-step process as follows:[25]

1. Describe the problem or difficulty.
2. Identify the "paradox" that underlies the problem. That is, what *conflict* is basic to the problem?
3. Identify or locate an analogy to the paradox. This is the "crucial step" for it forces novel or creative thinking.
4. Describe the "unique activity" or characteristic of the analogous circumstance (event, situation) as it relates to the paradox.
5. Equate the unique activity of the analogy to the problem or concern.
6. Produce a new solution or idea based on this equivalent.

To illustrate: The administrators of a once-small hospital wished its personnel to meet informally to discuss and share ideas as it once did. This was difficult to do because the hospital was no longer a small one. The price of bigness and success was the loss of the highly desirable informal lines of communication.

So Step 1, problem definition, tells us that there was a lack of informal meetings. Step 2 cites the paradox: Unless employee gatherings are "unorganized," they won't be effective. (Formal meetings are not very useful for authentic communication.) Step 3 entails the search for an analogy to the paradox. In this case one of gulls surrounding a fishing boat in a highly unorganized manner was produced. Step 4, the unique activity of the analogy, is identified as it relates to the paradox—the gulls are attracted to the herring boat by the accidental presence of good food tossed overboard by the boatmen. Step 5 requires finding an equivalent, in terms of the problem, to the gulls at the boat (the analogy). This equivalent was perceived as offering A-1 food at reasonable prices to the employees. Gourmet food was offered weekly in the

hospital cafeteria (Step 6), which drew employees together again.

The PCT procedure can be made more vivid to those participants applying it by setting up a worksheet as follows: Allow space at the top for the entering of "Problem Description;" this is followed by four boxes, each large enough to write in, labeled: "Paradox" (Step 1), "Analogue" (Step 2), "Unique Activity" (Step 3), and "Equivalent" (Step 4); and below the boxes provide a space to permit describing the "New Idea."

The Gordon Technique

In the "Gordon Technique"[26] (named after its developer William J. Gordon, Arthur D. Little, Inc., Massachusetts) the leader alone knows the exact nature of the problem to be solved. The leader utilizes six to eight experts, drawn from different fields, to bring their specialized knowledge (sales, personnel, finance) to bear on the problem. Why is the problem presented to the group not defined more precisely? To avoid premature judgments as to what the solution might be.

Expert leadership is critical since the group leader must stimulate creativity, give encouragement to the specialists, and lead them along a predetermined path.

This technique is hardly a fast process—a session may last as long as three hours, and several sessions may be essential. A second disadvantage is that there are problems in assembling all of the desired specialists since they typically have full schedules of their own.

Key Points

1. To obtain solutions (Step 3 in the model) to a problem, these techniques are useful: brainstorming, slip method, nominal group technique, the Delphi technique, idea writing, card posting techniques, client-centered approach, upside-down method, checklists, attribute listing, morphological analysis, forced relationships, analogy, and the Gordon technique.

2. Brainstorming, a now "classic" problem-solving tool, has been "updated" via such variations as reverse thinking, rotational contributions, integration procedures, using pauses, trigger sessions, eliciting far-out ideas, rolestorming, and altering the environment.

3. Whereas brainstorming depends upon group action and interaction, other techniques primarily tap individual creativity, e.g., the slip method, the nominal group technique, the Delphi technique, idea writing.

4. In the client-centered approach to problem solving, problem solving responsibilities in a group are di-

vided between the "owner" of the problem and the facilitator. The assumption is that very few problem owners can handle the many diverse tasks of problem solving.

5. In upside-down problem solving a problem is worked on by approaching it in opposite, nonconventional ways.

6. Certain techniques—checklists, attribute listing, morphological analysis—initiate idea *development.* These are in contrast to devices like brainstorming that encourage the free flow of ideas.

References

1. Van Gundy, A., "Try These Problem Solving Techniques in the Classroom," *Training/HRD* (December 1980), pp. 32–35.

2. Scharlatt, Harold, "Beyond Brainstorming," *Training and Development Journal* (August 1984), pp. 8–9.

3. "A Storm Of Ideas," *Training* (November 1985), p. 66.

4. Rickards, T., *Problem Solving Through Creative Analysis,* Gower Press, New York (1975).

5. "Group Techniques: Part 2, Alternatives to Brainstorming," *Small Business Report* (October 1981), pp. 15–17.

6. Crawford, C. C., *How To Make Training Surveys,* published by the author, Los Angeles (1954).

7. Murnighan, J. K., "Group Decision Making: What Strategies Should You Use?" *Management Review* (February 1981), pp. 59–62 and Messer, L. A., III, "Management Circles—An Idea Whose Time Has Come," *The Quality Circles Journal* (November 1981), pp. 35–36, describe the NGT.

8. For an account of the use of the Delphi technique to predict developments in the video field, see Vermilyea, D., "New Technical Developments in Video—A Symposium," *Educational and Industrial TV* (July 1980), pp. 23–24. For an account on the deliberations of a Delphi panel of 65 experts in the field of organization development, who were asked to forecast the impact of world and U.S. trends on the demand for OD in the coming 20 years, see Shephard, K. O., and Raia, A. P., "The OD Training Challenge," *Training and Development Journal* (April 1981), pp. 90–96.

9. Somers, Ken; Baker, Gus; and Isbell, Clint, "How To Use The Delphi Technique To Forecast Training Needs," *Performance and Instruction Journal* (May 1984), pp. 26–28.

10. The modified or group Delphi technique was presented to the Montgomery County, Maryland, group of the American Society for Training and Development, by Joseph Greenberg of George Washington University, on July 25, 1981.

11. Moore, C. M., and Coke, J. G., *Guide for Leaders Using Ideawriting,* pamphlet, National Training and Development Service for State and Local Government, Washington, D.C. (September 1979).

12. Van Gundy, A., "Try These Creative Problem-Solving Techniques in the Classroom," *Training/HRD* (December 1980), p. 33.

13. These ideas were presented by Eric Baron of Synectics, Inc., at the 1981 Annual Conference of the American Society for Training and Development, Boston. For an overall summary of Synectics' ideas, see Prince, G., "Creativity and Learning As Skills, Not Talents," *The Phillips Exeter Bulletin* (June–July 1980), pp. 1–12; this article is by the founder of Synectics, Inc. A detailed account of the Synectics process is given in (a) Prince, George, M., "The Operational Mechanism of Synectics," in Parnes, Sidney J.; Noller, Ruth B.; and Biondi, Angelo M.; *Guide to Creative Action*, Charles Scribner's and Sons, New York, 1977, pp. 155–160 and (b) Ulschak, Francis L.; Nathanson, Leslie; and Gillian, Peter, G., *Problem Solving: An Aid to Organizational Effectiveness*, Addison-Wesley Pub. Co., Reading, Mass., 1981, pp. 67–83. For a journalist's breezy account of her participation in a Madison Avenue Synectics session, see Kanner, Bernice, "Birth of A Nation: Brainstorming For Avon," *New York*, June 18, 1984.

14. The ideas were brainstormed by a group that was using "second order" strategies, per Kim Barnes of Lawrence Livermore Laboratory, California, in a presentation given at the American Society for Training and Development Annual Conference (1979), St. Louis.

15. Parnes, S. J., "Idea-Simulation Techniques," in *Guide to Creative Action,* New York, Charles Scribner's Sons (1977), pp. 193–200. (This article appeared originally in the *Journal of Creative Behavior,* Vol. 10, No. 2 (1976).)

16. Mariotti, J. J., "Checklists in Problem Solving," *Management Review* (August 1971), pp. 52–54. The article appeared originally in *Management Advisor* (May–June 1971).

17. For a four-column matrix, dealing with the generation of ideas about ways to reduce serious accidents, see Tagliaferri, L., *Creative Cost Improvement for Managers—A Self-Teaching Guide,* New York, Wiley and Sons, Inc., New York (1981), p. 114.

18. Gordon, W. J. J., "On Being Explicit About Creative Process," in *Guide to Creative Action* by

Parnes, S. J., Noller, R. B., and Biondi, A. M., Charles Scribner's Sons, New York, 1977, pp. 172–174. The article originally appeared in *The Journal of Creative Behavior* (1972), Vol. 6, No. 4.

19. Hochschild, A., "Emotional Labor in the Friendly Skies," *Psychology Today* (June 1982), p. 14.
20. Parnes, S. J., Noller, R. B., and Biondi, A. M., "Personal Analogy," in *Guide to Creative Action,* Charles Scribner's Sons, New York (1977), p. 103.
21. Parnes, S. J., Noller, R. B., and Biondi, A. M., "Creativity Through Personal Analogy," in *Guide to Creative Action,* Charles Scribner's Sons, New York (1977), p. 123.
22. Gordon, W. J. J., "On Being Explicit About Creative Process," in *Guide to Creative Action,* by Parnes, S. J., Noller, R. B., and Biondi, A. M., Charles Scribner's Sons, New York (1977), p. 173.
23. Prince, G. M., "The Operational Mechanism of Synectics," in *Guide to Creative Action,* by Parnes,

S. J., Noller, R. B., and Biondi, A. M., Charles Scribner's Sons, New York (1977), p. 158.
24. The material herein is drawn from "The Hidden Productivity Improvement Weapon for Manufacturing Management," a report (undated) on the use of special productivity improvement teams, prepared by PROFITCO, The Advanced Cost Reduction and Productivity Service Group, Pittsburgh. PROFITCO president Jerry D. Brooks also described the work of the productivity teams in "Pretend You're a Drop of Oil . . . Don't Laugh Until You Look At The Results," *33 Metal Producing* (March 1982), pp. 60–63.
25. Cookman, G., "The Trainer's Guide to Problem Solving," *Northeast Training News* (June 1981), pp. 8, 9, 16.
26. "Group Techniques: Part 2, Alternatives to Brainstorming," *Small Business Report* (October 1981), pp. 15–17.

SELECTING AND IMPLEMENTING A SOLUTION

To put one's thoughts into action is the most difficult thing in the world.

—Johann Wolfgang von Goethe (1740–1832), German poet, dramatist, novelist, and philosopher

Plans are only good intentions unless they immediately degenerate into hard work.

—Peter Drucker, management authority, consultant, writer, and educator

In the prior two chapters we learned about the first three steps (skill areas) in the problem-solving process: "How to define the problem," "How to generate data about the problem" and "How to generate solutions or ideas for resolving the problem." In our final chapter on problem solving we will learn "How to choose among alternative solutions" (Step 4) and "How to plan and implement the solution" (Step 5). We will also be introduced to a number of additional approaches to problem solving.

How to Choose Among Alternatives (Step 4 in the Problem-Solving Process)

Quite often participants in the training/problem-solving situation have a need to decide among a variety of possible courses of action. Typical situations in which the need for choices might arise are these:

☐ In an in-house management development seminar there may be a need to rank, on a priority basis, the importance of management problems that have been identified.
☐ In a team building session the group may wish to select a solution to a problem from several alternatives available to it.
☐ In a time management workshop participants may be asked to rank in order of their severity the "time wasters" they encounter. (Action plans are then developed to deal with them.)
☐ In a career planning workshop participants may wish to choose among career alternatives, job opportunities, etc.
☐ It may be desirable to sort out (prioritize) ideas which were produced in a brainstorming session.

Of course, a simple way for the group to make choices is through voting. Let's take our brainstorming situation for example. The participants may be asked to indicate by a show of hands which of the brainstormed items, posted on the flipchart, they favor. The idea receiving the most votes is "Number One," meaning it is the number one problem to be tackled or the best solution among the many offered.

But voting, unfortunately, may not produce the best answer if there is a need to make more careful distinctions among the alternatives. If finer discrimination is appropriate, the group can be aided via the use of various ranking and rating procedures, either with or without criteria, to facilitate the process. It should be stressed that the purpose of "the numbers" which are generated and displayed is not to decide things quickly or arbitrarily, but to encourage thought and discussion of the available options.

Ranking Procedures Without the Aid of Criteria

At times a group may wish to rank certain items *in order of their importance*, e.g., sources of time wasting identified in a time management course, ideas that came out of a brainstorming session, or the value of various employee motivators. The ranking can be aided by a system of point assignments.

A simple procedure to rank needs, problems, or other data is as follows:

1. Provide group members with an individual worksheet, such as the one shown in Figure 12-1.
2. Instruct each participant to enter from the flipchart onto the worksheet the problems that had been previously identified by the group. Since this is a priority ranking, the most serious problem is entered on the top of the worksheet and is thus given a ranking of 10; the least serious problem is entered on the bottom of the worksheet and is given a ranking of 1; all other items are ranked in accordance with this system, i.e., from 10 to 1.
3. Assume our group (of seven participants) has been actively engaged in a team building session. They have ranked individually their problems, as previously described. They are now ready to enter and consolidate their individual rankings onto a group worksheet. Their worksheet might look like the one shown in Figure 12-2.

Ranking Procedures Using Criteria

Note that in the previous ranking process criteria are not provided to the participants. Rather, their judgments are based on individual and consolidated group perceptions as to the importance or priority of the problems under review. To sharpen the decision-making process, criteria for ranking identified problems may be provided. For example, these three criteria may be used:

☐ Predominance, prevalence, or frequency of problem (widespread character)
☐ Criticalness, seriousness, or severity of problem (impact)
☐ Amenability or vulnerability of problem to resolution (success likelihood)

Note: Some groups may wish to add other criteria such as cost.

The identified problems can be evaluated using this criteria via a five-point scale (1—low; 5—high), as shown in Figure 12-3.

In the preceding example we used specific criteria to help us decide on priorities for identifying our problems. In the following example we use criteria to choose

Individual Ranking Sheet

Problem Area	Values for Ranking
	10
	9
	8
	7
	6
	5
	4
	3
	2
	1

Figure 12-1. Example of a ranking sheet for use by individual participants.

Group Ranking Sheet

Problem Area	Individual Member Rankings	Total Value of Rankings	Group Ranking
Policies unclear	9-7-3-5-7-5-7	43	3
Policies absent	5-4-10-9-4-2-1	35	5
Gaps in product line	8-10-9-4-3-1-9	44	2
Staffing	4-6-7-3-2-8-10	40	4
Relations with field	7-5-2-2-9-4-2	31	7
P.R.	6-2-4-1-8-3-8	32	6
Slippage in MBO program	10-9-8-10-10-3-10	60	1
Staff meetings	2-3-1-7-5-9-4	31	7
Teamwork	3-1-5-8-1-6-5	29	8
"Meetingitus"	1-8-6-6-6-7-6	40	4

Note:
1. *The MBO program was deemed to be the most important problem, receiving a 60-point total and thus a number 1 ranking; team work received a total of 29 points and the lowest ranking—number 8.*
2. *While this weighting system uses a maximum of 10 points, we could also have used a ranking of 7 through 1 or 5 through 1.*
3. *There are two ties in the rankings, 7 and 4.*

Figure 12-2. Example of a completed group ranking sheet rating the importance of previously identified problems.

Problem	Frequency	Severity	Solvability	Total Weight
1. Tardiness by clerical staff	2	3	3	18
2. Absence of policy on overtime	2	4	5	40
3. Customer complaints	5	4	3	60
4. Breakdowns of office copier	3	4	2	24

Note:
1. *The process entails multiplying the numbers from left to right, thereby providing a heavier weighting factor. If the numbers were merely added, the differences among the four totals would not receive the same importance and prominence.*
2. *At this point we are choosing our problems for resolution, but we are not solving them as yet.*

Figure 12-3. Example of a ranking sheet using a weighting system to prioritize significant problems.

Decision-Making Matrix

Alternative	Cost	Completion Time	Impact	Basic Learning	Total Points
Home study	5	2	1	5	13
One-at-a-time attendance	1	1	4	2	8
Consultant-developed course	2	5	5	5	17
In-house course	5	5	4	5	19

Note: *Weights have been added rather than multiplied across the columns. Accordingly, point totals are fairly close to one another. A multiplication of the four factors would produce much more varying point totals: home study, 50; one-at-a-time attendance, 8; consultant, 250; in-house, 500.*

Figure 12-4. Example of a decision-making matrix.

Cross-Comparison of solutions

Solution	A	B	C	D	E	F	Totals
A	X	B	A	D	A	A	3
B	B	X	B	B	B	B	5
C	A	B	X	D	E	C	1
D	D	B	D	X	D	F	2
E	A	B	E	D	X	F	1
F	A	B	C	F	F	X	2
Totals	3	5	1	2	1	2	14

Note:
1. *When an item is compared with itself in the grid an X is put in the space.*
2. *The process entails judgment but not criteria to facilitate those judgments.*

Figure 12-5. Example of a matrix for comparing solutions or alternatives with one another.

among several courses of action available to us. For example, let's assume a decision has to be made concerning the launching of a supervisory training program. The possible courses of action are home study, attendance on a one-at-a-time basis at various outside (external) courses, conduct of a course by a consultant, and an in-house conducted program. Criteria to evaluate these four approaches, per the group, are:

1. Cost
2. Rapidity of completion time for the participants
3. Impact (learning level)
4. Basic learnings for everyone.

A grid or matrix, as in Figure 12-4, can be readily constructed, using a five-point rating system to assess each possibility. One is low or unfavorable; five is high or very favorable.

In passing, we might mention the procedure shown in Figure 12-4 was used by an insurance company to select a producer to make a training film. Five possible producers were evaluated (via a ten-point scale) on the basis of these criteria: estimated production costs, professional efficiency in film production, and overall film-making quality (creativity, visual and sound elements). Each alternative is subject to what a member of this company calls "test of preferredness in grids."[1]

Another way of systematically assessing options or alternatives is to compare each one against the others. That is to say, solution A can be compared to solution B, C, and D, then solution B can be compared to solution A, C, and D, and so on. A grid or matrix, as in Figure 12-5, can facilitate the comparison process.

Predicting Success

Decision making, as opposed to problem solving, typically is concerned with future consequences or, putting it

another way, the probability of success. To quote management authority Peter Drucker on the distinction between problem solving and decision making:[2]

Well, you solve a problem so that you don't have to make a decision. Every time you solve a problem you try to "restore" the process to where you know it should be. So that you don't have to make a decision. You make a decision when you want a change, and a decision therefore creates a new set of circumstances. It is focused on the future. Solving a problem is almost, really, looking back. This is the way it should be and it no longer is. So let's go back to it. In fact, problem solving can be greatly overdone because it creates a fear of change. Managers have to learn to see in change an opportunity; and not to ask how do we get back to where we were, but what is the new optimal stage. And so a decision has consequences; it changes the environment and the situation. It focuses on making things happen in the future. You do that when you make the most critical of all decisions, the *people* decisions—how to promote somebody, to move somebody, to let somebody go. You do it when you make a decision to buy a house and move out of the one you're in. And a decision therefore has a risk and an uncertainty, but it also creates an opportunity.

In respect to on-the-job decisions, we know that investing in a new product line, buying new equipment, selecting an executive for a key post, or embarking on a particular employee-management relations policy all have important consequences for the future. Therefore, these decisions must have a high likelihood (probability) of succeeding.

To aid in measuring success probability, one prominent management consultant and author, Edward Roseman, uses this formula:

Desirability (of alternative) $\times$ Probability of success = Expected value (of the decision).[3]

As an example of how the formula works, let's assume we are conducting a career planning workshop and our participants have to choose a wise course of action among several career alternatives. One of them is a young woman with a newly-earned Ph.D. in industrial psychology. Her career options are these: teaching in the business school of a small college in the midwest, a personnel research job with IBM, a consulting position with a newly formed consulting firm, establishing herself as an independent consultant, and a training job with a multinational firm.

The young woman sets up a weighted decision-making matrix along the lines shown in Figure 12-6, using a modified version of the Edward Roseman model. Note that the weights shown are percentages of 1.00. A weight of 1.00 would be a maximum weighting, indicating an extremely strong feeling concerning "desirability" or "success probability." In general, by quantifying the alternatives and success data, one can put the possible decision in better perspective.

Prediction of success also can be aided by using a number of nonquantitative approaches including:

Success-failure analysis. With this technique participants brainstorm conditions for both success and failure. A T-column, with the headings "What Will Guarantee Success" and "What Will Guarantee Failure" can help sharpen the issues.

Devil's advocate technique. Participants are asked to focus on failure: In what ways can this solution (decision, idea, course of action, alternative) be less than successful?

If there is a possibility a higher body—board of directors, a legislative group, a higher echelon—may ask this question before it approves the decision, it may be desirable to role play this eventuality. Several participants may assume the role of board members who ask searching, "negative" questions about the proposal.

Reality testing. Here we are concerned about success in the real world—"Will it really fly?" A T-column, with the headings "Our Expectations" and "Our Concerns" can facilitate the analysis.

Risk analysis. The analysis of possible risks to be encountered and means to meet them can be helped with a T-column with headings "Anticipated Risks" and "Ways of Overcoming the Risks."

In general, since a decision is concerned with future consequences, it is essential to give thought to negative eventualities that may arise once the decision is implemented. To do otherwise is to ignore the real world. The trainer who raises such questions is providing extremely worthwhile assistance to the participant group. For more details on this procedure, see "Risk Analysis," pages 16–17.

How to Plan and Implement the Solution (Step 5 in the Problem-Solving Process)

After a problem is "solved," that is, a course of action is decided upon, the problem-solving process is hardly over. Why not? Because steps must be taken to *implement* or *activate* the solution. In effect, the group is concerned with questions such as these: How will we implement the decision? Who will be responsible for which aspect of the implementation plan? Will we need outside resources? When are the various phases of implementation to be completed? Is there a sequence for these phases? What conditions will exist so we will know "we are there?" Who is to be informed of the decision and the implementation plans?

The reader will note that these questions are merely an expansion of the journalist's six questions: Who? What? Why? When? Where? How? Responses to the six questions may provide the data needed for good plan implementation. The six questions may also stimulate other questions, too.

To ensure that planning proceeds in an orderly way, a control sheet or chart for time and another one for responsibility (who is responsible for what) are very useful. Sample charts relating to a marketing plan, are depicted in Figures 12-7 and 12-8.

Another procedure is to brainstorm the concerns entailed in implementation, write each idea on a $5'' \times 8''$ card with a felt-tip pen, and post them on the wall with masking tape. Then rearrange the cards for chronological implementation.

Card-posting procedures, previously discussed under Step 3: Generating ideas about a problem for its resolution, may also be used in the implementation phase (planning for action) of the problem-solving process. For example, it may be desired to work through, on a step-by-step basis, how a particular action plan is to be carried out. A procedure for this is to have participants list (via brainstorming) on large cards the steps to be considered in such planning. For example, if the action plan relates to the launching of a new sales campaign, steps

Success Prediction Matrix

Option	Desirability of Option	× Success Probability	= Expected Value of Option
1. Teaching	.25	.75	.188
2. Research	.50	.75	.375
3. Trainer	.70	.75	.525
4. Consultant with firm	.65	.50	.325
5. Independant consultant	.75	.25	.188

Figure 12-6. Example of a weighted matrix for predicting success, based on the Edward Roseman formula.

Activities	Jan. 15	Jan. 31	Feb. 15	Feb. 28	March 15	March 31
1. Hiring						
2. Training						
3. Promotion						
4. Trade shows						
5. Press releases						
6. Budget						
7.						
8.						

Figure 12-7. Example of a planning chart for ensuring proper scheduling.

Activity	Joan	Pat	Kim	B.J.	Chris
Hiring					
Training					
Promotion					
Trade Shows					
Press releases					
Budget					

Figure 12-8. Example of a planning chart for ensuring that project assignments are clearly specified.

such as space (magazine) advertising, direct mail efforts, exhibits at trade shows, TV and radio ads, press releases, hiring of new personnel, and training of new sales personnel have to be considered. The cards can be posted on the wall and repositioned in relation to desired time frames. The names of those responsible for each step also can be entered on the cards. In effect, the posted cards would provide a PERT chart (Program Evaluation and Review Technique) depicting a complete action plan. The chart could be photographed with a camera using a self-developing film and copies made on a photocopier and distributed to all concerned.

Additional Approaches to Problem Solving

Several added approaches to problem solving follow. They have not been included in the prior material since they cut across or overlap our five-step problem solving model. These techniques are:

☐ Rotational problem solving
☐ Past/present/future approach
☐ Using the journalist's six questions
☐ Personal needs analysis
☐ Problem solving for quality control
☐ Quality circles
☐ Maximizing idea power at meetings

Rotational Problem Solving (PSR)

Problem Solving Rotation (PSR)[4] is a highly participative and original problem-solving device involving movement, ideation, individual and team effort, and recognition. It works as follows:

1. With a normal-size group of about 20–25 participants, appoint four "problem solvers." (A smaller group may utilize only three problem solvers.)

2. The four problem solvers are given a short, written statement about a problem in need of resolution. The problems are different, meaning there are four problems.
3. The other group members become "advisors" and are teamed-up into four advisory groups—A, B, C, D. They are positioned at four different points in the training room.
4. Problem Solver One goes to Advisory Group A for ideas, guidance, advice, etc. about the assigned problem. Simultaneously, Problem Solver Two goes to Advisory Group B about the problem and so on, until each problem solver has contacted the four advisory groups for inputs. (Visits to the four advisory groups should take about 30 minutes in total. In this time frame, visits have been made to all four advisory groups and the latter have worked on, or advised on, four problems.)
5. The four problem solvers are given several minutes to summarize and digest the inputs they have garnered.
6. The four problem solvers form a panel and each gives a five-minute report on his/her solutions, recommendations, conclusions, etc.
7. The advisors interact with the problem solvers, quizzing them about their reports.
8. The advisors vote (secret ballot) on the "best" solution.
9. The problem solvers vote on the most helpful advisory group.

Steps 8 and 9 are designed to provide recognition for quality accomplishment.

Past/Present/Future Approach

Problem solving can be aided if groups can agree on these key issues:

☐ Where we are (current status of events)
☐ What happened (causes) to get us there

☐ Where we go from here (establish new goals)
☐ How we can get there.

Note: No mention is made of *who* did what to get us there. Avoidance of blaming people is essential to prevent defensive behavior from arising. When people are preoccupied with defending themselves, they can hardly engage in constructive problem-solving behavior.

Using the Journalist's Six Questions

The journalist's five W's and H—who, what, when, where, why, and how—can be used as a framework to analyze a problem and then to resolve it. The procedure calls for problem analysis via the journalist's six questions and then a reworking of the situation via a new set of responses to the six questions. An example follows:

Problem Analysis

Who: Safety personnel in Region 3 office.
What: Late (two weeks) submission of monthly safety reports; also, data often incomplete and hard to interpret.
When: Due tenth of each month.
Where: Due at corporate level.
Why: Data basic to overall coordination of safety program. Region 3 not aware of how data is used at corporate level; also absence of positive reinforcement for prompt, accurate submissions; deadline not realistic for Region 3.
How: Problem has become aggravated because we, at corporate level, have tolerated incomplete submissions.

Problem Resolution

Who: Safety personnel in Region 3 office and at corporate level.
What: Need to shift to new behavior: timely submission of safety reports.
When: Change reporting date to twentieth of month since other activities at Region 3 office make it difficult to meet our deadline of the tenth.
Where: Initiated in Region 3 office; submitted to corporate level.
Why: Data are basic for continuing program review.
How: The change can be facilitated by having two key Region 3 staffers work in corporate office for four weeks to get corporate viewpoint as to importance of report; the change in behavior can be maintained via positive reinforcement, i.e., provide praise for timely reports and for work done well as reported in those reports.

To generate data about each of the six questions, these techniques may be used:

☐ Brainstorming by the total group
☐ Small group work (buzz groups)
☐ Assignments to individual participants, such as in a quality circle that may have six members
☐ Assignments to dyads or triads

Investigating a problem situation. The journalist's six questions can also be used to form a check list to use in investigations; e.g., to investigate an accident, a theft, an employee fight, an incident of employee insubordination, etc. Thus, the six questions are used as a guide to ferret out systematically vital information as follows:

Who: The name(s), job titles, branch or department, etc., of the person(s) involved in the incident. Similar data on witnesses, those reporting the incident, etc., should be collected.
What: Description of incident, event, accident, loss, injury. Photos may be used for added detail.
When: Time of event or incident (date, time of day).
Where: The scene of the event should be clearly described: in or outside of the building; on what street; on what floor; in an office, shop, lab, cafeteria, hallway, stairwell, restroom.
How: What took place, what was the beginning event(s) and its end.
Why: Causative factors—why did the event take place?

Problem Solving for Quality Control

A particular system in an organization—a bank, a warehouse, a customer service office—may be established with great care and cost. Yet, all too often one or more of its basic procedures may be ignored in whole or in part. The result: The intended payoff from the system is not realized. This undesirable result occurs despite the fact that everyone knows that a system is no better than the degree of "respect" it receives. One bank (Irving Trust Company, New York) was concerned about the lack of quality in its telecommunication operations due to the failure to observe the procedures required by its system. It thus set up a study group on quality measurement. These procedures were used by the facilitator:

1. At the first meeting a description of the system's boundary and its workflow was provided. These questions were raised and answered:

   ☐ At what point are inputs received?
   ☐ When is it finished with outputs?

☐ What major charges (unit operations) occur from input to output?

☐ How are these unit operations divided into subtasks?

2. After the description of the workflow all possible deviations in quality were listed on a sheet of paper by group members on an "auto-brainstorming" basis.

3. Each person then stated aloud a deviation from his/her list.

4. The process was repeated until all deviations were reported and recorded on the flipchart. This listing was done without comment to save time.

5. Those deviations that were not clear were clarified.

6. Participants were given a packet of $3'' \times 5''$ cards and asked to select the eight most important deviations and to mark them on a priority basis. Of the 122 deviations identified, 22 were deemed to be the most significant.

7. The session coordinator then led a discussion on the deviations. Numerous improvements came out of the discussion. Seventeen were proposed, top management later reducing that number to eleven measures. Actions to produce improvement included more training for some operators, rescheduling working hours, reducing the action time on a cable from three to two hours, and rearrangement of the workflow.

It is to be noted that measuring the quality of the system's operations took place over a four-week period. But it only took about 12 hours of management time.[5]

Quality Circles

Using ideas developed in the United States about participative management, the Japanese (since 1962) have made significant industrial strides with the aid of the quality circle. So we now have the interesting phenomenon of American business executives going to Japan to see how an *American* idea can be implemented successfully. In any case, quality circles are being rapidly introduced into U.S. plants, offices, hospitals, etc.

Basically, a quality circle is a problem-solving unit composed of 8–12 employees who volunteer to do the job. They concern themselves with quality, safety, maintenance, cost, waste, faulty equipment, poor procedures, and the like. They meet one hour per week to work on problems that they have identified themselves. When they have solved their problem, they present their solution formally to top management officials for review and possible approval.

Quality circles not only can save organizations money and aid efficiency and profitability, but they can augment employee morale and self-esteem and provide a worthwhile social experience.

To be effective, the quality circle should operate in a company that already has a participative climate. In the absence of appropriate understanding and support by management, quality circles can hardly be anything but short-lived.

Another must for the success of the quality circle is training:

☐ Training of circle leaders in group dynamics, team leadership, communication, and motivation as well as in using problem-solving tools.

☐ Training of circle members in the purpose and functioning of the circle plus such practical problem solving tools as brainstorming, Pareto diagrams, cause and effect analysis, Four-M approach (manpower, materials, machinery, method), check sheets, check lists, histograms (vertical bar chart showing frequency of occurrence), and graphs. They also learn how to make presentations to management on their recommendations.

Another form of the quality circle is the "pyramid" developed by the U.S. Air Force. It is designed to permit the solving of problems that are broader in scope than those which are undertaken by the typical quality circle. It is a "super-circle," drawing on members in two other circles. Thus, if there are work problems such as distribution between two units or shops, the pyramid works on them.[6]

Note: In Japan quality circles may be composed of outside suppliers and company personnel. This is the model for the quality circle which goes beyond the one-shop level.

How big an impact can a quality circle make in an organization? One quality circle practitioner, E. J. Metz of General Telephone and Electronics, Stamford, Connecticut,[7] responds to this question by pointing out that a quality circle can only hope to solve a small proportion of an organization's problems. His reasoning is based on the fact that problems are of three types:

☐ Type I problems are appropriate for quality circles to solve since they have fairly complete "control" over them.

☐ Type II problems are influenced by quality circles only in part because control rests with others elsewhere in the organization. As a circle matures, it can take on Type II problems, working cooperatively with outside line and staff people who can aid in solving the problem.

☐ Type III problems are those over which the circle has neither control nor influence.

Metz asserts that 80% of an organization's productivity-quality problems are not Type I and must be solved by management action. In effect, these higher level problems result from coordination matters, management policies, product design, vendor-relation practices, etc.

Metz thus proposes the "verteam" circle to work on the broad, Type III problems. What is a verteam circle? It is a vertically structured problem-solving unit. It is a heterogeneous rather than a homogeneous work group and may meet for extended periods rather than for only one hour per week. Its problems come from top management rather than from the circle, and in general it is more closely allied to upper levels of management and may be integrated into and reinforce other improvement efforts such as organization development and quality of work life.

How successful the basic quality circle and the verteam will be in the United States remains to be seen. In fact, Robert E. Cole, an expert at the University of Michigan on Japan and quality circles, asserts that only about one-third of Japanese circles have been effective. And given the less-than-participative nature of most American organizations, a wait-and-see posture would seem to be very appropriate.[8]

A recent general review of the status of quality circles indicates that not all companies have been able to sustain their interest in them. Causes for their demise range from lack of management understanding and support to lack of demonstrable cost savings. In some cases the name has been changed to employee involvement team, worker participation group, continuous improvement process, and quality communication circles. Membership in the International Association for Quality and Participation Circles (formerly the Association for Quality Circles) totals over 6,000, a fairly stable figure.[9]

Since quality circles and similar productivity teams don't succeed (or even survive) merely because they have been established, team leaders should maintain/invigorate their teams via these kinds of approaches:[10]

☐ *Secure management recognition.* The use of these techniques can show achievement: show before and after results of a project; ask line managers to attend team sessions on occasion; publicize results via newsletters and graphic displays in work areas; seek out commendation memos and other praise from top management.

☐ *Emphasize on-going individual development.* To perk up member interest over time, devices of this sort merit use: evaluate the team's strong points and areas in need of improvement; invite other team leaders and specialists from various parts of the organization to input new ideas; work on new problems in excess of current capabilities ("stretch"); develop new projects around new member skills; spot check other teams to broaden perspectives; tap the skills of experts and specialists to stimulate interest.

☐ *Share leadership.* The team leader should rotate leadership roles among the team; let the team set its own goals and select its own problems; share information fully.

☐ *Provide rewards and recognition.* Since the organization rather than the team leader controls the formal reward system, the leader should rely on nonfinancial incentives such as praise, certificates and letters of commendation, pins, etc.; show how the team's efforts impact on organizational productivity and/or quality; stress value of their cooperation with the organization; point up value of the team experience to future job/career possibilities.

Study Groups

One of the devices used in Japan for greater productivity is the Study Group.[11] It has been transplanted to the United States in a growing number of companies. It entails the meeting of managers from different functional areas one to three hours per week to define and resolve productivity problems. Some examples are: how to install the "Just-In-Time" inventory system, quality improvement, participative management, waste reduction, how to install a new technology. Typically, managers read a book on a topic of concern and collectively bring to the study group the theoretical material of the text to a practical level that all share. The meetings are results oriented, and are not a bull session of griping and blaming others for creating problems.

The key to the success of these learning experiences is that it comprises observation/problem definition, theoretical learning (the book discussion), and *action*. Unlike the usual office meeting, where there is a presenter who has information which others don't have, here all have a common fund of knowledge since they all have read the assigned book. This increases the vitality and pace of the discussion and raises the potential for locating a workable solution.

To set up a study group, these steps should be followed:

1. Define the problem.
2. Secure *volunteers* from the affected departments (engineering, finance, marketing, R&D, production, possibly personnel). Obviously, it helps considerably if the plant manager attends, too.
3. Recommend a book (or let the group select one) relating to the problem.

4. Select a group leader/facilitator or let the group select its own.
5. Schedule a suitable time for the weekly meetings which may continue for 2–5 months to resolve the problem.
6. Discuss the book and apply its ideas to the identified problem.
7. Secure several solutions to the problem.
8. Select the best solution.
9. Plan implementation of the solution. Consider the use of spin-off groups to study specific applications of the new concepts.
10. Take corrective action.
11. Evaluate results upon the agreed=upon date of project completion.

Another allied reading and discussion technique is used by The Woodlands Group, a group of trainer/consultants and other high-level trainers who meet quarterly for networking purposes. Their procedure is as follows:[12]

☐ *Individual reading.* Articles (one or more), a book or a report is assigned for reading. Enough time is allowed in advance to permit preparation for the discussion. Reading is not done at the session. Particular assignments are given arbitrarily, randomly, or voluntarily. A ground rule is that at least three people should have accomplished the reading. Several discussion questions are provided: "What are the major trends?" or: "What are the key leadership characteristics, per the author?" These questions are merely devices to focus attention and to stimulate thinking.
☐ *Small group analysis.* Groups are formed of those who have read the same article or book. They are given a task which will require a more comprehensive analysis of the material.
   Reporting. Each group sums up the main points of its discussion on flipchart. Members of all groups study these reports.
☐ *Major point examination.* New groups are formed of individuals who have read *different* assignments. They receive an assignment which focuses more on what the materials mean to the participants, e.g., "What leadership characteristics are critical for success in our company?"
   Reporting. Again, each group records its key points on flipchart.
☐ *Personal application.* Each person develops action plans to best meet personal needs.

The plus factors of The Woodlands approach are group pressure to read; learning becomes fun; it has great flexibility in terms of subject matter; learning can occur at several levels: informational, analytical, interpersonal, and group process. The major disadvantage: people may not carry through on their reading assignments, which dooms the session, of course.

SEA Formula. In any reading and discussion program some members will profit from guidelines of a general sort to assist them in "wrestling" with the assigned reading. If so, a practical and logical way to attack the book is to use the SEA approach: Significance, Evaluation, and Application. More specifically, these are:

☐ *Significance:* What is the author saying? His/her main thesis? Main arguments for his/her position? Is there a "call for action?" Why? *Note:* At this stage the goal is to grasp fully and objectively what is said or advocated, not to accept or reject ideas or proposals.
☐ *Evaluation:* How do I find the major thesis and arguments which are presented for it? Do I agree or disagree? Why? Did the author overlook anything? Where did he/she go "wrong," if he/she did? How does the material relate specifically to my experience?
☐ *Application:* Based on what I read, what should I (or the team or organization) do to capitalize on the author's ideas?

Note: An ideal arrangement, insofar as guidance to the reader is concerned, is to (a) encourage participants to use the SEA formula and (b) also provide them with questions, which focus more specifically on the content, for their use when they reach the Evaluation step.

Knowledge Circles[13]

To help people to work smarter, the Knowledge Circle is a useful device. As a complement to more formal classroom training, it provides a system to share one's knowledge with others. At these meetings short presentations—one to ten minutes long—are used to pass along tips, shortcuts, new ideas, and new approaches. Presenters of ideas may come from the immediate unit, other parts of the organization, or the outside. People who have just returned from training programs are good idea sources. For maximum learning, the short presentation should be followed by group discussion. Handouts should be provided, as appropriate.

Certain administrative/organizational/procedural details require attention for maximum success of the circle:

☐ Provide a leader who assumes responsibility for scheduling speakers, setting up meetings, documenting activities, and evaluating results. A volunteer leader works best since he/she will bring his/her enthusiasm to the operation.

☐ Although the Knowledge Circle can take place during the regular staff meeting, a special meeting time will demonstrate management commitment to the idea.

☐ Schedule meetings frequently enough to establish the concept in everyone's mind. Anticipate that the frequency will probably taper off as the volume of available ideas decreases.

☐ Circle size will depend on the number of people who have a need to know, to learn, and to share information. Thus meetings will vary in size. It is the leader's job to invite the "right" audience.

☐ Activities should be documented. Keep summaries of the meetings in a binder to serve as a permanent record and to orient new workers.

On-going evaluation is essential to determine Circle usefulness, i.e., whether job performance has improved or cost reduction has occurred. Calculate dollar savings wherever possible. Other less tangible benefits such as improved communication, better inter-group problem solving, improved team work, and greater job involvement may also accrue.

How to Maximize Idea Power at Meetings

In the pages that follow, several techniques are provided to maximize efficiency at meetings. By "efficiency" we mean tapping participants' ideas and converting them into specific solutions and/or action plans. The "jury technique" is particularly useful for a small group of about 12 "in-house" participants. The other three techniques—"idea reinforcement teams," "small group psychological reinforcement," and the "Phillips 66 method"—can be used with both small and large audiences at conferences, meetings, conventions, etc.

Problem solving via the jury technique. Problems that require quick action can be resolved properly via the "jury technique." By focusing on the "evidence," the technique can overcome tendencies toward "search-and-destroy," "find-the-villain," or "judgment-at-Nuremberg" strategies and proceedings, and other blocks to effective problem solving due to personality conflicts, status, domination (intended or otherwise) by "experts," and the heavy influence of the crisis situation resulting in too quick a decision. Here are its procedures:[14]

1. The top executive who will decide finally on a solution states the nature of the problem.
2. The top executive decides who can best contribute to the resolution of the problem and the implementation of a solution.

3. The top executive calls the problem-solving meeting, limited to 12 participants. They are encouraged to bring all necessary background material (memos, notes, statistics, reports).
4. The trainer provides the guide lines for an effective problem-solving effort:

   a. Each person states what he/she knows about the problem (the evidence).

   b. Each presenter is quizzed by the group about his/her ideas.

   c. The problem is redefined, as may be indicated.

   d. Small work units are formed to develop solutions. A recorder in each small group is designated to identify incomplete information and necessary follow-up action to secure missing data.

   e. The recorder consolidates all data to produce a problem definition and to identify subproblems and an appropriate action plan.

   f. Assignments are made to team members for the various agreed-upon action steps and for reporting on progress at the next meeting.

The principles of problem solving underlying this technique are these:

☐ Initial statements of problems tend to be improperly phrased due to a tendency to describe situations or symptoms.

☐ Freedom of inquiry by all participants is basic to effective problem solving.

☐ A friendly, supportive climate is also vital.

☐ All participants are of equal importance; everyone who has evidence to submit is an important person.

Idea reinforcement teams. On the assumption that far too many meetings and conferences produce much talk but little commitment to action thereafter, the "idea reinforcement team" technique merits consideration. Here are its procedures:[15]

1. Divide the total group into trios.
2. Provide each team of three with a packet of materials that when divided gives each participant two 5″ × 10″ notecards, one sheet of graph paper, and one sealed envelope. (The envelopes remain sealed until instructions to open them are given by the trainer or moderator.)
3. Ask each person to write on the notecards five or six points he/she got from the session.
4. Instruct each participant to create a visual on the graph paper that explains one of his/her learning points. Advise that stick figures, graphs, flow charts, or anything of an illustrative sort may be used.

5. Assign these roles to each team: presenter, prober, and observer. (The latter observes silently the effectiveness of the communication process.)
6. Tell the prober to open his/her envelope. The message therein advises on the attitude to assume, e.g., "Be hard to convince. Ask tough questions: 'Why do you think that?' 'How can that be used?' 'Why'"
7. Have the presenter tell the prober what he/she has learned. (Allow five to nine minutes for this.)
8. Have the prober respond per his/her written instructions in the envelope.
9. Call time and have the observer report (feedback) to the presenter and the prober the effectiveness of the communication process between them.
10. Encourage all team members to discuss the data generated therein.
11. Give a signal to the probers to interrupt the presenters and ask: "What *two* things do you plan to do about this?"
12. Have team members switch roles and repeat the above process two more times. In this way, all team members will have had a chance to function in all three roles.

The advantages of this procedure are these:

☐ Instant and total participation.
☐ Each team member is not only encouraged to think about his/her learning and plans for action, but also to listen to the ideas of his/her colleagues.
☐ Each presenter is challenged to "sharpen up" his/her plans for action.
☐ As a team effort, each member helps the others in their action planning.
☐ The team discussions become a form of peer pressure, augmenting the possibility that personal commitments will be acted on upon return to the job.

Small group psychological reinforcement. Two major barriers to meeting effectiveness are:

☐ Lack of full and meaningful participation
☐ A reluctance to nail down answers to specific questions and problems

To overcome these two problems, the "small group psychological reinforcement" technique merits consideration. Its procedures are these:[16]

1. Seat participants (six to eight) at round tables.
2. Provide each table with easel, pad, and felt-tip pen.
3. Instruct each group to select a recorder-reporter (RR).

4. The chairperson announces the problem in concise terms and requests suggestions thereon.
5. At each table ideas are collected and put on the easel pad. *Keypoint:* The name of each contributor is added to his/her idea. This provides motivation to the others, including shy persons, to contribute, too. People *do* like to see their names on the pad!
6. The chairman calls on several of the RR's to report their groups' ideas in full. Ideas may thus be seen as repetitive; but this is O.K. because by repetition they become imprinted in participants' minds. They psychologically reinforce their importance and adaptability.
7. The chairperson then calls on other RR's to add ideas not already reported on.

In general, the technique stimulates ideation at each table, it sets up a competition among the groups to produce ideas, and it elicits specific solutions to problems.

Phillips 66 method. A classic, easy-to-implement, idea-collection device is the Phillips 66 method, so named after J. Donald Phillips of Michigan State University. Originated in the Fifties, it works well with groups of 36, 66, or 666. Use these procedures:

1. Arrange chairs so that participants can readily form groups of six.
2. Ask three people to turn around so that they are in eye contact with three other participants.
3. Ask them to select a recorder.
4. Assign (or state) the problem.
5. Provide these instructions: "In the next six minutes come up with as many ideas as you can on the problem under discussion. The recorder is to write all of them down. In the last minute of your six minutes you are to select the better ideas. I will ask you to prioritize them at the five-minute mark. O.K., go to it."
6. Call time after five minutes and ask the group to rank their ideas in the order of their importance.
7. Collect the lists of ideas at the six-minute mark.
8. Depending on the nature of the meeting and time constraints, ideas may be posted on flipchart, discussed orally, or simply collected for later screening and analysis.

Note: Step one may be varied by having participants seated at tables or by counting off one through six. The latter procedure may be used if it is desirable to have people form new groups. The new teams can provide some invigoration, break up "cliques," and the like. The technique can be used to respond to a speaker or presentation; to obtain data from the participant group concerning needs, preferences, interests, problems, suggestions, attitudes, etc.; to explore various facets of a fairly complex problem by letting one or more groups discuss and analyze segments or phases of it; to react to a short handout.

Personal Needs Analysis

In various personal growth programs such as career development workshops, retirement planning sessions, assertiveness training, T-groups, and encounter groups it is desirable to help participants to focus on their needs for growth and how to take some action to meet their needs. The worksheet given in Figure 12-9 may be helpful for this purpose. It can be completed and processed in small groups.[17]

Participant	Major Concern (growth need)	General Course of Action	Specific Activities to Be Undertaken
Al	Dead end job; losing motivation	Seek out opportunities to secure new challenges, on and off the job	1. Ask boss for added responsibility 2. Seek transfer within organization 3. Start an advanced degree program
Amy	Dull existence; all work, no play	Seek out situations and activities which provide new stimulation	1. Join two or three groups 2. Take exciting vacations
Betty	Facing retirement; fear of future	Begin realistic planning now	Consider: 1. Second career 2. Academic work 3. Volunteer work

Figure 12-9. Example of a completed worksheet for helping participants plan for personal growth.

The worksheet obviously provides structure or a framework for the endeavor so participants can "think things through." It also emphasizes that as members of the small group "we're all in this together." By "together" we mean group members provide help, counsel, support, feedback, critique, etc. to one another, so that the end result is realistic and better than if one worked on one's problem alone.

Some Problem-Solving Principles

We have identified and discussed numerous techniques for and approaches to problem solving. We would be remiss, however, if we ignored the *importance* of certain principles/strategies basic to effective problem solving.

"Swiss cheese" principle. At times it may make more sense to work on *part* of a problem rather than to tackle the whole thing. Backing off a bit from "a monster" problem, i.e., one having many aspects or ramifications, may be the acme of practicality.

"Bleed-off" principle. When working on a long-term problem, it is helpful to point to short-term or more immediate gains or benefits. This will reassure those who authorized the project that their judgment was correct, for "pay-offs" are already apparent. The alternative—not being able to demonstrate any success—may very likely cause doubts and anxieties in the minds of the project's sponsors.

Success principle. A new group, for example, a quality circle, should tackle a relatively easy or "sure-fire" problem at the outset. This approach will establish the group's credibility with management and give group members confidence in their ability to succeed.

Studying the winners. Problem solving is more likely to succeed if we assess our successes as opposed to probing our defeats. To quote Robert L. Woodson, president of the Center for Neighborhood Enterprise, Washington, D.C.: "The only reason to spend your time studying failure is if you want to produce more failure. You cannot learn to produce success by studying failure. Every school, every neighborhood, no matter how dismal its circumstances, has successes. It's a mystery to me why we spend so much time crying over our failures and so little time trying to learn from our successes."[18]

Illogical thinking. Although much of problem solving depends upon thinking that is logical, orderly, sequential, and objective, many of the techniques presented in this book, such as brainstorming and imaging, help to encourage thinking which is non-conventional and fanciful. The ultimate horror of totally logical, left-brain thinking is epitomized by the incident involving the individual who, upon learning that most auto accidents happen within 10 miles of home, immediately decided to move to a new location!

Pilot runs. When conducting "demos" or pilot runs, it is wise to begin with two or more such projects. Why? Because if only one is started and some special circumstance beyond our control affects it adversely, we're out of business. Conversely, if two out of three "pilots" do work, we now have a successful track record and "are in."

Sampling. When collecting data about a problem, there's little point in engaging in "overkill"—as the saying goes, "drowning in data, but starved for information." Sensible data collection techniques will always consider the possibility of using simple sampling procedures. Depending on the problem, the sample can be random or systematic (e.g., every fifth or tenth item).

Causes vs. solutions. We have stressed in these pages the importance of gathering all the data we can about a problem, particularly its causes. However, in certain situations we may find that the continuing search for and assessment of causes may be nonproductive. To illustrate: Let's assume you or I find that our morning newspaper frequently is not at the front door as it should be. We want to learn the causes for this inconvenience. One training group brainstormed this problem and came up with thirty-five (!) possible causes—everything from theft by a dog, excess wind, dishonest/hostile neighbors, and shortages in delivery, to the newsboy donating the paper to the home for the aged, keeping samples to secure new customers, and selling "leftovers." However, since the causes for the missing newspaper are purely speculative, it is apparent that prolonged discussion of them is not very productive. It thus is essential to concentrate, instead, on *solutions*. The situation is akin to treating phobias—the causes, if not readily known, can be readily dispensed with. What is more important is to work out a program to teach the phobic new behaviors, i.e., by desensitizing the person gradually to his/her nonproductive fear.

Flipcharting. Flipcharts are a basic tool in problem solving. They encourage objectivity—data are collected and posted as opposed to possible finger-pointing or blaming others. Also, a visual display stimulates added ideas. Unlike the blackboard, the group can never run out of space to capture ideas, particularly if they are numerous as in a brainstorming procedure. Finally, the flipchart enables the group to "store" its ideas easily for use in later sessions.

Tangible results. The best measurements of successful problem solving are those that show tangible results: quality improvement; cost savings; reductions in waste, scrap, rejects, customer complaints, employee grievances, accidents, absenteeism; etc. Conversely, "soft" indicators of improvement such as change in attitudes, while interesting and useful, are not likely to receive the same degree of acceptance by upper-level management.

Some Do's and Don't's

Groups can solve problems effectively if they avoid these six pitfalls:[19]

Failure to identify the real problem. Often groups reduce their problem-solving capability by working on *symptoms* instead of the problem. Dealing with a symptom will, at best, provide short-term results. Remember, symptoms tend to recur; problems which are solved do not.

Failure to identify problem ownership. In other words, whose problem is it? Sales? Production? Service? Personnel? "Solving" the wrong group's problem only produces resentments, noncooperation, charges of meddling, etc. Once we know who assumes responsibility for the problem, we can work with that person or unit in resolving the difficulty.

Failure to identify all possible alternatives. This may be due to sloppy thinking, impatience, bias (predisposition toward a solution), or whatever. But regardless of the cause, high quality decisions require a good look at the choices.

Failure to create a written plan for implementation. No solution is better than the plan developed to activate it. This means attention (getting agreement) on who does what, how, and when. Use the flipchart to record group members' responsibilities for their piece of the action plan. Visibility helps to avoid misunderstandings about responsibility.

Failing to monitor the implementation. The best laid plans of groups often go awry due to various factors—illness, pressure of new events, unanticipated delays, unforeseen "bugs" that arise, etc. The solution: Appoint a monitor, coordinator, or trouble-shooter to stay on top of things. The alternative is slippages, bottlenecks, disappointments, frustrations, finger-pointing, and defensiveness ("that wasn't my job").

Failure to use a trained resource person or catalyst. As is apparent from everything that has been presented in this chapter, effective problem solving is dependent on the intelligent (appropriate) use of a good variety of techniques and procedures. The properly trained facilitator can help a group immeasurably whether we are talking about ensuring that the problem is defined at the outset, that it is subject to force field analysis (or other cause-effect analysis), that it is brainstormed (or "ideated" in some way), that all alternatives are really considered, and that a plan for implementation is developed and monitored.

So much for pitfalls. The other and more positive side of the problem-solving coin is what we can do in the training situation to ensure that we train our participants well. Here are some pointers:[20]

Use a problem-solving model. Participants need to work from a model, a conceptualization, a process so that they can check themselves at the various stages in the problem solving process. We have suggested a five-step model, but yours can have as many steps as needed. The Problem Solving Center in New York uses four steps: understanding the problem, devising a plan, carrying out the plan, and evaluating the results.

Solve participants' problems. This approach ensures full participant involvement, provides participants with something they can use immediately, and acquaints participants with one another's work.

Build upon problem presentations. Using live, challenging (unsolved) problems, the trainer can help participants zero in on each aspect (stage) of the problem-solving process. The idea is to slow down the action and make them do the job on a step-by-step basis, rather then permit replication of the hurried, global approaches used ordinarily on the job.

Encourage sequential questioning. Have participants ask questions of one another on each step of the problem-solving process. This will make for increased participation plus an internalization of the notion that solutions must await exploration of the earlier stages.

Assign written exercises about participants' problems. This procedure will aid in consolidating participant knowledge and skill about problem-solving techniques.

Encourage the use of "figurative" techniques. Introduce participants to analogy and metaphor. For the analogy, start them off with phrases like: "This thing reminds me of _____" or "This thing can be compared to _____." For the metaphor, use this starting phrase: "The (key person or object) is (another person or object)." Example: "The inventory system is a vehicular fuel system." The analysis picks up easily enough from the fuel system metaphor.

Key Points

1. To decide among alternatives (Step 4 in the model), ranking procedures are helpful. The ranking may be done with criteria developed by the group or without any criteria.
2. Procedures may also be used to predict the success of one option (decision) over another.
3. The last step in the model—planning and implementation—may be aided by time and staffing assignment charts.
4. Other more general approaches to problem solving are these: rotational problem solving, past/present/future approach, the journalist's six questions, personal needs analysis, quality circles, study groups, knowledge circles, and ways to maximize idea power at meetings.
5. The best problem solving follows principles and procedures such as these: use of pilot runs, sampling, flipcharting, "Swiss cheese" and "bleed off" principles, tackling easy problems first, moving appropriately from causes to solutions.

References

1. Carspecken, P., "How to Pick a Producer for Your Training Film," *Training and Development Journal* (December 1977), pp. 28–29.

2. "Peter Drucker on the Manager and the Organization," *Bulletin on Training* (March–April 1977), p. 4.

3. Roseman, E., *Confronting Nonpromotability: How to Manage A Stalled Career,* American Management Associations, New York (1977), pp. 234–235.

4. Developed by Weiss, K. D., Laredo State University, and reported in *Training and Development Journal* (September 1978), p. 27.

5. Latzko, W. J., "Quality Circles Won't Work Without Quality Control," *Bank Administration* (December 1981), pp. 23–26.

6. *Productivity* (March 1982), p. 10.

7. Metz, E. J., "The Verteam," *Training and Development Journal* (December 1981), pp. 78–85.

8. Dr. Cole's views on the problems of transplanting the quality circle to the United States are given in "QC Warning Voiced by U.S. Expert on Japanese Circles," *World of Work Report,* (July 1981), pp. 49–51.

9. Geber, Beverly, "Quality Circles: The Second Generation," *Training* (December 1986), pp. 54–61.

10. Miskin, Val, and Gmelch, Walter H., "Quality Leadership For Quality Teams," *Training and Development Journal* (May 1985), pp. 122–129.

11. "Middle Management: Making The Grade Through Study Groups," *Productivity* (July 1984), pp. 1–3.

12. Belcher, Forrest R., "About This 'Cognet' Business," *Training* (May 1985), p. 94.

13. James, Randolph, "'Working Smarter' Through Knowledge Circles," *Performance and Instruction Journal* (July 1986), pp. 7–11.

14. Devine, D. W., "The Jury Technique: Will the Real Problem Stand Up?" *Personnel* (September–October 1976), pp. 25–30.

15. Clark, C. H., "Teams Reinforce Ideas," *Successful Meetings* (June 1973), pp. 122–123.

16. Jones, J. E., "Structure Your Meeting for Success," *Meetings and Conventions* (January 1976), pp. 44, 57.

17. For ideas on how to "pep up" one's life, see Carlisle, M. W., "Is Your Fun Too Much Work?" *Parade* (October 11, 1981), pp. 26–27. The worksheet is adapted from a chart in the article.

18. Quoted in the column by William Rasberry, "Studying Success," *The Washington Post* (March 10, 1986).

19. Bledsoe, J., "When Solving Your Problems Here Are Six Pitfalls to Avoid," *Training/HRD* (May 1977), p. 86.

20. "Six Tips to Help Improve Your Problem-Solving Training," *Training/HRD* (October 1979), pp. 10, 16.

Recommended Reading

Ackoff, Russel L., *The Art Of Problem Solving*, New York, John Wiley and Sons, Inc., 1978.

In an anecdotal, humorous way, Ackoff explores problem solving and creativity and explains why many of our attempts at problem solving go awry.

Dyer, William G., "When Is a Problem a Problem?" *The Personnel Administrator*, June 1978, pp. 66–71.

Dyer distinguishes between problems and "felt needs," the former being a condition below standard and the latter being a situation where one or more people "hurt" enough to take some action on it.

Gryna, Frank M., Jr., *Quality Circles: A Team Approach To Problem Solving*. AMACOM, American Management Associations, New York, 1981.

This research study of the status of the Quality Circle in the United States. Covers history, benefits, determining feasibility in an organization, design, training, implementation, evaluation.

Ingle, Sud, *Quality Circles Master Guide*. Prentice Hall, Inc., Englewood Cliffs, New Jersey, 1982.

This is a comprehensive treatment of the subject by an early practitioner in the field.

Ingle, Sud, and Eitington, Julius E., *Implementing Quality Circles: Trainer's Manual and Leader's Handbook*, BNA Communications Inc., Rockville, Maryland, 1985, looseleaf, 179 pages.

These materials serve as a guidebook for Quality Circle leaders who need to know how to train QC members and to conduct QC meetings. *Note:* A QC member's workbook of 107 pages is also available.

Maier, Norman R. F., "Leadership Principles for Problem Solving Conferences," *Michigan Business Review*, May 1962.

This presents ten principles for problem solving including the admonitions to: direct effort toward solving surmountable problems, use *available* facts even when inadequate, recognize that the starting point of a problem is richest in solution possibilities, increase problem-mindedness and delay solution-mindedness, learn that disagreement can lead to hard feelings or to innovation, diagnose for facts vs. feelings, recognize that solutions suggested by the leader tend to be improperly evaluated.

Murnighan, J. Keith, "Group Decision Making: What Strategies Should You Use?" *Management Review*, February 1981, pp. 55–62.

This discusses and critically compares various group decision-making methods including the unstructured group meeting, brainstorming, statistical aggregation, the Delphi technique, and the nominal group technique.

Osborn, Alex, *Applied Imagination*, Charles Scribner's Sons, New York, 1960.

This is a classic work on problem solving, particularly on the technique of brainstorming.

Parnes, Sidney J., Noller, Ruth B., and Biondi, Angelo M., *Guide To Creative Action*, Charles Scribner's Sons, New York, 1977.

A rich source book of short readings and practical exercises this covers the vast field of problem solving and creativity.

Parnes, Sidney J., Noller, Ruth B., and Biondi, Angelo M., *Creative Actionbook*. Charles Scribner's Sons, New York, 1976.

This is an exercise book to accompany *Guide to Creative Action*.

Rawlinson, J. Geoffrey, *Creative Thinking and Brainstorming*, John Wiley and Sons, Inc., New York, 1981.

This treats (1) barriers to creative thinking and how they can be removed, (2) how to organize and evaluate brainstorming sessions, and (3) the do's and don't's of brainstorming.

Ulschak, Francis L., Nathanson, Leslie, and Gillan, Peter G., *Small Group Problem Solving: An Aid to Organizational Effectiveness*, Addison-Wesley Publishing Company, Reading, Mass., 1981.

This presents an overall problem-solving model that considers both technical and human factors in small group problem solving. It also treats in individual chapters these specific problem-solving techniques: synectics, nominal group techniques, systems analysis, force-field analysis, and brainstorming.

TEAM BUILDING: OVERCOMING THE "LONE RANGER" SYNDROME

Coming together is a beginning; keeping together is progress; working together is success.

—Henry Ford (1863–1947),
American industralist

People acting together as a group can accomplish things which no individual acting alone could ever hope to bring about.

—Franklin Delano Roosevelt
(1882–1945),
thirty-second U.S. President

There is nothing good or bad per se about a group. A group can be a roadblock to progress, enforcing 'group think' and conformity upon its members, paralyzing decision-making processes, and smothering individual initiative. Under other conditions, a group can be a powerful synergism of talents, strengthening its members, speeding up the decision-making process, and enhancing individual and personal growth.

— Rensis Likert (1903-1981),
director of the Institute of
Social Research,
University of Michigan

Trainers who have been delivering management training for some time may find that it is essential to move into team building. This is a logical development since "conventional" management training is concerned only with the dissemination of management concepts and individual skill development. Conventional training does nothing about resolving the real problems of work teams or helping managers who interact on the job to communicate and relate better to one another. And if the trainers don't move in this desirable direction, management may nudge them into it. Hence trainers should prepare themselves to become team builders or facilitators.

Team building is an organized effort to improve team effectiveness. It may relate to defining and clarifying policies/goals; to reviewing and refining procedures; to seeking out ways to be more innovative and creative; to improving management practices in such areas as communication, decision making, delegation, planning, coaching, career development, and incentives; to improving relationships between team members; to improving external relations (with customers, suppliers); to improving relations with other work teams; and to improving products and/or services.

In a sense team building draws upon the athletic model for its basic concepts. These concepts include the assumptions that performance must be continually critiqued, that the team can't rest on past accomplishments, that a team must constantly strive for greater teamness, that a team must be willing to engage in introspection and feedback (receiving as well as giving), and that such values as openness, trust, spontaneity, mutuality, sharing, caring, risk taking, and experimentation are paramount.

Team building typically begins when the team leader realizes that there are blocks to team effectiveness, that the team is not hitting on all cylinders, that improvement or change is desirable, and that help along those lines *is* wanted. Note that this is not the same as the team leader wanting team development so that the team leader's will can be imposed more fully on the group. In the latter case team building would be wasted effort, for such a leader's concept of a team would be one where members were subservient rather than creative, independent, questioning, etc.

Team building also is not likely to succeed if it is done because another department is doing it or because someone at a higher level directs that it be undertaken.

A very useful form of team building is the "transition team build."[1] Its purpose is to facilitate the entry of a new manager into an on-going operation. Each manager has a lot to learn about the new team and vice versa and, obviously, the sooner the better.

The manager wishes to learn of member strengths and weaknesses, their temperaments, possible interpersonal issues, the degree of teamness which exists, the team's history, current operating goals, priorities, and problems, etc.

Similarly, team members want to remove uncertainties concerning their new leader's management philosophy and style, personality, expectations, "hot buttons," and the like.

Some organizations regard the transition team build as so important that they require it to take place whenever a manager is assigned to a new post.

Team building may also take place following a major reorganization, a merger or an acquisition, and severe staff cutbacks. It may also be triggered by new organizational requirements such as significantly added responsibility, a change in mission, and new programs such as cost reduction or quality improvement. A highly critical report resulting from a communications, climate, or morale survey may also be an indicator of the need for team building.

A new plant, office, or special team project can also profit from team building before actual start-up. Its objectives are: to clarify mission, policies, priorities, and expectations generally, as well as to get acquainted more meaningfully and to make a good start on the development of authentic relations among team members.

One way to understand team building better is to consider what it is *not:*

☐ It is not something that can be accomplished successfully by every manager or team leader. Sharing the leadership and decision-making roles, listening, a willingness to receive as well as to give feedback, supporting and praising others as opposed to blaming people, and creating a climate for openness are skills and attitudes not all managers possess. In other words, "leader readiness" is a key concept for successful team building.

☐ It is not likely to be effective if all members of the group are not committed to the idea. Lip service to team building by one or more members will vitiate the effort.

☐ It is not only for the work team "in trouble." All work groups can improve their effectiveness.

☐ It is not a one-shot affair. Initial sessions must be supported by continuing follow-up meetings. It is a long-term investment for unit or group health.

☐ It is not a T-group (sensitivity training). Although the facilitator may draw upon certain techniques and activities that are used in such training, the basic thrust is toward work improvement rather than improvement in interpersonal competence.[2]

☐ It is not a panacea. It cannot overcome problems that relate to the larger system such as insufficient resources, an ineffective reward system, poor leadership at the level above the work team, an ineffective organizational communication system, or lack of cooperation by other work units.

☐ It is not an easy thing to accomplish. Hard work, patience, a willingness to invest the necessary time, risk taking, experimentation are some of the ingredients of successful team building.

☐ It typically is not something that can be done well without a trained facilitator. Some managers may be able to "pull it off" on their own, but they are few in number. In essence, a neutral observer of the group—the facilitator—is an indispensible adjunct to the total process. The facilitator's role as a catalyst, standard-setter, challenger, issue-raiser, processor, arbitrator, and the like is what makes things happen meaningfully.

☐ It is not a process that is intended to create dependence on the facilitator. In fact, the proof of a facilitator's effectiveness comes when the group no longer needs the facilitator

As a final observation, what distinguishes team building from more conventional group effort in the workplace is that is has a *dual* concern:

1. The work per se (goals, policies, priorities, procedures, problems, products, services).
2. An appraisal of the group itself as it functions to do that work (group process). Although the emphasis on work vs. the emphasis on process will vary with (a) the needs of each group, (b) the group's ability and willingness to receive feedback about itself, and (c) the facilitator's style, the primary emphasis, typically, is on work improvement.

Regarding item 2, there are three member-related issues that will determine whether a group striving to become a team will actually become one. They are:[3]

☐ *Membership:* Am I in or out? (The more "in" we feel, the greater our cooperation and zeal and vice versa.)
☐ *Influence:* Do I have any power and control? (This relates to maintenance vs. loss of self-esteem.)
☐ *Personal growth:* Will there be opportunities to use, develop, and expand my needed skills and resources?

Preliminary Work

Prior to the first session, it is essential for the facilitator to gather data about the work team. This can be done via:

☐ Interviews with team members (for one to one and one-half hours)

☐ Questionnaires
☐ Questionnaires supplemented by interviews (preferred over method 2)

The gathering of such data will serve these purposes:

☐ Provide some "feel" for the group—their personalities and their problems, needs, hurts, reservations, hopes, and dreams.
☐ Provide the facilitator with a chance to meet the team members and vice versa (if interviews are conducted).
☐ Make team members aware that this is a serious, data-based training effort.
☐ Provide data that can be introduced into the group for its analysis.

The best way to begin an interview is to state clearly who you are, your relationship with the boss, why you're doing this, and what ground you hope to cover.

Data to be collected in the interview can fall logically into these broad categories:

☐ General questions
☐ Task (work) elements
☐ Interpersonal factors
☐ Process factors
☐ Systems influences

General questions may follow these lines: What are the group's key problems? What are the group's major strengths? Its major weaknesses? Its opportunities? What one thing would make the group more effective than it is? How do you feel about being a member of this group? What, if anything, would make you more effective? What are your major satisfactions/dissatisfactions on the job? What would you like to see happen in the team building session that would make it a worthwhile venture for you?

Task or work-related questions may assume these forms: What are the goals of the team? Are they clear? Logical? Current? Attainable? Are any goals absent, as you see it? Are there any policies, either current or absent, that affect team effectiveness? Is the team planning minded? Are priorities clear? Are there any procedures that are hindering effectiveness? Is your own job clearly defined? How do you know when you've done a good job?

Interpersonal factors may be probed with questions like these: How do you relate to the team? Do you feel you are part of it? How would you describe each team member? Who is most influential? Are there any members who produce conflicts? If so, how do they get resolved? Who do you work with the most? How sound is this relationship? How is your relationship with your su-

perior? What one thing would strengthen it (or make it even stronger)? How would you describe your boss as a leader? What is your boss' influence up the line?

Process factors relate to how the group goes about doing its work. These kinds of questions should illuminate this area: How are decisions made? What is the nature of your input in decisions? Are problems faced up to? How would you characterize communication in your team? Do people level with one another? Do people trust one another? Is this a creative or a conforming group? How effective are staff meetings? How effective are other problem solving meetings? How is conflict handled? Is it welcomed or smothered? In what kind of climate does the team operate?

Systems influences relate to broader aspects of the group's culture that influence behavior. Questions worth asking are these: How effective/adequate is the information system? What is the nature of the reward system? Does real accomplishment get rewarded? What would you say about the nature/adequacy of the pay system? The training system (growth opportunities)? The career development/promotion system?

A problem that is likely to arise in the interviews is the offering of data by a team member with constraints. That is to say, the interviewee may offer data "just so it is kept in confidence." In this circumstance the trainer has the obligation to make it very clear that while a request to treat the *data source* as confidential is O.K., the issues presented cannot be treated that way. In other words, there is little point in listening to team problems that cannot be reported back to the team.

Once all the data have been collected, what do you, the facilitator, do with it? You organize it so it can be presented logically and meaningfully to the group. You do not try to interpret it; the task is left to the group. Why? Because it is *their* data and it thus is *their* responsibility to deal with it. They may elect to use it or to ignore it. But that's the team's prerogative.

Also, the data are not to be shared with anyone before the team building effort begins. The data are *group* property and must be treated as such. So questions from the team leader or anyone else to the facilitator such as: "What have you been finding so far?" or "What did George have to say?" must be politely turned away on the grounds of confidentiality and/or incompleteness.

Starting the First Session

Team building is both difficult and important. It thus merits the best possible atmosphere/location for its proceedings. A motel/hotel or conference center away from town is extremely helpful. This "cultural island" retreat is essential for getting away from the usual job/family pressures and distractions and for permitting total concentration on the team building task.

The core or initial effort should be planned to last two or three days. It is a good idea to begin things with a social or cocktail party the first evening. This should be followed by dinner and the opening session of two hours or so.

The first session is a crucial one. For at this time team members are eager to learn answers to questions such as these:

- ☐ Is this going to be a serious effort or are we just going to go through the motions?
- ☐ Will I be put on the spot in any way?
- ☐ How candid can I be? Or should I just "play it safe?"
- ☐ What is the facilitator like? Is he/she the boss' stooge? Will he/she take sides?
- ☐ How eager are the boss and others to learn about their own shortcomings?
- ☐ Can *this* group really be helped?

Recognizing, then, that participants do have concerns, anxieties, and misconceptions, one way to start is with an opener such as "Hopes and Fears." Using a T-column, ask the group to list candidly its greatest hopes for and worst fears of this training effort.

Going to the right column first—the worst fears—we may expect responses such as "go over same old stuff;" "reinvent the wheel;" "waste time;" "make an ass of myself;" "be put on the spot;" "open up 'wounds' (old and new) unnecessarily."

By getting the fears out at the outset, we are candidly recognizing that it is legitimate and logical to have some doubts about the program. The fears need not be processed. Recognizing that they exist is a step forward.

If it is desired to process this material, a good way to do this is to establish subgroups—one or more being assigned this task: "How to make those hopes realized;" the other subgroups dealing with: "How to overcome these fears."

One of the fears that is certain to be expressed is that of being too frank or too open. A question may also arise about the impartiality of the facilitator—is he/she a stooge or spy for the boss, top management, or the personnel office? Since these questions are "trust" issues, experienced facilitators try to meet them head on. You may thus say: "I can't tell you how much you should level and express your feelings. It's your decision to decide how much to say. But based on my experience with these kinds of training programs, I must say to you that whether we succeed or fail depends on what each of you does here—how willing you are to say what you think."

As to the positive side—"the hopes" or possibly "fondest fantasies"—we may get responses such as: "solve all of our tough problems;" "improve coopera-

tion;" "remove blocks to communication;" "set realistic goals;" "improve profitability;" "strengthen our product line."

Another "safe" way to start is to approach things on a highly positive note. Thus, an assignment to several subgroups, or possibly to a fishbowl group, is to respond to this question: "What is our team particularly good at? What are our strengths?"

The data may be posted on flipchart and "reality tested." A second, logical task then might be to ask the reverse of the above question: "O.K., we know now what we're good at. What aspects of our team functioning could be improved upon?"

An obvious alternative to the prior approach is to have subgroups develop a T-column on both effective and less-than-effective capabilities (The Things We Do Well vs. The Things We Do Less Than Well). The data are posted and then discussed and critiqued in the total group.

An easy, low-key way to start is to have subgroups develop data that respond to these questions: What behaviors should team members engage in to produce teamness (build the team)? What behaviors should team members avoid lest they hurt teamness?

Note: The data requested is adequately general in character and not pinpointed at any one member of the team. The data may be posted on a T-column (Behaviors That Help vs. Behaviors That Hinder).

Another way to start is to break the group down into subgroups, each of which develops a list of problems facing the team. Some facilitators term this a "bug" list. The data that emerge—essentially a problem census—is then prioritized and becomes the team's agenda.

Things can begin, too, by taking an MBO (Management by Objectives) approach; that is, current overall goals can be posted and discussed as to their relevancy, adequacy or comprehensiveness, clarity, reachability, tie-in to those of horizontal units, etc.

Another "safe" way to start is to have the team experience a training program together, for example, on time management. A number of the topics that are treated in such a course relate to all team members as a working unit, e.g., defining key results areas (major responsibilities), conduct of meetings, the interruptions problem, delegation by the boss, the possible establishment of a quiet period. Stress management is another training activity that may have team development implications.

Another low-key, low-threat way to start is with an exercise that relates to team work, group decision making, etc. The NASA Exercise[4] is a useful one for this purpose for it shows how group judgment is superior to individual decision making. Or the Broken Squares[4] exercise may be used as a learning experience concerning cooperation.

Of course you may provide your own small group exercises on subjects such as:

□ Trust—What behaviors by the team (members and leader) build trust; what behaviors reduce trust.
□ Cooperation—What behaviors increase cooperation; what behaviors reduce it.
□ Teambuilding—risks vs. benefits.

Or the group may be asked to fantasize: What would things be like if we could all work well together? Or they may be asked to respond to a question such as this: What do you want for *you* as a result of our work here?

Still another way to start is with the completion of an instrument which tells the group how its members feel about current "teamness." The data are quickly tallied and can serve as the basis for much of the agenda for the day. This approach is recommended only for an advanced group, i.e., one that is really ready to move into an analysis of sensitive but basic team issues. The data that were gathered via questionnaires in advance of the program also may serve as a starting point for a team that is "ready to move."

A start on generating data can also be made via "fun-type" activities such as using Tinker Toys. Thus the total group may be divided into two or three small groups and given this task: "Build a representation of what the team is really like." In one program the small groups constructed the following: two forts with big cannons; a large tower with an object pointed out the window upward, to symbolize that "decisions are made in space;" a boat in disarray.

The point of suggesting alternate approaches is to indicate that there is no "best way" to start. What is "best" for one group may not be suitable at all for another. What is "meat and potatoes" for one group may be "high threat" for another. Hence the need to know the group, its leader and its problems quite well. Sizing up the group and its tolerance for approaches and data that confront them with its own functioning is a major art of team building.

A key rule: Wait for team readiness to "introspect." Rushing or forcing such analysis will only blow it. So timing is basic to interventions that confront the group with its own behavior.

It is also a good idea to propose a set of "ground rules" early on for the proceedings. These may include the following:

1. No blaming. Instead, talk about opportunities, challenges, problems, difficulties, bottlenecks, restraints, etc.

2. Don't talk about people who are not in the room.
3. When questioning or speaking to a team member, make comments directly to the person. For example, in lieu of saying "But she is always late with her reports" or "I have this problem with her," state "I have this problem with you, June. . . ."[5]

You may also wish to ask if other ground rules should be added to this list. This may produce suggestions such as responding to phone calls only during breaks or lunch, no smoking at sessions, full-time attendance by everyone (assuming this ground rule has not been clearly stated before the retreat). Other possibilities, which may emanate from the trainer, are to avoid interrupting a speaker, resolving issues by consensus rather than voting, and avoiding "plops." (A plop occurs when someone makes a statement and no one responds to it: the comment, then, simply plops to the floor, totally unrecognized. A likely reaction to the plop: "They don't seem to want my ideas. So I won't give them any.")

One way to emphasize teamness, with particular emphasis on shared leadership, is to also suggest a procedure of rotating the chairperson role on a two-hour or half-day basis.

Core Activities in the Team Building Session

Day One

The first day of the team building session is designed to develop a collaborative/supportive climate and tone for the total program. Hence the need to use openers to help team members ease into things (see "Starting The First Session"). The learning at this early stage is concerned with what an effective team is like, openness (leveling) and trust; feedback, both giving and receiving; assessing team functioning; and identifying problems and developing an agenda therefrom.

Note: In a certain sense the nature of the tasks the team works on in the morning of Day One is not too significant. What *is* significant is that the team is doing the tasks together—developing rapport, respect for one another, supportiveness, trust, intimacy, cooperation, warmth, etc.

In Day One a great deal of introspection is going on: "Who are we? What kind of place (organization) are we working in? What is our mission? What philosophy underlies our mission? What kind of collaboration do we need and what kind do we have? What are our strengths and weaknesses?"

For a team that has been experiencing confusion over responsibilities, the management responsibility/account-

ACCOUNTABILITY CHART

Job Duties	President	Marketing Vice Pres.	Financial Vice Pres.	Managing Vice Pres.	Field Sales Manager
1. Manages corporation to achieve corporate goals.	P				
2. Establishes and estimates overall operating policies.	P	C	C	C	
3. Establishes overall company financial, sales & production goals.	P	C	C	C	N
4. Prepares quarterly operating statements.	N			A	
5. Maximizes sales volume.	S	P			C
6. Supervises field salespeople.		S			P
7. Operates plant to produce quality product at minimum costs.	S	N		P	
8. Determines inventory levels.	N		C	C	
9. Purchases capital equipment.	A		A	C	
10. Administers employee benefit program.	D	C		C	

Key to Chart

S = must *supervise* (but not perform) the work, including planning, organizing, and coordinating it; maintaining contact with workers; training and instructing employees.

P = must *perform* the work, including making decisions related to getting the work done.

N = must be *notified* of actions and decisions of the person who performs the work.

A = must *approve* of actions and decisions.

D = must *decide* on any matter when an internal conflict arises.

C = must be *consulted* on an advisory, non-binding basis prior to actions and decisions.

Figure 13-1. Example of an accountability chart. Source: "Accountability Charting Using Job Descriptions," *Small Business Report* (June 1979), p. 17. Reproduced with the permission of the publisher of *Small Business Report*, Monterey, California.

ability guide[6] is useful. It takes the form shown in Figure 13-1.

The chart may reveal a lack of delegated authority, overlapping responsibility, failure to assign responsibility for an activity, failure to appreciate one another's roles, etc. Obviously, these problems must be resolved on a team basis and the results should be ones that team members find logical, equitable, and generally worth supporting.

The chart may be begun on Day One and possibly refined the next day or back on the job.

Closing Day One. In the course of the first day's work (including the prior evening's post-dinner, two-hour opener), considerable progress should have been experienced by the team. Members should be speaking more freely, a number of real issues should have been identified, the team should have a sense of where it is going, and the group may even begin feeling a degree of teamness.

One way to wrap things up is to have the group complete and process (tally, analyze, discuss) the instrument "My Assessment of Group Functioning," Appendix 42.

Another way of finishing the day is to have everyone jot down responses to the two questions on the worksheet given in Appendix 43. The data should be posted on flipcharts and they may be either processed the night after dinner or carried forward as the agenda item for the start of Day Two.

Another exercise that might be used is called "Catastrophe, Anyone?"[7] It entails the anonymous writing by each group member of the sensitive topics that others (not themselves) would be too reluctant or embarrassed to discuss publicly. The lists then are posted on newsprint, ranked according to payoff if discussed openly, and the top four or five items are subject to this prediction and discussion by the group: What "catastrophes" are averted by avoiding these issues? The exercise tends to help allay fears about discussing these *assumed* to be sensitive issues.

In general, by the end of Day One the group should have reached the stage where it is willing to take some risks in analyzing and discussing its problems as well as its own functioning. If the group is not ready for self-appraisal, it obviously cannot be done and should be deferred. Its desirability, however, should be explored by the facilitator with the group.

Day Two

A good way to start the second day is to "reality test" feelings about the all-significant first day, for Day One is the stage-setter, the climate-establisher, the communication channels-opener. If progress in these areas has not been made, the team is not really ready to move into its main tasks.

Tests of readiness for "movement" may be accomplished via various activities: a fishbowl exercise; completion and analysis of an instrument about teamness; asking people to move to one of three positions in the room (a "human continuum") representing their feelings of minor, moderate, or considerable progress. These feelings about progress or movement should be subject to team processing if the "reading" is low or only moderate. Also, additional work to improve climate and trust may be essential. If the trust problem revolves around the leader, this issue has to be resolved or there is little point in continuing the team development process.

If the group is "with it" on Day Two, they will dig in and identify problems realistically, establish goals and priorities, review and alter policies as necessary, and develop action plans to meet goals. They will also begin work on relationships (see the discussion of role negotiation in the section that follows). Decisions may also be made concerning time frames for future meetings. At these later dates action plans would be reviewed for progress/completion and such additional input as may be deemed necessary would be given.

Depending on the "contract" as to time, an evening session may be held on Day Two. Additional business also may be conducted on Day Three, either for a half or full day.

Note: The above description of team building has assumed that the entire team has "closed shop" and has taken off for a two- to three-day retreat in a "cultural island" setting. However, a team may also work on its problems on a less intensive basis. For example, the U.S. Public Health Service uses the Rubin, Plovnick, and Fry model[8] and has the team meet once a week (for two hours) for eight sessions. It covers these topics in that time period:

- ☐ Mission/priorities
- ☐ Roles and responsibilities
- ☐ Decision-making process
- ☐ Staff meetings
- ☐ Rewards and recognition
- ☐ Interpersonal relations
- ☐ Performance standards (includes "where do we go from here")

The "spread-out" approach helps the team to digest and use what it learned and thus make connections with the real world. It also overcomes such problems as "reentry" and "exhaustion" which may accrue over the long weekend at the cultural island.

Tools for Team Building

Lecturettes

At early stages in the team building program short talks may be given on topics basic to the team building process such as the feedback process including descriptive vs. evaluative feedback; the Johari window[4] and consensus for group decision making. Or various models relating to management may be introduced, such as Herzberg's Motivation-Hygiene Theory, McGregor's Theory X and Y, Likert's Systems 4, The parent-adult-child model of Transactional Analysis, Maslow's Hierarchy of Needs, etc.

Consensual Problem Solving

While all work units solve problems using one technique/approach or another, the team-oriented unit accomplishes this *consensually*. That is to say, the work on resolving problems is done on a mutual consent basis. *Note:* Consensus means the fullest possible opportunity for each team member to contribute his/her ideas. Agreement comes about by "talking things through," not by voting. The latter process tends to create winners and losers and thus detracts from the development of teamness. Also, voting, all too often, is done prematurely, i.e., before everyone is fully clued in to the alternatives, including the pros and cons of each.

Let's use the three-step problem solving model by Dave Quinlivan, Solution Finders, Inc., Vancouver, British Columbia, to develop this concept more fully.[9] The steps are data gathering, problem solving and action planning.

1. *Data gathering.* The group collectively attempts to define its problems. Obviously, agreement in problem definition is basic to moving on to the next two stages. In fact, a common cause for difficulty in agreeing on a solution (stage 2) and on an action plan (stage 3) is that real consensus was not established in respect to problem definition.
2. *Problem solving.* At this stage alternatives are developed, explored, and a solution is chosen. The selection is accomplished not via bargaining, compromising, accommodating, acquiescing, or fiat, but on a "win-win" basis—i.e., what is best from a team standpoint.
3. *Action planning.* Here the group looks at the potential impact of the implementation of their agreed-upon solution. They consider obstacles and opportunities offered by an action plan. If consensus is utilized at all of the above stages, *commitment* for implementation of an action plan is very certain. Conversely, if there has been limited participation/involvement/discussion, commitment will have to depend on the leader's authority.

If the model is introduced to the group early on by the trainer, he/she can make reference to it as the group works on its problems. The trainer's role is not to become involved in the content of a particular problem, but to provide guidance on the *process* that is used in problem solving. The trainer's monitoring should be concerned with (1) adherence to the model in sequential fashion, e.g., action plans are not to be developed before the problem is defined, and (2) encouragement of the fullest possible participation at all three stages of the process.

Subgroups

These are useful for generating considerable amounts of data, which then can be compared critically. The smaller group size not only aids participation because of its more intimate and thus open character but also, in a low-key way, creates a friendly competition.

Instrumentation

To enable the group to look at itself and its functioning, various instruments may be used. A number of them are given later.

Fishbowl

At times, various issues can be discussed advantageously by dividing the total group into two smaller groups. One group serves as the discussant group, the other group functions as observers. The discussion phase may last 20 minutes or so and then roles are reversed. At this point the ideas of the first group are discussed and enlarged upon. The fishbowl, as a small group device, provides greater participation, novelty, a change of pace, a chance to build on and/or critique the ideas (content) of others, etc. It may be also used for purposes of group process; i.e., the observers (outer ring) may give the discussants (inner group) feedback about their behavior, both as individual participants and as a group.

Role Negotiation

This is a technique to clarify and improve *work* relations between two team members so that they can do their jobs better. At times, however, it may result in or relate to the improvement of *interpersonal* relations as well. Typical work-related problem areas are the need for added or more timely information, meeting deadlines, coordination matters, scheduling concerns, and eliminating actions or behaviors that produce bottlenecks, tie-ups, delays, and uncertainty.

The following dialogue is an example of negotiating changes in interpersonal behavior between a boss and a subordinate:

Subordinate: I wish you would listen to me more when I'm in your office instead of shuffling your papers.

Boss: I wish you would come to the point more directly when you present me with a proposal.

In general, the idea is to talk through expectations so that misunderstandings are removed and mutual cooperation is secured.

The procedures for conducting a role negotiation follow:

1. Pass out the form in Appendix 44 to each member in quantity so that everyone can prepare a form on everyone else, or have members copy the three statements in the worksheet off a flipchart.
2. Members complete their forms on all the other team members, including the boss.
3. The facilitator asks for a volunteer "to start us off."
4. The volunteer then teams up with another team member and discusses his/her form.
5. After the negotiation is worked through the same two negotiators reverse roles.

Note: Although the negotiations can be done privately in dyads, it is more effective if the negotiations are conducted publicly. The reason for the public sharing is that it allows everyone to know what is going on for everyone else may be involved in the problem, too.

A caution about role negotiation: It is not recommended for use with a team that has a lot of conflicts. In this circumstance it will only produce a great deal of wrangling and little forward movement.

Relationship Recourse

Another way to encourage exploration of member relationships is to:

1. Have each member draw on a flipchart a circle, segment it, and then label each segment with the name of the other team members, including the boss.
2. Enter in each segment a percentage representing the strength of one's relationship with the other members. A perfect relationship rates 100%. (See Figure 13-2.)
3. Explain the basis for the assigned percentages and what behaviors on the part of the other parties would permit raising them to 100%.
4. Encourage team members to really level with one another. You may wish to say something like this: "You may feel that it is wiser and safer to give everyone a rating of 100%. But if you do, you may be losing out on a real opportunity to make things more satisfying for you over the long haul. And glossing over less than solid relationships certainly won't build a strong and open team. There may be some risks here, but in my experience the benefits far exceed the risks." *Note:* Some groups may find it helpful to work through their concerns by using the Risk Analysis procedure given in Chapter 2, pages 16–17.

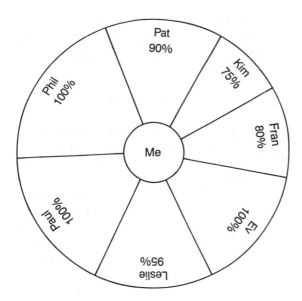

Figure 13-2. Example of a circle representing relationships.

Brainstorming

The group may be asked to brainstorm ways it can improve its communication effectiveness, how to improve the product line, how to make regularly scheduled staff meetings more useful, or how to improve cooperation. One group brainstormed "Obstacles to Team Effectiveness" and came up with 78 items! The team then spent six two-hour sessions to explain and clarify the items.[10]

The staff meeting improvement problem is often fertile ground for group ideation. One managerial team that I worked with brainstormed it and produced this batch of ideas in a short seven minutes:

Invite secretary to attend regularly
Rotate minutes-taking chore
Limit time to 1 hour
Meet twice weekly for 45 minutes
Make them luncheon meetings
Meet in a nearby restaurant
Meet in a bar
Use an observer to monitor how we do
Distribute minutes next day
Rotate chairmanship as we've been doing here
Invite Mr. Williams to attend occasionally (the boss' boss)
Invite experts from other departments to talk to us
Use a flipchart as we've learned here
Meet in a conference room (rather than in Chris' office)
Serve coffee and cake
Serve fruit juice
Invite an employee to attend each time

Use meetings to solve problems as well as to give information
Prepare an agenda in advance (secretary to coordinate)
Ban smoking
Get more comfortable chairs
Invite our consultant to attend to see how we're doing
Ban telephone interruptions
Latecomers pay $1.00 fine to go into coffee fund
Introduce short cases for added management training
Fine anyone $2.00 who gives a "put down" to someone
Assign someone to call attention to "plops"

Using Metaphors

As an activity to facilitate climate building, the group may be asked how it sees its functioning, using such metaphoric images as:

☐ A car, for example: "a Mercedes without a motor;" or "a Ford Escort—small, but up-to-date, perky and efficient;" or "a very old Oldsmobile—we always seem to be running out of gas."

☐ An animal, for example: "We're an ostrich, not seeing what's going around us;" or "We're an old pussy cat when we should be a tiger;" or "We're a bear in the spring, living on previously accumulated fat."

Force Field Analysis

This tool involves an enumeration (identification) and analysis of forces—favorable and unfavorable—at work in any problem solving situation. Analysis of the forces will make for a more sophisticated resolution of the problem.

Note: For additional information on the following topics, see the chapter as indicated: instrumentation, Chapter 9; fishbowl, Chapter 4; brainstorming, Chapter 11; metaphors, Chapter 10; force field analysis, Chapter 10.

Conflict Management

Groups which are active, energetic, and concerned inevitably will have differences among their members. But disagreement can lead to creativity—watch the sparks fly!—or to hard feelings. The trick in team management is to encourage the former and to soft-pedal the latter.

Management consultant Robert Lynch of L. M. Miller & Company, Atlanta, believes that groups should learn about and post on their meeting wall this three-step procedure to manage conflict:

1. *State your case.* Each party to the conflict states his/her side of the issue objectively. Inflammatory words like "always" and "each time" are taboo.
2. *Investigate the other's case.* This is the critical step. People tend to misuse their time allotments:

much of it goes into defending positions and all too little of it into *listening*.

3. *Shift the focus to identify other options.* A good statement for this is: "I have heard you, I know where you are coming from. You have heard my position/preferences. Why don't we collectively see if there are other options which merit our consideration?"

These steps set a new tone, unfreeze people from their rigid positions which they have already stated over 20 times, and permit new ideation and consideration of alternatives.[11]

In sum, disagreement should be accepted as normal and useful rather than being smothered. It should be brought out into the open and managed for innovation/creativity. Controversy can unleash high interest, stimulation, excitement, enthusiasm, challenge, exploration, participation/involvement, and ultimately new, worthwhile directions. Candid airing of differences can also lead to greater respect for others and stronger team cohesion.

Personality Preference Indicator

To help team members understand themselves and their colleagues better, and thus to value more varied views, a personality indicator, e.g., the Myers-Briggs Type Indicator, may be used. The MBTI can provide data to enable each person to look at the styles team members use to take in and process information, communicate, and solve problems and make decisions. Style indicators can help members (1) to learn of their own style and how they interact with others having the same and different styles, (2) to value different styles with their unique attributes, and (3) to understand the total group better.[12]

Play Time

Opportunities should be found for play, fun, and relaxation. The purpose of the recreating is not only to provide a change of pace and to loosen people up, which in themselves are highly desirable goals, but, more importantly, to afford team members the opportunity to experience one another in another setting and thus appreciate their own attributes and dimensions. ("She's really a smashing tennis player.")

Play time may be scheduled between 4:30 and 6:00 p.m., with a possible evening session following dinner. Or, if the group works the full day and doesn't opt for an evening session, the recreation can take place before a later dinner. Some activities can take place after dinner, too.

Outdoor activities—tennis, softball, running, hiking, swimming—are best, weather permitting. Indoor activi-

ties may encompass ping pong and billiards. Watching Monday night football and beer/soft drink drinking on a group basis also has cohesion-building potential. If dinner at the motel is not a must (i.e., there are no contractual arrangements for it), a small motorcade to a more distant and more desirable restaurant would also be a fun thing.

Note: The trainer should anticipate assuming the role of "recreation director" or participants may simply drift off to watch TV in their rooms on an individual basis. This means learning about available recreational facilities, and announcing "up front" the desirability of having some play time together as an added but vital part of the team building process. Also the trainer should be careful in the planning, organizing, and implementation of play activities to ensure that competition does not get carried back into the learning situation.

Instrumentation

At various points in a team building training program, the facilitator can help the group to look at its own functioning via instruments covering:

☐ "Teamness" (Appendix 45)
☐ The communication process (Appendix 46)
☐ The decision making process
☐ Group creativity/innovation (Appendix 47)
☐ Leadership (Appendix 48)
☐ Cooperation
☐ Trust
☐ Goals and policies (Appendix 49)

Other, more specialized instruments may also be used relating to:

☐ Conduct of meetings (Appendix 50)
☐ Time management
☐ Individual growth and development

The facilitator may also wish to use a simple rating scale to assess "satisfaction" with the proceedings, particularly that of Day One. The procedure for this is as follows:

1. Just before the morning break, say to participants: "It might be helpful to us if we took the temperature of the group—a reading concerning our satisfaction with our proceedings up to this point."
2. Then draw a scale on the flipchart, as follows

1	2	3	4	5	6	7
Lo						Hi

3. Tell participants: "Jot down on a piece of paper your rating, fold it, and pass it forward. O. K., I'll read the scores aloud and, Pat, will you average them, please?"

4. Pat gives the group an average score of 3.5, the facilitator marking the scale appropriately.

5. Then say: "We'll be taking these readings as we go along and I'll post them on the flipchart on this wall." You point to a flipchart sheet that has either of the formats given in Figures 13-3 and 13-4.

SATISFACTION RATING CHART

Time	Average Score
Day 1 Break A.M.	3.5
Lunch	**4.0**
Break P.M.	**3.8**
End of day	**3.5**
Day 2 Break A.M.	**5.0**
Lunch	**5.0**
Break P.M.	**4.0**
End of day	**5.5**

Figure 13-3. Example of a chart that indicates group satisfaction by using team averages.

Figure 13-4. Example of a graph using team averages to show team satisfaction.

Depending on how things seem to be going, you may ask the group if they wish to talk about their average score. This may be the first score or a later one. In effect, this intervention is an attempt to secure candid comments about how the group is progressing.

A group that is quite open may raise this question itself. Also, it may prefer to do the rating publicly rather than anonymously. The anonymous procedure obviously is "safer" for a group that has not yet developed a high degree of openness and trust.

Incidentally, the term "satisfaction" may be questioned by one or more participants, either when asked to give a rating or if a discussion is made of the rating. You may turn the question back to the group and ask them to define it or simply say it relates to how we feel about "progress" so far.

In general, the rating of satisfaction is significant not for its "accuracy," but for the idea that the group has been challenged, possibly for the first time in its history, to assess its own functioning.

The group may also be given a more elaborate rating form to complete at noon or towards the end of the first day. This form would help to assess the group feelings about team work from a number of standpoints. The data would be tallied and averaged and fed back to the group. A sample form is given in Appendix 48.

Evaluation of the Team Building Effort

As every trainer knows, management training is far easier to deliver than it is to evaluate. This follows since after a management development seminar or workshop, all return to their original environment where the pressures to perform in the "old" way tend to undo the new learning and the best of participant intentions.

Team building, on the other hand, is a lot harder to pull off successfully than it is to evaluate. For if the team development has succeeded, the results will be quite apparent in terms of both "soft" (attitudinal) and "hard" (quantitative) data.

Giving Feedback

It is (or should be) obvious from what has been said in the prior pages that a key to success in teambuilding is the ability to give feedback effectively. The instrument in Appendix 51 might be used to appraise one's prowess as a giver of feedback. While the use of the form may be beneficial if used totally on a "self-help" basis, much more significant results will ensue if it is processed in, say, trios. The triad will provide the intimacy and safety needed for sharing and the external motivation (via two other team members) to stay with the task fully.

The instrument should be used at a stage in the program—midway or later—where participants realize clearly why they are here and the importance of giving feedback properly.

Let's consider, then, soft data or indicators of how people feel about team work one to six months after the training is completed. We can use various attitude survey instruments to measure change and current satisfaction with the new way of doing things. We can ask team members how they feel about "teamness" in general or various aspects of it such as cooperation, communication, climate, creativity, problem solving, decision making, leadership, trust, and clarity of goals.

We can also secure harder data in terms of specific and measurable end results. Here are some indicators:

☐ Roles are clearly defined.
☐ Goals are established by the team and are clear to everyone.
☐ Policies have been established or revised.
☐ Procedures/systems have been set up to make operations efficient.
☐ Study groups/task forces are established and are readying action plans to implement decisions agreed to in the team building sessions.
☐ A schedule is set up for continuing team building sessions.
☐ When the team meets, quite often process matters are examined rather than ignored or taken for granted.
☐ Relations with external groups are improved.
☐ There is less dependence on the trainer, who may not be brought in very much or at all.
☐ Delegation is greater (deeper and more authentic).
☐ Greater opportunities for training (professional growth) are taking place.
☐ Group decision making is a norm.
☐ Costs have been reduced.
☐ Turnover may be reduced.
☐ Budgets are adhered to.
☐ Service to customers is better.
☐ Profitability (if a profit center) is improved.
☐ New and better products/services are being introduced.

Key Points

1. Supervisory and management development, however effective, can only deliver improvement in individual skills. If the broader management concern of effective work group functioning is to be addressed, team building has to be undertaken.
2. Team building must start with full understanding and support by the team leader. This means a candid facing up to key problems, a true desire for participative management, and a willingness to receive feedback about one's own functioning as a leader.
3. Team building has to proceed with careful groundwork in the form of interviews/questionnaires by the trainer to secure data about the team's functioning. Data collection relates to work problems, process factors, interpersonal relationships, and system impacts.
4. Typically, the initial team building effort takes place for two to three days, away from the demands and routines of the office.
5. Early team building activities are designed to establish rapport, mutuality, trust, open lines of communication, and so on.
6. As the team building program develops, the group begins to look at its own functioning, goals, policies, relationships, barriers to effectiveness, etc.
7. Typical training tools that are used include small group work, fishbowls, dyads, triads, instrumentation, role negotiation, brainstorming, feedback (giving and receiving), etc.
8. A successful team building effort results in a positive resolve to "do better." This takes the form of concrete action plans to meet key problems head on.
9. Follow-up sessions generally are necessary to keep the resolve alive.
10. The best team building effort is one wherein the work team is able (learns) to function effectively with little or no dependence on the trainer.

References

1. Looran, James, "The Transition Meeting: Taking Over A New Management Team," *Supervisory Management* (September 1985), pp. 29–36.
2. Woodman, Richard W., "Team Development Versus T-Group Training," *Group and Organization Studies* (June 1980), pp. 135–143.
3. Weisbord, Marvin R., "Team Effectiveness Theory," *Training and Development Journal* (January 1985), pp. 27–29.
4. The NASA and Broken Squares exercises are in Pfeiffer, J. W., and Jones, J. E., *A Handbook of Structured Experiences for Human Relations Training,* Vol. I, University Associates Publishers, Inc., San Diego, 1969. For a vivid description of how the Broken Squares worked in one team building session, see Hines, W. W., "Increasing Team Effectiveness," *Training and Development Journal* (February 1980), pp. 80–82.

5. Johnson, Cynthia R., "An Outline for Team Building," *Training* (January 1986), pp. 48–52.
6. For a detailed discussion of this tool, see Miller, N., "The Accountability Chart—A Tool for Team Building," *Personnel* (November–December 1977), pp. 51–56.
7. Steel, F., and Jenks, S., *The Feel of the Work Place: Understanding and Improving Organization Climate,* Addison-Wesley Publishing Company, Reading, Mass. (1977), p. 163.
8. Rubin, I. M., Plovnick, M. S., and Fry, R. E., *Task Oriented Team Development,* McGraw-Hill Publishing Company, New York (1978).
9. "Involve Your People In Organizational Team Building," *Training and Development Journal* (July 1987), pp. 73–74.
10. Hines, W. W., "Increasing Team Effectiveness," *Training and Development Journal* (February 1980), p. 79.
11. Lynch, Robert, "The Shout Out Among Non Team Players," *Training* (January 1986), pp. 48–52.
12. Cooper, Colleen R., and Ploor, Mary L., "The Challenges That Make Or Break A Group," *Training and Development Journal*, pp. 31–33.

Recommended Reading

Cooper, Colleen R., and Ploor, Mary L., "The Challenges That Make Or Break A Group," *Training and Development Journal*, April 1986, pp. 31–33.

The writers discuss procedures to help groups accomplish their work effectively: introductions, agendas, ground rules, voting vs. consensus in decision making, the use of personality preference indicators such as the MBTI. Of particular interest from a team building standpoint is dealing with two prime issues: (1) Purpose ("What business are we in, anyway?") and (2) SWOT Analysis (What are our strengths, weaknesses, opportunities, and threats?).

Goodale, James G., "Employee Involvement Sparks Diagnostic Conferences," *Personnel Journal*, February 1987, pp. 79–87.

The article presents an account of a team building effort entailing diagnostic analysis by *employees*. The employees discussed problems in their departments, causes of poor communication and teamwork, and recommended changes and improvements.

Dyer, William G., *Team Building: Issues and Alternatives,* 2nd edition, Addison-Wesley, Reading, Massachusetts, 1987.

This is a comprehensive treatment of the subject covering rationale, methods, implementation, design options, special situations such as the new team and the complacent team and interteam conflict.

Fordyce, J., and Weil, R., *Managing With People: A Manager's Handbook of Organization Development Methods*, Addison-Wesley, Reading, Mass., 1971.

The book treats in detail the many technologies for developing teams and bringing about change. Coverage extends from methods of data collection to methods for the conduct of team building sessions.

Margerison, Charles; Davies, Rod; and McCain, Dick; "High-Flying Management Development," *Training and Development Journal*, February 1987, pp. 38–41.

The article describes how an Australian airline developed crew members (generally regarded as technicians rather than managers) by sharpening their *management* skills. The reason? Team management in the cockpit is essential to flying a modern jet airliner. Joint training in decision making, communication, conflict management, etc., is a must, particularly if the crew is to cope effectively in pressure situations.

Miller, Barry W., and Phillips, Ronald C., "Team Building On A Deadline," *Training and Development Journal*, March 1986, pp. 54–57.

The article discusses a successful team building effort among warring project managers in an Ohio electric utility company.

Reilly, Anthony J., and Jones, John E., "Team Building," from Pfeiffer, J. William, and Jones, John E., *The 1974 Annual Handbook for Group Facilitators*, University Associates Publishers, Inc., San Diego, 1974, pp. 227–237.

This covers the whole sequence of team building including its goals, consultant's role, role of games and simulations, issues, effective problem solving, planning the team building session, coaching the team leader, conducting the session.

Weisbord, Marvin R., "Team Effectiveness Theory," *Training and Development Journal*, January 1985, pp. 27–29.

A long-time management consultant and team builder presents an insightful overview of team building concepts and procedures.

Woodcock, Mike, *Team Development Manual*, John Wiley and Sons, New York, 1979.

In addition to general background about how to improve team performance, this provides 45 activities (exercises) and 9 lecturettes for facilitator use in the training situation.

Woodcock, Mike, and Francis, Dave, *Organization Development Through Team Building: Planning A Cost Effective Strategy*, John Wiley and Sons, New York, 1981.

This is not a how-to-do it book, but rather a tool to think through whether you should do team building. Some factors the book suggests you consider are whether poor team work is a significant problem, whether the organization's culture supports it, team readiness, skill available to do the job.

Woodcock, Mike, and Francis, Dave, *Unblocking Your Organization*, University Associates Publishers, Inc., San Diego, 1978.

This contains numerous activities (exercises, instruments, etc.) useful for the team building facilitator.

"Nurses Build A Multi-Shift Team," *Training and Development Journal*, October 1984, pp. 14–15.

This brief article describes how nurses on a 24-hour, 3-shift schedule developed an effective work team. One interesting end-product: a statement of agreement about what the manager will do (e.g., give more positive feedback) and what the manager will ask the staff to do (e.g., "remind me that you need more information," "remind me when I'm being abrupt").

THE IN-BASKET EXERCISE—HOW TO CONDUCT AND DESIGN IT

Many persons might have achieved wisdom had they not supposed that they already possessed it.

—Seneca, Roman Philosopher and author (B.C. 4?–65 A.D.)

The in-basket exercise is a management simulation designed to provide skill practice in problem solving and decision making. It is composed of a set of 15–20 items, more or less interrelated, which have to be acted upon in a relatively short time frame under considerable pressure.

The completed in-basket is subsequently analyzed and discussed by the group, thereby giving the participants an opportunity to receive feedback about their prowess as decision makers. The feedback also may point up strengths and weaknesses in other leadership/managerial skills such as communication, motivation, delegation, planning, time management, etc.

What might participants "wring" out of an in-basket activity in the way of specific learning or benefits? The following are typical end results:

1. Skill in problem solving and decision making should be strengthened. More specifically, participants are challenged to note the interrelatedness of items awaiting action, to respect the importance and urgency of problems (prioritizing), and to take appropriate (logical) action in a short time period.
2. They may also learn that it is all too easy to over-emphasize, under-emphasize, or overlook various elements with relate to the decision-making process.
3. Conceptually, the should learn that there is no "best" way to handle (decide upon) a managerial problem. This learning comes about through exchange and discussion of the actions taken.
4. The importance of utilizing staff in working on day-to-day problems also comes through quite clearly.
5. Coordination of matters with colleagues and superiors is also a possible learning.
6. Managing one's time wisely is also likely to be a learning.
7. New managers may be expected to learn about the kinds of problems they are quite certain to encounter, as well as how to go about resolving them.

Working With The In-Basket

To appreciate more fully how participants operate in relation to the in-basket, let's examine the situation which exists when the in-basket is first encountered in the exercise.

Typically, the participant, in the role of manager, is about to report for duty on a new job. The new assignment has come up suddenly. He/she is to succeed someone who has just been transferred, retired, died of a heart attack, etc. The visit to his/her new office is very brief—60–90 minutes, sometimes 2 hours. Why the short visit? Because he/she has to catch a plane to go to headquarters to work on a special project, or to attend an important conference, or take a field trip, or attend a three to four day management seminar, etc.

What is the purpose of the visit to the new office? To check the in-basket to see if there is anything which may require attention (must be "handled") before going off on the required trip.

When does the visit to the office take place? Unfortunately, at a time when no staff members are available— Sunday evening, Saturday afternoon, possibly a weekday morning at 7:00 a.m., Friday evening at 5:30 p.m., or the like. (As we said, this is just before flight time so one cannot dally.)

And what are the conditions under which one attacks the in-basket? Not only are there no staff members present because of the time of day, but typically the secretary has just gone on annual leave or is hospitalized ("I'll be back in a week. Sorry I wasn't there to help you."). Also, the manager's immediate assistant has just been killed in a private plane crash; the telephone switchboard is unmanned and inoperative or is simply out of order; the file cabinets are locked; the photocopier is in a locked office, which means that one cannot make copies of any items to take along for further study, but must act now.

So what do all these harrowing circumstances add up to for our manager, as decision maker?

1. The pressure is on!
2. The in-box must be examined in a short time frame (one to two hours).
3. No one can be reached now for advice or to give oral instructions.
4. Instructions to staff, if any, only can be given in the form of short notes, either scribbled on the in-basket item or written on slips which are clipped or stapled to it.
5. All action is taken solely on the basis of the information in the in-basket, even though there may be information voids, irrelevant facts, conflicting information, and the like.

Are these limitations and pressures contained in the simulation likely to produce a feeling that this is not a very realistic situation? Not at all, for managers typically work with the in-basket and often find themselves in pressure-laden situations. Also, the problems themselves are plausible.

The In-Basket Exercise—Advantages and Limitations

An in-basket has a number of advantages, including:

1. It can provide participants with materials for analysis which are marked by a high degree of realism. What is more "natural" than for a manager to "attack" an in-basket?
2. It is a truly inexpensive form of training for managers. Most trainers should be able to study the guidelines for the construction of an in-basket exercise described herein, plus the models provided here and elsewhere, and create an engrossing and high-impact learning tool. (Of course, the trainer should have experienced the in-basket activity, too.)
3. It is a flexible tool and thus can be used in a variety of ways: as the basis for a rather comprehensive management training program or as an adjunct to such a course; for general and/or more specialized managers; with or without small group work in the evaluation phase of the activity. Also, the content (examples) may be closely work-related or more general in character; the individual analysis and group evaluation phases may be separated, timewise, e.g., several days later.
4. Since the basic work-analysis of the in-basket is done on an individual basis, there is no problem of self-consciousness arising among participants. Other management training techniques such as role playing and certain exercises may present this problem for some managers.
5. It helps to "pep up" the training program.

Some limitations of the in-basket are these:

1. The total time of the in-basket activity is fairly extensive. While the individual processing of the in-basket is ordinarily limited to one hour or so, the subsequent group-in-action work (analysis phase) takes two or three hours. (On the other hand, the time investment is worthwhile if real learning ensues. In fact, some trainers may argue that the long time element is what gives the activity its impact.)
2. For the trainer, considerable detail is involved in preparing and reproducing letters, memos, etc., to give them an authentic look. Also, large amounts of materials have to be carefully assembled; for example, visualize an in-basket of 15–20 items for 15–20 participants. Obviously each packet of items must be complete and assembled in its appropriate order. Duplicates must be avoided.

3. The moderator/facilitator must be skilled in working with groups as well as have the creativity, logic, perseverance, and management (or other) knowledge to develop an interesting, challenging, and technically sound in-basket. Not all trainers might meet these multi-faceted qualifications. (Of course, in-basket materials can be purchased from publishers of training materials. They also may be found in books.)

How to Design Your Own In-Basket

While in-baskets may be obtained from various publishers, you may wish to tailor-make your own. This procedure will allow you to include problems typical of your own organization. The greater realism of and interest in such materials should help to augment participant learning. Also, by avoiding the off-the-shelf product, you may keep your costs down. Of course, a printed in-basket from a publisher may look "superior" to your own.

In any case, here are the steps you should follow if you wish to design your own in-basket.

Step 1: Study Several In-Baskets

This procedure will give you a feel for their general thrust, style, format, tempo, etc. These materials are available in books and from publishers of such materials. Colleagues may also be helpful in this regard.

Step 2: Selection of Subject Matter

In designing an in-basket for managers, you have these choices as to subject matter:

☐ *General character.* The items in the in-basket can be *general* in nature, i.e., applicable to and of interest to *all* managers, regardless of their organizational affiliation. Our goal in this situation is, of course, to provide practice in analyzing and resolving management problems. In other words, just so there is a good mix of problems, with enough elements of complexity, challenge, pressure, realism, interrelatedness, etc., the precise nature of the actual items in the in-basket matters very little, if at all. Our assumption, here, is that all managers, whether general or more specialized (e.g., finance, engineering, etc.), regardless of who their employees may be, will identify with and learn from the problems presented in our in-box.

Thus we could have items related to personnel management, budgets, public relations, customer relations, communication, production, safety, marketing, etc., all of them relating to a fictitious organization.

This type of in-basket would fit in well in a general management seminar, a leadership program, and so on, either in-house or one available to the general public.

☐ *Specialized character.* We could also design our in-basket to have these special appeals:
1. To managers in particular organizations such as banks, hospitals, various state, federal or city government agencies, schools, manufacturing plants, retail enterprises, etc.
2. To managers engaged in particular job specializations such as engineering personnel, finance, manufacturing, R & D, etc.

☐ *In-house character.* In this type of in-basket we select carefully the items in it, by subject, because our goal is to present opportunities to deal with and thus learn about typical in-house problems, e.g., our marketing matters, our personnel concerns, our budgeting problems, our customer complaints, our vendor relations, and other problems peculiar to the operations of our enterprise or organization.

Step 3: Selection of In-Basket Topics

Now that we know the general character and direction of our in-basket, we are ready to select specific in-basket topics. A good way to do this is to meet with a committee composed of several knowledgeable, training-oriented management officials. They can give us guidance concerning the emphasis our in-basket should take—problems relating to finance, production, human relations and communication, marketing, customer and vendor relations, community relations, etc.

Specific items for the in-basket may be drawn from actual problems encountered in dealing with other managers, employees, suppliers, customers, etc. Or they may be "invented," drawing on our general familiarity with the problems involved. The in-baskets of colleagues may also provide us with models for adaptation.

Step 4: Guidelines For A Quality In-Basket

Our in-basket can be provocative of thought, challenging and realistic or it can be received with a "so what?" reaction. To ensure the former response, attention to these skill pointers should be given.

☐ Strive for a good "mix" of items, i.e., have an in-basket which has:
1. Crisis-type items (one or two); these are items which give the in-basket interest, challenge, excitement. (Position-wise, they could be placed at the middle or near the end of the in-basket and suddenly loom very significantly.)

2. Other substantive items, i.e., real problems of considerable magnitude or complexity. Examples: budget matters, complaints, personnel concerns, etc.
3. Interrelated items, i.e., those which affect or are affected by items 1 and 2 above.
4. Distractors or chaff, i.e., items which in themselves are minor and can be handled fairly easily. Of course, the chaff may be indicative or symptomatic of poor organizational functioning; e.g., Why is not the secretary handling routine items? Why are anonymous complaints on personnel matters, in sealed envelopes, coming here? Why are subordinate managers dodging run-of-the-mill decisions or engaging in incomplete staff work?

☐ Strive for realism. This should be done not only with the selection of high-interest, relevant topics, but in the use of language and style contained in the items. Variety in written style will aid realism.
☐ Try to avoid repetitive items. They provide little added challenge and are likely to turn the participants off. So if there is a fair amount of chaff in the in-basket, at least vary such materials.
☐ Use a mix of formats for the items: memos, letters, informal notes, reports, telephone slips, possibly telegrams, etc.
☐ The use of humorous names on the in-basket items should help to keep participants chuckling and "loose." Some examples are Edward Euphoria, Miles A. Way, I. M. Vigilant, Gordon Knott, John Nagg, John Sharp Quill, Otis B. Joiner, Y. B. Close, R. U. Meek, E. Z. Mark, John A. Quickwit, Rise N. Fast.

Fun-type names should be related to the role or character of the particular person. For example, an overly ambitious management trainee might be called E. Gore Beevore. Or an autocratic manager might be called Tigh Wrant.
☐ For added realism and help to the participant, include such aids as an organization chart and a calendar.
☐ The in-basket should be self-contained. That is, the problems being presented in all the items should be "workable," to varying degrees, based on the information provided. Of course, relevant information concerning a problem often may be contained in two or three interrelated items rather than in just one. Or the nature of the item may be such that the participant also may have to "invent" information (make his/her own assumption about the facts).
☐ A workable in-basket may have 15–25 items, depending on (1) the time available for the analysis and (2) the complexity of the items themselves. An in-basket having considerable "chaff" obviously would have more items than one having mostly relevant ones.

☐ The "traditional" practice of creating a situation where there is no staff available for help, no telephones, no photocopier, etc., is essential. It ensures that decisions are made on all items. "Cop outs" such as "I'll check this out with personnel before I do anything at all" are thus avoided.

Step 5: Sequencing the In-Basket Items

Part of the challenge for our participants in attacking their in-basket is to be able to separate the wheat from the chaff; the urgent and demanding items from the inconsequential; the interrelated items from the independent ones; the old from the new (are we watching our dates?); the significant and symptomatic from the commonplace (are there bottlenecks, delays, crises, poor team relations, timidity-prone individuals, etc., possibly indicative of a less-then-well organization?).

Hence, a well-constructed in-basket will not only have items such as the above in it, but the items themselves will be arranged carefully to give the *appearance of randomness*. In this way, the manager's skill in winnowing out, prioritizing, and "inter-relating" is tested and hopefully developed.

"Randomizing" the in-basket items also provides for realism and a change of pace as well. An in-basket of "heavy stuff" without a "break" would be a bit much.

Step 6: Try to Experience an In-Basket Yourself as a Learner

The wise trainer will try to become acquainted with the in-basket via a personal experience before he/she attempts to construct one. Why? Simply because there are considerable nuances and complexities built into a good in-basket. The personal experience will help you to appreciate fully those elements so that your in-basket will "hang together."

A Sample In-Basket

To appreciate better the anatomy of the in-basket exercise, we have provided one.*

Provide each participant with:

☐ Twenty-five sheets from a notepad similar to that shown in Figure 14-1.
☐ Ten blank memos as shown in Figure 14-2.
☐ The instructions shown in Figure 14-3.
☐ The organizational chart in Figure 14-4.

---

* *All memos, letters, and other handouts for the in-basket exercise may be copied directly or retyped to fit on regular 8½" × 11" paper.*

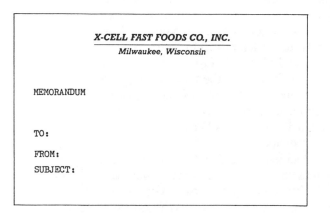

X-CELL FAST FOODS CO., INC.
Milwaukee, Wisconsin

You've Never Had A Better Reason To Eat Away From Home

Figure 14-1. Sample of a sheet of a note pad to be provided to in-basket exercise participants.

X-CELL FAST FOODS CO., INC.
Milwaukee, Wisconsin

MEMORANDUM

TO:

FROM:

SUBJECT:

Figure 14-2. Sample memo to be used in in-basket exercise.

☐ The calendar in Figure 14-5.
☐ The memos found in Figure 14-6.

Comments on the In-Basket Problems

In the paragraphs that follow, we offer an analysis of the various items in the in-basket. The comments should not be regarded as "perfect school solutions." Rather, they present ideas on how these cases or incidents might be handled. It may be anticipated that group members will come up with other approaches, many being very innovative and highly workable as well.

It is suggested that the trainer record carefully participant solutions to the various problems for use with other groups at a later date. In this manner, one can amass a good set of management knowledge which can be shared with other participants.

Note: The best procedure is to go through the whole box to spot "must do" items and to bring related items together, *before* acting on anything.

☐ *August 13 Memo*—Give secretary a note to send condolences to Fran Beck's spouse. Secretary won't be back until August 23, but this is not a rush item.

☐ *Telegram*—Some options: (1) Ask your subordinates via notes to them to work as a team and check out quickly other possible equipment deliveries. Put the same note on all staffers' desks and tell each to join with the others to work on this. (2) Cancel the EQUIPMENT CONFERENCE. This can be done via a note to a subordinate—put it on his/her desk and ask that action be taken to notify all regions of this.

Note: That a staff exists, and thus is available to provide help, is indicated by memo of July 5th from the Personnel Officer which summarizes leave taken by all employees of the Branch of Operations.

Note that you cannot use your secretary to relay this message for she won't be back until Monday, August 23, at the earliest. An interesting question: Could the boss' (the company president's) secretary be used to help out on this and other urgent matters?

☐ *August 8 Letter*—Routine—tell secretary via note to respond with a letter of appreciation, for your signature. Also give secretary a note to send a copy of letter to the Regional Director for transmission to the restaurant manager concerned. *Note:* No hurry; this can await your secretary's return.

☐ *August 11 Memo*—Prepare note to secretary: "Sorry you're out, see you when you return, etc. Please keep in touch so we'll know when to expect you back." *Note:* Secretary will not be there when you come back on Thursday, August 19; she hopes to be back on August 23, however.

☐ *August 10 Memo*—Give note directly to all your staff members to meet as a team and for them to select the trainers. (*Note:* Action is needed now since the training is coming up quickly, August 30 and 31. Also, as headquarters staff members they should know how to work this out with the regional offices quite well.)

☐ *August 9 Memo in Sealed Envelope*—A serious item. Since you'll be going to Region 1 soon, you can save it for that time. Give yourself a note to do that. You may also wish to meet with your staff about this. (*Note:* Visit to Region 1 office is likely, per item of July 14. Also, an old memo—March 29—reports on high operational costs in Region 1.)

☐ *August 6 Letter* (Diabetes Letter)—Options: (1) Give a staffer a note with instructions to attend for you.

(text continued on page 229)

Instructions to Participants

You are about to participate in an in-basket training experience. You have a packet of materials which simulates those found in the in-box of Ken Fixx.

You are Ken Fixx. You have just been promoted from the field to the position of Chief of Operations, X-Cell Fast Foods Co., Inc. (Congratulations!) X-Cell is a nation-wide chain of fast food restaurants, headquartered in Milwaukee, Wisconsin.

You were told initially to report for duty in Milwaukee on Monday, August 16. However, on Friday, August 13, you were told, instead, to report to a team building session in Wild Woods Conference Center, near Houston, Texas, on Sunday evening, August 15.

You decided to visit your new office in Milwaukee before going on to Houston. Although you only have an hour and one-half before you catch your plane to Houston, you thought you might at least check-out the in-basket. In this way you might be able to get on top of a few things, maybe make some photocopies of items worth taking along for further study on the plane. (By copying items, rather than taking originals, you leave the in-basket intact for others, such as your assistant, the boss' secretary and/or your own, who may have need for certain items.)

You also hope to phone your secretary and assistant chief at their homes to let them know you've arrived and to say hello, and possibly to get background on some of the in-basket items. Also, you would like to let them know you won't be back until Thursday (August 19) due to the Houston team building session.

As you check things out in the office, you quickly learn that the switchboard is unmanned and calls can neither be made nor received, that the two file cabinets which might have provided you with background about some of the in-basket items are locked, and the photo copy machine is also locked. (You probably wouldn't know how to start this model even if it weren't locked.)

Given these circumstances, here are your instructions:

You are to examine the in-basket items and decide how to deal with all of them.

All the actions you take are to be written out. You have a memo pad, a notepad, paper clips and a stapler to help you on this. You can draft memos to your secretary or anyone else or give yourself notes. If you wish, you may write notes on any of the in-basket items themselves.

To sum up:

- You are Ken Fixx.
- This is Sunday, August 15, 12 P.M.
- You have 1 hour to act on the total in-basket. (The plane leaves in 1½ hours.)
- You must write down every action you take.
- Assistance from anyone is not available at all; you're entirely on your own.
- You can only work with the materials on hand. (A calendar and an organization chart are included as your aids.)
- No materials are to be taken to Houston.
- You will be back in the office on Thursday noon.
- If you're thinking that this is a heck of a way to start a new job, well, you may be right! But, then, as a former U.S. President once said: "Life is unfair."

Figure 14-3. These instructions should be distributed to all participants.

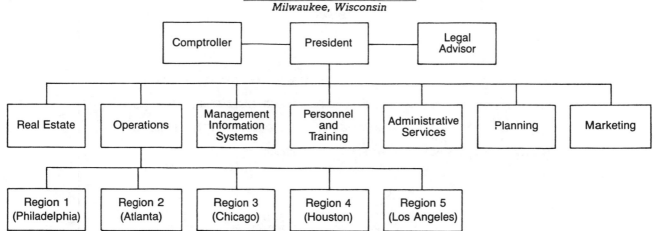

Figure 14-4. The organization chart for the in-basket exercise.

July						
S	M	T	W	T	F	S
				1	2	3
4	5	6	7	8	9	10
11	12	13	14	15	16	17
18	19	20	21	22	23	24
25	26	27	28	29	30	31

August						
S	M	T	W	T	F	S
1	2	3	4	5	6	7
8	9	10	11	12	13	14
15	16	17	18	19	20	21
22	23	24	25	26	27	28
29	30	31				

September						
S	M	T	W	T	F	S
			1	2	3	4
5	6	7	8	9	10	11
12	13	14	15	16	17	18
19	20	21	22	23	24	25
26	27	28	29	30		

Figure 14-5. The calendar needed by in-basket exercise participants.

X-CELL FAST FOODS CO., INC.

Milwaukee, Wisconsin

August 13

MEMORANDUM

TO: Ken Fixx, Chief of Operations

FROM: Reg Leader, President

SUBJECT: Your New Appointment

Welcome aboard. I'm sure you can help us here at Headquarters a great deal.

You probably haven't heard the bad news, but your immediate assistant, Fran Beck, was fatally wounded in a hunting accident last week. I'm sure you would have wanted to attend the funeral since I understand you know him pretty well.

We'll have a talk in detail about your responsibilities as soon as things settle down. In the meantime, just dig in as all of us are doing here.

Figure 14-6A. This and the following figures show the material to be used for the in-basket exercise.

```
                              TELEGRAM
                                                        August 13

   TO:  CHIEF, BRANCH OF OPERATIONS

   RESTAURANT EQUIPMENT TRAILER IN ACCIDENT YESTERDAY.  DOUBTFUL IT WILL

   ARRIVE IN TIME FOR DEMONSTRATION AT NEW EQUIPMENT CONFERENCE, THIS WEDNES-

   DAY.  CAN YOU MAKE OTHER ARRANGEMENTS FOR THIS EQUIPMENT WITH APPROPRIATE

   MANUFACTURERS?  TWENTY-FIVE PEOPLE DUE TO ATTEND.


                                        LEE GOODE

                                        REGIONAL DIRECTOR
                                        REGION #4
                                        HOUSTON
```

Figure 14-6B.

```
                                        1800 Dill Street
                                        Los Angeles, California
                                        August 8



   President
   X-CELL FAST FOODS CO., INC.
   Milwaukee, Wisconsin



   Dear Sir:

       My wife and I arrived at your Los Angeles restaurant #7 on July 20
   near closing time.  We ate our meal and in our hurry to leave, I left my
   briefcase which had some very important business papers.

       I needed those papers for a meeting early the next day.  To our sur-
   prise, one of your employees, who lived near our neighborhood, delivered
   the briefcase to our home the next morning at 7:45 A.M.

       We thought this was a very considerate act and felt compelled to
   write to you about it.  We can assure you that your employee has made us
   a friend of your restaurant chain for life.

                                        Sincerely,

                                        Mr. and Mrs. B.N. True
```

Figure 14-6C.

FROM THE DESK OF
Kim Rogers, Secretary/Operations
_____

August 11

Dear Mr. Fixx:

I am very glad to learn that you will be heading up Operations. We have a lot of problems, as you may know. But with your reputation as a trouble-shooter, we should be in great shape shortly.

I have been called away to Orlando, Florida. My mother has just been hospitalized with a bad back. I have to make arrangements to take care of my younger brother and sister (ages 6 and 9) and help out at home until mother can come home.

I would say I should be back by Monday, August 23, assuming all goes well.

I hope I am not inconveniencing you too much.

Kim Rogers
Kim Rogers

Figure 14-6D.

X-CELL FAST FOODS CO., INC.
Milwaukee, Wisconsin

August 10

MEMORANDUM

TO: Burton Quagmeyer, Chief, Operations Branch

FROM: Win Learnwell, Corporate Training Officer

SUBJECT: Coaching and Counseling Course

Our plans are firming up for the Coaching and Counseling Course. All we need to do to get moving on this is your appointment of two trainers from each of our five regions. They will be responsible for training supervisors in their respective regions.

The training is set for the last two days of this month. We have three University resource people lined up to train the trainers at that time. The trainer course will take place in Chicago.

Do you see any problems with any of this?

Figure 14-6E.

X-CELL FAST FOODS CO., INC.

Milwaukee, Wisconsin

August 9

MEMORANDUM

TO: Burton Quagmire, Chief, Operations Branch

FROM: Bobby McGee, Assistant Manager, Restaurant #4, Boston

SUBJECT: Management at Restaurant #4

   I don't know how much you know about management at Restaurant #4 here in Boston, but things are really bad. Morale is low; turnover is high; the boss plays favorites; costs are up because of wasted food and failure to observe energy regulations.

   I know I'm out of channels in writing to you, but the regional office doesn't seem to know what's going on. The Regional Director visits here fairly often, but the boss wines and dines him and generally snows him. The only reason we're making a profit is because we're near the two schools (public and private high schools). With half-way decent management we could do a lot better.

Sorry to have to bring this up in this way, but in view of the circumstnaces, I didn't feel I could go directly to anyone in Region 1.

Figure 14-6F. This item came in a sealed envelope marked "Personal and Confidential," addressed to the Chief, Branch of Operations. The trainer should provide an envelope for this item. Place the memo in it and seal it.

**SOUTHERN WISCONSIN
DIABETES ASSOCIATION
Madison, Wisconsin**

August 6

Burton Quagmeyer
Chief, Operations Branch
X-CELL FAST FOODS CO., INC
1219 Glendon Dr.
Milwaukee, Wisconsin

Dear Mr. Quagmeyer:

   Just a note to indicate that we are glad that you will represent your organization at our planning meeting here in Madison on August 20.

   Nationally, some 600,000 people will be told this year that they have diabetes. We have our share of that number in Southern Wisconsin. So I know you will want to attend the meeting to help our campaign get launched well.

   We shall look forward to seeing you at the kickoff meeting.

Sincerely,

R.W. Felton

R.W. Felton
President

Figure 14-6G.

X-CELL FAST FOODS CO., INC.

Region #4 Office
Houston, Texas

August 2

MEMORANDUM

TO: Burton Quagmeyer, Chief, Branch of Operations

FROM: Lee Goode, Regional Director

SUBJECT: New Equipment Demonstration and Conference

As the host for the New Equipment Demonstration and Conference, I wish to tell you we're all set to go.

As I've been telling anyone who will listen, this conference is a darn good thing. We need to update our kitchen ranges, dishwashers and other small equipment items as well.

I expect the demonstration restaurant equipment trailer to arrive here August 11 or 12. We can check everything out with plenty of time to spare for the August 18 Conference.

I have lined up two reps from each of the five regional offices plus several restaurant facility managers in each region. This should be a total group of about 25 keenly interested people.

We'll keep you posted on the results of all this.

Sorry you couldn't make it to Houston.

Figure 14-6H.

X-CELL FAST FOODS CO., INC.

Region #2 Office
Atlanta, Georgia

July 26

MEMORANDUM

TO: Burton Quagmeyer, Chief, Branch of Operations

FROM: Val Sanders, Regional Officer, Region 5

SUBJECT: Proposal for Conference of Regional Officers

It's been over two years since we last had a Regional Officers' Conference. Problems are piling up and a good week-long discussion on these matters should help us a lot.

We'll be glad to host the conference here in Atlanta. Just give us enough lead time so we can do the job properly.

Figure 14-6I.

X-CELL FAST FOODS CO., INC.
Milwaukee, Wisconsin

July 23

MEMORANDUM

TO: Burton Quagmeyer, Chief, Operations Branch

FROM: R.V. Reddy, Chief, Administrative Services Branch

SUBJECT: Security in Urban Restaurant Facilities

    I think we have to take another look at the security problem in our big city facilities. Our break-ins are running well ahead of last year and the year is only about half up.

    Since we purchased the heavy safes, on our recommendation, we haven't been losing any money between 11 P.M. and 7:00 A.M. But there have been break-ins for food after we close up at 11 P.M., and hold ups at night (9:00 to 11 P.M.) are increasing.

    We can plug most of these leaks, but cost will be a big factor to consider.

    How about exploring this further at lunch soon?

Figure 14-6J.

X-CELL FAST FOODS CO., INC.
Milwaukee, Wisconsin

July 20

MEMORANDUM

TO: Chief, Branch of Operations

FROM: Comptroller

SUBJECT: 5-Year Plan

    At our next meeing of our planning group, August 23, 9:00 A.M., we will get into the actual numbers - revenue projections, expenditures, the whole bit.

    You should be prepared to give the other budget team members your data for their review.

Figure 14-6K.

X-CELL FAST FOODS CO., INC.
Milwaukee, Wisconsin

July 14

MEMORANDUM

TO: Burton Quagmeyer, Chief, Operations Branch

FROM: Kyle Pyle, Chief, Planning Branch

SUBJECT: Food Industry Conference

I intend to take in the fast food industry conference in September. The agenda features several sessions dealing with economic and social trends affecting our functions. I would be delighted to have you join me.

      Place: New York City
      Dates: September 20-22

Let me know and I'll have my secretary register and hotel both of us at the same time.

While we're in the East we might also visit the Philadlephia Regional Office. Is this O.K.?

Figure 14-6L.

CITY MANAGEMENT ASSOCIATION
MILWAUKEE, WISCONSIN

July 12

Burton Quagmeyer
Chief, Branch of Operations
X-Cell Fast Foods Co., Inc.
1219 Glendon Dr.
Milwaukee, Wisconsin

Dear Burton:

Since your organization has been going ahead full blast on Quality Circles (at least two of your regions are gung-ho on this), I thought you might want to share your Q.C. experience with our group.

Could we "sign you up" to handle the September meeting? This would be a good start for our fall programming.

Let me know of your acceptance so I can get notices out. (We meet the fourth Thursday of the month.) We may invite the Madison Chapter to attend and make this a joint meeting.
Regards.

Cordially,

Dee Scission

Dee Scission

Figure 14-6M.

X-CELL FAST FOODS CO., INC.

Milwaukee, Wisconsin

July 9

MEMORANDUM

TO: Burton Quagmeyer, Chief, Operations Branch

FROM: Mann Powers, Chief, Personnel and Training Branch

SUBJECT: Turnover and Absenteeism at Restaurant Facilities in Major Cities

I thought you would be interested in personnel turnover and absentee rates in our big city operations. They are about twice the rates of our other operations. The figures are for the first 6 months of this year.

	Turnover	Absenteeism
Atlanta	15%	10%
Chicago	18%	12%
Philadelphia	20%	11%
Los Angeles	22%	13%
Pittsburgh	19%	15%
Boston	24%	10%

May we discuss this? The figures are disappointing considering that we pay well and all our supervisors have had that one week course in supervision.

Figure 14-6N.

X-CELL FAST FOODS CO., INC.

Milwaukee, Wisconsin

July 5

MEMORANDUM

TO: Burton Quagmeyer, Chief, Branch of Operations

FROM: Mann Power, Chief, Branch of Personnel

SUBJECT: Leave Summary, Branch of Operations

The data below summarizes annual and sick leave taken (full days only), January 1 - June 30, by staff members of the Operations Branch, corporate headquarters:

	Annual	Sick
Burton Quagmeyer, Chief	10	1
Fran Beck, Assistant Chief	6	2
Jacques Frost, Operations Specialist	12	1
Wilde Oates, Operations Specialist	15	4
Sarah Chance, Operations Specialist	5	0
Kim Rogers, Secretary	10*	7
V.R. Tell, Clerk-Typist	3	3

* Plus 4 days LWOP

Figure 14-6O.

July 1

Burton Quagmeyer
Chief, Operations Branch
X-CELL FAST FOODS CO., INC.
1219 Glendale Dr.
Milwaukee, Wisconsin

Dear Mr. Quagmeyer:

I am writing to you for the last time. And if I don't get an
appropriate cash settlement I shall have to bring suit about this.

Your waitress in the Newark restaurant, No. 7, dropped that tray
of dishes on my neck last March and I haven't been able to move it
properly since.

If you are a reliable company at all, you will see to it that my
claim is taken care of without further delay.

I assure you that my next letter will be from my lawyer's office.

Very truly yours,

Les Payne

Les Payne

Figure 14-6P.

X-CELL FAST FOODS CO., INC.

Milwaukee, Wisconsin

July 1

MEMORANDUM

TO: Burton Quagmeyer, Chief, Operations Branch

FROM: Lotta Land, Chief Real Estate Branch

SUBJECT: Disposal of Urban Properties

This memorandum is to encourage further thinking on the problem of
our big city restaurants. (See my memoranda of March 6th, May 12th
and June 15 on the same subject). These operations have good volume
but, as you know, they suffer from high turnover of personnel, vandalism,
break-ins, high waste ratios, and huge property taxes and so on. Their
annual net profit is always marginal compared to our other operations.

But the big thing is that the properties could be sold at a very
handsome price and we could use that money to relocate elsewhere in
those metropolitan areas. We could go to locations where customer
parking is available, labor is more dependable, and have facilities
which are up to the standard of most of our other successful operations.

I have asked your support before (see prior memos) to set up a
task force to really study this problem. I believe strongly that we should
move on this now.

Figure 14-6Q.

X-CELL FAST FOODS CO., INC.

Milwaukee, Wisconsin

June 30

MEMORANDUM

TO: Burton Quagmeyer, Chief, operations Branch

FROM: Mann Power, Personnel Officer

SUBJECT: Employee Orientation

I am setting up a special team to study employee orientation at all our facilities and in the regions and to make recommendations thereon.

Could we have one of your staffers serve with us for 3 or 4 days, starting, August 23?

We'll be meeting in the Region 5 office for this.

Thank you.

Figure 14-6R.

X-CELL FAST FOODS CO., INC.

Milwaukee, Wisconsin

June 15

MEMORANDUM

TO: Burton Quagmeyer, Chief, Operations Branch

FROM: Robin Well, Chief, Marketing Branch

SUBJECT: New Product Line

Our consultant group is about ready to bring in its report. They seem to be ready to propose some serious changes in our evening menu.

I don't think our equipment at the facilities could do the job.

You may want to check this out with Operations Specialist Wilde Oates who has been keeping up on this possible development.

Glad to discuss further.

Figure 14-6S.

X-CELL FAST FOODS CO., INC.
Milwaukee, Wisconsin

June 5

MEMORANDUM

TO: Burton Quagmeyer, Chief, Branch of Operations

FROM: Reg Leader, President

   I don't know whether or not you are thinking about another Regional Officers' meeting. I don't believe we've had one for three years now.

   We do have the funds to handle the travel, pay for outside speakers, etc.

   If you were to hold it early in November my schedule would permit my attendance for practically all of the first day.

Figure 14-6T.

X-CELL FAST FOODS CO., INC.
Milwaukee, Wisconsin

May 22

MEMORANDUM

TO: Burton Quagmeyer, Chief, Operations Branch

FROM: Win Learnwell, Corporate Training Officer

   Evidence is accumulating that   MBO (Management by Objectives) is really working well in only one region - Region 2. I think the training we did on it two years ago got things off to a good start. But, somehow, the enthusiasm seems to be waning.

   We could do the training bit again, but I think the problem is deeper that that.

   Can we discuss soon ?

Figure 14-6U.

X-CELL FAST FOODS CO., INC.

Milwaukee, Wisconsin

March 29

MEMORANDUM

TO: Burton Quagmeyer, Chief, Operations Branch

FROM: Sandy Mandee, Comptroller

    We have just completed a study of costs of restaurant operations
by region. While one might expect some differences to exist, there
really are some astounding differences in the operational figures among
the five regions. Region # 1 is particularly bad in almost all the indicators we use.

    We have the printouts, any time you want to go over them with me.

    Some of this data might be worth discussing at a future Regional
Officers' Conference.

Figure 14-6V.

X-CELL FAST FOODS CO., INC.

Milwaukee, Wisconsin

January 15

MEMORANDUM

TO: Burton Quagmeyer, Chief, Branch of Operations

FROM: Reg Leader, President

SUBJECT: Regional Operations Programming

    My recent trip around the regions produced these items of interest
for the Operations function:

    1. There's some question whether our managment development program
for restaurant managers is doing what it was set up to do - namely,
better human relations.

    2. Equipment breakdowns and equipment obsolescence seem to be on
everyone's mind.

    3. A meeting of the Regional Officers seems to be overdue. Wasn't
the last one held some $2\frac{1}{2}$ years ago ? If so, you may wish to look into
this.

Figure 14-6W.

```
                                          ┌─────────────────────────────┐
                                          │   X-CELL FAST FOODS CO., INC.│
                                          │     Milwaukee, Wisconsin     │
                                          │  ─────────────────────────── │
  615 Smallwood Dr.                       │ Burton Quagmeyer:            │
  Boston, Mass.                           │                              │
                                          │ Please look into this.       │
  January 5                              │                              │
                                          │    Thanks.                   │
                                          │                              │
                                          │    Reg Leader                │
  President                               │                       2/15   │
  X-CELL FAST FOODS CO., INC.             │  ─────────────────────────── │
  Milwaukee, Wisconsin                    │ You've Never Had A Better Reason To Eat Away From Home │
                                          └─────────────────────────────┘
  Dear Sir or Madam:

  This letter is to let you know that I was never so shocked and insulted
  in a restaurant in my life.  Several of your employees were openly
  soliciting tips on December 24.  They had a soup bowl on the counter
  with quarters in it and a sign near it which said:  "FOR OUR XMAS CHEER.
  THANK YOU."  I passed by the bowl without tipping, however, and really
  received some dirty looks.

  I thought you should know about this which is why I am taking the trouble
  to write to you.


                                          Sincerely,

                                          J.M. Straight
                                          J.M. Straight


  P.S.  This incident occurred in Restaurant #4 in Boston.
```

Figure 14-6X.

(text continued from page 215)

(2) Give a staffer a note to call R. W. Felton and express regrets, that you're brand new on the job and will be out of town until Thursday afternoon so August 20 can't be handled.

☐ *August 2 Memo*—Just put with telegram on the disabled truck problem. No action to take on this, if telegram is being acted on.

☐ *July 26 Memo from Atlanta, Re: Need for Regional Conference*—There are two other items on this from the President. Put on agenda for your next staff meeting. Advise staff to be thinking about this.

☐ *July 23 Memo*—Give secretary note to: (1) set up a meeting at an appropriate date and (2) give you pertinent back-up material.

☐ *July 20 Memo*—Give your staffers a note to do preliminary work on this, if nothing has been done as yet. Tell them you'll meet with them to discuss this on your return. (*Note:* The meeting is on Monday August 23 and Ken Fixx comes back on Thursday, August 19.)

☐ *July 14 Memo*—Have secretary, via a note, indicate to Pyle that you'll attend. Also, ask secretary to have Pyle arrange for the visit to Philadelphia Regional Office. (*Note:* The personal item in the sealed envelope talked of trouble in a Boston restaurant and that the Region couldn't be counted on to correct a bad situation.) You may also ask secretary to learn whether other staff members may wish to attend the New York City Conference. Tell secretary to tell them that you will discuss their recommendations on this with them.

☐ *July 12 Letter*—You can attend or have a staffer do it, depending on: (1) your interest in this topic and (2) your anticipated workload. (*Note:* Have you committed yourself to go to the Philadelphia Regional Office, after the September 20–22 conference in New York? See letter of July 14 in this regard.)

☐ *July 9 Memo*—Ask secretary to arrange for an early meeting with Personnel Officer Powers. *Note:* There are interrelationships with other items: (1) Memo of July 1 from Chief of Real Estate Branch re: urban facilities and (2) a supervisory training program is also present here. There is also a training program in the memo on May 22 from the Training Officer. The President's memo of January 15 talks about ineffective results of prior human relations training.

☐ *July 5 Memo—Note:* This is the first written indication that there is a staff to aid the Chief, Branch of Operations. No action required, this is just informational; although the secretary seems to be using all types of leave to the fullest.

☐ *July 1* (Complaint Letter)—Route to Legal Advisor for review and recommendation.

☐ *July 1 Memo from Chief of Real Estate Branch*— Have secretary arrange for meeting with staff to discuss the task force idea. *Note:* Other items related to urban facilities are: (1) Memo of July 9 on turnover and absenteeism and (2) Memo of July 23 on security matters.

☐ *June 30 Memo*—Give staff a note to meet with you the first thing, on your return, to discuss this. You want to cooperate, but you don't know who is the best person to serve on the Task Force, who is free to serve, etc. *Note:* You return on Thursday, August 19 and the Task Force begins its work on Monday, August 23 in Los Angeles.

☐ *June 15 Memo*—Give to your staffer, Wilde Oates, with a note to discuss when you return. *Note:* This may be a team matter, but you probably should discuss with Oates first.

☐ *June 5 Memo*—The big boss is pushing for a regional meeting in November. He had mentioned it earlier, too, in the Memo of January 15. The Atlanta Regional Office is also interested in such a meeting, per memo of July 26. Memo of March 29 also suggests such a meeting. Action: Ask boss' secretary, via a note, to meet with him on this at his convenience.

☐ *May 22 Memo*—This may be an agenda item for the November Regional Officers' Meeting. You may wish to discuss this first with your boss and then with the Personnel Officer and the Training Officer.

☐ *March 29 Memo*—A complex problem. First action: Have staff join you to study printouts. Second: Establish as an agenda item for the November Regional Officers' Meeting.

☐ *January 15 Memo*—In view of date, probably no need to respond on this memo. The training item should be picked up for action along with other training items. The equipment item should be resolved by the August 18 equipment conference. And you are working on the Regional Officers' Conference.

☐ *February 15 Note from President Forwarding Complaint Letter of January 5*—Since nothing was done on this January letter, it may be that it is too late to reply

since an investigation would have to be made first. This would take more time. Perhaps the letter should be carried along to the Philadelphia Regional Meeting for discussion. Certainly the Regional Director should advise the Restaurant Manager, facility #4, to "watch it" this coming Christmas. But recall, too, in enveloped, personal memo of August 9th from Boston restaurant facility #4, that the Asst. Manager thought things were poorly managed at the facility and the Regional Office in Philadelphia wasn't doing anything about it.

Group Processing of Completed Work

Participants typically experience learnings by taking action on the 15–25 in-basket items. They may become more aware of communication, staff utilization, public relations, managing in a crisis, prioritizing, etc. But the more profound learning eventuates from the exchange of views with fellow participants in a permissive atmosphere, concerning the "best" way to handle a given item. One's reasoning to explain a given action taken may be challenged frequently by the group. One may find that the thrust of an item may have been missed in whole or in part, that one worked too rapidly or too carelessly, and the like. Of course, as in case study, there typically is no "best way" to treat an item. This, in itself, is a significant learning. Yet, one can learn that there are "better" ways of getting the job done or (solving a problem) than one may have initially imagined.

Nature of Responses

One of the purposes of the in-basket activity is to gauge the extent to which the participants, as managers or would-be managers, are acting appropriately. As an obvious example, a routine personnel matter hardly calls for a group meeting; similarly, an instruction from one's boss to "look in on this personally" is certainly not a delegatable item.

In other words, for the manager the learning is that there are a *range* of possible responses to each action item in his/her in-basket. These include, in addition to making a decision:

1. Taking no action at all—the timing may be wrong, there may not be enough information upon which to act, there may be no urgency involved, the problem may cure itself in time, etc. But one must have a reason for inaction.
2. Instructing one's secretary to act.
3. Asking the secretary for additional information.
4. Instructing a staff member to act on the item.
5. Instructing a staff member to see you about the matter.

6. Calling a group meeting, at a later date, to work on the problem.
7. Asking the group to work it out among themselves (group decision).
8. Contacting a peer for advice, information, to resolve a conflict, etc.
9. Asking one's boss for guidance, advice, etc.
10. Contacting someone on "the outside" for information, clarification, etc.
11. Returning the item to the originator for his/her action ("Do what you deem appropriate").

As to choice of media of communication in acting upon the items in the in-basket, the manager has various options:

The manager can write instructions in the form of notes, write/dictate memoranda, arrange for one-on-one meetings, call for a group meeting, etc. These meetings are not conducted immediately since typically the manager is alone in the office (Friday at 5 p.m., Sunday after 6 p.m., a week day at 7:30 a.m., etc.). Rather, they are designed to take place when the manager returns from the "trip."

In respect to the calling of meetings, we might suggest that the effective team manager may also encourage the staff to meet on a problem alone as a group. They can study the problem and then recommend, as a group, the "best" course of action. In some cases, they may act collectively without the boss, the latter agreeing in advance to abide by their decision.

Group Analysis

The total group may analyze participants' in-basket decisions or actions in various ways. A common procedure is simply to begin with the first action item and discuss it collectively. This approach works out fairly well in a small group, say, 8–12 members.

In a larger group, the use of small group methods is preferable. Let's assume that we have 16 participants in our in-basket activity. We can assign them to four groups of four members each. The teams are asked to swap completed in-baskets for analysis, as follows:

Team A ⇄ C
Team B ⇄ D

Each team is given either the rating schedule in Figure 14-7 or the rating form in Figure 14-8 to appraise and rate all the items in the in-basket. Be certain to advise the participants that the point scores are a tool to aid in the analysis; that they are not the analyses themselves.

In-Basket Rating Schedule

As a team, you are to review each completed in-basket action. You are to agree on points to be assigned to each action taken, as follows:

5 Points—The action taken is logical/rational/reasonable in all significant respects. *Note*: It may not be the action you would take, but it is a very appropriate solution, one which you can respect fully. The odds are very high that it should succeed.

4 Points—The action taken is quite effective. It is not as persuasive/logical/appropriate an action as might have been taken, but it is certainly a workable one. The odds are in its favor for success.

3 Points—The action taken is acceptable; hardly creative and may have some questionable or risky aspects to it. But it is one that merits a try.

2 Points—The action taken is very marginal or questionable. The odds against its success are considerable. One or more key elements have been overlooked or not considered appropriate.

1 Point—This appears to be an inappropriate response. The proposed action has little chance of succeeding and is very wide of the mark.

Figure 14-7. The in-basket rating schedule for reviewing in-basket solutions.

The teams are also given the In-Basket Item Comment Sheet shown in Figure 14-9. It calls for the making of entries, for reference and discussion purposes, about each item. The writing of statements concerning the analysis of the items in the in-basket will help to sharpen the thinking involved.

Summarizing the Experience

After all in-basket items have been analyzed and discussed, the trainer should extract from the group what they learned. One way to do this is to use "The Circular Whip" technique—i.e., whip around the room and secure one statement of learning from each participant and post their responses on the flipchart.

The process may be repeated two or three times until all significant points have been recorded. Typically, we may anticipate responses such as the following:

☐ Delegation (details were coming to the top)
☐ Time management
☐ Communication
☐ Peer relations
☐ Importance of indicators of malfunctioning in the organization

In-Basket Rating Form						
Elements in Decision Making	N/A	1 (LO)	2	3	4	5 (HI)
1. Pertinent facts were fully considered						
2. Timing was considered						
3. The problem rather than the symptom(s) was treated						
4. The decision considered the context which underlies it (climate, interrelationships, etc.)						
5. Future consequences of the decision were considered						
6. Interpersonal factors (human impacts) were considered						
7. Resources of others (boss, staff, peers, etc.) were utilized						
8. Implementation aspects of the decision were considered						
9. Inaction rather than action was taken appropriately						

Using a 5-point scale (1 is low and 5 is high), analyze and discuss each action taken on all in-basket items. Use the nine-factor criteria for effective decisions in rating the actions taken. Agree, as a team, on the point scores you assign to the factors relating to each completed action. As an illustration of how the scoring might go, let's assume you were totally impressed with the logic/reasoning/appropriateness of all actions taken on, say, 20 items. If each action taken were deemed "perfect," it would receive 45 points (9 elements @ 5 points = 45). And if all 20 in-basket items received 45 points, the total in-basket score would be 900 points (45 × 20 items = 900).

Figure 14-8. The in-basket rating form used to assess the decisions made on an in-basket item.

☐ Importance of setting priorities (was the in-basket to be "attacked" as the items appeared, grouped, or what?)
☐ Need to avoid handling problems piecemeal (interrelationship of items)
☐ Importance of observing dates
☐ Pressure of the in-box or in-basket
☐ The nature of the managerial job (for a new or future manager)
☐ Managing in a crisis

The above learnings may be referred to or commented upon, in summary fashion, to wrap-up the exercise.

Summary

The in-basket exercise is a simulation of the kinds of activities which managers and, possibly others, face (or

In-Basket Item Comment Sheet	
Item #1	
Item #2	
Item #3	
Item #4	
Item #5	
Item #6	

Figure 14-9. An in-basket comment form should allow enough space to comment on each in-basket item.

are likely to face) on the job. It is designed to improve their capability to solve problems and make decisions, particularly where problems are quite interrelated and have significant time implications.

In-baskets work well because they provide realism, challenge, fun, and significant learning. A possible disadvantage is that they do take considerable time.

Although the in-basket typically has followed a single format, there is no reason why one cannot be creative and develop new approaches to and uses of the in-basket exercise. Also, while the in-basket ordinarily is used for management training, it would seem that the technique could be adapted to non-managerial training as well. For example, after basic or "theoretical" training, a bank clerk could engage in an application activity using the in-basket approach. It could provide exposure to the varied transactions likely to be encountered in a typical banking day. This type of activity could be conducted on either an individual or a group basis.

Key Points

1. The in-basket exercise is a simulation which, because of its very nature, managers (and others) can relate to readily.
2. Managers can develop a variety of skills from the in-basket activity including problem solving and decision making, time management, utilization of

staff members, coordination with other units, crisis management, etc.

3. The in-basket exercise is a flexible tool and can be used in a variety of ways to develop managers and others.

4. Although in-basket exercises may be purchased or found in books, the trainer may wish to design his/her own to meet better the needs of the participant group.

5. While the initial analysis of an in-basket is accomplished on an individual basis, that analysis should be subject to further small group analysis. This procedure allows for learning from the approaches to in-basket problems taken by one's peers.

6. In-basket analysis can be aided via rating forms and rating schedules.

7. Although the "best" in-basket entails the use of "real" memos, letters, reports, etc., an alternate format is to present incidents, events, problems, etc., in summary form.

8. In addition to management training, an in-basket can be used to provide training in report writing, training of tellers in a bank, etc.

Recommended Reading

Burchett, Terri, "In-Basket Cases Keep Policies In Line," *Personnel Journal,* May 1987, pp. 61–65.

This article describes the use of the in-basket technique to orient/train managers in personnel policies, e.g., regarding overtime, disciplinary action, sexual harassment, vacation policy, reference requests on former employees, etc.

Daly, Andrew A., "In-Basket Business Game," *Training Directors Journal,* August 1960, pp. 8–15.

Presents an in-basket of 11 items, including instructions to the participants.

Engle, Herbert M., *Handbook of Creative Learning Exercises,* Gulf Publishing Company, Houston, 1973.

Chapter 9 describes the in-basket in detail and tells how to develop such materials. Chapter 10 presents two complete in-baskets, one of interest to business managers, and the other to professional managers in the public and non-profit sector.

Ferner, Jack D., *Successful Time Management: A Self-Teaching Guide,* John Wiley and Sons, Inc., New York, 1980.

The Appendix contains a 20-item In-Basket exercise concerned with daily planning. Chapter 12 discusses the in-basket in general and specific terms. Skill practice relates to setting priorities, organizing time in a weekly planning guide, delegating, planning a meeting, accumulating similar tasks.

Gilson, Thomas Q., "A Look At The In-Basket—A Realistic Technique for Selection and Training," *Management of Personnel Quarterly,* Autumn–Winter 1962.

Provides an overview of the in-basket technique, shows sample memoranda, provides a system of scoring responses, and discusses its use in selection as well as development.

Joyce, Robert D., "In-Basket Training for Engineering Managers," *Educational Technology,* January 1970, supplement, pp. 20–26.

Describes an in-basket exercise to broaden engineering managers. Topics covered by the 40 incidents (memoranda): promotion policies, performance evaluation, project assignments, employee sharing on projects, interdepartmental conflicts, interpersonal rivalries, design problems, customer and vendor relationships, turnover, morale, communications.

Joyce, Robert D., "In-Basket Programs—How to Make Them, How to Use Them," *Training in Business and Industry,* February 1971, pp. 40–44.

Provides guides to the creation of one's own in-basket and procedures to conduct the program.

Kemerer, Richard, and Wahlstrom, Merlin, "How To Develop and Use In-Basket Simulations—A Case Study In The Selection of Bank Managers," *Performance and Instruction Journal,* May 1984, pp. 6–8.

While in-baskets typically are used for training managers and others, they also may be used for personnel appraisal and selection purposes. This article describes the latter use in a Canadian bank.

Nylen, Donald; Mitchell, J. Rubert; and Stout, Anthony (Eds.), "Decision Making Under Pressure in the In-Tray," in *Handbook of Staff Development and Human Relations Training: Materials Developed For Use in Africa,* NTL Institute For Applied Behavioral Science, Washington, 1967, pp. 153–170.

Provides a 16-item in-basket including general instructions to conduct the activity.

OTHER KEY GROUP-IN-ACTION TOOLS

Retention is best when the learner is involved.

—Edward Scannell, director,
University Conference
Bureau, Arizona State
(quoted in *Meeting News*,
January 1980)

In the prior pages we presented a variety of issues, techniques, and methods that relate to working with small groups. In the following pages we will discuss several additional areas of concern that are significant to effective group training, both small group and total group. They are:

☐ Pre-work
☐ Seating
☐ Movement
☐ Flipcharting
☐ Humor and fun
☐ Props for empathy
☐ Handouts
☐ Using silence

Pre-work

At times it is desirable to provide participants with an assignment in advance of the first session of a training program. The basic principle behind the pre-work concept is that the more the participants bring to the training situation the more they will carry away from it. Thus, the more participants can prepare themselves for the learning experience ("early entry"), the more effective—easier, quicker, more profound—it is likely to be.

Pre-work also has these advantages:

☐ It alerts participants early on that the forthcoming learning is a two-way street—that participants and the trainer have *joint* responsibilities for the success of the training effort.
☐ It indicates that the learning experience will be an active, involving one, rather than just another passive training exposure.
☐ It provides an early opportunity to understand the nature of the course or program.
☐ It sets a professional tone for the course: "Hey, these people really mean business. Why they're putting us to work before we even get to class. Maybe this *will* be worth coming to."
☐ It stimulates interest, provokes curiosity, provides involvement, and thus encourages motivation.

In general, pre-work helps establish the right kind of expectations by participants.

When to Assign Pre-work

Pre-work, as a training tool, is most effective when it is fully integrated into the overall learning design. Here are some guidelines for the trainer for using pre-work.

It is basic (relevant) to the course, i.e., it is something that must be done on the job before attendance at the training session. For example, you might have participants

☐ Keep a time log as a prelude to analysis and discussion in a time management workshop.
☐ Complete an instrument to produce data for subsequent analysis in a leadership training course.
☐ Identify work problems related to the forthcoming training.
☐ Read a rather complex case that will be discussed in class.

It is essential to assemble on-the-job materials or acquire other data to be used in the course. For example:

☐ In a course on effective writing, the participants select and bring to class copies of letters, memos, reports, etc. of a type specified by the trainer.
☐ Participants visit a plant, office, gallery, school, museum, store, etc. prior to attending a course that treats a topic related to those locales. (Be sure to provide guidelines so the trainees know what to look for.)
☐ In preparation for a management development seminar, participants prepare a "minicase" on an assigned aspect of leadership or a current management problem.
☐ Participants bring in pertinent "live data" and added perspectives about the subject by interviewing their bosses or peers.
☐ Participants bring to class items culled from the media relevant to the topics to be discussed, e.g., newspaper or magazine articles, editorials, photos, book reviews, ads.

It is desirable to provide participants with subject-matter background prior to class attendance. For example have participants:

☐ Read one or two articles that explore nuances of the MBO (Management by Objectives) process prior to attending the MBO course *per se.*
☐ View a film or videotape or listen to an audio-cassette that sets the stage for the course. (This presumes appropriate equipment is readily available, etc.)

It is considered worthwhile to motivate (excite, interest) participants about the course in general or the first session in particular. For example:

☐ In advance of a public speaking course, provide participants with an article that challenges them to become a better formal presenter.
☐ In advance of a course on communication, present participants with one or more models and accompanying text which point up the complexities of the communication process.
☐ In advance of a course on improving one's dictation skills, provide participants with (a) data concerning the economics (potential dollar savings) of good dictation plus other benefits (e.g., making life easier for one's secretary) and (b) a short exercise or two to check out certain principles of good dictation.

When *Not* to Assign Pre-work

Although the preceding paragraphs point up the value of pre-work, it, nevertheless, is a tool that should be used only with considerable forethought. In the absence of such care, one may anticipate negative effects toward the training effort. More specifically, pre-work is not recommended when:

☐ The participant group is an extremely busy one (e.g., upper-level managers, those who are subject to considerable travel) and thus not likely to cooperate. Of course, insistence by the head of the organization that all participants are to do the pre-work may prove to be a helpful motivator.
☐ The participant group possesses limited educational background (e.g., blue-collar foremen) and is uncomfortable with the somewhat "academic" course requirements that may be entailed in pre-work.
☐ There is insufficient time to get the materials to the participants to complete the assigned tasks.
☐ The tasks can more properly be completed in class (e.g., due to the complexity of the instructions or the initial need to involve the group).
☐ The benefits of pre-work are only marginally advantageous to a particular training effort. As one anonymous sage put it: "If it ain't broke, don't fix it."
☐ Past experience with a particular participant group indicates that pre-work is quite certain to provide a negative reaction.
☐ Top management may not be sympathetic to activities which connote "training overload."

Some Skill Pointers in Assigning Pre-work

Successfully completed pre-work is likely if attention is paid to these skill factors:

☐ Provide an explanation in writing concerning the reason for the assignment. Remember that participants, especially busy ones, may resent the idea of doing tasks outside the training situation. In fact, some may even object to attending the training program in the first instance.

☐ If practicable, meet with the group to explain the pre-work assignment. This procedure is very essential to secure cooperation from the participants in a "must do" situation, e.g., keeping a time log in preparation for an intensive time management course.

☐ Keep assignments simple and brief. One easy-to-do task is clearly preferable to two or three assignments that may take considerable time to complete.

☐ Provide clear-cut written instructions concerning the conduct of the assignment. Conduct a "field-test" to ensure that your meaning is being communicated clearly.

☐ As applicable, facilitate the execution of the assignment by providing simple forms or worksheets. For example, see the worksheets on delegation in Appendix 52.

Despite your best efforts to plan and organize your pre-work activity, one or more participants may not have completed the requested assignment. So what do you do? Some possible answers:

☐ If the assignment is not too complex and thus not time-consuming, one possibility is simply to take time for it to be done as the first order of business. The assumption here is that the completion of the assigned work is basic to the learning from the course.

☐ Another possibility is to have the "delinquent ones" try to participate as well as they can; e.g., in the case of a time log that was not done, the participants may attempt to reconstruct the work week or at least a work day on a memory basis (admittedly a poor procedure) or at least make an effort to recall some of their daily problems in managing their time.

A final caution regarding pre-work: Be sure that you process any pre-work you assign. Pre-work that is not used actively in class will have only limited value. Maximum benefit accrues from sharing and discussing the assigned work.

Seating to Facilitate Participation

Seating of participants is important for these reasons:

☐ It can facilitate participation.
☐ It can energize the group.
☐ It communicates the trainer's philosophy of adult learning and training style.

A meaningful approach to seating is to think in these terms: How much involvement of participants do I want? How much movement should take place to facilitate that involvement? Let's discuss, then, three situations: *low*

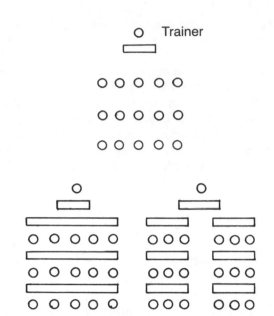

Figure 15-1. Seating configurations for low participant involvement.

participant involvement, *moderate* participant involvement, and *high* participant involvement.

Low Involvement

Seating configurations for low involvement are given in Figure 15-1. The physical set-up obviously is very formal. The tables themselves (sometimes desks are used) contribute to a stilted, highly traditional classroom atmosphere.

Note that the course conductor is in a position of authority, seated behind a table or standing behind a lectern. Communication is intended to flow primarily from the front of the room to the rear—one-way communication. Lateral communication, i.e., inter-participant communication, is not deemed to be important. In effect, the trainer is in complete control of the instructional process. The trainer is active, and the participants, if we can use that term, are passive. All (or nearly all) the knowledge or wisdom is presumed to reside with the trainer.

If we could secure comments from our participants they might say to us: "Looks like we're back in that old high school/college lecture hall." "I hope the trainer doesn't forget the break."

In short, what we have operating in this situation is an instructional effort underpinned by "the funnel theory" of learning—"just pour it in and they'll get it." Probable impact/retention is limited or low.

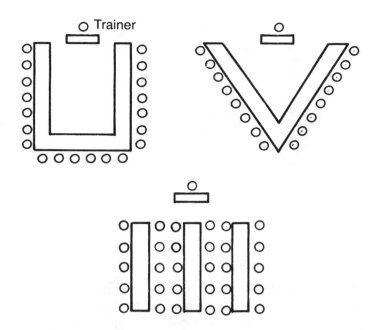

Figure 15-2. Seating configurations for moderate participant involvement.

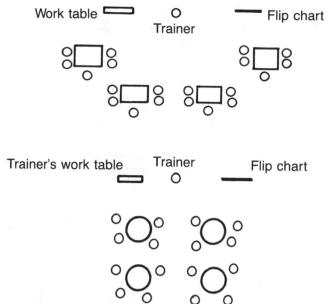

Figure 15-3. Seating configurations for high participant involvement.

Moderate Involvement

Seating of participants for medium or moderate involvement is given in Figure 15-2. In the U, V, or I setups, the instructor is, again, very much in control. However, these configurations are designed to have some participant interchange. Also, with movable chairs "buzz grouping" should be possible, even if only done occasionally. In general, there is an assumption that participants can learn from one another, at least in part. Much of the learning still depends upon one-way communication devices: lectures, slide talks, films, handouts, etc.

If participants have been exposed entirely to lecture-hall learning atmospheres, these configurations would be regarded by them as "a step forward." Their observation might be: "The trainer is in charge, but we do have the opportunity to have some exchange." Probable impact/retention is fair to good, depending on opportunities for participant interaction provided by the instructor.

High Involvement

Seating configurations for high participant involvement may assume these forms:

Use of several square, rectangular or round tables. In these configurations, shown in Figure 15-3, the trainer serves primarily as a resource person or facilitator. While he/she does not work directly with the group, the emphasis is on small group work. In fact, the major re-

source in this learning experience is the small group. Note that the trainer has a work table to his/her *right*; merely having a chair in the front of the room reduces the social distance between the trainer and the participants. The trainer also has a flipchart, a symbol of informal learning, to his/her left. The trainer is in a position to move around the room, auditing and helping the teams at the tables as may be necessary. Short talks, rather than lectures, stimulate/generate the small group work.

Use of a single square or round table. In this configuration, shown in Figure 15-4, the trainer joins the group and assumes the role of catalyst/facilitator/resource person. The trainer deliberately reduces his/her status to encourage full and free interaction among participants and between participants and the trainer. The atmosphere is informal, relaxed, participant-centered. Everyone is

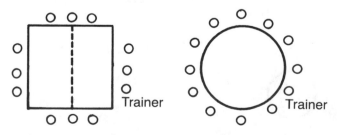

Figure 15-4. Other seating arrangements for high participant involvement in which the trainer joins the group.

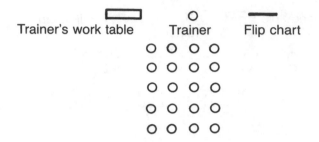

Figure 15-5. Diagram of a lecture hall arrangement as a prelude to a highly informal seating configuration.

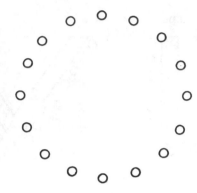

Figure 15-7. Diagram of the circular, table-free arrangement, which, by also involving the trainer, is designed for maximum informality and high involvement.

concerned with exploration, problem solving, critique, discussion, etc.

Flexible, no-desk/table seating. In this approach, the trainer may start the group off in lecture array, as in Figure 15-5. However, this apparently neat and tidy arrangement is short-lived. After a few short comments, or none at all, the group is "put into action" very quickly via dyads, triads, buzz groups, fishbowls, stand-up activities, movement, etc. And the neat configuration with which things began, hardly, if at all, returns. In fact, the room typically remains in informal, relaxed disarray, with the participants at times communicating from buzz group positions or even an informal U-shaped circle, as in Figure 15-6.

The use of many participant configurations—that is, dyads, triads, buzz groups, etc.—is facilitated by movable chairs and the absence of desks or tables, which inhibit ready movement of the participants. If notebooks have been distributed, they are used for occasional writing tasks.

The trainer's role, obviously, is to set the stage for a variety of activities, get the group into action, secure

data from the small groups, role players, etc., record the data on flipcharts, as necessary, and work with the group to interpret (analyze, summarize) its experience.

Use of a circle without the tables. In this configuration—Figure 15-7—the trainer joins with the group on a more-or-less peer basis. The assumption is that "we're all here to learn together." This is the hallmark of advanced forms of experiential learning (T-group, encounter group, team building). The atmosphere is totally informal, and as the group matures, it becomes warm, egalitarian, supportive, caring, spontaneous, and highly trusting. Thus, the trainer's highest skill is to create an environment where everyone can work/learn well together. Note that tables—the trainer's and the participants'—are discarded to accent informality, to eliminate the traditional classroom atmosphere, and to stimulate the freest possible flow of communication.

The probable impact/retention of learning in these four configurations is high, at least for most participants. Satisfaction with the trainer and the training process should also be high.

Seating for Larger Groups

Various meetings, conferences, symposia, etc. may be attended by fairly large groups. "Large" may be defined as a group of more than 25–30 participants, including audiences of several hundred people. Despite their size, certain kinds of participation still are possible. Proper seating can contribute to such participation. Several examples to trigger your own thinking about appropriate seating configurations for at least some participation and involvement follow.

Panel discussion for an audience of 50–75 people. A helpful arrangement—Figure 15-8—is to use a "theater in the round" approach. Assume, then, that we have four

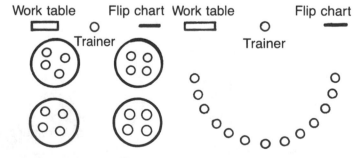

Figure 15-6. Diagrams of seating arrangements for high involvement that can flow from the lecture hall arrangement.

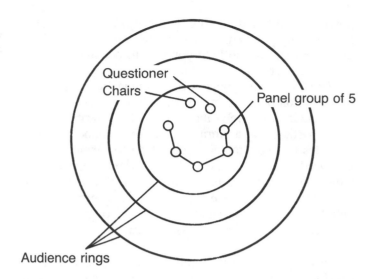

Figure 15-8. Diagrams of "theater in the round" seating for a large group.

panelists and a moderator. We can place them in the center ring, with two or three added rings or clusters around them for the audience. Two empty chairs can be added to the center ring for use by audience members who wish to ask a question of a panel member. The ground rule is that a question may be posed to one or more panelists by taking an empty chair, a follow-up question or two also is permitted, and then the questioner relinquishes the chair to another audience member. The use of the second chair for another audience participant expedites the movement of the questioners in and out of the inner ring. *Note:* An aisle should be provided for easy entry into the inner ring.

The use of this configuration gives everyone a sense of being near the action—no one is in a rear row. While the number of questioners is limited, as in any large audience, it still is possible for audience members to identify with the questioners and thus feel a certain degree of involvement in the proceedings.

Lecture for an audience of several hundred. An audience of 100–500 people can be involved to a degree despite a lecture-type situation. One way to do this is to use large round tables which seat 8–10 people. For example, a group of ten (or two groups of five) can "buzz" on an assigned topic or question and report back its conclusions to the total audience. Not all groups may be able to report back, but a small number, selected randomly, can. It is also possible, with proper instructions, to have several "team" role plays at each round table—two role players and one or two observers per team. *All* at the round table participate in the role plays.

In the traditional lecture hall set-up small group work is possible if the chairs are movable. Participants simply turn their chairs around to form groups of four or six.

Round tables are preferred to lecture-hall style since they allow for the development of much more rapport. In fact, by reducing the number of participants at the round tables from ten to say, seven or eight, even greater intimacy is possible.

Use of an Outside Facility

If you are using an "outside" facility such as a hotel, motel, conference center, a school or other public building, some suggestions are offered to help you to cope with Murphy's Law (i.e., if anything can go wrong, it will. Seasoned trainers will say that Murphy was essentially an optimist!)

☐ Inspect the facility in advance, if at all possible. It may be too small to move chairs and people around once you have your work table, a registration table, a coffee table, a motion picture screen, a movie projector, one or two flipcharts on easels, and a coat rack in the room. There also may be posts to limit your usable space. Remember that when you ask a nontrainer if the space is "large enough," his/her perception of "large" is quite different from yours. Hotel/motel sales personnel particularly are accustomed to fitting 50 people, lecture hall style, into a small room. They may also wish to save the bigger rooms for other clients in case such requests should arise.

☐ Arrive early on the morning of the training. It is a good bet that no one has communicated to the set-up crew what your needs and expectations really are. For example, they may have set up the room with tables which you did not request. Or they have a mammoth blackboard instead of a compact easel and flipchart. By arriving early, you may be able to rearrange the room as you wish, get rid of unwanted items such as lecterns and tables, accomplish your other preliminary tasks, keep your frustrations down, and be able to greet your early arrivers in good humor.

☐ A possible way to secure "compliance" with your request is to provide the hotel's coordinator with a diagram of your proposed room set-up.

Seating Management

In addition to concern with seating configurations, the trainer opting for high participation will give attention to these issues:

Seat "ownership." Since a body at rest literally tends to stay at rest, we many anticipate that participants will try to acquire "vested rights" in the seats that they took at the outset of the course. It is your job to overcome this "squatter's rights" tendency. Why? Two reasons: We don't want people getting too comfortable and routinized; rather, we want to keep them in a free-flowing, more active, energized, and motivated state. New seating locations provide an opportunity to work with and get to know other participants, to learn how they see things.

Seating changes can be brought about via:

☐ The "count-off" approach. In this way the ones, twos, threes, etc. will team up.

☐ A statement at the end of the first day to this effect: "Tomorrow we'll be working with new partners. So when you come in in the morning, please take a chair at another table."

The buddy relationship. Participants often tend to gravitate toward and team up with someone they know. Or they may ally themselves with the person with whom they came to the course. Sitting next to a buddy undoubtedly is comfortable and anxiety reducing. But the purpose of the training program is, again, to meet new faces, to encounter new views, to attempt to enter into the world of someone one knows less well or not at all, to develop a relationship with "a stranger." Again, it is your job to undo the buddy seating relationship.

Chair count. If the program calls for 15 people to attend, don't set up seating for 20 to 30 people. Instead, limit the number of chairs to the number expected. In this fashion, when participants sit down they will be certain to acquire "a neighbor," either immediately or shortly thereafter. And if a coat rack is provided, there will be no need to "neutralize" a chair by someone draping his/her coat over it.

Flexible seating. Try to have a training room with comfortable, but lightweight chairs. Chairs should be light enough so that anyone can push or carry a chair to a new location for role plays, fishbowls, small group work, etc.

Seating instructions. All too often, participants assigned to dyads, triads, or buzz groups will assume seating configurations that ignore the need to be on an eyeball-to-eyeball basis with fellow participants. Face-to-face contact is essential, of course, for good communication. Hence, the trainer must insist politely that dyadic partners "eyeball" it and that buzz groups sit in a true, tight circle rather than in a half-moon or even an elliptical configuration. One way to do this is to ensure proper seating *before* assigning the task. To the reluctant ones, simply say: "Would you please try to eyeball it? I assure you that you'll be able to communicate a lot more effectively if you can look at one another."

Seating position by the trainer. Whenever possible, the trainer should operate informally by using a chair as op-posed to standing up before the group. By being seated, and drawing your chair close to the group, you will reduce your status and help yourself to become "a member" of the group.

The table issue. Trainers of the nonexperiential, low-participation bent are inclined to place chairs around tables. Their rationale is that it provides a writing aid, it gives participants a storage area for notebooks, and it provides a comfortable resting place for arms, elbows, and tired heads. However, the experiential trainer sees tables only as providing added clutter and formality to the training room. The extra impediments certainly don't help to form fishbowls and small groups or to allow participants to move their chairs to corners or other locations for role plays.

Certainly if writing is minimal it can be accomplished readily enough on a notebook. If it is a "heavy" part of the course, tables are indeed warranted. Notebooks can be placed easily enough underneath one's chair on the floor, and as for resting one's elbows and head on the table, comfort of that sort is hardly the energizing we wish in the dynamic training room.

In general, tables add to formality; they give the training room more of a traditional classroom flavor. Do we really want that?

The auditorium problem. Sometimes you may find yourself in an auditorium setting, complete with chairs bolted to the floor and a stage with lectern. Obviously, an informal atmosphere and small group work are not easy in this situation. What to do? First, you should learn of the nature of the facility before the actual training day and consider whether it is worth doing the training there. Second, if small group work is desired, it still can be done in one of two ways:

☐ Have participants stand and have every other row turn around to face those behind them. Groups of four to six are then possible. (Participants will find it very difficult to work in small groups while seated.)

☐ Use adjacent break-out rooms, if available.

The smoking problem. In recent years it has become customary to divide the seating opportunities into smoking and nonsmoking categories. This certainly is a considerate way of doing things. However, it cannot be done in the type of seating I advocate. For with movement and the changing composition and size of small groups, the smokers and nonsmokers typically become intermingled. One trainer deals with the problem by announcing at the outset of the workshop various ground rules, including a ban on smoking. As to his rationale for such action, he advises the participants that he cannot provide them with excellence for the three days involved if he is subjected to smoke. However, he makes the rule more palatable to the smokers by scheduling frequent, short breaks. Also, he advises the smokers that they may leave the room at any time if they find they must smoke.

Movement

This is a training device to keep participants alert and energized. In general you should opt for those techniques that require participants to "rearrange" themselves, e.g., fishbowls, role plays, certain exercises, field trips, and in-plant visits. Some other forms of movement that can be used follow:

Icebreakers

Depending on the group, course objectives, and so on, it may be desirable to start things off by getting participants "into motion." This approach will communicate at the outset that your program is indeed going to be a "live one." Here are some examples:

Envelope Enigma
Simply put all participants' name cards or tent cards (folded cards that once set up look like tents) in a box. Let the participant select a card randomly from the box. Instruct the participant to move around and locate the person whose name is on the card. Then the participant exchanges personal data with the other participant: name, goal for the course, etc.

Values Billboard

The procedures for this are:

1. The trainer posts on a flipchart (or provides a handout of) a list of values such as the following:

   ☐ To be a good citizen
   ☐ To achieve above average financial success
   ☐ To help mankind
   ☐ To develop a reputation in my field
   ☐ To help my family grow and be happy
   ☐ To have worthwhile friends
   ☐ To have the opportunity to apply my creativity
   ☐ To be a physically able person
   ☐ To be a good neighbor

Note: The trainer may substitute other values. Limit the number posted to seven or eight.

2. On a sheet of paper or preferably a flipchart sheet (with felt-tip pen) have the participants rearrange (prioritize) the values as they see them. (A variation is to let participants drop two values and prioritize the others, if nine or ten are given.)

3. Then have everyone stand up, mill around, display their "billboard," find a partner, and discuss the values.
4. The partners share (discuss) their values with one another for several minutes.
5. The trainer calls "time" and asks everyone to find a new partner. Finding a new partner is accomplished two or three times.
6. Wind up the activity by "processing" the action: What did you learn? Anything about anyone? About yourself?

Trust Walk or Blind Walk
Begin by pointing out that: "The success of our program depends on participant participation. But participation depends upon *trust.* To symbolize the importance of trust, let's conduct a trust walk. Is there anyone who doesn't want to participate? O.K., here are our procedures:

"Find a partner, preferably someone you don't know at all or don't know very well. In your pair, decide who will be the leader and who will be the follower." (This step can also be done randomly by having every one call out "one" and "two," with the "ones" automatically becoming the leaders and the "twos" the followers.)

"The followers are to close their eyes. The trust walk is done *silently*—nonverbally.

"When I give the signal, the leader will steer the follower around the designated area. The leaders should try to make the trip as interesting as possible and should do so safely. Remember eyes closed, followers, since you trust your leader to ensure that no harm befalls you. Let's walk around, then, for five minutes or so." (The time period can be 15–20 minutes in an experiential program that emphasizes sensory awareness and where the outdoors is available to feel trees and rocks, smell flowers, etc.)

"O.K., let's stop our walks and process the action. Followers: How did you feel? Anxious? Fearful? Dependent? Trusting?" (Secure several responses.)

"Leaders: How did you feel about your role and responsibility? Concerned? Silly? Responsible?" (Secure several responses.)

"Was a system of communication established? Was trust accomplished to any degree? Any general comments or reactions from anyone?"

Several key or skill points to make the trust walk an effective experience are:

☐ Keep it voluntary. Don't put pressure on anyone to participate. This would defeat the whole purpose of the exercise—building trust.
☐ Limit the use of this activity to groups oriented toward experiential training.

☐ Stress the nonverbal or silent aspects of it. This behavior is typically hard for participants to grasp. (I sometimes facetiously tell the group, "I generally say that nonverbal means no talking and I always have difficulty communicating this idea.")

☐ To make the experience worthwhile, the walk should take at least five minutes. Tell them that you will signal them when the five minutes are up, and that if they quit sooner they won't get much out of the experience.

☐ Be certain to provide time to process the action. People *do* want to talk about this unique experience.

The trainer should be ready to adapt the trust walk experience to the needs of the group; e.g., with a sales training group the processing of feelings can be shifted to a discussion of how the *customer* feels in a selling transaction. Or are we only concerned with our feelings as salespeople? Also, how do we develop trust with a prospect or customer?

I Am

On a sheet of paper or, preferably, using felt-tip pens on a flipchart sheet have participants develop a comprehensive list of nouns that describe themselves. Stimulate their thinking by giving them a partial list about yourself:

I am a:
☐ Father
☐ Husband
☐ Neighbor
☐ Beer drinker
☐ Lover
☐ Trainer
☐ Movie goer

Then have each participant find a partner and exchange data. The process may be repeated once or twice with a new partner.

Hum Fun

To get acquainted, participants are given the opportunity to team up in trios or quartets via the humming of well-known songs.

1. Type or write the names or titles of three or four well-known songs on 3″ × 5″ cards. The number of cards and participants should be limited to 12–16. The songs may be drawn from such categories as Irish songs, folk songs, popular oldies. For example, with 12 participants 4 cards might have typed on them "When Irish Eyes Are Smiling," four others might have typed on them "Let Me Call

You Sweetheart," and four others "I've Been Working On The Railroad."
2. Distribute the 12 cards randomly.
3. Instruct participants to *hum* their song, mill around, and try to team up with others who also are humming their song.
4. When the trios or quartets are formed, have them exchange data about themselves. It is essential to limit the number of participants to 12–16 since with a larger number "teaming up" would become too difficult in a hum-filled room.

Find Someone Who . . .[1]

This icebreaker is particularly useful for people in a stranger group. Provide participants with a sheet of paper which contains 10–15 items relating to their work (see the following). Allow two lines per item so that entries can be made readily for all items. On the top of the sheet write in large letters with a felt-tipped pen: "Find Someone Who . . ." Immediately below, provide these instructions:

Directions: Find someone who can sign one of the lines on this form, with name, company, and phone number. Each person can sign your form up to two times only. You cannot sign your own form. Once your entire sheet is completed, jump up and down and shout: "I win!"

Here are the items which may appear on your form:

☐ Forms a one-person department
☐ Lives at the shore
☐ Is a first-timer at this conference
☐ Really understands quality circles
☐ Knows a lot about management development programs
☐ Teaches time management
☐ Has a great idea for avoiding burnout
☐ Knows all about career ladders
☐ Has a great idea for motivating employees

Note: Anticipate a lot of "noise" because of the many simultaneous conversations of the total group. Also, the preceding questions were used with a trainer group. Other groups would require other items on their forms.

Note: For additional icebreakers, but not necessarily ones entailing movement, see Chapter 1.

Standups

It is very desirable to get people to stand in place and engage in some type of physical movement or activity. Several examples of such activities follow:

Signups

Post to the wall several (five to seven) signs. Ask participants to "sign up" with the sign that relates most closely to themselves. Sample topics:

☐ Leadership styles (e.g., team management; totally participative; moderately participative; somewhat participative; happy ship; strictly business; management by objectives)

☐ Off-the-job interests (e.g., totally outdoors; totally indoors; mostly outdoors; mostly indoors; equally indoors and outdoors)

Then have participants, on a stand-up basis, introduce themselves and talk about the sign they selected and how they relate to it.

Value Clarification Activity in Leadership[2]

An opener, designed to clarify values in a leadership session, can help people to feel comfortable by having them get up and move around. It utilizes these procedures.

1. Take four large index cards, number them 1, 2, 3, and 4, and post them in the four corners of the room.

2. Write these (or other appropriate) questions on the flipchart:

   ☐ *Who would you prefer to be your leader?*
   1. One who has vision
   2. One who has compassion
   3. One who communicates well
   4. One who is judicious

   ☐ *Where would you like to work?*
   1. Disneyland
   2. IBM
   3. Your own organization
   4. American Red Cross

   ☐ *What do you most value in an employee?*
   1. Loyalty
   2. Creativity
   3. Thoroughness
   4. Interpersonal skill

   Note: The above questions used by the trainer reflected the spirit of the class she was conducting.

3. Cover up the four sets of questions and unveil them, one set at a time.

4. As you uncover each set of questions, ask participants to walk to the number representing their choice. When everyone is at a corner, ask them to discuss, standing up, why they made their choice

and to share their values with the class. (Anticipate that the involvement and sharing of insights and perspectives will generate a lot of enthusiasm and a deeper understanding and interest in the leadership area.)

Armfold

To make the point that habits are hard to break (overcoming resistance to change) give your group this assignment while they are standing:

"Fold your arms.

"Raise your head and glance at the ceiling.

"Make a mental note concerning how your arms are folded, such as the right arm is placed over the left.

"Now reverse the position of your arms." (Most people find this awkward to accomplish).

Ask: "Was this hard to do? Why?" (Answer: strength of habit. Say: "If we can't break a *physical* habit very easily, we can hardly expect to break one that is of an ingrained intellectual or emotional sort. So in trying to change habits (or a learned behavior) of others, be prepared for resistance. People obviously are now doing something which is satisfying to them, so why should they change?")

Note: The activity may also be accomplished via clasping and unclasping of hands.

Break

To introduce the coffee break in an active and fun way, give your participants these instructions:

"Stand up.

"Extend your arms forward, the palms facing one another.

"Clap your hands together, separate them, and everyone yell: 'Break'"

This procedure may be used again from time to time.

Instant Interaction

Start the first session (possibly a formal one) with instant interaction by everyone. Say to participants:

"Is everyone comfortable? Good.

"O.K. Stand up, please.

"Turn to your neighbor and talk for three to four minutes about _____.

"O.K., what did you come up with?" (Secure a few comments.)

"Good. Let's take our seats, again."

Power Play

In a session concerned with power, open things up by asking for several volunteers to come forward. Have the volunteers introduce themselves to one another, if they are strangers, and talk briefly about possible program (course, session) benefits. Then ask the volunteers how they felt about coming to the front of the room. Also, ask: "Why did you do it? To make an impression? To co-operate? Or what? Did you consider that you ran the risk of looking foolish?"

Then turn to the audience: "*All* of you participated in this activity. How? Because you made a decision *not* to volunteer. Are you glad or sorry about your decision?" (Secure feedback from nonvolunteers.) "To sum up: This activity relates to two important dimensions of power: *visibility* and *risk-taking*. If you participated, you acquired power; if you did not participate, you didn't acquire it."

Meditation in Motion

Meditation in the training situation is intended to relax participants and/or to establish a quiet, pensive mood. A helpful way to look at meditation is not to regard it as a means of *leaving* where we are but, rather, as a technique to become *aware* of where we are, i.e., taking our environment inward. Two exercises for meditation follow.

Have participants:
1. Form a circle (8 to 20 participants are a workable group), away from the chairs, with everyone standing.
2. Put their left foot forward.
3. Close their eyes.
4. Sway their body gently back and forth (20–30 seconds).
5. Halt the motion (eyes still closed), and return their left leg to its original position.
6. Put their right foot forward.
7. Sway their body back and forth (20–30 seconds).
8. Return their right leg to its original position.
9. Keep their eyes closed for another 10–20 seconds, palms facing the floor, head slightly bowed.
10. Open their eyes and return to chairs.

Another format for a stand-up meditation is to have participants:

1. Form a circle, everyone standing.
2. Put their left foot forward and close their eyes.
3. Extend their arms to the left.
4. Gently move their arms and develop a gentle, rhythmic, circular motion (30 seconds).
5. Return their left leg to its original position, cease the arm motion, and put their arms down.
6. Extend their arms to the right (their eyes are still closed).
7. Gently move their arms to form a circular motion again (30 seconds).

8. Return their right leg to original position, cease the arm motion, and put their arms down.
9. Bow their head, their eyes still closed, palms now at the side and facing downward (10–20 seconds).
10. Open their eyes and return to chairs.

Energy Check

At various stages in the program day you may want to check the "energy level" of the group. If so, ask participants:

"Will you stand up, please?

"Let's see how energetic/vigorous we are at this point. Let's sing out 'E' in an increasing crescendo.

"Let's sing out 'I,' and louder this time.

"Let's sing out 'O', really loud now.

"Was it fun? Yes? Let's hear it?" (Applause)

Note: The larger the group the more the impact, of course.

Group Hum

In an experiential training program, the following icebreaker may be useful to relax participants as well as to set a desirable tone or mood. Procedures are:

1. Ask everyone to stand up and form a circle. This may be a single circle or several circles, depending on group size.
2. Instruct them to close their eyes, take their partners' hands, and exercise a firm, friendly grip.
3. Have everyone take a deep breath and then exhale out loud with an "ommm."
4. Then ask everyone to take *three* deep breaths and exhale each time with a loud "ommm."
5. Ask participants to please be seated.

Note: If this icebreaker is used with a fairly large audience, the "ommm" is quite impressive and probably will be rendered more loudly each time.

Ball Toss

This is an active, fun-type icebreaker; it also encourages creativity. Procedures are:

1. Form a circle of 5–8 participants, everyone standing.
2. One person tosses an imaginary ball to another participant, calling out that person's name prior to making the "toss."
3. Repeat the process until everyone's name has been called out.
4. When the last person in the circle has "received" the ball, he/she may transform the ball into another object (e.g., a wallet of $100 bills, an egg, a TV set).

Note:

1. When one tosses the ball or other object, it should be done with gestures, vigor, and verbal comments ("Dotty, here's that ball. Look out. Here it comes!")

2. Two or three tosses of different objects are adequate to familiarize everyone with participants' names.

3. This activity may be done with one or more groups operating simultaneously.

4. If several groups are playing, anticipate that your training room will be filled with totally loud and friendly responses.

Mobile Continuum

Participants can be asked to position themselves at various points in the training room to indicate their attitudes, feelings, etc. on various issues. For example, in a session concerned with the explanation and exploration of assertive behavior provide a continuum for participants to assess their degree of assertiveness. Procedures are:

1. Post on opposite walls of the training room the two flipcharts as shown in Figure 15-9.

```
┌─────────────────────┐   ┌─────────────────────┐
│ Very willing to     │   │ I'm highly reluctant:│
│ execute this task,  │   │ makes me very        │
│ I'm very comfortable│   │ uncomfortable        │
│ with it.            │   │                      │
└─────────────────────┘   └─────────────────────┘
```

Figure 15-9. Examples of flipcharts for use in a "mobile continuum."

2. Ask participants to stand up and position themselves mid-way between the two walls bearing the two flipcharts.

3. Read aloud statements such as the following, one at a time:

   ☐ Ask the boss for a raise above the average being doled out.

   ☐ Attend an office party in our building where I know several people but don't have a specific invitation.

   ☐ Confront a "tough" colleague about his/her continuing lack of cooperation.

   ☐ Ask the boss for the day off after Thanksgiving, knowing that the office will be understaffed and

the boss has already expressed oral disapproval of such requests.

   ☐ Speak frankly to a colleague who annoys you with his/her put-downs and other assorted hard-hitting humor.

   ☐ Remind a very capable staff member, who doesn't like feedback, that his/her reports are often late and that this behavior has to stop.

   ☐ Return an inexpensive electrical switch that isn't functioning too well to the hardware store, although you probably abused it on installation.

   ☐ Tell a colleague that you don't really care to listen to the gossip he/she regularly provides.

   ☐ Tell a subordinate who likes to take up your time with trivia that you don't have that kind of time.

   ☐ Tell the boss that the proposed new office arrangement, that he/she personally designed, will cause many new problems.

   ☐ Inform a peer that he/she has a personal hygiene problem on hot summer days.

4. After each statement has been read, ask participants to position themselves at an appropriate point between the two signs, regarding the signs as a five-point continuum. (Give them these instructions: "If reluctant, go to or near the appropriate sign; if willing, go to or near the other sign; if undecided, take a mid-room position between the two signs.")

5. After all statements have been read, "process" the activity. Ask participants what they noticed about their behavior. Anticipate answers such as: "I was timid in a fair number of situations," "I was surprised at the variety of positions everyone took, some like mine, some quite different."

Shifting to Right Brain Thinking

Formal inputs, if abundant or prolonged, are quite likely to put participants into a highly intellectual or left-brain frame of mind. If you would like participants to shift gears, i.e., move from left brain thinking (logical, rational) to right brain (spontaneous, creative) thinking, the following fun-type activities, in succession, can contribute positively to such a goal.

Start things off by telling participants: "We've had a lot of heavy intellectual stuff. We now want to get into a fun-type, creative mood. So let's do some things that will help us to do that."

Group Gibberish

Have participants move all chairs to the walls and take standing positions. Then instruct them to mill around the room, talking loudly at their colleagues in gibberish. Stop the activity after three or four minutes.

Guided Imagery

Have participants stand in a circle, close their eyes, and reflect on a highly imaginative bit of imagery such as the following: "You are on a space ship. You are enjoying a voyage into outer space. You pass breath-taking galaxies; you can almost reach out and touch the moon. Suddenly you see another space ship. It is larger than yours, emitting bright, colorful lights. It is trying to hook up with your ship. You now see. . . ." (Have participants continue the imagery, going around the circle until everyone has contributed to it.)

Exercises

Be on the lookout for and utilize exercises that require some movement or physical activity. Several examples follow.

Praise Bombardment

1. Have participants move the furniture to the walls. Then ask your participants to form two lines, everyone facing someone in particular. (The double line may have as many as 10–15 pairs. In a small room, two sets of double lines may be more appropriate.)
2. Designate the two lines "A" and "B." Tell the participants that: "We are going to conduct an experiment in giving and receiving praise. Those in line A will give their partner praise for five minutes—this can be on anything: appearance, dress, smile, performance in the program so far, performance on the job (if one knows of it), etc. Those in line B are to listen, 'drink it in', but *not* to respond orally."
3. Process the experience. Ask questions such as these: How did you feel about receiving praise? (Secure several responses.) How did you feel about giving praise? (Secure several responses.) Any other observations? Conclude the exercise by pointing out that in our culture it's very difficult for many people (supervisors, parents) to give praise (positive reinforcement). Also, some people have difficulty receiving praise. They may "discount" it by saying things like: "Oh, it wasn't much." or "Oh, I've had this dress a long time." or "Aw, shucks, anybody could have done it."
4. In some situations it may be desirable to reverse the roles and let those in line B become the praise givers. In this case, have people acquire a new partner. Another variation, which should be used carefully, is to reverse the procedure and let those in line B give negative feedback to their new partners.

This will make the receivers uncomfortable, pointing up the destructive effects of negative reinforcement, even in an exercise situation.

Trust Fall

This is an exercise involving physical activity and contact as well as movement. Here are the procedures:

1. Have participants form a very tight circle of about eight participants.
2. Ask for a volunteer to enter the inside of the circle.
3. The volunteer is to stand in a stiff, erect way, eyes closed, and to fall back on a signal from the trainer.
4. The participants in the circle then gently move the volunteer around the circle.
5. Ask for other volunteers to enter the circle and engage in the trust fall.
6. Process the action: Did you trust the group to catch you? How did it feel to be moved about? Did the activity affect or improve group cohesion?

Note: Pairs (one on one) may also conduct the trust fall, but the receivers must be physically able to cope with a falling, inert body.

Frame Game

1. Select a topic you wish your participant group to focus upon, e.g., leadership, values, praise, delegation.
2. Develop a set of statements, about four or five per participant, and type them on $3'' \times 5''$ cards. The statements should be so written that participants will find that some statements are acceptable philosophically and some are not.
3. Give each person a set of cards (four or five).
4. Instruct participants to review their cards, stand up, find a partner, and exchange their cards. The exchange is designed to "perfect" one's set of cards, that is, to get rid of those which are undesirable or even repugnant.
5. Have each participant repeat the process of exchange with a new partner some five or six times.
6. Have participants meet in small groups to discuss their cards—the ones they like and the ones they don't.
7. Process the activity after the small group work.

Note:
1. A variation of this activity is to let the participants develop the statements and print them on blank cards. A possible topic is ideas about motivation.

Figure 15-10. Graphic presentation of the "frame" concept.

2. "Frame" simply refers to the concept of a frame, vehicle or format, which you use to "plug in" any topic you wish, as illustrated in Figure 15-10.

Role Play

Have participants, in pairs, role play a supervisor who approaches a subordinate who is on a scaffold. (Use a chair to simulate the condition of height.) The problem: The subordinate has failed to use a heavy safety belt as required by safety regulations.

Networking

If one of your goals in a supervisory (or other) training program is to encourage post-program support (networking), have participants do the following:

1. Provide data along the lines suggested in the worksheet in Appendix 53, i.e., help wanted/help offered. The data may be written on a flipchart for easy reading.
2. Post the flipchart sheets to the wall.
3. Move around the room to inspect the posted sheets, entering their name and phone number to offer and/ or request help.

Note:
1. This exercise may be presented as an icebreaker or at other stages in the program.
2. The large sheets may be retained on the wall so that data may be entered throughout the program. At program's end, the participants may retrieve their sheets from the wall.

Resource Rotation

If you have 5 or 10 resource people—experts on a particular subject—and you want your total audience (25–50) to sip at the learned cup of all or most of them, you can accomplish your goal via this procedure:

1. Set up 5–10 "stations"—round tables are best if you have them. Post a large card on a two or three foot post which labels the name of the resource person and his/her specialty.
2. Ask your participants to go to the expert of their choice. Let them know, of course, that they will have a chance to visit with the other experts, too.
3. Let each expert interact (talk, advise, answer questions) with his/her group for some 15–20 minutes, depending on the number of stations and available time as well.
4. When the allotted time is up, blow the whistle and ask people to move to another location.

Note: The ratio of stations to participants should be based on the size of the participant group. Ideally, each expert should have the opportunity to communicate with five to ten participants at any one time. Of course, the actual number of people who visit a particular station or table will depend upon participant needs and interests and possibly on the "prestige" of the resource persons as well. To prevent an "overflow" at one table and limited visitation at another, set up a ground rule that no more than x number of participants may visit a table at any one time.

Other Opportunities for Movement

Be on the alert for various ways to secure movement of participants. Some examples are:

☐ Although it may not always be possible, it is helpful to have lunch at a "removed" location. Similarly, coffee should be served outside or away from the training room so that at least some movement is required. (Of course, many trainers will prefer to have the coffee close at hand to conserve time.) In passing, we should note that there is nothing "sacred" about the twice-a-day coffee break. Why not, then, consider shorter, more frequent breaks, say, five for the training day? Remember, it is highly unusual for people in their normal situation to sit in one place for considerable periods of time without some movement. So why should we make training a less-than-normal experience for our participants?

Also, in a "cultural island" setting, consider arranging the schedule so that free time for recreation is available between 3:30 p.m. and 5:30 p.m. Then hold an evening session after dinner. Try to limit the pre-dinner cocktails so that everyone is able to come back for work after dinner!

☐ Encourage participants to take different seats each day. Although this is not movement in the physical sense such as the activities just described, this procedure will help to break up "the comfort" of the routine. Explain to the participants why you are asking them to do this, of course: "You'll learn more if you interact with someone you don't already know. It may not be as comfortable, but it may help your learning."

On the subject of seating, it should be apparent that activities involving movement can best be engineered if (1) chairs are movable (avoid the heavy "executive" type chair or the fixed seating of auditoriums), (2) desks or tables are not used unless essential for considerable writing (most people can do their minor writing chores on a notebook), and (3) the room is adequately large and "loose." If projectors are in use, be certain that their electrical wires are not likely to be tripped over.

☐ Allow participants to leave their locations to enter data on flipcharts and to post flipcharts on the walls.

☐ Consider permitting participants to re-fill their cups or glasses at any time, rather than insist that they wait until the break. This freedom to move about will help to provide an informal atmosphere. Inform them at the outset that such movement is O.K., unless, of course, you find it too distracting. (*Note:* Some of the distraction can be reduced by having the beverage table *inside* the classroom, thereby eliminating the opening and closing of doors.)

☐ Use one wall for a "running" mural for participants to record in an artful or graphic way their initial reactions to the program, learnings during the day, and final reactions.

☐ In the evaluation of completed training, have participants position themselves with a group with which they identify; e.g., with those who learned a lot, with those who learned to a moderate degree, or with those who feel they learned minimally. Process briefly the feelings of those in each group about their degree of learning.

A final, "contemporaneous" aspect of participant movement: The trainer and the group needn't worry about establishing smoking and nonsmoking sections in the training room if participants are continually rearranging themselves in small groups, pairs, trios, role playing teams, etc. The movement makes such segregation impractical.

You, as trainer, should use movement in as many ways as possible:

☐ You should move among the small groups (discussions groups, role playing teams) to garner impressions, reactions, live data, etc., as opposed to standing "above and beyond" the action. This movement will also help

to show that you want to be one of the group, not the traditional pedagogue.

☐ You can position yourself at *different* points in the room when exercises, games, fishbowls, etc. are processed. The discussion can be led from the *new* position in the room.

☐ You can work with two sets of flipcharts set 15–20 feet apart, thereby creating movement for yourself.

☐ You can post flipchart sheets on the wall.

Flipcharting

Flipcharts, also called newsprint, are an indispensable tool for the trainer and the participant group. (In fact, some would say that the three main tools of a trainer/facilitator are flipcharts, felt-tip pens, and masking tape!) Flipcharts can be used to advantage in several ways:

☐ For inputs from (or by) the trainer, prepared on a pre-session basis. (These should be few in number lest one take the program away from the participants.)

☐ For inputs from the group at large. The data may be obtained by the trainer from various participants or from spokespersons representing small groups.

☐ For inputs (or reports) from small groups that have been entered on the flipchart by either group members or a recorder appointed by the small group.

☐ For inputs by a dyad or triad, working on an assigned project such as steps to implement a plan or project back on the job (e.g., a new quality circle program).

Obviously, our major concern is with the last three procedures, since they actively involve individuals and the group by securing and posting their ideas. Trainer-prepared flipcharts, conversely, are *didactic* rather than participative tools.

Purposes

The use of flipcharts—which I call "flipcharting"—is best done when all the big sheets, produced by the group with the aid of the trainer, are posted to the walls for the full life of the course, space permitting. (I recall a workshop that I conducted for new trainers wherein the group was asked late in the day the following question: "I've been posting these flipcharts on the wall all day. Why have I been doing this?" Came a reply from one participant: "You're doing this because all facilitators like to do this!" In another program a participant advanced this reason: "Because you don't have a wastebasket!") Flipcharting, then, is designed to accomplish the following purposes:

☐ To provide reinforcement to what is said orally by the trainer and the participants.

☐ As a visual aid, it can augment retention significantly.

☐ To serve as a ready and indisputable source of reference to what was said previously.

☐ To aid in note taking.

☐ To help the latecomer or absentee to "catch up" with things.

☐ To encourage participation. It provides an opportunity to get one's ideas displayed before the entire group.

☐ To provide participants with pride in accomplishment (recognition, reward) relative to their contributions. After all, the *participants* made the flipcharts. In a sense the trainer only served as a "scribe" for the group. (Of course, the trainer also may have posed the "right" questions, sharpened the issues, encouraged participation, and condensed the verbiage, besides doing the actual writing.)

☐ To create a sense of atmosphere. ("This is not just a classroom or a training room. It is a workroom, *our* workroom; for it is our work that is on the walls.")

☐ To record progress. By posting the flipcharts in sequence, everyone has a running record of what has been accomplished. In some cases a pattern of results may be evidenced. (Depending on the need, it may help to date the sheets.)

☐ As an aid or control for the trainer so that he/she can see that his/her coverage is on the right track, i.e., reaching the goals.

☐ To aid in a reviewing session or course activities that have been completed.

☐ To serve as a role model for all those in attendance, especially managers. It is hoped that some day all managers will have a flipchart in their offices (and regard it as their key problem-solving tool) instead of the usual fancy desks, chairs, sofas, and other assorted status symbols.

☐ For the trainer, who can take the sheets back to the office, the flipchart can serve as notes for future sessions or as a basis for reviewing and redesigning the program, either in whole or in part.

Skill Points

To help you do a good job of flipcharting, here are some skill points:

☐ Use the largest size paper to provide maximum visibility and clarity.

☐ Start with a new pad of paper to avoid the nuisance of having to install a new pad midway in a presentation or while recording group data. (Or have a second easel handy.)

☐ Use the broad-tipped marking pens to ensure maximum clarity.

☐ To ensure visibility, avoid writing on the bottom of the flipchart sheet. This caution is particularly important if you are using a lecture hall seating arrangement.

☐ Pen a welcoming statement (e.g., "Welcome to _____" or simply "Good Morning") and/or graphic (e.g., a round, happy face on the visible flipchart pad). Why should people have to stare at an empty flipchart pad for 15–20 minutes while they wait for things to get started?

☐ As recorder for the group, be sure that you are capturing participants' ideas as opposed to replacing them with your own. Check with the idea presenter whenever you are in doubt.

☐ Share the recording chore with a participant from time to time. (*Note:* If you are perceived as *the* leader, it may be desirable to share the leadership role to help set a more democratic learning atmosphere.)

☐ Consider using two flipcharts. This will provide you with the opportunity to move around and, as may be helpful in some cases, allow you to compare the data on the two flipchart sheets.

☐ Another use of two flipcharts is as a time saver: use one for previously prepared material; use the other for fresh data generated by the group.

☐ Make liberal use of the T-column. It is an invaluable tool for pointing up comparative and contrasting data and has considerable value whenever two columns are required (e.g., in risk analysis).

☐ Use a flipchart sheet as a visual reminder to respond to questions or issues that were deferred. The "back-burner" flipchart will "keep the trainer honest" and assure participants that their postponed points will be dealt with.

☐ The flipchart can serve as a basis for post-session or post-course participant-prepared handouts. (Remember, the data belong to the participants.) This can be done in one of two ways:

1. Have your secretary type up the flipchart ideas from the big sheets for next-day or post-course distribution.

2. Take a self-developing picture of flipcharts you want participants to retain. Four such photos can be posted on a single sheet of paper and run through a copying machine to produce multiple copies. (You may wish to follow the camera procedure for your own use; it will eliminate the need to carry back to your office the large and clumsy newsprint sheets.)

☐ Try to conduct your training in rooms that have a lot of usable wall space. Rooms with a wall of windows, drapes, or paintings are poor training rooms for they frustrate attempts at flipcharting.

☐ Post flipcharts with masking tape. Unlike cellophane tape, it will not remove paint.

☐ Try to secure a large enough training room so that you can post the completed flipcharts without climbing over people. As an alternative, post the sheets during breaks, lunch, or role plays—times when participants will not be near the walls.

☐ Try to print or write legibly, i.e., in large size with bold letters.

☐ Use multicolored markers. They heighten interest and aid retention. But be certain to avoid weak colors such as yellow, light orange, or pale red.

☐ If possible, use water-based, nontoxic markers. This type does not bleed through the paper onto other sheets.

☐ Don't let a flipchart remain on the easel for it serves as a distractor. Either flip the sheet over, post it on the wall, or discard it.

☐ If a fair number of flipcharts have to be distributed for participant use, you can "economize" by cutting the large sheet vertically in two halves. Also, rather than providing each group or team with a full roll of masking tape, consider wrapping some around the large section of the felt-tip pens.

☐ One way to provide small groups with flipcharts is simply to hand them several sheets. Another way is to post on the wall two or three blank sheets, with masking tape, at several points in the room. These points would be the areas where the small groups would meet and write on the flipcharts. Felt-tip pens may be distributed to the participants or affixed to the wall in advance (next to the flipcharts) with masking tape.

☐ Use a single color of pen for each major topic, theme, or unit. Thus, if four main subjects are covered, the flipcharts would be written in four colors. Color coding is designed to facilitate the search for particular references. Another use of color is to point up data gathered *before* the course, such as information from customers, from employees, from the participants themselves, or from superiors.

☐ Consider posting a flipchart on the wall labelled "Unfinished Business." Advise participants to enter items on it at any time when it is apparent that some need is not being met. The flipchart may have subcategories on it such as "More Of," "Additions," "Needs Clarification," etc., to help participants better describe their needs vis-a-vis themselves and the course. You may wish to tape a pen to the wall for convenient use.

☐ At various points in the program (session, course), ask participants to walk around the room to review the flipcharts. This procedure may be particularly helpful if a detailed or comprehensive evaluation form is to be completed at program's end and a "reminder" about course coverage would be useful.

☐ If your writing is a bit hard to read, you may wish to consider one or more of these approaches: Let an associate or participant write for you; print rather than write; use lined flipcharts if there is a problem in writing in a straight line; use larger-size flipcharts with king-size, felt-tip pens.

☐ If you have a flipchart pad, but no easel, you can use the wall as a writing and display board. The procedure is to tear off a batch of sheets from the big pad and tape the sheets to the wall. Each flipchart sheet is placed just above the one underneath it. The tape is placed on the two sides (horizontally) of the sheet, at or near the top, rather than on the top of the sheet (vertically) as is normally done to post the big sheets to a wall.

☐ At times an exercise, game, or other activity may have the participants in small groups in different parts of the training room. In processing (analyzing) the completed action, it may be desirable to have the participants stay with their small groups rather than returning to their more conventional group-at-large configuration. If so, move the flipchart pad and easel to an adequately central point in the room and lead the discussion from that new, more visible location.

☐ Try to talk to the audience rather than to the flipchart. If, while entering data, you have a comment for the group, simply stop writing, turn completely around and make your statement.

While flipcharts are "standard" equipment in most organizations, some still shy away from them. Trainer/consultant Patricia A. McLagan cites an incident involving an organization which told her prior to the training that "the group won't go for it." She replied that she would not use them throughout the process. But she insisted on using them to document participant input and as a tool to help the group reach decisions. The result: What the group "wouldn't stand for" turned out to be one of the most successful sessions they ever had.[3] *Moral:* Stand for your principles concerning the use of flipcharts, but modify them to avoid alienating the sponsor or client.

Humor and Fun

Learning that is enjoyable, fun-filled, and humor-based is always easier to take than that which is super-serious, deadly, and dull. If we, as trainers, can put our participants in a relaxed, receptive, child-like mood via laughter and fun, the training experience will be a joy for everyone concerned. Humor, enjoyment, and learning are not antithetical to one another.

By humor we don't merely mean dusting off a lot of old jokes, projecting them intermittently and mercilessly on your participants or trying to entertain them in other ways. The trainer is neither a stand-up comic nor a supper club M.C. Rather, we have in mind the use of the sophisticated techniques advocated and employed by educator/trainer and humor authority Dr. Joel Goodman. He favors the use of the following eight "E-lettered" devices:[4]

☐ *Environment.* First, build a humor-laden atmosphere via a bulletin board that has cartoons, funny quotations, poems, and/or photos. Your participants can check these out before the start-up, at breaks and after lunch, garner a few chuckles from them, and interact a bit more easily with fellow participants.

☐ *Enter.* You may wish to start a session by sharing a personal, humorous anecdote or funny incident illustrating the program's theme. (At one time I conducted EEO workshops. I began things by recalling an incident that had occurred at a large EEO conference that I had attended. The speaker made the point that treating all racial and ethnic groups with dignity and respect was not a new concept. To buttress his observation, he asked the audience if anyone knew who had said: "I never met a man I didn't like." As if on cue, a guy in the back of the room yelled out: "Elizabeth Taylor." The crowd roared. The speaker, of course, was quoting American humorist Will Rogers. This true incident always got a big laugh from my workshop groups.)

One trainer finds that her use of humor is the best way to relieve tension—the group's and her own. She thus may start out by saying something like this: "We've got eight hours worth of training to squeeze into two, but with a group that learns as fast as this one, we should still have time for a 10-minute break and a chess game. Well . . . perhaps not chess, but maybe checkers." She garners a lot of laughs thereby and simultaneously communicates some key information: There's a lot to cover, they're smart, the class will run two hours, and there will be a break. She may also use other humorous devices such as showing a cartoon on an overhead transparency or posting a trivia question to be answered at session's end.

In the warm-up phase of the first session you may wish to make a point about the need for participation by everyone. I often pass out the following statement as an encourager and chuckle producer:

NXXDXD VXRY MUCH!

Xvxn though my typxwritxr is an old modxl, it works quitx wxll xxcxpt for onx kxy. Thxrx arx 46 kxys that function wxll xnough, but just onx not working makxs thx diffxrxncx.

Somxtimxs it sxxms that our group is somxwhat likx my typxwritxr, not all thx kxys arx functioning propxrly. You may say: "Wxll, I am only onx pxrson. It won't makx much diffxrxncx." But, you sxx, thx group to bx xffxctivx nxxds thx activx participation of xvxry pxrson.

So thx nxxt timx you think you arx only onx pxrson and that your xffort is not nxxdxd, rxmxmbxr my old typxwritxr and say to yoursxlf, "I am a kxy pxrson and am nxxdxd vxry much."

☐ *Ear Ye, Ear Ye.* Use the "circular whip" (whip around the room) and let each participant share a funny joke, quotation, or perspective on the work at hand. Not everyone may have something to contribute, but all would have had the opportunity to do so. (In one workshop that I ran on delegation one of my participants defined it as "deliriously dodging the drudgery which you can unload or dump on someone else.") This device, obviously, encourages listening to one another as opposed to the trainer alone, as well as loosening people up.

☐ *Exercise.* Look for ways to introduce humor into training exercises. For example, when I introduce brainstorming to a group, I have them practice it via a listing of uses of a somewhat ridiculous object, e.g., a pair of mixed socks, an old tennis ball, or a live elephant; or listing causes of particular phenomena, e.g., fleas on my dog or my frequently missing a.m. newspaper. Humor, in these instances, is also mind-stretching, a means of encouraging creativity.

A fun thing to do when participants seem to be suffering from the "blahs," discontent, or disappointment, is to engender some robust laughter via this simple procedure:

1. Ask everyone to stand up.
2. Staring straight ahead have everyone say: "Hee, hee, hee." Start low and repeat it several times, each time increasing the volume until a loud roar is produced.
3. Then turning heads to the right, have everyone say: "Ho, ho, ho." Repeat, this time turning to the left side. With each "Ho, ho, ho," start low and finish robustly.
4. Ask: "How are you feeling now? 'Good'? Let's hear it. Let's hear it again."

You can have a lot of fun by doing two things: (1) provide humorous tasks/activities and (2) convert the activity or exercise into a competitive event or game. For example, I may have two or more groups compete in the identification and listing on flipchart of certain metaphors. The team which has the greatest number of metaphors is the winner. A small prize will add energy and fun. Allow 10–15 minutes for the small group work. Two possible topics are metaphors using "body parts" or "animal references." You can start the groups off by providing these examples:

☐ *Body Parts Metaphors:* "I can't stomach that"; "I'm all ears"; "foot in the mouth"; "pain in the neck"; "get off my back"; "he's a headache"; "they're dragging their feet."
☐ *Animal Metaphors:* "It's a dog's life"; "dog eat dog"; "clever as a fox"; "bull in the china shop"; "quiet as a mouse."

The "archeological game" will also create a lot of fun-filled rivalry (see page 100).

When small groups have to select a leader and you wish them to do this randomly, rather than having them assign the task to the same person, you can provide some fun criteria for the selection. For example, the one who has the most $10 bills in his/her wallet or purse; the one who was most recently promoted; the one who has the brightest colored ball point pen; the one who came here from the farthest distance.

☐ *Exaggerate.* By stretching examples and demonstrations to the point of hilarity, you can make your point well. For example, I have trained managers in how to conduct the annual performance review. I had two of my participants act out (a demonstration role play) all the horrors of a really third-rate appraisal interview. They used a script I provided. I also selected role players whom I thought could really ham it up and get a big kick doing so.

☐ *Engage.* Provide activities which involve movement and fun. For example, I have found that the icebreaker "The Ball Toss" (page 244) raises the decibel level considerably and loosens people up with laughter. The University Associates' *Handbook of Structured Experiences for Human Relations Training*, Vol. 5, #149, describes a number of "Energizers: Group Starters."

☐ *Enhance.* The key to "good" humor is that which enhances participants' readiness to learn. In other words, you want humor that encourages laughter with people, not at them. This means avoiding put-downs, stereotyping, ridiculing, demeaning, playing practical jokes.

☐ *Extend.* As trainers we want to transfer or extend the new learning to the back-home situation. Dr. Goodman offers several suggestions. One is to use a humorous "chain." After the workshop ends, the person on the top of the group's roster sends a humorous item (cartoon, quotation, joke) to the next one on the list and so on. Another is to develop a "jargon dictionary," e.g., "It's under consideration," "I agree with you, but . . ." Third, during the workshop appoint a "court jester" on a rotating basis, each of whom is responsible for providing a

fun thing, e.g., a humorous skit which serves as a lampoon of the course, some art work which has some fun with certain course concepts, etc.

Dr. Goodman's eight "E" concepts also should trigger interest in looking for devices which:

● Kid the instructor (yourself)
● Kid the subject matter
● Kid about the facility or food being provided, especially if it is high calorie or monotonous. (This may be a sensitive area, however.)

But one "no, no" is to kid the organization and/or its hallowed traditions or the professions or specializations in which your participants work. These are cultural taboos and, if violated, they may backfire badly. If the participants do this on their own, that's O.K., of course.

If you want to use a lot of fun-type activities, the materials of University Associates, Inc. (see page 116) will be of interest to you. These abbreviated titles indicate their fun-potential: wooden blocks, riddles, Tinker toy bridge, coloring book, towers, poems, greeting cards, limericks, slogans.

Props for Empathy

When developing interactive, experiential activities—games, exercises, role plays, etc.—try to think in terms of heightening or intensifying the experience with the aid of real-life, everyday objects. Typically, cost is minimal or even nonexistent, but these objects can produce a great impact on participant learning and retention.

The "trick" is to ask yourself questions concerning the proposed simulation. The following are some example situations that lend themselves to the use of props:

☐ *In an activity on eye safety, how can we vivify the effect of the loss of sight?* Have participants put a cotton ball over one eye and tape it in place with masking tape; or have them wear a pair of glasses with one lens masked over.
☐ *How can we demonstrate the effect of carelessness around fast-moving machines?* Allow participants to run a weiner through a machine to show what it can do to a finger.
☐ *How can we show the great value of wearing the hard hat?* Use the before and after method in a demonstration that is not likely to be forgotten. First, drop a heavy object such as a bowling ball or an item in the work place on a round watermelon. Let your participants observe the ensuing crunch, squish, and squirt. Then repeat the drop on a new melon, this time placing a hard hat on it.

☐ *How can we simulate an injury to an arm?* Have everyone bandage their arm and wear a sling.

☐ *How can we drive home the importance of the tactile sense to perform certain tasks requiring acute finger dexterity, such as threading a needle?* Provide participants with surgical gloves.

☐ *How can we give added empathy to the execution of a given role, e.g., in black-white communication?* Provide black and white masks to the role players and use the role reversal technique.

☐ *How can we augment identification with a given occupation in an exercise or role play?* Provide appropriate costumes, e.g., a doctor's smock; a laborer's hard hat; a police officer's badge; a truck driver's cap.

☐ *How can we sensitize customer contact personnel to the concerns of older customers?* Have the employee/trainee don eye glasses smeared with Vaseline to limit vision, stuff cotton in his/her ears to reduce hearing, and have them wear rubber gloves to impede writing ability. These procedures were used by the American Bankers Association[5] in its member banks and the Florida Power and Light Company.[6]

Note: According to the ABA, older people hold 68% of all bank deposits and their checking account balances average 25%–50% higher than the other age groups.

☐ *In a role play (or other activity), how can we increase empathy for the handicapped?* Have role players use a wheelchair.

☐ *How can we simulate a telephone pole on which a maintenance person is working?* Use a chair to stand on. (In a group exercise all who are linemen would stand on a chair.)

☐ *How can we show the "connectedness" of the self to all its components, i.e.,*
1. *The physical self*
2. *The intellectual self*
3. *The emotional self*
4. *The sensual self (includes all the "holes" in the body, i.e., eyes, ears, nose, mouth, navel, genitals, nipples, skin)*
5. *The interactional self (the way one reacts with others)*
6. *The nutritional self (relates to solids and liquids for physical growth)*
7. *The contexual self (sound, light, air, color, movement, space, time influences, our being)*
8. *The spiritual self (which may or may not be related to religion)?*

After a short talk on this topic, ask a participant to come to the front of the room. The participant is the "I" or "the self." Tie a rope around that person's waist. Then call up eight participants, one at a time, each representing the various parts of the self. As each "part" comes up front, tie the rope around that person's waist. Have all of them mill around to demonstrate how the self is pulled in various directions by its component parts. Then instruct the self to "get control"—not let each part lead a life of its own—and to tell each part what it must do to help connect or integrate self.[7]

Using Handouts

Handouts are vital training aids. Their proper selection and use can enrich a program and thereby enhance the learning experience. The checklist in Figure 15-11 is designed to assist you, as a trainer, to re-think your use of handout materials and thereby augment your instructional effectiveness.

One trainer[8] suggests that handouts passed out in class may become a distraction and consume time unreasonably. He thus suggests alternate procedures: pass them out when participants arrive, or just before a break or, in some cases, use overhead transparencies instead. To simplify their distributions, he places them on a rear table with a sign which reads: "Take one from each pile."

I would suggest that a good guideline to follow in distributing handouts is to only pass out in mid-session those items which are to be used immediately; e.g., worksheets, check lists, instruments, quizzes, cases, and the like.

Using Silence

As trainers, we typically expect our participants to be active and energized and to engage in all kinds of verbal activity—interviewing, conferring, discussing, challenging, critquing, questioning, responding, initiating, interpreting, summarizing, reporting, and so on. There are numerous instances, however, when the training situation is better served by silence. Here are several such examples:

☐ Role players are given instructions about their roles and asked to enact them. It will be helpful to the role players if they are given several minutes to reflect silently about the nature of their role assignments and how they propose to execute them (their strategy). Certainly, as a minimum, silent reflection will aid in reducing possible anxieties and thus strengthen the enactments.

☐ Small groups are given an assignment. Again, the opportunity to think through its significance on a quiet basis will be helpful to the participants. They can ask themselves: Do I understand the instructions? How

---

Handouts—Help, Hindrance, or Happenstance?

General   No   Yes

1. Do I regard handouts as aids or tools rather than just "throw aways?" — —
2. Do I choose handouts carefully and opt for quality rather than quantity? — —
3. Do I constantly up-date and enrich my handout files? — —
4. Do I think in terms of *variety* of formats and uses: outlines, charts, graphs, models, cartoons, poems, quotes, cases, articles, question sheets for films, instruction sheets for exercises, editorials, self-quizzes, topic summaries, etc.? — —
5. Do I plan their use carefully? — —
6. Have I secured permission to reproduce copyrighted materials? — —
7. Do I use handouts at *all* stages of the course: 1. *Pre-Session;* 2. *In-Session;* 3. *End-of-Session;* 4. *Post-Session?* — —

A. Pre-Session   No   Yes

1. Do I utilize pre-work materials for one or more of these reasons: — —
   a. To establish early contact with the participants — —
   b. As a "motivator" — —
   c. As a topic introducer — —
   d. To bring everyone up to a common level of understanding of a topic — —
   e. To facilitate entry from the job to the classroom — —
   f. To save time — —
2. Is there a *plan* to tie advance work to *specific* class activities? — —
3. Do advance readings, exercises, etc. consider carefully trainee interests and needs? — —
4. Are instructions re advance work clear and goal-oriented? — —
5. Time factors:
   a. Will the materials be received early enough to work on them? — —
   b. Will the participants' schedules allow for pre-work? — —

B. In-Session   No   Yes

1. Do I provide participants with a bulky notebook of materials "for effect" rather than for actual class use and benefit? — —
2. Are all or most sessions supported by handout materials? — —

3. Do I provide *outlines* so participants can have an *overview* of an activity or the total course? — —
4. Do I hand out materials to advance the session rather than to compete with it (e.g., extensive reading in class of handouts is to be avoided.)? — —
5. Do I pass out more items at any one time than people can digest? — —
6. Do I tap participant motivation via:
   a. Participant-prepared handouts (i.e., assembly and reproduction of ideas developed by participants in their small groups or general sessions)? — —
   b. Encouraging trainees to bring in pertinent materials which can be reproduced for the total group? — —
7. Do I provide in writing key points or summary statements of talks, learnings from exercises, complex ideas, etc.? — —
8. Do I "imagineer" handout distribution (e.g., put an item on everyone's chair during the break)? — —
9. If I use handouts extensively do I try to evaluate their effectiveness? — —

C. End-of-Session   No   Yes

1. Have I provided any materials for backhome reading? — —
2. Have I pointed up the importance of take-home materials so they are seen as reference items rather than "throw aways?" — —
3. Have I allowed enough class time for distribution of final take home materials? — —
4. Should all take-home materials be distributed to everyone or, alternately, might they be placed on a table for optional selection? — —
5. Have I facilitated storage (via notebook, folder or envelope) and retrieval (via dividers) of handouts? — —

D. Post-Session   No   Yes

1. Do I think in terms of *follow-up,* of stimulating participants via handouts provided 1, 3 or 6 months *after* training's end? — —
2. Have I considered contacting course "graduates" re additional materials they might wish to receive? — —
3. Can handouts developed in class by participants be made available to other segments of the organization? — —

Figure 15-11. Use this checklist to rethink your use of handout materials. (Prepared by J. E. Eitington, *Bulletin on Training,* July/August 1977, page 6. Used with special permission from the copyright holder, BNA Communications Inc., 9439 Key West Avenue, Rockville, MD 20850. Further printing or reproduction without specific permission of the publisher is prohibited.)

should our group proceed? What outcomes should we strive for?

☐ Individual participants are asked to complete an instrument. The basic work, of course, is done silently. Silence aids the twin processes of *introspection* (how do I see my attitudes, beliefs, values, perceptions, behavior) and *reflection* (making meaning out of the material I have developed/discovered in introspection). The silence inevitably triggers the desire to share verbally what was learned or to seek out the learning from one's colleagues.

☐ Meditation, performed silently, provides participants with an opportunity to experience a change of pace so as to regroup psychologically. It can help to renew one's energies and to get in touch with feelings that may be hard to reach while one is in an active, verbal state.

☐ Nonverbal exercises can aid participants to achieve a new awareness based on the use of the other senses; they can help to set a particular mood; and they can produce a change of pace and encourage a deeper contemplation.

☐ In a group discussion or team building session that is marked by an impasse (creative block), fatigue, or possibly conflict accompanied by the expression of unusually strong feelings the trainer may ask the group to "disengage" from the task by taking a silent "time out" for two or three minutes. These moments of silence should help to restore energy, good humor and creativity, chart a new course, and the like.

☐ After a profound, highly impacting film, allow participants to reflect quietly for a minute or two on what they have experienced, rather than disrupting the mood by embarking on its discussion immediately.

Long-time trainer/consultant Dugan Laird also suggests that trainees need "silent, introspective time . . . time to put a new information into perspective . . . time to contract with themselves about how they will apply their new skills . . . how they will measure their effectiveness in doing so . . . how they will overcome the inevitable obstacles to change. Such commitment requires an unpressured environment of which silence is one key ingredient."[9]

The trainer can also use silence constructively in other ways; e.g., after posing a question to a group one should wait patiently for a response. The silence may be "painful:" but if the group understands that you intend to wait them out, someone in the group will break the silence.

In a T-group, which is a special training situation, of course, participants may lapse into silence for various reasons ranging from extreme caution about revealing feelings to fear of embarrassment for saying something

inappropriate or "stupid." The skilled trainer accepts the silence and waits until someone says something. Not everyone can endure silence for any length of time. (Actually, the silent periods seem longer than they really are.) If the group seems completely bent on "clamming up," the trainer may break the silence with a comment of this sort: "We seem to be in a silent mood which is fine if you find it helpful. I have the feeling, however, that there are many things which could be said, that we have many feelings which are going unexpressed. For starters, would anyone care to explain this silence? Why are we doing it? What does it mean? Is it helpful to group progress? How are we feeling about it?" Questions of this sort are certain to get the group going again.

And in management development programs, particularly in time management, managers (and others) should be encouraged to adopt the practice on the job of having a "quiet period" each day. An hour of silent contemplation for planning and considering major issues, as opposed to dealing continually with the demands of the telephone, the in-box, visitors, meetings, and assorted conflicts and crises, cannot but help make one more calm and thus more effective.

Other opportunities back home to use silence are while engaging in the communication process, particularly in the all-important act of listening, and while coaching and counseling.

All in all, silence is a potent and valuable tool. The effective trainer should understand its potentialities and utilize it appropriately along with the many other techniques available.

Key Points

1. Pre-work is a useful device for involving participants "early on," that is, before the formal training program begins.
2. While pre-work has a number of advantages from a learning standpoint, it should be used judiciously. Time constraints and reluctance by the participant group should be considered carefully.
3. Keys to the effective use of pre-work are course relevance, a presession meeting to explain purposes and procedures, avoidance of pre-work overload, and the use of forms, instruments, etc. to facilitate assigned tasks.
4. Seating is a vital factor to consider if you want to facilitate your approach to participative training.
5. The key element in effective seating is to avoid formal, classroom configurations in favor of flexible, free-flowing seating.
6. Desks and tables should be used only if considerable writing is to take place.

7. Movement is helpful in keeping participants alert, alive, active, and energized.
8. Movement may accrue from training activities per se as well as from program management, e.g., walking in a dyad to lunch.
9. Flipcharting is useful for capturing participant inputs, as an aid for reinforcement of what was said, for giving participants recognition for their contribution and accomplishment, for giving the training room a working look or atmosphere.
10. As part of the overall training design, include experiences which provide fun and humor. A light, relaxed classroom climate is a positive aid to learning.
11. Physical objects (props) can be used to heighten the learning experience. By engaging in physical contact with objects that relate to the subject matter, the participants can be made more fully aware of the learning to which they are being exposed.
12. Handouts are much more than materials which participants can cart home in their heavy notebooks. Look at them as learning tools and consider their use on a pre-session and post-session basis as well as during sessions.
13. Use silence to heighten training experiences such as role play, fantasy, guided imagery, viewing of a profound film, etc., and to overcome impasses in problem solving or conflict situations.

References

1. Askins, Nancy, Director of Educational Development, Shore Memorial Hospital, Somers Point, New Jersey, used this icebreaker at the 1986 National Conference of the American Society for Training and Development with a group of 75–100 people.
2. Wangler, Joan S., "What Do Leaders Value?" *The Torch*, Newsletter of the Washington, D.C., Metropolitan Area Chapter of the American Society for Training and Development (November 1986), p. 11.
3. "What Do We Need To Know About A Group Before Designing Training For It?" *Training and Development Journal* (September 1984), p. 19.
4. Goodman, Joel, "Using Humor In Workshops," in *The 1983 Annual for Facilitators, Trainers, and Consultants,* J. William Pfeiffer and Leonard E. Goldstein, editors, University Associates, Inc., San Diego, 1983, pp. 137–141.
5. Reported in *Modern Maturity* (October–November 1986), p. 16.
6. Reported in *The Wall Street Journal* (August 12, 1986), p. 1.
7. The last example, concerned with connectedness of self, is based on a presentation by Dr. Virginia Satir at the Annual Conference of the Association of Humanistic Psychology, Washington, D.C. (July 23, 1982).
8. Dunnit, Ben N., "To Pass Around Or Not To Pass Around—Is It Worth the Distraction?" *Training News* (October 1983).
9. Laird, D., "Uses of Silence," *Training News* (September 1982), pp. 5–6.

Recommended Reading

Broadwell, Martin M., "Seating Arrangements," *Training,* July 1975, pp. 18–19.

The article discusses the best way to arrange a room, the effect of crowding, student preferences, whether to assign seats.

Eitington, Julius E., "Seating Arrangements and Participant Learning," *Bulletin on Training,* March/April 1978, pp. 4–5.

This relates various forms of seating arrangements to trainer style, trainer philosophy, classroom atmosphere, possible trainee attitudes, and impact on the learning process.

Facilitator, G. F., "Dead Men Don't Use Flip Charts," *Training*, February 1984, pp. 35–40.

A tongue-in-cheek article pointing up the many advantages of the flipchart over the highly sophisticated electric and electronic a/v devices.

Greenberg, Jerald, "The Role of Seating Position in Group Interaction: A Review, with Applications for Group Trainers," *Group and Organization Studies,* September 1976, pp. 310–327.

This summarizes experimental research on seating positions and relates it to advice for the trainer, e.g., how physical layout influences participation, how different group activities are facilitated by different seating arrangements, why tables should be avoided.

Koneya, Mele, "Privacy Regulation In Small and Large Groups," *Groups and Organization Studies,* September 1977, pp. 324–335.

Research is reviewed to show that seat location is associated with verbal interaction rates and visual accessibility among and between group members and leaders.

Smith, Homer, "Communicating With A Flip of the Chart," *Sales and Meeting Management,* July 2, 1984, pp. 90–98.

The article discusses advantages of flipchart work, what to put on a pad, and techniques for best use.

Stone, Donald, and Stone, Alice, "The Administration of Chairs," *Public Administration Review,* January–February 1974, pp. 13–25.

The authors' thesis, presented with humor, is that "not the persons or subject, but the arrangement of chairs determines the success of a meeting."

Suessmuth, Patrick, "The Psychology of Classroom Seating," *Canadian Training Methods (CTM) The Human Element,* August 1980, pp. 63–64, 66.

This uses questions and puzzles (problems) to help the reader develop new ideas about seating.

INVOLVING PARTICIPANTS IN FILM/VIDEO

If you see in any given situation only what everybody else can see, you can be said to be so much a representative of your culture that you are a victim of it.

—S. I. Hayakawa, general semanticist and former U.S. Senator from California

Film Versus Video

In our discussion we will use the word "film" to include video as well. The rationale for using film and video interchangeably is that both media are forms of one-way communication; both impart ideas to a passive learner. And as will be indicated, the real learning occurs via the group-in-action devices that the trainer employs to involve the learner fully.

Of course, there are certain technical (nonsubstantive) differences between the two media:

☐ A film has the advantage of impacting a high-quality picture every time it is shown. It is not subject to loss in color fidelity due to electrical interference or improper set adjustment as is video. Also, it can be shown with no loss of fidelity to large audiences (although a special lens is required in a very large room). However, new, large TV screens of good quality are now overtaking this advantage of film.

☐ Video, on the other hand, has a number of advantages. For one thing, there is no need for the careful threading of a projector—just insert the video cassette, and you're off and running. For another, there is no projector noise. Also, rewind and reverse actions can be executed simply and rapidly. Finally, the room need not be darkened, thereby permitting note taking or using handout material. And if you have a video camera, you can make your own videotapes for play back.

Film captures large scenes—the outdoors, crowds, panoramic views—better than video. Conversely, video can provide a feeling of greater intimacy for one-on-one interactions and small group scenes.

Uses of Films

The film (video) is a valuable training tool. It is used widely by trainers and expected universally by participants. However, we should recognize that the film, despite its popularity, is essentially a form of one-way communication. It is a carrier of information, like the lecture or the panel discussion. Hence the need for the trainer to exploit a visual presentation properly so that participants have opportunity for full involvement in the learning process. In the pages that follow, we shall present a variety of techniques that the trainer can use to secure such active participation.

Before we do so, however, it might be helpful to ask ourselves this basic question: Why do we, as trainers, use film? Or, putting it another way, what specific values or benefits do films actually have? They are beneficial in many ways in that they:

☐ Can hold attention easily, far more effectively than a book or a speaker.
☐ Provide a quick way to get a story across. Because of a film's careful planning and organization, a lot of learning can be packed into a 20–30 minute film (or even into a minute or two if the trainer uses a vignette from the film).
☐ Offer a great deal of realism. Filmed incidents, events, situations, interactions, etc. bring the viewer as close to real life as is possible.
☐ Tap the visual sense so vital in much of our learning. The visual material is supported or reinforced by the sound, of course.
☐ Provide a high-impact, high-interest learning experience. Participants can readily be involved emotionally in many dynamic situations: conflict, cooperation, missed signals, vexing problems, unresolved relationships, misunderstandings, frustrations, aspirations, successes, failures, etc.
☐ Allow the case or problem to be presented in all its dimensions, something that the lecture or printed page cannot do.
☐ Allow for identification (or nonidentification) with characters in the film who serve as role models.
☐ Provide an immediate group experience, since all participants see the film at the same time. The story becomes "group property." That is not to say that everyone sees (perceives) the film's events and characters in the same way. In fact the opposite—varying perceptions—is more likely. But it is a *common* experience, unlike a previously assigned case or article, which may or not be read by everyone who comes to class, and which if read may be hazily remembered or forgotten.
☐ Provide an opportunity for discussing perceptions. As people project themselves into the film, they read different meanings into it, all of which is grist for the "discussion mill" and a basis for real learning.
☐ Allow for standardization; that is, repeated presentations by the trainer—to the immediate group or to other groups—are always the same in all vital particulars. And, of course, the message is the same even if the film is shown by different trainers.
☐ Are expected by participants in our visually-oriented culture. Consequently, people readily relate to them.
☐ Vary the pace of the training day, particularly if it is a "heavy" one.
☐ Illustrate concepts and situations that can't be observed or appreciated very readily, e.g., how to deal with an angry customer.

☐ Provide an opportunity to "meet" and learn from an expert or authority in a given field.
☐ Can "humanize" an expert who may appear in them.
☐ Provide a worthwhile training experience at a relatively low cost per participant. Most films have a relatively long shelf-life, which helps to keep costs down.
☐ Are extremely versatile; that is, they can be used as a program opener to provoke thinking about the topic about to begin; to reinforce a given topic or presentation; to set the stage for other training activities (exercise, game, role play); to demonstrate a skill (how to lift properly or to conduct a meeting); to alter attitudes (on controversial subjects such as sexual harrassment); and to help summarize a session or program.
☐ Are a uniquely flexible and versatile tool for the trainer. That is, various training activities may be conducted *before* the film/video showing, *after* its showing, and even *midway* or at other points in the course of its presentation. These strategies are developed in more detail later.

To put the use of films into proper perspective, we should add that films should *not* be used to fill in a "blank spot" in the program; to offset the effect of a weak or marginal instructor; because it is the "prestigious" thing to do; to provide entertainment; to fill in for a resource person who didn't show; to give the trainer some free time; etc. A film is a training tool; it should thus be used appropriately.

Also, while films have many advantages they also have some decided limitations.[1] These include an emphasis on passive rather than active learning (unless the trainer does something about this); realism may be lacking, with artificial and exaggerated situations being presented to make the major points; individual differences may be ignored for not everyone will perceive the content with the same relevancy; too many examples of inappropriate or undesirable behavior may be shown.

Other disadvantages/limitations are that they can't readily transfer somewhat idealized materials (in the film) to the participant's here-and-now world; nor can it lead a group discussion, i.e., serve as a substitute for an insightful, provocative and enthusiastic trainer.[2]

Previewing

A fundamental rule in using films is to always review it before you present it. This vital procedure will avoid unwanted surprises to you and your participant group as to its relevancy and quality. Additionally, part of your planning for a given session entails designing activities that will actively involve your participants in the film's content. (See "Post-Film Activities.") You can only design relevant activities if you have seen and reflected on the film. In sum, a film isn't merely something you show. Rather, it is a *tool* which you use with purpose and care.

It is a good idea to involve several people in the previewing process—a colleague(s), your boss, two or three supervisors or managers, or possibly several people who would be representative of your client/participant group (e.g., if you were showing a film on customer relations invite several customer relations personnel to your preview). Your objective is to garner multiple reactions about the film's pertinency, quality, and overall suitability. Multiple judgments should provide adequate assurance that your participants will find the film a helpful learning tool in relation to course objectives.

In your preview session you will want to:

☐ Note parallels and contrasts to the real (work) world and your own in-house situation as well.
☐ Note major questions/issues which the film *raises*.
☐ Note questions/issues which the film *answers*.
☐ Note significant incidents, events or situations which you will wish to emphasize.
☐ Look for opportunities to exploit the film properly. (See "Post-Film Activities.")

It is also a good idea to preview the film twice. You are very likely to observe certain things which were not evident on the first viewing.[3]

Introducing a Film

In today's complex and demanding training world, you can't simply load your projector, tell the group that a film is coming and "let 'er roll." Your participants will expect and need much more, too. Your job, then, as an introducer of the film is to:

☐ Provide an opening statement which will challenge and excite your participants. ("You are about to see a film about a manager who came into a plant besieged by numerous production and morale problems, and how he gradually turned things around so that his plant became the best producing plant in his company.")
☐ Tell them what to look for in both a general and particular way so that they can transfer the incidents observed in the film to their own job situations.
☐ Point up areas that may be outside the group's experience or possibly have an element of controversy or ambiguity.
☐ Anticipate and defuse possible negative reactions by candidly stating at the outset that they will see something which they may not like or agree with.

☐ Overcome almost certain complaints about the film's age. Be candid about it being an older film. Ask them to zero in on the key learning points and not to get too hung up on the older cars, dated dress and hair-do's, and so on. Assure them that other groups have found the film helpful despite its production date.

All in all, your objective in your introduction is to set positive expectations and encourage the rendering of full attention.

Post-Film Activities

An effective way to exploit a film is to put a group into action following their viewing of it. Some ways of doing so follow:

Dyads

The simplest, quickest, and most effective way to involve participants with one another (and the subject) is to ask them to join with someone else to form a pair. The "someone else" may be on one's right, or left, or in front, or behind, or elsewhere in the room if a "new" partner is to be secured. The pairs may then be asked to respond to a general, open-ended question for five to ten minutes. The result is instant interaction and conversation. Some examples of easy-to-respond-to, open-ended questions that permit the participants full leeway to "pick up the ball," discussion-wise, on their own are these:

☐ What was the most significant learning in the film for *you*? or What are the lessons to be learned from the film?
☐ Why do you suppose the filmmaker produced this kind of film? What was he/she trying to accomplish?
☐ What did you like or not like (agree-disagree with) in the film?
☐ What did the film omit or overlook, if anything?
☐ Was the film a balanced presentation of the problem?
☐ If you were to redo the film, what approach would you take?
☐ How do the film's ideas square with your own experience? or What is significant to you from the standpoint of your current job?

Specific questions, rather than general ones, may also be used. Some examples:

☐ With what characters could you identify in the film?
☐ With what character could you *not* identify?
☐ Do you feel the policy regarding promotion is a sound one?

☐ Comment on the company president as a decision maker (or as a delegator, communicator, planner, time manager).

☐ What are the implications of the film for team management (or for customer relations, intercultural awareness, problem solving, creative selling)?

☐ What are the risks in taking the course of action the police officer did?

Triads

When a somewhat greater variety of inputs than is possible in the dyad is needed, the trio works well. While the trio is less intimate than the pair, it is still conducive to a high degree of interaction. The assignments can take the same form as those just suggested for the team of two.

Buzz Groups

Groups of four to six can be asked to "buzz" on any question or issue that the film points up. Or the groups may be asked to frame a question to which another small group or the total group can respond. Buzz groups typically provide a good diversity of viewpoints. Hence a good technique is to ask them to *agree* on some aspect of the film's content; e.g., the three main learning points, the wisdom of the sales manager's course of action, the nature of the communication process at work, the correctness of the salesperson's approach to closing the sale, the role of the secretary.

Note: In "putting the group to work" following the showing of the film, you have two options. You can start the pairs, triads, or small groups "to buzz" immediately *or* a more "reflective" approach to the assignment of tasks may be taken. In the latter instance, you may say: "O.K., you've seen the film. Let's take two minutes to sit back and reflect on what we've experienced."

The rationale for the second approach is that, at times, participants are prodded into reacting verbally before the full impact of the film's message has actually settled in. The two-minute reflection period makes sense particularly when a group has seen a film with a great deal of impact, such as when considerable emotionality has been presented or a theme such as prejudice has been treated.

Brainstorming

Groups of six to ten can be used to generate multiple ideas about or solutions to a problem raised in a film, for example, how to make our promotion plan (or career development plan, performance review plan, compensation plan) more effective; how to motivate persons who have reached a plateau in their career; how to improve communication in an organization (or *our* organization). Two or three groups can brainstorm the assignment simulta-

neously. Each group must have a recorder (scribe) to capture the ideas on a flipchart.

Role Play

If a film points up a problem of an interpersonal sort, you may ask for two (or more) volunteers to see how they would handle the problem. This may relate to coaching, counseling, performance review, discipline, employment interviewing, a sales interview, etc. The purpose of the role play enactment is to explore alternative, more effective ways of resolving the one-on-one difficulty that the film highlighted.

Using a Fishbowl

The fishbowl, or group-on-group observation technique, is a means of involving participants in a novel, high-interest way. Procedurally, you:

1. Assign participants to two clusters, an inner one (Group A) and outer one (Group B). Five to eight participants in each group are workable groups.
2. Give Group A a discussion assignment (10–20 minutes) based on the film. Group B observes and listens silently.
3. After time is up, switch the groups so that Group B now is in the fishbowl. Have Group B develop the topic further, including an analysis of Group A's conclusion and observations.
4. Reverse groups again, if appropriate. A shorter time-frame may be used on the second go-around.
5. Sum up conclusions of the total activity.

Contracts for Reentry

If a film is used at program's end to solidify or reinforce learnings, you can then plan for back-home activity. For example, if the closing film stresses the importance of team action or team development, participants may be asked to develop an action plan (or contract) to improve the functioning of their team.

Pre-Film Activities

Whereas the post-film assignment is designed to exploit the film after it is seen, the pre-film assignment or activity is designed to set the stage for the visual presentation. Some examples:

Group-at-Large Participation

Various tasks can be given to the total group for individual completion prior to the film viewing. The data generated by these tasks can be discussed as a prelude to seeing the film. Begin by giving everyone small cards or a sheet of paper to record their responses on. Some example tasks are:

☐ Ask participants to enter on a $3'' \times 5''$ card some quantitative data, such as a percentage estimate of one's listening efficiency, or the amount of discretionary time (as opposed to reaction time) one has at one's disposal, or how good a delegator one is using a 100-point scale, etc. Collect the cards, have someone quickly tally the results, and discuss their implications. Then run the film. The "live" data can be referred to again in the post-film discussion session.

☐ Have everyone jot down a definition pertinent to the subject, such as job enrichment, coaching, counseling, innovative marketing, or support systems. Record a number of the definitions on a flipchart, discuss them briefly, run the film, then refer back to definitions after the film. Check to see if anyone wants to alter their definition.

☐ Have everyone come up with one basic principle or technique to aid in closing the sale, collect the cards, post ideas to a flipchart sheet, comment on the ideas, run the film, then refer back to flipchart, comparing ideas in the film.

Small Group Work

In a unit on the role of the supervisor in the orientation process, kick things off by having small groups develop two kinds of laundry lists. You might say something like:

"Groups One and Two, come up with the things the effective supervisor should do to make the new employee's first day a rewarding one. You have ten minutes for this."

"Groups Three and Four, come up with the things, you as a supervisor might do, if you were so inclined, to really 'louse up' the orientation process for that new worker. Do this in ten minutes."

Post group reports to a flipchart. Then tell the group that: "We will now see a film which shows a supervisor orienting a new worker. Let's see how well we predicted what our supervisor might do."

After running the film, check off the things done by the orienting supervisor on both the positive and negative lists.

In effect, the small group work, the list development, and the effort at "prediction" were interest generating or attention-getters. They involved the participants *in advance* of the film by exciting them or raising their anticipation level.

Role Playing

If a one-on-one problem-solving situation or interview is to appear in the film, it may be desirable to let two participants role play that interaction. The enactment can then be compared with the one seen in the film.

The role playing activity can also be organized along more formal lines, that is, giving it a good deal of struc-

ture. The advantage to this approach is that learning points are "buttoned down" more tightly.

1. In a session on interviewing (coaching, counseling, discipline, employment, discharge, performance appraisal) conduct a role play.
2. Have the role players provide a self-critique of their interview. Have them list on a flipchart the things they felt went well and those that could have been strengthened. (A group critique may also be employed if the participants wish the added feedback.)
3. Then show a film that presents an interview of the same type as was role played.
4. Have the role-playing participants review their lists in relation to the film and report to the total group on them.
5. Secure group critique as may be helpful.

Using Viewing/Listening Teams

The trainer can heighten interest in a film by giving small groups or teams an assignment *in advance* of seeing the film. The rationale for this procedure is that by giving participants responsibility for a task in conjunction with the forthcoming film, they are certain to be "tuned in" rather then "tuned out." Viewing becomes purposeful rather then "loose." These assignments may be specific or general.

Specific assignments. The viewing/listening teams may be asked to look for such elements in the film as:

☐ Leadership styles
☐ Decision making procedures
☐ Communication processes
☐ Techniques used to close a sale
☐ Handling of customer complaints
☐ Climate of the organization

After the film has been shown, the teams meet to discuss their assignment and then have a spokesperson report back on group findings.

The assignments may be treated in various ways: all teams may be given the same assignment; each team may be given a different assignment; one-half the teams may receive one assignment and the other half another one; etc.

General assignments. Teams may be asked to function in these capacities:

☐ *Question-raisers.* "Look for something that raises or stimulates a question in your mind."
☐ *Clarifiers.* "Look for something that is presented in a hazy way and requires clarification or amplification."

□ *Agreers.* "Look for something you really agree with, like, or identify with."

□ *Disagreers.* "Look for something that you can't buy; possibly something that even turns you off."

□ *Appliers.* "Look for principles or techniques that you can implement readily on Monday morning when you return to your jobs."

After seeing the film, the teams meet to discuss their assignments and report back their conclusions or recommendations.

Point-of-View Teams

Another form of the viewing-listening team is to have teams observe/listen from a given frame of reference (e.g., top management, first-line supervision, employees, the personnel office, the comptroller) or from the views of production vs. sales; or headquarters vs. field; or line vs. staff; or senior personnel vs. newcomers; or men vs. women; or adults vs. teenagers.

Committee Work

In advance of the film showing, assign teams pertinent readings or discussion topics. This may be done on a pre-work (or homework) basis. Discuss the pre-work assignment in class *prior* to showing the film. The pre-work and in-class discussion, in effect, sets the stage for the film and the post-film discussion.

Incident Application

In advance of the film showing have participants jot down on a sheet of paper an incident, event, or situation pertinent to the forthcoming film's content. Some examples participants might include are:

□ An incident where they helped a customer with a problem and really got turned on because of it.

□ An incident where they got something important done, not because of authority but because of the ability to influence the situation.

□ An event or situation involving delegation which really paid off.

□ An instance where persistence in follow-up produced a "big" or otherwise important sale.

Then run the film and have participants form small groups to share and compare the significance of the recorded incidents in relation to the film's message. Secure reports from the small groups concerning what was discussed and learned.

Another way of treating incidents is as follows:

□ Have everyone describe on a card an incident, event, or happening related to the subject matter of the ses-

sion (e.g., one half of the group may be asked to describe an incident in their career wherein their growth was encouraged and one-half of the group can describe an incident where growth was discouraged); collect incidents and randomly select and read aloud several of the positive and negative incidents; draw some tentative generalizations and then run the film; refer back to the incidents in the post-film discussion.

Note: In the previous examples, specific training techniques were suggested to be used, either on a pre-film or post-film basis. It should be obvious that the same techniques—fishbowls, brainstorming, role plays—if used one way (e.g., pre-film) could also be used the other way (e.g., post-film),too.

Stop-Film Technique

We have indicated previously that proper exploitation of a film calls for a group involvement either before or after a film viewing, or possibly at both times. Added involvement is also possible via the "stop-film" technique. This simply entails stopping the film at one or more appropriate points and putting the group to work discussing the film up to that point.

Some films have the stop-film technique (also known as "viewer participations") built into it by the producer. But there's no reason why you can't stop a film at logical points without such guidance.

Some examples of stop-film use are as follows:

□ In the film *Twelve Angry Men* the film may be stopped by the trainer at various points to allow participants to *predict* which person will now shift his position from "guilty" to "not guilty."

□ In the film *The Eye of the Beholder* the film may be stopped at midpoint and the group asked: "What is your impression of Michael Gerard based on what you now know about him?" This film has a stop-film point provided by the producer.

□ A film may be stopped to allow participants to discuss the action (or decision) a manager should take in light of the facts presented up to this point.

□ In a film having separate wrong-way/right-way sequences, the film may be stopped after the wrong-way presentation to allow participants to propose the right-way course of action. Their solutions can then be compared with the film's solution.

As a summation of these examples, be on the lookout for stop-film opportunities that relate to:

□ *Prediction:* What is likely to happen? Who will do _____?

□ *Decision:* What would you do? What decision will _____ make?

□ *Perception:* How do you see the sales manager (or the organization, or the situation, or _____'s prospects) at this point?

The rationale for the stop-film technique is:

□ It allows for discussion when the issue is "hot;" that is, before the group "here and now," rather than sometime later.

□ It prevents information overload, particularly if a film is fairly long and meaty.

□ It gets attention. ("Hey, she stopped the film!")

□ It creates suspense. ("I wonder what the rest of the film is like.")

□ Most importantly, it converts a one-way communication device into a participant-involving medium.

Other Aids and Approaches

There are a variety of other aids that can ensure participant involvement with film presentations. The following discusses some of these other approaches.

The Vignette

Ordinarily we take a film as the producer prepares it and show it in its entirety. There is no reason, however, why we cannot merely show a pertinent segment of it—a vignette or film clip. By isolating a particular vignette, we may actually achieve a greater participant impact than by showing the full 20 or 30 minutes of film. Vignettes which run for only one and a half to three minutes can be quite powerful. They can present an incident, a problem, a case, an interview, etc., all of which require participant reaction, analysis, or problem resolution. The vignettes can be exploited via pre-film or post-film devices as previously described.

Of course, a short case or problem also can be prepared on videotape on a "tailor-made" basis to meet the needs of a particular group. Thus, one writer cites the use of "trigger tapes" to train student teachers to handle discipline problems, an area of special concern to a new teacher. The procedure used was to query experienced teachers concerning typical classroom discipline problems. Nine problems were chosen (note passing, tardiness, drugs, falling asleep, rebellious attitude, etc.) for preparation of tape simulations. Cards were also developed containing background data concerning the children shown in the taped situations. The two-minute tapes present a role-played incident on an open-ended basis. At the conclusion, the teacher must make a decision.

Trigger tapes also can be used for in-service training of experienced teachers for discussions of classroom management.[4]

Prediction

A helpful way to involve participants is through the device of prediction. Three examples of the use of prediction in working with films are as follows:

□ A new employee is being pressured by two senior workers to "join" with them in holding down production. The new worker seems to favor "rate busting" because of his economic needs and he feels that hard work will be noticed. The vignette presents the forces working on the new worker to "join with the boys" and the forces to "join up" with management. At this point the trainer may stop the projector and asks: "Which way will the new worker go? How many think 'with management'? How many 'with the boys'? O.K. let's watch the rest of the film and see what happens." Another vote may be taken after more footage is observed to see if there is a shift in participant opinion.

□ In the film classic *The Eye of the Beholder*, the trainer may stop the film after several film characters have met Michael Gerard and have commented upon him. The trainer then asks: "How do you see Michael now?" Adjectives are supplied by the group and put on flipchart. "O.K., we're going to learn now how Michael sees himself. How do you predict Mike will present himself? Let's get some other adjectives."

□ The group may be shown a scene involving a fall from a ladder resulting in a serious injury. The trainer may ask the group for possible causative factors. Responses by group members—leaning too far, insecure feet of the ladder—become predictions. These are "checked out" with the next film sequence, which reports on the actual investigation of the accident. The trainer may then ask for suggestions concerning how to prevent this kind of accident. Ideas may be offered, such as tying the ladder to increase stability, which, again, are predictions. The trainer returns to the film to see how the problem is actually handled, thereby validating the accuracy of the predictions.[5]

Prediction, at times, may pose "a threat" to some participants. Consider the following set of circumstances. After viewing a filmed sequence presenting an unresolved problem, the trainer may ask a participant: "What would you do in this situation?" For some participants this may present them with a threatening situation. Why? Because not everyone wishes to display his/her "ignorance" before the total group. One way to get the participant "off the hot seat," so to speak, is to phrase the question in less personal items, for example: "What will the person in the film do next?" In essence, by asking for a prediction of *someone else's* behavior, the trainer can turn a high-threat situation into one having little or no anxiety.[6]

Threat can also be minimized or eliminated by having predictions made in (and by) small groups or by several individuals in the total group. No particular attempt need be made to identify the predictors. Consequently, the concern of threat is not present as may be the case in the one-on-one situation.

Note: Reference has been made to having participants predict the action that will take place in a film. The prediction may relate to the film, in general, *before* it begins as well as to sequences in it *as the film progresses*. For example: A film may show the orientation of a new worker. As a means of stimulating interest, the trainer may ask one small group to list the elements that make for effective orientation and another group to list the things that a supervisor might do if he/she wished to really mess up the orientation process. Both sets of data are posted to a T-column on a flipchart, the data serving as a prediction of the behavior to be observed in the film. After the film has been seen, the group checks off the items on the flipchart in relation to the observed behaviors.

Film Discussion Aids

If the film displays a form such as a sales call form, a model, an instrument, a diagram, or a chart with key points, the trainer should reproduce these aids, if possible, and distribute them to participants. (This is subject to copyright restrictions, of course). These aids present pertinent ideas, which, on film, pass by all too quickly. Also consider distributing other aids such as an organization chart that may be in the film's leader's guide.

Wherever practicable, the participants should be given the opportunity to work with these materials. For example, a film on team management may show the characters in it discussing an instrument that facilitates the rating of team effectiveness. Why not let the participants rate their own work teams and discuss the results with their colleagues in the training group?

Nonverbal Approach

At times it may be worthwhile to have participants analyze the nonverbal communication in which characters in the film engage. If so, simply turn off the sound and have the group analyze the silent interaction.

Another approach, allied to the above, is to show certain vignettes in the film in two ways: first, *without* the audio portion, the audience hypothesizing or predicting what was said; second, presenting the vignette with both

sound and picture, and then discussing why the predictions were or were not "sound."

Of course, the trainer can also do the reverse—that is, turn off the picture and just present the sound track. This might be done with very powerful dialogue, the participants creating their own images of the interaction taking place.

Using Viewing Worksheets

Participant involvement with films can be augmented by using viewing worksheets. They are passed out to participants *before* the film begins. The structure of the worksheets helps to stimulate and channel observation and thinking about the film. Three such worksheets are presented in Appendices 54, 55, and 56. The first is essentially an open-end aid to note taking; the second two direct the participant to specific elements in the film. Allow time after the viewing to complete the form (five to ten minutes). Data entered on the worksheets can be shared in small groups after the film viewing.

Using Question Sheets

Questions to the small groups for pre-film or post-film discussion may be reduced to writing. The advantages to the participants of the written format are these:

☐ They are more likely to be easily understood than an orally presented question. Why? Because they can be read at one's own reading pace and even reread, if necessary. Also, since the trainer has taken the pains to write them out, the odds are that they will be carefully phrased and concisely written.

☐ They may be taken home as a post-course reference.

Advantages also accrue to the trainer. They are these:

☐ The writing process encourages more careful thought as to what should be asked.

☐ Instructions to the small groups are simplified and systematized. Thus, the trainer need merely say: "Group One take question one; Group Two take question two."

☐ It is available for future reference in the course of program planning or revision.

An example of a question sheet is given in Figure 16-1.

Another form of the question sheet is one that asks participants to respond in writing to certain questions. Two forms of the question sheet are as follows:

1. *Post-film*. Participants are given the question sheet, post-film, and are asked to complete it and then meet in small groups to discuss their answers.

```
                  Understanding Our Relationships
                     Questions for Discussion

1. What is the role of feedback in a healthy relationship?

2. What place does support have in a successful relationship?

3. How is conflict handled in a relationship that works well?

4. Comment on the importance of trust in a successful relationship. How can it be
   developed if it is weak or lacking.

5. Is openness an element in a good relationship? Are there any limits to it? If so,
   what might they be?
```

Figure 16-1. Example of a question sheet for stimulating pre-film or post-film discussion.

2. *Pre-film.* Participants are given a question sheet *in advance* of the film showing, are asked to read the questions and to focus on them as they view the film. They are encouraged to make entries on the question sheet as the film evolves and to complete their answers to the questions at film's end. Again, they would meet in small groups to discuss their answers.

Examples of two question sheets are given in Appendices 57 and 58.

Developing Question Sheets

Questions given to participants should be challenging in nature. They should provoke significant thought, adding a worthwhile dimension to the film viewing and analyzing process. You can prepare "good" questions if you recognize that:

1. Questions can serve different functions and thus take different forms.
2. Questions can assume a hierarchy of complexity; that is, we can rank questions as to how simple or involved they are.

Questions, then, may take these forms or levels:[7]

☐ *Factual level.* Some examples are:
  • Who were the main characters in the film?
  • Why did Alexandra refuse the promotion?
  • What guidelines did the expert in the film offer for effective communication
  • How do the general manager's and the president's views on discipline differ
  • What causes burnout in a customer relations job, per the film?

☐ *General level.* Some examples of questions that are general and thought-stimulating and take an open-ended form are:
  • What does the film seem to be telling us?
  • Is there more than one theme in it?
  • What's the most significant point made in the film?
  • How does this film relate to our own experience?
  • Would you like to work for the comptroller?
  • Would you like to supervise Allen and Jean?

☐ *Analytical level.* Here we involve the group in an analysis of:
  1. What is going on—the characters' reactions, motivations, feelings, attitudes, values, support systems, conflicts, frictions, rivalries, dependency tendencies, defenses, styles of leadership (communication, delegation, selling).
  2. Processes and systems in the organization such as the communication system, the reward system, authority vs. the power of the informal organization, the decision making processes, team work, innovation, creativity, leadership-followership, setting objectives. Typical questions relative to this are:
  • Who seems to have the power in Division X?
  • How would you describe McBride as a leader?
  • Is the company subject to the problem of "yesterday's bread-winners?"
  • What does the corporate level seem to expect of its divisions?
  • Can you describe and evaluate the organization's system for "self-appraisal?"
  • What kind of stress factors seem to be at work in Division X?
  • What is the real source of conflict between the two branch chiefs?

☐ *Application level.* At this level we move beyond an attempt to analyze or interpret the action and interaction pertaining to the individuals, the groups and the total organization depicted in the film. We now wish to see if we can *apply* our learnings from the film and its subsequent discussion to a higher level—prevention of undesirable, situations, improvement of our own policies and practices, etc. Sample questions include:
  • What significance does the film have for our job situations?
  • What are the implications for our long-range planning system?
  • How would we go about utilizing these principles with our customers?
  • How would organization renewal or organization development aid the company in the film and our own organization as well?
  • How does an MBO program relate to all the problems we saw?

- How important is openness and trust? Do *we* have it? To what degree? How can we increase it?
- Is our organization vulnerable to the same set of external forces we saw in the film?
- Do we have (or need) an early warning system to avoid these and other oversights?
- Do these ethical factors relate to us at all?
- What do you think the business environment will be like in the next five to eight years? What problems will this pose for us?
- How could we go about changing the attitudes of *our* employees?
- Should we be working on team building in the same way as the group in the film did?
- How can we apply these concepts of discipline to our kinds of workers and situations?

Participant-Prepared Questions

Although the trainer ordinarily presents questions to the group after a film viewing, at times it may be desirable to reverse this responsibility. The task, then, for the participants working in small groups, is to frame several questions to which the other teams or the total group are to respond.

Summary Sheets

One way to "button down" learnings from the film is to provide participants with a handout that lists the key ideas or learnings that emerged from it. It's a good idea to go over these pointers or principles with the participants to ensure understanding. Also, you should take notes about the reactions to the discussion so that you can revise and enrich the sheet for use with future participant groups.

Adjectival Description

1. After showing the film, have each participant jot down on a sheet of paper two or three adjectives that describe *all* the main characters in the film.
2. Then have participants meet in small groups to develop composite descriptions that are to be written on a flipchart and posted on the wall.
3. Test the "validity" of the descriptions via total group review and discussion.

Note: A variation is to ask each small group to develop a composite description of only *one* character.

Planning for Multiple Film Use

At times the training design may call for the use of several films. Or an off-the-shelf audio-visual program may be built around a group of films. In such cases it is desirable to vary the techniques used to "exploit" the films. This approach will augment participant interest in the films and the training as well.

Let's assume, then, that we are working with a six-film series. As part of our planning of ways to "kick off" and generally work with each film, we might use the ideas suggested in the following list. The list will encourage us to think systematically about diverse ways to enrich each film presentation.

1. *Post-film, dyadic discussion*: "Turn to your neighbor and discuss and agree on the most significant learning for you from the film."
2. *Post-film, small group assignment*: Ask each group a different question, such as: "What turned you on; what did you really like?" "What raised a question in your mind about what you saw?" "Was there something in the film you are somewhat reluctant to accept?"
3. *Post-film fishbowl*: Have the participants discuss what was learned or the implications of the problem under review.
4. *Pre-film, small group assignment*: Relate the tasks to the film's subject matter. "Group One look for and report back on the most significant ideas on planning. Group Two, look for and report back on the most significant ideas on decision making."
5. *Post-film, group-at-large discussion:* Use general questions such as: "Any reaction?" "Significance?" "Do you agree?" "Disagree?" "Do you buy it all?" "Any omissions?"
6. *Post-film, group-at-large discussion:* Use specific questions such as: "What did the expert in the film say about product liability?"

Participant Reactions to Film Content

In various workshops for trainers and in other contacts, I have been asked how to deal with or respond to troublesome or "negative" reactions that participants may have to certain films or portions thereof. Some of the trainers' most common questions, along with my answers to those concerns, follow:

☐ *"But we work in a hospital."* How do you as a trainer, respond to trainees who work in a given occupational setting (e.g., an office) and thus assert they can't identify with an unrelated setting (e.g., a factory)?

This is a classic "problem," but one principally aired by inexperienced trainers. These suggestions generally help: First, you should use your introduction to the film to "defuse" in advance such possible objections. Specifically, you should point out that the setting the participants will see is different from theirs, but that "this shouldn't matter too much because our goal is to study managerial behavior to understand better management principles and processes (or sales techniques, or communication processes, or leadership styles) not the nuts and bolts of the industry depicted in the film. So as you watch the film, relate the incidents in it to your own job situation."

Ordinarily, these introductory comments should quiet such criticism. If complaints persist, you can also point out that "just as a student in a Michigan law school may study a California case to extract the legal principle involved, so, too, managers study management cases regardless of their source. In any case, other management (or supervisory) groups have used this film without difficulty, so I don't think this will cause any problem at all for you." You can point out, too, that if a case is "organization- (or industry-) specific," all too often participants get distracted by the minutiae (technology, policies, regulations) of the job or industry portrayed, hence "outside" filmed cases are desirable. Finally, it's simply too expensive to try to produce a film for every job or industrial situation. In general, the alert, interested, and flexible participant will transfer successfully the learning from the "abstract" film to his/her job situation. Conversely, and at a deeper level, the inability to make the transfer may indicate resistance to the training. If participants find the message unsettling, they may understandably discount it by quibbling over the setting or the occupations presented in the film

☐ *"This is a 'racist' (or 'sexist') film."* How do you deal with a trainee who complains that a film is "racist" or "sexist"?

1. Listen carefully to the participant's complaint as to its logic or validity. If it is an older production and there are no women, blacks, or other minorities in managerial or professional roles, obviously the complaint is based on fact. All you can say to the participant is something along this line: "You are quite right. But you have to consider when the film was made."

2. If the complaint is somewhat less than "logical," e.g., "In the opening stage-setting shots, there are no women operating the big cranes in the pipe yard," it is your job to try to elevate the conversation to a more logical plane. You thus might say: "What you say is correct. But there is a woman in a key managerial role throughout the film (or film series). There also are blacks in important roles in the film, too. I believe that showing women and minorities in important roles, such as in manage-

rial positions, is more significant than showing them in traditional blue-collar roles, don't you?"

3. It is also possible, at times, to turn a complaint into a plus element. For example, in the British film *Blowing Hot and Cold*, the production manager uses the term "Jap." Use this incident as an opportunity for the participant group to discuss the implication of the comment in relation to prejudice. In effect, the racial slur can become grist for the discussion mill.

☐ *"Hey, this film is a dozen years old."* What is the best way to handle complaints about an old or older film? The message may be lost on participants because of the age of the film in which styles of clothing, hair, cars may, indeed, be "dated."

You might respond to a complaining participant by saying: "Yes, there's no question that it is an older film. But the message is still worthwhile." You can use the film successfully by introducing it carefully. That is to say, point out to the group at the outset that the film is an older one, that the costuming and cars are a bit "dated," but that the content, nevertheless, is still highly valid. Advise the participants: "Don't get too concerned about such details, but concentrate on the principles and techniques the film is pointing up." This candid type of introduction should "defuse" in advance possible noncontent-type objections. Some older films are "classics" and should be so designated along with a statement such as: "Thousands of participants have seen this film since 1965 and have found it quite helpful."

In most cases, a challenging film-related assignment will stimulate participant thinking about content as opposed to peripheral items in the film.

☐ *"This film runs too long."* If you are concerned that participants in all likelihood will like the content, but will be turned off by the film's length, you could use some of the following suggestions to overcome this problem.

1. Use certain (not all) of the vignettes in the film.
2. Stop the film midway or at any other logical break point and introduce a group-in-action activity.
3. In some instances the lecture portions, if any, can be dropped.

Another possibility, of course, is to try to locate another film on the same subject that is somewhat shorter.

☐ *"This film is hardly realistic"* (or *"too far out"* or *"too idealistic"*). What is the best way to deal with extremely negative comments about a film made by a participant?

It is to be expected that some participants may overreact to a film or some portion of it. But is this a "disaster"—something to be feared? Will these negative comments "frighten off" the "positive" thinkers? Hardly.

An *extreme* comment is actually grist for the discussion mill. An effective way to deal with the negative thinker (probably one who is merely engaging in "attention-seeking" behavior) is to turn the comment back to the group in this fashion: "Does anyone else have any other thoughts on this point?" The odds are that the extreme comment will draw the opposite (more favorable) reaction. Why? Simply because fair-minded people find it hard to sit idly by when far-out, unfair over-reactions are expressed.

Remember, too, that diversity of opinion indicates that the film is live, provocative, disturbing, and thought-provoking—something every alert trainer is always looking for.

☐ *"The film failed to discuss . . ."* What do you do or say when participants point out gaps or omissions in the film?

You should realize that no film will discuss every conceivable aspect of a subject. If another substantive point should be made, there's no reason why a participant or the trainer can't make it. That is part of the trainer's job. The film is designed to present certain issues, to get some thinking in motion, to spark discussion. It can only set a groundwork for exploration of other related issues; it cannot serve as a substitute for such exploration.

Thus you might say to the participant: "You are quite correct. The film does not delve into that aspect of the problem. I'm glad *you're* making that point."

Remember the film is essentially a springboard for group discussion, so there's no reason why participants/ or the trainer cannot bring up added points. By so doing, all parties would be expanding upon the significant points already contained in (or made by) the film.

☐ *"Too much lecture in the film."* Ideally, films should use the medium properly and be highly dramatic. However, at times a worthwhile film may have one or more somewhat lengthy "talking-heads" scenes in it.

So when trainers tell me: "The concepts are excellent, but our audience will be turned off by the excessive lecture," I offer this response: "I'm glad you feel your participant group will profit from the ideas in the film. However, even if the formal inputs are long, your skill as a trainer can help to make the film a valuable learning vehicle. By using the problems, questions, and exercises in the Leader's Guide (or workbooks), or some of your own, you can provide the participants with a change of pace—a break from the lecture aspects of the film."

Other possibilities are:

1. To use the vignettes, if any, and omit or reduce the film's lecture portions
2. "Break up" the film, rather than running it straight through, and provide practical work or discussion at strategic stop-film points.
3. To use an alternate film on the same topic

Useful Scenes From Popular Movies[8]

Movie: Monty Python and the Search for the Holy Grail
Scene: Captain giving instructions to nincompoop guards
Use: Active Listening (clarifying and confirming)

Movie: Monty Python and the Search for the Holy Grail
Scene: Knight asking peasants to figure out if a woman is a witch
Use: Problem solving

Movie: Lost in America
Scene: Albert Brooks in boss' office, thinking that he's getting promoted
Use: Transactional Analysis (from adult mode to child mode)

Movie: Lost in America
Scene: [same scene]
Use: Career management (making assumptions about getting a promotion)

Movie: Modern Times
Scene: Company president turns on spy-screen and shouts out orders
Use: Management style

Movie: Airplane
Scene: Two black guys talking jive. Subtitled
Use: Cultural and language barriers in communications

Movie: The Karate Kid
Scene: Coaching boy by having him wax car, paint fence, etc.
Use: Coaching techniques

Movie: The Caine Mutiny
Scene: Queeg stating how he solved the stolen strawberries mystery
Use: Problem solving—using same old methods to solve all problems

Movie: Take the Money and Run
Scene: Virgin Starkweather applying for a job and getting interviewed
Use: Interviewing and selection skills

Movie: The Great Dictator
Scene: (Hitler) and (Mussolini) racheting up their chairs
Use: Communications—positioning, territory

Movie: 12 O'Clock High
Scene: [The whole movie]
Use: Situational Leadership

Movie: Five Easy Pieces
Scene: Jack Nickolson ordering breakfast in the diner
Use: Communication skills; Transactional Analysis

Movie: Teachers
Scene: [The whole movie]
Use: Train-the-trainer (commitment to performance improvement)

Movie: Patton
Scene: Opening speech
Use: Leadership style

Movie: Patton
Scene: [same scene]
Use: Making effective presentations

Movie: Pee-Wee's Big Adventure
Scene: Pee-Wee calls a meeting to discuss his stolen bike
Use: Managing meetings/agendas

Movie: 2001: A Space Odessey
Scene: Dave lobotimizes HAL. HAL apologizes for being bad
Use: Recognizing the feelings of others

Key Points

1. Films have many virtues—everything from providing realism and a great deal of information in a short time frame to the fact that they are very much in tune with our film/video culture.
2. Nevertheless, films are a form of one-way communication. The trainer, therefore, must exploit them properly to ensure participant involvement.
3. Films can be made participative via pre-film, stop-film and post-film activities. Numerous techniques in each category are available to the trainer.
4. Added approaches to dynamic film use include the vignette approach, trigger tapes, prediction, film-discussion aids, the nonverbal approach, worksheets, question sheets, summary sheets, and adjectival description.
5. If more than one film is used in a program, it's a good idea to vary the techniques that are used.

6. Films, as a training tool, must relate to learning objectives. They should not be used as "filler," to entertain, or for other nongermane reasons.
7. Be sure to preview the film/video while planning and again just before using. The first screening is for making sure it is appropriate and that you have the necessary materials to supplement the film. The second review is to be sure it is the correct print (if rented) and is in good shape.
8. Consider carefully how you introduce a film. Use your introduction as a means of providing interest and motivation and to defuse in advance possible negative reactions and comments.

References

1. Nolan, J., "The Use and Misuse of Films in Management Training," *Training and Development Journal* (March 1980), pp. 84–86.
2. Faris, John P., "How To Use Films In Training," *Training and Development Journal* (May 1984), pp. 108–110.
3. Eitington, J., "How To Preview A Film," *SM* (Sales Meeting Magazine) (January 1972), pp. 41, 99, 101–102.
4. Zeimet, E. J., Miller, K., and Turner, P., "Trigger Tapes—A Tool for Teacher Education," *Educational and Industrial Television* (March 1975), pp. 43–44.
5. Lowry, C. R., "Sensitivity to Safety Taught by Videotape," *Educational and Industrial Television* (July 1977), p. 22.
6. Levine, S. J., "Prediction—New Tool for Videotape Involvement," *Training* (April 1974), pp. 25–26.
7. Based on material developed by Eitington, J. E. (Ed.), *Bulletin on Training* (September–October 1979), p. 8.
8. This list was distributed by Mitch Mitchell, Training Specialist, Training Department, Hewlett Packard, San Diego Division, San Diego, California 92127-1899, at the 1988 Annual Conference, National Society for Performance and Instruction, Washington, D.C., April 8, 1988. The list was part of a presentation paper for his session entitled: "Dagwood, Penthouse, and Patton: Using Offbeat Resources to Spice Up Your Seminars and Workshops."

MAXIMIZING PARTICIPATION AND LEARNING IN THE CASE METHOD

The real voyage of discovery consists not in seeking new lands, but in seeing with new eyes.

—Marcel Proust (1871–1922),
French novelist

In a day when the industrial training world employs so many involving (experiential) and exciting training methods (role plays, dyads, buzz groups, fishbowls, in-baskets, exercises, games, simulations) the case method (also called the case study method and the case discussion), at least in its classic form, is hardly the most glamorous of training methods. Nevertheless, it *is* a student- or learner-centered method and has many advantages over such one-way communication devices as lectures, films, and panel discussions.

The case method is an age-old teaching device, having taken through the ages such familiar forms as fables and parables. By way of more modern historical note, the case method was developed and used at Harvard University in the 1880s. First used in the business school, it spread to other schools of the university and to other universities. In time it entered the industrial training scene where it was used extensively in management training in conjunction with the traditional lecture method.

Advantages and Disadvantages

The *Management Development Casebook,* prepared by the Veterans Administration,[1] cites twelve advantages in using the case method. The method is advantageous in that it:

1. Is personal. It puts the burden of thinking on the members and arouses their interest by making them active rather than passive participants.
2. Is real. The members examine situations that have actually occurred.
3. Is specific. The members deal with specific facts and events rather than with generalities. The method brings about the recognition that formulas and principles are of little value in specific situations and that each situation requires its own understanding and reaction.
4. Places the members in a group situation. It provides opportunities to work cooperatively and with satisfaction within the group, and gives some feeling for the importance of the group.
5. Establishes a strong give-and-take. Members must justify and defend their own views and, at the same time, must try to comprehend and use the contributions of others.
6. Brings about a recognition by the members that other people look at situations in different ways, that other people have problems similar to their own, and that other people have difficulty in solving these problems.
7. Produces a realization that the types of problems discussed do not have a single subject or a single answer.

8. Develops judgment and ability to think independently and more maturely.

9. Provides experience for performing essential parts of the supervisory or administrative task. It enables members to develop the habits of analyzing a situation, using factual knowledge, formulating a program of action, and making decisions. And it provides this experience without risk to the members or to the organization of which they are a part.

10. Brings about a better understanding of human behavior, and increased sensitivity to causes behind behavior, and an awareness of the necessity for seeking these real causes. The members realize that people tend to have feelings, sentiments, and beliefs which are not logical, which are important to them, and which have to be considered. They also see more clearly how their actions affect the behavior of others.

11. Increases skill in communication. Members learn how to listen better. They also improve their ability to convey ideas.

12. Reduces fixed attitudes, such as "all redheads are hotheads" and "fear makes people work harder." It produces changes in attitudes and outlook and develops a willingness to see problems from all points of view.

The *Casebook* also listed these disadvantages: The case method

1. Does not actually provide *real* experience. While the case method uses real situations, there are a number of aspects in which it lacks realism. Participants do not have actual responsibility for the decisions they make. The facts are presented; the members get little practice in seeking and recognizing facts and relationships. Because it may not be feasible to present all of the available facts, the situation may be oversimplified. The printed case doesn't convey many subtle but important overtones of human personality and conduct. The members don't experience the successive interactions which are a part of real experience.

2. Is incomplete. It does not proceed to the process of carrying out the decisions and checking on the results.

3. Sometimes overemphasizes the making of decisions. In real life action may not be justified or a particular solution may not be feasible.

4. Takes a more skilled discussion leader than do other methods. It is easier to "tell" than it is to phrase questions which will stimulate discussion and keep the discussion on the track. It takes great self control for a leader to refrain from giving his own views. A lecturer can select the questions which he will discuss; in the case method the leader cannot anticipate all the questions which may be raised.

5. Is different. Not only that, but it is radically different. Participants usually feel frustrated at first when they find there are no specific conclusions, answers, or recipes. Some may find the idea of thinking for themselves to be new and even terrifying.

6. Is slow. The discussion and deliberation which this method requires naturally take more time than the types which pass on "the word." Usually it takes some time to get past the frustration period mentioned in 5.

7. Is not adaptable to all employees.

8. Presents greater opportunities for the "eager beavers" to monopolize the discussion.

9. Is more difficult to integrate the results of this method with specific operating practices.

10. Is not useful when the primary purpose is the transmission of facts.

11. Can be a waste of time and effort, if not used properly.

In *executive* development programs the case method has these special benefits:[2]

☐ Participants (executives) can assume the position of and identify with the real-world manager and are challenged to make decisions and action plans.

☐ Retention of concepts used to solve real-world problems is increased.

☐ Skills in appraising situations and applying concepts are developed as opposed to only learning theoretical, textbook ideas.

Special disadvantages accrue in using cases in *executive* development programs:[2]

☐ The written case does not convey fully the complexity of a management situation.

☐ The participants don't have the opportunity to collect and sift the data which aid in identifying significant trends and organizational climate. (The case writer does this.)

☐ The case lacks immediacy. It is essentially a historical document.

☐ Since the participants are not involved in the actual decisions, they will not experience the uncertainty of decision making or the risks associated with it.

Assessing the pluses and minuses just cited, one can safely say that it is a useful training method, a *participative* method, but hardly the most exciting and profound training method available today. However, maximum return from its use can be achieved by (1) varying the format of the cases and (2) providing supplementary training devices to exploit a given case more fully. The bulk of this chapter will be concerned, then, with these two "enriching" approaches to case study.

The Case Study—A Potpourri of Formats

In the pages that follow we will present the case study in many forms. In doing so, our selections are essentially representative rather than exhaustive. All of the formats, however, have the same purpose—to get the participants *to think*.

The Classic Harvard Case

In classic case study, participants are given a comprehensive case. It is drawn from a real situation and is very well-researched. While no case writer can capture *all* the facts, there generally is enough data for analysis. In fact, the discussion leader may ask in response to participant requests for more facts: "But are you using the facts you already have?"

Because of the length of the Harvard case, participants must spend considerable time (two or three hours) in preparation for the case discussion session. The discussion itself is very nondirective, the trainer's role being that of catalyst, encourager, climate-setter, devil's advocate, issue-sharpener, "referee," etc. rather than that of expert, lecturer, authority figure, and the like. The trainer's technique to start the discussion is a simple question: "What seems to be going on here?"

The group typically will identify a good many issues in the case since it is so comprehensive and ramified. A major goal is for participants to see the "big picture," the interrelatedness of events, the internal and external forces at work, the role of personality in decision making, etc. Learning takes place in large part by listening to the divergent views of the group. A major learning is that there is no single or "best" solution to a case, and indeed, sometimes there may be no answer at all.

Due to the length of the Harvard-type case, industry tends to use much shorter cases. Few managers have the time or motivation to engage in the preparation required by such cases. This chapter presents examples of the kinds of cases used in industrial training.

The Short Case

A case need not be long to excite participant interest and encourage creative efforts at problem resolution. This is exemplified by the following case and the many

creative, high quality solutions regarding it that were developed by participants in several separate sessions.

The Case of the Undesirable Job

A meat packing plant has a job that is marked by extremely high turnover. Employees rarely stay more than three or four months. Some workers leave after only two weeks. Absenteeism and tardiness are also high. The reason? The duties are repetitive, tedious, dirty, smelly, and generally low status. Typical tasks include readying the garbage for removal, sweeping and mopping floors, scrubbing walls, cleaning several restrooms, and hosing down garbage cans. The volume of the work is such that "free time" is generally available, ranging from 45 minutes to nearly 2 hours daily depending on the workload as well as the pace of the worker.

Assume you are the Personnel Officer of this plant. What might you do to extend in a fairly significant way the period of time in which the employee stays with the company?

Some solutions:

☐ Job-design-type approaches

1. Mechanize the job to remove as much of the "dirty work," monotony, fatigue, etc. as possible.
2. Ensure the availability of high-quality materials and equipment that will minimize job irritations.
3. Enrich the job with higher-level duties and responsibilities, if at all possible, either on the job or elsewhere in the organization. *Note:* Free time is available for this.
4. Another approach, taking into consideration normal turnover, would be to utilize that employee's time with training for higher-level positions. He could be a "spell" man, as they call them in industry (replacing regular employees who must take a short personal break during group operations).
5. Distribute or rotate tasks so the same person doesn't have to do it all the time.

☐ Recruitment-type approaches

1. Spend as much or more time interviewing for these positions as you do for others. Don't hurry through this interview just because it is a low-paying job. The rule here is: If you don't interview properly the first time, you'll have to the second time or the third time. . . .
2. Selectively interview only those people who may find this type of job rewarding and interesting; that is, someone who will regard the job as a promotion.

3. When you find a likely candidate, completely explain to and if possible show the prospect what the job entails. Be candid about job drawbacks.

4. If the candidate is still with you at this time, explain in a very honest, truthful way the importance of the job as it relates to what your organization does.

5. Selectively hire a person who is psychologically more able to take the unpleasantness of the work. (This is the only approach that will work in some situations.)

6. Be certain to hire someone who has all the physical characteristics needed for the job.

7. Hire a retarded individual who is able to function in a regular job environment. You may consider that people are leaving because it is beneath their capabilities and insults their personal senses. They may be overly qualified for that type of work.

8. Recruit a college student who would relish the free time for study.

☐ Motivational approaches

1. Treat the position as an "entry job" and move the employee to other work as soon as possible.

2. Add incentive by allowing the person to leave when the job is done and still get paid for the full shift.

3. Have constant contact and communication with that particular person. Help make the job important by checking often as to the employee's progress or problems. (Most often these jobs are relatively low paying and easy to forget, except every several weeks when you are rehiring a new "body.")

4. Ask the employee from time to time what could be done to make the job less unpleasant or more rewarding. Don't hesitate to repeat the question even if you don't strike "paydirt" the first time or two. Certainly some employees will appreciate the fact that you asked!

5. Don't hesitate to give sincere praise for tasks well done.

Note: I developed this tri-partite classification of the solutions on a post-discussion basis. However, it would be good training technique for the trainer to have the participant group classify their suggested solutions, posted on the flipchart, as to JD (job design), R (recruitment) or M (motivational) approaches. This would allow the group to see its tendency to propose "across-the-board" or one-or two-category solutions.

The Incident Process

The incident process, like the short case, was a reaction to the lengthy Harvard-type case with all its complexities, long advance preparation time, long discussion periods, and the like. Developed by Dr. Paul Pigors, a retired professor of industrial relations at M.I.T., and Faith Pigors, the incident process is used to teach managers to collect a full set of facts before making a decision.

In this method the participant group receives a short account of an incident, which can be read and digested quickly. The incident typically involves the need for the manager concerned (meaning the participants) to make a decision. However, before the manager decides, it is essential that one have as full a set of facts as possible. And how does one get these added facts? One must ask you, the trainer, for them. Thus, group members, in the role of the decision maker, must raise questions of a fact-seeking nature such as:

☐ What is the organization like? (The trainer will then distribute organization charts to everyone, assuming the trainer has them stockpiled.)

☐ What is the company's financial condition? (The trainer will likely provide a statement containing financial data.)

☐ Is there additional information on the performance record of the senior engineer? (Again, such data may be forthcoming.)

☐ Is there a policy concerning promotion in the company? (If available, this too, will be provided .

If the trainer cannot answer a question with a data sheet, he/she will simply indicate that: "We don't have any information on that point."

To illustrate how the process works, let's work through the following real-life incident.

Observing The Lennon Vigil[3]

You are Mary Ames, manager of a variety store. It is Sunday, 2 P.M., December 14, 1980. Betty Carnes, one of your cashiers, decides to bow her head and stop work. She did this to observe the ten-minute silent memorial to the late rock star John Lennon. The vigil had been requested by the former Beatle's widow upon Lennon's murder. In explaining her behavior, Betty simply said that: "John Lennon stood for peace and love, and that's what's important." As a consequence, some customers waiting in a long Christmas-time line stalked out.

Assume you are Mary Ames. What action do you take, if any, respecting Betty?

As indicated, the group will need to garner more facts before a decision is reached regarding Betty. Presumably they would raise questions such as the following:

☐ What is the performance record of Betty Carnes and what is her tenure at the store? (Betty, a high school senior, is a part-time worker. Presumably she would not have a great deal of seniority.)

☐ Did any other clerks also engage in the silent vigil? (Another cashier and a stock clerk did, but only for a couple of minutes according to management. Betty stated they also observed the ten-minute work stoppage.)

☐ How many customers out of what total left the store because of Betty's action? (Some left; we don't know how many were in the store at the time.)

☐ Did Ms. Ames order Betty to return to work? (Yes; but Betty did not.)

☐ What is company policy regarding insubordination? (Any action, including discharge, is acceptable.)

☐ What disciplinary action was taken regarding the other two clerks? (They were reprimanded.)

Thus far we have dealt with the first two steps of the incident process; namely,

Step 1: The incident (available to participants in writing)

Step 2: The fact-finding process

Assuming the available facts have been obtained, the participants are now ready for the third step, namely,

Step 3: The issue. Here the trainer tries to get the group to define the major issues and sub-issues, if the latter exist.

Step 4: The decision by the manager. The trainer asks participants to write their decision, giving reasons therefor. The statement is turned in and those with like decisions form discussion groups. In our case on the Lennon vigil possible decisions by the manager could be these:

1. Fire Betty Carnes (which is what happened, and thus the case hit the newspaper).
2. Reprimand or possibly suspend Betty. (Two other employees were merely reprimanded since they only took a couple of minutes out.)
3. Explain the situation to the customers, request their cooperation and ask them to wait the ten minutes.
4. Pass out fruit juice to the waiting customers.
5. Ask the customers to join in the silent vigil.
6. Take over for Betty for the ten minutes involved.

Note: What might appear to be a simple case, could, nevertheless, have at least six solutions. The reader may think of others, too.

When the discussion groups are formed, they choose a chairperson who will also be their spokesperson. The spokespersons briefly debate their positions. The group-at-large then compares critically the reasoning of the several groups. This phase of the process is completed by the discussion leader telling the group what the actual or real-life decision was. (Betty was fired.)

Step 5: Evaluation. In the final step, the broader issues of the incident are examined in depth. This is the pay-off point, that is, where the real learning takes place. Questions such as these are considered: How could this incident have been prevented? What might the long-range effects of the firing decision be on customer relations and relations with the rest of the workforce? Would Ms. Ames' superiors feel the incident was handled properly?

The incident process has several benefits including:

☐ The short case gets the group into action quickly.
☐ It obviously teaches the manager to respect facts and to seek them out in full before making a decision.
☐ It involves the participants to a high degree. The debate aspect is generally a fun thing and the question-posing aspect of the process is usually a fast-moving activity.
☐ It sharpens up one's skill in decision making. Note the emphasis on reaching a sound decision.

On the other hand, we should recognize these limitations or disadvantages, too:

☐ It is a highly trainer-oriented activity. In fact, some critics say it unwittingly teaches dependence on the leader or trainer. Certainly much of management training today endeavors to deemphasize the importance of the leader's role and to discourage adulation of the all-powerful, all-knowing, authoritarian leader. This is done to provide a democratic-participative role model for the participants.
☐ The process is more suited for low- to mid-level managers rather than executives because of its emphasis on fact gathering. In the real world top officials rely on subordinate managers for fact collection, concerning themselves with the broader, strategic aspects of the decision-making process.
☐ The process also lends itself best to short cases of limited complexity, again making it less suitable for executive groups.
☐ In the questioning process the more bright and verbal participants take over, leaving others in the group to serve as spectators.
☐ The questioning process may fail to elicit certain elements or issues. Thus, vital factors in the case may be overlooked.

□ The debate on particular points in the case may become so lively that the groups become polarized around their positions.

Action Maze[4]

An action maze is a highly structured group activity relating to problem solving and decision making. It is a form of case study, but goes beyond it in its complexity, i.e., it is highly programmed. Here's how it works:

The trainer gives the participants a written case. It not only states the problem, but also provides options in respect to its possible solution. The group discusses these alternatives and then agrees on a solution. They can then ask the trainer for another "frame" which explains the *consequences* of the decision they chose. They also receive more alternatives and the process goes on.

To illustrate, let's take this problem which requires resolution:

You have a secretary—Kim Biles—who has been taking advantage of her position and has been abusing leave privileges: frequent late arrivals, long lunch periods about once per week, and use of sick leave in excess of others in like jobs. The problem is complicated by the fact that Kim has been around over three years, knows the job very well, and is an unusually fast, helpful, cheerful, and competent worker. You have received several complaints from staff to the effect that Kim "seems to be getting away with murder." Your action is (select one alternative):

C—*Counsel* Kim on the abuse of the leave regulations.
S—Invite Kim to your *staff meeting* where a general discussion will be held on leave abuse. Hopefully, Kim will get "the message."
L—Lay it on the *line*. Tell Kim in no uncertain terms that things have gone far enough.
N—*Do nothing*. Kim will probably come around in time. Kim is too valuable an employee to risk "turning off."

The group selects one of the options, e.g., "N." They are told what happens (consequences) as a result of their decision: "Kim doesn't 'shape up' as you had hoped. In fact, two months later you can see that things have gotten worse. So you must now make one of the following decisions . . .", etc.

Each decision the participants make produces particular consequences. If high quality decisions are made, the group receives sets of more desirable choices. Bad choices garner less desirable alternatives. In the latter case, there is always one good choice in the new set so that the group can still work its way out of the maze.

A variation on the above procedure is to let small groups form on the basis of their preference for a particular alternative in the first round. Each buzz group, then, has to work its own way out of the maze.

The strong points of the action maze are that the participants have to debate their choices (as in case study), they get to learn the consequences of their decisions (unlike case study), and they have a lively time working their way out of the maze. On the down side are the difficulty of developing well-thought-out sets of decisions for each step of the maze and the time consumed in class to advance through all the frames or steps. Also, some small groups may get "lost" in the maze and, if time runs out, be frustrated due to lack of closure.

Note:

1. The Action Maze requires a more comprehensive file of materials than any other case study approach.
2. It may begin with an incident rather than a case. This is particularly helpful when one of the learning objectives is for the participants to learn how to ask the right questions to get the kinds of information they are usually given in a case.

The Mousetrap Technique

The mousetrap technique is designed to point up to participants that their thinking about organizational problems and issues may be marked by various forms of faulty reasoning—engaging in rationalizations, tolerating double standards, ignoring inconsistent enforcement of rules, overlooking the significance of the leader as a role model, confusing personal and societal values, arguing for standards to follow practice rather than vice versa, etc.

"The Gambling Case," which follows, is adapted from a case used some years back by the Navy Department's Civilian Personnel Division in Washington, D.C., in its leadership training program. This program was concerned with leadership and such issues as ethics, values, authority, discipline, and standards.

As will be apparent from the three situations presented below, as part of "The Gambling Case," the learning objective is to sharpen thinking concerning leadership by example, toleration of double standards, and inconsistent rule enforcement. The case raises the question whether standards should follow actual practice or vice versa and challenges the all-too-easy rationalization that practices may be acceptable simply because "everybody does it" or "it's done all the time."

To overcome these usual rationalizations, the mousetrap technique is used in this case. Three quite different situations are presented, but each calling for acceptance or denial of the same set of standards. Participants readily commit themselves to situation one, unaware of situation 2; they further commit themselves to situation 2, unaware of situation 3. Each commitment makes it extremely difficult to avoid enforcing the next situation without being patently inconsistent.

All three situations should be discussed in one session, lest the impact of the participants' inconsistencies becomes lost. Situation 1 (but not the other two situations) may be given to participants for advance reading or pre-work.

The Gambling Case

Situation 1

You are Fred Blair, chief of administration in Big City Hospital. This morning you are faced with a perplexing situation. It seems that last evening four hospital attendants were caught playing cards for money. Their excuse was that they were playing on their supper period, as they often do. Ordinarily no money is wagered, but since it was pay day they decided to set up some small stakes. They were playing just ten minutes past their supper period when they were spotted accidentally by a patient who promptly reported their gambling activity to the shift supervisor.

The four men have been with the hospital for periods ranging from five to eight years. Three have above average performance records; the fourth has a history of intermittent absenteeism and was involved in a gambling incident several years ago and received a reprimand as a first-time offender. One of the three good performers admits to having urged the others to play for money.

The hospital has a clear-cut schedule for all disciplinary offenses. The section on gambling specifies the following penalties:

1. *Gambling*
   a. First Offense
      Minimum: Written reprimand
      Maximum: Suspension for 10 days
   b. Second Offense
      Minimum: Suspension for 10 days
      Maximum: Discharge
2. *Promotion of gambling*
   a. First Offense
      Minimum: Suspension for 10 days
      Maximum: Discharge
   b. Second Offense: Discharge

As Fred Blair you have to decide:

1. Do you enforce the no gambling rule?
2. If so, do you treat all four men alike?

Situation 2

A week after the problem with the four card players, Fred Blair had an irate visitor in his office—Vina Dixon, chief dietitian of the hospital. This dialogue ensued:

Ms. Dixon: I'm here to find out who's running my department.
Fred Blair: What?
Ms. Dixon: I'm tired of people coming into my department and hassling my employees to buy raffle tickets.
Fred Blair: Hassling?
Ms. Dixon: Oh, sure, they say it's voluntary and it's always for a worthy cause—underprivileged kids, volunteer firemen, church groups, and so on. But that isn't the point.
Fred Blair: The point is . . .
Ms. Dixon: That people are promoting gambling on official time and on city property, too.
Fred Blair: Which has been going on since the year one . . .
Ms. Dixon: Exactly. And I'm here to put a stop to it.
Fred Blair: How will you do that?
Ms. Dixon: By calling a spade a spade rather than a shovel, Mr. Blair. This is *gambling,* not charitable soliciting; and I hereby bring formal charges of promoting gambling against Supervisory Nurse Betty Burns.
Fred Blair: You mean official charges . . .
Ms. Dixon: Exactly. Here's my memorandum which has all the details. Now what are you going to do about it?

You are Fred Blair. What should you do about the charges presented?

Situation 3

A month later Fred Blair has another visitor. It is Tommy Edmonds, a branch chief who reports to Blair.

Tommy: You'll want to get in on this one.
Fred: What one?
Tommy: You know, the Super Bowl is on next week and we've got our usual pool on. Only this time the ante is higher and we got twice as many "investors." A big pot is really shaping up.
Fred: Uh, I'm not sure . . .
Tommy: Come on, you've always played and have hit more winners than the rest of us. Give us a chance to get some of that green back. How about it?

You are Fred Blair. How do you respond?

Wrong Way-Right Way

Fran's Request of Pat

Fran is administrative officer in the Information Division with a responsibility for, among other things, renewing subscriptions to magazines, newspapers, newsletters, etc. Although subscription items number about 2 dozen, some 50–60 other items are received regularly on a complimentary basis. These "freebies" come from two sources: (1) various publishers who wish to secure ads for their publications and (2) as a result of subscription-exchange arrangements made by Pat, editor of a management newsletter. All freebies are routed directly to Pat by the mail room.

As Fran sees it, it is not always clear when an invoice to renew a subscription should be honored since there are so many freebies coming in. Fran decides to talk to Pat about the problem. Pat is not always the easiest person to deal with.

Sequence A—The Wrong Approach

Fran: Pat, I'd like to talk to you about that subscription problem again.

Pat: What subscription problem?

Fran: The one I mentioned last summer—this business of the renewal notices.

Pat: Don't know anything about it.

Fran: But I asked you to give me a list of all freebies.

Pat: You did?

Fran: Yes, I did.

Pat: Well, maybe you did. But what do you need the list for anyway?

Fran: You get all the freebie magazines and papers, don't you?

Pat: Sure. So what?

Fran: Well, sometimes I get a bill for a renewal of a subscription when we've never subscribed to it. That's why.

Pat: Well, if you have a question about paying the bill why don't you just look in your file?

Fran: I do. But sometimes a receipt for a subscription gets misplaced and I don't know whether we actually subscribed or not.

Pat: Why not ask the person who's interested in the publication, they'll know whether they actually ordered it or not.

Fran: That's just what I want to avoid. I don't want to heckle people about something that I ought to have information on.

Pat: Or you could ask me. I know the one's we get free on an exchange basis and most of the others, too.

Fran: Most?

Pat: Yeah, most. I'm not a computer.

Fran: Well, how about giving me a list of all the free ones so there's no slip-up.

Pat: Seems like a lot of coolie labor to me. Can't you just keep a good file on your subscriptions? What you bought you bought. If you have no record of it, it's a freebie. Simple.

Fran: You're giving me a hard time.

Pat: Look. You're trying to get me to prepare a report for you on something that's totally your problem.

Fran: You're not willing to cooperate . . .

Pat: Why not ask the mail room to compile a list for you? They know what comes in.

Fran: This is ridiculous. I'm going to see the boss about this.

Pat: You're making an issue out of very little.

Fran: I need this information, and you're not cooperating.

Pat: O.K., I'll get that list for you. But I'm not guaranteeing it's going to be one hundred percent accurate.

Fran: When will you have it?

Pat: Come on. I said I'll get it, so I'll get it. As soon as I can.

Fran: O.K., but if I have to remind you again I'm going to the boss instead.

Discussion question: What did Fran do improperly?

Sequence B—The Right Approach

Fran: Hi, Pat. How are things?

Pat: Good. But busy. Real busy.

Fran: Well, then I won't take much of your time.

Pat: Be sure you don't.

Fran: I'd like your help on a little problem, Pat.

Pat: I'm good at the *little* ones. Shoot. What is it?

Fran: Well, as administrative officer they expect me to pay the bills.

Pat: Yeah, I know that.

Fran: But sometimes I get a bill that I shouldn't pay, or at least I'm not certain if we should honor the invoice.

Pat: So?

Fran: So I don't want to authorize payment on something that is doubtful or at least should be checked into before it's okayed. Why waste the company's money?

Pat: Makes sense.

Fran: I was hoping you'd agree.

Pat: So where do I fit into this?

Fran: Glad you asked. Here's the way you can help. What if—I'm only asking "if"—starting tomorrow you kept a running list of every freebie publication you get?

Pat: Wait a minute. We get a lot of them here. I don't want to do a lot of research.

Fran: I'm with you on that. *No* research. Just jot down the name of each publication *as it comes in.* No checking back into history.

Pat: I guess I could do that. But you're sure your own file of paid invoices won't give you the dope you need?

Fran: Good question. Most of the time it's O.K. But other people use the file and sometimes invoices get borrowed or misplaced or something. In any case my file isn't one hundred percent accurate.

Pat: Well, if all I'm to do is record the titles of the publications as they come in . . . You don't need all the other stuff like addresses, and frequency, and rates. . . .

Fran: Heck, no. Just the titles. Simple as that.

Pat: Well, they won't be in any special order, then, so the list won't be the easiest to use.

Fran: Good point. What if—another "if"—you jotted down each title on a three by five card, just dumped 'em in a box or brown envelope and eventually let me have them. I'll sort 'em out alphabetically, and the list will be perfect to match against any invoice I'm not sure about. If you get the magazine free I don't pay the invoice.

Pat: When do you want the list?

Fran: Whenever you feel you've captured all the titles.

Pat: A two-month cycle should give me a chance to record every title we get.

Fran: Good. Today's the 12th of May. What if I checked back with you on, say, July 20th?

Pat: Fair enough.

Fran: And one more thing.

Pat: Yeah?

Fran: You're an easy person to get cooperation from.

Pat: (smiling and obviously pleased) I guess you caught me in a weak moment.

Discussion question: What did Fran do that made for success?

The Multiple-Case Technique

An interesting and worthwhile variation on case study is to present for analysis three or four cases on a given problem area. This affords participants the opportunity to compare critically the events of and principles in the several cases. A variety of cases can help to ferret out and firm up a set of allied concepts, which a single case may not be able to do as well.

The four short cases that follow are designed to stimulate thinking concerning proper managerial outlooks toward appraisal and development of their employees.

Case 1: The Day and Night Scholar

Mary Evans, a young professional worker in the Management Analysis Office, presented her boss, Tom Tuff, with a proposal to take two management courses at the university, which is located in walking distance of the office. One course would be taken during the day on company time (an hour on Monday, Wednesday, and Friday) and the other evenings on her own time. (Cost was not particularly at issue, since the company paid in full for job-related university courses if the employee received a grade of "C" or better.)

Tom's immediate response to the request was this: "If you've got *that* kind of time, maybe there's a lot of other things you ought to be doing around here."

Case 2: The Toastmaster Membership Case

You are Bill Brown, operations manager. You have five supervisors who report to you. One of them, young Hank Peters, approaches you about his possible regular attendance at a toastmaster's club meeting during working hours. You have no objection to the toastmaster idea, but the club meets for its luncheon meeting every other Friday at noon and Bill has to leave early (around 11:15 A.M.) to get to his meeting. Bill has been very active in the Toastmaster's Club and is now its president. Hence his need to arrive early to be sure everything is set up and "in order," to greet arriving members, to greet guests from other clubs, etc.

The difficulty that arises for you is this: Your weekly staff meeting takes place from ten to about noon. You like this period because you generally have lunch with your staff right after the meeting. You have found that going to lunch with the group on a once-a-week basis helps to maintain rapport and good communication with all concerned. These Friday meetings fit into your schedule very well and, besides, they enable you and your team to plan and coordinate certain things for the following week.

Case 3: Appraisal By Surprise

Bill Arndt is a member of a personnel management evaluation team that visits military installations to assess the effectiveness of their civilian personnel management programs. At large installations the total team of five evaluators conducts the analysis; at smaller units two or three team members may do the assessment job. The team chief, Frank Nels, does not always join the team, particularly at the smaller civilian personnel offices.

It is performance review time and Frank is completing his discussion with Bill about his performance for the year.

Frank: Something that I would like to bring up is your interpersonal relations with the personnel people with whom you interact.

Bill: Oh, something wrong?

Frank: Well, not exactly. But I thought I'd bring it up and see what your reaction is.

Case No. 4: Appraisal By Default

Arch Bricker is a young foreman in the maintenance yard. He recently attended a supervisory training course. One of the topics discussed in depth was performance review. He thus expected his supervisor, Superintendent Dan Oakes, to call him into his office at the end of the year to review the year's work, discuss strengths and weaknesses in performance, discuss development needs, etc. However, several months went by after year's end, and Arch was not called in for the annual performance review discussion.

Arch decided to bring the issue up informally with Dan. So one evening he approached Dan in the parking lot and said: "Boss, I'm ready for my annual appraisal whenever you are." Dan looked at Arch in wonderment: "How's that? Appraisal? You're putting me on! The fact that you're still here at the end of the shift means that you've gotten your appraisal."

The Filmed Case

A worthwhile variation on the written case is the case presented on film or videotape. Its advantages are:

☐ It can present the problem with a realism that the written case can rarely equal. Seeing and hearing "live" characters present their personalities and problems is an extremely helpful way for the participant to get "cued in" as to what is really going on.

☐ It can encapsulate and simplify ideas and events so that participants "get the message" with relative ease.

☐ It enables participants to identify (or "dis-identify") more readily with the characters and events presented in the film because of its live, dramatic character.

☐ It is particularly helpful to those who have difficulty gaining ideas from a printed page.

☐ Reading of the case in advance of the session or in class is, of course, made unnecessary. It thus enables the group "to get into action" quickly, thereby saving on preparation time. Also, typical problems such as not having read the case, having read it too quickly, or not remembering it too well are eliminated.

Using Audiotape

A case may also be presented on audiotape. This may be desirable in order to:

☐ Vary the format

☐ Highlight the dialogue of the case's characters

☐ Present participants with more of the feelings of the principals in the case, something that the conventional written case may not communicate as well.

☐ Provide added realism via the spoken language, e.g., to communicate a regional accent, a halting manner of speaking, a commanding (or indecisive) tone of voice, male vs. female voices, sarcasm, possibly certain sound effects (cars, clocks, typewriters, machinery).

As a cautionary note, the audio case should be relatively brief for most of us have a limited aural attention span—too much input and our minds will wander. A case length of about ten minutes or less is adequately listenable. In some cases it may be desirable to play the tape a second time.

A limitation of the case on tape is that it cannot present nondialogue type material very well. A solution to this problem, of course, is to draw on the best of the two worlds—use the written word for background material and the tape for dialogue.

The Live Case

An interesting variation on traditional case study is the live case. This entails bringing into the training room a top-level personage (e.g., a company president, a bureau chief of a government department, a key university official) who presents a live case or problem to the participant group. By "live" we mean a problem currently being worked on, possibly one that is really "bugging" the organization.

The case can be presented to the group at large by the "outside" executive for immediate response and interaction, or preferably, small groups can be formed for initial framing of questions and subsequent attempts at "solving" the problem.

The live case has considerable appeal to participants since they are dealing with a current, unresolved problem rather than a "stale" one from a casebook; the case is presented "in person" by a key (often prestigious) official and, in some cases, he/she may bring along other company representatives to provide added insights about the problem; they have the opportunity to develop case data further by live interaction with the official, thereby overcoming the frequent complaint in case study work "that we don't have all the facts;" and they can "reality-test" their solutions with the authoritative "on-the-spot" case presenter. In essence, it provides splendid opportunities for the dynamic and more satisfying aspects of two-way (rather than one-way) communication.

It is also possible to have the official present the case from his/her office via an audio (or even video) teleconference hook-up if a personal appearance is not practical. Procedurally, this would (should) entail two separate interactions—the first for the presentation of the problem and possibly a question period immediately thereafter to establish a fuller understanding of it; the second (possibly the next day or at a later date) to present participant solutions to the official and to secure reactions (feedback) thereon from the official. Typically, participants work in small groups to develop solutions or decisions.

If the participant group is a knowledgeable and sophisticated one, the presenting official is quite likely to be "surprised" at the creative solutions presented. If this positive reaction (praise) is communicated to the participants, they would be reinforced (rewarded) psychologically for their "digging in" to the case so well. Of course, the participants do not expect that their suggestions will necessarily be adopted. Nor is the official obligated to implement them.

General Electric, at its Management Development Center, Crotonville, New York, has developed another format for what they call the "living case." Their idea is to have participants work on a major, unresolved challenge facing the company, instead of focusing on something that happened in the past. Their case is not a single document, but a collection of data—similar to what managers have for their regular analysis—for sorting through and organizing.

To illustrate, a live case was developed by a University of Pennsylvania business school professor and the Crotonsville staffers. They interviewed key individuals and assembled significant documents. Their "big picture" topic concerned magnetic research to advance medical technology via better images than X-rays and CT scanners. It is also a tool to study basic inside body cells, a means of signaling diseases like cancer well before symptoms appear.

At the Center the participants were divided into four groups—two to develop a marketing strategy based on the introduction of a high-end medical product (just described) and the other two to work with a low-end product. After presenting their preliminary recommendations, the four groups discussed them with their colleagues and executives from the Center and the GE Medical Systems Business Group. They used these discussions as a basis for development of final recommendations that went to top management.

As GE sees the value of live case study, it familiarizes participants with the kinds of decisions they actually will

make as well as experiencing them with the risks, ambiguities and pressures facing managers who have to introduce a new technology.[2]

Citing a Personal Case

The Case of the Partying Conferees

A group of school officials from Mid-Area School District attends annually a professional conference for one week at an out-of-state location. Jane R., one of the group, finds that her fellow participants (three males and two females) seem to be more interested in "partying" than in attending conference sessions. She has the feeling, too, that although several of her colleagues have spouses back home, there seems to be an interest in "pairing off." Also, much of the group's conversations and jokes are very suggestive and "off-color." Jane R. doesn't want to be a "wet blanket" and wants to be part of what is, of course, her professional group. But at the same time she is here for the conference and, besides, has a loving husband back home.

What would you do if you were Jane R.?

Note:
1. After the case has been thoroughly discussed by the group, move into a more personal level by asking participants to relate similar pertinent incidents from their own experience.
2. This particular case relates to problems of assertiveness, possibly sexual harassment, peer pressure, self-development, etc.
3. Since the technique asks for personal incidents, one has to know the nature of the group. That is, are they willing to share personal incidents? Also, the sharing obviously is more likely to be acceptable to the participants at a later rather than at an earlier stage of the program.

Citing an Allied Case

The Case of the Simple Cover-up

A corridor in the basement of a large office building led to the company cafeteria. Unfortunately, at one point in the concrete corridor a four-inch pipe protruded just above ground level. The pipe was large enough to be visible, but inevitably employees who were distracted by conversation, preoccupied, or simply in a hurry tripped over it. New employees were almost certain to stumble over the pipe at least once. Employees in wheelchairs and those with visual problems also had a hard time with the pipe.

Management tried many remedies to cut down on the tripping-type accidents: posting a notice on the wall near the pipe, issuing warning memoranda (generally after a mishap), painting the protuding pipe a bright color (different colors were tried), rerouting traffic (quickly abandoned because this proved to be a nuisance), encouraging supervisors to remind employees from time to time about the hazard, etc. The problem was finally solved when a legally blind employee who stumbled over the pipe suggested putting a gently sloping wooden ramp over it.

The case illustrates how a rather simple *change in the situation*—as opposed to more complex attempts to *change people's behavior* via signs, memos, and lectures—solved the problem instantly and for everyone and for all time.

Task assignment: Have participants relate an incident from their own experience where a change in behavior was accomplished by working on the situation (as in this case) as opposed to working on the person via the usual lectures, signs, warnings, reprimands, memos, bulletin board notices, etc.

Using Participant Cases

A worthwhile variation on the conventional case study method is to introduce several participant-developed cases for group analysis. The advantages of this approach are these:

☐ Greater participant involvement and interest in a truly live case.
☐ The cases are quite certain to be "complex" and thus challenging. Why bring in a case that lends itself to ready resolution?
☐ Increased responsibility by participants to contribute materials for the learning experience, with a corresponding reduction in dependency on the trainer who ordinarily "does it all."

Training-wise, a good design is to ask the participants who bring in their cases to identify people who can best help them to analyze and resolve the problem presented. In this way, they are being encouraged to seek out (assess) the most knowledgeable resources in the group, a concept they should carry back to their jobs. Those who are not "chosen" by the case presenter to work in a small group should form other small groups. Solutions then can be compared—the "expert" small group vs. the others.

If a format has been provided to analyze problems, such as a multistep problem solving model, cases may be analyzed along those lines.

The Participant Modified Case

Another way to overcome the problem of trainer-prepared or trainer-selected cases that typically lack immediate relevance, is to allow the participants to *modify* the "canned" case. They can supplement or substitute the usual trainer-supplied information with data specific to the challenges and problems they now face. In essence, they direct their own learning and problem solving by drawing on their experience and applying their knowledge to current situations and actual personalities.

If you take this real-world application to case study, you may have to notify your participants in advance (a pre-work assignment) with instructions concerning the information they need to gather. For example, in a case involving selling a boss on a "radical" idea, the participants will have to gather data on their bosses' leadership styles—communication patterns, tendencies toward (or against) innovativeness, problem solving and decision making approaches, etc.[5]

The Rating Approach

Another way to vary the case method and to stimulate discussion considerably is to provide specific statements regarding the significance of the case and have participants express their agreement-disagreement with the statements using a prescribed rating scale, as given in Appendix 59.

Advice from the President

The Key Brands Chain Stores has its headquarters in Philadelphia. Each year six to eight promising young supervisors are brought into headquarters from the field for six months of management training. The purpose: "broadening." While at headquarters these "management interns," are subject to rotational assignments, take one or two university courses on management, attend various institutes or workshops that relate to their career objectives, attend the president's weekly staff meeting, attend other "big picture" meetings, work on a group project, meet regularly as a group with the trainer to discuss problems of the organization, and write reports periodically on their training experiences.

When the six months of training are over, the trainees typically return to their original assignments in the field. However, one or two of them may be assigned to headquarters or to a regional office upon completion of the training. The training seems to do what the organization expects in terms of broadening, but new assignments for everyone do not materialize immediately. In fact, the trainees may return to their old jobs for two to two and a half years before they receive a new assignment. In effect, most graduates of the program are "stockpiled" for future upward assignment.

Because of the delay in "capitalizing" on their training, the trainees typically feel "lost and abandoned" after returning from Philadelphia. In fact, recently a number of the graduates of the program felt strongly enough about the problem to write the following letter to the company President:

Dear Mr. Rogers:

We appreciate greatly the training we received at headquarters some two years ago. It was a fine program and hardly a week goes by that we don't apply something of what we learned in Philadelphia.

We do feel, however, that as time goes by we are getting out of touch with things and are losing some of the "big picture" we have received. We thus thought it would be helpful to us if we could be assigned to our respective regional offices for two weeks for special assignment, once or twice a year. This procedure, if adopted, would not only help us, but would protect the company's large investment in our training.

Sincerely yours,

Matt Thomas (6th Mgt. Intern Program)
Henry Briggs (6th Mgt. Intern Program)
Elaine Woods (7th Mgt. Intern Program)
Nat Spencer (7th Mgt. Intern Program)
Al Knowles (7th Mgt. Intern Program)

Upon receipt of the letter, the president entered this notation on it: "Why can't the training department work up a good correspondence course on management for these trainees?" The letter then was routed to the chief administrative officer and the personnel director, both of whom added to the president's note: "I concur." The letter then went on to the Training Department. The director of training, on receipt of the letter, had a strong reaction to it.

Memo From The Boss

A memorandum from the boss which demands, complains, or criticizes unfairly is always a headache for the receiver. If used as a case, it can challenge participants to take notice and to react in one form or another. A healthy form of reaction is to develop and consider one's options as opposed to acting precipitously and possibly aggravating matters. Possible options are these: do nothing, grin and bear it, and engage in soothing self-talk: "This, too, shall pass"; respond with a memo to defend one's actions or position; visit the boss in his/her office to explain things or to confess error and assure the boss it won't happen again; and so on. Obviously the actual action taken will depend on the nature and gravity of the "offense" as well as the personalities of the two parties involved.

A sample "Memo From The Boss" case follows. Note the case is very brief and contains background about the circumstances relating to the memo as well as the memo itself. Questions to the participants follow the case.

Memo From The Boss: "Quality Circle Overtime"
You are the facilitator for a group of quality circles in your company. You recently worked with one group that got so engrossed in their problem solving that they ran over the allotted time by some 30 minutes. (Meetings run for one hour per week, one-half of it on company time, the other half on the QC member's lunch time.) Your boss, who is not really sold on quality circles, sent you this scorching note:

The Quality Circle time has gotten completely out of hand. These meetings are for *one hour* only. Today we lost the production time of eight workers.

This abuse will lead to disqualifying a circle. You are responsible for keeping it on track and to observe the rules.

Jim

Questions: What is the likely impact on the receiver? If you were the facilitator what would you do? What are your options? Which would you select? Why? Would you show the letter to your participants? Why or why not?

The Ranking Approach

A good way to involve and "excite" participants is to have them rank possible solutions to a case on an individual basis and then let them discuss their rankings in small groups. They should be asked to agree, as a team, on their rankings. After the small group work, secure feedback from the teams concerning their key rankings—i.e., which were first, second, and last. Secure the teams' reasoning for their rankings.

A sample case follows.

The Case of The Successful Training Director
Pat Teal, Training Director for High-Tech Diversified Products, Inc., has been on the job some 18 months. The training program, as Pat found it, consisted of employee orientation and an occasional skills training course. At the outset, Pat identified a strong need for management training and promptly planned, organized, and implemented a series of highly successful management training workshops. The workshops of 18–20 managers were conducted in out-of-city locations, ran for five full days,

relied heavily on group-in-action methods, and achieved rave notices from the participants and the regional directors who had sent their managers to the training.

The company president was informed of Pat's successful work and now wants to "ride" on Pat's success. Specifically, he wants Pat to provide the same kind of training to some 150–175 managers and others who will be attending the company's bi-annual, three-day management conference in Las Vegas this coming summer. The big boss has also invited various outsiders to attend, too, such as suppliers, trade association officials, and business journalists. Several new products are to be unveiled at the meeting. In other words, the president sees this conference as a big sales-motivation-PR opportunity rather than intensive management training as Pat has been providing. Pat appreciates the president's enthusiasm and praise for her work, but knows that one can't replicate the workshops' success under the extravaganza-type conditions which will prevail at the national conference.

You are a close colleague of Pat, doing similar work in another company. Pat has contacted you for advice in respect to the alternative strategies that might be considered in coping with the company president's request. These strategies are listed below. Rank them in the order in which you would recommend them to Pat. (No. 1 is most recommended; no. 10 is least recommended.)

Possible Approaches For Pat Teal:

1. Why argue with your own success? Just try your best to give the big boss what he wants.
2. A key department head, who has an "in" with the president, is aware of the problem and sees it as Pat does. In fact, he said: "What's the use of providing the training if it won't be any good?" This official would probably intercede for Pat, if asked. Why not arrange a meeting with the big boss, your ally, and yourself, explain the facts to the president, and ask him to "cool it"?
3. Confront the president on a one-to-one basis and candidly explain to him that a large, PR-type conference in Las Vegas will not accomplish what your small group training programs can do in a "cultural island" setting.
4. Secure advice and assistance from a consultant who specializes in making large group meetings and conferences effective and go ahead and participate in the big bash.
5. Call a special meeting of the Training Advisory Committee to explain the problem and try to get their support for a strong negative recommendation on the president's idea.

6. Ask your boss, the VP for Human Resource Management, to run "interference" for you. (*Note:* The VP's major strengths are in the areas of recruitment and benefits, rather than training.)
7. Write a detailed memo to the president. Explain the basis for your reservations and suggest alternatives such as having two or three nationally known speakers talk to this rather large audience, rather than trying to conduct genuine management training.
8. Since you are on excellent terms with several regional directors as a result of your training, ask one or more of them to intercede for you.
9. On the assumption that this is the kind of "support" a training program hardly needs, start looking for another job.
10. Get off the hook by suggesting that the management training to be provided at the conference be turned over to the Management Department at Local University for their execution. Let them get the credit or the brickbats.

Using a Letter

The following two cases use a letter to stimulate discussion. The first case, "Shopping For An Ice Chest," is a rather simple one, dealing with the very common problem of sales clerks in a department who are weak in both product knowledge and customer relations.

The second case, "The Case of the Bureaucratic Manager," is more complex. It asks the participants to identify and deal with problems of bureaucracy in an academic setting. This letter writer (or complainant) raises two issues: refund policy and the provision of information of a "perishable" sort on a promotional brochure that is made available to prospective enrolees in a noncredit course in a community college. Both issues have public relations implications. These complaints actually were handled via a letter of apology to the complainant (see a third letter) plus an invitation to the complainant by the president to accompany him to a Rotary Club luncheon, a unique public relations gesture. In addition, management at the college presumably has to deal with a somewhat arrogant, inflexible bureaucrat in its ranks.

Shopping For An Ice Chest

John L. Quinn
President
Lincoln-United Stores, Inc.

Dear Mr. Quinn:

My wife and I had the misfortune to shop in the River Oaks suburban store last Friday night. We were in the camping department and saw two clerks there, but apparently they couldn't see us. Or at least so it seemed after a 15-minute wait.

We finally approached one clerk and he said to us: "Sorry, but I'm still on my supper hour. You'll have to talk to someone else." So we approached another clerk and asked her if she was familiar with the ice chests. She replied: "Oh, sure. What do you want to know?" We asked: "What is the difference between these two ice chests? They look the same, but this one costs $7.50 more." She replied: "Well, it if costs more it *must* be the better one." Not being satisfied with her answer, we asked her if anyone else might know more about the chests. She said: "Oh, yes, my supervisor." So we asked her if we could talk to him. She replied: "Sorry, but he's not on the floor right now." And when would he be back? "Gee, I don't know."

At this point another clerk came to us and said: "May I help?" Relieved, we said: "By all means." Again, we went through our questioning about the relative merits of the two ice chests. Would you believe that all he could tell us was that *both* chests were very good. Why? Because he owned *both* of them *himself*!

So we went across the street to Kelly's and were waited on promptly, got decent answers to our questions and bought a moderately-priced ice chest of high quality having all the features we required.

Do you think we should return to Lincoln-United Stores? We have some big doubts.

Sincerely,

Mr. and Mrs. Ben Grayson

Small group assignment: Assume you are the company president, Mr. Quinn. What action do you take, if any?

Bureaucratic Manager

Dr. Herman Peters
President,
Central Community College

Dear Dr. Peters:

Since you are the top-level administrator of your organization, I am certain that you are concerned acutely with both high-level instruction by your faculty and sensitive, flexible administration by your subordinate managers. I thus wish to call to your attention to what I consider to be an instance of inflexible, arrogant, and bureaucratic management by one of your management officials. The facts, as I perceive them, are as follows:

1. I enrolled in a Central College Community Services course entitled "Independent Counsulting: Is It For You?" The course was scheduled to meet on Saturday, February 13.
2. The announcement on the yellow brochure said the class was to be held at "Wiley Square." When I arrived at the college campus I asked several students where I could find Wiley Square. No one knew. I went to the guard's office and made the same inquiry. None of the three guards knew, although one of them thought it might be "somewhere in Hinton." One guard made several phone calls to secure the needed information, but this was Saturday and no one was available.
3. I decided to return to my home. My wife decided to call the instructor at his home, possibly his wife or a family member might know where the course was being given. She actually reached the instructor at his home (someone else was pinch-hitting for him), but he couldn't provide specific information either.
4. On the following Monday I called Mrs. Watt, the Registration Supervisor of Community Services. I told her the brochure did not indicate where Wiley Square was. She agreed with me and readily admitted that they had goofed in their placement of the information. It seems that the brochure *did* have the requisite information, but on the *reverse* side of the registration form!! Hence, once the form was sent in to the college, the student no longer had this vital information in his/her possession.
5. I asked Mrs. Watt for a refund of my $17.00. But apparently life is not that simple. I had to write a letter to her to justify the refund! O.K., this is a small bit of bureaucracy, certainly not Mrs. Watt's fault, so I wrote her a detailed letter. She was quite certain that I'd get the refund since the college had goofed.
6. I received a letter dated February 26, from Mr. John May, assistant dean for management services which denied my request!
7. I called Mr. May (on Tuesday, March 2) who turned out to be as arrogant, inflexible, and supercilious a bureaucrat as one might find. He told me in no uncertain terms that the student is expected to be "responsible" and "adult" in preparing to arrive for his class. He also told me that since the information *was* on the form, I should have read it early on instead of waiting until the class morning to find out where the class was. He even gave me a far-fetched analogy about preparing *in advance* to locate a theatre which one might attend. Question: Do all your bureaucrats tell your student/citizen/customers *when* to prepare for their arrival, *when* to read the announcement? A bit much, I'd say. Mr. May also implied that since only $17.00 was involved, this was really a minor matter. I told him it was a matter of principle and that I could get along O.K. without the $17.00. In general, Mr. May would not concede any possible error on the college's part, despite the obvious careless place-

ment of the school location on the registration form.

To sum up:

1. Location information on a brochure must be placed in a *permanent* position. Perishable information is equal to none at all. I happen to be in the training business, our company conducting various public seminars. We learned a long time ago about proper, helpful placement of the location data. It should *never, never* be put on the back of a registration form which has vital information on the reverse.

2. Even if the customer were only half right, a helpful and sensitive firm provides a refund for purposes of good will and good customer relations. My company provides refunds if a customer has *any* reasonable complaint. If we didn't, we wouldn't be able to continue to serve the public. Is a public bureaucracy above a reasonable (and logical) request of a citizen/customer?

I don't wish to make a federal case out of this, although I am tempted to write the local newspapers and/or my representative about this. Before I do so, however, I shall await your considered reply.

Thank you for your interest in dealing with bureaucracy in your organization.

Sincerely,

I. Rayte

Dear Mr. Rayte:

Your letter of March 8 has been received by the college president, who is concerned about the issues you have raised and has asked me to respond. We are indeed interested in dealing with behavior such as you experienced. I enclose your refund check and apologize.

Your approach to the question of brochure design and placement of critical information is correct in my view; your comments on the issue of refunds are also well taken. Be assured that the dean of community services will be following through on these matters.

Although I am sorry it has been necessary for you to write the president, I appreciate your taking the time to do so.

Sincerely,

Rhee Lee Syncere
Academic Vice-President

Using an Editorial

Beef Over the Delly
The *Daily Blade* carried the following editorial:

If you've been reading our news columns of late you know that city officials are blocking a liquor license sought by a delicatessen in the New Square Shopping Plaza. Their rationale: Sale of wine and beer in community shopping centers inevitably attracts young loiterers, hot rodders, unruly partyers, and other assorted nuisance makers, causing annoyance to merchants and shoppers alike. In fact, the granting of such a license to a pizza parlor recently in the Elmark Shopping Center has already netted fourteen disorderly conduct complaints to the police.

City Councilperson R. U. Stern has been quoted as saying: "We don't want to hurt a legitimate, hard-working businessman. And we know the present owners are good citizens and responsible business people. But the ready availability of beer and wine just creates headaches we'd as soon do without."

As for the delly owners, they say their small carry-out will "go under" if the Board of License Commissioners denies them the license. Says co-owner Bill Wines: "Beer and wine are economic necessities. If we don't get the license we'll just have to give up the store. All we're trying to do is to earn a fair living and give the people in this area a chance to shop for our kind of foods without driving six and one-half miles to get it."

To complicate matters a bit more, Mayor Edgar Bruntovitall cites a state law which bans liquor licenses to a store within 700 feet of a school, church, or government-sponsored youth center. The delly is opposite such a youth center. However, the Board of License Commissioners can (but by unanimous decision only) grant the license up to within 300 feet. The mayor hopes the board will follow the intent of the state law to the letter.

As for us, we see this as a "damned if you do, damned if you don't" kind of case—the kind of decision Solomon would have relished (no pun intended) and our elected officials sink their teeth into all the time. Our only thought at the moment is that before the decision makers decide, they should stop for a thick corned beef on rye at the delly in dispute, savor each warm morsel and contemplate its potential added goodness if it could be washed down with a cold beer or two.

Questions for Discussion

1. What is the main issue or problem here?
2. How would you decide the case so that the community is well served?
3. What is the role of city management in a case of this sort?

Dialogue

Improving the Weekly Staff Meeting
Pat Cane, department chief, has asked his assistant, Melissa Blunt, to discuss ways of improving the weekly

staff meeting that is attended by eight branch chiefs. This dialogue ensues:

Pat: Melissa, you've got a lot of good ideas about management. What do you think we should do to improve our staff meetings?

Melissa: Hey, wait, boss. I'm not that much of an expert on that.

Pat: Well, we keep getting little digs about how dull they are and how much time they take. And you know as well as I do that some of the branch chiefs keep looking for excuses to skip 'em whenever they can.

Melissa: I suppose there is a problem . . .

Pat: Sure there is. So let's be frank. What would *you* do if you were me?

Melissa: Umm. Umm. I might turn the problem over to the group. In a sense it's their meeting, you know. Why not let them . . .

Pat: Whoa, wait a minute. We don't want to stir up all the animals over this, do we? Can't we just make some simple changes without getting everybody all riled up?

Melissa: I suppose that's true. How about rotating the chairmanship among everyone? This would get them all in the act and . . .

Pat: Hey, wait a minute. Why half of 'em couldn't run a meeting properly. Why we'd be running those meetings even longer than we do now.

Melissa: I just thought . . .

Pat: Besides we got enough trouble already with some of them acting as if they're ready to take the place over. Naw, that'd never work.

Melissa: Yeah, I guess that's a little far out.

Pat: Glad you see it that way. Anything else?

Melissa: As I said, I'm not an expert on this stuff. But what if we could cut down on everyone reporting what they've been doing all week and use the time instead to work on some of our problems . . .

Pat: Oh, we couldn't do that. People want to know what's going on. That would cause more of a problem than we have now.

Melissa: I suppose you're right. But what if everyone just prepared a short written statement about the events of the week and we passed them around? Then we could use the time for some real problem solving.

Pat: You mean we're not solving our problems now?

Melissa: Oh, no, I didn't mean that . . . It's just that . . .

Pat: Sure. Well, it's nearly lunchtime and I've got that meeting downtown and I'm running late already. Why don't you give it some more thought and we'll talk some more about it another time. And keep the ideas as practical as you can . . .

Melissa: Sure, thing, boss—real practical.

Questions for Discussion:

1. What is (are) the real issue(s) here?
2. Does Pat really want help on the "problem"?
3. How well did Melissa read Pat's attitudes about staff meetings?
4. If you were Melissa how would you have responded to Pat's request?
5. If you were Melissa how would you respond should Pat bring it up again?
6. How open is Pat to feedback?
7. How would you characterize the climate in this department?
8. Would Pat and the department be just as well off if they eliminated staff meetings? If you were Melissa would you consider recommending this course of action?
9. What can managers do to "pep up" staff meetings?
10. What are the implications of this case for participative management?

Monologue

Jeffery Bates Returns from the General Management Course

"Man, these management training courses are really something. I've been to three of them now and they all tell you the same thing—delegate more, communicate more, listen more, involve people in decisions more, develop subordinates more, and on and on.

"Who doesn't know all that? As if a manager doesn't do all that anyhow!

"Boy, if I followed all the behavioral science stuff these bushy-eyed trainers teach, I'd never get the work out. If they knew of the pressures for production and control of costs I get from the bosses, all the paper work I have to do, my having to deal with other managers who want everything their own way, my supervising employees who complain about the work and the pay and everything else, and my working for a boss who's never got time to listen to some of your problems . . .

"Yeah, I wonder how many years of management experience these trainers have. Probably nowhere near my twenty-two, if they have any at all.

"And the worst part of it is these younger managers. They keep buttering up these trainers by picking up all their jargon about motivation and group decision making, and beating that drum about hiring more women and minorities . . . Gad, what a farce . . . They're not doing any more of this newer stuff than I am and they know it. They just want to look smart in class. Well, they can put on that up-to-date act all they want to. I've been managing a lot longer than they have and neither they nor these trainers are going to get old Jeff to change anything that he's been doing."

Questions For Discussion

1. Is Jeff consistent in his statements?
2. How do you see Jeff as a manager? Is he strong, weak, effective?
3. Is Jeff typical of most managers you know?
4. What is Jeff's major problem, if any? What are his strengths, if any?
5. Does Jeff have a good fix on his own motivations, needs, values? The needs or values of others with whom he regularly deals?
6. Should people like Jeff be sent to management training courses? Why or why not?
7. Would you be willing to work for a man like Jeff? Why or why not?
8. If you were Jeff's boss and wanted to "upgrade" and "update" him, how would you go about it?
9. What kind of future, career-wise, do you see for Jeff?
10. Are behavioral science ideas compatible with "getting the work out?"

Note: The monologue is a variation of the case study format. It creates or communicates a certain mood, a depth of feeling, which the usual form of case study does not. It gives the participants a chance to get "inside the head" of the principal character in the case.

The Decision Analysis Approach

Depending on the group's and your training goals, it may be desirable, at times, to present participants with a case and several possible solutions to it. This would entail asking the participants to do either one or both of the following:

1. Analyze the pros and cons of *each* given decision, including its possible future consequences if implemented.
2. Come up with *another* decision that would be *superior* to those suggested at the end of the case.

The rationale for this approach is that there is:

☐ A need to concentrate on the decision-making process as opposed to other aspects of case study such as agreeing on facts and identifying the issues involved.
☐ A need to teach the manager, as a decision maker, to be deliberate rather than precipitate. The best way to overcome tendencies to make snap judgments is to slow the manager down by insisting that he/she weigh the pros and cons of all possible decisions.
☐ A desire to challenge the participant, to be creative, to break new ground. This is done by asking participants to come up with a solution "superior" to those already presented.

To illustrate the nature of this variation of the case study method, here is a short case accompanied by several solutions to it.

The Request for A Salary Increase

You are Lance Adams, controller for the Blue Bag Independent Food Stores. Your firm operates six supermarkets in a large metropolitan area. You are 52 years old, a professionally trained accountant and have been with the firm 8 years now. You report to a vice-president and realize that in a relatively small firm a promotion to other or "better" work is not very possible. So you expect worthwhile pay raises to be forthcoming each year. However, the raises that have come have been "token," nowhere near actual cost-of-living increases. In fact, you wonder if any raises would be forthcoming at all if the nonmanagerial employees, who are subject to a collective bargaining agreement, were not getting annual increases. As a result, you see yourself falling behind, each year, in terms of real income. Also, it seems unfair that you have not been rewarded for the experience you have gained on the job. Certainly you are more valuable to the company now than you were when you started eight years ago.

The company has an annual performance review system but it is largely a "paper" plan. There is no job evaluation or salary standardization plan for managers. Information about managerial salaries is kept very secret—so it is hard to know what others are earning.

You have brought up this matter of a worthwhile raise twice with your boss—once at a staff meeting and once at performance review time. In response to the first request, the boss said: "We'll have to talk about it." But he never did. When you brought it up at performance review time the next year, he "finessed it" by telling you he was giving you an increase that seemed surprisingly good; but then when you got back to your desk he called you on the inter-com to tell you he had made a mistake in his figures and the actual increase turned out to be the usual minor one. You are pretty well convinced that there is going to be a tough stand by your boss on this pay issue.

As you now see it, you have these options:

1. Try to "fight fire with fire"—try to out-maneuver the boss with a strategy superior to his.

2. Try to present an ironclad case for a real raise.
3. Make an "end run"—go to the company president with your problem, bypassing your boss entirely.
4. Look around quietly for another job.
5. Drop hints that you have been approached for employment by a couple of other companies in recent months.
6. Team up with two other managers who have the same problem and try a "united front" approach.
7. Grin and bear it and take *early* retirement at age 62, per company policy.

Analyze and reduce to writing each of these solutions as to its strengths and weaknesses and possible future consequences. Then, either select one of those decisions or arrive at one of your own. In either case, give a full justification for the course of action you propose to take.

Benefits-Risk Approach

The Children at Work Case

Management in a large publishing firm has called this problem to the attention of its employees:

"Increasingly, employees have been bringing small children to work with them for a day or a part of a day. In most instances the reason is the unexpected nonappearance of a baby-sitter. Management is impressed by the determination of the employees to come to work in such cases. But the distraction caused by the presence of small children—and it's usually more than their parents realize—is neither fair to other employees nor conducive to a good work environment. There have been many complaints from employees and supervisors alike on this matter. This practice has never been approved in a formal way.

"Accordingly, we are issuing this policy: Any employee who comes to work with a child (for more than a brief visit) should be sent home, using personal leave or leave without pay."

Assignment to trainer: Have participants use a T-column to list the risks and benefits of management's decision. After they have completed the T-column, have them answer the questions presented in the worksheet in Appendix 60.

Using Judicial Cases

In case study work our cases typically are drawn from problems encountered in organizational life: marketing, production, finance, interpersonal relations, safety, organization, general management, and so on. And these cases are ordinarily presented with all of their many ramifications with neither organizational identification nor any indication as to their actual resolution.

At times, however, the need for greater credibility may necessitate the use of cases drawn from court actions. This is particularly true in the area of sexual harassment, where it is essential to demonstrate the serious nature of potential liability for the organization and employees as well.[6] In such cases the actual organization involved, the decision, and the liability assessed, if any, would be presented.

Similarly, in training salespersons to understand and respect the potential legal implications of their actions, actual court cases may be used. We have reference to such potentially troublesome areas as the delivered product being below agreed-upon quality standards, misrepresentation (e.g., regarding use of the product), extra charges added without the purchaser's knowledge, kickbacks, delivering a brand other than the one agreed upon, giving favorite customers price concessions, violating the contracted-for delivery date, slandering a competitor, and failure to warn a buyer of potential hazards in using a product.[7]

A Case For Self-Review Purposes

This case is designed to provide an opportunity for self-evaluation and review of material that has been previously discussed in class or has been read on an individual basis. The technique is designed to help participants "button down" pertinent details about a problem situation. Unlike our other cases, it is not intended to broaden outlooks, encourage explanation of alternate courses of action, or call attention to management implications.

The County-Wide Illness

You are the county health officer. Several adults and children have requested treatment at various hospitals in the County for an illness marked by these *initial* symptoms: listlessness, a slight fever, and influenza-type aches and pains. Typically, by the third or fourth day an eruption appears on the wrists and ankles.

Assignment to trainer: Have participants answer the questions in Appendix 61. After the pairs have discussed and compared their answers, pass out the answer sheet for total group discussion.

How to Develop Case Material

Cases and material to prepare cases may be obtained from many sources. These include:

☐ Case books
☐ Articles in training, personnel, and management journals
☐ Articles in newspapers and magazines

□ The experiences of colleagues
□ Problems presented by lecturers at conferences, workshops, and training sessions
□ Organizational events
□ Personal experiences

However, quite often the trainer requires a case that must be integrated with a specific learning objective and is not readily available from these sources. Under these circumstances, you must develop your own case. Bradford B. Boyd[8] offers these six steps as guides to developing the tailor-made case:

1. *Decide on the principle(s)* you wish to have the case point up. This first step obviously is the most critical one.
   Example: Delegation may not work because of forces at work among subordinates, not necessarily those in the boss.
2. *Establish a situation* that demonstrates the principle. This requires us to draw upon our experience with typical problems and problem individuals.
   Example: Delegation goes awry because subordinates fail to keep the boss posted as they are getting into "deep water."
3. *Develop appropriate symptoms*. These may be positive or negative or both types of symptoms, whichever best illustrates the principle we plan to teach. Here we seek out incidents and situations which are symptomatic of the attitude expressed in Step 2.
   Example: "The boss might punish me if I give him the bad news." "He'll learn about it in time." "Maybe the situation will get better." These attitudes are rationalizations to avoid having to share with the boss one's inability to carry out the assigned delegation.
4. *Develop the characters*. They can be those who are doing things right or doing them improperly. Characters, of course, are plentiful. We need only bring them to life by giving them names, titles, responsibilities, attitudes, values, perceptions.
   Example: Jennifer Bayliss is a section chief in the Operations Department. She has a tendency to procrastinate about things and blame others for her problems.
5. *Write the case*. Here we develop fully the pertinent details surrounding events, problems, and personalities, all of which are the specific building blocks for the case.
6. *Provide questions*. This is to guide participants' thinking about the problem presented and is the vehicle to reach the principle involved.

It may be desirable, in writing the case, to think of situations where a role play could develop from the case discussion. This will provide added interest in and insight about the problem presented. It should also be remembered that the best case is one that is marked by realism, a certain amount of conflict, somewhat strong personalities, and avoidance of unnecessary detail.

In developing a case use this checklist to ensure that it will be of high quality to be effective as a learning tool:

___ 1. Subject matter is realistic, i.e., use of believable situations, events, circumstances, difficulties.
___ 2. Facts are presented sequentially, clearly and briefly.
___ 3. Facts are adequate to resolve the case.
___ 4. Characters are believable and interesting; avoids "Attila the Hun" and "Robin Hood" types which are extreme and thus unrealistic.
___ 5. Includes conflict or friction points among the characters.
___ 6. Unnecessary detail is avoided.
___ 7. The case is open-end; solutions are neither given nor implied.
___ 8. Multiple solutions are quite possible (no one best answer).
___ 9. The case is short enough so that it can be read quickly in class.
___ 10. The case is very likely to provoke a lively discussion or debate.

Learning from Cases

Although a case is a learning device designed to point up certain principles to participants, it is not unusual for the trainer to receive a complaint such as this: "Why don't we discuss cases drawn from our own organizational or industry setting?" You can respond in a number of ways to this "classic" complaint.

First, you should point out that the case is a tool for learning, and its origin or location is really not too pertinent. What *is* pertinent is the learning we can extract from it in terms of principles, concepts, processes, forces at work, etc. This is similar to the law student who uses cases to "learn the law" to develop legal reasoning ability and who could not care less whether the cases used come from Maine, Maryland, Texas, or Oregon. So whether the managers are wearing hospital smocks, three-piece suits, or fire chief's uniforms is really of no great importance. A meaty case is still the main thing!

Secondly, using a case that is "organization specific" may actually produce boomerang effects—participants may get "hung up" on particular details of organizational structure, organizational policy, various in-house rules, regulations, and procedures. By using a "culture free" case, participants can concentrate on the case per se and not be detoured by incidental elements in it.

Thirdly, quite often an "outside" case may be richer in learning potential because of its superb context (realism, conflict), the way it is written, and the personalities portrayed in it.

Finally, if the case is in a film format it obviously is too costly to produce your own case.

All in all, most participants accept the case for what it is—a tool for learning. They thus are able to "internalize" the learning despite its being somewhat abstract in relation to one's particular job situation. Persistent inability to transfer classroom learning to the job may well indicate resistance to what is being taught, e.g., the staunch nondelegator may endeavor to "pick the case apart" rather than state publicly that he/she disagrees with the delegation concepts that the case advocates.

Using the In-House Case

In the preceding paragraphs we presented a number of reasons why the "outside" case is preferable to the in-house one. However, there may be special circumstances where the in-house case would be preferred, such as in the issue of sexual harassment.

According to the EEOC (Equal Employment Opportunity Commission) guidelines, an organization can limit its liability when it is involved in sexual harassment cases by demonstrating that it did take "immediate and corrective action." Thus, if cases have occurred and the organization has already taken appropriate disciplinary action on them, such cases merit introduction into the sexual harassment training program. The cases should be presented anonymously, of course. The use of these cases would show the company's concern for a harassment-free work environment plus the fact that disciplinary action is taken promptly and appropriately.

In a sensitive area such as sexual harassment, the in-house cases will have high impact since the participants are learning about situations involving some of their fellow workers.

The "best" in-house cases on sexual harassment are those marked by:[6]

☐ Across-the-board fairness, i.e., where discipline was extended to both managerial and nonmanagerial employees.
☐ Pocketbook impacts, i.e., demonstrating how pay checks are affected (via discharge, demotion, or suspension).
☐ Broad subject-matter coverage, i.e., cases that deal with those relating to an "intolerable working environment" as well as with demands for sexual favors in relation to employment, promotion, etc.

Note: If an organization has not had any disciplinary cases in this area, it may have to draw on the experience of other companies. If so, the cases would, again, be presented as "live" ones, albeit less indigenous.

Techniques to Maximize Learning From Cases

Using Small Groups

In the lecture method participant learning comes from "the wisdom" that is heard (and presumably "absorbed") from "on high," from the expert. In case study, conversely, learning comes from what one analyzes, discusses, advocates, defends, and listens to; in short, learning (or wisdom) accrues from interaction with peers.

In traditional case study participants and the trainer often arrayed themselves around a table for good eye contact and generally better communication. They also assumed this configuration to emphasize that all concerned were "equals." All of which was true enough, except that the more verbal and aggressive ones become "more equal" than their fellow discussants. This competition for "air time" obviously becomes most acute if the group is quite large. If the group were composed of 25 participants and the session ran 2 hours (120 minutes) and everyone actually had equal opportunities to participate, per person participation time would be less than five minutes. This figure is exclusive of added time consumed by trainer inputs.

Because of this participation problem, trainers in time began to employ small group methods as a major means of attacking the case. This can be done in one of several ways:

☐ Hold a group-at-large discussion to be certain that everyone agrees on the facts and issues involved. Then have the participants break into small groups of four to six persons to come up with a solution to the problem. Solutions or decisions are then reported back to the total group for further discussion.
☐ Alternatively, the total group could be divided into small groups immediately with instructions to respond to the trainer's usual opening query of: "What seem's to be going on here?" Then the groups could report their conclusions on that question to the large group, endeavoring to secure agreement on the facts and issues, and then return to the small groups for the problem resolution phase of the work as in the preceding procedure.
☐ If the case has specific questions for discussion (see the following discussion on "Focused Analysis"), specific questions could be assigned to various small groups for discussion and feedback to the total group.

A variation on this technique would be to have individual participants develop their responses to the questions in writing prior to entry into their small discussion groups (see the discussion on "Using A Worksheet" later). More specifically, the procedures are as follows:

1. Have participants read the case in class.
2. Have each person jot down his/her responses to the assigned (focused) questions.
3. Form small groups to discuss and agree on their responses to the assigned questions. (Answers may be written on flipchart.)
4. Ask each team to select a spokesperson/responder to answer questions from the other teams. *Note:* Keep the groups "intact" while the discussion is going on to establish clearly who the responder is responding for.
5. As trainer, wrap up the discussion by highlighting responses to the questions which were assigned. Alternately, you may ask for volunteers to provide such summary responses.

Note: Twenty-seven "Thought Questions" are given in Figure 2-1. They may help you to stimulate discussion, either total or small group.

Focused Analysis

In classic case study participants are put into action via such general questions as: What seems to be going on here? Is there a problem here? If so, what is it? What are the issues we should be cognizant of? The theory here, of course, is that providing specific questions encourages too much dependency on the trainer; for what is preferred is that participants attack the case on a totally open-end basis.

Alternatively, and depending on the learning objectives and the group's needs, it may be quite desirable to provide participants with more structure in the form of specific questions on which they should focus. For example, the following short case on delegation may take this focused format:

Rationalizations About Delegation
In a management seminar a participant told the group about his attempts to get his dad, who ran a small metal fabricating plant, to "loosen up" and delegate more. He cited these conversations with his dad.

Son: Dad, why don't you make it easier on yourself and let someone else do the maintenance on those machines?

Dad: No one has had the experience I've had taking care of them.
Son: Are you saying you're the only one who can maintain them?
Dad: Oh, sure, there are others who can do the job, too.
Son: Then why not let them do it?
Dad: They *could* do it. But how do I know they'd do it *right?*

And another conversation went as follows:

Son: You took the *full* two weeks vacation and the plant is still there.
Dad: I really missed the plant.
Son: I can understand that. But you've got to get away now and then.
Dad: But what if something comes up while I'm away?
Son: Did anyone call you while you were away?
Dad: No.
Son: So they didn't *need* to call.
Dad: Since they didn't have my number, how do I know they didn't *try* to call me?

Questions for discussion:

1. Why may managers be reluctant to delegate?
2. Assume you had a subordinate manager working for you who was "weak" at delegating. How might you change his approach to delegation?
3. One way to encourage delegation by managers is to acquaint them with proper "control" procedures? What might some of these be?

Note that the preceding questions took a specific focus, i.e., they dealt with reluctance to delegate. It is also possible, however, to provide a broader or multifocus. We thus could explore this case in respect to other dimensions of the management job, e.g.,

☐ *Communication:* Would you say it is hard or easy to communicate with Dad? Did the son seem to have the kind of relationship with Dad that made authentic communication possible? Was Dad interested in feedback about his prowess as a manager?
☐ *Motivation:* Assume everyone has a "need" system. What was Dad's? Is it possible to bring about a change in Dad's (or anyone's) need system? If so, how might this be done?
☐ *Managerial Grid®:* Using Grid concepts, what were the leadership styles of Dad? His son?
☐ *Johari Window:* How did people in the plant see Dad? Did Dad see himself as others did? Or did Dad have serious "blind spots?"

☐ *Coaching:* How would you see Dad as a developer of people? If you were working for Dad what problems would you see arising between you?

Another form of focus is to "learn from failure." Thus, participants zero in on the mistakes or failures contained in a given case. The written case may be followed by questions such as these:

☐ What went wrong?
☐ How or why did Marie fail?
☐ What were Marie's principal mistakes?
☐ Was the series of errors inevitable?
☐ How could the failure (crisis, emergency) have been prevented?
☐ How could Andy have avoided getting into this jam?
☐ What are the company's chances for survival?
☐ How can Miss Benedict establish a plan or procedure to deal with future emergencies (contingencies, disruptions, crises)?
☐ Was there any learning in the organization as a result of these unsuccessful events?
☐ Is it possible to learn from failure? If so, how?

Still another focused approach is that of *empathic analysis.* Here we ask the participants to put their feet in the shoes of the case's characters and respond to questions such as these:

☐ How would you have handled this incident (situation, problem, crisis, event) if you were the district manager?
☐ Assuming you were the head of the company _____.
☐ Could this situation have been prevented? If so, what would *you* have done?

It also would be useful to the group to analyze a case in terms of the *forces* at work that produced the problem:

☐ Those in the persons, including leaders, peers and/or subordinates
☐ Those in the group
☐ Those in the organization (its structure, values, policies)
☐ Those in the world at large (if applicable)

As a final example of focused analysis, the psychological/psychoanalytical model developed by industrial psychologist Harry Levinson merits consideration. Dr. Levinson provides these key questions for case analyses:[9]

☐ Where is the pain? (That is, who is most upset by the behavior?)
☐ When did it begin? (Cases with a long history are less amenable to mangerial intervention.)
☐ What is happening to affection?
☐ What is happening to aggression?
☐ What is happening to dependency?
☐ What is the nature of the ego ideal? (This relates to self-appreciation, self-perception, self-aspirations and their realizability.)
☐ Is the problem solvable? (Some problems have to be lived with.)
☐ If so, how?

Introducing a Role Play

Management cases typically present situations involving poor communication, conflict, resistance to change, role confusion, unrealistic values, fuzzy goal setting, and the like. Added insight into these interpersonal dynamics may be secured by acting out the roles of the personalities presented in the case. This may be planned in advance by the trainer or it may be structured on an *ad hoc* basis. In the latter instance a participant may trigger the role play by saying: "If I were the manager and Terry were working for me I would _____." At this point the trainer interrupts and says: "Fine. Rod you be the manager. Fred you be Terry. Fred is in your office and _____."

Introducing Brainstorming

Brainstorming, as role playing, can be planned in advance or introduced as the situation seems to call for it. For example, in the prior delegation case, you could have the group brainstorm control procedures a manager could use to ensure that delegation is proceeding as intended. Typical "controls" might be periodic written reports, computer print outs, briefs at staff meetings, planned inspections, spot checks, informal chats.

Personalization

After discussing the formal case, greater insight into the issues raised might be obtained by asking participants to volunteer data or examples drawn from their personal experience. Thus, in the delegation case, participants could be encouraged to share instances, past or preferably present, of their own reluctance to delegate.

Using a Worksheet

A case may be presented in worksheet format. This entails providing the particulars of the case as usual plus

The Case of the Non-Team-Playing Peer

Len Thompson is a relatively new member of the personnel office. He was recently brought in to head up all matters pertaining to recruitment and placement. In a meeting with his boss Rex Ross, the personnel officer, Len dropped a comment to the effect that Arch White, the training officer, did not seem very interested in the new career management program he (Len) was developing.

Several days later you (Arch White) are in your boss' office on some business, and Rex unloads this bombshell:

Rex Ross: Len tells me that you don't seem to be interested in the new career management plan he's working on.
Arch White: What?
Rex Ross: That's what he implied.
Arch White: Where did he get that idea? I've always said we needed that program to complement our overall training and development program.
Rex Ross: Um . . .
Arch White: This really beats anything.
Rex Ross: Well, I thought you'd want to know how he feels.

You leave the boss' office, both stunned and puzzled. The next day you return to your boss' office to try to button down Len Thompson's statements to the boss. You also let your boss know that Len's statement really irritated you. Rex Ross, however, doesn't provide you with any more specific information, merely repeating what he said yesterday. You leave your boss' office wondering what kind of a team player Len Thompson is.

Case Study Assignment Sheet

1. You are Training Officer Arch White
   a. What action, if any, do you propose to take?

   _____
   _____
   _____
   _____
   _____
   _____

   b. What are the reasons for your action?

   _____
   _____
   _____
   _____
   _____
   _____

2. Small group assignment: Agree, as a group, on the best course of action Arch White should take.

   _____
   _____
   _____
   _____
   _____
   _____

(Note: You will have the opportunity to present your approach to the group at large.)

Figure 17-1. Example of a case presented in a worksheet format.

an opportunity for the individual participants and possibly the small groups to reduce their conclusions to writing. The advantages of this more structured approach are:

☐ Offering conclusions in writing requires more careful thought.
☐ Everyone is more certain to participate. (People can "cop out" even in a small group.)

An example of a case presented in this format appears in Figure 17-1.

Using Fishbowls

The fishbowl, or group-on-group observation, can be used to increase both involvement and excitement in the group. At any of the various stages of the case study discussion, the trainer can divide the total group into 2 smaller groups—one to discuss the case and the other to observe and listen to the discussants. After 20–30 minutes the roles can be reversed, with the outer group becoming the discussants and the inner group the observers. On the second go-around the discussion can cover both the groups' own ideas about the case and its reactions to the comments of the first group.

For best results, the discussion group should have no more than eight people.

Added Skill Pointers

The following guidelines and cautions will help to ensure a high-quality learning experience for your participants:[10]

1. Choose cases carefully to meet course objectives.
2. Allow sufficient time for your group to read the case thoroughly before you start the discussion. Skip lengthy cases unless they can be read on a prework basis.
3. One practical way to begin is to have a group member to summarize the facts and main issues in the case. Check to see if there is agreement with this presentation.
4. Anticipate resistance to the case method by some participants who are more comfortable with *the* answer. Part of the learning, of course, is that in management there typically is no one "best" or "right" answer. Also, managers must learn to become comfortable with ambiguity.
5. Avoid taking away the participants' opportunity to think by providing answers, or worse, "*the* answer."

Evaluation of Participants

If the group wishes to evaluate its behavior as a group, it can employ various devices for this. These include the use of a sociogram to diagram participation, a role observation chart to record assumption of task and maintenance roles, and a check sheet to assess problem solving behavior.

Key Points

1. The case study method is our oldest training technique for achieving trainee participation.
2. Its major limitation is that it is somewhat intellectual and academic in its approach, i.e., it merely involves an analysis and discussion of someone else's problem—and often in a large group setting at that.
3. Also, it is not as involving as newer participative training devices such as exercises, games, simulations, role plays, or instruments.
4. In using case study the trainer should seek out formats that make for greater participant interest, such as using letters and editorials, dialogue, filmed cases, the live case, personal cases, and the rating approach.
5. The filmed case has greater realism than the printed case. It is "easier to take" and eliminates the need for prior preparation (pre-work).
6. Although cases may be acquired from outside sources such as books and magazines, the alert trainer will be on the lookout for incidents, events, and problems that can be converted to case materials of particular interest to the participant groups.
7. In writing cases, structure them so that they have the potential to point up principles/issues you deem pertinent. Develop "strong" characters and include adequate conflict in their interactions to ensure interest and realism.
8. Since the traditional group-at-large approach to case study allows for only limited participation and has an "academic" cast to it, use other devices with it to ensure greater involvement—small group work, role plays, fishbowls, brainstorming, or focused analysis.

References

1. *Management Development Casebook,* Training Guide TG 5-16, Office of Personnel, Veterans Administration, Washington, D.C. (1958).
2. Andrews, Eugene S., and Noel, James, L., "Adding Life To The Case Study Method," *Training and Development Journal* (February 1986), pp. 28–29.

3. Based on an Associated Press news item which appeared in *The Washington Post* (December 17, 1980) with a Lake Ronkonkoma, New York, dateline. The names of the persons in the case have been changed.

4. This description is based on the author's experience with the Action Maze technique plus the incisive observations contained in (a) Broadwell, Martin M., *The Supervisor As An Instructor*, 3rd edition, Addison-Wesley Publishing Co., Reading, Mass., 1978, p. 194 and (b) Laird, Dugan L., *Approaches To Training and Development,* Addison-Wesley Publishing Co., Reading, Mass., 1978, pp. 143–144.

5. "Training Away Work Place Problems," *Training and Development Journal* (November 1987), pp. 18–19, which describes suggestions submitted by Michael Shahnasarian, ISFA Corporation, Tampa, Florida.

6. Kronenberger, G. K., and Bourke, D. L., "Effective Training and Elimination of Sexual Harassment," *Personnel Journal* (November 1981), pp. 879–883.

7. "Selling and The Law," *Industrial Distribution* (October 1981), pp. 38–41.

8. Boyd, B. B., "Developing Case Studies," *Training and Development Journal* (June 1980).

9. Levinson, H., *Psychological Man,* The Levinson Institute, Inc., Cambridge, Mass. (1976), pp. 135–138.

10. "Case Method: Tips," *Government Training News* (August 1984), p. 8.

Recommended Reading

Amistead, Colin, "How Helpful Are Case Studies?" *Training and Development Journal*, February 1984, pp. 75–77.

The article covers types of case study, criteria of a good case, pros and cons, learning objectives, and writing cases.

Andrews, Kenneth R., (Ed.), *The Case Method of Teaching Human Relations and Administration,* Harvard University Press, Cambridge, Mass., 1953.

A now classic reference work on the case study, the book features a collection of papers by those who taught and conducted research in human relations at the Harvard Business School.

Boyd, Bradford, B., "Developing Case Studies," *Training and Development Journal,* June 1980.

This presents a six-step method for writing cases to fit the special needs of one's course or program.

Glover, John D., et al., *The Administrator: Cases on Human Aspects in Management,* 5th edition, (Richard D. Irwin, Inc., Homewood, Illinois, 1973.

This is the "granddaddy" of case books that emanated from the Harvard Business School. The book was originally published in 1949 by two Harvard Business School professors, John D. Glover and Ralph M. Hower. It was titled *The Administrator: Cases on Human Relations in Business* and went through several revisions under that title.

Green, Thad B., and Cotlar, Morton, "Do Filmed Cases Improve the Case Method?" *Training and Development Journal,* May 1973, pp. 28–31.

This is a research report that concluded that "presenting case materials on film does improve the case method. Although the film did not promote greater transferability, those students using film-based simulation demonstrated a superior performance in comprehension of management principles and concepts, and a more realistic understanding of the environment in which the manager interacts."

Hennecke, Matthew J., "Case Studies: A New Approach," *Training and Development Journal*, March 1983, pp. 70–71.

The author shows how to overcome a problem of case study—namely, its remoteness from the participants' real world. The answer? Use "individualized" case studies which include the participants' own staff, peers and bosses.

McCarthy, John J., "The Case Method," *Sales Training,* January 1977, and "A Case Handling Technique," *Sales Training,* March 1977.

A long-time sales trainer shows how case study can be applied effectively to sales training.

McNair, Malcolm P. (Ed.), *The Case Method At the Harvard Business School: Papers By Present and Past Members of the Faculty and Staff,* McGraw Hill Book Company, New York, 1954.

This is a work devoted to the broad application of case study, e.g., marketing, production, control, economic aspects of business, and advertising. (Note: The book by Andrews, cited earlier, was concerned solely with teaching human relations via the case method).

Pigors, Paul, and Pigors, Faith. "Learning Through Experience in Leadership Training," *Office Executive,* October 1955, pp. 1–3.

This is a description of the incident process by its founders.

"IF YOU MUST LECTURE . . ."

The biggest enemy to learning is the talking teacher.

—John Holt, educator and author.

A prominent newspaper columnist—Colman Mc-Carthy of The Washington Post—was invited to speak to a journalism class while he was visiting the University of Iowa. He noted very quickly that many of the 40 students were taking notes, obviously responding to the usual professorial imperative of "covering ground." So he asked them if they would join him in an experiment. He gave them these instructions: "Stand up. Leave the building. Stand on the curb for 15 minutes and count all the red and green cars that pass. Then come back to answer questions."

When the students were half way down the hall, he called them back. He then posed these questions: Didn't anyone think it was stupid to count red and green cars? Why didn't anyone ask the objective of the "experiment"? Do you let your profs push you around this way? Since it was raining, why didn't someone say he/she didn't want to get wet?

Of course, the aim of the experiment was not merely to down-grade note taking. It was about passivity and coercion, the long time enemies of learning and the permanent assaults on students. He wished to point up to the students that they are in school to learn by questioning and to get their questions answered. Also, they should question oppressive authority and ask whether the university is giving them their money's worth. If not, said Mr. McCarthy, let the professors count red and green cars in the rain. And let them take notes, too, for "there's ground to be covered."[1]

The Lecture—A Problem-Laden Technique

More than any other training method, the lecture has been continually cussed and discussed. Newer, more involving methods have certainly moved the lecture off "center stage." Here are some of the many charges levied against it:

☐ It is dull, boring, and thus a waste of time.

☐ It makes the learner passive.

☐ It causes a loss of motivation, curiosity, and creativity.

☐ Since it is a one-way communication device, the presenter can hardly tell whether the message is coming through.

☐ It has a high "tune out" and "turn off" potential.

☐ Participants may not be able to seek a necessary clarification because of the size of the group, time constraints, the lecturer's "flow," the presumed embarassment of interrupting, etc.

☐ It ignores varying listening rates of participants.

☐ The formal presentation may be poorly planned and organized.

☐ The delivery itself may be poor.

☐ The speaker may "talk down" to the audience.

☐ It "endorses" the authority figure concept, something that is not appreciated in a democratic culture.

☐ Retention is very low—much is lost in 24 hours, most of the rest is lost thereafter.

☐ It is archaic as a teaching device. Socrates, who lived around 450 B.C., sensed this. Hence his development of the Socratic method, which entailed asking a series of well-planned questions to lead his learners to the "ultimate truth."

☐ It ignores the old adage, "The mind can absorb only as much as the seat can endure."

Lecturing, of course, is the way professors teach in the colleges and universities. But this approach is hardly a model for the alert and sophisticated trainer. In fact, a former academic teacher, now a professional trainer, Don M. Ricks, president of Industrial Writing and Communications Consultants Ltd. of Calgary, Canada, candidly stated why he wouldn't hire "academics" as instructors in his company. Here are his well-articulated objections:[2]

☐ They know little about how adults learn. They even pride themselves "in *not* knowing how people learn."

☐ They have a limited range of instructional skills, knowing little of modern audio-visual and group-in-action devices as discussed in the preceding pages. Also, their instruction is often mind-bending (manipulation) rather than mind-liberating.

☐ They teach the wrong people, i.e., they "play" to the bright students, the ones who need help the least.

☐ They teach the wrong things, i.e., the students are overburdened with detailed content as if they were to become instructors in the field. Most academics have limited experience in these vital roles: setting directions, answering questions, providing feedback, and helping the learner define objectives and solve problems.

☐ As "experts" they are reluctant to surrender "ownership" of learning, thus shortchanging students by withholding vital content from them.

☐ They have too much confidence in words, despite the well-known fact that listeners have short attention spans and poor retention rates. Academic teachers often get trapped by the beauty of their own voices and drone on and on.

☐ They hesitate to trust learners, preferring control over them rather than providing general guidance and direction.

☐ They have a limited understanding of the effects of their own behavior. They thus overlook the need to display such desirable qualities as openness, receptivity, confidence, and interest, all key elements in establishing a sound instructor-student relationship.

☐ Finally, they simply misunderstand their primary function—to induce change. They ignore the fact that learning is intended to bring about a change in knowledge, perception, or behavior, not to "expose" people to information or to "cover" a subject.

Regardless of whether one accepts this indictment of those who live (and die?) totally by the lecture method, Ricks' statements do point up that one can all too readily become enamored with communicating from "on-high" to the detriment of participant learning.

Not all observers, certainly, see the lecture as evil or even as a necessary evil. For example, Donald B. Miller, program manager of human resources, for IBM in San Jose, California, sees it quite positively:[3]

The growth activity to which we have been most exposed is the lecture. We sometimes wonder about its effectiveness; however, when it works we can grow as a result of the exposure. A good lecture is one which engages our attention, sharpens the differentiation between alternative actions, and motivates us to new experience, or aids us in internalizing the information. A good lecture gets us emotionally involved. A good lecture presents material in a way which captures our involvement and interest. A good lecture disciplines our use of time and our actions in a way we cannot or have not done for ourselves.

When to Use the Lecture

The issue, of course, is not whether the lecture is totally bad or is, on occasion, helpful. Rather, our concern, as trainers, is: When does its use make sense? When is it most appropriate? The late Donald Bullock, who was responsible for marketing training development with the C & P Telephone Company, Silver Spring, Maryland, offers these guidelines to help trainers decide when "lecture-driven instruction" may be adequately useful:[4]

☐ The instructor has the need to present his/her ideas to the group. (Not a trivial consideration, says Bullock.)

☐ The lecture is the most convenient and cost-effective means to disseminate material.

☐ Concepts are to be given inductively and the expected varied responses of the group can only be responded to by the instructor.

☐ In a nonlecture-type program occasional lecturettes (short talks) may provide a worthwhile change of pace, reduce boredom, etc.

☐ Participants' needs to ask questions or to comment can best be met in a typical lecture-type format. (Conversely, the need may not be met well in a nonlecture or participative mode.)

☐ A demonstration of equipment or a job aid may require a lecture-type explanation, i.e., so that key points or features are highlighted.

☐ A high-status person or skill in delivery is deemed essential to ensure the credibility of the information or instruction.

☐ The content or material changes so frequently that an "up-date" can only be handled via formal input by a lecturer.

Giving the Lecture Polish

Since the lecture is so problem-laden, a lot of advice is constantly being doled out to lecturers in hopes that they will give a "good" talk or a "stimulating" lecture. Some of this advice includes the following:

☐ Know your subject.

☐ Prepare well—use a tape (audio) recorder for practice.

☐ Study yourself "in action" via videotape.

☐ Over-prepare.

☐ State your objectives at the outset. Remember, participants are eager to learn very early on the answer to this question: "What's in it for me?"

☐ Use visual aids; but make certain they can be read easily.

☐ Watch your techniques of delivery; use voice variation, gestures, movement, and pauses; vary the tempo; abandon the lectern or podium; etc.

☐ Maintain eye contact.

☐ Use humor, anecdotes, examples, analogies.

☐ Use handouts.

☐ Breathe properly.

☐ Don't read from a manuscript; use general notes only.

☐ Introduce surprise.

☐ Enunciate carefully.

☐ Exude confidence, sincerity, conviction.

☐ Exude energy, enthusiasm.

☐ Don't turn down an opportunity to speak before a group; practice is invaluable.

☐ Watch your beginnings—get interest at the onset.

☐ Watch your closes—give them a message they'll remember.

☐ Try to get feedback about your performance.

☐ Join a speaking-improvement group such as a toastmaster's club to upgrade your skill.

☐ Avoid "uh's" and "ah's."

☐ Know your audience—their interests, perceptions, expectations, background.

☐ Assess and reassess your audience in the course of your presentation, and make adjustments as necessary.

☐ Quit on time.

☐ Dress properly.

☐ Personalize your talk: talk about yourself, your experience, your "goofs".

☐ Use a lot of "you's" for audience rapport.

☐ Include practical material ("how to") in your talk.

☐ Avoid "heavy" statistics; instead, speak generally about quantitative items.

☐ Use everyday language; avoid pomposity.

☐ Try to speak in a conversational tone of voice.

All of this is useful information—except for one thing: it relates only to how well the person "up front" should and can perform. Unfortunately, the well-intentioned advice has little bearing on *how well the learner will learn.* In other words, the answer to the lecture problem—and anyone who has suffered through lectures in classrooms and training rooms can enumerate scores of such problems without too much prompting—is not just to make better lectures, but to work on ways to involve the group. Certainly, sophisticated trainers would agree that the lecture, at best, is a necessary evil. But on the assumption that the lecture, despite its many demerits, is here to stay, some means of making it more palatable and productive for the participants in your programs are presented.

Securing Participation at the Outset

Although participative approaches can be used at various stages in a talk or lecture, it's a good idea to get your audience into the act at the outset. This procedure will establish rapport immediately with the group. They will, in effect, say thankfully to themselves: "Hey, this person isn't just going to talk *at us* for the full hour. Sure looks like a lively deal coming up." By putting the group to work you will also relax yourself and do a better job as a speaker.

Here are some examples of activities to involve the group *before* the lecture is launched.

Pre-work: Reading

Give your conferees an advance reading assignment and have them discuss it in class before the formal presentation.

Audience Answers

Involve your participants on their arrival by having them enter data on flipcharts. Procedurally, post three sheets to the wall or use three separate easels with flipchart pads on them. In the former case, also tape several marking pens to the wall, one next to each flipchart sheet for ready use.

Assume your session is related to "Delegation and The Manager." You might label your three flipchart sheets as follows:

Review the sheets before you start the session and make reference to the data from time to time as you conduct it.

Note: Since the participants may not be aware that they are to contribute to the flipcharts, you, a colleague, or a participant should call this task to their attention as they arrive.

Pre-work: Case or Problem Analysis

Give participants a short case, incident, or problem in *advance* of the talk. Ask them to come to class with a possible solution. Use the case discussion as an introduction to the formal lecture or talk.

Problem Census

At the outset, elicit from the audience areas of special interest, problems, or concerns that they hope will be covered in the session. Post them on a flipchart and then check off those that will be dealt with in the formal presentation. This procedure will give the audience an assurance that at least some of their problems and interests will be addressed, as well as provide for "instant" participation.

Problem Swap

Assign participants to small groups, have them introduce themselves to one another and then give them this *individualized* assignment to discuss for two minutes: What is the major obstacle you encounter in _____ (introducing change, securing cooperation, selling product X, improving employee safety)? Then have participants put their problems on 3" × 5" card (each group member puts his/her problem on a card) and share the problems in their groups for five minutes. Hand out a

large 5" × 8" card to each group. Have the groups spend five minutes deciding on the one "best" problem in the group and write it on the large card. Collect the big cards and switch them among the groups. Then have the groups take ten minutes to answer the problem on the card they received. Then say "O.K., let's get some reports from several groups. Who wants to start? State the problem you have and your group's answer to it."

Interest Inventory

Ask your audience to respond to questions such as these:

☐ What is your interest in this topic?
☐ Why are you here?
☐ What do you hope to take back?
☐ When this session is over, what will have made it successful?

You can ask the participants to respond to questions of this sort on an individual basis or, better still, in pairs or small groups of three to five persons.

Incident for Involvement

Ask everyone to jot down on a sheet of paper a real-life incident, problem, or event that relates to your topic. Ask several people to share their incident or problem with the total group. A variation is to use small group work to select the "best" examples before sharing them with the total group.

Problem Probe

Begin things by assigning to small groups a short problem, case, or incident. Secure feedback and discuss it; then begin your talk.

Exercise Excitement

Start things off with a short, simple, exciting, and involving exercise, puzzle, or game. It should be pertinent to the topic and make the point in relatively short order.

Anxiety Reducer

Quiet all concerns about a possible dull lecture by commencing the session with an interest-stimulating instrument or quiz. If appropriate, collect data from the "test" and feed it back to the group. Reference may be made to this data at one or more points in the talk, as appropriate.

Structured Note Taking

Ask the group to draw the tri-column that follows on a sheet of paper.

Talk Monitor Chart

I Accept/Agree	I Reject/Disagree	I Have This Question

Then tell them to use the chart as a guide to note taking and that at a point roughly midway in the session you will have them "process" their notes with a neighbor (or a small group).

Flipchart Fill-up

In advance of the session's start, place a sheet from the flipchart and a felt-tip pen on each table. To start things off, assign a task to the various small groups and then have them post their "products" on the wall. The task may involve a definition, the development of a list, the making of a statement about something by means of a drawing, etc.

Present vs. Preferred States

Start things off by asking your audience to break down into small groups and for 10–12 minutes address themselves to these two questions, applicable to almost any group's concerns:

☐ What is the *current* or present state of affairs?
☐ What would you see to be the preferred or *ideal* state of affairs?

Note: Each small group could address itself to both questions, or as a variation, one half of the small groups could deal with the first question and the second half with the latter question.

Secure feedback from the small groups and put it on flipcharts. Post the flipcharts on the wall for later reference.

Quiz the Expert

Post on a flipchart three or four major concerns or problem areas with which your talk will deal. Give all group members several 3″ × 5″ cards and have each of the participants come up with *one* question for each of the problem areas. Retrieve all the cards for topic (problem) one, then for topic two, topic three, and topic four. Return the grouped cards to the small groups for sorting, consolidating, and prioritizing. Then ask for questions from the small groups on all the major areas of concern (for 10–20 minutes). It is not necessary to try to respond to all the questions.

The Two-Step

Give participants a two-stage assignment. For example, to introduce a talk on leadership, have participants list (on the left side of a sheet of paper) three to six individuals, past and present, who might be considered significant leaders or "heroes." Then, on the right side of the paper, list two to four characteristics about these individuals that "justify" the leadership label. Other two-step assignments: cause-effect; risk vs. ways of overcoming the risk; perception: mine vs. theirs; etc.

Thought Stimulator

As soon as people sit down, have them respond in writing to a set of incomplete statements. The questions may be on a prepared form, on the flipchart, or on an overhead projector slide. Examples of such statements for a lecture on time management are:

1. The biggest problem(s) managers have in managing their time is _____.
2. The big time wasters in any organization are _____.
3. If I had total control of my time I would _____.

When the question sheets are completed, secure random responses to those questions or use small groups to process the data before feedback is secured.

Mid-Talk Interventions

As the prior section indicated, it is both desirable and practicable to involve participants *before* a formal talk, lecture, or lecturette. It may also be desirable to put the group into action as the formal presentation proceeds. If so, the devices below should prove helpful.

Challenge Rank

Give participants a handout of, or post on a flipchart, a list of "challenges" (or problem areas, difficulties, concerns). Have them rank the challenges as to importance or intensity. Then secure feedback from the group, via a show of hands, concerning the rankings. ("How many ranked 'field relationships' No. 1? No. 2? Why?").

Film Excerpt

Use a brief film vignette either as an opener (thought stimulator) or at a later point in the presentation. Process the data with the aid of small groups.

Defining Dyads (Pairs)

Have participants turn to their neighbor to meet for several minutes to define an issue; to frame a question;

to present a reaction, observation, or comment. Remember, in a dyad *everyone* plays!

Buzz Groups

Use small discussion groups at one or more points in the presentation to react, to problem solve, to form questions, to apply learnings to job situations.

Participant Survey

Run a quick survey via slips, questionnaires, or show of hands to produce live data pertinent to the topic from the participant group. Use an associate to tally written data. Then feed it back in summary form to the audience.

Participant Assignment

Give the audience (via small groups) a specific task. Example: "Here is a common house brick. Come up with eight ways the brick could be used in your home or office. Be as creative as you can! The sky is the limit! Let your imagination soar." "Think up a number of things you can do to _____" or: "Jot down the three most important ways (techniques, methods, procedures) you see to achieve this objective (or end result)."

List Development

Have the group develop a list on a given topic ("Come up with a 'laundry list' on _____."

Structured List

By adding a bit of structure to a "list assignment," via a handout such as in Appendix 62, you can encourage participants to "dig in" more.

Test Tease

Give the audience a short quiz or use an instrument as an attention getter or interest stimulator. Discuss the results briefly.

Listening Teams (with Topic)

Assign participants to listening teams (four to five participants) in *advance* of the presentation. Then assign to the small groups particular issues or questions that they are to reflect on as the talk is given. At mid-point or at talks's end, have the small groups discuss their assigned questions in light of the formal input. Have a spokesperson from each group report back the small group's conclusions to the group at large.

Listening Teams (General)

Provide listening teams with these prepresentation assignments:

"Group One you are *the questioners*. You might respond by saying, 'We heard you say _____ and wondered if _____' or 'Your statement on _____ triggered the thought that _____.'

"Group Two you are *the clarifiers*. You might say, 'We were not clear (or were confused about) _____.'

"Group Three you are *the disagreers*—not the disagreeables, but the disagreers. Your response might be 'We would question your assertion that _____.'

"Group Four you are *the agreers*. You might say, 'We were turned on by your statement (or idea) concerning _____.'

"Group Five you are *the appliers*. Your response might be 'We see an opportunity to put to work your idea concerning _____.'"

As in the previous suggestion, provide opportunities for the teams to respond to their assignments.

Puzzle Fun

Provide participants with puzzles as a stimulator or to make a point. (Puzzle materials may be toothpicks or other physical items such as matches; the puzzle may be written on the board, passed out as a handout, or communicated orally.)

Didactic Enactment

Work into the presentation a demonstration role play. This can be done informally, with the role players working from general role instructions, or more formally with the role players working from a complete dialogue script. Example: How *not* to conduct an appraisal interview. Secure audience comments as to what was done improperly.

Role Play

The ideas in a talk can be made more meaningful by having the entire group act them out. Giving participants "skill practice" is practical in a large as well as in a small group. For example, I was a participant in a lecture-type session on equal employment attended by some 250 people. We were in a hotel ballroom seated at large round tables, ten to a table. We received this assignment: "Break into trios. One person will assume the role of an applicant applying for a secretarial job. A second will be the boss who is hiring the secretary. The one playing the secretarial role preferably should be someone who has never been in that role in real life. A third person will be an observer. (I assumed the role of the job applicant and acquired considerable insight and empathy about this type of recruiting situation.) The observer provided feedback about the role plays. Our configuration at the tables for the role plays was as shown in Figure 18-1.

Similar role plays could be employed in situations involving prospect-salesperson, police officer-citizen, counselor-counselee, coach-trainee, and boss-subordinate roles.

Figure 18-1. Diagram of how role playing teams could position themselves at a large round table.

POINT MADE IN TALK	MY RELEVANT PERSONAL EXPERIENCE
1	
2	
3	
4	
5	

Figure 18-2. Example of a handout to aid participants in relating points made in the lecture to their personal experiences.

Voluntary Vignettes

Have participants take a sheet of paper and jot down an incident, instance, or event of which they were a part. A variation is to use a more structured approach by providing them with the handout shown in Figure 18-2.

The personal incidents may be shared in dyads, triads, or small groups of four to six persons or with the group-at-large.

Feedback Fest

Stop midway in the presentation and ask for feedback or reactions: "Have I said anything that makes sense? How do *you* see what I've been saying?" The response may be obtained on an individual or, preferably, a small-group basis for *full* audience involvement. A variation is to do one of the following:

☐ Ask orally: "What points have I made so far that cause you to have some reaction—good-bad? Agree-disagree? Practical-impractical?" Secure responses.
☐ Ask for a response in writing: "Put down the three most important ways, techniques, methods, steps you see as needed to achieve this objective." Then secure feedback.

☐ Ask for a show of hands in response to these kinds of questions: "How many agree? Disagree?" "How many believe it's workable?" "How many have had that experience?" "How many had that kind of supervision?" "How many have tried this procedure at least once?" Ask the hand-raisers to provide a few particulars about the queries posed.

Problem Analysis

Assign a problem or case during or after the talk for small group discussion and resolution.

Definition Dare

Have the group jot down a definition of something: leadership, motivation, time, job enrichment, democracy, communication, coaching, etc. Then have several participants read the definitions back to the group at large for discussion.

Handout Helps

Pass out handouts at critical points in the presentation and discuss them with the group. The handouts may be a conceptual model, graph, chart, list of principles, set of concepts, etc. Along with your "straight" handouts, you may wish to pass out a cartoon that makes a relevant point. Prove to the participants that learning need not be dull.

Photo-Object Display

Use photographs, physical objects, etc., to illustrate points and excite interest. For example, one speaker used a photo of the Mona Lisa to make an analogy to an effective supervisor. He asked the group: "What is it about this painting which turns people on?" When he elicited the answer of her ambiguous smile, the instructor then made the point that a supervisor can challenge people by presenting an assignment with adequate ambiguity, that is, low structure and few guidelines.

Deep Think

Hold a short meditation period to encourage reflection, spark creativity, relax tensions.

Fanciful Fun

Use fantasy to stimulate interest and ideation. For example: "You are at the bottom of the sea. You notice a large coral covered cave. You are attracted to the cave. You enter it and you encounter. . ."

Tap Participant Creativity

Ask the group to take a sheet of paper or newsprint and draw a picture (a graphic or illustration) that symbolizes in art form the topic or a problem (e.g. leadership, the organization, communication). Collect a number of them and share with the total group, or post all of them on the wall.

Conjecture Challenge

Stimulate audience response and creativity by the "What if . . . " approach. "What if you had a perfect organization (or supervisor)? What might those attributes or characteristics be like?" "If you could set all the goals (or standards) for this project (or program), what would they be?"

Participant Presentation

In advance of the talk or lecture ask one or more audience members to make a short statement or give a brief presentation on the topic. This will provide the audience with a change of pace. However, individual presentations can be "deadly." After all, you may merely be substituting one lecturer for another. So try to give the presenter some advance coaching, if at all possible. This should prevent a dull, rambling, semi-coherent presentation. Some added answers to this problem are to select able presenters only, to keep the reports short (three to five minutes), and if more than one presenter is used, to scatter the presentations throughout the talk.

Movement and Muscles

Assign a task requiring participants to leave their "safe" locations and to stretch a muscle or two in the process. For example, a college statistics instructor[5] asked his students to arrange themselves on the floor on a straight chalk line according to an assigned score. They immediately found themselves in the classic normal or bell-shaped curve. He then asked how they felt and those in the well-populated middle responded "crowded." He then went out to the three standard deviations and the one student there reported her feelings of "loneliness." The result from a learning standpoint: enhanced recall becomes possible, not only because of cognitive images, but with muscles and visual memory of distances.

Chair Fare

Midway in your talk, do what one creative speaker did: ask everyone to stand and lift up their chairs. Several found a dollar bill posted on the bottom of their chairs! The speaker then made his point: "You have to get off your butt to make a buck!"

Pick a Panel

Call on several participants to serve as panel discussants, summarizers, and debaters. Then have the entire group interact with panelists.

Panel Probers

Instead of the audience asking questions of the panel—the usual procedure—have the panel ask questions of the participants. The purpose is to define, clarify, narrow, and/or zero-in on issues, concerns, learning, and unresolved questions.

Action Plan

At session's end, provide participants with "A Guide For Action" worksheet which has questions such as these on it:

☐ As a result of this session I will _____.
☐ The forces favorable to my action plan are _____.
☐ The forces unfavorable to my action plan are _____.
☐ I can overcome these limiting forces by _____.

Q & A Period

Use an extensive (as opposed to a brief) question and answer period at talk's end, thereby minimizing lecture time considerably.

Question Reversal

Turn a question back to the audience: "I have some ideas on this subject. But I think it would be more useful if we got some *participant* reactions to the question."

Using The Question-And-Answer Period Effectively

A question and answer period has these primary purposes:[6]

☐ To check understanding and retention.
☐ To correct misunderstandings and misperceptions.
☐ To learn of knowledge gaps that require attention.
☐ To learn of possible resistances to the learning.
☐ To check the extent to which the material presented met needs.
☐ To provide a chance to discuss and apply the new learning.
☐ To serve as a means of reemphasis or summary.
☐ To point up possible added help the learners may need to be able to apply what was learned.

Note that all of these stated purposes relate to the furthering of genuine learning goals. Conversely, if the question and answer period is conducted "Because there's some time left over," or "It's the courteous thing to do," or "The boss expects me to do it," or "It's a good way of cutting down on 'prep time' for the lecture period," then the odds are that the benefits to the group will be minimal.

The question and answer period is a traditional way of involving participants. It will not, of course, involve everyone, particularly if a large audience is present and time is limited. But besides the lack of opportunity, many participants hesitate to ask a question for fear of "looking bad" in front of others. In various ways our culture tends to produce a reluctance to ask questions, to stifle natural tendencies toward curiosity. Thus, according to social psychologist Caryl Marsh,[7] children learn very early on the following "don'ts" which often are carried on to adult life:

☐ Don't ask questions, especially of strangers. Why not? It's impolite and could be dangerous.
☐ Don't risk asking questions that may embarrass someone or bare his/her ignorance.
☐ Don't ask questions that may challenge someone's authority or may be perceived as belligerent.
☐ Don't show your own ignorance by asking a stupid question.
☐ Don't bother busy people with questions.

Trainers may also have "inner restraints" that may subtly inhibit participants from questioning them, says Dr. Marsh. These include:

☐ An actual dislike of being questioned.
☐ A fear of showing one's ignorance or being "bested" by a participant.
☐ A fear of exposing something of which one may be ashamed.
☐ A fear of discussing "painful" subject matter.
☐ A reluctance to share knowledge representing personal or group power or a fear of accidentally revealing something confidential.
☐ A feeling of fatigue, time pressures, and a resentment against those who ask questions that waste time.

These fears were expressed by docents (tour guides in an art museum) who were interviewed for an experiment on the encouragement of visitor questions conducted by Dr. Marsh. Her interviews also revealed the circumstances that encouraged the asking of questions. If an authority figure—parent, aunt, uncle, teacher,—served as a role model who exhibited and encouraged curiosity, the willingness to ask questions "rubbed off" on the docents as children.

Marsh's museum experiment on the encouragement of questions required the docents to use two potent techniques in their work with museum visitors: *modeling* and *extended wait-time*. Modeling entailed *asking the visitors questions* that they (the visitors) wanted to ask but felt constrained to do so. This procedure, it was found, encouraged the visitors to ask more profound, interpretive questions rather than routine, factual ones. The wait-time procedure entailed waiting *six* seconds after a profound question was asked of the visitors. Prior research with elementary school teachers had indicated that the teachers who used a wait-time of three seconds for the first student to respond to a question produced more interpretive questions and more frequent questions as opposed to those who waited only one second.

The results of Marsh's experiment were dramatic. On tours *before* the experiment the visitor group asked about seven questions per tour, most of which were "safe" questions such as "Is the artist still alive?" But on the experimental tours, where the docents asked interpretive questions ("Why is this art?"), the visitors in turn asked seven times more interpretive questions per tour.

The research in the elementary school situation and that of Dr. Marsh in the museum indicate clearly that the trainer can hardly treat the question and answer period lightly. Certainly the question and answer period is an integral part of the learning (and lecturing) process. It, therefore, should be approached properly. Here are some skill pointers to ensure an effective Q & A period:

☐ A good way to effectively communicate that you really want questions is to leave a good block of time for that purpose at lecture's end. For example, if your session is 90 minutes long, leave 30 minutes for questions. Better still, divide the time equally. Nothing is more ineffective and irritating than for the instructor to say: "We've just about used up our time." (Question: Why did you?) "So we'll only be able to take a couple of questions." If you "can only take a couple of questions," you may be saying (or be perceived as saying):
   "My material really wasn't that profound or provocative. So why should I expect anyone to want to explore this stuff further?"
   "Those clods out there aren't bright enough to have more than a question or two anyhow."
   "My anxiety level is such that I don't care for any heckling."
☐ Provide 3″ × 5″ cards or a question form to participants to encourage the posing of questions. These procedures are ways to overcome the "embarrassment" of questioning a speaker before others.
☐ Respond to the questioner by name, if at all possible. ("John, has an interesting question. . . . ") The questioner and the audience will appreciate your attempt at personalization.

☐ Anticipate a possible lag in the posing of questions. If you do this, you won't panic over the silence. Instead, you can use the pressure of the silence to elicit a question from the group. The audience will probably be uncomfortable with the silence (unlike yourself!) and this will soon provoke a question. *Skill pointer*: The wait will *appear* longer than it actually is. If the silence won't break after you have given it a fair trial, you have two alternatives:

1. You can ask the audience a question to get things going again.
2. You can call it quits ("Thank you, I enjoyed working with you . . . " or "If there are no more questions, let's move on to . . . ").

☐ Avoid "windy" responses. This will give you more time to answer other questions as well as reduce the "yawn factor" by the group.

☐ Don't try to field every question yourself. Instead, toss back a question now and then to the group. Say something along this line: "I've got some ideas on that one. But I think it would be more helpful if we got some other views on this."

☐ Treat irrelevant questions graciously. Invite the questioner to see you at the break or after the talk. ("That's an interesting question, but I'm not sure everyone is interested in that area. See me after the session and we'll talk about it, O.K.?")

☐ Don't let any one person monopolize the question period. Instead, try to involve different participants. In a large lecture hall, select questions from different parts of the room.

☐ If you can't answer a question, admit it. Bluffing your way through a phoney response won't aid your credibility. You may wish to ask for help from the audience in some circumstances. ("I can't respond to this one. Can anyone help us on this?") Or offer to get the answer later.

☐ If there is a likely possibility that the question was not heard (large or noisy audience, poor acoustics, low voice of questioner) or not understood by the audience, repeat it before responding. Better still, *rephrase* it so that the questioner (and the other participants) will know you understood the question and are interested in it. Your paraphrasing of the question is preferable to asking the participant (or someone else) to restate it. Why? Because if you ask the participant to restate or repeat it, the obvious assumptions are that either you didn't understand it or it was poorly phrased. Of course, if you really didn't understand the question be candid about it. ("I'm sorry. I failed to catch your question. Could you try me again, please?")

☐ In responding to questions, make certain you show the interrogator that you feel good about his/her query. ("That's a very pertinent question," or "Your question has some profound implications," or "I'm glad you raised that point.") Positive reinforcement is a tremendous way to keep the questions coming to you.

☐ Avoid irritating your questioner with sarcastic responses, putdowns, argumentation, and other attempts at "one-upmanship." The cardinal rule is that you can't win an argument with a participant. The audience will swiftly rally to that person's side (the questioner is "one of them," you know) and the questions from the others will dry up fast.

☐ If possible, secure questions from participants *in advance* of the formal session. This type of pre-work will not only get people into the act very early on, but will provide a stimulus for others to pose questions in your question period. *A skill point:* Provide the question request form for this, as shown in Appendix 63, as an enticer and encourager.

☐ If time runs out and it appears that there still are a good number of unanswered questions, you may wish to leave the Question Request Form, as shown in Appendix 63, with your name and mailing address on it. This procedure will allow those who are "unsatisfied" to forward the form to you, and you can dictate responses on it later on.

Using an Audience Panel

An interesting way to elicit questions from a large audience is to establish a "participant question panel." A panel of three to four participants can pose the questions, with one of the panel members acting as moderator. To ensure that the panel works well, they should do enough "homework" so that they can ask questions with both insight and dispatch. In some cases, and if practical, you may wish to meet with the panelists in advance of the session. This will help preparation and ensure a smooth operation in the questioning period.

Asking Questions of Participants

In addition to responding to participant questions, don't hesitate to use some of your lecture time to ask the training group (or audience) questions. This approach will help to provide added involvement in the instructional process. However, before you pose a question to the participants, you should have a "good fix" on what constitutes a good question.

Most formal presenters would agree that a good question has these characteristics:

☐ *Brevity.* Long, windy, and wordy questions overload people's intake valves; they are sure-fire ways of creating confusion and thus turning participants off. So keep them "lean" and short.

☐ *Clarity.* Your question should zero in on one point alone. Overly-ambitious, multifaceted questions will only produce frustration, not thought.

☐ *Pertinence.* The question should be targeted to the subject being discussed. Session "enrichment" to the instructor runs the risk of being perceived as "out of the ball park" (out of context) by the participants.

☐ *Challenge.* Worthwhile questions are those that cause thought and provocation, and encourage creativity, evaluation, interpretation, comparisons, contrast, synthesis, reassessment, and the like. Accordingly, questions that only tax participants' memory banks are to be avoided.

In respect to questions that "challenge," trainers Patrick Suessmuth and Marit Strengels suggest that there are essentially three types:[8]

☐ *Convergent*—brings together facts to form a fact or theory. For example: "Based on the behaviors you saw in the film, what principles of motivation can you develop?"

☐ *Divergent*—Evokes interpretation, explanation, and translation. For example: "How would you explain the firm's reluctance to abandon 'yesterday's bread-winners' in its product line?"

☐ *Evaluative*—Requires the making of judgments (via exploration and analysis) about the facts presented. For example: "How would you characterize the company president as a team leader? As a coach? As a communicator?"

Suessmuth and Strengels also make a distinction between *closed* and *open* questions.[9] The former merely seek information, identification, confirmation and thus do not really encourage active participation. For example: "What did Peter Drucker say about delegation?" "What are the different types of job evaluation plans now in vogue?" "Would you say job enrichment is preferred to job enlargement?" Conversely, open questions, which don't "box people in" and thus cause more active involvement, take these forms:

☐ *Subjective question*—What is your thought on the values of the young worker? Can we assume that management was correct in this case? Is "directive" leadership best in a situation that _____?

☐ *Objective question*—What elements make for an effective performance review system? What distin-guishes successful employment interviews from unsuccessful ones?

☐ *Problem question*—Given the climate that exists in many organizations today, what are the prospects for a viable organization development program? What is the best way to mount the career ladder in your case, given those difficulties? How would you go about delegating a particular responsibility (e.g., P.R.) when you know your boss is vitally concerned about this area?

Another essential form of questioning is that which relates to *follow-up* or *probing*. This type of question enables you and the group to learn what is on the participant's mind. Suessmuth and Strengels offer five reasons to use a probing question:[10]

☐ *To clarify an answer.* At times a participant may offer a response that definitely requires clarification. A good way to do this is to ask another participant to re-state what was said. A good, low-key clarifying probe for this is to say: "What did Emma mean by _____?" and sum up what was originally said. The restatement on your part is essential since it is a sure bet that a significant number of the group didn't hear (listening failure) the answer in the first place.

☐ *To justify an answer.* By asking "Why?" or "Why that?" you are augmenting the group's critical awareness.

☐ *To refocus an answer.* This is essential to getting the discussion back on track.

☐ *To expand an answer.* This is easy to do. Merely express puzzlement and wait. Or you can simply ask: "Could someone develop that thought for us?"

☐ *To redirect the answer.* This means involving other participants in addition to the original respondent. There is, of course, a natural temptation to move on to the next question once a response is secured, but we may be overlooking an opportunity to get others into the act. They may have some other insights on the issue, too, which can enrich the discussion.

Paul Mills and Bernard Roberts, partners in a New York City communications skill firm, offer seven types of probes—essentially skill pointers—to encourage a participant to keep talking:[11]

☐ *Non-verbal probes* such as a nod of the head or a smile.

☐ *Short verbal probes* such as "Uh, huh?" "Yes?" "I understand?"

☐ *"W" (or journalistic) word probes* (who, where, when, what, why, how) which elicit a great variety of information, for example: "What does that mean?" "Why did it develop as it did?"

☐ *Statement probes* such as "Tell me more" or "I would appreciate it if you could expand on that point."

☐ *Echo probes* which entail a repetition of some of the participant's words.

☐ *Reflective probes* wherein one changes the words but retains the meaning.

☐ *Specialized reflective probes* whereby one implies more than the participant actually intended, e.g., "You feel *very uneasy* about taking this up with your boss?"

It should also be mentioned that the basic skills one needs to keep the ball in the participant's court and thus to learn how the participant sees his/her world, are these: good listening ability, patience, an inviting style, and avoidance of argumentation and one-upmanship. A suggestion: Study the talk show hosts. You'll note that the better ones show a great deal of interest in what the participant has to say. They are neither enamored with their own voice nor their own wisdom. Since they truly want the other person to get into the act and have his/her say, they present an encouraging, low-key, questioning style.

How To Elicit Responses—Skill Pointers

If the learner learns best by active involvement in the learning process, we should think in terms of techniques to engage the learner, i.e., getting him/her to respond. Training House, Inc., Princeton, N.J., offers these eight techniques to secure responses of all our participants:[12]

1. Present the question. Wait 10 seconds. Restate the question. Give everyone a chance to develop a response. Then select someone to respond.
2. Provide some questions which everyone can answer, e.g., why might employees be reluctant to assume delegated authority? or what is a significant barrier to presenting ideas to the boss?
3. For more complex, thought-provoking questions, have everyone prepare a written response. Circulate, read a number of responses, and then call on one or more participants.
4. Provide a question which requires a guess or estimate, e.g., what is the last thing you should do when making a decision? which activity consumes the greatest amount of a manager's time?
5. Provide a handout having questions and space for the answers. Have the group prepare their answers in writing and then secure responses.
6. Provide a pre-printed response sheet which requires completion during the session; e.g., entering words or phrases on a flowchart or checklist.
7. Distribute a self-quiz to get a quick reading on knowledge, skills or attitudes. Secure responses via oral reports, show of hands, or slips of paper on particular items.
8. Present a question which is likely to polarize the group, e.g., how many believe money is the most important motivator for managers? for secretaries? for assembly line workers? for computer programmers? Ask for a show of hands to get responses.

Added skill points:

1. In most cases participants will respond voluntarily or enter into things with a little encouragement. If you do call on someone at the outset ("Can you help us on this, Pat?"), this will break the ice and others will then respond reasily. To ensure that others do enter in, simply ask: "Any other thoughts on this?" or "How else might this be done?"
2. Involve the shy participant by calling on him/her occasionally to field an easy question or one in which he/she has special knowledge or experience.
3. If you wish everyone in the group to respond to a given question, use the "circular whip" technique (see page 36).

Involving Individuals

The techniques to secure participation *before* the talk starts, as previously described, relate to the involvement of the *total* audience or group. It also may be desirable to involve actively *one or two* participants in the program for various purposes. Some examples follow:

☐ Appoint various individuals to execute these special roles:

1. Stretch monitor—This participant stands up and calls "stretch" whenever he/she feels it's needed.
2. Handout distributors
3. Card collectors (the cards have participant-prepared questions or comments on them for response by the speaker)
4. A timer (if needed)
5. Jargon stopper—This assignment entails standing up or raising one's hand when an unexplained or undefined concept, word, or phrase is used by the lecturer or a fellow participant.
6. Card-carrying member—Appoint four or five participants to display large posters bearing key points or topics in large print. The procedure may be used at the outset to indicate overall topic coverage, possibly midway in the lecture to summarize or highlight points already made, or at talk's end as a

Message is in the receiver	Watch your wording
Make EGO appeals	Anticipate resistance

Figure 18-3. Example of posters displayed by participants to highlight key points made by a presenter.

summary. As an example of the summary at the end of a talk on persuasive communication and/or selling, the four posters shown in Figure 18-3 might be used.

☐ Conduct a demonstration role play involving yourself and a participant or two participants (e.g., on a sales problem or a disciplinary problem).

☐ Have two participants conduct an impromptu interview that may set the stage for your comments as speaker (e.g., the difficulty of introducing change in an organization, or how to deal with a mid-career manager who has "plateaued out").

☐ Have one or more participants present a short report on a previously assigned topic.

Key Points

1. Although audience/participant groups respond tepidly to lectures, this method is still widely used by trainers, instructors, and teachers of all sorts.
2. The greatest weaknesses of the lecture method are that lectures are boring and hard to take and retention is low.
3. The strong point of the lecture method is that it is a "quick and dirty" way to impart information to others.
4. The lecture method is something of an anachronism in light of everything we know about adult learning and the communication process.
5. Much advice abounds on how to give a better lecture. However, a lecture is a lecture . . . is a lecture . . . is a lecture.
6. While the idea of improving the techniques of lecturing is O.K., a better approach to meeting a

training need is to ask whether another more dynamic method is available.

7. If one must lecture, one should at least start things off in a participative way.
8. Participative devices used midway in the talk are also helpful.
9. The question and answer session, another "must," can be made productive by *modeling* and *extended wait-time*.
10. Asking the participant group questions and involving individual participants in various ways helps, too.
11. Finally, the trainer is well advised to think in terms of lecturettes and short talks if a lecture is really necessary.

References

1. McCarthy, Colman, *The Washington Post* (October 31, 1987).
2. Ricks, D. M., "Barriers to Industry—A Successful Trainer Tells Why He Doesn't Hire Academics," *Instructional Innovator* (January 1981), pp. 11–13.
3. Miller, D. B., *Personal Vitality,* Addison-Wesley Publishing Company, Reading, Mass. (1977), p. 129.
4. Bullock, D., "Lecture-Driven Instruction," *National Society for Performance Improvement Journal* (April 1980), p. 15.
5. Hartson, David, "Orchestrating The Teachable Moment," *Training News* (February 1984), pp. 6–7.
6. Bradford, L. P., "Are There Any Questions?—How to Plan the Question and Answer Period," *Adult Leadership* (July–August 1952), pp. 5–8.
7. Marsh, C., "Opening the Way for Questions," *Northeast Training News* (October 1980), p. 8.
8. Suessmuth, P., and Strengels, M., "Training Ideas Found Useful: Questions, Answers and Socrates," *Canadian Training Methods* (March–April 1971), p. 26.
9. Suessmuth, P., and Strengels, M., "Wake Them Up—Ask the Right Questions," *Training in Business and Industry* (May 1972), p. 33.
10. Suessmuth, P., and Strengels, M., "The Follow-Up Question," *Training in Business and Industry* (February 1974), p. 41.
11. Mills, P., and Roberts, B., "Learn To Guide And Control Discussion," *Successful Meetings* (March 1981), pp. 96–97.
12. "Eight Techniques for Eliciting Responses," *News 'N Views* (Training House, Inc., Princeton, N.J.) (March/April 1984).

Recommended Reading

Broadwell, Martin, "In Defense of the Good Old Lecture Method," *Training/HRD,* August 1976, pp. 25–26.

After citing the pros and cons of the lecture method, the author presents a way to overcome its drawbacks; namely, by delivering a "programmed lecture" wherein participants are given problem-solving activities to work on as the lecture proceeds. This procedure keeps learners accountable for results and provides a meaningful goal and a reason to listen.

Brown, David S., "The Lecture . . . And How to Make It More Effective," *Training Director's Journal*, December 1960, pp. 17–22.

This provides pointers to improve the lecture method, particularly when the lecturer is from "the outside." Key points: Help the lecturer understand his/her role and the audience's composition; help him/her in the planning for the lecture; discuss and evaluate the lecturer's contribution.

Feldman, Michael, "Planning For An Indirect Training Style," *Training and Development Journal*, October 1982, pp. 79–81.

To overcome liabilities which accrue from a training style relying on the lecture approach, the trainer can involve participants via use of trainee experiences, use of trainer questions, use of previous trainee statements, positions, and opinions, and use of past, prevailing, and possible future trainee feelings and attitudes.

McCarthy, John J., "The Lecture Method," *Sales Training*, June 1976, pp. 22–23, 34–40.

This lists and compares the advantages and disadvantages of the lecture method. The article also provides tips concerning ways to maximize the use of an outside speaker.

Milcal, Paul J., "Socratic Is More Emphatic," *Training/HRD*, March 1981, pp. 58–59.

This recommends the use of the questioning approach to increase learner interest, involvement, rapport with the presenter, and retention of learning.

Tagliere, D. A., "Questions: Use Them to Help Others Discover Ideas," *Sales Meetings*, January 1972, pp. 45, 90–92.

"Inquiry learning" is accomplished via questions on cards given to participants plus encouraging participants to ask questions of their own.

Thiagarajan, Sivasailam, "In Praise of Impromptu Instruction (And Some Practical Tips on How to Do It)," *National Society for Performance and Instruction Journal*, April 1980, pp. 8–9.

Presenters can augment their effectiveness if they know their subject matter, plan and organize the presentation, prepare for adjustments in the plan should this be necessary, conduct a trial run with a member of the target population, avoid note cards to ensure spontaneity, demonstrate ideas by using participants, avoid being trapped by tangential issues.

Vinci, Vince, "Eleven Ways to Hold Your Audience's Attention," *Meetings and Conventions*, May 1974, pp. 83–84, 142–146.

Key points: Zero in on a *universal* interest of your group, think "big" when using visuals and gestures, ask questions, use participants' experiences, try to develop and use a "theatrical" style, relate all activities to your theme, repeat intermittently the main message of your presentation, look for and use new approaches, provide inputs which require the use of more than one sense, use special appeals or motivators, secure participation.

USING PARTICIPATIVE METHODS TO EVALUATE TRAINING

Education is what survives when what has been learned has been forgotten.

—B. F. Skinner, leading American exponent of behavioral psychology

The classic model of training evaluation requires the trainer to consider evaluation as taking place at *four* levels:[1]

1. Participant reaction level (attitude or feeling regarding satisfaction-dissatisfaction).
2. Learning (observable or measurable behavior change) in the classroom or training situation.
3. New or changed behavior (performance) on the job.
4. Measurable impact of the training on the organization, e.g., increases in productivity, sales, quality, profitability and reductions in cost, waste, scrap, accidents, grievances, absenteeism, customer complaints.

It will be noted that as we move from Levels 1 to 4 the data become more objective and thus more meaningful. Most training, however, is evaluated only at Level 1 since that information is quite easy to obtain. Conversely, evaluation at Levels 3 and 4 requires much more work and sophistication (ideally, before and after techniques coupled with experimental and control group procedures) and thus is left by the trainers to the researchers and statisticians.

Participant Reaction Level

Participant reaction data, which only report attitudes and feelings, obviously are not "hard" data; that is to say, they don't attempt to measure changes in behavior or performance. In fact, research psychologists and others typically use such terms as "happiness data" and "whoopie sheets" to describe the usual self-report feedback rendered by enthusiastic and grateful participants. The enthusiasm, they say, is almost certain, given an adequately interesting and active program, hotel/motel food, a friendly trainer, a chance to get away from the usual office routines (and even the family in some cases), and a chance to have a few drinks with old buddies.

Nevertheless, participant reactions are still useful information for these reasons:

☐ They are easy and economical to gather and certainly better than no data at all.
☐ They do meet the trainer's need to know how well his/her efforts have been perceived. (Trainers have egos that require stroking, too!)
☐ Certainly management also wants to know how well the training is being received by the participants. If the trainees don't like it, there's little point in supporting it.

☐ If the trainees are not satisfied with the training, the likelihood is that is will be ignored in whole or in part. Conversely, if the training is deemed to be worthwhile, there is at least a possibility it will be applied. Thus, it is desirable to know what the satisfaction-dissatisfaction ratio is.

☐ They can be a guide to program improvement.

In the paragraphs that follow, a number of involving, group-in-action methods to collect participant data are described. They are easy to apply and are intended to serve as a supplement, *not* a substitution, for questionnaire-type data. Questionnaires are important for they permit the garnering of participant reactions in a *systematic* way. The trainer is thus able to learn, for example, that 75% of the trainees felt that learning for them was "high", 15% learned at a "moderate" level, 5% learned in a "minor" way, and the other 5% were "not sure." The trainer may also learn that a majority of the participants favored small group work over lectures, the day was too long, and the ventilation was poor much of the time.

As to group-in-action methods of evaluation, they serve these useful purposes:

☐ They stimulate trainee thinking about personal learning. Group interaction is an effective means of opening new avenues of thought about the completed training experience and the need for growth or improvement.

☐ The participant's ideas or questions about the program can be "checked out" (reality tested) with others. Conversely, the questionnaire procedure, if used alone, requires preparation of responses in total *isolation* from one's peers.

☐ Aside from personal learning, ideas for program improvement (methods, administration, facilities) can be obtained.

☐ If the training program is a highly participative one, evaluation procedures that involve participants are a logical way to conclude the training effort.

The best evaluation design, then, at the reaction level, is to use this *paired* approach:

1. *Begin* with the collection of data via group-in-action methods.
2. *Finish* with the administration of a formal questionnaire. Some trainers may wish to use a "fun-type" questionnaire, such as in Appendix 64. (Need training always be grim?)

The following paragraphs offer "how-to-do-it" suggestions for a number of group-in-action evaluation techniques.

Self-Appraisal

Assign participants to dyads, triads, or buzz groups of four to five participants, and have them discuss their learning in one of the following ways:

☐ *Open-end assignment.* Ask participants to respond to two critical questions such as these: Where do you think you "are" now? Where do you think you "were" when you started?

☐ *Expectations.* Ask participants to respond to these paired questions: What were your expectations for this course? To what degree were they met?

☐ *Course objectives assessment.* Ask participants to assess and discuss their learning in relation to stated course objectives.

☐ *Individual goals assessment.* On the assumption that participants were asked to state specifically their learning goals at the outset (on a sheet of paper, on a form, on a flipchart sheet), have them discuss the degree to which their goals were met. *Note*: In some situations, such as in a time management course, the goals may be both personal and organizational.

☐ *Sentence completion approach.* Provide participants with a sentence completion form, such as the one in Appendix 65 for individual completion and subsequent discussion in small groups.

To maximize the benefits from any one of the five self-appraisal and small group activities just listed, encourage participants (secure volunteers) to share the nature and extent of their new learning with the total group.

Circular Whip

For a quick, easy-to-accomplish assessment about participant learning, form a circle (maximum of 15) and "whip around" it, each participant making a statement concerning the one most significant learning in the course for him/her. This procedure readily generates considerable data about group learning. It is particularly helpful to encourage the "reluctant dragons" to admit that they, too, learned something!

The statements offered by participants may be subject to total group discussion, depending on course objectives and time limits. They may also be used as a "lead in" to the completion of the formal questionnaire, which elicits more comprehensive and systematic data concerning program reactions.

Note:

1. The statements to which the participants might respond in the whip activity could take one of these forms:

   ☐ The most significant thing to me in this program was _____.

☐ What I intend to apply (or do) on the job as a result of this course is _____.

☐ I now see (or understand) that _____ _____.

☐ I intend to do less of _____.

☐ I intend to do more of _____.

2. Following the use of the circular whip to secure statements about individual learnings, the group may be asked (one statement per participant, again) for ideas to strengthen the program.

Using the Fishbowl

With the aid of the fishbowl or group-on-group observation technique, all participants can be involved in a group assessment of the completed training. The procedures are as follows:

1. Decide the evaluation area that is to be discussed. Typical assignments: What did we learn? What did we like about the course and what did we not like (or strengths and weaknesses of the course)? What would have helped to make this course (even) more effective? How can we apply the learning "back home?"

2. Divide the total group into smaller discussion groups of six to eight participants. Two or three fishbowls may be conducted simultaneously.

3. Let the inner group (Group A) discuss the assigned topic for 15–20 minutes with the outer group (Group B) observing.

4. Let Group B switch places and roles and now become the discussant group; Group A is now the observing group. Group B's task is to comment on the observations or critique developed by Group A as well to respond to the question assigned to Group A.

5. As an optional procedure, repeat Steps 3 and 4 an additional time.

6. Allow time for a final, group-at-large discussion.

Using Movement: Discerning Learning Categories

☐ Ask group members to stand and then position themselves at one of three points in the room representing high learning, moderate learning, and limited or minor learning. In effect, this is a "human continuum." Then ask for volunteers (two or three per location) to explain why they assigned themselves to their particular learning category.

☐ In a highly experiential program, ask everyone to stand up. Then ask *one* group member (a volunteer will do) to "sort" or "assign" the total group into three categories (at three locations in the room): those who learned a great deal, those who learned a moder-

ate amount, and those who learned relatively little. In effect, this is an exercise in giving feedback. Ask group members to be seated at their new locations and to hold a group-at-large discussion on these "assignments."

Note:

1. This technique may not be appropriate for the "novice" trainer for it entails skill in "group process."

2. The assumptions in this activity are that there is a small participant group; that everyone now knows everyone else quite well including their degree of learning; that giving and receiving feedback is an appropriate part of the learning process.

Using Art

☐ Have group members informally develop a "running mural" (on flipcharts) about the course, starting the first morning and carrying through to the final session. The mural, as an art form, requires that statements be made only in graphic, illustrative, diagrammatic, or pictorial form. *Note:* This may take considerable wall space.

☐ Have group members in an intensive management seminar respond in a graphic or illustrative way to the data requested in the triangle shown in Figure 19-1. The art work is to be completed *twice*: at the outset and at program's end. The idea is to have participants note any difference in their perception about leadership, communication, etc.

The first completion of the triangle may be treated as a personal thing and simply filed away until program's end. At that time both "artistic" renditions, i.e., pre- and post-course, may be discussed in pairs or trios.

Figure 19-1. Example of a geometrical figure for eliciting data from participants about pre- and post-course perceptions.

Individual Course Critique

☐ *Posting technique.* Ask participants to take a sheet of paper and jot down their reactions to the course or program in three categories: *content* or subject matter, *methods,* and *administration.* Then have participants post their ideas to three flipchart sheets on the wall bearing those category headings. Lead a general discussion about the total group's posted ideas.

Note: To speed up the posting operation, have two or three separate sets of the three flipcharts available to participants.

☐ *Individual Role Play.* Toward the end of the program, provide participants with a task assignment sheet such as the one in Appendix 66.

Note:

1. The rationale for this activity is that it forces the participant to think through carefully what the course was trying to accomplish, what was learned, etc. In effect, it provides an opportunity to create a personalized *summation* of the total learning experience.

2. In a small group of 8–12 *all* participants should be asked to give their presentations. In a larger group ask for six to eight volunteers to do this.

3. Encourage the listening participants to applaud the presenters after their talks.

Small Group Course Critique

☐ At program's end, divide the total group into small group evaluation or critique teams. Give one or more groups this assignment: What suggestions do you have to improve *course content?* Give a second group (or set of groups) this assignment: What suggestions for course improvement do you have that relate to *training methods?* Give a third group this assignment: What suggestions do you have to improve this program *other than* in the areas of content and methods? Consider course length, course administration, physical conditions, trainer effectiveness, etc. After the small group work, secure reports orally and post the main ideas on flipcharts.

☐ In an extended (long-term) program, set up evaluation committees at the outset to assess and report back on course effectiveness. The reports should be in writing and summed up orally to the total group. Be sure to provide guidelines to the teams concerning the course elements to consider in the evaluation process.

☐ One way to wrap-up a program is to have everyone stand up and form a circle. Ask participants to close their eyes and think of what the experience has meant to them. Allow about a minute or two for this. Now ask participants "to come back" and describe the completed training in *one* word or phrase. (Anticipate words/phrases such as "informative," "eye opening," "challenging," "not sure.") In an experiential training program the question may be posed as follows: "Using one word, what are you *feeling* now that the training is over?" (Possible responses: "exhilarated," "helped," "fulfilled," "sad.")

Learning (Changed Behavior) in the Classroom

As previously indicated, participant reactions are always of interest and, given an intelligent and well-organized training effort, generally comforting to the trainer. However, the validity of "happiness ratings" is very much on the low side insofar as real learning is concerned. A better measurement is of the actual learning that has taken place in the classroom. Here we find out not only what participants feel, think, or believe, but what they now can *do* differently as a result of the training. We can accomplish such an assessment in several ways.

☐ *Observation.* It is possible to note differences in performance levels when participants engage in activities such as:

1. *Writing letters*—Samples brought into class at the start of the training can be compared with letters (and reports) produced after the training; or the new letters can be checked against the criteria advocated by the training program.

2. *Delivering talks*—In public speaking training the before and after performance can be appraised via videotape or by ratings prepared by the participants and/or the trainer.

3. *Role playing*—How one coaches an employee, deals with a reluctant customer, interviews a job applicant, etc., can be appraised, again, on a pre- and post-training basis and/or in relation to course standards. If the role plays have been videotaped, further substantiation is possible.

4. *Case study*—How participants attack (analyze) problems presented in cases, on a before-and-after basis, can provide evidence of change (new learning). The change data may be gathered on an observational basis (somewhat subjective, of course) or via the preparation of pre- and post-course written case analyses.

5. *Field trips*—How well participants collect and analyze data, based on criteria or principles developed in the classroom, is another indicator of actual learning.

☐ *Action plans.* The nature of action plans or contracts— i.e., commitments to engage in a new behavior—can indicate the degree to which the training has been internalized. Of course, pledges and promises are not necessarily the same as on-the-job performance, but they are a hopeful sign. Also, with the right type of follow-up by the trainer and reinforcement by the participant's boss, plans for change are quite likely to be fulfilled.

☐ *Attitude surveys.* Although changes in attitude obviously are not "hard" data as much as changes in performance or behavior, attitude changes do indicate, nevertheless, that a change has taken place. Thus, if a training program is designed to reduce bias or prejudice toward certain groups, before-and-after attitude surveys are helpful to reflect that change. It is hoped that new attitudes will be carried over to the job situation and be reflected in new on-the-job behavior. Again, supervisory and/or organizational support for the new attitudes are essential to implement and maintain them.

Change in On-the-Job Behavior

Change in observable behavior in the classroom, as previously described, is an indicator that the new learning *may* be carried over to the job. However, this is hardly conclusive evidence. What is needed is "harder" data about actual on-the-job performance such as:

☐ Implementation of action plans producing measurable/observable change.
☐ Supervisor's day-to-day observations concerning changed behavior.
☐ Employee reports concerning behavior change in their bosses.

The two sections that follow provide some pointers concerning how supervisors can be encouraged to support and monitor possible behavior change.

Involving Supervisors in the Evaluation Process

Far too many participants attend training programs in which there is little or no involvement by their bosses. That is to say, their supervisors may not really know why *their* subordinates are going to the training, what the specific goals of their courses are, what was actually learned at the courses, and how the new learning may be applied to their jobs. The following procedures are suggested to get supervisors more fully "into the act" and thus help them to overcome their abdication of responsibility.

The form in Figure 19-2 is designed, first, to secure the understanding of both the supervisor and the participant as to the nature and value of the course's major (high impacting) goals. *Both* parties are thus asked to

identify high-impacting goals and to rank and discuss them as to their value or importance *before* the training begins. Secondly, following the completion of the training, the supervisor is expected to talk to the subordinate about the realization of course goals in the training situation and the development of action plans to implement course learnings. Involving the supervisor in a postcourse discussion should be a logical procedure once the supervisor has identified, ranked, and discussed course goals with the participant on a pre-course basis.

Involvement of Supervisors through Group Audit Sessions

With proper planning and organizing, the key "clients" (participants' superiors) who authorize the training can be involved fully in its evaluation. The following is a system to provide this involvement.[2]

Step 1. Invite the clients to a two-session audit (or evaluation) program.

Step 2. At the first session (one hour), explain the overall program. Ask the clients to gather data concerning program results. They, obviously, are best positioned to note and collect data (via discussions with participants, performance observations, etc.) on how the completed training affects their operations. Tell them that they will work in teams at session two, comparing critically their collected data.

Step 3. At session two (about four hours) the clients, in small groups or teams, are asked to do two things (in about one hour):
  a. List (on flipcharts) positive results and prioritize them.
  b. List (on flipcharts) negative or unachieved results and prioritize them.
  Note: By keeping program weaknesses separate from its strengths, clients can zero in more readily on program areas requiring improvement.

Step 4. Conduct a general session (three hours) with all client teams who report back on their data. This sharing of data (all flipcharts are posted on the wall) gives the clients a fuller set of data for their subsequent evaluation.

Step 5. A consolidation (in general session) is made of all the teams' lists, one list for strengths and one for weaknesses. Priorities are also established.

Step 6. The trainer who is concerned with the particular program reacts to the lists.

Step 7. The program administrator indicates the nature of and timetable for the necessary follow-up action.

Evaluation meetings of key training programs, as just described, should be conducted at least annually.

Value of Goals—A Pre-Course Assessment

Learning Goals in Customer Relations Course:	Identification of Major or High-Impacting Goals (Use check mark)		Weighted Goal Assessment (Use a % for each goal; total must = 100%)		Weighted Assessment After Joint Discussion (use % re each goal)	Goal Accomplishment: Participant's Post-Course Assessment (use % re each goal)	Joint Development of an Action Plan (Check when completed)
	Per Participant (1)	Per Superior (2)	Per Participant (3)	Per Superior (4)	(5)	(6)	(7)
1. Improved product (or service) knowledge		√		25%	20%	30%	
2. How to deal with frustrations	√		25%		15%	80%	
3. How to handle difficult customers	√		60%		20%	95%	
4. How to handle customers to ensure repeat business		√		40%	30%	50%	
5. How to be a more effective member of the customer relations team		√		25%	10%	95%	
6. How to keep up enthusiasm (prevent "burnout")	√	√	15%	10%	5%	90%	
			100%	100%	100%		

Note
1. Differences in pre-course assessments (columns 1–4) are to be discussed and "negotiated" (column 5).
2. Participant's post-course assessment (column 6) is to be discussed with one's superior and an action plan is to be developed for each goal as may be indicated (column 7).
3. Complete the form in duplicate—one copy is for the participant, one copy is for the superior. (The trainer may also want a copy.)

Figure 19-2. Form for involving supervisors in setting goals for subordinate training and in evaluating the training after it is completed.

Measurable Impact of the Training on the Organization

Evaluation of training at this level—the bottom line or pay-off level—is not accomplished through group methods such as those suggested for the prior three levels of evaluation. Rather, since "hard" data is desired—e.g., increased profitability/productivity; increased sales; better service to customers; reductions in cost, waste, errors, defects, turnover, absenteeism, customer complaints, grievances —pertinent information is obtained from records and reports including those already produced systematically.

Daily Pulse-Taking

The best training takes place when participants regularly evaluate what they experience. This is desirable from several standpoints:

☐ It forces the participants to think about what they have learned and how it can be applied to their jobs.
☐ It gives the trainer feedback so that he/she knows how well the training is being given and received—what is deemed valuable, what is not—and thereby permits the making of program adjustments to the extent practicable. The alternative is to wait until program's end

for the feedback. By then, it obviously is too late to improve things.

Assessment of Participant Learning

To encourage thinking and *public* statements about what was learned, this procedure may be followed:

1. Ask participants to write quickly ("auto-brainstorming") on a piece of paper "the ten learning points for you from today's work."
2. Then conduct a "round robin," asking each of them to select the one item from the ten they had identified in Step 1 and to report it orally to the total group.

Good assessment procedures also call for participant introspection about what the participant plans to do about training needs that the program may uncover. Accordingly, the Daily Self-Assessment of Learning sheet given in Appendix 67, may be of value. It may be administered in any one of the following ways, depending on your training philosophy:

☐ It may be retained by the participant on a private basis. Although the assurance of privacy may encourage candor in its completion, without the stimulus of at least some discussion with another participant the likelihood of it being merely tucked into the notebook and forgotten is quite great.
☐ It may be shared in a pair or trio. This procedure should provide some motivation, where needed, to overcome what might just be a paper exercise. The pair or trio approach will provide a good degree of privacy, too.
☐ Upon completion, one writer suggests that the form may be handed in to the trainer.[3] A code number, selected by the participant, is used to ensure both anonymity and candor. The next morning the trainer reports back on the forms before returning them. The idea is to let the total group hear how others intend to use the new learning, thereby expanding and/or reinforcing the interest in self-improvement.

Assessment of Program Effectiveness

At the end of Day 1 of a three- to five-day program, it may be desirable to secure feedback from the participants concerning "how things went." To do this, the trainer can draw a five-point continuum on the flipchart and ask participants to respond to the several points on it by a show of hands. Examples of items for the continuum are given in Figure 19-3.

Figure 19-3. Example of scales that can be used in an evaluation procedure involving the flipchart.

Another way of using the continuum is to place it on a wall. The five degrees may actually be posted via flipchart sheets at five wall positions or just pointed to in a general way: "'Strongly Agree' is here;" "'Agree' is here;" etc. Then let participants position themselves *physically,* in relation to the five degrees, to indicate their reaction or feeling about a given evaluation question.

Another approach to the daily critique is to give participants the guide sheet given in Appendix 68 and follow these procedures:

1. Participants individually complete the form.
2. Small groups consolidate the individual data on flipcharts.
3. The group at large discusses the small group reports.

If it is desired to gather data about the day's work in a more systematic and quantitative way, the participant questionnaire given in Appendix 69, may be of value. The data should be summarized, reported back to the participants the following morning, and discussed with them.

One trainer reports the use of a daily close-of-business evaluation session wherein the trainers meet with trainee representatives for 20 to 30 minutes. The areas of evaluation include pace; problems with materials (too easy? too hard? poorly organized? instructions unclear?); small groups interaction problems (nonparticipators, dominators, personality conflicts); problems with the instructions from the trainer; housekeeping or environmental needs such as temperature and break procedures.[4]

Some trainers may prefer to use the last half-hour of class time for this *joint* critique because of its importance. In any case, the advantages of the participant-trainer critique are:

☐ Participant input can enrich the critique process. Visualize the trainers discussing an aspect of the day's work that needs strengthening and, after considerable discussion, one of the trainers says: "Let's get a participant view on this issue. I don't think that we, as trainers, have all the answers on this issue by any means."

☐ Participants have the opportunity to observe a democratic model for critique—one that stresses feedback from participants, as opposed to the program conductors only listening to themselves.

☐ Participants are provided with an added opportunity for participation. There is a feeling that they have at least some "ownership" of the training program.

A final procedure: Call attention to a flipchart sheet on the wall entitled "Unfinished Business" with three catagories on it: "Want More Of," "Needs Clarification," and "Additions." Advise the group they may go to the flipchart and enter their ideas on it now, at day's end, or anytime tomorrow.

The Participant Group—A Self-Appraisal

A fascinating activity for a participant group is to examine its own culture, that is, the norms that govern its behavior and thus give the group its unique personality and identity. This analysis is particularly helpful and appropriate in an experiential training program, where much of the learning comes from the group's own experience and appraisal of it.

The exercise that follows should be given at the end of a fairly intensive training program, typically of four days or more. If it is done sooner, the group may not have enough data about itself for meaningful analysis.

Understanding Social Norms: An Exercise

Background information for trainer. Every social institution—organizational, family, school, church, recreational—has a system of social norms. Norms, of course, are the *unwritten* rules—the "O.K.'s" and the "no-no's"—that govern the behavior of the members of the social group. For example, executives don't pack a lunch although it is O.K. on occasion to eat at the desk;

secretaries refer to their bosses as "Mr. _____" rather than by their first name; the lab people, but not the sales personnel, may dress informally.

Norms give an organization order, predictability, stability. On the other hand, norms may not really help productivity or creativity (e.g., disagreement with the boss is taboo). They persist nevertheless, because they are seldom questioned.[5]

Procedure.

1. Introduce briefly the concept of norms, using the prior information or similar data.
2. Break the total participant group into small groups of three to five persons.
3. Give the following instruction to the small groups: "To help us understand the concept of social norms more fully, let's consider our class as a social system. Let's analyze the norms that have developed in this classroom. For example, the smokers have been assigned to the right side of the room; neckties are worn only to dinner. So your task in the next 20 minutes is to identify as many norms as you can that influence our behavior in this classroom. O.K.?"
4. The small groups meet for 20 minutes.
5. Secure data from the small groups and enter on flipcharts.
6. Post the flipchart sheets on the wall.
7. Set up a tri-column on a flipchart as in Figure 19-4.
8. Working from the posted data that have been developed by the small groups, ask the group at large to classify the norms into the three groupings. (Sample answers have been provided.)
9. Ask the small groups to meet again for 10–15 minutes, giving them this assignment: "Should *on-the-job* group norms be analyzed? What are the advantages of such an analysis, if any, and the risks, if any?"
10. Secure small group reports and enter on a T-column the advantages and risks discussed.
11. Hold a general discussion of the significance of the exercise.

Key Points

1. Evaluation of training may be conducted at the (a) reaction level, (b) classroom (change in behavior) level, (c) on the job level, and (d) organizational level.
2. While participant reactions are essentially "soft" or subjective data, they do tell us how satisfied par-

NORMS IN OUR CLASSROOM

Helpful to Learning	Not Helpful to Learning	Neutral
O.K. to disagree with trainer.	Everyone takes same seat all week.	Slow return from coffee break and lunch.
Use of first names exclusively	People who came together stay together	Profanity is used.
	Holding back of real feelings (by some)	

Figure 19-4. Example of a tri-column used in an exercise on understanding social norms.

ticipants are with their training, what they feel they learned, how the course may be improved, etc.

3. Participant reactions may be obtained via both group-in-action methods and individually prepared questionnaires.

4. Participant reactions may be obtained via various group-in-action devices including self-appraisal, the circular whip, the fishbowl, movement, art, and individual and group critique.

5. Learning accomplished in the classroom may be ascertained via observation, review of proposed action plans, and attitude surveys.

6. Learning transferred to the job may be ascertained via study of implemented action plans and supervisory and employee reports.

7. Impact of the learning on organizational effectiveness may be measured via "hard" data such as reports on productivity, sales, costs, defects, and turnover.

8. The best evaluation procedures are those that involve "the clients"—i.e., managers and supervisors at appropriate levels in the organization.

9. Evaluation concerns should extend to daily pulse taking as well as end-of-course assessments. This procedure will enable changes in the program as may be necessary and practicable.

References

1. Kirkpatrick, D. L., "Techniques for Evaluating Training Programs," a four-part series beginning in the November 1955 issue of the *Training Director's Journal.*

2. Coffman, L., "An Easy Way to Effectively Evaluate Program Results," *Training and Development Journal* (August 1979), pp. 28–32, and "Successful Training Program Evaluation," *Training and Development Journal* (October 1980), pp. 84–87.

3. Murtha, T. J., "Make Your Course Evaluation Work," *Training and Development Journal* (July 1979), pp. 50–51.

4. Stevenson, G., "Evaluating Training Daily," *Training and Development Journal* (May 1980), pp. 120–122.

See Steele, F., and Jenks, S., *The Feel of the Work Place: Understanding and Improving Organization Climate,* "Social Norms and Organizational Climate," Addison-Wesley Publishing Company, Reading, Mass. (1977), Ch. 4, for additional background on norms.

Recommended Reading

Brinkerhoff, Robert O., "Making Evaluation More Useful," *Training and Development Journal,* December 1981, pp. 66–70.

This is an overall and very current view of evaluation based on the Evaluation Training Consortium project founded by the U.S. Office of Special Education. The author is director of the ETC project.

Phillips, J. J., *Handbook of Training Evaluation and Measurement Methods,* Gulf Publishing Co., Houston, (1983).

This is a comprehensive source book to aid the trainer in evaluating the training effort. The book shows how to evaluate management and supervisory training (tough areas to assess) in addition to skills areas. Essential statistical approaches are treated in understandable ways.

HOW TO OVERCOME THE TRANSFER PROBLEM

Nothing is more terrible than activity without insight.

—Thomas Carlyle (1795–1881),
Scottish essayist and historian

The art of teaching is the art of assisting discovery.

—Mark Van Doren (1894–19–),
American poet, critic and
editor

Up to this point we have been introduced to (or possibly reacquainted with) a broad range of training techniques. All of these devices are designed to facilitate the acquisition of new concepts and skills so that our participants will be more effective when they return to their jobs. As trainers, however, we must ensure that the training really "takes," that it gets "glued in" to the job. Participants thus need meaningful opportunities to apply their learning to:

☐ Work-related problems in the training situation
☐ And more importantly, their work when they return to their jobs

In the following pages, therefore, we will discuss these pertinent topics:

☐ Program design for effective transfer.
☐ How to make application activities in the classroom effective.
☐ Formats of application activities, i.e., observation-assessment, practical (hands on) assignments, role playing, and using worksheets.
☐ Contracting (developing action plans), both pre-session and at program's end.
☐ Skill retention in management training.
☐ Additional ways to aid transfer of training to the job.
☐ Conducting follow-up sessions.

Program Design For Effective Transfer

Concern with transfer begins *before* the training starts—with design—not after the participants have gone back to their jobs. This means that the trainer must so operate that all parties concerned—management, bosses, trainees, and trainers—are totally clear as to the specific behavioral results which will ensue from the training. Only under these circumstances can the application of the new learning to the job be tracked. For if we are fuzzy about what is to be done on the job at training's end, we can't pinpoint the true success of the new learning.

Trainers/consultants Dana G. and James C. Robinson properly point out that skills are likely to be transferred to the job when both the learning experience and the work environment are in sync about desired end results. They thus suggest that all concerned be aware of and use this formula: L E × W E = Results.[1]

"L E" stands for *learning experience* and "W E" refers to *work environment* of the returning learner. The trainer obviously can affect the former and line management influences the latter. Line management's role is to produce an environment that supports, reinforces, and rewards the learner for applying the newly mastered skill or knowledge provided by the trainer.

To understand the formula in full, note that if either multiplier merits a zero, the final result is also a big goose egg. So how can the trainer ensure that the environment supports the training endeavor? By looking for barriers to transfer in the work environment, and then reporting that data back to management, the clients, or sponsor of the course or program for their corrective action.

The barriers to skill transfer, per the Robinsons, fall into three distinct categories:

☐ *The learner.* Because of personal values and concepts about how the job should be performed, he/she might reject the course's values and concepts. Or, alternately, may lack confidence to use/apply the new skills.

☐ *The learner's boss.* The boss may not coach the learner as to how to use the new learning or may not reinforce the learner if he/she applies what was learned. Also, the boss may not serve as a proper model for the learner. In effect, any of those behaviors or attitudes may nullify what was accomplished in the training room.

☐ *The organization.* The learned skills may receive a punishing response when applied in the back-home work environment; e.g., if customer relations reps are paid on the basis of the number of orders taken, the skill of dealing with customer concerns/complaints, which may double the time spent with the customer, is not likely to be performed very often. Hence the need for a drastic alteration by management of its prevailing reward system. Or learners may be inhibited to perform their new learning because of time constraints, inappropriate/incompatable policies or procedures, or lack of authority to act. Or feedback may not be provided about how the application of their new skills actually affects results.

Making Classroom Application Activities Effective

In our work on exercises we learned that they may vary greatly as to format, involvement, novelty, time consumption, realism, intensity, and degree of work-relatedness. In the application session (or application activity), however, *all* training work is totally work-related and thus is marked by the highest possible degree of realism. In such sessions, then, participants are presented not only with activities that have "face validity" as to realism, but also activities that are readily perceived as intrinsically relevant to the work itself. (This does not always mean, unfortunately, that application-type activities are universally applauded by the participants.

In fact, they may be resisted because they hit "too close to home." Unfortunately, not everyone wishes to undergo the painful process of introspection that relates to the improvement of one's work.)

In the pages that follow we will suggest a number of application-type activities. They can be worked on by the participants in one of several ways:

☐ *Totally individual work.* This may be desirable when the assignment relates to work that is highly specialized. In such an instance hardly anyone else can offer help or comment constructively on what was done.

☐ *Team assignment.* Certain learnings can best be accomplished via a group or team effort. The assumptions are that several participants, working together, can provide a broader variety of inputs on the task, augment motivation and support, learn to work well with others, etc.

☐ *Individual work followed by small group work.* This may be done in pairs or small groups of three to five participants. The assumption in this instance is that one or more persons, as neutral reviewers, can provide certain insights that the preparer cannot. Why not? Because the preparer of the material is often "too close" to it, too emotionally or ego-involved with his/her own accomplishment. Thus, objective "outsiders" can aid the preparer of the material by offering helpful feedback or raising questions about the completed assignment: Is it on-target, practical, realistic, cost-effective, complete, policy-based, future-oriented, understandable, likely to meet resistance? A good training design for this type of application assignment is the following:

1. Assign participants to trios. *Note:* The smaller the work team the greater the likelihood for candid sharing. Hence, I favor work in trios or even pairs as opposed to larger work teams.
2. Tell the participants that they are being assigned to small work teams (trios) to share completed work and to elicit help about the activity from the other team members. Advise them that the assumption here is that three heads are better than one—that *team* analysis can ensure that proposals are marked by the maximum degree of realism and practicality.
3. Instruct the teams that each participant will present his/her work for review, critique, and assistance by the other two team members. All participants, then, assume the roles of presenter and reviewer (or helper). *Note:* The time for each presentation and receipt of feedback thereon will vary with the complexity of the assignment. If each presenter has 30 minutes the total critique session will take 90

minutes; if each presenter has 20 minutes, the team's work can be completed in one hour.)

4. Remind the participants that in their role of reviewer they are to be as helpful as they possibly can. Similarly, advise the presenters that here is a splendid opportunity to get feedback from two other objective, knowledgeable participants.
5. Assign participants to relatively noise-free locations. If separate training rooms are not available, locate the teams as far as possible from one another in the regular training room.
6. Keep track of the elapsed time. Provide a ten-minute warning as to the imminent close of the application session.
7. Secure small group reports concerning the learning from the activity. This group-at-large sharing should enrich the total experience.

Formats of Application Activities

Application activities in the training situation can assume a variety of formats. Here are several:

Observation-Assessment

Participants and participant teams can be given practical observational assignments; e.g., to conduct a safety inspection of a given work area or operation and to prepare a report thereon; to study the operation of the admissions desk at a hospital and to recommend improvements therein; to observe the operation of the complaint desk at a large department store and write a report thereon.

Note: For true experiential learning, the observers must analyze, suggest improvements, make recommendations, etc. Observation without actual involvement will produce only limited learning.

Practical Assignments

"Learning by doing" or "hands on" assignments may include:

☐ Developing a job training plan for a new subordinate
☐ Developing various checklists, e.g., to aid in conducting a safety inspection of one's work area, to help in orienting a new worker, or to assist in dealing with contingencies (unexpected events, emergencies, crises)
☐ Making a critical job inventory[2] for one's area of supervision
☐ Preparing a job safety analysis of one or two jobs that one supervises[3]

☐ Developing a plan to enrich a subordinate's job
☐ Developing a list of customer objections to certain of our products and coming up with creative ways to deal with the objections
☐ Having a team of management trainees work for a specified time in a shop or office, select a management, administrative, or operational problem for study, and then make recommendations thereon
☐ Giving oral reports if it is desired to augment skills in talking before groups

Management training courses typically entail the delivery of considerable conceptual material. Why not, then, redress this imbalance and have the participants also focus on on-going management practices that, for example, influence climate and creativity in the organization? This may include such topics as the career management plan, the suggestion system, the MBO plan, the tuition aid plan, the communication system, and the productivity of staff meetings.

In a training program for logging-camp supervisors of a Canadian lumber company, the trainers took a radically results-oriented approach and decided to abandon "education" for intervention.[4] Although the program was intended to teach the usual management training topics such as planning work, giving directions and feedback, setting short-term goals, and promoting communication and team work, the program they actually built focused on a pressing company problem instead—reduction of hauling costs. All training activities and exercises, management support, and follow-through zeroed in on the cost problem. The results were these:

☐ One camp closed three weeks ahead of time
☐ Hauling costs were reduced 5%
☐ Unit hauling costs decreased by 4%–6%
☐ 20% more wood was stored at the river bank
☐ Task-related radio communications increased from 30% to 90%

The intended managerial skills were learned while engaging in the practical work. As a consequence, the trainer concluded that it is far wiser to concentrate on limited material, practice, and application than on a lot of "standard" concepts and theory. Their program, then, was marked by these principles:

☐ Relate the training to organizational goals, priorities, and the system's real performance demands.
☐ Focus on short-term productivity improvements, drawing on immediate problems.
☐ Gear it to the participants' needs and capabilities.
☐ Build-in mechanisms to ensure real-world success experiences with the training techniques applied.

Role Plays

Role plays that are job-oriented are ways of applying principles and concepts to actual work situations; e.g., a customer service representative who has to deal with an irate person; an airline hostess who has to "calm down" passengers who may be anxious, angry or possibly inebriated; a salesperson who has to deal with certain customer objections; a police officer who has to "break up" a violent family argument; a supervisor who has to deal with a troubled employee; a supervisor who has to conduct a performance review discussion with a marginal worker.

Using Worksheets

Presented in Appendices 70 through 80 are a number of worksheets (also called guidesheets) for the conduct of application sessions. The "structure," which the worksheets provide, is designed to help participants "zero in" more precisely and quickly on their assignments. An important factor in the psychology of the worksheet is its motivating force; that is to say, to the extent that one is presented with an incomplete form, one is motivated to complete it.

The reader will note the worksheets exemplify the wide array of formats that may be used. Some of them may be used "as is;" others may be adapted to meet your own training circumstances. The important thing is to develop your thought processes to think in "guidesheet terms," thereby creating and providing practical and challenging application assignments to your participants.

Interim (Post-Session) Action Plans

As we will discuss later, a training program should end with a positive resolve in the form of participant action plans to do something concrete and worthwhile with the training experience upon return to the job. However, it *also* may be desirable to encourage thinking about the application of learnings at the end of particular sessions or possibly at the end of each training day. If so, guidesheets such as the ones in Appendices 81 through 84 may be given to participants for completion.

To increase the likelihood of commitment to action plans, provide five or ten minutes for preparation of the plans in class plus a similar time period for discussion of them in pairs or trios.

Note: End-of-session or daily action plans should help to set the stage for the development of a comprehensive action plan on a major problem at the end of the course or program. If mini-contracts are worked on each day, they should help develop the "mindset" for the final one.

Contracting at Program's End

On the assumption that the training effort has brought about various changes—acquisitions of new skills and concepts; new ways of looking at bosses, peers, customers, the organization, oneself; and new resolves to perform or manage better—there obviously is a need to help participants to convert the new learning and determination into concrete plans for action on the job.

Changing one's behavior in the back-home situation is hardly a simple task. Realistically, there are many forces at work that can undo the best of a participant's good intentions to change. These include a return to the usual job pressures, possible lack of support from superiors, passage of time, the vanishing of support and pressure from the participant group and the trainer, and the absence of opportunities to communicate with others who have shared the training experience. All of these indicate quite clearly that there must be a formal, all-out effort to plan for new behavior on the job. Procedures to accomplish this come under the general heading of "contracting." This entails the development of specific action plans to convert the classroom learning to concrete and realistic job application.

An action plan, then, is a commitment to engage in a new behavior resulting from the impetus of the training experience. It often can be quite simple, entailing no more than a self-pledge such as in Figure 20-1.

MY ACTION PLAN

As a result of the training I plan to:
1. Hold staff meetings regularly (every Wed. at 9:30 a.m.).
2. Appoint an assistant with full authority to act for me while I am away.
3. Use praise more liberally to reward and motivate subordinates.

Figure 20-1. Example of a self pledge that could be used as an action plan.

The action plan may also have more "specifics" such as proposed dates of accompishment, how the plan will be implemented, who else will have to be involved in the plan (possibly one's boss, subordinates, peers), and criteria to tell whether the plan is working well or not.

Guidelines for an "application session" to accomplish the necessary contracting are given in Appendix 85. Note that the steps that participants are to take in developing their action plans are provided in specific detail. Also, the action plans are submitted to peers for critique and augmented commitment. The trainer may wish to modify the forms given in Appendix 85, to meet better the needs of the participant group.

The contracting idea, although pedagogically sound, is not universally accepted by program participants. Expect, then, resistance in the form of "lip service" to the idea (just going through the motions) or possibly verbal objections: "I could do a better job of this back on the job where I can give it more thought." "Should we be taking up our valuable time in class to do this when we could be learning more of the subject?" "I don't have the information that I need; I've got it back home."

Since the principle of application in the classroom to aid transfer to the job is a sound one, the trainer must insist that practice in the training situation is an integral part of the training process.

How to Help Contracts "Take"

To ensure that participant contracts are carried out as pledged, the observance of these guidelines should be considered:

Early commitment. Secure commitments for goals (action plan) as early as is practicable. In some cases this may be *before* the formal training program begins. Identifying goals early will provide the fullest possible thinking about them in relation to program inputs. Recognize, however, that in other cases participants may have to acquire "insight" from the program itself before meaningful goal setting is possible. This is particularly true in personal growth programs, leadership development, and the like. Also, with certain participants it may not be desirable to "push" for action plans until the training is completed. Premature requests for work on action plans may raise anxiety levels unnecessarily and interfere with the hoped-for learning.

Realistic goal setting. Recognize that as in the case of any goal setting effort, targets (for improvement) must be clearly defined, limited in number, reachable, time-specific, voluntarily arrived at, and organization/boss supported (as necessary).

Group discussion. Provide opportunities for discussing completed plans with fellow participants. One's colleagues obviously can be useful as helpers, critics, reality-testers, support-givers, etc. Equally important is the vital role of group discussion as a stimulus to commitment. The reader may be familiar with social psychologist Kurt Lewin's research in World War II which pointed up so dramatically the impact that discussing a potential course of action may have upon the discussants.

Lewin's research involved the U.S. Department of Agriculture's concern with getting the American housewife to purchase less popular but highly nutritious cuts of meat such as liver, heart, kidneys, and sweetbreads. A change in eating habits was deemed essential by the government since the regular cuts were going to the military in great quantities. Dr. Lewin, then at M.I.T., set up a number of experiments with Iowa housewives that entailed these procedures:[5]

1. Lectures were given to three groups of housewives on the desirability of buying the organ meats. The lectures were accompanied by recipes for their preparation plus patriotic appeals (good nutrition was essential to keep workers productive in the war materiel industries). There was no group discussion of the information provided.
2. Three other groups received the same information as the first three groups and, in addition, were given an opportunity to discuss the data among themselves.

Lewin's staff followed up on the buying and serving behavior of the housewives. The following shows the results of their research:

Lecture method: 3% acted on the information (served the less-popular cuts)

Lecture plus discussion: 32% served the less popular cuts

Note that the lecture-plus-discussion group was ten times more effective than the lecture-only group. This is not to say that everyone acted as hoped for—only 32% actually did try out the less popular cuts of meat. But the difference in the behavior of the two groups was so large that it has been considered a breakthrough in the social sciences, particularly in the area of group dynamics.

One might ask: Why did group discussion work so dramatically? Peer pressure, i.e., a feeling of group identification developed. Visualize the housewives talking about the new information and one of them possibly saying to the others: "If you're willing to try it, so am I." In other words, the group discussion had an encouraging or reinforcing effect on their decision to act. Note that although the decision made was an individual one, that is, it was carried out in the meat market without the presence of the group, it nevertheless, represented a commitment to the group which was honored thereafter.

In passing, we might add that good politicians understand the power of the group and the importance of *public* commitment. They thus organize neighborhood "coffees" in people's homes during election campaigns to build up support for and commitment toward their candidates (or candidacy).

Monitoring procedures. Give adequate thought to monitoring or enforcement procedures. From the trainer's standpoint, action plans can be implemented and followed-up in different ways and with different degrees of effectiveness:

☐ Provide participants with the necessary forms and procedures and encourage them to develop an action plan when they return to their jobs. This is the "hope and promise" approach and few will do much about it. Job pressures in the back-home environment will scuttle most good intentions.

☐ A better procedure is to allow time for the preparation of the action plans *in the class.* At least a plan will have been developed. Implementation is another matter, of course.

☐ A still more effective procedure is to have the action plans developed in class *and* then have them discussed and critiqued for realism in triads. This will provide some reinforcement for possible back-home implementation of the plan.

☐ The best procedures entail some follow-up of action plan commitments. Some possible ways of doing this are as follows:

1. Collect the completed action plans and mail them back to participants, two to four weeks after the training has been completed, with an encouraging letter or memo.
2. Have the action plans prepared in duplicate, collect one copy of them, and mail the plans back to the participants 30 days after the training as a reminder of their commitment in class.
3. Contact participants via questionnaire or interview concerning accomplishment of the action plan.
4. Assemble participants in a group situation 30 days after the training to discuss their progress and problems in implementing their action plans. Pressure by the thrust of the post-training effort, plus that of one's peers, should optimize results.
5. "Wire in" the participants' supervisors into the action planning and reviewing process for maximum results. The theory here is that people are more likely to respond to what is *inspected* rather than merely *expected.* But note: While this procedure may be helpful in many cases, this is not universally so. For example, some participants may have an improvement goal that they consider too personal to discuss with their boss. Others may feel that they do not want to "confess" weaknesses to their superior, particularly if the latter is one who

is not particulary sensitive to others, or with whom a trusting relationship has not been established.

Regardless of the particular follow-up procedure employed, the important thing is to keep up the momentum (enthusiasm, commitment) achieved in the training situation.

Peer monitoring/networking. Another approach to monitoring is to ask the participants to pick another person, one with whom they ordinarily do *not* work closely, to keep in touch with them on their contract or action plan. The person selected is given a copy of the action plan and agrees to contact its preparer within 30 days or so to ascertain progress.

By committing oneself to another person (and indirectly to the rest of the group and the trainer) to carry through on the action plan, motivation to achieve this goal is stimulated and enhanced. In other words, a commitment to someone else is much greater than a promise to one's self. A side benefit of this procedure is that it establishes lines of communication among persons who might not ordinarily be in any direct contact.[6]

Difficulties questionnaire. Consider conducting a survey of program graduates to ascertain specific difficulties in living up to contracts and secure suggestions concerning ways to overcome such difficulties. *Note:* This procedure would be employed only if overall implementation of action plans was deemed inadequate.

Contracting: Behavior Modification Approach

Another form of the action plan is personal contracting using behavior modification procedures; that is to say, it uses the "baseline" data collection approach (before and after measurement) and positive reinforcement to reward any behavior change. Of course, the reinforcement is self-administered rather than applied by an outside source as in a true "behavior mod" effort.

The change effort may relate to either work-related or personal-type changes, or both. By work-related changes we mean such quantifiable areas as production, downtime, cost, errors, customer complaints, waste, scrap, absenteeism, tardiness, accidents, and grievances. By personal changes we are talking about changing habits of smoking, eating, exercising or improving one's family life (via helping children with homework, doing home chores, reducing nagging behavior, giving one's spouse or children positive reinforcement).

Here is a ten-step procedure given to program participants who wish to participate in the "Behavior Change Project." The system was developed by K. A. Moody, manager, General Management Development of U.S. Steel in Pittsburgh.[7] Basically the "Behavior Change

Project" asks participants to provide data (via a simple form) on these questions or steps:

1. *Targeted or terminal behavior.* Cite specific end results to be achieved, i.e., what conditions will exist when the goal is met?

2. *Beginning or entering behavior.* What is the current state of events in respect to the problem of concern? (Cite current weight, number of cigarettes smoked daily, number of times praise is given to spouse each day, cost of production, accident rate.)

3. *Reinforcers for the change.* What are the benefits to you and the person changed? Make separate lists.

4. *Set up a graph or grid to measure the change over time.* On the vertical axis indicate changes in quantity; on the horizontal axis show changes over time. The time measurement can be daily, weekly, monthly. A terminal date should be indicated. *Note:* The starting point or current behavior is referred to by the behavior mod people as "baseline." For example, if one wishes to change a smoking habit, the baseline may be 40 cigarettes smoked per day. The measurement idea, which gives one feedback about progress toward the goal, is basic to the change process.

5. *Consider special reinforcers to reward progress;* e.g., special rewards may be given to oneself at the one-fourth, one-half, three-quarters mark, or other stages of accomplishment.

6. *Anticipated obstacles to progress.* What factors or events may derail your plan? (List.) How will you meet these impediments to progress?

7. *Securing outside help.* Who can help you meet your goal? In what way? What rewards shall you give them?

8. *Plan maintenance.* How can you prevent fading or slippage of the new behavior, once it is attained? What added reinforcement is essential?

9. *Enter baseline data.* This means recording data on the grid (see Step 4) concerning the point of departure from the baseline. Enter data regularly concerning progress toward terminal behavior.

10. *Evaluation.* Did you succeed? If not, why not? Should the original plan be revised? Are new reinforcers necessary? Any problems in data collection? What was your major learning? How do you feel about your accomplishment?

Ensuring Skill Retention in Management Training

Management training presents special problems in skill retention for transfer to the job. Relapse rates can be as high as 90% says Robert Mark, professor of management, University of Massachusetts. A key reason for the fadeout phenomenon, says Dr. Mark, is that many of the complex behaviors taught and learned in management training comprise numerous *support skills.* Unfortunately, the "trained" manager may lack some of these skills. For example, leadership concepts may be well understood in the classroom, but the manager may not have acquired the time management skills required for its proper execution. Or the manager may learn the "whys" and "hows" of delegation, but may be uncomfortable with the authority aspects of it, such as giving orders or actually "letting go." Or, to resolve conflicts successfully, the manager may lack the requisite skill of active listening. Other vital support skills are assertiveness and stress management.

A way to help participants understand the vital role of support skills in the retention process is to have them identify the "high-risk" situations back home that may vitiate application of the new learning. If they can become aware of the vulnerability of a new skill to relapse, they can then discover clues to help them diagnose support skill deficits.

To diagnose needed support skills and to develop a modus operandi to increase long-term skill retention, Dr. Mark proposes adoption of the "Relapse Prevention Model" in management training. The RP Model identifies potential causes of training failure by using data from past personal relapses as feedback to make one sensitive to possible future slips back home. Slips are not to be regarded as indicators of inadequacy/incompetence/weak will, but as valuable data for the prevention of future difficulties.

In effect, for the new skills to survive the treacherous work environment, the participants must learn (1) to anticipate job realities, (2) to expect impairing emotional responses to temporary failure, (3) to recognize the need for development of support skills, and (4) to learn to cope with little or no reinforcement from the organization. The RP Model, then, operates on the assumption that retention of learning is aided if the unpredictability of the work environment is reduced and if vital strategies of *self-control* can be provided (by the training) and learned.

In respect to point 4, managers must be trained to realize that skill retention and application is basically a matter of self-management. Even if highly busy bosses up the line were interested and wanted to be supportive, in the last analysis execution of the new behaviors will be self-motivating, lonely, and private events. For example, no one but the manager can wrestle effectively with all the interpersonal dynamics and nuances of the delegation process.

The key steps in behavioral self-management (relapse prevention strategies) are:

1. *Anticipate and monitor potential difficulties.* Learn to control events via a sensitive early warning system, i.e., to anticipate harassers, trouble spots, or high risk situations.
2. *Increase rational thinking.* Expect and manage irrational thoughts and emotions which play hob with rational skill building.
3. *Diagnose and practice support skills.* Learn to identify skill shortcomings and acquire and practice appropriate support skills. A review of disruptive patterns is essential, e.g., a tendency toward perfectionism.
4. *Provide consequences.* Learn to provide one's own consequences (rewards) for the new behaviors since the environment probably won't (and can't) provide them. Set specific rewards for both short and long-term accomplishment.

To implement the RP strategies, Dr. Mark states that three steps are required:

1. The manager chooses an appropriate skill he/she wishes to retain, e.g., using group decision making. *Note:* It should be described in operational (observable or measurable) terms so that a slip can be readily noticed. Thus, a goal, in this instance, might be one weekly group decision.
2. The manager applies the above four-step relapse prevention strategies (the RP Model) to his/her on-the-job situation.
3. The manager predicts in detail the circumstances of the first set-back. In effect, this is use of "relapse imagery" so that when the predicted negative scenario comes on screen at work, it is no surprise, less disruptive, and much more manageable.

In sum, the RP Model provides a systematic means, a methodology, to identify possible skill-threatening situations and tying them to possible support skills which can be learned in the training situation.[8]

Additional Ways to Aid the Training Transfer

To ensure that the training really "takes," these devices and approaches merit consideration:

Pre-Training

☐ Involve the participant's boss *before* the training begins. Encourage supervisors to nominate their subordinates to training programs based on mutually agreed-upon development needs to learn as much as possible about the course, and to set goals for learning by the subordinate.

One writer[9] utilizes a two-step program to ensure full supervisory involvement:

1. *The trainer conducts negotiations with the supervisor.* Course or workshop objectives plus on-the-job expectations after the training is completed, should be discussed with the supervisor for about 20 minutes. It helps if the supervisor is shown a performance or behavior model, i.e., what will be done by the participant (subordinate) post-training. Not every supervisor may "buy" all aspects of the model. In such a circumstance, the trainer should promise to mention such objections in the workshop. In any case, a promise should be secured from the supervisor for *active* support/reinforcement of the parts of the model he/she does accept.
2. *A pre-course meeting between the supervisor and the trainee is required.* The meeting must be held to discuss the workshop's performance model, its objectives, and the anticipated benefits from the training. It is desirable to secure some "evidence" that the discussion actually took place. This may take the form of signatures of both parties on the objectives statement or a memo from the supervisor summarizing their discussion of the workshop and the boss' expectations of the workshop.

☐ Secure support for the training from participants' superiors via appreciation sessions and help in planning the training, or better still, have the superiors experience the training before their subordinates do.

☐ As appropriate, have an entire unit, section, or department attend the same training. Attendance may be on a joint basis (vertical training) or in separate sessions. The end result should be the acquisition of a common set of concepts, procedures, "language," etc., so that mutual reinforcement of the new learning is an easy and natural thing to do.

☐ Make your training "research-based," i.e., collect information via interviews, questionnaires, and operating data and use these inputs (need data) as bases for course design and post-training follow-up.

☐ Have participants identify in *advance* of class one or two problems they will work on in the program. Use pre-work procedures for this purpose.

☐ Use other pre-work assignments such as completing a self-assessment quiz; gathering data for a report to class; studying an assigned case or problem; interviewing a key figure who is knowledgeable about some aspect of the course; teaming up with another participant to work on an assigned project.

☐ Advise participants in advance of the training session to bring their calendar (desk or wall type) with them for it will be used in the contracting phase (action planning) of the program. This is not only a practical way to record "good intentions" on a time-frame basis, but communicates at the outset that the course has a high expectation that contracting must be taken seriously by the participants.

In the Classroom

☐ Consider the use of "spaced learning," i.e., break up the training with one or more opportunities to return to the job to reflect upon and try out the new learning.

☐ In a management training program, introduce live data on managerial practices from the participants' subordinates. This may relate to communication, coaching, team work, rewarding good work, etc. Secure managerial self-assessments on the same behaviors and compare them with those of the subordinates. Wherever subordinates are more critical of the manager's behavior than the manager is, the latter obviously has a need to study the feedback carefully and possibly initiate such changes as may be indicated.[10]

☐ To overcome possible trainee discouragement upon return from training, ascertain problems and obstacles that might prevent proper performance of the new learning. A fishbowl exercise may be useful for this purpose. Then organize accordingly, based on the data from the participants.

☐ Overlearning, i.e., practice beyond the point of mastery, may be helpful to ensure the learning of vital skills, approaches, or concepts, e.g., learning a foreign language or, in a restaurant setting, learning how to make special desserts or breads.

☐ Use guided imagery to help the learning really "glue in." Mental rehearsal via vivid mind pictures is very helpful, e.g., how to close a sale with an undecided customer or how to deal with a highly angry person.

☐ Train participants to look for cues, signals, or trigger mechanisms to take immediate action. Examples: heavy or repeated absences on Monday and Friday over a six-week period indicate the need for a meeting with the employee to review the leave record; in technical areas various sounds, lights, smells, or readings on gauges may serve as action alerts; in a factory setting a particular percentage of the re-work or customer complaints may point up the need for added quality control measures.

Post-Training

☐ Involve the participant's boss *after* the training. Encourage supervisors to sit down with participants upon their return from the training program to assess what was learned, to discuss how the new learning can be "plowed back" into the on-going operation, and to establish specific goals to capitalize on the new learning.

Data about the results of supervisory follow-ups should be obtained by the trainer via personal visit, written report, or questionnaire. The latter written procedures may be essential if many supervisors are involved or the supervisors are located away from the trainer's office. Should supervisors be tardy or derelict in submitting their evaluation reports, a tactful phone call along this line should jog the delinquent ones: "We're going through the evaluations for the safety course, and we don't seem to have your report form. Would you care for another copy?"

☐ Where action plans are developed in class, consider structuring them so that the participants' bosses are involved in their review and follow-up.

☐ Encourage participants' supervisors to reward psychologically (positive reinforcement) the new learning upon its performance. ("Charlie, I'm glad to see you're lifting just as they taught you in the training course.")

☐ Provide participants with handy "tools" or performance aids to facilitate application of the learning, such as checklists, plastic overlay data wheels, flow charts, formulae, tables, guidesheets, question lists, diagrams, models, reminder cards, and wall charts.

☐ Discuss with the training committee transfer problems, either those anticipated before the training is given and/or those that arose after the training had been completed.

☐ Keep in touch with participants via periodical articles, possibly a newsletter, or occasional questionnaires to produce data that is then shared with all concerned.

☐ If practical in a geographical sense, try to bring course graduates together for an "alumni reunion." This might be both a social and a work-oriented activity. Where reunions or class "get-togethers" take place, the trainer might meet with the group, at least initially, to help in its organization.

☐ As appropriate, team up two course graduates to form a "buddy system." This procedure should provide mutual help, motivation, and support.

☐ Encourage those who are trained to keep diaries or other records of their experience in applying the training. Then visit with the participants, either on an individual or on a group basis, to ascertain problems, if any, in applying what was learned.

☐ Provide and publicize the availability of follow-up resources such as audio/video cassettes, print materials, visitation services, and assistance via telephone and letter requests.

☐ Use course graduates as instructors/trainers in future courses. This procedure will serve to continue their interest and involvement in their initial learning.

☐ Encourage course graduates to form a "network" or post-training support group to keep in touch after the formal training is over. Suggest they appoint a secretary-recorder to keep the participant roster current insofar as names, addresses, and phone numbers are concerned.

☐ Think long-term rather than short-term participant involvement. By keeping the participants in a "continuing" state of training, the likelihood of the training "becoming part of them" and more of a "way of life" is increased. For example, to teach public speaking skills, opt for participation in a toastmaster's club rather than for attendance at a public speaking course, either in-house or college. Similarly, in time management training a long-term program (four months), entailing keeping a time-log (pre-work) and three post-workshop follow-ups conducted at monthly intervals is preferable to a quickie one- or two-day seminar.

In this latter connection, the concept of follow-up training should be considered wherever practical. This topic is covered in more detail in the section, "Conducting the Follow-Up Session."

☐ Provide participants with pertinent rules to govern their behavior on the job. While many behaviors are subject to contingency shaping, not all are. Hence the need to provide rules for self-monitoring of behavior. For example, the rule "always wear your seat belt" is very much worth learning. Why? Because there's no need to learn to use seat belts by experiencing the result or consequence of *not* having worn them.[11]

☐ Consultants may be trained and utilized to follow-up and to offer help and encouragement to seminar graduates. A carefully controlled evaluation study (via the use of experimental and control groups) of a seminar for church leaders indicated that the participants who were part of the consultation system improved their attitudes toward transfer of training from the seminar setting. The consultants contacted their "clients" over an eight-week period via personal meetings, phone conversations, and letters. The research also indicated the clients appreciated these consultative contacts, the special attention being regarded as helpful, and not an intrusion. The consultants' contact also provided the seminar conductors with information regarding the ac-

tual transfer occurring between the seminar and real-life applications. In some cases transfer was hindered because of work demands. A salutary by-product was that the consultants themselves increased their own enthusiasm for and use of the seminar materials.[12]

Conducting the Follow-Up Session

The follow-up session is an excellent technique to:

☐ *Prevent fadeout.* Time, of course, is a major factor in our forgetting what was learned. Unless the new learning is practiced on the job regularly, a significant percentage of loss is inevitable. In essence, then, the refresher session is essential to reinforce or help "glue in" what was learned.

☐ *Introduce new, related material.* In this manner, we can build on what has already been learned and experienced. This approach will enrich the participants' initial training experience.

In a given refresher training session, the goal may be to accomplish either or possibly both of these goals.

In the refresher training session the trainer obviously has to decide on "agenda ownership." That is to say, should it be built entirely by the trainer or should it be left to the participants, either in whole or in part? Of course, there is no "best" answer to this question. But it is obvious that to the extent that we can involve the participants in agenda building, the greater the likelihood of acceptance of the training. Certainly, in the refresher training we are trying to meet participant needs. Also, since the basic program has already been experienced, it would appear adequately logical to expect our participants to be able to decide on agenda items.

The Participant-Developed Agenda

If it is decided to secure participant input for the agenda, this can be done in various ways.

☐ A short, pre-session questionnaire having questions such as the following might be used:

1. List one or two successes in applying learnings from the course.
2. Cite any difficulties you may have encountered in your attempts to implement what you learned in the course.
3. What subjects or topics should we cover in our follow-up session?
4. When the follow-up session is completed, what should have happened to make it a success for you?

Answers to these questions can be tallied and analyzed and become the building blocks for the agenda. It should be recognized, realistically, that responses to the pre-session questionnaire may well be spotty or even "overlooked" by practically everyone. Hence the need to be prepared to do the agenda-building job as the first order of business in the follow-up session itself.

☐ The development of an agenda in the follow-up session may be done via small groups or general (group-at-large) inputs. An interesting way to accomplish this with the total group is to ask all participants to take the following "fantasy trip:"

"It is the morning after the follow-up session. A good friend asks you a number of very penetrating questions about it. In discussing it with your friend, you suddenly find yourself saying: 'Gosh, I wish we had covered _____ in our session."

Let's assume that our fantasy procedure, used for a supervisory training course, produced the following nine agenda items:

1. How to handle irrational people
2. Communication problems: up-down, parental approaches, generation-gap aspects
3. How to motivate the person on a "plateau"
4. How to use confrontational skills
5. How to use the skills I have acquired in a "heated" situation (as opposed to abandoning them under pressure)
6. Group meetings: why hold them, how to conduct them, etc.
7. Mutual expectations; standards setting: how to go about it
8. How to enter onto a new supervisory position
9. How to give reinforcement (positive feedback)

Our next procedure is to have our participants rank *in writing* the above nine items in order of priority. Then rankings can be aided by this weighting procedure:

Choice #	Weight (Votes)
1	4
2	3
3	2
4	1

Note that we are asking only for four choices since we can't handle all topics.

You then ask all participants to call out their *votes,* starting with each person's Item 1 on the list. You total the votes aloud for each item. This might give us the following array of scores:

Agenda Item Number	Number of Votes (Weight)
1	8
2	29
3	18
4	9
5	0
6	3
7	3
8	6
9	10

The agenda items with the highest scores, our top four items, become the agenda. This would be agenda items 2, 3, 9, and 4.

The Trainer-Developed Agenda

In the preceding paragraphs we discussed agenda setting by the participants on the assumption that this was the vehicle to meet their needs. There may be other circumstances, however, when the trainer necessarily decides upon the agenda. For example, if the program concluded with the development of action plans for back-home implementation, it is essential to check back to see how well and to what extent these plans were carried out. In effect, the action plan reviews automatically become the agenda. In this circumstance it is the trainer's job to structure the agenda to facilitate the action plan discussion/review process.

An example of a trainer-developed agenda is one used in a time management course:

Activity 1: Use fishbowls to allow participants to talk about successes, near successes, problems, etc., in implementing their action plans. The discussion may relate to defining key responsibilities and setting priorities, time improvement plans, job improvement plans, delegation, meeting improvement, etc. Note that the discussion/sharing at this point is intended as warm-up, "re-entry," motivation, rather than as a means to "nail down" any specifics of the action plans.

Activity 2: One of the action plans is selected for intensive review/discussion/sharing. This is done as follows:

1. Each person indivdually reviews his/her action plan for five or ten minutes.
2. Small group work (in pairs preferably) is done to share and help one another (25–40 minutes).
3. Reports from the small groups to the total group on what was learned or accomplished in the small groups are given.

This activity can be repeated twice again using other topics.

Activity 3: Use the "circular whip" technique, i.e., whip around the room, having each participant state the most significant learning from the program *as of now.*

Activity 4. Have participants complete individually the two worksheets given in Appendices 86 and 87. Then process them in trios and secure feedback from the several teams.

Note: The activities proceed from the general to the specific. Also, the last activity, particularly the second worksheet, makes a positive bridge with the back-home situation by asking for further reflection about on-the-job problems.

Key Concepts for Follow-Up Sessions

In planning and conducting the follow-up session, these key ideas should be of value:

☐ In planning your session, think in terms of learning *enrichment:* "What can we provide our participants that will augment, upgrade, consolidate, reinforce their skill and/or understanding?" Then ask: "How should I design the program so that learning enrichment will actually take place?"

☐ Training methods used are certainly important. But in another sense *what* is done or *how* it is done is less important than the fact that *something is being done* to keep things alive. The key point of it all is that the organization, through the follow-up session, is saying: "We think the training you have experienced is so important that we want to be certain it is not subject to fade out. In fact, we're willing to take you away from your very important jobs for so many hours to prevent this."

☐ Give careful thought to the length of the follow-up session. It may be two hours, a half day, or a full day. But the time frame decided upon should be used in a totally productive way. Participants should not leave the follow-up session with the feeling that it was just "busy work."

☐ Any work to be completed by the participants before the follow-up session should be spelled out in precise detail and subject to a written reminder before the session takes place.

☐ Anticipate that in the interval between the regular and follow-up session some participants will forget to bring along their notebooks, workbooks, worksheets, etc. Accordingly, be prepared to provide extra materials as may be needed. If a participant fails to complete or bring an assignment, little can be done about it. One "solution" is to have that person function as a "consultant" to the other participants in his/her small group.

☐ Don't be surprised if there is a certain amount of "fallout" insofar as attendance is concerned. Time intervenes, people become involved and busy again with their jobs, interest may diminish a bit. Thus the forces at work for full attendance are inevitably under attack by these competing counter-forces. Some possible solutions to the problem:

1. Involve the participants' bosses in the follow-up session planning, thereby securing their support.
2. Announce the program at the outset as a two-faceted, totally integrated training activity—the initial workshop plus the follow-up session.
3. Stress the importance of action plans in the very first announcement of the program and thereafter whenever practicable. Indicate that the all-important action plans will be reviewed and discussed in the follow-up session. Stating it another way, avoid leaving the impression that the follow-up session is an "add on," an optional extra, or something that is merely "nice to do."

☐ A simple but effective way to start is with a "success story." The objective is to keep things at a high, positive level. The procedure is to whip around the room, each person citing a tangible accomplishment as a result of the course or program.

☐ Be certain to close the session on a high note, too. One way to do this is to ask each participant to "testify" concerning what has been learned to date or possibly respond to this question: "My next step in this program is to _____."

Instrumented Follow-Up

Follow-up may also be conducted via instrumentation. This approach is useful:

☐ To encourage continuing introspection after program's end. The instrument may be used in conjunction with a follow-up session if one is conducted or it may be used in lieu of such a session.

☐ When a formal follow-up session may not be practical due to distance (dispersion of participants), time pressures, or other reasons.

A copy of an instrument for follow-up purposes is given in Appendix 88.

Key Points

1. Think of transfer as a key consideration in designing a training program. If transfer becomes a post-course afterthought, the problem is compounded unnecessarily.

2. To ensure transfer of training, application activities that involve the learner fully are essential.
3. Application activities may relate to individual work, small group work, or a combination of these two approaches.
4. Application activities may assume these forms: observation-assessment, practical work, role playing, and using worksheets.
5. Action plans or contracting are essential to ensure that what is learned in the classroom will be applied to the job.
6. Action plans may be developed by participants on either a post-session or a post-course basis, or both.
7. The best contracts entail early commitment, realistic goal setting, small group review and discussion of action plans, monitoring/follow-up procedures, "wiring in" the participants' supervisors into the process, etc.
8. Behavior modification techniques may be employed to ensure that contracts are properly developed and "enforced."
9. Transfer may be aided by numerous techniques including pre-course planning with supervisors, appreciation sessions for management, team or vertical training, pre-work, having participants introduce their own problems into class work, journalizing, post-session meetings with the participants' supervisors and involvement of the training committee, networking, reunions, and expanded rather than compressed time frames for the training.
10. Follow-up sessions are useful to prevent fadeout and to build on initial learnings.
11. Instruments may be used as part of the follow-up process.
12. Glueing in of *management* training can be aided by use of the Relapse Prevention Model.

References

1. Robinson, Dana G., and James C., "Breaking Barriers To Skill Transfer," *Training and Development Journal* (January 1985), pp. 82–83.
2. Sources of information are accident reports, maintenance and quality control records, and interviews with employees and other supervisors and various plant engineers.
3. For an excellent article on how to conduct a Job Safety Analysis (JSA) see L. C. Smith, "The J Programs," *National Safety News* (September 1980), pp. 74–75.
4. "Build Better Managers With Short-Term Performance Goals," *Training/HRD* (February 1981), pp. 70, 75.
5. Lewin, K., "Group Decision and Social Change," in Swanson, G., Newcomb, T. M., and Hartley, E. L. (Eds.), *Readings in Social Psychology,* 2nd edition, Holt Publishing Company, New York (1952).
6. Siegel, S. R., "Improving the Effectiveness of Management Development Programs," *Personnel Journal* (October 1981), pp. 770, 772–773.
7. "Behavior Change Via Personal Contracts," *Bulletin on Training* (November–December 1976), p. 4.
8. Mark, Robert D., "Self-Managed Skill Retention," *Training and Development Journal* (January 1986), pp. 54–57. *Note:* The self-management strategies presented herein are adapted from Marlatt, G. A., and Gordon, J. R., (Eds.), *Relapse Prevention: Maintenance Strategies In The Treatment Of Addictive Behaviors,* Guilford Publications, New York, 1985.
9. House, R. S., "Increase Training Benefits," *National Society for Performance Improvement Journal* (June 1982), pp. 14–15.
10. "Training Managers to Rate Their Employees," *Business Week* (March 17, 1980), pp. 178, 183.
11. Brown, M. G., "Understanding Transfer of Training," *Performance and Instruction Journal* (March 1983), pp. 5–7.
12. Ott, Stanley E., and Russell, James D., "Consultation As A Means Of Improving Post-Seminar Performance," *Performance and Instruction Journal* (June/July 1986), pp. 20–21.

Recommended Reading

Baker, Richard A., "In Search of Relevance—Weaving On-The-Job Reality into Supervisory Training," *Training News,* July 1983, pp. 6–7.

This describes the use of projects selected jointly by participants and their bosses to be accomplished on the job after the training is completed.

Brown, Mark G., "Understanding Transfer of Training," *Performance and Instruction Journal,* March 1983, pp. 5–7.

Since much of our behavior is governed by rules (as opposed to those behaviors that are contingency-shaped), the author advocates that the trainer provide learners with rules so as to maintain the new behavior learned in class. His guidelines: don't teach "false" rules; require participants to frequently repeat rules; teach participants to observe their own behavior and give themselves positive feedback when rules are followed and negative feedback when rules are ignored.

Feldman, Michael, "Successful Post Training Skill Application," *Training and Development Journal,* September 1981, pp. 72–74.

This suggests attention be given to needs analysis, full organization support for the training, pre-program activities to motivate trainees, post-program support groups, and contracting as means to ensure transfer.

Leifer, Melissa S., and Newstrom John W., "Solving the Transfer of Training Problems," *Training and Development Journal,* August 1980, pp. 42–46.

Contracts, discussion of obstacles to successful implementation of the new learning, support groups, delayed evaluation, refresher courses, follow-up handouts, and training incentives are means to aiding transfer.

Mahoney, Francis X., "Targets, Time and Transfer: Keys to Management Impact," *Personnel,* November–December 1980, pp. 25–34.

This recommends the substitution, at least in part, of "working meetings" in lieu of training sessions. By working on relevant targets or issues transfer will be facilitated.

McNamara, J. Regis, "Why Aren't They Doing What We Trained Them to Do?" *Training/HRD,* February 1980, pp 33–36.

This is a uniquely well-thought-out and practical account of the many factors which help/hinder the transfer of training to the job. The article stresses the importance of "consequences" as a factor in anticipating whether the new training will actually take place on the job.

Michalak, Donald F., "The Neglected Half of Training," *Training and Development Journal,* May 1981, pp. 22–28.

This provides numerous suggestions for "maintenance of behavior" after the training is over including skill practice, letter to self, total department attends, buddy systems, positive reinforcement by the boss, etc.

Sedlik, Jay M., Magnus, Arlene K., and Rakow, Joel, "Key Elements to An Effective Training System," *Training and Development Journal,* July 1980, pp. 10–12.

To ensure that training objectives are accomplished in the real world, the authors propose the use of five systems: developmental, internal training, performance, installation, and evaluation/modification. The article offers practical tools for successful application including transfer exercises, job performance aids, and the trainee progress record.

Seiler, Clarence J., "Let's Put 'Management' Into Management Training," *Training and Development Journal,* September 1981, pp. 68–70.

The author outlines a comprehensive program to ensure that a management training program really pays off back on the job.

Siegel, S. R., "Improving the Effectiveness of Management Development Programs," *Personnel Journal,* October 1981, pp. 770, 772–773.

This discusses various procedures for and issues in contracting, including motivation, when to request it be done, voluntary vs. involuntary aspects, and success in contracting.

Spitzer, Dean R., "But Will They Use Training on the Job?" *Training/HRD,* September 1982, pp. 48, 105.

To prevent "training entropy," the author suggests 12 approaches: personal action planning, group action planning, multiphase programming (intersperse the training with work), the buddy system, performance aids, recognition systems, training trainees as trainers, use of signed contracts, post-training resource access, follow-up questionnaires, follow-up phone calls and visits, follow-up session.

Tauber, Mark S., "Supervisory Skill Development," *Training and Development Journal,* September 1981, pp. 49–54

The author's answers to the question: "What happens after they have been trained?" are reunions and supervisory support groups (networks). Procedures to make these activities effective are discussed.

Trost, Arty, "They May Love It, But Will They Use It?" *Training and Development Journal,* January 1985, pp. 78–81.
Involving the learner, trainer, and trainee's boss, before, during, and after the training is essential for effective transfer.

Zemke, Ron, and Gunkler, John, "Twenty-Eight Techniques For Transforming Training Into Performance," *Training,* April 1985, pp. 48–63.

This detailed article describes and groups transfer techniques into five strategies: pre-training, good training, transfer-enhancing, post-training, and finessing.

ANCILLARY ISSUES AND TECHNIQUES

Learning without thought is labor lost. Thought without learning is intellectual death.

—Confucius (551–479 B.C.), Chinese ethical philosopher and teacher

A number of added concerns for the trainer are discussed in this chapter. All of them relate to the broad area of participative training. Specifically, we will discuss these topics:

☐ Program design
☐ Need determination
☐ Selecting training methods
☐ Climate
☐ Augmenting trainer competency
☐ How to become a participative trainer
☐ Co-training
☐ Broadening the trainer base for management training
☐ Vertical training
☐ Terminology for the training effort

A Participative Approach to Program Design

All training programs begin with a determination of need. The more reality-based ones, however, involve as many knowledgeable parties as possible in the need assessment process. This might include the program participants, their bosses, other knowledgeable officials, and if it is a management or supervisory training program, their subordinates, too. Upper levels of management also may be helpful. In sum, need determination, if conducted in a professional and sophisticated way, is a highly participative process. In fact, it would not be an overstatement to assert that to make the need determination in isolation from the recipients and beneficiaries of the training is to court disaster. Why? Because one runs the risk of providing great training, but on nontargeted subjects or problems.

To the extent practicable, we, as trainers, should convert the identified needs into behavioral or terminal objectives. Thus, if the need is to learn about MBO (Management By Objectives), the behavioral objectives or outcomes may be:

☐ To identify or establish key responsibilities
☐ To set annual targets
☐ To develop or identify indicators of accomplishment, so that both the boss and the subordinate have an agreed-upon understanding about what to look for to measure progress toward the accomplishment of each goal
☐ To conduct quarterly reviews of progress toward goal accomplishment

Again, these learning outcomes should be set up in conjunction with those who sponsor the course and expect results from it.

And if determining needs and setting up of behavioral objectives have been accomplished, evaluation of the completed training will proceed logically. Also, course sponsors will assist in the evaluation process, in the form of postcourse feedback, since the sponsors were in on the training "from the ground floor." The operative maxim is that people support what they helped to create. We should also consider:

☐ Designing the program for small group learning. A program or course for 10–15 participants can achieve the rapport, warmth, intimacy, caring and sharing— all ingredients of a relaxed, participative atmosphere conducive to learning—which a group of 25 or more cannot.

☐ Using a design matrix so that we can see at a glance the overall nature and structure of the course and the degree to which participative rather than one-way communication devices have been employed. (A de-

sign matrix has the hours of instruction on the left side of the paper in a vertical column; the other related columns, also vertical, show subject or topic, method of instruction, resource person(s), aids or materials used in the session, post-session handouts, if any, etc. An example of a design matrix appears in Figure 21-1.) In respect to the latter point, we, as course designers, must continually ask ourselves: What is an acceptable ratio of lecture-talk-film to bona fide participative techniques for *this* particular program? Can we alter the ratio to favor *involving* activities?

☐ The length of the total course. Adults react negatively to a course that is loaded with filler and thus is too long, or to one that is too hurried and just scratches the surface of the subject.

☐ The nature of the training day. Although lunch and breaks are "givens," with a little imagination we may

Subject: Developing our Listening Skills

Time	Topic	Method	Resource Persons	Aids	Handouts
9:00–9:20	Assignment: What Problems do we have as listeners?	Small group work (10 minutes); general discussion (10 minutes)	Fran & Pat	Flipchart	
9:20–9:30	Results of Poor Listening	Film viewing	Fran & Pat	Film: "Listen, Please"	
9:30–9:45	Assignment: Re Film: What is the main learning from the film?	Pairs to meet	Fran & Pat	Flipchart	
9:45–10:00	Causes for poor listening	Lecturette	Pat	Flipchart	"The Poor Listener— Causes and Cures" (periodical article—15 copies)
10:00–10:15	Your skill as a listener— self-assessment	Quiz—individual work	Fran & Pat	Instrument (15 copies)	
10:15–10:30	BREAK				
10:30–11:00	Learnings from the quiz	Trios to meet	Fran & Pat		
11:00–11:15	ditto	Reports from trios and general discussion	Fran & Pat		
11:15–11:30	Exercise: "Restatement"	Total group in a circle	Fran & Pat		
11:30–11:45	Active Listening	Lecturette	Fran	Flipchart	
11:45–12:00	Q & A period summary	Total group discussion	Fran & Pat	Flipchart	"Active Listening—Key To Better Communication" (Staff paper—15 copies)
12:00–1:00	LUNCH				

Figure 21-1. Example of a design matrix.

be able to structure a more appealing and invigorating day. For example, in a three- to five-day program, conducted in a "cultural island" setting, we may have a 3:00 p.m. to 5:00 p.m. recreation break and a highly participative session after dinner (from 7:30 p.m. to 9:30 p.m.). Lecture sessions after dinner are a "no-no."

☐ Not overlooking the possibilities of designing a pre-work activity into the program.

☐ Including icebreakers and/or openers, as appropriate.

☐ Considering whether the design includes opportunities for humor and fun via icebreakers, openers, art, music, puzzles, games, exercises, and movement.

☐ Examining our completed course design matrix to check whether greater impact may be achieved by switching certain activities. For example, ending the morning session with a potent film, game, or exercise may lead to further discussion of the activity at lunch. Or an end-of-day session may serve as a prelude (stage-setter) to a short evening assignment.

☐ Recognizing that the more "threatening" activities (role plays, fishbowls, certain types of movement) should take place later in the program. This caution assumes that we have participants who need to be "eased" into participative/experiential training.

☐ Including adequate "support" materials of an interactive sort, as appropriate, for each session, such as worksheets, checksheets, instruments, and quizzes to check for understanding. In this connection, I recall a management seminar at which I used trainer/educator Dr. Malcolm Knowles as a resource person. As we were waiting for the participants to assemble, Dr. Knowles was glancing at my nearby work table, which was completely covered with a variety of support materials. Pointing to the table I said, somewhat self-deprecatingly, "Lot of paper, eh?" Dr. Knowles looked up and said, "Oh, *no*. Those are all *tools."*

☐ Making provision for special interest groups to explore certain topics in depth, if appropriate. For example, in a time management course, participants may be grouped around problem areas such as delegation, meetings, telephone use, and use of one's secretary.

☐ Designing the program with opportunities to practice the skills that were introduced. Too many training programs present the skill/concept, but rush on before participants have "buttoned down" what was presented.

☐ Including follow-up sessions in the design to aide in "glueing in" the learning. In some cases the more practical work may be given at this time.

☐ Providing participants with take-home worksheets and other aids to enable them to apply what was learned in the training situation on the job.

☐ Asking: "Is the design cost effective?" Here we are talking about participant time away from the job; the trainer's time; and costs for outside resource people, audio-visual materials, facilities, support materials, off-the-shelf materials. etc.

☐ Getting another professional opinion on the final design, or better still, designing the program with a colleague. "Peer design" should prevent oversights, expose weaknesses and inconsistencies, and generally help to make for a richer, tighter program or course.

To sum up, the design of a training program is basic to program effectiveness. It is analogous to an architect's plan for a physical structure. Hence the need for care in developing the design. A broad, cooperative effort is a key to securing such care.

Determining Needs via Participative Methods

Every trainer knows that the training cycle begins with a determination of training needs. But what is not universally known—or at least not universally observed—is that training programs are more likely to be cost-effective and accepted if *both* the sponsors and recipients of the training participate actively in that need determination. If your philosophy of training is a participative one, here, then, are some ways of ensuring participative need determination.

☐ *Individual interviews.* Participants, their bosses, and other managers may be contacted to learn of *current* problems, difficulties, deficiencies, and possibly *anticipated* (future) needs. Interviews may be conducted with all program participants, as in the case of team-building sessions, or on a sample basis. Depending on the number of people involved, sampling may be essential since worthwhile interviews run 30 to 60 minutes or more.

☐ *Group interviews.* Small groups of four to ten participants may be interviewed to learn of their problems. This method obviously may lose some of the intimacy of the individual interviewing approach. On the other hand, it is a time saver and, the group interaction may trigger added data that the one-on-one method may not. Also, the validity of the data may be verified more readily in the group situation. Finally, by meeting with the participant group before the program begins, one can begin one's acquaintance with them and the group itself can begin to develop its identity.

A practical way to help the group zero in on a need is to use the modified critical incident technique developed by David S. Stein of Ohio State University.[1] Stein's procedure is as follows:

1. Provide participants with a stack of 3″ × 5″ cards.
2. On one set of the cards have participants list incidents/situations where they felt frustrated, underprepared, or ineffective.
3. On another set of cards have them describe the skills and/or knowledge that would have helped them to cope with these incidents.
4. Set up teams of three or four persons and provide them with packets of the two types of cards.
5. Have each small group identify five situations and corresponding skills necessary for improvement.
6. Secure team reports and screen them as to the identification of bona fide training needs. *Note:* Although problems due to lack of feedback about performance, the work environment, or management shortcomings are important and should be communicated to management, they are *not* training problems and thus cannot be met via training programs.

☐ *Survey procedures.* Data, when large numbers of persons are involved, may also be gathered via various survey forms or questionnaires. The survey approach has the twin advantages of broad or even full coverage of all concerned plus the potential for uniform analysis (standardization) of the data.

If one has a good general feel for the kinds of needs that exist, based on interviews with bosses and various participants, a rating scale may be developed and used to ascertain needs in a more precise way. For example, need data for a proposed communications course may be garnered via the rating scale shown in Appendix 89.

The survey form may also be "open end" and ask for a listing and prioritization of needs. This ranking approach is helpful when the trainer has little or no data about existing training needs. A form for this procedure is given in Appendix 90.

Data Interpretation

Regardless of how the needed data are collected from the participants, the data in summary form should be cleared with the operating officials or supervisors who are sponsoring the training. To avoid this step is a certain means of losing program support, program credibility, and assistance in the evaluation and follow-up phases of the program. One of the reasons post-program or follow-up sessions often are poorly attended by participants is the lack of commitment to the program by the program sponsors. Involvement in need determination is a key strategy to secure that commitment.

On-going Adjustments

Another aspect of need determination is the making of adjustments, to the extent practicable, in the on-going program. Thus it may be desirable to reserve the last half hour or so of each day to meet with participants to learn how well the program is meeting their needs or if new needs have emerged as a result of the training. Not all such needs, obviously, will permit program alteration. But to the extent that they can, participant input should be heeded and redesign procedures instituted.

Note: A good way to secure participant input is via a fishbowl approach.

Meeting Individual Needs

The data we now have collected, using the preceding procedures, are concerned with determining and meeting group training needs. On this basis, the trainer would proceed to develop the overall course. It is hoped that this course design would be general and flexible enough so that *individual* needs also could be recognized.

One trainer[2] uses an instrument (or survey form) on site to ascertain from the participants possible alternatives to the previously planned training. In effect, the participant input produces "a contractual agreement" with both parties pledged to work on the meeting of individualized needs. Mutual agreement on intended outcomes should improve greatly the likelihood of successful training. Of course, this procedure will require considerable skill by the trainer to adapt and revise established material and to utilize participant resources/experience for the modified design.

Meeting Special Needs

Most of our training programs operate on the assumption that all participants have the same needs. While this is generally a valid assumption, it may, at times, overlook the principle of individual differences. Obviously not everyone is cast in the same mold and not everyone has identical needs, interests, preferences, or problems.

One way to meet individual or special needs is to organize on a "two-track" system, at least part of the time. For example, let's assume that we are planning a course in leadership for quality circle facilitators and leaders. We thus design the bulk of our sessions around such topics as motivation, team work, power, values, communication, conflict, and stress. However, we may also wish to provide those who are interested with advanced quality circle problem-solving techniques. We thus can run *concurrent* sessions as follows:

☐ *Leadership track:* Small groups conduct "clinics" on leadership problems of quality circles.

□ *Problem-solving track:* Formal instruction is provided by the seminar leader on advanced quality circle problem solving techniques (as opposed to concern with leadership).

Multiple special interests can be met by organizing around problem areas identified by the participants. For example, in a time management course participants may have identified their major time management problems as delegation, interruptions, paperwork, meetings, or use of the secretary. We can meet these individual needs by establishing "special interest groups," with participants joining a small group of their choice. In these small groups participants share their concerns and endeavor to help one another to resolve their difficulties.

Note: In the two-track system the trainer decided on the optional topic; in the special interest group procedure the participants provided the topics based on their own problems.

Selecting Training Methods

Many of us, as trainers, have our favorite training methods and thus "know" what works best. However, we might do a better job of methods selection if we considered these principles:

□ Some methods are more effective and appropriate than others. Two independently conducted studies, both using like criteria employed by an earlier (1972) researcher, are pertinent. Nine training methods were evaluated; case study, conference or discussion method, lecture, business game, films, programmed instruction, role playing, sensitivity training, and TV lecture. These nine methods were evaluated as to effectiveness in relation to six training objectives: knowledge acquisition, changing attitudes, problem-solving skills, interpersonal skills, participant acceptance, and knowledge retention.

The two studies, based on trainers' perceptions as to effectiveness of various methods were as follows:

1. A study by Dr. John W. Newstrom, University of Minnesota, of 54 training directors working for the largest U.S. firms.[3]
2. A study by Linda L. Neider, University of Miami, of 191 A.S.T.D. members.[4]

The rankings resulting from the two studies are given in Table 21-1 in a combined table. Note that the responses (rankings) were not too different. A major difference did occur on the lecture (with questions) method. Newstrom reported low rather

Table 21-1
Perceived Effectiveness (on a Ranking Basis) of Nine Training Methods
for Six Objectives as Reported by Newstrom (A) and Neider (B)

Method	Knowledge Acquisition		Changing Attitudes		Problem-Solving Skills		Interpersonal Skills		Participant Acceptance		Knowledge Retention	
	(A)	(B)	(A)	(B)	(A)	(B)	(A)	(B)	(A)	(B)	(A)	(B)
Case study	4	4	5	4	1	1	5	5	1	2	4	4
Conference/ discussion method	1	3	3	3	5	3	4	3	5	1	2	3
Lecture (with questions)	8	2	7	6	7	5	8	6	8	3	3	6
Business games	5	8	4	5	2	2	3	4	2	4	7	5
Movie films	6	7	6	7	9	8	6	7	4	6	5	7
Programmed instruction	3	1	8	9	6	6	7	9	9	7	1	2
Role playing	2	5	2	1	3	4	1	1	3	5	5	1
Sensitivity training (T-group)	7	9	1	2	4	7	2	2	6	9	9	8
TV lecture	9	6	9	8	8	9	9	8	7	8	8	9

than high knowledge acquisition and low rather than high participant acceptance. Note, too, the following trainers' preferences as to methods:

- *Case study* was ranked high for problem solving skills (1,1) and participant acceptance (1,2). Note: Numbers in parentheses here and after refer to rankings in the Newstrom and Neider studies.
- *Conference/discussion method* was ranked high in both studies for knowledge acquisition (1,3), but only Neider found high participant acceptance (1).
- *Lecture (with questions)* received a high ranking for knowledge acquisition by Neider only (2).
- *Business games* received a high ranking for problem-solving skills (2,2).
- *Films* received mediocre to low rankings on all six objectives.
- *Programmed instruction* received high rankings on knowledge acquisition (3,1) and knowledge retention (1,2).
- *Role playing* received numerous high rankings on all objectives, although the two studies differed on knowledge retention (5,1).
- *Sensitivity training* received high rankings on changing attitudes (1,2) and development of interpersonal skills (2,2), but low rankings on knowledge acquisition (7,9), participant acceptance (6,9), and knowledge retention (9,8).
- *TV lecture* garnered low rankings—mostly 8's and 9's—on all six objectives. Since the lecture with questions fared somewhat better in rankings, it may be assumed that its two-way aspects accounted for the difference.

☐ Methods should be related to instructional objectives, e.g., knowledge acquisition, changing attitudes, developing problem-solving skills, or developing interpersonal skills. However, as we will see later, this "ideal" procedure may not always be practical.

☐ Methods may have to be selected in relation to organizational and/or participant acceptance. For example, many organizations will not permit the use of T-groups even though it is recognized in the literature and by many trainers as the best technique to use to change attitudes and to build interpersonal skills. Or, a particular participant group may resist role playing because it may prove embarrassing or object to games as being "too frivolous."

☐ A whole host of "environmental constraints" may also influence decisions concerning choice of method or instructional strategy. These are:[5]

1. *Money:* For example, it may be too expensive to "import" a trained facilitator to conduct T-groups or to use a video-telephone hook-up at nine points.

2. *Time:* A ramified business game or three role plays (supervisor, employee, observer on a rotational basis) may take too long.
3. *Staff:* Expert trainers may not be available to staff a given training program properly; hence, self-teaching methods may have to be utilized.
4. *Trainer philosophy:* A trainer may prefer T-groups, which are based on humanistic psychology, rather than programmed learning, which is underpinned by behaviorist psychology.
5. *Physical space and equipment:* A small room may work against the use of mass role plays enacted simultaneously.
6. *Class size:* One can hardly utilize fishbowls and certain games and exercises if the participant group has only six people in it.

☐ Certain methods are of minimal effectiveness unless supported by other ones. For example, a film presentation by itself can hardly be effective, hence the need to combine it with one or more methods such as a small group discussion or possibly a role play.

☐ Various methods may be combined to form an "instructional strategy." For example, "behavior modeling" uses a variety of techniques including an introductory talk to explain the skill area to be worked on; a videotape will then demonstrate the proper behavior to be learned (modeling). The participants then role play the skill in question per the model observed, critique the behavior via feedback (positive reinforcement is stressed) after the enactment, and engage in further skill practice via role playing.

Selecting Methods—A Case Example

To help the reader visualize how the trainer might go about selecting methods for a given unit of instruction, my experience in coaching may be of help. I was asked by an organization to conduct a session on "the appraisal interview." By raising many pertinent questions about the real supervisory problems prevalent in the organization, I concluded that the problem was much broader—that supervisors were falling down in their responsibilities as a coach. A session on coaching was thus recommended. The recommendation was accepted and I "auto-brainstormed" the supervisor's responsibility as a coach. This led to the conclusion that the effective coach had to be concerned, as a minimum, with these skill areas:

☐ Encouraging employee growth and development. *Note:* This skill area was placed on the top of the list to give emphasis to the idea that this was the most important aspect of the coaching job and that such tasks as assigning and reviewing work were more related to routine supervision rather than the broader concept of coaching.

☐ Upgrading performance of employees, i.e., bringing about a change in attitude/behavior. The idea was to encourage supervisors to utilize everyday events to do this upgrading. For example, a minor accident while backing up a truck could be dismissed with a "let's be more careful next time," or the supervisor could sit down with the careless employee and discuss safety practices in detail as well as the possible consequences of an accident. Similarly, in an office situation a poorly written letter could be returned with the necessary editing or one could discuss with the writer the "principles" that were overlooked or violated.

☐ Delegating responsibility. This is an area that not only encourages employee growth, but also brings about "invention." That is to say, if you or I as a supervisor do a particular task, even if we do it well, in all likelihood it will still be performed in the same way. But if we delegate the task, it is likely to be done differently, possibly in a novel and more effective way.

☐ Giving clear, specific, and complete instructions and guidance when assigning work.

☐ Conducting an effective annual performance review.

☐ Introspecting about one's prowess as a coach.

In addition, since all of these activites were *trainer-selected and developed,* it seemed desirable to have a "clinic" where the supervisors could introduce some of their own problems for resolution.

The grid (Table 21-2) was then set up to help design the desired learning sequence on coaching. In general, the approach is to design and provide a set of "stimulus materials" that will zero in on the specific learning objectives that have been pinpointed.

Climate

The "right" climate or atmosphere is essential for high participant learning. While "right" may be subject to a certain amount of debate, most trainers would agree that the following elements are basic ingredients of the climate we require:

☐ Pre-arrival factors
☐ Greeting of participants
☐ The learning facility/environment itself
☐ The trainer's style and behavior

The following sections discuss these elements of climate as well as what to do "when things go wrong."

Setting the Climate Before the Training Session

Ordinarily we think of climate in terms of what participants perceive once the training begins. However, what we as trainers do or fail to do prior to our participants' arrival at the training room door is also an influencing factor. Hence the need to pay attention to such preentry elements as:

☐ *Contact.* Do we send participants a letter of welcome explaining the program and its goals briefly; its location and how to get there, if necessary; daily hours; when the program ends; provisions for meals; clothes to wear; recreation possibilities? Remember, the letter, as the first contact with the program, begins immediately to set the tone for the program.

☐ *Pre-work.* Do we provide a pre-session assignment (through the mail) to involve participants early-on and to indicate that this is a real learning opportunity?

☐ *Pre-session get together.* Do we try to have a pre-session meeting to pass out a pre-work assignment? For example, in a time management program distributing a time log and providing instructions concerning how to keep it is a must. Or, in a management training program, do we open with a get-acquainted cocktail party the evening before the first morning session?

☐ *Need determination.* Do we consider the possibility that we can better meet participant needs if we learn of their problems before they arrive at class? In effect, their problems, needs, and ideas can aid us in our work on program design in general and in agenda setting in particular. Certainly, participant input will go a long way in setting high expectations as well as a climate of mutuality.

☐ *Calendar for contracting.* Do we ask our participants to bring along their calendars or appointment books for back-home action planning purposes?

Greeting Your Participants

Although climate is certainly established to some extent before participants arrive at the training room, a key factor in perception of climate is what takes place on arrival. Participants do have questions, even concerns, about what they will experience. ("I wonder what I'm getting into." "Will this be worthwhile?" "What's the trainer like?") By paying attention to the "meeting and greeting" aspects of climate, participants' anxieties can be quieted and their comfortable entry into the program facilitated. Some suggestions to do this follow.

First of all, try to provide easy-to-follow instructions concerning the location of the training room. A sign on the door or wall or one standing on the floor will help to

Table 21-2
Designing a Learning Sequence: Coaching

Skill Area and/or Activity	Rationale	Technique or Method	Specific Task or Assignment	Length of Activity
Encouraging growth	To focus attention on power, all of us, as supervisors, have. We can develop and "turn on" our people *or* discourage and "turn them off" and inhibit their growth and development	Small group work (trios); data generated by the trios to be posted on flipchart, compared and discussed	1. One set of groups to focus on experiences in career, school, home, etc. that *encouraged* growth 2. One set of groups to focus on experiences that *discouraged* growth	Work in trios: 10 minutes Feedback and posting: 15 minutes Discussion: 15 minutes Total time: 40 minutes
Upgrading performance—bringing about a change in attitude or behavior	To provide skill practice in challenging an employee to upgrade his/her performance	Role play (on a rotational basis so that each participant functions as coach, subordinate, and observer)	Three role plays, each of a different degree of difficulty. Typical cases: A young person with good potential is handicapping himself/herself by poor interpersonal skills; a senior supervisor is a good production person but weak on human relations skills	*Each* role play runs for 25–30 minutes; feedback and discussion also run for 25–30 minutes
Delegating responsibility	Delegation is a skill that can be sharpened. It is a skill basic to encouragement of growth and creativity of subordinates	Exercise: Analysis of one's job with the objective of delegating greater responsibility to subordinates: 1. Individual analysis of responsibility 2. Sharing in pairs or trios	Develop a chart listing major and minor responsibilities in Column 1, subordinates to whom responsibilities might be delegated in Column 2, and whether duties are delegatable now or require training in Column 3	Individual work: 30 minutes Sharing: 30 minutes Total group processing: 20 minutes
Assigning work	In absence of fully helpful instructions, employees may experience frustration, errors and/or low performance. But with proper guidance by the boss, employees can get the job done quicker, easier and more accurately	Exercise—Numbers: A Problem Solving Activity (given in *The 1978 Handbook for Group Facilitators,* University Associates, Inc., Publishers, p. 9)	To connect "miscellaneous" numbers on a worksheet. The task is completed five times, performance going up markedly when full information and assistance is provided.	Individual work: 5 minutes General discussion: 10 minutes
Conducting an annual performance review	Practice via role play can provide confidence and skill in the conduct of the interview	1. Film or video showing the proper way to conduct the interview 2. Role play to get skill practice	Conduct an annual performance review based on data provided by the trainer.	Role Play: 20–30 minutes Feedback from observers: 15 minutes General discussion of key points to conduct an effective interview: 15 minutes

(Table 21-2 continued on next page)

Table 21-2
Continued

Skill Area and/or Activity	Rationale	Technique or Method	Specific Task or Assignment	Length of Activity
Introspection of one's skill as a coach	Supervisors need to look inward to their coaching practices. This is a step toward improved/strengthened coaching ability	Instrument	Complete an instrument on coaching to assess one's prowess as a coach	Individual completion of instrument: 15 minutes Sharing of data: 30 minutes Group discussion: 15 minutes
"Clinic" on coaching skills	This is an opportunity to secure help on a coaching problem one may have	Small group work (trios)	Come up with one need you see you have as a coach; discuss it with your team, which will try to provide feedback, advice, and support on the problem; each member of the trio presents a problem or concern about himself/herself	Each person presents and discusses his/her problem for 20 minutes. Total time: 60 minutes Group-at-large discussion: 20–30 minutes

eliminate that anxious question: "Is this the place?" (*Note:* Not all groups may have this problem.)

Make it a practice to greet participants when they first arrive. People *do* like to feel welcome. To do this in a relaxed way, arrive early so that you have completed your preparation chores—checking out the room, setting up the projector, arranging your exercise materials and handouts, completing "advance" flipcharts, and the like. Try to recall your own feelings about the instructor/ trainer who was so busy with "setting up" that he/she didn't even have time to say "hello" to anyone. In this connection, it's a good idea to review the roster before participants arrive to get at least some "feel" for participants' names, titles, locations, etc.

If name cards are to be used, consider making it an informal, "do-it-yourself" procedure. Help people get rid of their anxieties by putting them to work. You may wish to say: "Would you please write your name on this card as you want to be called while you're here? This is your first participative act in our program!" (I prefer this procedure to the formality of preparing cards beforehand, which ordinarily doesn't allow for the use of nicknames. Another undesirable procedure is to have the trainer write the name on the card for the participant. This approach seems to carry an unnecessary tone of: "You look pretty helpless to me; since I'm in charge, *I'll* do it for you.") When the name has been written on the name card it's a good idea to repeat it aloud, both to please the name's owner and to help you to remember it. If the

name should have an unusually pleasant ring to it, you may wish to tell the participant about it.

If registration or "signing in" is required, notebooks or learning packets are to be passed out, or a roster of participants is to be distributed, try to make these procedures as "painless" and expeditious as possible. Use an assistant, if needed.

Suggest the use of the coat rack, as may be appropriate. Be certain of the location of the restrooms as opposed to: "I think it's somewhere downstairs." Avoid inappropriate humor such as: "I'm not sure whether they have one or not."

Consider having a welcoming, early morning (pre-session) coffee service available. This is a "natural" location, of course, for you to "mingle" with participants before things get started. Introduce yourself to anyone you don't know.

Create a warm and inviting atmosphere by having some lively music emitting from a table radio or cassette player. (Why let your participants stare uncomfortably at the wall, ceiling, or blank flipchart pad?) Also, the flipchart pad can be dressed up a bit with a cheery statement along the lines of Figure 21-2.

Remember, participants are trying to get "a fix" on you as a person. They are asking themselves: "Is he/she approachable or distant? Relaxed or harried? Friendly or aloof? Interested in others or detached? Warm or cold? Human or a machine? Your behavior is communicating something about you at the very outset. Ask yourself:

"Is the communication what I wish it to be?" Are you aware that over 70% of your communication is nonverbal?

Requirements for the Effective Learning Environment/Facility

Changing behavior and/or attitudes or imparting new skill and knowledge is hardly an easy process. Hence conditions for participant learning should be as close to "ideal" as is practicable. One vital condition is the facility. An ideal facility would pay attention to these concerns:

☐ *Physical appearance.* The physical set-up should help to create an atmosphere that supports the learning process. The ideal facility, then, is attractive, comfortable, bright, relaxing, clean, and generally "easy to take."

☐ *The training area.* The training space should be able to accommodate the nature of the training being offered. Thus, if audio-visual aids are being used, a room with pillars or posts which block visibility is taboo. If a good quantity of flipcharts are to be produced and posted on the wall, the room's wall space must be able to accommodate them. If movement, small group work, role plays, etc. are to be utilized, the room must be large enough to allow for such activity. As necessary, other breakout rooms must be avail-

Figure 21-2. An example of how to enliven a blank flipchart before a session begins.

able. If tables are used to form a U, there should be enough room for participants to enter and exit from their chairs easily.

Attention should also be paid to these factors: lighting; dimming or darkening capability for a-v presentations; comfortable chairs; temperature and ventilation; elimination of noise from fans, an adjacent kitchen (if in a motel), the street, competing meetings; the availability of tables if writing is to take place.

Telephones, wall clocks, distracting views from window areas (e.g., the swimming pool) are to be shunned. The use of a message board should help avoid telephone and personal interruptions. (Most of such calls can await a response at the break or lunch period.)

☐ *Physical location.* The training facility must be distraction-free. In-house training centers away from the usual location of the learner; out-of-town motels, hotels, or conference facilities; and other cultural island-type facilities thus are preferred. They help participants to forget back-home (job, family) concerns and permit maximum concentration on learning. Conversely, training "in-the-building," all too often, is subject to participants being pulled out for "emergencies" (whatever happened to delegation?), unwanted visitors, phone calls, temptations by participants to return to the office to "clean up" the in-box at breaks or lunch.

☐ *Participant comfort.* Every training program must provide adequate concern for "creature comforts." In a live-in facility, comfortable beds and good food, are a must. In any facility the usual morning and afternoon coffee/refreshments also are essential.

☐ *Accessibility.* Whether in town or away from town, participants should not be burdened with problems of reaching the location or anxieties about "getting home." The great popularity of a conference center—motels near airports—is a confirmation of this principle. Don't overlook providing instructions concerning how to reach the place. Participants also want information about such matters as parking.

☐ *Adequate support.* The facility should be able to provide the lubricants essential to a troublefree training operation—extra tables, flipcharts, a-v equipment, coat rack, wastebaskets, possibly a photocopy service. Also, cooperation is essential concerning the prompt delivery of coffee, and lunch. A cheerful, cooperative contact person representing the facility is certainly desirable.

☐ *Flexibility.* The facility should be amenable to special needs; e.g., an evening or early morning session; a change in the lunch period or coffee break; exercises that may deviate from facility norms, such as conducting a trust walk or building towers out of newspaper.

The Trainer as a Climate Setter

Mention has been made of the importance of the trainer greeting and mingling with the group before the program starts. The trainer can also help to set the right climate by concern with these added elements:

Clothing. Encourage the participants to dress informally in the advance notification to them about the program. Upon arrival, also encourage them to put their coats on the coat rack or on unused chairs. To the extent that *they* are made comfortable, they will help to make the atmosphere that much "looser." Similarly, you should abandon your academic stance by shedding the traditional suit coat. In fact, in certain situations other informal dress such as a sweater rather than a coat and tie may work well.

Personal introduction. If the group doesn't know you, tell them how you want to be called and something about yourself. Don't be a mystery person. But keep the "intro" pertinent, brief, and humble. The participants may be particularly interested in your relationship to this program: did you design it, experience it elsewhere, buy it off the shelf, revise it? Also, have you conducted it before? If so, how often?

Positioning. Where and how you position yourself in the classroom is also significant. Thus, being seated (at least part of the time) is preferred to standing; being seated or standing in front of a table is preferred to being behind it; varying one's positions in the room—to the left or the right side—is preferred to always being up front; letting participants present material "up front" while you are elsewhere is also good; sitting in a circle with the group, if at all practicable, is preferred to always being up front.

Flipcharting. Numerous tear sheets on the walls can help to give the training room a workshop atmosphere. Conversely, the blackboard up front tends to aid the traditional schoolroom look. *Note:* Several flipcharts containing key ideas may be posted on the wall in advance of the session.

Breaks and lunch. Beside the formal morning and afternoon breaks, intermittent one or two minute "stretch" breaks can help to create a "looser," more relaxed feeling. In respect to the lunch period, try to keep the group together so as to develop fuller group cohesion. Also, try to conduct the training away from the building so the lunch period isn't used to check out the in-box.

Using participant names. Try to address participants by their first names or nicknames. Advance study of the roster, using name cards and/or tent cards on tables will help you do this. If you are using icebreakers, join in so that you can get acquainted with at least some names and faces from the outset. I like to have people call me by my first name. How do you feel about this? If you like it, it's a safe bet your participants favor it, too.

Group size. Small group situations are basic for achieving high participation, involvement, comraderie, and learning. While larger groups (20–30 persons) can certainly be broken down into small groups with good results, intimacy and rapport among participants and with the trainer are more readily achieved with the smaller group (8–12 or possibly 15 persons).

Intimacy. The trainer who wishes to create a positive climate will seek out opportunities to get closer to the participants, to become a member of the group. Some suggestions are:

1. Mingle with participants at the break. Obviously you can't talk with everyone. But the fact that you are talking to one or more group members will be noted and appreciated. In effect, they will identify with the ones you are speaking to.
2. Be certain to join the group at lunch. If it is not an organized group lunch—and it should be, if at all possible—ask two or three participants if you may join them.
3. If it is a "live-in" program, join the group at breakfast, cocktails, and dinner as well.
4. Be particularly understanding and helpful to latecomers. If the late-arriving person has merely missed some introductory material, tell him or her: "Hi, welcome. You haven't really missed anything. We only had a warm-up exercise and the goals for the program are posted on that flipchart sheet." This will help to reduce the latecomer's anxieties and show the group that you do have empathy with *all* participants.

If the latecomer has missed some significant material, you may wish to make this statement: "We have covered some material which you will want to get checked out on. Would you please see me at the break (or at lunch) and I'm sure that I can fill you in pretty well on what took place. OK?"

Trust. Effective learning requires a high degree of trust in the training situation. Participants must feel that they can comment, question, challenge, disagree without fear of being criticized, attacked, or put down. Certainly, to the extent that the trainer can establish intimacy and rapport with the participants, they will feel free to express their thoughts and feelings.

What about the use of training procedures and techniques that relate to trust building? While such devices will not be a substitute for the trainer's behavior—actions do speak louder than words, and gimmicks, too—they may help if they are in context and perceived as sincere. In any case, here are two such procedures:

1. Conduct a trust walk at the outset to symbolize the importance of building trust (see the chapter on icebreakers).
2. Draw on a flipchart the following.

```
┌──────────────────────────────────┐
│                                  │
│        MEMO                      │
│        ─────                     │
│  To:  ALL PARTICIPANTS           │
│  From: Trainer (Add your name)   │
│  Subject: OUR PRIME GROUND RULE  │
│                                  │
│  There is no such a thing as a   │
│  stupid question, comment or     │
│  suggestion. PERIOD.             │
│                                  │
│  Note: The only really "poor"    │
│  question or statement is the    │
│  one you were reluctant to       │
│  offer!                          │
│                                  │
└──────────────────────────────────┘
```

Style. The most important factor in climate setting is the trainer's style. Key elements that will determine it are:

☐ Using icebreakers and/or openers.
☐ Listening with empathy; don't interrupt.
☐ Accepting an idea one may not agree with.
☐ Credibility—do you communicate frankly what you know and what you do not? Participants appreciate genuineness. Do you practice what you teach, especially if you teach interpersonal skills.
☐ Dealing with "difficult" participants in a respectful way.
☐ Dealing empathically with "slower" participants.
☐ A high energy level—one's energy/electricity, high or low, is very likely to rub off on the participants.
☐ Strong tendencies to utilize positive reinforcement (praise, recognition).
☐ Caring—do we recognize the training situation as an opportunity to make the participants, rather than ourselves, "look good?"
☐ Ability to learn with the group—every training experience is a learning opportunity for the trainer and must be so perceived by the group.

☐ Creating a supportive atmosphere where people feel free to take risks, where they act on the assumption that there are no stupid questions or comments.
☐ Being sensitive to the communication process, including participant body language and our own as well.
☐ Organizing the program and behaving in such a way that participants feel that they have "ownership" of the program. Some key questions: Who is spending valuable time away from the job? Who is here to learn? So whose program is it?
☐ Establishing at the outset participant expectations and trainer expectations and the degree to which they coincide.
☐ Establishing in your own mind your own role: catalyst/facilitator vs. lecturer/instructor/expert and then behaving consistently in that chosen role.
☐ Providing a fun-type atmosphere—need learning be dull, dreary, depressing?
☐ Providing for change of pace—recreation, a party, field trips, etc.
☐ Stressing opportunities for discovery rather than didactic learning.
☐ Making learning gradual/developmental—no one likes to be "pushed" nor are "uncontracted for" surprises appreciated.
☐ Securing feedback, to the extent practicable, about your own behavior—for the trainer, a training program should be a growth experience as well as a learning experience.
☐ Making oneself accessible for questioning after the session's or program's end.

When Things Go Wrong

Murphy's Law (if anything can possibly go wrong it will) is a fact of the trainer's life. Thus, we can anticipate that irritations will arise for us and our participants from unanticipated inadequacies in lighting, heating, ventilation, seating, acoustics, equipment, etc.

What do we do? Above all, we should avoid the "ain't it awful" trap. Instead, we should regard these contingencies as a challenge and engage in healthy coping behavior. Thus, if the air conditioning system fails and it is too hot, consider approaches such as these:

☐ Encourage people to adjust their clothing for comfort—remove ties, coats, possibly shoes and shirts, too, in a free-flowing experiential program.
☐ Encourage people to sit on the floor where they can relax and the temperature may be lower.
☐ Relocate to another room or to the outdoors.
☐ Hold frequent stand-up stretches and breaks
☐ Another possibility is to tell the group: "I'm feeling hot and tired as I know you are. But maybe we can

approach this problem via a contract—if you'll pay attention to (or cooperate with) the program, we'll try to do our best to help you learn from it. OK.?"

☐ Suggest to the group this approach: "Let's use our power to cool the room, to produce a breeze. Let's say in unison 'oooo oooo oooo.' Again, louder, 'oooo oooo oooo.' And a final time, much louder, 'oooo oooo oooo.' Now raise your arms over your head and wave them. Feel the breeze?"

☐ If it's really at the impossible stage, defer or cancel the session.

To test your coping ability, here's a problem for you: Assume you are invited to conduct an all-day training program for another organization. You neglected to ask about the precise nature of the facilities, and as it turns out to your dismay, you have to work in a medium-sized auditorium with fixed seats. You wish to use participative (small group) methods. What can you do to "salvage" the situation? Some answers follow:

1. Use dyads extensively—simply have people turn to their left or right.
2. Have participants move to the stage, aisles, rear or front of the room for small-group work on a stand-up basis.
3. If other chairs are available, bring them in for small group work.
4. Form quartets by having a pair turn around (not comfortable, but workable for a short task).
5. Better still, have everyone stand up for better eye contact.
6. Relocate to the hall *outside* the auditorium for stand-up, small group work.

Augmenting Trainer Competency

On the very valid assumption that the best trainer is one who is either training someone or training himself/herself, it makes good sense to work actively and systematically at your self-development. One helpful way to start is to list the areas that you might wish to explore and check off those of immediate need or interest. A suggested checklist, emphasizing "newer" subjects, appears in Appendix 91.

The goals of such training could be for:

☐ Introduction to the subject, that is, for background purposes
☐ personal development
☐ Development of a new competency so that one can provide the training to others, in-house

Obviously, the intended use of the new skill or knowledge will determine the intensity of the training undertaken (i.e., the nature and number of the courses or programs one would take).

It is to be noted that the check list deals with specific *content areas* relating to the training field (e.g., TA, MBO, time management). Similar self-development lists could be developed that cover

Trainer skill development, e.g., in public speaking (via a toastmasters club membership), writing, instrumentation, exercises and games, the systems approach to training, and consultation skills

Professional growth via participation in training and/or other management associations and societies

Broadening outlooks and interests via participation in community and civic affairs, college teaching, etc.

How to Become a Participative Trainer

Working with training groups in a participative way requires three components:

1. A strong philosophy that adults learn best when they are active rather than passive, challenged rather than talked at, involved rather than observing, and committed rather than detached.
2. Skill in the use of participative training methods, including a willingness to try out new ways of involving groups.
3. Concern with continuing personal and professional growth.

Element 1—a sincere belief about the worth of participative training methods—is a "given." We start from this conviction. If it's lacking, the requisite skills cannot be learned meaningfully.

Element 2—ability to use participative training skills—certainly can be acquired. The best prescription for this is to:

☐ Attend a basic course in instructional design and methods, paying particular attention to the participative aspects being presented.
☐ Attend courses in both supervision and management development. These are essentially "core" courses and cannot be overlooked.
☐ Seek out additional, more specialized training opportunities in such skill areas as role playing, instrumentation, exercises, games, and team building.
☐ Attend early on a personal growth laboratory. This is a must. This may be the T-group (sensitivity training), an encounter group or preferably both. Highly experi-

ential activities such as these will acquaint you with the "laboratory method" of training (the group learns from its own behavior), provide you with models of trainers who interact nondirectively but effectively with the participants, show you how participative training methods should be properly executed, introduce you to concepts vital in training work such as giving and receiving feedback, introspection, openness, caring, sharing, intimacy, spontaneity, the world of the affect (feelings), and experimentation. Most importantly, the laboratory experience should impact favorably on your growth as a person, for very few of us, especially if we work with adults in the training situation, can assume that we really understand ourselves—our needs, our motivations, our impact on others, our sensitivity to the feelings of others. A good T-group experience should help to clear away some of the psychological impediments all of us carry around with us.

Continuing professional growth (element 3) can be achieved by

☐ Attending specialized programs to learn such *content* as MBO transactional analysis, assertiveness training, communication, coaching, counseling, and stress management.

☐ Affiliation with appropriate professional societies that can continue your professional growth and development. Attend their chapter meetings and national conferences and read their journals. The "basic" society to consider is the American Society for Training and Development (ASTD), Alexandria, Va. Should your work tend toward the experiential/human growth areas, the Association for Humanistic Psychology, San Francisco, merits consideration, too. And if your interests are more oriented toward "hard core," performance-based, skills training and you use various educational technologies such as CBI (computer-based instruction), interactive video discs, etc., consider affiliation with the National Society for Performance and Instruction (NSPI), Washington, D.C.

☐ Enrollment in appropriate university courses, or even degree-type programs, might be explored if one lacks adequate grounding in the behavioral sciences/education. Programs that should prove helpful are psychology, organizational behavior, and human resource development.

If all of this seems like a tall order, the answer is that it is. For learning the training job well is not a quickie, overnight proposition. Rather, it takes dedication and continuing application. In fact, one might say that the best trainer is one who is "at it all the time"—either training others or training himself/herself. This follows

since the training field is a dynamic one that is constantly expanding, changing, and receiving inputs from the burgeoning behavioral sciences, education, and management fields. This quote from Pope John XXIII is pertinent to one's personal growth: "Always learn something new. This year, I am going to learn Russian."

Experiential training authorities Pfeiffer and Jones provide some added worthwhile advice:[6]

1. Build a repertoire of materials to use in design work, e.g., structured experiences, instruments.
2. Work with a variety of other facilitators. There is no substitute for experience with other professionals.
3. Seek out opportunities to work with *various* client groups.
4. Study other facilitators' designs.
5. Attend professional development workshops.

Cotraining: Some ABC's

Just as there is real merit in involving participants fully in the *learning* process, there also are many advantages to making the *training* process a team or coeffort. The ABC's regarding cotraining or team training, which are given below, should present the rationale for it.

Anxiety can be reduced significantly. A joint training venture, in which responsiblity is shared, has the potential to reduce the assorted stresses and strains entailed in planning and delivering the training. So why go it alone and court fatigue, anxiety, and even "burnout?"

Breaks and breathers become possible in the training situation. Cotraining gives the participants a "break" from the same trainer's face and pace. And with two persons doing the teaching/facilitating, you get a "breather" in terms of reduced load. You thus can return to the training task recharged and refreshed. Participants are quick to pick up trainer fatigue and may even enter on their evaluation forms such comments as: "The trainer seemed to run out of gas in the afternoon" or "It gets a little tedious working with one training person all day."

Copresenting can help to share the managing of cognitive tasks—monitoring audience reaction, keeping track of content, and managing time. While one presents, the other can assess the audience or plan modifications in the lesson or session. And should one trainer get off track, the other can help to make the needed correction. A duo also means greater availability for break-time chats with the participants.

Course content can become more varied, more enriched when more than one trainer is making inputs. This follows since the odds are that different trainers will have different competencies, different approaches, different interests, different emphases. Different material may thus be incorporated into the course at the outset, and in the training situation the trainers may provide different examples or illustrations about the subject matter. They may also respond to participant questions and comments from different vantage points.

Delivery of material can be more varied, which, as has been indicated, is easier on the participants. Two (or more) trainers are certainly an attention-getting device. Also, if one trainer is more comfortable with a given subject or topic, he/she obviously should handle that area. Two trainers are also useful if two groups have to be formed (e.g., in brainstorming, case study, setting up fishbowls) or if you need two trained observers to observe separate group activities.

Evaluation also may be improved with a more-than-one-person effort. This relates to both the planning and the execution of evaluation. Since program assessment is one of the toughest areas of the overall training job, the old adage of "two heads are better than one" merits heeding.

Feedback regarding one's performance, trainee relationships, and so forth is a major route to augmented professional competence. The observations of a colleague, in the form of a professional critique, are invaluable. And if an aspect of program delivery merits rehearsal, feedback from the cotrainer can strengthen such delivery.

Growth, both professional and personal, can be stimulated and enhanced. In the team training situation one certainly learns from the ideas and approaches of the other trainer. Also, one learns how to work cooperatively. Given the fact that both trainers very likely have different backgrounds and personalities, one must learn how "to work things out" and "how to give and take" with another professional person.

Handouts can be better conceived, developed, and evaluated via the multiple-judgment route.

Interaction with another competent, professional trainer can provide stimulation, confidence, encouragement to experiment and innovate, etc. The participants also benefit from the opportunity (or even challenge) to interact with another trainer having a different style, personality, pace, and possibly another viewpoint.

Judgments or decisions can be made in a more sophisticated way when more than one resource is employed.

Knuckling down is likely to be facilitated. When one goes it alone, there may be a tendency to defer, postpone, put things "on a back burner." This is understandable since all the motivation to do must come from within. Conversely, in a two-person training effort one is naturally encouraged by the other's presence to "get with it." If we may coin a phrase on this problem, we might say: "Pairs prevent pusillanimous procrastination."

Loneliness can be overcome. The best professional effort is one done in concert with a colleague. For this is the way one gets stimulation, encouragement, support, feedback, etc.

Modeling for participants becomes possible. When two trainers work well together, they establish a model of cooperation for the group. They can demonstrate that two persons with different personalities, styles, and views on various issues can work as a team. They can show how they handle disagreement, which may arise at times, with respect. ("George has worked in both the private and public sectors and thus sees the issue a bit differently than I do. I can respect his view, although my background is such that it's difficult for me to share it totally.")

New ideas, novel approaches are encouraged by the mix of backgrounds. Conversely, with a single background or perspective, plowing new ground is that much harder.

Options can be more readily identified, explored, and exploited by the team approach. The best decisions in any field, training included, come about through consideration of alternative or optional courses of action.

Pedagogical approaches and methods can be subject to greater variety based on dual interests and capabilities.

Questioning of what is planned and designed is facilitated. It's a lot easier to question someone else's ideas than our own. Though it is sad to relate, one's own ideas may be overly revered and thus may tend to become "chiseled in stone."

Reinforcement of certain views or issues may be needed from more than one source should participants resist the program's point of view. If so, the added trainer can help to provide that added reinforcement.

Support can be provided by a colleague at all stages of the program. No person, including the trainer, is an island. A trainer, too, needs praise, encouragement, and support. A "Hey, you really did a good job on that exercise. The group ate it all up," is always welcome. Support also encompasses sharing, caring, intimacy, and comraderie.

Triumphs are often best when they can be shared: "We really pulled it off. The best first day we ever had."

Unequalness, imbalance, inconsistency can be detected more readily when two professional minds are at work.

Visual aids can also be prepared and evaluated better via joint effort.

Weaknesses in all aspects of program development, delivery, and evaluation are more likely to be overcome by virtue of a second perspective.

X-cellence is more certain to be stressed when *two* professional trainers have to be satisfied with their results: "Dave, I don't think this is our best effort. We ought to take another look at the whole thing."

Yesterday is more likely to be abandoned. With time pressures to produce, one "critic" may well be content to leave things as they are. With the added set of hands and eyes, there should be a greater willingness to question what has been done.

Zest can be augmented when one can profit from the "sparks" which the other produces.

The above ABC's present the rationale for cotraining. However, we should recognize that there are circumstances when team training may not be desirable. For example:

☐ When one's boss expects clear-cut, fixed accountability for results and thus is not comfortable with "divided" or shared responsibility.

☐ When the *skill* levels of the trainers are highly dissimilar. In such a circumstance the more experienced or effective person is likely to have to "carry" the other trainer. And since the weaker person is not really a cotrainer, he/she can only end up looking "weak" in the eyes of the participants. (Of course, a trainer-trainee relationship often exists; but that is not a "cotrainer" relationship.)

☐ When the trainers' *philosophies* are strongly divergent. Although some difference in viewpoint has educational or training value, too great or frequent divergencies may confuse and frustrate the participants.

☐ When the *personalities* are quite diverse and thus are likely to produce conflict rather than cooperation.

☐ When the relationship is *not a fully cooperative one.* Hence, one person is forced to carry more than his/her fair share of the workload and do the minor or "dirty" jobs. There may even be quibbling about who "kicks" things off, who wraps it all up, etc.

☐ When there is genuine *rivalry* between the trainers. Visualize, for example, one trainer teasing or "putting down" the other in front of the participant group.

Organization development consultants Beverly Kaye and Betsy Jackson provide these examples of irritations and frictions which may arise between cotrainers:[7]

"But you said that *you* would bring the overheads."
"He didn't do a fair share of the pre-work detail."
"She tried to take complete control."
"He corrected me in front of the class."
"She used my favorite story."
"He played to the group instead of the learning objectives."

Kaye and Jackson also point up difficulties which may arise due to differences in skill levels of the cotrainers:

"She ignored the agenda."
"He threw us off our time schedule."
"She didn't process the exercises enough."
"He pre-empted my next lecture."
"She wasn't as prepared as she should have been."

However, there is a bright side to conflict and irritation between cotrainers. Kaye and Jackson state that they "may make us uncomfortable, but they may also keep us on our toes. For example, your feeling of competition with a cotrainer can sometimes heighten your performance level. Confronting control issues with a colleague may give you a chance to practice what you have preached in training sessions."

Recognizing that differences can arise between cotrainers, one trainer suggests that it is very important for the cotrainers to reach agreement on how they will handle these two issues:[8] (1) where the "non-performing" trainer will be located physically, i.e., up front, on the side or in the rear and (2) when and how to intervene during a session.

Note: The author's practice when in the non-performing mode: I take a back seat and try to keep silent unless my colleague calls for my added input.

Copresentation Formats[9]

The preceding paragraphs have discussed copresentation in its most common form—one trainer is "on" and the other is "off." Trainer/consultants Robert Garmston and Suzanne Bailey term this style "tag-team." This format is particularly useful for trainers beginning a cotrainer relationship. It is also useful when the material to be delivered is new to one or both parties. Other formats are described in the following.

Speak-and-Add. Both trainers are "on stage" simultaneously. One makes a statement, the other adds to or enriches it. One initiates and leads, the other supports. In general, this format permits the trainers to provide different insights, perspectives, experiences, and examples. However, one trainer is always "in charge," i.e., he/she makes the major decisions about content, when to move on, and the like.

Speak-and-Chart. One trainer presents content and elicits ideas from the group; the other records participant responses on the flipchart. The recording chore permits the trainer in the presenter role to devote full attention to his/her work with the participants.

Duet. This format provides the greatest challenge to the trainer pair for both are operating ensemble. (As metaphors, visualize a ballet duo or a singing pair.) There is a great deal of cooperating, sharing, drawing the other in, deferring to the other, listening, and showing of mutual respect. For the audience, the net effect is the observation of a fascinating, synchronistic style. No competition here; rather, the blending of the work of two individual trainers in a high-level, supportive team effort.

Broadening the Trainer Base for Management Training

While training departments routinely use instructors from the organization for professional/technical training, there is a tendency to avoid using line managers for management/supervisory training. The assumption is that teaching management skills and concepts is something that only "training professionals" can do properly. Thus, management/supervisory training becomes the exclusive province of the in-house trainer, possibly supported by outside colleagues, consultants, and academics.

There is no question that a good case can be made to *avoid* using in-house line managers for management/supervisory training. For one thing, they may not be oriented to participative training methods. For another, they may lack the "necessary" behavioral science background. Then, too, they may not have the time nor the interest to overcome such shortcomings. Given these circumstances, it is understandable why training staffs decide to "go it alone" in the management/supervisory training area.

On the other hand, the training staff that carves out a monopoly for itself on the delivery of management training runs various risks. These include being insulated from the real problems of managers; an inability to relate well to line people since their "worlds" are so different; a lack of prestige and credibility since the trainers may

never have worked on the line; being perceived as too theoretical, academic, and jargon-prone—visualize trainers bombarding participants with glowing references to Maslow, Skinner, McGregor, Likert, Herzberg, Bennis, Argyris, et al. and such terms and concepts as MBO, TA (transactional analysis), AT (assertiveness training), OD, OJT, TM (transcendental meditation), Johari window, perceptual screen, autotelic behavior, positive reinforcement, and right and left brain thinking.

Weighing the pros and cons of the issue, I feel that line managers *should* be active participants in the conduct of management/supervisory training. My reasoning is as follows:

Advantages For Participants

☐ Resistance to training can be reduced since the participants understand that it is a *line* product, that managers are involved in its design, delivery and evaluation. The course or program acquires a higher degree of *credibility* for them than for one which was developed in isolation by the training staff.
☐ Participants receive confirmation that the training effort is truly a company supported one. They thus are more willing to recognize its *relevance*.
☐ Participants are exposed to the values, style and management philosophy of senior managers. They thus receive a better understanding of the concerns of upper level management and can see better how decisions are made.
☐ Since managers will have worked on the development of training materials such as cases, simulations, and video models, the participants will learn from support materials which reflect corporate cultural realities.[10]

Benefits for the Line Manager

☐ Line managers so involved will broaden their perspectives. As long-time practitioners of the management art, exposure to a certain amount of management science, behaviorial science, educational theory, and the classroom itself will provide a good complement to that practical, on-the-line experience. As has been stated, "There's nothing so practical as good theory."
☐ For many managers it can serve as a good "shot in the arm." Being tapped to serve as a trainer should establish one as a "special person" and thus augment one's self-esteem. Being stretched to learn new skills and concepts and working with others in the training situation can serve as great motivators/energizers.
☐ It can increase the manager's visibility. He/she is now working on new program areas, is focusing on company-wide concerns, and is coming in contact with

other personnel he/she may have had little to do with previously.

☐ When the manager returns to the job, he/she will be enthusiastic about applying such classroom concepts as management by objectives, Systems 4 management, openness, and job enrichment. In effect, the person will become a more effective, progressive, participative manager. This improvement is likely to occur since the manager has been focusing solely on the management process, management skills, and management concepts for an extended period of time, say during a tour of duty of some three years or so. Teaching others to manage is a spur to better management of one's own functional area.

Procedures for Success

Of course, the keys to success with such staffing are careful selection of line managers for the training job plus serious attempts at their development. To ignore care in selection is to fall victim to what has been termed "the anyone can teach syndrome." Realistically speaking, not everyone can pull it off. While much of the training job is teachable and learnable, the would-be trainer has to bring to the job good interpersonal and communication skills, an openness to new ideas, a strong desire to help others to grow, an interest in a broad range of group-in-action training techniques (determined lecturers need not apply), and the like.

As to the training of the line manager in training techniques and concepts, the line manager has to be willing to invest the time and energy needed to begin developing new competencies. This means "going to school" at the outset to learn about the training job in a systematic way plus continuing attendance at workshops and professional training society meetings. The latter is essential to learning the subjects to be taught in the classroom and the training techniques to be used to deliver the content properly.

To ensure that our line managers who link up with the training program are successful, these procedures should be followed:

1. Think in terms of making the line manager an *addition* to the training staff as opposed to his/her becoming an intermittent instructional resource. (Of course, adding other managers to serve as trainers on an "as needed" basis is O.K., too.) *Note:* Adding line managers to the training staff obviously will require full support and approval of upper management as part of the organization's career development and training programs. Once management has given its blessing to the concept, the train-

ing staff will play an active role in the selection process, including suggesting standards and procedures for its implementation. Additionally, they can provide inputs (recommendations) to management concerning specific managers they would like to have join the training staff for a significant tour of duty.

2. Select carefully. Those who have reputations as highly competent managers, who are interested in a broad range of management ideas, who feel strongly about helping others to become more effective, and who have a flair for working effectively with others in group situations are to be preferred.

3. Analyze carefully the actual training competencies the new "hire" has. Plan an individualized development program to meet those needs.

4. Provide enough training opportunities so that the new trainer will function at a high standard as soon as possible. Provide enough coaching and counseling to provide motivation and to ensure success.

5. Ensure that the line manager's tour of duty in the training unit is long enough—some $2^{1}/_{2}$ to 3 years—so that the job can be learned well and that the manager can make a real contribution to it as well. Those who are merely interested in a "quickie" tour of duty are to be shunned.

6. Secure management support to make this type of assignment a much sought after career opportunity, one having high status, high visibility, and high opportunity to contribute to the success of the organization.

Gains For The Organization

☐ The expanded role of the manager can serve as an organization development intervention, a lever for change. For example, trainers Donna R. Christensen and Dennis C. Kinlaw report that in designing and conducting a performance appraisal workshop, the managers, as trainers, became so aware of the system's weaknesses that a whole new policy and set of guidelines were developed. A massive training effort for all employees was also provided.[10]

☐ Since more reality-based training is being provided, the organization's training effort will get more attention, more credibility, greater support at all levels, and thus more return on the training dollar.

☐ Managers so involved profit from an added developmental experience which should augment their managerial capability upon return to line work, and thus impact on overall organizational outcomes.

☐ Its image as a career-minded organization is enhanced since it is providing diversified, in-house developmental opportunities, as well as showing strong interest in and support of the training function.

Values For The Training Department

☐ It can augment the credibility of those who deliver the training. Line managers are worthwhile role models in the management training situation. Conversely, when trainers provide management training and have done little or no managing themselves, the training effort, understandably, may be suspect.

☐ It obviously can increase the size of the training staff. Most training units can profit from "extra hands."

☐ In planning or designing courses or sessions, the line managers detailed to the staff can serve as an excellent resource to reality test the proposed offerings.

☐ It can provide trainers with increased stimulation and learning by intimate contact with representatives of management.

☐ When the line managers return to their jobs they are likely to become advocates for the training function. This is one way for the training unit to get the support it always seeks and needs.

In summary, line managers should be involved in training other managers. If the task is approached properly, it can pay dividends to the participants, the managers, the training staff, and the total organization.

As a final point, the organization's culture must recognize the importance of line participation in its training program. The training assignments should be regarded as a prestigious, coveted career opportunity, with appropriate rewards and support provided to program participants.

Vertical Training

The trainer who is interested in broad participation is faced from time to time with a request to include a supervisor with his/her subordinates in the same training course. If both parties attend together, we have "vertical training." It is not an overstatement to say flatly that such joint attendance is not a very workable procedure. Why not? For two reasons:

1. The most serious objection is based on the fact that all too many supervisors, wittingly or unwittingly, will inhibit the paticipation of their subordinates. After all, who wants to "look bad" in front of one's supervisor? Or worse still, who wants to disagree openly with one's boss? Disagreement with another participant might not be too threatening, but disagreement with the boss becomes a matter of "high risk."

2. The inhibition to participate also works the other way. Bosses may not feel comfortable discussing their problems as a manager, their shortcomings, their "hangups," etc. in the presence of subordinates. Nor are they likely to relish any disagreement or feedback from them.

As a trainer, I have been "pressured" at times to include bosses with their subordinates in the same training activity. Sometimes an "assurance" is given that "it won't matter." Unfortunately, it does matter. Relatively few bosses can reduce their status enough to allow for full and free communication, either at work or in the training situation.

There are certain situations, of course, where vertical training can work. These are:

☐ In a *technical or skills training* course where everyone is learning new information or new techniques and problems of varying philosophies or perceptions, giving and receiving feedback and the like, are not involved. In fact, it may be desirable or essential that all concerned receive the new learning together since they will be applying it together.

☐ In a *team building* situation where the boss is *consciously* trying to build a better team, to improve interpersonal communication, and to improve the team's problem-solving capability it can work. But to be successful in this effort, the boss should be an employee-centered boss and have participated in some kind of feedback program such as an encounter group, the T-group (sensitivity training) or the Managerial Grid®. Also, the team building sessions should be aided by a trained, outside facilitator-consultant who can referee disagreements and encourage low-key feedback.

☐ There may be some instances wherein a boss is uniquely nondirective, open to new ideas and feedback, and nonstatus conscious without any prior training along his line. If so, the boss' presence may not prove to be an inhibitor to full participation by subordinates. (In my experience, however, this happy state is quite rare.) One approach to the problem is to call the high-status person aside, in advance of the program, level with him/her about the need to "low-key it." Suggest he/she play the role of a devil's advocate rather than expert, lest overall participation be inhibited. By presenting the problem as "a challenge," a few bosses may rise to the challenge and be an encourager rather than a smotherer of participation.

Terminology for the Training Effort

Is there any way to distinguish between workshops, seminars, institutes, conferences, symposiums, courses, and programs? And does it matter?

Let's take the second question first: "Does it matter?" Yes, it matters because participants should know in advance of their attendance how they will learn, how participative it will be, and what the trainers will expect of them before, during, and after the training experience.

To the extent that we use fuzzy language such as "seminars," "institutes," "courses," and we misuse the language by calling sit-and-listen type programs "workshops," we are not being fair to our potential participants. Remember, more and more people who attend training programs expect to be involved. Our choice of language to describe a training function, which communicates the degree of their potential involvement, thus should be accurate. Of course, the announcement concerning any training effort should state in specific terms the nature and degree of participation that may be encountered.

As to our first question about how to differentiate between the various terms used to describe training efforts, these definitions may help:

Workshop is a term used to describe an intensive training activity where participants learn primarily by doing. While there may be some formal inputs, these activities are relatively minor. The key idea is heavy participant activity and high interaction, stemming from the use of a good variety of participative training techniques. Typically, the emphasis is on learning new skills as well as new concepts. Application sessions and/or activities are used extensively. Sometimes those who announce or provide this type of training refer to it redundantly as a "hands on" workshop to communicate that participants will be highly active and involved.

Laboratory describes a training experience whereby people learn primarily from their own behavior. Such experiential learning activities as the T-group, the Managerial Grid®, encounter groups and the like are illustrative of laboratory learning/training. Team building may also be included in this category.

Seminar refers to a learning experience where knowledge rather than skill is to be gained. Thus, there are experts or resource persons (one or more) who provide inputs to stimulate discussion. The learning comes from listening and exchanging views with the experts and other participants. Attendees are expected to have subject-matter background and to be fairly active discussants rather than passive listeners. The group is fairly small (15–20 persons) so that views can be exchanged readily. Other than discussion, participative training devices are not used for the most part.

Conference is a learning experience wherein one or more of the following activities take place:

☐ Current problems may be examined with the idea of producing solutions about them.

☐ There may be some "motivational" and "clarification" efforts.

☐ New policies, goals, products, etc. may be presented.

Conferences are designed to accommodate all kinds of groups—sales, management, safety, headquarters-field—and come in all sizes (groups of 20–50, hundreds, or several thousand).

Conferences vary in the degree to which they are participative. The "better" ones make an effort to secure participant input via small group work plus reports from those groups.

Professional societies and trade groups also hold conferences. Since their audiences are often quite large, the attendees are recipients of lectures, papers, etc. and typically have little opportunity for participation in the proceedings. Occasionally, resource people, with imagination and concern for participant involvement, may devise ways "to put participants to work."

Symposium entails a presentation of several points of view by various experts. The audience typically is large and is one that listens primarily, although there may be some opportunity to pose questions to the experts. A moderator is used to introduce the speakers, to summarize, and to guide/control the questioning by the audience. Unlike the panel presentation, there is little or no interchange among the experts.

Forum is a distant cousin to a debate in that different and opposing views are presented to the audience. Typically, however, the presenters do not challenge one another in their views. The audience is encouraged to ask questions after all views have been heard.

Panel is akin to a forum except that there is interchange among the panelists (three to six persons). The audience may also have a chance to comment or to ask questions. The audience may be relatively small (20–25 persons), medium-sized (50–100 persons), or large (200–500 persons).

Institute is a term applied to a meeting of a specialized group. Typically it is a session of limited participation, using assorted lecturers for the most part. In my experience it is a pretentious term that few people really understand.

Courses, programs, sessions, etc. are "global" terms that tell us very little about the actual nature of the training event insofar as participation is concerned. If one wishes to be vague, for whatever reason, these are excellent terms to use in announcing the training effort.

If these terms appear confusing, it is probably because they are. I prefer to use the term "workshop" when a high degree of participation/interaction is involved. If the training effort is a "sit and listen" affair, conference and course are suitable terms. *Conference* would imply a general presentation of ideas by various experts and a *course* a much more formal and didactic experience.

Note: I prefer these definitions. Others, however, may favor different terminology.

Key Points

1. The design of a training program should involve the participation of colleagues, operating officials, supervisors, and employees as appropriate.
2. Some factors to consider in making the design are the use of behavioral objectives, use of small group learning, course length, the structure of each training day, pre-work, warm-up activities, use of support materials, meeting the needs of special interest groups, aids for back-home application.
3. Need determination should also be approached in a participative way. Individual and group interviews plus survey procedures are basic tools for this purpose.
4. To the extent practicable, the program should seek out individual or special group needs.
5. Methods for training should be selected carefully since certain ones are more effective/appropriate than others.
6. Method selection should be based on relationships to instructional objectives, likelihood of acceptance by the participants and/or the organization, environment constraints, and the supporting role of one method in relation to another.
7. Concern with climate is basic to a successful participant learning experience. Factors to consider include pre-arrival concerns, greeting or welcoming procedures, the total training environment including support available to the program, the style of the trainer, and contingency planning.
8. If you wish to improve your prowess as a participative trainer, appropriate training experiences should be undertaken. Laboratory training is one of them.
9. Cotraining or joint instruction can enrich the course/program for participants and add to the personal growth of the trainers.
10. Line personnel should be used extensively by the training department, even in programs relating to management development. This procedure benefits both the line and the trainers. Careful selection and considerable training of line trainers are basic to such a training effort.
11. Vertical or team training should be approached with caution. The need for "everyone to know" should be balanced against the problem of status, which the supervisor inevitably brings to the training situation.
12. Trainers should avoid fuzzy language in respect to announcing seminars, institutes, workshops, and the like. The terminology employed should relate to the degree of participation that will actually take place in the training situation.

References

1. Stein, D. S., "Designing Performance-Oriented Training Programs," *Training and Development Journal* (January 1981), pp. 12–16.
2. Miller, G. V., "Individualizing Learning Objectives," *Training and Development Journal* (July 1979), pp. 40–42.
3. Newstrom, J. W., "Evaluating the Effectiveness of Training Methods," *The Personnel Administrator* (January 1980), pp. 55–60.
4. Neider, L. L., "Training Effectiveness: Changing Attitudes," *Training and Development Journal* (December 1981), pp. 24–28.
5. Bell, C. R., "Criteria for Selecting Instructional Strategies," *Training and Development Journal* (October 1977), pp. 3–7.
6. Pfeiffer, J., and Jones, J. E., "Design Considerations in Laboratory Education," in *The 1973 Annual Handbook for Group Facilitators*, University Associates Publishers, San Diego (1973), pp. 192–193.
7. Kaye, Beverly, and Jacobsen, Betsy, "Tying Ourselves In Knots," *Training and Development Journal* (December 1986), pp. 28–33.
8. Rosenweig, Fred, "Co-Training," *Performance and Instruction Journal* (August 1987), p. 20.
9. Garmston, Robert, and Bailey, Suzanne, "Paddling Together: A Copresenting Primer," *Training and Development Journal* (January 1988), pp. 53–55.
10. Christensen, Donna R., and Kinlaw, Dennis C., "Managers Can Do It All—Or Nearly All," *Training and Development Journal* (May 1984), pp. 87–89.

Recommended Reading

Program Design

Bell, Chip, and Putnam, Tony, "Mastering The Art of Training Design," *Training and Development Journal*, May 1979, pp. 24–27.

This suggests that "the art of training design requires the logic of people" whereas "the craft of training uses the logic of machines." Attention to both aspects makes for good design, although the people orientation is the primary point of departure.

Nadler, Leonard, *Designing Training Programs: The Critical Events Model*, Addison-Wesley, Reading, Mass., 1982.

The book presents a model for the planning/design of training involving managers and supervisors in all its steps. The CEM covers these steps: identify the needs of the organization, specify job performance, identify learner needs, determine objectives, build curriculum, select instructional strategies, obtain instructional resources, and conduct training. Each step, per the model, is subject to evaluation and feedback.

Putnam, Anthony O., "Designing From The Logic of People," *Training and Development Journal*, May 1981, pp. 125–131.

This develops the relationship of people orientation to design in more detail (see previous reference), and it presents such principles as focus on the person not the program, pay attention to what causes "movement" for participants, provide the learner with material that is intrinsically interesting, and use "resistance" to facilitate movement.

Rogoff, Rosalind, L., "The Training Wheel: A Simple Model For Instructional Design," *Training*, April 1984, pp. 63–64.

The author suggests a common-sense design model consisting of four steps presented in a circular, sequential format: (1) Find out who, what and why (a combined needs assessment and audience analysis). (2) Define realistic objectives. (3) Design and implement instruction. (4) Fix what went wrong (evaluation).

Romines, Jack A., and Crump, Bill, "A Self-Examination for Training Developers," *Training and Development Journal*, July 1982, pp. 76–80.

Training program designers should ask themselves these questions: Why is training needed? Who is the training audience? What is the most cost-effective way to reach the training goal? When does the training need to be done? Where will it be given? How will you know if the goal was achieved?

Simpson, Donald T., "Are You an Informed Consumer of Training?" *Training and Development Journal*, December 1981, pp. 34–40.

In this article, which provides guides to purchasing learning packages, the author presents such design principles as examine your philosophy of how people learn, develop a model for the learning and design process, test the model, and compare existing programs against the model. The model, presented in diagrammed format, covers these stages: establish learning objectives, define subject matter, determine learning components of subject matter, determine complexity of subject matter, estimate learner resistance to subject matter, select appropriate methods, develop media to support methods.

Need Determination

Alexander, Anne, "Need Assessment for Planning Training Programs: A Participatory Method", *Canadian Training Methods (CTM): The Human Element*, February 1980, pp. 19–21.

This describes the use of a participatory method to determine needs. Participants were contacted for help in developing a questionnaire that they subsequently completed. Advantages and limitations of this method are discussed.

Miller, Gerald V., "Individualizing Learning Objectives," *Training and Development Journal*, July 1979, pp. 40–42.

The article raises and answers this question: "How do I, as a trainer, individualize when I have preset learning objectives to meet or a 'packaged program' to present?" The author's answer is to use individualized needs, which become a contractual agreement, and program adjustments to meet these needs.

Stein, David S., "Designing Performance-Oriented Training Programs," *Training and Development Journal*, January 1981, pp. 12–16.

This describes the use of a modified critical incident technique to uncover learning needs as employees see them. The needs sought for are clear-cut deficiencies in performance rather than "felt learning needs," thus making for cost-effective training.

Walley, John R., "Let Attendees Help Plan Your Meetings," *Successful Meetings*, September 1979, pp. 93–96.

The author explains how you can use agenda questionnaires to design sessions around problems, topics, and program expectations presented by participants prior to the meeting.

Climate

Bhatti, Tariq, "What To Do in the First Session of a Learning Event," *Canadian Training Methods*, February 1981, p. 19.

The author provides numerous pointers for getting started right, including tips on atmosphere, expectations, greeting participants, introductions, and conducting a needs assessment.

Finkel, Coleman, "The 'Total Immersion' Meeting Environment," *Training and Development Journal*, September 1980, pp. 32-39.

This identifies eight separate environments that require attention: the main meeting room, the break area, breakout areas, sleeping rooms, areas for socializing, dining rooms, recreation/exercise areas, and the facility itself.

Garry, William W., "Integrating Wellness into Learning," *Training and Development Journal*, July 1980, pp. 48-53.

The author suggests to the trainer that appropriate new areas for concern to facilitate the maintenance of learning capability are emotional stress, nutritional imbalances, and the inability to convert oxygen at necessary vitality levels. The latter physical fitness need can be met via vigorous exercise opportunities in the training situation.

Kennedy, William T., "Learning from the Learning Process," *Northeast Training News*, May 1981, pp. 18, 28.

This stresses the importance of humanistic factors in the training situation, including the trainer as a catalyst and the importance of a caring attitude, trust building, integrating participant needs into the course, and commitment.

Lefton, Robert E., and Buzzota, V. R., "Trainers, Learners, and Training Results," *Training and Development Journal*, November 1980, pp. 12-18.

This identifies and explores four major styles of trainer behavior: "tell-and-do," "take-it-or-leave-it," "let-me-entertain-you," "demonstrate-the-payoff." Basically, the styles in the authors' model range from Theory X to Y; this is must reading for the trainer who is particularly interested in assessing and honing his/her interpersonal skills and humanistic approaches.

Potamianos, Pete, and Crilly, Lynn, "Grade 'A' Instructor: How Do You Know One When You See One?" *Performance and Instruction*, June 1980, pp. 24-27.

This provides criteria, in textual and checklist form, to evaluate an instructor (not a trainer). The article is an interesting counterpoint to the highly humanistic standards for the trainer suggested by Lefton and Buzzota.

Toto, Joseph R., "Credibility—Key to Effectiveness," *Northeast Training News*, Feb. 1981, p. 18.

This presents keys to trainer credibility that range from learning participant names to dealing with conflict appropriately.

Cotraining

Miller, Gerald V., and Wilson, Patricia G., "Cotraining: A Synergistic Outcome," *Training and Development Journal*, September 1982, pp. 94-100.

The authors discuss the advantages of cotraining, the relationship between cotrainers and the steps in the development of an effective relationship. They focus on situations where experience levels differ widely, especially where one trainer is a content expert and the other a training expert.

Newstrom, John W., "The Dynamics of Effective Teaching," *Personnel Administrator*, July 1981, pp. 55-64.

This discusses the need for team teaching effort, the various formats for such teaching, potential problems, and the prerequisites for a collaborative effort.

Pfeiffer, J. William, and Jones, John E., "Cofacilitating," in *The 1975 Annual Handbook for Group Facilitators*, University Associates, Inc., La Jolla, Cal., 1975, pp. 219-229.

This discusses advantages, disadvantages, and ways to avoid pitfalls in cofacilitating. Also contains an interview guide sheet and a "cofacilitating inventory" to check out mutual compatibility.

Willems, H. A., "Comanagement: An Alternative to the 'Black Hole' of Management Development," *CTM (Canadian Training Methods): The Human Element*, December 1980, pp. 14-16.

Comanagement of training programs is examined in terms of its assumptions, assessment, and areas requiring attention (e.g., selection, relationships, sharing responsibility).

Broadening the Trainer Base for Training

Curry, Theodore H., "Why Not Use Your Line Managers as Management Trainers?" *Training and Development Journal*, November 1977, pp. 43–47.

Curry cites benefits which accrue to trainers and the organization by using line managers. Conditions for success and potential pitfalls are also presented.

Hilliard, Richard L., "How Travelers Trains Teachers," *Training In Business and Industry*, May 1974, pp. 39–41.

This presents details concerning an instructor training program designed to teach subject matter experts good training techniques.

Jackson, Charles W., "Managers As Trainers," *Training News*, May 1983, pp. 18–19.

This describes the training and use of line managers in a behavior modeling program for supervisors.

Kozoll, Charles E., "Finding The Trainers Among You," *Training and Development Journal*, July 1975, pp. 12–15.

This cites nine qualities/skills which the potential line trainer should have: empathy, honesty, patience, a controlled pace, democracy, purpose, ability to listen, respect for experience, and prestige. Kozoll also offers ten questions as guides to effective selection.

Sussman, Lyle, Talley, Edwin, and Pattison, Virginia. "Training Nontrainers For Training," *Training and Development Journal*, May 1981, pp. 132–136.

This describes a train-the-trainer training program which used training objectives designed to overcome concerns of the nonprofessional trainer.

GLOSSARY

ABC approach—A check list which serves as an aid in problem solving. Ideas, as stimuli, are offered in an A to Z format to provoke ideation.

Action learning—Learning is accomplished by doing and experiencing as opposed to listening, observing, reading, viewing (audio-visual materials), etc.; synonymous with experiential and discovery learning.

Action maze—A highly structured or programmed form of case study. The case includes alternative decisions to resolve the problem presented. Wise decisions will get the team out of its maze; poor ones will mire participants into it more deeply.

Action plan—A specific, concrete "blue print" to accomplish something on the job as a result of a given training experience. It is also known as a *contract*; the process is called *contracting*.

Activity—Generic term for participative training experiences such as exercises, games, role plays, small group experiences, and instrumentation.

American Society for Training and Development (A.S.T.D.)—The professional society of the training occupation headquartered in Washington, D.C.

Analogy—In problem solving, the use of a direct comparison of like things, concepts, or processes. See also *Metaphor, Direct analogy; Personal analogy;* and *Symbolic analogy.*

Application—Transfer of the classroom training to the job situation.

Application session—A formal (classroom) attempt to aid in transferring the training to the job situation.

Atmosphere. See *Climate.*

Attribute listing—A problem solving tool that entails identifying or listing all the attributes or characteristics of a problem, product, or process and then systematically examining them.

Behavior modeling—A form of structured role playing wherein participants enact roles as provided by "good" models. Critique is provided by the trainer and the group to ensure proper skill development. Positive reinforcement is stressed throughout.

Behavior modification—A system to influence behavior/performance/learning based on the assumption that behavior is a function of its consequences. In training, the receipt of positive reinforcement is deemed to be a significant consequence for the learner.

"Behind the back" technique—A way of discussing a completed role play. The role player being critiqued turns his/her back to the group, thereby facilitating the giving and receiving of the feedback.

Brainstorming—A basic and highly popular tool for group problem solving. It can be used to identify problems, to suggest causes for problems and to propose solutions for problems. The technique emphasizes deferred judgement and quantity to get quality.

Buzz group—A small group that works on an assigned task; its conversation produces a "buzzing" sound, hence the term.

Buzz words—Generalized words to describe a problem, such as "communication," or "morale," which no one really understands and which inhibit the problem-definition/problem-solving process.

Card posting technique—Although formats may differ, the basic idea is to generate ideas on slips or cards and post them on the wall for better visualization of them. Cards thus may be readily modified, removed, prioritized, grouped, etc.

Case method. See *Case study*.

Case study—A technique designed to give a group training in solving problems and making decisions. The leader's role is typically catalytic rather than didactic.

Check list—(1) An aid to memory to ensure that critical factors in either prevention or diagnosis of a problem are not overlooked. (2) Involves the use of "trigger words" to stimulate new thinking about a problem, product, or process.

Check sheet—A simple statistical (tabular) device for gathering data about a problem.

Circular whip—A participative device wherein the trainer whips quickly around the room to elicit ideas, decisions, and feelings from all participants in the group.

Client-centered approach to problem solving—Utilizes procedures to ensure that processes of idea generation (content) are not inhibited by faulty group process.

Climate—Atmosphere in the training situation that may affect training outcomes in a positive or negative way.

Conference—A training session providing the opportunity to receive current information about a problem area or to exchange views on pertinent problems. Its size may vary from a small group to a very large audience.

Continuum—(1) An array of ideas or concepts that, if read from left to right, provide a logical progression. Example: Styles of leadership, ranging from highly participative to highly autocratic. (2) An array of numerical values, ranging from low to high. Example: A rating scale of 1–7 concerning one's ability to listen effectively.

Contract or contracting. See *Action Plan*.

Cotraining—The use of two or more trainers; also known as team training. This approach has many benefits for both trainers and participants.

Cultural island.—A removed or isolated training location that enables participants to work and learn better, the distractions of the office or shop situation being absent.

Debate—A participant-involving technique, structured formally or informally, to generate varying viewpoints on an issue or problem.

Debriefing—Also termed "processing," "sharing," and "reporting," it is the final phase of an experiential activity. At this stage the trainer aids the participants to report back and interpret what was learned from the game, exercise, role play, etc.

Delphi technique—In problem solving, a consensus-seeking technique wherein ideas are generated individually and anonymously through the mail and "filtered" a number of times by the same participants. In a more "modern" version, the group is assembled and polled as to preferences; choices are still accomplished individually and without discussion.

Demonstration role play—An enactment of a problem situation by two or more role players, with the rest of the group functioning as observers who subsequently may critique or discuss the action.

Diary—See *Journal*.

Didactic teaching—Traditional approach to teaching or instructing, entailing the dissemination of facts, knowledge, information, manual skills, etc. Today, it is contrasted with *experiential* or *discovery learning*.

Direct analogy—In problem solving, entails the comparison of one thing with another. Essentially, it is a search for the similar. See *Personal analogy* and *Symbolic analogy*.

Discovery learning—See *Action learning*.

Dramatic skit—A demonstration-type role play presented to the group that closely follows instructions provided by the trainer. Its purpose is didactic as opposed to having an experiential growth orientation. See also *Personal growth enactment*.

Dyad (Pair)—A pair of participants who work together in the training situation. The dyad is a tremendous means of securing involvement, intimacy, rapport, sharing, etc.

Empty chair technique—A dialogue in a role play with an imagined person in an empty chair; the emotionality and insight is heightened by the single role player switching chairs and thus assuming *both* roles.

Evaluation—(1) The final phase of the training cycle. Its purpose is to assess training outcomes. (2) The last phase in a problem-solving activity such as brainstorming; *ideation* precedes evaluation.

Exercise—A structured training experience marked by a learning goal, high participation, structure. Its overall purpose is to generate data for participant analysis.

Experiential learning—Method allowing the learner to learn from experience; synonymous with discovery learning. Today, it is contrasted with traditional, didactic methods of instruction.

Facilitator—A trainer who functions in a way to allow participants to assume responsibility for their own learning. The term is in contrast to the more didactic instructor, teacher, lecturer, presenter, etc.

Facing chairs—A device to generate data about opposing positions on a problem, involving physical and verbal reversal of positions on the issue. The idea is to aid participants to "see the other side" by arguing for it.

Fade-out—Loss of what was learned, over-time, in whole or in part. See *Application.*

Fantasy—Creation of a mind picture by individual participants in response to a *general* (nonspecific) idea/topic provided by the trainer, e.g., "What if you were head of the company. . . ." See also *Guided fantasy; Mental imagery; Guided imagery;* and *Visualization.*

Feedback—Data received from or given to one or more participants concerning one's behavior, attitudes, and relationships, in the training situation.

Field trip—A planned visit to a given area, site, building, plant to study its operation in depth and to report back thereon. The field trip is typically a team project, although not universally so.

Fishbowl—Also known as clusters, this is a training device entailing a group-on-group activity, the inner group (A) serving as the discussion group and the outer group (B) the observation group. Typically, groups A and B reverse roles.

Five-M (5-M) Analysis—A structured format for problem solving (especially identifying causes) using the five factors of manpower, machinery, materials, methods, and money.

Flipcharting—Process of securing participant ideas, recording them on easel paper, and posting the big sheets on the wall; provides reference, recognition, motivation, atmosphere.

Focused analysis—In case study, discussants are provided specific issues for analysis as opposed to having the case presented to them on an open-end basis.

Follow-up training—The provision of additional or post-course training to add new material and/or reinforce what was learned in the regular training course. See *Application.*

Forced-choice technique—An instrument that asks the participant to choose between two statements, neither of which may be totally preferred. The choices typically produce a pattern on such things as on one's leadership style.

Force field analysis—A training device to assess the forces—favorable and unfavorable—bearing upon a problem.

Forum—Experts present diverse views, but do not challenge one another as in a *panel presentation* or a *debate.* Audience participation is limited to posing questions.

Forced relationships technique—A problem-solving device entailing the development of ideas in response to the stimulus of a new, even unrelated word, concept, or phrase.

Frame game—A type of game that is possessed of a framework or format, only requiring the trainer to "plug in" the *content* to that frame.

Game—An experiential training activity marked by a learning goal, competition, rules, scores or outcomes, and winners and losers. Games may be content-laden or be a "pure" game devoid of content.

Geometrics—An assignment, presented orally or via worksheet, that requests the participant to make an artistic, graphic, or illustrative statement in one or more squares, triangles, rectangles, or other geometric figures. It is intended to encourage introspection.

Gordon technique—A form of problem solving wherein a group of diverse experts are only given a general definition of the problem. The assumption is that a precise definition of the problem will result in premature solutions.

Group-in-action methods—See *Small group methods.*

Group dynamics—Process of interaction of a group at work; includes such processes as communication, goal setting, decision making, support giving, and leadership.

Group fantasy—A highly imaginative story development (mind picture) by the total group. The basic, general input may be provided by the trainer or a participant, the group then embellishes it to form a "far out" mind picture. See also *Guided fantasy; Group fantasy; Guided imagery; Mental imagery;* and *Visualization.*

Group role playing—A form of demonstration-type role playing utilizing a group rather than a pair of role players.

Guided fantasy—Creation of a "scenario" on the basis of a variety of inputs (questioning, channeling, encouraging) provided by the trainer, the latter working jointly with the participants. The initial input by the trainer is general rather than specific. See also *Fantasy; Guided fantasy; Guided imagery; Mental imagery;* and *Visualization.*

Guided imagery—On the basis of a *specific* picture or image provided by the trainer, each participant develops a mind picture; e.g., the trainer may offer the image of a waterfall, cave, or old house and ask the participants to go on from there. See also *Fantasy; Group fantasy; Guided fantasy; Mental imagery;* and *Visualization.*

Handouts—Also know variously as "passouts," "take homes," and "leave behinds," they are designed to provide added information, stimulation, and interaction, on either a pre-session, in-session, or post-session basis. Although they are a form of support material, the latter term has a broader meaning and typically includes participants' and leaders' workbooks and possibly text and film/video materials.

Icebreaker—Structured, content-free training activity designed to relax participants, get them acquainted with one another, and energize them. See *Opener*.

Idea reinforcement teams—A highly participative form of problem solving wherein each team member is required to listen to the ideas of the other team members and thereby develop the "best" solution to a problem.

Ideation—In problem solving, the process of creating ideas as in a brainstorming session. The ideation phase is kept distinct from the evaluation phase to encourage the free flow of ideas.

Idea writing—Also known as "brainwriting," this entails individual ideation in writing followed by written comments by colleagues in small groups. A total group discussion of all small groups' ideas concludes the operation.

Ideographs—Symbolic pictures used in lieu of written notes, e.g., in giving a speech.

Imaging—A tool in problem solving wherein a problem is assumed to be solved and one imagines or visualizes the conditions that existed *before* the solution was created. Also, conditions may be visualized that *will* exist when a problem is solved.

In-basket exercise—A highly structured activity simulating an in-basket. Individual analysis of and decision on the items in the in-basket may be supplemented by group feedback on one's decisions. Learnings from the activity are designed to augment skill in decision making, delegating, coordinating, time management, etc.

Incident process—A variation of case study wherein the discussion group is provided with a brief incident and then must ask the trainer for additional data. When enough facts are garnered, teams are formed to debate a solution to the problem.

Informal role playing—Develops as the need arises in the training situation and thus is unplanned, unstructured, unwritten, and unrehearsed.

Inner advisor—Technique used in guided imagery by a participant to tap his/her "wisdom" buried below one's usual level of awareness.

Institute—A meeting of a specialized group wherein "experts" are the primary sources of information. (The term, generally vague in meaning, is often used interchangeably with forum, symposium, conference, and panel discussion.) Audience participation is typically limited.

Interaction—Dynamics among participants, including communication patterns, relationships, role assumptions, etc.

Introspection—A looking inward at one's attitudes, beliefs, values, perceptions, behaviors. See also *Reflection*.

Instruments—Tools used in instrumentation. See *Instrumentation*.

Instrumentation—A technique for experiential learning using various scales, inventories, check lists, questionnaires, continua, etc. designed to elicit data about individuals, teams, groups, or the total organization.

Journal or journaling—A device for the capture in writing of one's feelings, attitudes, and values as one undergoes a given set of experiences. It is intended to give one insight or self-awareness about one's motivations, behavior, etc.

Journalist's six questions—Entails the use of the questions *who? what? when? where? why?* and *how?* to resolve a problem.

Jury technique—A form of problem solving entailing the search for the real problem and full evidence rather than for villains or scapegoats.

Jury trial—Mock or simulated trial designed to give participants insight into a particular problem area, e.g., "trying" a supervisor who avoids conducting annual performance appraisals.

Laboratory training—See *T-group*.

Learner-centered training—A training situation wherein participants are given the opportunity to assume responsibility for their own learning. See *Experiential learning; Didactic teaching*.

Learning contract—See *Action plan*.

Learning packet—Materials provided participants essential for the learning experience.

Learning sequence—A systematized approach to session design entailing a listing in grid or chart fashion the following elements: skill area/activity to be worked on, training method, specific task or assignment, rationale for the assignment, and time for all tasks.

Lecturette—Short talk designed to prevent boredom from setting in; in experiential learning trainers/facilitators typically give short inputs rather than full lectures.

Lecture method—A didactic instructional method, involving one-way communication from the active presenter to the more or less passive audience or trainee group.

Listening teams—See *Viewing-listening teams*.

Live case—A case or problem of a current nature presented by a manager to a training group; to be distinguished from the usual "canned" or already-described case.

"Magic wand" technique—A form of fantasy in which the participant is given total power to mold, change, or control a given situation, event, relationship.

Meditation—A silent, relaxing activity designed to encourage psychological regrouping, renewing one's energies, getting in touch with one's feelings, etc.

Mental imagery—Creation of mind pictures by one's self on command, i.e., the stimulus is internal rather than external. See also *Guided imagery; Fantasy; Group fantasy; Guided fantasy; Visualization*.

Metaphor—A tool in problem solving in which a word or phrase in used as a reference to suggest a resemblance to something else, e.g., the ship of state. See *Analogy*.

Mirror technique—In role playing, wherein a member of the group or the trainer mirrors the feelings of another role player. It is particularly useful when the original role player is experiencing a block or impasse.

Mock trial—See *Jury trial*.

Model—A conceptualization designed to present a rather complex body of information or ideas in a relatively easy-to-understand way. Examples: The Johari Window; Maslow's Hierachy of Needs.

Monologue—A form of case study, entailing thoughts projected by one person.

Morphological analysis—An idea-generating technique that entails relating several variables of a problem to aid in finding a new solution.

Mousetrap technique—A form of case study, involving multiple situations, designed to point up that participant thinking may be inconsistent, rationalizing, and tolerant of a double standard.

Movement—An approach to training that departs from the usual static situation in which participants are typically placed. Its rationale: Movement keeps the group active, alert, energized, "loose," creative.

Multiple case technique—A form of case study involving the analysis of several related cases or incidents.

Multiple-choice instrument—An instrumented format requiring the participant to select the one statement of three to five given statements with which he/she agrees. Typically, the choices produce a pattern, such as of one's managerial style.

Multiple group role playing—The use of small groups or teams to resolve a problem having multiple characters. In this format, *all* participants "play" regardless of group size.

Multiple role playing—Role playing formats that permit all participants to engage in role plays at the same time. See *Demonstration role play*.

Multiple role taking—The assumption of a single role by two or more participants. The objective is to generate more data about the problem, relationships, preconceptions, etc.

Need determination—The primary step in the training cycle utilizing available productivity data, interviews and/or questionnaires.

Networking—A post-program effort by participants to "keep in touch" so as to lend support to one another and to help learning "glue in." See *Application*.

Nominal group technique—A tool for problem solving entailing individual, silent work. Interaction is purposely limited so that ideation will not suffer due to premature evaluation or social pressure.

Observer—A nonparticipant member of the group who observes and reports back on activity in a role play, game, exercise, small group, fishbowl. The rationale: An "outsider" can see behavior more objectively than the person engaged in the activity.

Opener—Structured, content-oriented training activity designed to ease participants into the formal program. See *Icebreaker*.

Organization development (OD)—The use of planned interventions to augment organizational effectiveness and health. Typical interventions: team building, data collection, MBO, quality of work life.

Panel presentation—Panelists with diverse positions exchange views, the audience having an opportunity to pose questions to them.

Pareto's analysis—The 80/20 principle used in problem solving (20% of the effort contributes to 80% of the results). It tells us how to separate the significant few from the trivial many.

Pareto diagram—Bar chart used to show graphically the major problem or major causes for a problem.

Participant-centered learning—See *Learner-centered learning*.

PCT (Purposeful Creative Thinking) approach—A form of analogy used to solve problems. It entails identifying the paradox or conflict basic to the problem, locating an analogy basic to the paradox, and then producing a new solution or idea based on the equivalent.

Personal analogy—In problem solving, one takes on the identity of an object or person—"gets inside of it"—to understand it better and thus change or improve it. See *Direct analogy* and *Symbolic analogy*.

Personal growth enactment—A demonstration-type role play acted out with few or no guidelines, subject to group critique. See also *Dramatic skit*.

Personal shield—An icebreaker that asks participants to respond in writing to six (self-disclosing) questions that appear on the shield.

Phillips 66 method—A device to enable groups of six participants at a meeting or a training session to produce ideas or solutions relative to a problem. Ideas are generated in the first five minutes and prioritized in the last minute of the six-minute time allotment.

Point-of-view team—A small group that is instructed to listen/view from a given frame of reference, e.g., that of field personnel. See *Listening/viewing team*.

Prediction—By asking participants to predict an outcome in a film/video, how a particular character will behave in it, or the nature of a concept before it is explained, we excite interest and involve participants early on.

Pre-work—An assignment to participants in advance of the training. Its rationale: Advance preparation will facilitate one's easing into the program, stimulate curiosity about it, augment motivation.

Problem census—In problem solving, a listing of problems by a group. It may be done via brainstorming, the slip method, buzz groups, or general (total group) discussion.

Processing—See *Debriefing*.

Profile—A procedure to show at a glance the significance of data presented on a rating scale. It also permits comparisons between different time frames, individuals, groups, etc.

Projective technique—On the basis of pictures provided by the trainer, the participant projects himself/herself and his/her feelings into the stimulus. It is a means of "dredging up" or projecting feelings or attitudes that may be difficult to bring forth via more conventional methods.

Props—Physical objects used in the training situation to augment participant insight into or empathy with the program's content; e.g., a participant may ride in a wheelchair to appreciate the problems of a handicapped person.

Psychodrama—See *Role playing*.

Pulse taking—Assessment of participant feelings about a given session or a full training day. It is useful for making adjustments in the training program as may be warranted or practicable.

Puzzles—A fun-type form of experiential learning that is designed to stimulate participant curiosity, creativity, and a problem-solving orientation. In some cases puzzles are used "just for fun."

Quality circle—An employee group consisting of six to eight volunteers who identify and resolve a problem and recommend a solution to management. Problems may relate to quality, waste, cost, bottlenecks, safety, etc.

Question sheet—By giving participants a list of questions, as opposed to presenting them orally, the trainer can ensure their comprehension to a significant degree. The sheet also simplifies the question assignment process to the participants and can serve as a reference tool.

Rating scale—An instrument, assuming many formats, designed to permit the participant to express degree or strength of feeling about an issue, behavior, attitude, value.

Recorder—One who records and thereby provides a summary of small group ideas, conclusions, and recommendations to the total group. The recorder may be an active participant as well as a reporter for the small group.

Reflection—A process, following introspection, wherein we make meaning out of the material we have developed/discovered via introspection. See *Introspection*.

Reinforcement—(1) Praise or encouragement of the learner's performance so as to augment his/her interest, motivation. (2) Provision of added learning tasks or data so as to aid the comprehension and/or "glueing in" of the training. See also *Application*.

Resource person—A knowledgeable person who provides content for the training effort (session, course).

Responsibility/accountability chart—A control sheet or chart to pinpoint who is responsible for what and when; useful in team building and in implementing an agreed-upon decision or action plan.

Risk analysis—Using a T-column, the problem-solving group highlights risks and ways of overcoming them. Typical problems: promoting women to upper-level jobs, delegating, engaging in team building.

Role clarification. See *Role negotiation*.

Role negotiation—A technique used in team-building programs to clarify and improve work and/or interpersonal relations between two team members. Each party in the negotiation tries to learn what the other expects more of and less of and what is expected to remain the same.

Role playing—A training technique in which participants act out and thus experience real-life roles and situations. It is both a form of simulation and experiential learning.

Role reversal—A role-playing technique wherein one role player "reverses" and assumes the role of another. The purpose is to acquire empathy and insight concerning the feelings, attitudes, and values, of the other person.

Rotational problem-solving technique—Entails the visits of several problem solvers to the "stations" of several expert advisors, the former gathering ideas from the latter. Each problem solver consolidates the ideas he/she has garnered and reports back to the total group on them.

Scatter diagram—A statistical procedure in problem solving designed to show graphically the relationship between two sets of data.

Seminar—A training effort dependant primarily on the expertise of knowledgeable resource persons. Participants generally have the opportunity to exchange views with the experts. The participant group is typically limited in size for discussion purposes.

Sentence-completion instrument—A tool for individual and/or group analysis. It involves using open-ended statements completed by participants to disclose feelings, attitudes, values, perceptions, behavior.

Seven S (7-S) analysis—A structured format for problem solving (determining causes) using these seven factors: structure, strategy, systems, superordinate goals, skills, style, and staff.

Simulation—A training activity designed to reflect reality. It may range from a role play and an in-basket exercise to a mock military invasion.

Simulation-game—A training activity akin to real life marked by such game attributes as competition, scores, outcomes, winners, and losers.

Slip method—A problem-solving tool wherein participants list individually on 3″ × 5″ slips ideas that relate to problem identification, causes for problems, or solutions to problems.

Small group methods—A term used to describe the use of small groups in identifying and solving problems. These are also known as *group-in-action methods*.

Small group psychological reinforcement—A problem-solving technique designed to secure maximum participation and pinpointed solutions to problems. Several groups are put in competition to produce better ideas.

Sociogram—A diagram which plots interpersonal relations/communication in a group, e.g., who talks to whom, how frequently one contributes, how frequently one receives.

Soliloquy—A form of role play in which the single role player talks aloud about his/her problem, role, attitudes, values, relationships.

Spaced learning—By experiencing the training over longer time periods, learning is presumed to "glue in" better. See also *Application*.

Spokesperson—A person who presents the ideas of his/her team or small group to the group at large. (The spokesperson may be appointed by the small group, a procedure preferable to appointment by the trainer or by self-appointment.)

Spontaneous role playing—Uses problems or situations that the participants themselves provide; also known as "live" or "hot" role playing. See also *Informal role playing*.

Spread sheet—A chart, on flipchart, used by the trainer to capture data from several role plays. It allows comparison of the results of the several enactments. Also used to display data from exercises, games, and so forth.

Stop-film technique—A procedure entailing the stopping of a film/video at any one or more points; the group then discusses what took place or possibly predicts the next action or final outcome.

Structure—Term used to indicate boundaries, guidelines, or limits provided by the trainer. For example: A game is structured; A T-group is basically unstructured.

Structured analysis—Entails the use of a structure or set of guidelines to aid in attacking (determining causes of) a problem. See *Five-M analysis*.

Structured role play—One that is well planned, typically including the use of written role play instruction sheets, observers, possibly pre- and post-role play guide sheets, etc. The idea is to keep things "on track" and reduce participant anxieties.

Subgroup. See *Buzz group*.

Symbolic analogy—A problem-solving technique using words or phrases that are placed in combat or conflict with one another. A key word from the problem statement triggers the analogy. See *Direct analogy* and *Personal analogy*.

Synectics—A theory or system of problem stating and problem solving based on creative thinking. It involves free use of metaphor and analogy, informal interchange within a carefully selected group of individuals of diverse personality and areas of specialization. See *Client-centered approach to problem solving*.

Symposium—Presentation of several points of view by several experts. Since audience participation is minimal, large groups may be accommodated.

T-column—A two-column device placed on flipchart/blackboard by the trainer to help participants better see the comparisons and contrasts of issues or problems.

Team building—A training effort designed to augment a work group's effectiveness. The "agenda" may relate to the work (goals, policies, procedures), group processes, and/or interpersonal relationships.

T-group—A form of unstructured training wherein participants learn about the impact of their own behavior or the behavior of others via feedback from the group. Also known as sensitivity training and laboratory training.

Think sheet—A worksheet assignment to introduce a topic, session, or course. It encourages the participant to reflect on the pertinent subject matter.

Total group role playing—A role play in which everyone has a role at the same time; it thus becomes a simulation such as role playing a civil defense disaster. See *Simulation*.

Trainer—Term used to describe a learner-centered conductor of a course or program. See also *Facilitator*.

Trainer-centered learning—A training situation in which the trainer assumes responsibility for the learning process. See *Learner-centered training*.

Training cycle—Encompasses the four phases of training: determination of need, design of the program, delivery of the program, and evaluation of results.

Transfer—See *Application*.

Triad (trio)—A group of three participants functioning as a team or small group. Although less intimate than the dyad, it brings to bear more ideas on a task or problem.

Trust walk—Also known as "blind walk," this exercise is designed to "loosen up" participants and develop "trust" among them. It may also be used to heighten sensory awareness.

Unstructured training—See *Structure*.

Upside-down problem solving—Unconventional solutions to a problem may be obtained by abandoning "common sense" and thinking in opposite terms.

Value analysis—A group problem-solving tool to refine, reengineer, and replan a product or service so as to reduce its costs of production.

Vertical training—Involves participants of two or more levels in the same organization. An acceptable procedure if all who work together *must* learn together. More typically, training with one's boss present inhibits participation.

Viewing-listening teams—By giving small groups an assignment in advance of seeing a film, the trainer secures their commitment to "look" with seriousness and purpose.

Note: If only a lecture is involved, the teams are called listening teams.

Vignette—A short segment of a film/video used to present a problem or situation for discussion. Quite often the vignette may have considerable impact, particularly if it is well selected, i.e., directed toward a particular problem situation.

Visualization—Working from actual events, relationships, etc., either past or present, the participant recalls and interprets it. Example: an incident involving an early supervisor who influenced one's career for the better. Feelings about the event, persons involved, etc., are expressed freely. See also *Fantasy; Guided fantasy; Group fantasy; Mental imagery;* and *Guided imagery*.

Warm-up activity—A training procedure, such as an icebreaker or an opener, designed to start things off and set the proper climate. See *Icebreaker* and *Opener*.

Whip. See *Circular whip*.

Workshop—A "hands on," highly participative training effort wherein participants learn by doing. Typically the group is small enough to ensure adequate rapport and intimacy.

Worst-case scenario—A form of fantasy used to explore the worst that would happen should a given event occur and feelings related to the event. Its purpose is to get out of one's system all the fear and anxieties surrounding a possible happening.

Wrong way-right way—A form of case study, utilizing two cases, to illustrate a preferred action, behavior, or decision.

Yes-no instrument—A relatively simple instrument that asks the participant to agree or disagree with the statements or questions included therein. A scoring device generally accompanies the quiz.

APPENDICES

WORKSHEETS AND TRAINING TOOLS

The materials in these appendices take the form of worksheets, task assignment sheets, check lists, instruments, note taking sheets, evaluation forms, and the like. They are basic tools for the trainer interested in putting his/her participants to work—a key approach to discovery learning.

Most of these forms may be used in the training situation "as is." Others require a degree of modification to better meet the reader's needs. It is suggested that these forms be studied carefully so as to develop a mind set toward the regular use and development of such learning tools.

APPENDIX   1

FINDING FELLOW HOBBYISTS

Gardening_____	Skiing_____
Motor boating_____	Bicycling_____
TV watching_____	Swimming_____
Fishing_____	Beer drinking_____
Movies_____	Horseback riding_____
Antique cars_____	Bridge_____
Reading_____	Flower arranging_____
Mountain climbing_____	Meaningful trips_____
Jogging_____	Local sports (pro, college)____
Waterskiing_____	Tennis_____
Woodworking_____	Sailing_____
Raquetball_____	Motorcycling_____
Crocheting_____	Golf_____
Collecting (coins, stamps, etc.)_____	Gourmet cooking_____

APPENDIX   2

YES, I HAVE PREFERENCES

1. State (in the U.S.)   _____

2. City (in the world)   _____

3. Soup   _____

4. Entree   _____

5. Beverage   _____

6. Dessert   _____

7. Movie   _____

8. Book   _____

9. Opera   _____

10. Symphony   _____

11. Athletic team   _____

12. Color   _____

13. Bird   _____

14. TV program   _____

15. Vacation, type of   _____

16. Movie actor   _____

17. Tree   _____

18. Flower   _____

]9. Outdoor activity   _____

20. Indoor activity   _____

APPENDIX   3

AID FOR DISTRACTION BANISHMENT

When we come to a workshop such as this, it is difficult to leave behind our "real world" concerns--unfinished work or new projects at work, relations with others, family matters, recreational and social interests, financial needs, the car, and so on.

Since reflection on these outside matters won't help our concentration in this workshop, let's see if we can banish them, at least symbolically. A simple way to do this is to list candidly below the major ones:

1.

2.

3.

4.

5.

Now fold this sheet of paper, place it in the envelope provided, seal the envelope, and write on the outside your phone number (or any other number) as an identification code. We'll return the envelope to you at program's end.

APPENDIX   4

PROGRAM HOPES AND PERSONAL CHANGE

1. My hopes and expectations for this seminar are

2. If my superiors could change me, they would

3. If my peers or associates could change me, they would

4. If my subordinates could change me, they would

APPENDIX   5

SESSION OPENER

1. My highest skill as a _____ (manager, trainer, salesperson) is

2. My biggest accomplishment in the last 12 months has been

3. My goal(s) for the next 12 months is (are)

4. My goal(s) for the next 5 years is (are)

APPENDIX   6

SESSION STARTER

1. When I am at my communication best I

2. When I am at my communication worst I

APPENDIX 7

INTROSPECTION REGARDING MY MANAGERIAL JOB

Draw anything that comes into your mind in the three boxes below. Let yourself go!

Organization	Leadership

Me and My Job

APPENDIX   8

WHERE DO I GO FROM HERE

My Job Satisfactions	My Job Concerns
A New Job Should Provide	Action Steps for a New Job

APPENDIX 9

HOW I SEE DECISION MAKING

(Check one of the two boxes below)

1 ☐	2 ☐
Managers make the wisest decisions when they:	Managers make the wisest decisions when they:
o Collect appropriate facts o Assess the facts o Develop alternate solutions o Choose among the alternatives, weighing the pros and cons of each o Communicate clearly the basis for the decision to the staff o Communicate clearly the need for all concerned to support the decision and the implement it fully and promptly	o Recognize the complexity of a problem o Collect appropriate facts, using group resources as necessary o Work with the staff to discuss facts, develop alternatives, weigh alternatives, and decide on a single course of action o Plan for action with the group

I checked box 1 ☐ 2 ☐ because:

APPENDIX   10

PROBLEM CENSUS

What are the major problems (blocks, barriers, obstacles) you see that keep you from doing the quality job you would like to do?

<u>Procedure:</u>

1. We will provide you with several 3" x 5" slips.

2. List no more than four or five problems.

3. Write one problem only on each slip. Try to state the problem briefly for ease of tallying.

4. If you do not have any major problems, write "no problems" on one slip.

5. Omit signatures.

6. Meet in small groups to discuss the problems.

7. Collect the slips.

8. We will classify and tally the responses and give you a summary report today or tomorrow.

APPENDIX 11

WORKSHEET: MOTIVATORS

Supervisors have many means of encouraging or unleashing motivation. List some ways you can think of below. Use the reverse side if you need more space.

1._____   11._____

2._____   12._____

3._____   13._____

4._____   14._____

5._____   15._____

6._____   16._____

7._____   17._____

8._____   18._____

9._____   19._____

10._____   20._____

APPENDIX 12

HELP-HINDERED GROWTH INCIDENT

A. Describe a situation or incident wherein your superior, past or present, so behaved as to discourage your growth.

Describe your feelings about the incident at the time.

Describe your feelings about the incident now.

B. Describe a situation or incident wherein your superior, past or present, so behaved as to facilitate your growth.

Describe your feelings about the incident at the time.

Describe your feelings about the incident now.

APPENDIX   13

POST-PROGRAM CONSULTATION

I am currently experiencing this problem and would appreciate your thoughts on it:

Name_____

Title_____

Address_____

My recommendation(s) is (are):

Trainer:_____

APPENDIX 14

GROUP OBSERVATION SHEET

You will shortly be observing the behavior of a group engaging in an assigned fishbowl activity. Here are some things you may wish to look for:

1. <u>Getting started.</u>

   Was the group clear about its task? If not, did the participants attempt to redefine it?

   What method or procedures did they use to attack the problem?

   How was the method adopted? Through the insistence of one dominant person? By group consensus (that is, talking it through without voting)? By voting? By default?

2. <u>Group behavior.</u>

   What was the energy/enthusiasm level of the group?

   Was there high interest in the problem?

   What was the participation pattern? Did some play it safe and hold back? Did all participate with adequate consistency? Was there a dominator? Did people really listen to one another? Did anyone interrupt others consistently?

   What was the trust level in the group? Did members share feelings openly? Were members supportive (did they show concern, caring, etc.) of one another?

   Was the group marked by high esprit de corps, cohesion?

   Was there a leader in the group? If so, did this leader help or hinder progress?

3. <u>Decision making.</u>

   Was a decision reached? If so, how?

   Was the decision arrived at through consensus, bulldozing, voting, bargaining, or what?

   Were members satisfied with the decision?

APPENDIX 15

INDIVIDUAL MEMBER OBSERVATION SHEET

In addition to observing overall group behavior, you may wish to observe the behavior of one or more individuals in the group. If so, here are some things to look for:

Participation (frequency, quality)

Support giving (encouraging, praising, inviting others to comment)

Undesirable behavior (arguing; using sarcasm, putdowns, inappropriate humor)

Assumption of leadership roles (helpful--defining the problem, summarizing, checking for consensus; nonhelpful--dominating, bulldozing, monopolizing the available air time)

Listening (as opposed to interrupting, daydreaming, faking listening)

Sensitivity to other members views, concerns, feelings, values

Use of nonverbal behavior (body language such as withdrawal, showing interest smiling, head bobbing, tensing up, flushing, winking at another participant)

APPENDIX   16

DAY 1

Workshop Activities	Course's Stated Learnings (Objectives)	Learnings for Me	Possible Action Plan
A.M. 1. 2. 3. 4. 5.			
P.M. 1. 2. 3. 4. 5.			

APPENDIX 17

HIERARCHY OF NEEDS

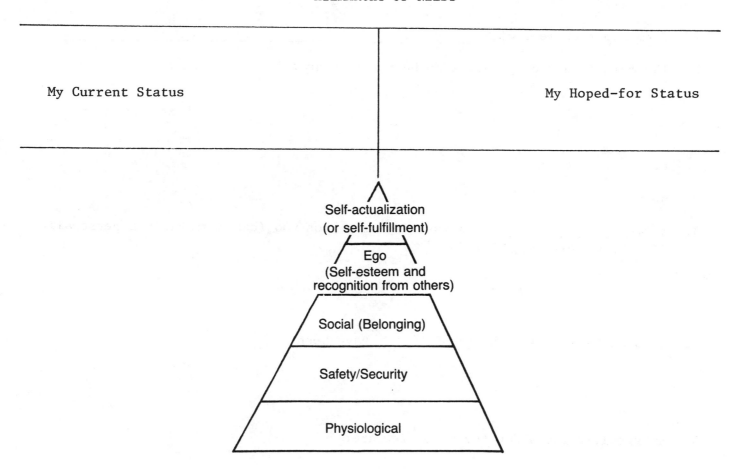

My Current Status

My Hoped-for Status

Self-actualization
(or self-fulfillment)

Ego
(Self-esteem and
recognition from others)

Social (Belonging)

Safety/Security

Physiological

APPENDIX   18

GUIDE SHEET TO PLAN FOR THE INTERVIEW

1. I am about to meet with _____

2. The main issues or problems to be resolved are:

    a.

    b.

    c.

    d.

3. I see _____ as the kind of person who (consider his/her personality, skills, accomplishments, etc.)

4. My past relations with _____ have been

5. My specific goals for the interview are:

    a.

    b.

    c.

6. I plan to use the following strategy in the interview:

7. A possible alternate or backup strategy is:

APPENDIX   19

GUIDE SHEET FOR THE OBSERVER

1.   Strategy used by (cite name)_____

   Effectiveness of the strategy

1	2	3	4	5	6	7
Lo						Hi

   Basis for my rating:

2.   Strategy used by (cite name)_____

   Effectiveness of the strategy

1	2	3	4	5	6	7
Lo						Hi

   Basis for my rating:

3.   Was any agreement reached?   YES_____   NO_____

   Explain your answer:

APPENDIX 19 CONTINUED

4.   As I saw the interview

Role Player	Strong Points (Effective Behaviors)	Behaviors That Could Be Strengthened
A		
B		

5.   Circle the word below that describes the character of the relationships that should exist after the interview:

Worse   Unchanged   Stronger

Explain the basis for your answer:

APPENDIX 20

CHECK SHEET FOR THE OBSERVER

ELEMENT	NO	YES	NOT SURE
1. Did the supervisor attempt to put the subordinate at ease?			
2. Did the supervisor show interest in the subordinate?			
3. Did the supervisor define the problem (objective of the interview)?			
4. Did the supervisor provide specific examples of the problem?			
5. Did the supervisor listen to the subordinate?			
6. Did the supervisor attempt to learn about causes of the problem?			
7. Was there a mutual problem-solving rather than blaming approach?			
8. Did the supervisor use questions rather than rely upon flat assertions?			
9. Did the supervisor propose an action plan?			
10. Was an action plan agreed upon?			
11. Will relations between the two parties be stronger?			

APPENDIX 21

ACTIVE LISTENING--A RATING SCALE

As you watch the role play, rate the customer relations person (or supervisor, or teacher, or parent, etc.) concerning his/her use of active listening techniques. Note: Active listening is an effective way to help others to clarify their thinking and thus start them on the road to resolving their own problems, dificulties, concerns, etc.

1. Use of body posture (e.g., leaning forward) and eye contact to show interest.

```
         1       2       3       4       5       6       7
     Ineffective                            Highly effective
```

2. Use of encouraging words (e.g., uh huh, yeah or yes) and head nods.

```
         1       2       3       4       5       6       7
     Ineffective                            Highly effective
```

3. Use of inviting, open-ended questions.

```
         1       2       3       4       5       6       7
     Ineffective                            Highly effective
```

4. Restatement of what is said to show real listening and understanding.

```
         1       2       3       4       5       6       7
     Ineffective                            Highly effective
```

5. Checking to clarify what was said.

```
         1       2       3       4       5       6       7
     Ineffective                            Highly effective
```

6. Summing up at appropriate points what was said.

```
         1       2       3       4       5       6       7
     Poorly done                             Skillfully done
```

APPENDIX 22

GUIDE SHEET FOR SELF-CRITIQUE OF THE INTERVIEW

1. My primary objective in the interview was

2. I would characterize the interview as (circle one word or phrase):

    Highly successful Successful Partially successful Indeterminate Unsuccessful

    The reasons for the this circumstance are:

3. The things that I did well in the interview were:

    a.

    b.

    c.

    d.

    e.

4. The interview would have been more effective had I:

    a.

    b.

    c.

    d.

    e.

5. I anticipate that future relations with the other person, as a result of the interview, will be (circle one item):

    Stronger   Weaker   About the same

APPENDIX   23

CONTRACT FOR WORK IMPROVEMENT

My Key Tasks/Responsibilities (List 6-8)	Possible delegation 1. Enter names of staff. 2. Check tasks appropriately.				Comments (e.g., training or controls to be provided)
1.					
2.					
3.					
4.					
5.					
6.					
7.					
8.					

APPENDIX   24

MY STYLE AS A MANAGER

Instructions to Trainer

Have participants complete the following quiz and then assign them to groups of three or four to discuss their results.

Most participants will probably recognize that a pattern emerges from the quiz: that is, certain answers define one as "Theory X" and others as "Theory Y." If you wish to provide participants with a "score card," you can give them the following data:

Theory X: Items 1a; 2a; 3b; 4a; 5b; 6b; 7a; 8b; 9b; 10b; 11a; 12b; 13a; 14a; 15a; 16a; 17b

Theory Y: The opposite of the above

Rather than cite a numerical score as to what constitutes Theory X or Y, suggest that participants look for tendencies--that is, whether they are mostly X or mostly Y. If someone is in the middle, it would seem to indicate that a clear-cut management philosophy has not as yet developed.

Note: Some individuals may complain about the forced-choice format. All you can do is agree that, yes, it is hard to choose in certain cases. But that is the purpose of this format--to force one to declare oneself by <u>choosing</u> between two possible alternatives.

It may be desirable to make the perhaps obvious point that the quiz points up one's philosophy of management. It does not necessarily reflect one's on-the-job behavior. In our culture Theory Y behavior is widely espoused: its practice is not as widespread. Hence, considerable self-deception may be at work here.

MY STYLE AS MANAGER

Quiz

For each of the 16 paired statements below, select the one item in each pair that best fits with your attitudes and philosophy of management. There are no right or wrong answers so just choose the ones that make the most sense to you. In some cases it may be a bit difficult to make a choice. If so, just pick the one item of the two that is more acceptable to you.

You will have a chance to discuss your answers with other participants in this program.

1. a. All of us have our limitations due to heredity, background, experience, age.

   b. People are in a constant state of becoming; they are continually growing, learning, adapting.

2. a. For most people the big motivators on the job are money and status.

   b. I see people as motivated by many work satisfactions: pride in accomplishment, a sense of contribution, new challenges, a worthwhile association, and the like.

3. a. It is important to me to supervise my employees so that there is a strong bond of openness and trust among us.

   b. I believe it is essential to supervise my employees so that the usual manager-subordinate relationship is properly maintained.

4. a. I expect people who work for me to exhibit the fullest degree of loyalty. This is something every employee owes his/her employer.

   b. I expect people who work for me to have full opportunities for the exercise of their creativity. If they receive this opportunity, I don't need to worry about their loyalty.

5. a. My job as a manager is to encourage subordinates to develop goals to which they can fully commit themselves.

   b. As a manager my job is to establish goals that are clear cut so that there are no misunderstandings about what, when, and how much are expected.

6. a. I find that people prefer work assignments that keep them alert, growing, and challenged.

   b. I find that people prefer work assignements that have clear-cut limits and do not make too great demands on their capabilities.

APPENDIX 24 CONTINUED

7. a. The job of a manager is to so manage that mistakes and errors are kept to a bare minimum.

   b. The job of a manager is to encourage maximum freedom in the performance of one's tasks.

8. a. I see employees and managers alike as people who have the potential to create and contribute for the betterment of the organization.

   b. I find that much of the drive and creativity in an organization comes from its managerial group.

9. a. I find that people respond positively to praise and recognition. Hence I am liberal in granting it.

   b. One can go overboard in praising people, for it can all too easily be misunderstood and backfire.

10. a. I find that people in organizations are seeking opportunities for self-direction, prefer limited guidelines, and wish for real opportunities to participate in decisions wherever they can.

    b. I see people in organizations as quite content to follow directions from capable leaders who assume responsibility for results.

11. a. I believe it is important to select capable people, to expect a full day's work for a full day's pay, and to treat your employees in a firm and fair way.

    b. I see myself as a person who is responsible for tapping potential and unleashing creativity in all my subordinates.

12. a. People require the fullest possible communication to carry out their jobs and to feel they are part of the team.

    b. Information is a tool and a resource for the manager. To over-do its dissemination is the mark of a weak manager.

13. a. My job as a manager is to prescribe duties and responsibilities clearly and fully.

    b. I prefer to assign tasks in a general way so that my employees have considerable leeway in carrying out their assignements.

14. a. The best motivators are firm and fair treatment, adequate pay, and clear-cut rules about discipline.

    b. The best motivators are praise, close relationships, and constantly challenging assignments.

15. a. People who work for me know where they stand in the way of assignments, pay, and promotion.

    b. People who work for me expect to be "turned on" by freedom in executing their assignments.

16. a. The job for any manager is to supervise so that employees' natural resistance to change is overcome.

    b. I see employees welcoming change provided that they have been involved in initiating that change.

17. a. I find that it is far more desirable to comment on tasks that are done well than to call attention to mistakes.

    b. I believe that it is essential to call attention to errors, even small ones, lest these mistakes turn into ingrained habits.

APPENDIX   25

CHECK YOUR I.Q. (IMAGINATION QUOTIENT)

Interpret the following:

1. ⎡ SAND ⎤

2. MAN
   ──────
   BOARD

3. STAND
   ─────
   I

4. |R|E|A|D|I|N|G|

5. WEAR
   ────
   LONG

6. R
   ROAD
   A
   D

7. CYCLE
   CYCLE
   CYCLE

8. T
   O
   W
   N

9. LE   VEL

10. KNEE
    LIGHT

11. DEATH/LIFE

12. ECNALG

13.   0
    ──────────
    M.D.
    Ph.D.
    D.D.S.

14. ii   ii
    O   O

15. DICE
    DICE

    CHAIR

16.

17. T
    O
    U
    C
    H

18. GROUND
    ──────
    FEET
    FEET
    FEET
    FEET
    FEET
    FEET

19. MIND
    ──────
    MATTER

20. HE'S/HIMSELF

21. GEGS
    GGSE
    EGSG

22. K I C K

Source: Unknown.

APPENDIX 25 CONTINUED

Answer Sheet

1. Sandbox

2. Man overboard

3. I understand

4. Reading between the lines

5. Long underwear

6. Crossroads

7. Tricycle

8. Downtown

9. Split level

10. Neon light

11. Life after death

12. Backward glance

13. Three degrees below zero

14. Circles under the eyes

15. Paradise (pair of dice)

16. High chair

17. Touchdown

18. Six feet underground

19. Mind over matter

20. He's beside himself

21. Scrambled eggs

22. Onside kick (as in football)

APPENDIX 26

ICEBREAKER

Complete the statements below and then discuss them with a partner, preferably someone you do not know very well or at all.

1. My favorite flower is_____

2. The best movie I've ever seen is_____

3. My favorite soft drink is_____

4. My favorite alcoholic beverage is_____

5. My favorite entree is_____

6. The sport I like best is_____

7. The best President we have ever had is_____

8. The musical instrument I enjoy the most is_____

9. The TV program I really like is_____

10. My favorite U.S. corporation is_____

11. My favorite government agency is_____

12. For a real vacation, the place to go is_____

13. The most appealing feminine first name is_____

14. The masculine first name I most prefer is_____

15. If I could choose any pet, I would have a_____

APPENDIX 27

SELLING AN IDEA TO THE BOSS

A Self Test

	YES	NO
1. I try to prepare the ground in advance of presenting a formal or full-blown proposal.	☐	☐
2. I do my homework properly--I get the facts, present alternatives, show pros and cons of each alternative, etc.	☐	☐
3. As part of my preparation I conduct a "dry run" on someone else--a subordinate, a colleague, my spouse-- who serves as a tough devil's advocate.	☐	☐
4. I pay attention to the boss's schedule. I try to see him/her when I know there won't be an obligation to hurry.	☐	☐
5. I pay attention to timing. I present the idea when it fits in with the concerns of the organization and/or the boss.	☐	☐
6. I try to involve the boss in the presentation so that there is two-way communication.	☐	☐
7. I use graphics, visual aids, etc. wherever I can be- cause people respond better to a formal presentation and something they can see.	☐	☐
8. I consider the boss' view. I know the boss' interests, values, orientation, and I start from there.	☐	☐
9. I try to stress "what's in it for him" as opposed to presenting the boss with an idea in the abstract.	☐	☐
10. I try to tie in my proposal to on-going programs and past successes so that there is a comfortable link with the past.	☐	☐
11. I try to make clear what the risks and what the chances of success are.	☐	☐
12. I anticipate possible objections or doubts and am pre- pared to respond to them.	☐	☐
13. I am prepared to respond to the possible question of "who else is doing (or using) this?"	☐	☐

APPENDIX 27 CONTINUED

		YES	NO
14.	I avoid putting my boss on the defensive or making him/her lose face or causing him/her to appear poorly informed, unrealistic, overly conservative, etc.	☐	☐
15.	I avoid arguing or debating. I avoid giving the impression that I alone have the right answer or the most of the available wisdom.	☐	☐
16.	I present realistic end results and avoid exaggeration or over kill.	☐	☐
17.	I try to make it clear how we will know if the plan or idea is successful and when we can anticipate results.	☐	☐
18.	I increase the possibility of my boss' acceptance of the idea by including a trial or pilot run in the overall proposal.	☐	☐
19.	I make sure that the boss rather than myself will get the credit for the proposal.	☐	☐
20.	I prepare myself for rejection. While I strive for success, I can accept the fact that the boss may defer judgment or give an outright "no."	☐	☐

<u>Scoring</u>

Give yourself 5 points for each "YES" answer.

<u>80 points and above</u>: You go to the top of the class! You are very sensitive to your boss as a person and to his/her needs. You certainly know how to present an idea well.

<u>70-80 points</u>: You have a good working knowledge of what it takes to get an idea across.

<u>60-70 points</u>: You have a fair knowledge and set of skills in selling your boss on an idea.

<u>Below 60 points</u>: Don't be surprised if your efforts at selling an idea frequently backfire. Try to sharpen up your skills before your next proposal up the line.

APPENDIX 28

GIVING EMPLOYEES FEEDBACK

A Self Test

Respond to the items below with a "yes" or "no." Be as frank as you can. The quiz will give you a "reading" on your skill in and attitudes about one key area of communication--that of giving feedback to your employees.

	YES	NO
1. Do you avoid giving employees feedback about their performance?	___	___
2. Do you avoid giving employees negative feedback since employees often do not like to hear this?	___	___
3. Do you try to give feedback about performance by comparing the employee with other employees?	___	___
4. Do you avoid giving employees praise, since they are often embarrassed by it?	___	___
5. Do you criticize the person rather than the action or the behavior?	___	___
6. Do you give criticism on a number of items at one time?	___	___
7. In giving feedback do you ignore the employee's sensitivity or receptivity to it?	___	___
8. Do you give feedback long after the incident (or behavior) has occurred rather than immediately?	___	___
9. Do you feel it is more important to communicate your view than to listen to your subordinate's point of view?	___	___
10. Is your purpose in giving feedback to prove that you are right as opposed to getting at causes for behavior?	___	___
11. Do you tend to slip in a criticism between two layers of praise?	___	___
12. Do you give feedback to subordinates when you are angry or upset?	___	___
13. Does your feedback often involve sarcasm or "put downs"?	___	___
14. After you give feedback, do you avoid checking for understanding, since people should get the message easily enough if they really want to?	___	___

APPENDIX 28 CONTINUED

YES   NO

15. Do you tend to interrupt your subordinates while they are responding to your feedback to them?

                ___   ___

16. Do you give feedback to others without worrying too much about your future relationship with them?

                ___   ___

17. Do you feel that it is more important to point up mistakes than it is to indicate how to correct them?

                ___   ___

18. Do you feel it is more important to give feedback than to receive it?

                ___   ___

19. Do you prefer to give feedback to employees in writing rather than orally?

                ___   ___

20. Do you give criticism to employees in both public and private locations?

                ___   ___

Scoring*

The above test items are designed to stimulate your thinking about this business of giving feedback to others. Now that you have discussed the quiz with your fellow participants, you undoubtedly have a better idea about the topic in general and your own needs for improvement in particular.

The preferred response to all quiz items is "NO." Accordingly, give yourself five points for every "YES" answer. You can use the following table as your guide to your skill as a giver of feedback.

20 points and below: Your understanding of and skill in giving feedback is very good.

20-30 points: You have a satisfactory ability to give feedback.

30-40 points: You have a fair ability to give feedback.

Above 40 points: You are probably in very deep water. Develop some new skills before you go back in.

*You may want to give scoring information after participants have discussed the quiz items with their fellow participants.

APPENDIX   29

MY TIME MANAGEMENT PRACTICES

Answer the questions below as candidly as you can. Your responses will give you a profile concerning your use of time.

		YES	NO
1.	I start each day with a daily set of goals.	☐	☐
2.	I set aside a solid block of uninterrupted time each day for accomplishment of tasks.	☐	☐
3.	I review regularly (three to six months) the authority delegated to my staff.	☐	☐
4.	I rarely take work home evenings or weekends.	☐	☐
5.	I use my secretary fully so that we are a two-person team.	☐	☐
6.	I find it difficult to make efficient the meetings I conduct.	☐	☐
7.	My current telephone habits are a significant cause of wasted time.	☐	☐
8.	I find it somewhat difficult to prevent interruptions from taking place.	☐	☐
9.	I would be a more efficient manager if I learned to say "no."	☐	☐
10.	One phrase that describes my work situation is "being on a treadmill."	☐	☐

Scoring

a. Give yourself 2 points for all the answers in the first five items you answered with a "NO."   _____

b. Give yourself 2 points for all the answers in the second five items you answered with a "YES."   _____

c. Your total point score is   _____

14 points and above: Your time management practices are in need of a major overhaul.

8-12 points: Your management of time is only fair.

Below 8 points: Your time management practices are very good; you should have little difficulty in overcoming the few shortcomings you now have.

APPENDIX 30

MY CAPABILITIES AS A DELEGATOR

A Self Test

This test is designed to help you assess your prowess as a delegator. Simply answer "yes" or "no" to all the questions. Please be as candid as you possibly can be. You will have a chance to discuss your responses with your fellow participants.

1. Do I avoid holding on to the tasks I like to do or feel comfortable with?

2. Do I avoid getting bogged down in "administrivia?"

3. Do I avoid taking work home regularly?

4. Do I so manage that I avoid being constantly on a "treadmill?"

5. Do I avoid falling in the trap of letting my subordinates delegate "in reverse," that is, to me?

6. Do I avoid tendencies to redo my subordinates' work to ensure that it is right?

7. Do I feel it is unimportant to convey the image that I am a hard, tireless worker?

8. Have I ever analyzed my job so that I really know how, where, and on what I am spending my time?

9. Do I really know how I should be spending my time?

10. Am I actually spending my time as I, as a manager, should be?

11. Do I recognize that delegating to others involves my living with uncertainty, even ambiguity?

12. When I delegate do I specify how much authority the delegate has to do the job?

13. Do I tolerate a certain amount of error in the things my subordinates do as the price I have to pay for delegation?

14. Do my subordinates feel free to act within their delegated authority?

15. Do I see and use my secretary as part of a two-person team to get the job done easier?

16. Do I use delegation as a tool to "turn on" my people?

17. Do I see delegation as a means of helping my staff to grow, develop, and achieve higher self-esteem.

APPENDIX 30 CONTINUED

18. Do I see delegation as a tool to force innovation, because if I allow my subordinates to do something, the odds are that they will do it differently than I would have?

19. Do I have a workable or reasonable number of people who report to me so that I am not suffering from supervisory overload?

20. Do I use controls to monitor delegated authority, that is, to spot problems before they develop.

Scoring

To assess your delegation prowess, give yourself five points for every "yes" response.

Above 80: You are a top-notch delegator. (I and many others would like to work for you!)

70-80: You are now doing an adequate job of delegation. (With a little more thought and effort you could be in Group 1!)

60-70: Your delegation capability is only fair. (Some added work on it is quite desirable.)

Under 60: Look out! Your delegation philosophies and practices have probably caught up with you. (But you now know what is needed to improve.)

APPENDIX 31

MY SKILL AS A LISTENER

A Short Quiz

Listed below are 15 statements that relate to one's ability to listen to others. Rate each item by placing a dot in the appropriate box. Try to be as candid as you can in making your rating.

When you have rated all the items, take a straight edge and draw lines to connect the dots. This will give you a profile of your capabilities as a listener. Obviously the more your profile leans toward the right, the more capable a listener you are.

Element	Never	Seldom	Occasionally	Frequently	Always
1. Do I listen for feelings, attitudes, perceptions, and values as well as for facts?					
2. Do I try to listen for what is not said?					
3. Do I avoid interrupting the person who is speaking to me?					
4. Do I actually pay attention to who is speaking as opposed to "faking" attention?					
5. Do I refrain from "tuning people out" because I don't like them, disagree with them, find them dull, etc.?					
6. Do I work hard to avoid being distracted from what is said by the speaker's style, mannerisms, clothing, voice quality, voice pace, etc.?					
7. Do I make certain that a person's status has no bearing on how well I listen to him/her?					
8. Do I avoid letting my expectations--hearing what I want to hear--determine or influence my listening behavior?					

APPENDIX 31 CONTINUED

9. Do I try to read the "nonverbals" the speaker presents--inflections, gestures, mood, posture, eye contact, facial expression, etc.?						
10. Do I work hard at overcoming distractions (sounds, noises, movement, outside scenes, etc.) that may interfere with good listening?						
11. Do I tend to "stay with" speakers who may be hard to follow--those who are slow in their speech or whose ideas are poorly organized or who tend to repeat themselves, etc.?						
12. As a listener do I use nonverbal communication (eye contact, smiles, occasional head nods, etc.) to indicate that I wish to hear more?						
13. Do I tend to restate or rephrase the other person's statements when necessary so that he/she will know that I understood?						
14. If I have not understood, do I candidly admit to this and ask for a restatement?						
15. Do I avoid framing my response to what is being said while the other person is still speaking?						

APPENDIX 32

MY C.S.Q. (CUSTOMER SERVICE QUOTIENT)

The 15 statements below relate to working with and providing service to customers. Rate yourself on each item, using the following scale: Often--5; Sometimes--3; Rarely--1; Never--0.

_____1. I try to learn all I can about our products (or services) so that I can really help our customers.

_____2. I try to size up the customer so that I can get on the customer's wave length.

_____3. My philosophy of customer contacts is that the "customer always comes first."

_____4. If I can't answer a customer's question, I try to get help from another employee or my supervisor.

_____5. I really try to be friendly and courteous toward all customers.

_____6. I respect the cutomer's need to take enough time to make a sound decision.

_____7. I am willing to work with a customer past my quitting time, if necessary.

_____8. I avoid showing irritation with customers, no matter what.

_____9. I work hard at producing "repeat" business from customers.

____10. Customers see me as a person with whom they like to do business.

____11. I always speak highly of our products (or services).

____12. I avoid saying negative things about our competitors.

____13. I will refer a customer to a competitor if we don't have the right product.

____14. I avoid "chit chatting" with other employees in the presence of customers.

____15. I willingly help my fellow employees as may be necessary.

Scoring

Scores can range from 75 points to zero. If you are very close to 75, you are a top-notch, professional, customer-service person. Your organization is fortunate to have you on its staff! If you are somewhere in the middle range, you should go over the quiz again and see where you can profit from personal improvement. Should your point score be on the low end, you'll want to do a lot of introspection or soul-searching about your current behavior. Try to bring about some real changes before your bosses have a go at it first!

Note to trainer: After the group has processed the data in trios, you may wish to ask participants to call out their scores, enter them on a flipchart, and secure a group average.

APPENDIX   33

AS I SEE MYSELF

1. When people talk about "high achievers," I would say that I

2. What I do best in my work is

3. What I would like to do better in my work is

4. Back home on the job people see me as

5. My greatest skill as a manger (or supervisor) is

6. My greatest need as a manager (or supervisor) is

7. When I get angry I

8. When I make a mistake I

9. I feel most alone when

10. What I expect of other people is that

11. What I feel most disappointed about in life is

APPENDIX 33 CONTINUED

12. What I feel most disappointed about in my job is

13. What I feel most disappointed about in my boss is

14. After an argument with another person I usually

15. In respect to "leveling" or being candid with others I

16. My reaction to my given name is

17. As a group member I generally

18. At cocktail parties I

19. What bothers me the most about the way the world seems to be going is

20. The feelings (emotions) I can express most easily are

21. The feelings (emotions) I find difficult to express are

22. If I could have anything in the world that I wanted I

APPENDIX   34

MANAGEMENT DEVELOPMENT--OPENERS

A management development seminar causes us to think (or perhaps rethink) about our jobs, our careers, ourselves, our values, our organization. The statements below, which you are to complete, should help you to get started on this. Try to be as candid as you can in making your responses. After you have completed this form, find a partner with whom to share your answers.

1. My biggest achievement in my career has been

2. If I could redo one aspect of my career I would

3. If I had to state what the two most important things about leadership are, I would say

4. My greatest satisfaction in my job is

5. My biggest irritation in my job is

6. If my boss could change me he/she would

7. If my subordinates could change me they would

8. If I could change my organization I would

9. If I had the power to change myself I would

APPENDIX 35

AS I SEE THE COACHING PROCESS

Complete the following statements as you see them. There obviously are no right or wrong answers. You will have an opportunity to discuss your responses with a colleague.

1. What is most important to me about communication is

2. What I find most difficult in the area of motivation is

3. What I find troublesome in the delegation process is

4. What I find most troublesome in the decision-making process is

5. The easiest part of the decision-making process for me is

6. In introducing change I find that

7. My feelings about helping subordinates grow and develop are

8. The best way to unleash creativity in my subordinates is by

9. To have a truly effective management team one's subordinates must

10. To have a truly effective management team the team leader must

11. My feelings about loyalty of staff are

12. My feelings about giving praise to subordinates are

13. When I receive praise I generally feel
    and respond by saying

14. My feelings about giving subordinates support are

15. The one thing that separates effective from less-than-effective coaches is

APPENDIX 36

AS I SEE YOU

1. You seem to be the kind of person who

2. When we first met what I liked about you was

3. When we first met what I was not sure about you was

4. A contribution you have made in this program is

5. I see you as a person who could

6. As a two-person team I sould see our strengths as

7. As a two-person team what I would not be sure of is

8. I you were my boss I

9. If you worked for me I

10. If you and I were colleagues we

11. What I am not sure we could talk about freely is

12. On a 100-point scale, I would rate our "sympatico" as _____ because

APPENDIX 37

MY APPROACH TO PROBLEM SOLVING

Ten problems are presented below, each having seven possible solutions. For each problem select the one best solution, as you see it. You will have a chance to discuss your solutions with your fellow participants.

Problem 1. Tom, a member of your staff, is an average performer. He is neither poor nor outstanding--just adequate. A recent problem with Tom is that he is typically tardy to your Wednesday, 11 a.m. staff meetings. Tom is not that big a contributor to these meetings, but his lateness doesn't seem appropriate.

A. Lay it on the line. Simply remind Tom when he arrives late that these meetings start at 11 a.m. promptly.

B. Treat it as a team problem. Take it up with the total group when other team problems are being discussed. Others may be as annoyed as you are.

C. Not a big deal. He's probably seeking attention, so why worry about it? In time he'll probably "come around."

D. Change the meeting time to 8:30 a.m. when the workday starts. Since the organization is strict about the morning arrival time, this should force Tom's prompt attendance to the meeting.

E. While talking to Tom on other business, close the conversation with this statement, "Oh, by the way, Tom, I know you're busy and get wrapped up in things, but could you please try to make our next staff meeting on time? Thanks."

F. Whenever Tom does arrive on time or close to 11 a.m., compliment him (after the meeting) for his efforts to attend promptly.

G. Point out to Tom how his lateness hurts group creativity: "Tom, we need your good thinking on our problem solving. If you are late, we are deprived of your helpful input."

Problem 2. You have seven section supervisors who report to you. Each is in charge of a group of young women who operate sewing machines. One supervisor, Williams, has been having considerable trouble with his people--you are not only getting complaints about his lack of tact, but you find that absenteeism, quits, waste, rejects, etc. are all high in his section. Some of these productivity problems exist in the other sections, too, but to a relatively minor degree. All sections do the same work and have the same layout, except that William's area is much more crowded so that Williams doesn't have a separate office as the others do.

APPENDIX 37 CONTINUED

A.   Try to counsel your supervisor--ask him to show more consideration to the young women.

B.   Invent a reason for a reassignment and move Williams to a staff job where he won't have as much contact with people.

C.   Talk to him about his problem and then compliment him whenever you see or learn of his handling someone in the proper way.

D.   Tell Williams what you expect in the way of standards. Either he gets his "indicators" (absenteeism, waste, etc.) up or you will have to take some direct action.

E.   Discuss these productivity and human relations problems with all your section chiefs to see if some practical solutions can be arrived at.

F.   You decide not to move too precipitously. After all, only one of seven supervisors is a problem, and your outfit overall is doing O.K.

G.   You decide to reassign some of William's employees to the other sections, take some machines out, and build a small office for Williams on the shop floor.

Problem 3. You are in charge of a factory that assembles electrical appliances for the kitchen. In the last three months there has been a noticeable drop in quality and productivity.

A.   Since this is the first bad quarter in the last seven, you decide to take a "wait and see" approach to this.

B.   You decide to visit more often with people on the floor and ask them about things they like to be asked about--the kids, the garden, their bowling scores. The friendly touch never hurt anyone.

C.   You decide to work on some changes in the system--better lighting, new soldering guns, and giving each worker full responsibility for assembling a given unit of equipment.

D.   You decide to set up several quality circles--these are special units of employees to identify productivity and quality problems and to make recommendations to management about them.

E.   You meet with your foremen to find out what people-type problems they might be having and what can be done about them. You are afraid that indifferent or overly demanding supervision might not be getting the employee cooperation you need.

F.   You tell your foremen very clearly that production and quality are their responsibilites and you expect results--and "no ifs or ands about it."

G.   You grant praise very clearly and fully to your supervisors and to employees, too, whenever a job is well done, a quota is met, etc.

APPENDIX 37 CONTINUED

Problem 4. You are the supervisor of a large warehouse that has a pipe protruding up from the floor. It's a pretty obvious pipe, although occasionally someone does trip over it. They do this absentmindedly or when they are in a hurry.

A.   You give people praise when you see them walk carefully over the pipe.

B.   You regularly issue reminders to all concerned about the pipe. The reminders are especially strong after a tripping incident, and you always have several warning signs on the walls nearby.

C.   Occasionally someone does complain about the pipe, but you always point out that it is a really big pipe, it is painted bright yellow, and mishaps are minor, few, and far between--really not a big deal.

D.   You decide to have the building engineer build a platform, ramp-style, over the pipe.

E.   You call your foremen together to discuss what might be done to be sure no serious accidents occur because of the big pipe.

F.   You embark on an employee safety program including frequent changes of posters, reminder notices in pay envelopes, movies, etc. The program emphasizes safety in general and the pipe problem is mentioned quite often.

G.   You decide to hold an employee safety slogan contest with a really big ceremony and cash prize for the "best" slogan as decided by the Safety Committee.

Problem 5. Your people leave their lights on in the storage room, tool room, etc. at close of business, despite repeated requests to help save energy.

A.   You call everyone together and ask for ideas on saving energy.

B.   You give your people strong statements on saving energy. This is done via a "pep talk" at a special group meeting, a memo, and a notice on the bulletin board.

C.   You turn the lights out yourself as necessary; no point in hassling people about everything all the time.

D.   You give employees feedback regularly, in chart form, on energy use, costs, etc. You also compliment them on any improvement in costs.

E.   You install automatic controls that shut off the lights in the rooms in question, five or ten minutes after quitting time.

F.   You follow this procedure that you heard worked in another plant: You have your assistant turn out the unwanted lights and then send out "Thank you" memos from time to time, praising people for their cooperation.

APPENDIX 37 CONTINUED

G.   You politely request cooperation whenever you come across a "guilty" party.

Problem 6. You are the superintendent of the warehouse. Employees from time to time lift improperly and end up with various back and groin injuries. You can't understand why these injuries occur, since all employees were trained in the proper lifting procedure six to eight months. You have six foremen who report to you.

A.   Train your foremen in positive reinforcement procedures--that is, have them praise a worker anytime he/she lifts properly. But they are <u>not</u> to criticize poor lifting techniques at all.

B.   Get an increase in budget for some new equipment to help out on lifting heavy items.

C.   Have Personnel put a reminder notice about lifting in everyone's pay envelope every so often.

D.   Have your foremen tell their employees in no uncertain terms to lift properly whenever they see a failure to do it right. You also follow this course of action.

E.   Call all your foremen together to discuss the problem and to come up with practical ways of dealing with it.

F.   Instruct your foremen to request the cooperation of their employees in lifting properly and to remind workers that they could injure themselves.

G.   Show a film on lifting that has some really "gruesome" scenes in it, showing the results of the failure to follow proper lifting procedures.

Problem 7. One of your subordinate supervisors has expressed concern about lax attention to proper dress standards. This is a large customer service office with regular personal contact by employees with the public.

A.   You decide to call everyone concerned to a meeting to get full employee input concerning dress--What are the current standards? Do they best meet the needs of employees and customers? Can we draft a "code" that everyone will be willing to live with?

B.   You believe all standards should be observed; on the other hand there seem to be only a few of the younger employees who take advantage of the situation now and then. You will probably talk to them when you can get around to it.

C.   You ask your assistant to write a memo to all employees on the problem. You ask him to cite a couple of complaints from the public that he presumably received over the phone. The "complaints" are not real, but they certainly could have occurred and, in any case, will make the office's concern clear.

APPENDIX 37 CONTINUED

D.   You ask your supervisors to compliment employees whenever they dress properly.

E.   You call all your supervisors together and make it very clear what the dress standards are and what their responsibility is in this regard. You advise them that you expect to make spot inspections on this matter starting Monday.

F.   You call a low-key meeting of all employees, give them a gentle reminder of dress standards and the vital reasons for them, and request their fullest cooperation.

G.   You decide to inaugurate a program of company-supplied outfits (four in all), all in good taste, really chic-looking, and interchangeable so that considerable variety in dress is possible each day and for each person.

Problem 8.   Your boss expects you to deal with a perennial employ relations problem-- too much tardiness.

A.   You call everyone together and tell them what the problem is, what the rules are, and what disciplinary action you intend to take for offenders.

B.   You call everyone together, point out quietly that your boss has called this problem to your attention, and say you would like everyone to please cooperate so that no one will have to be put on the spot about this.

C.   You issue the usual annual memo about tardiness, absenteeism, use of public telephones for private business, and the like.

D.   You decide to "work" on the late-comers by complementing them when they are early, on time, or even a minute or two late. You tell them you appreciate their efforts to get here on time. To those who are late five or ten minutes you express your appreciation for their efforts to get here because "all hands are really needed aboard."

E.   You decide to recommend a system of "flex-time" to your boss.

F.   You call everyone together to talk about the problem. Your aim is to see if the group can develop standards concerning arrival time that everyone--employees and management--can live with.

G.   You decide to rearrange the location of your desk to near the windows so that you will be in a position to see who is coming into the parking lot and when, of course.

APPENDIX 37 CONTINUED

Problem 9. You are the head of an office that has the constant need to protect various documents your employees work with. However, of late there are indications that a worrisome number of people are lax about security matters.

A.   You feel breaches of security are too important a matter to be ignored, so you call everyone together and give them a warning--lax security will be a basis for dismissal, with no exceptions and no further warnings.

B.   You ask the guard to double check all security safes and file cabinets every night.

C.   You adopt a procedure of complimenting people who put classified documents into the safe during lunch and at night as opposed to leaving them on their desks.

D.   You decide to call all employees together to discuss current security procedures as to their adequacy and to develop such plans for tighter security as may be indicated.

E.   You beef up security by increasing lights outside and inside the building, tightening up procedures on the entry of nonemployees into the building, improving the system for the registration of classified documents, etc.

F.   You call a meeting of all employees, compliment them generously on their adherance to all standards and procedures, thank them for their past cooperation on everything, and in the middle of the meeting give everyone a gentle nudge about the importance of security.

G.   You call an employee meeting expressly for the purpose of reminding people about security procedures. There is no complaining, no finger-pointing, and no threats, just an appeal to everyone's mature and "adult" side of themselves. A short, friendly, and frank question and answer period is held, too.

Problem 10. You are head of the Operations Branch. You and various members of your staff are having difficulty getting the cooperation you require from the people in Finance. The Finance Branch is located in another building across town.

A.   You take the head of the Finance Branch out to lunch with some frequency to really "butter her up."

B.   You get the help of the Training Department to hold a "confrontation" session to help clear the air about difficulties--past and present.

C.   Since your boss, a V.P., also supervises Finance, you go to him to get his help in getting Finance in line.

APPENDIX 37 CONTINUED

D.   You call up the head of Finance whenever they do something cooperatively and compliment her and her staff on it.

E.   You let the matter ride, since these things generally right themselves in time.

F.   You work out a move, which is quite possible, to their building, because a lot of misunderstandings and mix ups are a result of a lack of direct contact and communication.

G.   You start to work actively on improving interpersonal relations with the Finance people and request your staff to do the same.

Note to Trainer

After the participants have completed their individual work on the quiz (about 20-30 minutes) divide them into small groups (3-5) to discuss their solutions. Allow one hour for this. Then pass out the scoring sheet. After they complete the scoring, pass out the "Definition of Problem-Solving Styles" sheet. Then hold a general discussion of the exercise.

APPENDIX 37 CONTINUED

Self-Scoring Sheet

For each of the ten items that composes the quiz, circle the letter that represents your choice as to the best course of action. Then add up the number of responses in each column.

Problem	T	BM	S/S	HR	D/D	M	T/LF
1	B	F	D	E	A	G	C
2	E	C	G	A	D	B	F
3	D	G	C	E	F	B	A
4	E	A	D	F	B	G	C
5	A	D	E	G	B	F	C
6	E	A	B	F	D	G	C
7	A	D	G	F	E	C	B
8	F	D	E	B	A	G	C
9	D	C	E	G	A	F	B
10	B	D	F	G	C	A	E
Column Totals							

After you have tallied each column, read the definitions that follow. They will interpret for you your tendency to choose one or more problem-solving styles in respect to problems involving people.

APPENDIX 37 CONTINUED

Definition of Problem-Solving Styles

T is your tendency to operate as a Team Leader. You thus involve your staff in efforts at group problem solving and group decision making when problems seem to involve the team.

BM is your tendency to use Behavior Modification procedures; that is, you provide sincere praise (positive reinforcement) on proper performance. You generally do not comment on below standard performance. Also, wherever possible you use a data collection approach to give people objective feedback on their performance. Talking with people about the problem may precede the giving of praise and/or data about performance.

S/S is your tendency to approach problems in a Situational/Structural context; that is, you try to change the situation or system as opposed to attempting to influence people's behavior directly (e.g., via various lectures, coaching, memos).

HR is your tendency to use Human Relations approaches, which means you try to elicit cooperation by talking things over, being firm and fair, creating an adult atmosphere of mutual respect, etc. Your concern for people may exceed your concern for production, at times.

D/D is your tendency to lay it on the line in a Direct/Directive way. No nonsense, no timidity, no hesitation, but "damn the torpedoes, full steam ahead" is your philosophy and way of acting on a problem. Firmness gets both respect and results.

M is your tendency to get results through Manipulation of people. This is often a less-than-direct approach and at times even a bit less than honest. By outmaneuvering people or "finessing the situation," you get results you want and avoid a lot of confrontation, complaints, etc.

T/LF is your tendency to be Tolerant/Laissez Faire of people and situations. You certainly don't want to confront people, and you believe in "letting sleeping dogs lie," since situations often work themselves out.

APPENDIX 38

FORCE FIELD ANALYSIS

INSTRUCTIONS FOR COMPLETION OF PROBLEM DIAGNOSIS

1. Think of a current problem phenomenon, or difficulty that you would like to see changed, corrected or improved upon.

2. Enter the problem in the top box on the worksheet (diagnosis sheet).

3. On the right side of the diagnosis sheet list all the forces at work that are preventing the change you desire from taking place. These are the <u>restraining</u> forces.

4. On the left side of the diagnosis sheet enter all the forces at work that are pushing for the change you favor. These are the <u>driving</u> forces.

5. After you have completed the Force Field Analysis assess the driving and restraining forces at work and complete the questions below.

    A. My change strategy is to

        /_/ Increase the driving forces

        /_/ Weaken the restraining forces

        /_/ Do both of the above

    B. Explain the rationale for your strategy.

    C. Explain how you will go about implementing your strategy

APPENDIX 38 CONTINUED

FORCE FIELD ANALYSIS

Cite objective, goal, target, problem, need:

DRIVING FORCES

RESTRAINING FORCES

[FORCES FAVORING THE CHANGE]

[FORCES RESISTING THE CHANGE]

(EQUILIBRIUM OR CURRENT STATUS)

APPENDIX   39

5-M ANALYSIS

Difficulty (problem, obstacle)	Manpower	Machinery	Methods	Materials	Money
1.					
2.					
3.					
4.					
5.					

APPENDIX   40

SOME WAYS OF LOOKING AT LEADERS AND LEADERSHIP

If a leader (or manager) were a:

A. Politician he/she would

B. Gardener he/she would

C. Athletic coach he/she would

D. Captain of a ship he/she would

E. Newspaper publisher he/she would

APPENDIX 41

ORGANIZATIONS--AN ANALYSIS WITH THE AID OF METAPHOR

Group 1: If an organization were a <u>zoo</u>, it would be like (or have these characteristics or consequences):*

Group 2: Think of an organization as a <u>garden</u>. What would its characteristics or
consequences be?

Group 3: Think of an organization as a <u>train</u>. What would its characteristics or
consequences be?

Group 4: If an organization were an <u>orchestra</u>, it would:

Group 5: If an organization were a <u>human body</u>, it would:

Group 6: If an organization were a <u>community</u>, it would:

*The assignment could be given with greater specificity by stating the questions this
way: If an organization were a <u>zoo</u>:
The managers would_____. The employees would_____. The most common
problems would probably be described as_____.

APPENDIX 41 CONTINUED

Some Possible Answers to the Metaphor Questions

Zoo Metaphor

Sense of territoriality
Passive behavior
Compartmentalization--
  walls separate everyone
Sexual harrassment (!)
Bosses (the keepers) vs.
  workers (the animals)
Aged animals, past their
  prime, are kept on
No communication between
  groups (of animals)
Tangible rewards alone
  produce results
Short-term perspective

Train Metaphor

Survival problems
Off the track often
Late; slow freight
All going in one direction
  toward a fixed goal
In need of modernization

Garden Metaphor

Test soil, prepare soil, seed
  it, nurture it
Get rid of weeds and bad
  plants
Symbiosis
Environment is the key
Seasonal emphasis

Community Metaphor

Gossip abounds
Pride (or conflict)
Order
The other side of the
  tracks
Hard up for cash

Orchestra Metaphor

One-man band
Be in harmony
March to same (or different)
  drummer
Off key
Toot own horn
Beat its drum for _____
Out of tune with _____
Hearing the words but not
  the music
Hit a high note (or a sour
  note)
Be up-beat

Human Body Metaphor

Eliminate waste
Avoid that tired feeling
  (or have it)
Flex its muscles
Hide its skeletons
Get gray, old, fat, and flabby
Keep lean
Be healthy
Need a regular check up

APPENDIX   42

MY ASSESSMENT OF GROUP FUNCTIONING

1. My participation thus far has been:

```
  1      2      3      4      5      6      7
(LO)                                      (HI)
```

2. The degree to which my ideas have
    been listened to is:

```
  1      2      3      4      5      6      7
(LO)                                      (HI)
```

3. My role in the decisions we have
    made is:

```
  1      2      3      4      5      6      7
(LO)                                      (HI)
```

4. The degree to which members are
    willing to be open is:

```
  1      2      3      4      5      6      7
(LO)                                      (HI)
```

5. The degree to which members listen
    to one another is:

```
  1      2      3      4      5      6      7
(LO)                                      (HI)
```

6. The degree to which the team/group
    is really working together is:

```
  1      2      3      4      5      6      7
(LO)                                      (HI)
```

7. The degree to which we have faced
    up to our problems is:

```
  1      2      3      4      5      6      7
(LO)                                      (HI)
```

8. The degree to which we are reach-
    ing our goals (our progress) is:

```
  1      2      3      4      5      6      7
(LO)                                      (HI)
```

9. My satisfaction with my member-
    ship in this team is:

```
  1      2      3      4      5      6      7
(LO)                                      (HI)
```

10. I predict the degree of group
    functioning as a team six months
    from now will be:

```
  1      2      3      4      5      6      7
(LO)                                      (HI)
```

11. My satisfaction with the role
    of the facilitator in the group
    is:

```
  1      2      3      4      5      6      7
(LO)                                      (HI)
```

APPENDIX 43

QUESTIONNAIRE--END OF DAY ONE

1. What did I <u>not</u> say today that I should have?

2. What did the group <u>not</u> discuss today that it should have?

APPENDIX   44

FORM FOR ROLE CLARIFICATION/NEGOTIATION

To:

From:

I need more of:

I need less of:

I need the same of:

APPENDIX 45

A RATING SCALE TO ASSESS TEAMNESS

Criteria	Strongly Agree 5	Agree 4	Undecided 3	Disagree 2	Strongly Disagree 1
1. Cooperation: "Team members work well together."					
2. Communication: "Our ability to give and receive necessary information is one of our strengths."					
3. Goals: "Goal setting is truly a team activity."					
4. Creativity: "Innovation is encouraged and rewarded."					
5. Conflict: "Disagreements are faced up to and worked fully through."					
6. Support: "Praise, recognition, etc. are given enthusiastically."					
7. Mutual respect: "Team members show appreciation to one another and avoid sarcasm, put downs, etc."					
8. Commitment: "Everyone is dedicated to furthering team goals."					
9. Atmosphere: "The climate is such that people are willing to put forth their best effort."					
10. Cohesion: "Team members see themselves as a tight-knit group."					
11. Pride: "People feel good about being a team member."					
12. Decisions: "Everyone has the fullest opportunity to participate in decisions that affect the group."					

APPENDIX 45 CONTINUED

		Strongly Agree 5	Agree 2	Undecided 3	Disagree 2	Strongly Disagree 1
13.	Openness: "Everyone is encouraged to say what is on his/her mind without fear of reprisal."					
14.	Trust: "Team members feel that no one in the group will take advantage of them in any way."					
15.	Assessment: "The team reviews its own functioning regularly on a frank and open basis."					
16.	Identification: "I feel that I am treated as a full member of this team and feel very much part of it."					
17.	Leadership: "Our team leader is a key to our effectiveness."					
18.	Feedback to leader: "The boss is very open to suggestions about the improvement of his/her performance."					

APPENDIX 46

A RATING SCALE TO ASSESS TEAM COMMUNICATION

Criteria	Strongly Agree 5	Agree 4	Undecided 3	Disagree 2	Strongly Disagree 1
1. Team members listen to each other.					
2. The team leader listens to all group members.					
3. Everyone feels free to level and to be candid with everyone else.					
4. All team members "check things out" with all concerned before action is taken.					
5. Constructive feedback is given freely to group members to improve their functioning.					
6. Broad participation is strongly encouraged at all group meetings.					
7. No one uses a disproportionate amount of the available "air time" at group meetings.					
8. People are available to secure information needed.					
9. Information is shared willingly and no one hoards information.					
10. Information of interest to team members, such as information on new policies, new projects, and pay, is not categorized as "secret."					
11. Information about one's performance is communicated regularly and candidly by the team leader so that there are no surprises at performance review time.					
12. Team members are not afraid to give the boss the "bad news."					
13. We communicate well with other groups in the organization.					

APPENDIX 47

A RATING SCALE TO ASSESS TEAM PROBLEM SOLVING/CREATIVITY

Criteria	Strongly Agree 5	Agree 4	Undecided 3	Disagree 2	Strongly Disagree 1
1. Problems are met head on rather than "swept under the rug."					
2. Problems are regarded as challenges and opportunities rather than headaches.					
3. A striving for innovation/ creativity is a part of the team's way of life.					
4. Broad participation is a basic tool of team problem solving.					
5. The team's climate is concerned with the big picture rather than with nitpicking new ideas to death.					
6. Conflict/disagreement are utilized for purposes of creativity and ideation.					
7. Delegation is regarded as a tool for innovation					
8. The team leader regards the team as a constructive problem-solving force.					
9. As appropriate, problems are solved with the total team on a consensus basis.					
10. Group members present and discuss their ideas rather than defend them.					

APPENDIX 48

MY PERCEPTIONS ABOUT MY BOSS

The following 15 statements describe relationships between you and your boss. For each statement, provide a rating, using a 7-point scale: 1 is low or weak; 7 is very high or strong. The scores will be tallied for the total group so that your boss will receive an average score for each item and an indication of the number of low scores (1's or 2's) and high scores (6's or 7's).

1. ____Shares information about goals, policies, procedures, etc.

2. ____Listens to any ideas I may have.

3. ____Delegates fully so that I can get my job done on my own.

4. ____Involves me in decisions which affect me and my work.

5. ____Uses the team to solve problems and make decisions.

6. ____Encourages innovation and creativity.

7. ____Establishes a climate such that our best efforts are put forth.

8. ____Establishes an attitude of trust.

9. ____Provides praise for a job well done.

10. ____Provides support so that I feel good about myself.

11. ____Shows confidence in my abilities.

12. ____Provides opportunities for my growth and development.

13. ____Provides feedback about my performance regularly so that I know where I stand.

14. ____Is approachable and friendly.

15. ____Seeks and accepts feedback about his/her behavior.

APPENDIX 49

A RATING SCALE TO ASSESS EFFECTIVENESS OF GOAL SETTING

Criteria	Strongly Agree 5	Agree 4	Undecided 3	Disagree 2	Strongly Disagree 1
1. Team members work as a group to set goals that pertain to the total group.					
2. Individual goals are worked through on a mutual basis between the team leader and the appropriate team member.					
3. Our goals are marked by clarity.					
4. Our goals are marked by reasonableness.					
5. We try to introduce a "stretch" element into our goals so that we are constantly upgrading our performance.					
6. We set goals for personal growth and development as well as for the work.					
7. Our goals are revised as new circumstances arise, on a joint basis (leader/group; leader/team leader).					
8. Once goals are agreed upon, everyone concerned is given full authority to execute them (deep delegation).					
9. Progress on established goals is reviewed at least quarterly.					
10. Nonaccomplishment of goals is subject to discussion/critique, not punishement.					
11. Goals are assigned and reviewed for results/accomplishment rather than for details of execution.					
12. Goals are reviewed at year's end to plan better the next year's work as well as to learn what was done.					

APPENDIX 50

MEETING MANAGEMENT

(Circle the appropriate degree for each statement as you have experienced it.)

1. Objectives of our meetings are: Fuzzy 1   2   3   4   5   6   7 Clear

2. Meeting objectives are reduced
   to writing wherever helpful: Rarely 1   2   3   4   5   6   7 Regularly

3. Meetings start on time: Rarely 1   2   3   4   5   6   7 Always

4. Meetings finish on time: Rarely 1   2   3   4   5   6   7 Always

5. Time at our meetings is used: Poorly 1   2   3   4   5   6   7 Extremely well

6. Participation at our meetings
   is: Narrow 1   2   3   4   5   6   7 Broad

7. The way members listen to
   one another is: Casual 1   2   3   4   5   6   7 Intense

8. Plops (ignoring a member's
   idea, hence it "plops" to the Strongly 1   2   3   4   5   6   7 Strongly
   floor) are rare: Disagree   agree

9. The atmosphere, insofar
   as it encourages Dull 1   2   3   4   5   6   7 Exciting
   creativity, is:

10. Support/encouragement/praise
    recognition of member Miserly 1   2   3   4   5   6   7 Generous
    contributions are:

11. In our meetings we search for
    solutions, not scapegoats: Rarely 1   2   3   4   5   6   7 Regularly

12. Meetings produce decisions: Rarely 1   2   3   4   5   6   7 Regularly

13. Decisions made at meetings
    are subject to follow-up. Uncertain 1   2   3   4   5   6   7 Rigorous

14. Evaluation (critique) of
    how we conduct our meet- Never 1   2   3   4   5   6   7 Frequently
    ings is undertaken:

APPENDIX   51

FEEDBACK--MY SKILL/ATTITUDE PROFILE

Place a dot in one of the five boxes for each element stated below. Then connect the dots. This will give you a profile on your prowess as a "feedback giver." Elements graded below 4 are those that indicate more "work" is needed on your part to become a fully effective giver of feedback.

When I give feedback do I consider these elements?	Strength of skill or attitude				
	1 (LO)	2	3	4	5 (HI)
1. The observed behavior--improvability: Do I consider that it is something over which the recipient has control? Do I have a reasonable expectation that he/she can change his/her behavior as a result of the feedback?					
2. The observed behavior--specificity: Is my feedback to the other person typically specific rather than general? Based entirely on observed/experienced (hence factual) data?					
3. The observed behavior--verifiability: Is my feedback of the sort that I and others can verify its validity?					
4. My motivation: Am I aware why I am doing this? (To help? To support? To ridicule? To punish? To look "smart"?					
5. Nature of my feedback: Does it stress the positive side of things as well as the negative?					
6. Volume: Am I careful to avoid "feedback overload"? (This element relates to zeroing in on a limited number of "critical" behaviors as opposed to doling it out on "everything.")					
7. Style: Does it tend toward the descriptive or nonevaluative rather than the evaluative or judgmental? (Nonevaluative feedback entails the expression or description of one's feelings: "When you behave this way, I feel..." or "When you behave this way, I have difficulty meeting my deadline." Evaluative feedback assesses or comments, usually critically, on the other person's behavior: "You argue all the time at our staff meetings" or "You louse up the total operation by ignoring the deadline you agreed to.")					

APPENDIX 51 CONTINUED

	1	2	3	4	5
8. Empathic aspects: Does my feedback tend to be gentle, caring, friendly, considerate, as opposed to hardhitting, crude, rude?					
9. Timing: Do I consider whether the feedback recipient is ready, interested, and receptive to the feedback?					
10. Locale: Do I consider whether it is best given in a private or public setting (that is, in which place will it work best).					
11. Impact on receiver: Am I aware of how well it will be understood? Do I consider whether it will create defensiveness or that it might create a "get off my back" reaction?					
12. Understanding: Do I assure myself that the feedback I gave is actually understood by asking the recipient to restate it? Do I recognize that "emotional blocks" may interfere with understanding?					
13. The relationship: Do I consider whether giving feedback will improve or weaken the relationship or leave it unchanged? (Will it build bridges or walls?)					
14. Two-way flow: Do I try to elicit feedback on my behavior as opposed to solely giving it to others?					

APPENDIX   52

ADVANCE ASSIGNMENT: MY PROBLEMS ON DELEGATION

Worksheet A

As managers we often find that we want to delegate certain tasks to subordinates, but there are barriers to such attempts. In the space below list as many reasons as you can why delegation is not always practicable. An example is provided.

1.   Reluctance by subordinates to assume more responsibility.

2.

3.

4.

5.

6.

7.

8.

9.

10.

APPENDIX 52 CONTINUED

Worksheet B

For each of the barriers to delegation you listed in Worksheet A, see if you can provide a solution to the particular difficulty you identified.

1. Solution a. Fully explore attitudes involved

            b. Coach and counsel as necessary

2. Solution a.

            b.

3. Solution a.

            b.

4. Solution a.

            b.

5. Solution a.

            b.

6. Solution a.

            b.

7. Solution a.

            b.

8. Solution a.

            b.

9. Solution a.

            b.

10. Solution a.

            b.

APPENDIX   53

Name_____Title_____

Department_____Phone number_____

1. I have these skills and will be glad to give help on them:

    a.

    b.

    c.

    d.

    e.

    f.

2. I can use help on:

    a.

    b.

    c.

    d.

    e.

    f.

APPENDIX   54

AID TO NOTETAKING

Significant Ideas in Film/Video	I Question This...	Ambiguities and Omissions

APPENDIX   55

MONITORING ACTIVE LISTENING--A CHECK LIST

Observe the listening skills of _____ in the film. Whenever he/she exhibits an aspect of active listening, check the "Yes" column. When a principle of active listening is ignored or violated, check the "No" column. Your checkmarks should provide a comprehensive pattern of _____'s listening.

Element or behavior	No	Yes	Not Sure
1. Used "body language" to communicate interest (such as leaning forward).			
2. Used body language to show understanding (e.g., head nodding).			
3. Used encouraging words/phrases ("I see," "Uh huh," "Yes," etc.) to encourage free flow of conversation.			
4. Maintained eye contact much of the time.			
5. Used open-ended questions to encourage the other person to expand fully on his/her feelings.			
6. Listened quietly, refraining from interrupting, taking over, etc.			
7. Used the restatement technique to encourage communication.			
8. Sought clarification when statements were not totally clear.			
9. Summarized at various points in the conversation.			

Notes:

APPENDIX 56

PERFORMANCE REVIEW INTERVIEW

Guidesheet for Film Observation

Skill pointers to make a performance appraisal interview effective	Behavior shown in film (cite examples)
Friendly opening--puts employees at ease; established rapport.	
Explains purpose of interview at outset.	
Quiet, private setting, no interruptions.	
Goals are reviewed.	
Boss gets down to specifics.	
Boss listens to employees actively (paraphrases, nods head, smiles, says "uh huh").	
Agreement as to accomplishment of each goal is secured.	
Boss uses praise (positive reinforcement).	
Goals are developed for the next year.	

APPENDIX   57

FILM--<u>IMPROVING RESULTS THROUGH TIME MANAGEMENT</u>

Post-Film Discussion Questions

The film suggests that time management is basically "work improvement." What is meant by this?

The film stresses that effective time management in an organization requires the total team to work on it. How do you see this issue?

What ideas on time management does the expert (John Humble) present at the end of the film?

APPENDIX   58

FILM--<u>PETER DRUCKER--MANAGING TIME</u>

Questions to Aid in Film Viewing and Post-Film Discussion

What behaviors did company president Lansing exhibit that indicated an unawareness of how he was managing his time?

What results might we expect from Lansing's time management practices?

What approaches does Drucker offer for better management of one's time?

APPENDIX 59

ADVICE FROM THE PRESIDENT--RATING SCALE

Using the following key, rate each of the statements below as to your agreement-disagreement with them: a--strongly agree; b--agree; c--neutral; d--disagree; e--strongly disagree. Circle your response.

1. The trainees are showing their imaturity by being so impatient. a   b   c   d   e

2. The trainees are an ungrateful bunch. a   b   c   d   e

3. The trainees have put their finger on a real weakness in the program. a   b   c   d   e

4. The president really gave the training director two problems: the one in the letter and what to do with the president's proposal. a   b   c   d   e

5. The president's proposal missed the boat. The trainees don't want a correspondence course-- they simply don't want to be overlooked. They want more "visibility," more of a chance to "keep current" and "stay sharp." a   b   c   d   e

6. Correspondence training for managers is probably the poorest way to train them. a   b   c   d   e

7. The training director's two superiors are "yes men." a   b   c   d   e

8. The management intern training program is not well understood by those above the training director. a   b   c   d   e

9. The training program is not well supported by top management. a   b   c   d   e

10. A task force should be set up to study the training program in all its ramifications. a   b   c   d   e

The discussion leader will assign you to small groups to discuss your responses. This will be followed by a group-at-large discussion.

APPENDIX 60

CHILDREN AT WORK CASE

Worksheet

Now that you have listed the risks and benefits, how would you appraise management's decision? Is it a "good" one? Is it likely to work?

Would you have handled the problem differently? If so, how and why?

APPENDIX 61

<u>THE COUNTY-WIDE ILLNESS</u>

You are the County Health Officer. Several adults and children have requested treatment at various hospitals in the County for an illness marked by these <u>initial</u> symptoms: listlessness, slight fever and influenza-type aches and pains. Typically, by the <u>third or fourth day</u> an eruption appears on the wrists and ankles.

Provide the answers to the following questions:

1. What is the name of this illness?

2. How is this desease acquired?

3. How soon after contact with the source do symptoms occur?

4. What are the preventive measures people should take to avoid becoming victims to the disease?

    a.

    b.

    c.

    d.

5. What is the appropriate treatment for the disease?

6. As County Health Officer, what should you do to help others from succumbing to this disease?

After you have finished answering the above questions, team up with the person next to you to discuss your answers.

APPENDIX 61 CONTINUED

<u>ANSWER SHEET</u>

1. Rocky Mountain Spotted Fever

2. It is transmitted through the bite of ticks. More specifically, Spotted Fever is caused by an organism called <u>rickettsia</u>. Ticks become infected by biting dogs or wild animals which carry this disease agent. If a tick then bites a human (or an animal) it can transmit the disease to it. The tick bite is painless and thus can escape detection by the victim.

3. Within 3 - 10 days.

4. a) Learn to recognize ticks

   b) Know how to remove them. (If attached to the skin, remove very slowly with tweezers. Then touch the bitten area with disinfectant or iodine.)

   c) Inspect children and pets daily for bites.

   d) Avoid tick-infested locations. (They usually inhabit woody and bushy areas.)

5. The disease usually responds to antibiotics, if administered early. Vaccine is recommended only for those who must frequent infected areas and are subject constant exposure to ticks. The vaccine must be repeated annually to be effective.

6. Issue a warning to all rural and suburban residents, vacationers, picnickers, campers, sportsmen, etc. to be on guard against tick bites. Cite the nature of the initial symptoms so that the victims will report for treatment promptly.

APPENDIX   62

INCREASED PRODUCTIVITY--HOW CAN IT BE DONE?

Organizations (and supervisors) are very much concerned about augmenting productivity. In the space below, list as many methods and techniques as you can to accomplish this. Remember, the only limits are those that you impose upon yourself. So, let your imagination soar!

1.	21.
2.	22.
3.	23.
4.	24.
5.	25.
6.	26.
7.	27.
8.	28.
9.	29.
10.	30.
11.	31.
12.	32.
13.	33.
14.	34.
15.	35.
16.	36.
17.	37.
18.	38.
19.	39.
20.	40.

APPENDIX   63

QUESTION REQUEST FORM

For the session on _____ to be

held on _____

1. I have the following question:

2. My interest in this question is due to (or based upon):

APPENDIX 64

OPINIONNAIRE--HOW I FEEL ABOUT THIS COURSE

This form is designed to learn about your feelings toward various aspects of the course you have just completed. Check the appropriate picture to indicate the degree of satisfaction you wish to express for each item. Your feedback will help us to develop a more effective course for future participants. Added written comments may be given on the reverse side of the page.

1. Length of course
   Comment:

2. Content (subject matter)
   Comment:

3. Pre-work
   Comment:

4. Talks/lecturette
   Comment:

5. Films and discussion
   Comment:

6. Small group work
   Comment:

7. Exercises/games
   Comment:

APPENDIX 64 CONTINUED

8. Handouts
   Comment:

9. Evening sessions
   Comment:

10. Outside resource people
    Comment:

11. Training staff
    Comment:

12. Organization of course
    Comment:

13. Physical facilities
    Comment:

14. Overall benefit from course
    Comment:

15. How other participants might react to
    this course
    Comment:

16. Additional comments

APPENDIX   65

END-OF-COURSE REACTIONNAIRE

What I learned most in the course is:

What I still need to learn more of is:

What I will have difficulty in applying is:

My overall feelings about the course are:

If I were asked by a close friend how I saw this course, I would say:

APPENDIX   66

COMMUNICATING THE PROGRAM TO OTHERS

You now have been through most (or all) of the program. You should have a pretty good idea of its major components and possible benefits to participants. Assume that you wish to explain the program to your colleagues (or to field personnel or to the key personnel of another plant or office) so that they, too, will be motivated to attend. Jot down several key reasons why their attendance might be beneficial to them. You will have a chance to present your talk containing those ideas to the total group (three minutes).

APPENDIX   67

DAILY SELF-ASSESSMENT OF LEARNING

1. As a result of today's training, I now realize that I have a need for:

   A.

   B.

   C.

2. I see meeting these needs by taking these action steps:

   For Need A I will:

   For Need B I will:

   For Need C I will:

APPENDIX   68

What Might Have Made the
Session More Effective?
(Please Be Specific)

1.

2.

3.

What Concerns Do You
Have About the Session?
(Please Be Specific)

1.

2.

3.

What Did You Like
About Today's Session?
(Please Be Specific)

1.

2.

3.

APPENDIX 69

DAILY END-OF-SESSION QUESTIONNAIRE

1. Please rate today's activities on the scales below. The data will be summarized and reported back to you at tomorrow's meeting.

Activity

1. Talk on _____

```
 1     2     3     4     5     6     7     8     9    10
LO                                                    HI
```

2. Small group work on_____

```
 1     2     3     4     5     6     7     8     9    10
LO                                                    HI
```

3. Exercise on_____

```
 1     2     3     4     5     6     7     8     9    10
LO                                                    HI
```

4. Film on_____

```
 1     2     3     4     5     6     7     8     9    10
LO                                                    HI
```

5. Role play on_____

```
 1     2     3     4     5     6     7     8     9    10
LO                                                    HI
```

6. Simulation on_____

```
 1     2     3     4     5     6     7     8     9    10
LO                                                    HI
```

2. My overall reaction to the day's training is:

3. The training could be made more effective by:

APPENDIX   70

SUPERVISOR–SUBORDINATE PERCEPTIONS

A. List the areas or ways in which your subordinates could improve or strengthen their communication with you:

1.

2.

3.

4.

B. List the ways your subordinates might feel you could improve your communication with them:

1.

2.

3.

4.

C. What actions can you take to overcome the communication deficits you listed in A above:

1.

2.

3.

4.

D. What actions can you take to overcome the communication deficits you listed in B above:

1.

2.

3.

4.

(Note to trainer: Similar lists could be developed on other subjects: e.g., delegation practices--what I delegate well vs. what subordinates might expect of me in the way of delegation; motivation--what turns me on vs. what motivates my subordinates; performance appraisal--the problems I see in it vs. the problems my employees may see.)

APPENDIX   71

PROBLEM SOLVING AND DECISION MAKING

Step 1.   Problem definition:

Step 2.   Main facts bearing on problem:

Step 3.   Possible solutions (options) to problem resolution:

      a.

      b.

      c.

      d.

Step 4.   Evaluation of alternatives:

      Solution a
      Pros:

      Cons:

      (Continue this process--pros and cons--for each possible solution.)

Step 5.   Selection of solution (also explain why this one was chosen):

Step 6.   Implementation (planning for action)

      Who is to be notified of the decision?

      What are the action steps for implementation?

      1.
      2.
      3.
      4.

      Who is to assume responsibility for

      Action Step 1
      Action Step 2
      Action Step 3
      Action Step 4

Step 7.   How will this plan, when completed, be evaluated? How will we know when
the need has been met?)

APPENDIX 72

PROBLEMS AND ACTION PLANS

Form A--Overcoming Communication Problems

Problem	Action Plan

Form B--Overcoming Communication Problems

Problem	Causative Factors	Action Plan

APPENDIX 72 CONTINUED

Form C—Overcoming Communication Problems

Problem	Causative Factors	Action Plan	Forces Favorable to Action Plan	Possible Resistance Points

APPENDIX 73

PERFORMANCE IMPROVEMENT ANALYSIS

Name of Employee_____

Part A

Analysis of Current Performance

Employee Exceeds Standards in These Duties	Employee Meets Standards in These Duties	Employee Is Below Standards in These Duties
1.	1.	1.
2.	2.	2.
3.	3.	3.
4.	4.	4.

Part B

Employee Performs These Duties Below Standard	Agreed–Upon Plan to Help Employee Meet Standard
1.	1.
2.	2.
3.	3.
4.	4.

APPENDIX   74

TIME WASTERS

Part I

Time Wasters I Encounter in My Work	Frequency (Infrequently, I; Often, O; Regularly, R)	Severity (Lo, Medium, or Hi)	Degree Controllable (None-N; Somewhat-S; Considerable-C; Total-T)

Part II

List Time Wasters You Rated C or T	Action to Be Taken to Correct Condition

APPENDIX 74 CONTINUED

Part III

Candidly list the things you <u>may</u> do that waste the time of others; then indicate necessary corrective action.

Using the Time of Others

Ways in Which I Waste Time of Others	Procedure to Overcome Such Activities
1.	1.
2.	2.
3.	3.
4.	4.
5.	5.

APPENDIX 75

TIME AND YOUR SUBORDINATES

Bosses often get "trapped" into doing their subordinates' work for them. Check the rating form below to indicate the way you deal with such efforts by staff members. Enter dots in the boxes on the left side if you rarely engage in the practices cited and on the right side if you typically perform them. Then connect the dots for a profile on your skill in securing "completed staff work."

Practice	1 (Rarely)	2	3	4	5 (Typically)
1. When subordinates ask: "What do I do on this?" I reply: "What do you recommend?" rather than tell them what to do.					
2. When memos, reports, letters, etc. prepared for my signature require editing, I return such items for rewriting rather than try to "clean them up" myself.					
3. I encourage submission of final copy rather than rough drafts.					
4. I insist that subordinates meet deadlines on reports, projects, etc. so that I don't get caught up in a crisis situation and have to "pick up the pieces."					
5. I insist that my subordinates present their proposals in complete form so that all I need do is indicate approval or disapproval.					

APPENDIX 76

TIME AND YOUR MEETINGS

Meetings are notorious for their tendency to waste participant's time. Please complete the three columns below. They should help you to deal with problems at meetings.

Meetings I Have Attended in the Last 60 Days (Consider staff meetings, your own, your boss', committee meetings, special meetings, task forces)	Two of the Most Severe Problems I Noted at These Meetings	Action I Can Take to Overcome or Reduce the Frequency or Severity of the Problems
1.	a. b.	
2.	a. b.	
3.	a. b.	
4.	a. b.	
5.	a. b.	
6.	a. b.	
7.	a. b.	

APPENDIX 77

TIME AND YOUR BOSS

If I were to ask my boss: "What do I now do that uses your time unnecessarily?" he/she would probably reply:

1.

2.

3.

4.

5.

If I were to ask my boss: "What extra things might I do to conserve your time?" he/she would say:

1.

2.

3.

4.

5.

Note to participants: Consider discussing this guidesheet with your boss after you return to the job.

APPENDIX 78

TIME AND YOUR SECRETARY

A versatile and competent secretary is a key to the effective use of managerial time. List below the ways in which he/she can help you to save time. (Some examples: fielding of phone calls; following up on work assignments to staff; arranging meetings.)

Note: Secretarial dissatisfaction and turnover often are related to the fact that their bosses do not give them adequate responsibility.

1.   11.

2.   12.

3.   13.

4.   14.

5.   15.

6.   16.

7.   17.

8.   18.

9.   19.

10.   20.

APPENDIX   79

DELEGATION PLANNING GUIDE

Major Responsibilities	Not Delegable at All (State why)	Delegable Now (Check)	Delegable with Added Training of Staff (Check)
1.			
2.			
3.			
4.			
5.			
6.			
7.			

Minor Responsibilities			
1.			
2.			
3.			
4.			
5.			
6.			
7.			

APPENDIX   80

HAZARD IDENTIFICATION AND CONTROL

Now that you have completed the course on safety, here is a practical assignment to help you apply what you have learned.

I. Individual work

Analyze two jobs in your unit as to (1) hazards that may exist in them and (2) appropriate safety procedures essential to controlling these hazards. (30 minutes)

Hazard Potential and Control

Job A	Principal Tasks	Possible Hazards	Accident Control Measures
1.			
2.			
3.			
4.			
Job B	Principal Tasks	Possible Hazards	Accident Control Measures
1.			
2.			
3.			
4.			
5.			

II. Small group work

In teams of three, review and discuss each job analysis, offering suggestions to one another to strengthen the proposed accident control procedures. Each presenter will have 20 minutes to present his/her plan and to receive feedback and help on it from the other two team members.

III. Group-at-large-discussion

After your trio has completed its work, your trainer will hold a general discussion about it: What was learned? How helpful were the helpers? Is it easy to help others on their plans?

APPENDIX   81

COMMITMENT TO MYSELF

End of Session Plan for Action

Based on the learnings from the session (or training day) just completed,
I intend to do more of:

I intend to do less of:

I intend to continue doing:

APPENDIX 82

POST SESSION ACTION PLAN

Key Points of Session	Key Points Applicable to My Development Needs (Check)	Action I Intend to Take
1.	1.	1.
2.	2.	2.
3.	3.	3.
4.	4.	4.
5.	5.	5.
6.	6.	6.
7.	7.	7.

APPENDIX   83

ACTION PLAN

My Needs for Improvement	My Plans for Improvement	Quarterly Follow-Up (Add comments)	
		First Quarter	Second Quarter
1.			
2.			
3.			

APPENDIX 84

CONTRACT WITH MYSELF

My major area (opportunity or need) for growth is:

My action plan related to the above is:

APPENDIX 85

APPLICATION SESSION

RELATING COURSE LEARNINGS TO ON-THE-JOB PROBLEMS

I. Purpose

The final phase of this program is designed to give you an opportunity to apply the concepts and skills that you have learned to an actual on-the-job problem of your choice. This should provide real and lasting meaning to your training experience. It will also provide you with a maximum return from your investment of time and effort in the classroom.

II. Procedure

A. Select a topic about which you have genuine concern; that is, a problem area that requires some worthwhile improvement or remedial action. The problem may relate to a management concern, an operational matter, an administrative change, a plan for self-improvement, an improvement in relations with others (boss, subordinates, peers), etc. It may involve overcoming a deficiency or meeting a new challenge or opportunity. You alone know where a real need for change or betterment exists.

B. Individual work (60 minutes): Use the three-part Application Worksheet to help you work through the details of your problem-solving activity.

C. Small group work (60 minutes): You will be assigned to a team of three (two other participants and yourself). Each of you will have the opportunity to present your problem and plan for action to the other two members for review, critique, feedback, and counsel. Each presenter will have 20 minutes to secure help from the other two participants. Remember that although this is your problem, objective "outsiders" can be of real help, because they may see things that you, because of your immediate involvement, may have overlooked. As a minimum, they will help sharpen the issues for you and make you think through more fully the realism of your action plan.

APPENDIX 85 CONTINUED

Application Worksheet

I. Defining my problem

1. I have carefully reviewed my "back-home" situation, and the problem area I would like to see improved relates to:

2. I am concerned about the above stated problem because:

3. The major facts that relate to my problem are these:

II. Seeking a solution

1. The elements of my problem most amenable to change are:

2. The elements of my problem least amenable to change are:

3. I would use these indicators to consider the problem satisfactorily resolved:

APPENDIX 85 CONTINUED

4. The forces that I see as unfavorable to (blocking) the hoped-for change are:

5. The forces I see as favoring (supporting) the change are:

6. The solution I see to my problem is:

III. An action plan to implement my solution

    1. I see the time frame for the plan to be operative as follows:

    2. I will need the assistance of these individuals to implement the plan:

        Name_____   Task_____

        Name_____   Task_____

        Name_____   Task_____

        Name_____   Task_____

    3. I will need to communicate the plan to:

        Name_____   About_____

        Name_____   About_____

        Name_____   About_____

        Name_____   About_____

    4. I intend to follow up and evaluate the success of the plan by doing the following:

APPENDIX   86

TIME SAVINGS

As a result of my participation in the training program, I estimate my weekly time savings to be _____ hours per week.

This time savings has come principally from:

The time I have saved has enabled me to:

APPENDIX   87

TIME-THIEF ANALYSIS

Based on all the work I have done on time management, both in and out of class, I would say my most serious time robber right now is:

Time-wise, I would say this "time theft" adds up to _____ hours_____ minutes per week.

Two possible ways to cut down on that time loss are:

1.

2.

APPENDIX   88

MY COMMUNICATION SKILL

A Self Appraisal

Use the following rating scale to rate your communication attitudes/behaviors at various time intervals in relation to this training program: 1-rarely; 2-occasionally; 3-somewhat frequently; 4-frequently; 5-regularly or usually.

Element	Prior to Training Session	At End of Training Session	60-Day Follow-Up	120-Day Follow-Up
1. I understand that my frame of reference is not necessarily that of the receiver of my message.				
2. I recognize that the receiver may interpret a message differently because of his/her attitudes, values, experience, needs, etc.				
3. I recognize that the meaning of a message is in the receiver, not in the message.				
4. To ensure that my message is fully understood, I ask the receiver to restate it (elicit feedback).				
5. I restate things to the other person so he/she knows that I understood what was said to me ("You are saying that...").				
6. I accept responsibility for a message of mine that is misinterpreted by the receiver.				
7. When listening to someone else I try to "tune in" for feelings as well as facts.				
8. I try to avoid the use of "emotional" words, those that may irritate or inflame the other person.				

APPENDIX 88 CONTINUED

Element	Prior to Training Session	At End of Training Session	60-Day Follow-Up	120-Day Follow-Up
9. I recognize when others are communicating a fact, an assumption, or a value judgment.				
10. I recognize when I am communicating a fact, an assumption, or a value judgment.				
11. I try to state things in a "tentative" way so that others are drawn into the communication effort.				
12. I pay attention to the body language of those communicating to me.				
13. I am aware of the congruency between my nonverbal behavior and my verbal communication.				
14. I use full eye contact when communicating with others.				
15. I maintain warm, friendly relations with others to aid communication with them.				
16. I use praise freely so as to get closer to people, thereby aiding communication with them.				
17. I try to level with others so as to ensure authentic communication.				
18. My employees are willing to speak freely to me, to question my decisions, to give me the "bad news," to debate an issue fully, etc.				
19. I recognize that my status as a supervisor/manager may inhibit communication with me				

APPENDIX   89

SURVEY OF NEEDS FOR PROPOSED COMMUNICATIONS,
COACHING, COUNSELING COURSE

For each topic below, please circle the number that best expresses your need for it. (Number 1 is low and 5 is high.)

Improving communication with subordinates	1	2	3	4	5
Improving communication with peers	1	2	3	4	5
Improving communication with the boss	1	2	3	4	5
Conducting the appraisal interview	1	2	3	4	5
Counseling with a problem employee	1	2	3	4	5
Counseling for career development and planning	1	2	3	4	5
Improving assertiveness skills	1	2	3	4	5
Coaching for improved performance	1	2	3	4	5
Improving listening skills	1	2	3	4	5
Dealing with my anger	1	2	3	4	5
Improving effectiveness of group meetings	1	2	3	4	5

Note to trainer: The items in the above list merely could have been checked off by participants. However, this procedure would not provide us with data on strength or depth of need.

APPENDIX   90

SURVEY OF NEEDS

Please list below the topics you wish to have covered in the course. Your number one listing is the most important to you. Your number ten is the least important to you.

1.

2.

3.

4.

5.

6.

7.

8.

9.

10.

APPENDIX 91

SELF-DEVELOPMENT--A CHECK LIST FOR TRAINERS

Course or program	For my background or orientation (to keep up with my field)	For my personal growth (self-development)	To develop needed expertise to introduce the program into my organization
Assertiveness training			
Assessment center			
Behavior modeling			
Behavior objectives			
Behavior modification			
Career planning			
Change (introducing it, managing it)			
Communication			
Coaching			
Competency-based education			
Conflict management (intergroup relations)			
Counseling			
Creativity			
Cross-cultural training			
Experiential learning			
Equal Employment Opportunity			
Group dynamics			
Guided Imagery			
Internal consultant			
Interpersonal skills			

APPENDIX 91 CONTINUED

	For my background or orientation (to keep up with my field)	For my personal growth (self-development)	To develop needed expertise to introduce the program into my organization
Life planning			
Management by objectives			
Managerial grid			
Matrix management			
Models for management			
Negotiation skills			
Neuro-linguistic programming			
Nonverbal communication			
Organization development			
Problem solving			
Quality circles			
Quality of work life			
Stress management			
Systems theory			
T-group (sensitivity training)			
Team building			
Time management			
Transactional analysis (TA)			
Values clarification			
Women in managment			
Other_____			
Other_____			

APPENDIX 92

UTILIZING INSTRUMENT LEARNINGS FOR CHANGE -- MY ACTION PLAN

Now that you have completed your discussion of the data you produced on the instrument (self-quiz), you will wish to capitalize on your learnings from it. You can do this by completing carefully the Action Plan below.

1. My principal learnings from the instrument are:

   a.

   b.

   c.

2. In light of the above, I plan to do the following <u>more often</u>:

   a.

   b.

   c.

3. In light of the above (item 1), I intend to do the following <u>less often</u>:

   a.

   b.

   c.

4. I see these possible roadblocks to accomplishing these changes:

   a.

   b.

   c.

5. I can overcome these barriers to change by doing the following:

   a.

   b.

   c.

INDEX

A

ABC approach, 155, 347, 358
Accelerated learning, 47, 57
Accountability chart, 202
Action learning, 132, 358
Action maze, 276, 358
Action plans (learning contracts), 9, 60, 108, 141, 261, 304, 314–315, 320, 323–326, 328, 330, 358
Alumni reunion, 328
American Society for Training and Development (A.S.T.D.), 338, 347, 358
Analogy, 159, 162, 176–179, 195, 358
Application. *See* Transfer of learning.
Application session, 321–323, 358
Art, using, 4–5, 51–56, 64, 303–304, 313
Association for Humanistic Psychology, 347
Atmosphere. *See* Climate.
Attribute listing, 174–175, 358

B

Behavior modeling, 86–89, 358
Behavior modification, 175, 325–326, 358
Behind the back technique, 84, 358
Blind (trust) walk, 4, 241–242, 345, 365
Brainstorming, 95, 108, 154, 158, 162, 165–168, 176, 182, 185, 194, 205, 261, 293, 358–359
Burnout, model, 63
Buzz group. *See* Small group work.
Buzz words, 152–153, 359

C

Card posting, 172–173, 185–186, 359
Case method, 271–296, 359
  action maze, 276, 358
  advantages, 271–272, 338, 339
  allied case, 281–282
  audio tape, case on, 280
  benefits-risk approach, 289
  brainstorming, using, 293
  decision analysis, 288–289
  developing cases, 289–290

dialog, 286–287
disadvantages, 272
editorial case, 296
evaluation of participants, 295
executive development programs, in, 272. *See also* Live case.
filmed case, 280
fishbowl, using, 295
focused analysis, 292–293
Harvard case, 273
in-house cases, using, 291
incident process, 274–276
judicial cases, using, 289
letter as a case, 284–286
live case, 280–281
memo from the boss, 283
monologue, 287–288
mousetrap technique, 276–277
multiple case technique, 279–280
outside cases, learning from, 290–291
participant modified case, 282
participant cases, using, 282
personal case, 281
ranking approach, 283
rating approach, 282–283
role playing, using, 293
self-review case, 289
short case, 273
small groups, using, 291–292
worksheet, using, 293–295
wrong-way—right-way, 278
Check lists, 155, 174, 187, 290, 322, 359
Check sheet, 155, 359
Circular whip, 36, 112, 312–313, 331, 359
Client-centered approach, 173, 359
Climate, 10, 340, 342–343, 359
Conference, 353, 359
Continuum, 142–143, 206–207, 245, 317, 359
Contracting. *See* Action plans.
Cotraining, 347–350, 359
Crises, dealing with, 345–346
Cultural island setting, 343, 359

D

Debates, group, 34–36, 359
Definitions, producing, 29–30, 262, 303

Debriefing, 359. *See also*
    Reporting.
Delphi technique, 170–172, 359
Design matrix, 335–336
Diary. *See* Journaling.
Dramatic skit, 69–70, 359
Dyad, 14, 26–28, 114, 161,
    260–261, 328, 346, 359

E

Empty chair technique, 83, 359
Evaluation, 112, 311–319, 359
    case study, in, 295
    daily pulse taking, 316–318
    group self-appraisal, 318
    levels of, 311
    role playing, of, 84–85
    supervisory involvement in, 315
Exercises, 107–120
    books containing, 116–120
    characteristics, 107
    examples, 108–115, 200,
        246–247
    formats, 107
    planning the, 115
    sources, 108
Experiential learning, 132–136
    design principles, 134–135
    forms, 133–134
    objectives, 133, 359
    processing, 135–136
    traditional learning and,
        132–133

F

Fantasy, 42–45, 109, 152–153,
    201, 330, 360
Facilitator, 2, 199–200, 360
Facing chairs, 35, 360
Feedback, 108, 206–207, 303, 360
Field trip, 37, 314, 360
Film, 258–270
    advantages, 258–259
    case study and, 280
    dynamic use of, 109, 338–339
    introducing a film, 260
    multiple film use, 267
    negative reactions, dealing with,
        267–269
    prediction, 263–265

pre-film activities, 261–263, 266
previewing, 259–260
post-film activities, 260–263
question sheets, 265–267
ranking of value, 338–339
stop-film technique, 263–264
summary sheets, 267
video vs. film, 258
viewing worksheets, 265
vignettes, using, 264
First aid training, 27, 252–253
Fishbowls, 14, 26, 39–42, 64,
    261, 295, 313, 330, 337, 360
    configurations, 39–41
    limitations, 41–42
    openers, as, 8
    uses, 41–42
Five-M analysis, 158, 360
Flipcharting, 194, 248–250, 301,
    343, 344, 360
Focused analysis, 292–293, 360
Follow-up sessions, 320, 329–331,
    336, 360
Forced-choice instrument, 146,
    360
Force field analysis, 111,
    156–157, 205, 360
Forced relationships, technique,
    175, 360

G

Games, 9, 94–103, 338, 339, 360
    administration, 97
    advantages, 96–97
    conversion to exercise, 103
    definition, 94, 360
    design of, 97–98
    when to use, 97
Geometrics, 5, 8, 53, 55, 313, 360
Goal setting by participants, 7, 109
Goodbye, saying, 37–38
Gordon technique, 179, 360
Group fantasy, 42, 360
Guided fantasy, 42, 360
Group role playing, 76, 360
Guided imagery, 45–47, 55–56,
    246, 360
Guide sheets. *See* Worksheets.

H

Handouts, 253, 254, 303, 360
Hierarchy of needs, 61–62, 110

Humor and fun, 250–252, 312,
    454–455

I

Icebreakers, 1–6
    benefits, 3
    definition, 1, 361
    evaluation of, 6
    examples
        art mart, 4
        ball toss, 244
        cardswap, 4
        distraction banishment, 6
        dyad, 26
        early grades, 5
        envelope enigma, 241
        group creation, 6
        group hum, 5
        hobby hunt, 5
        hum fun, 242
        I am, 242,
        instant interaction, 243
        instrument as, 145
        interviews for introductions, 3
        know your sign, 4
        me: yesterday, today and
            tomorrow, 5
        name cards, 6
        nicknames, 5
        past, present and future, 5
        my personal shield, 3, 54
        preferences, 5
        puzzle fun, 5
        shoe in, 5
        strength billboard, 92
        trust (blind) walk, 4, 241–242
        values assessment—consensus,
            4
        values billboard, 4, 241
        wallet waggery, 6
Icebreakers and openers, 1–3
    classifications and cautions, 11
    definitions/differences, 1
    planning their use, 2
    purposes, 2
Idea reinforcement teams,
    191–192, 361
Ideation, 166, 361
Ideawriting, 172, 361
Ideographs, 54, 361
Imaging, 162, 361
In-basket exercise, 211–233, 271,
    361

Incident process, 274–276, 361
Incidents, personal. *See* Personal incidents.
Influence vs. authority, 33, 63
Informal role playing, 68, 69, 361
Inner advisor, 46, 66, 361
Institute, 353, 361
Instrumentation (quizzes), 139–150
  advantages, 139
  case study, in, 282
  definition, 139, 361
  design of, 147–148
  disadvantages, 140
  evaluation of major types, 148–149
  follow-up training, in, 331
  formats, 140
  how to use, 141, 206–207
  participant prepared, 108, 114, 147
  profile, 143, 363
  scoring, 147
  sources of, 140–141
  team building, in, 206–207
  types, 142–146
  when to use, 8, 140–141, 206

J

Journaling, 59–61, 64, 66, 328, 361
Journalist's six questions, 162–163, 173, 187, 301–302, 361
Jury technique, 191, 361
Jury trial, 36, 361

K–L

Knowledge circles, 190–191
Laboratory training. *See* T-group.
Large groups, 13–14
Leadership in small groups, 20, 25
Leadership style, 62–63, 112, 301
Learning contracts. *See* Action Plans.
Learning sequence, design of, 340–342, 361
Lecture method, 291, 297–310
  advantages, 298–299
  definition, 361
  lecturette. *See* Lecturette.
  polish, adding, 299

  participation in the, 299–304
  problems with the, 297–298
  question and answer period, 304–308
  seating and, 236, 239
  when to use, 298–299
Lecturette, 14, 203, 304, 361
  by participants, 304
Left-brain thinking. *See* Right-brain thinking.
Line managers as trainers, 350–352
List development, 30–32, 108, 174–175, 200, 262, 302
Listening teams, 15–16, 302, 361
Live case, 280–281

M

Management by Objectives (MBO), 34, 334, 347
Managerial Grid, 94, 352, 353
Meditation, 244, 303, 361
Mental imagery, 42, 47–48, 109, 361
Metaphors, 159–162, 195, 205, 362
Methods, selecting, 338–339
Mock trial. *See* Jury trial.
Models, working with, 61–64, 109, 362
Monitoring in small group work, 18–19, 25
Monologue, 287–288, 362
Morphological analysis, 175, 362
Movement, 241–248, 313, 317, 343, 362
Mousetrap technique, 276–277, 362
Multiple case technique, 279–280, 362
Multiple choice instrument, 146, 362
Multiple group role playing, 76, 91, 362
Multiple role playing, 72–74, 245, 362
Multiple role taking, 84, 362
Music, using, 57–59

N

National Society for Performance and Instruction (NSPI), 347

Need determination, 336–338, 362
Networking, 27, 247, 325, 329, 362
Nominal group technique, 170, 362
Nonverbal behavior, 113, 265

O

Observers
  definition, 362
  in fishbowls, 39–40
  in role playing, 74–75
  in small group work, 17–18, 26
Organization development (OD), 46, 362
Openers 6–11, 112
  definition, 1, 362
  benefits, 6
  examples of
    aerial animation, 10–11
    anxiety reducer, 300
    armfold, 243
    audience answers, 299
    check your I.Q., 152
    climate setting, 10
    commitment continuum, 7
    definitions, producing, 29–30
    dyadic analysis, 9
    exercise excitement, 300
    fears and fantasies (hopes and fears), 200, 201
    fishbowls, 8
    flipchart fill-up, 301
    garnering goodies, 9
    geometrics, 5, 10, 53, 313, 360
    goal analysis, 7
    hopes and change, 7
    incident for involvement, 300
    individual goals, 8, 113
    inspiring the uninspired, 8
    instrument as opener, 145
    interest inventory, 300
    introducing the program, 9–10
    learning contracts, 9
    list development, 30–32
    power play, 244
    pre-work, 8
    reading, 299
    case or problem analysis, 300
    present vs. preferred states, 301
    problem census, 9, 300, 363

problem description, 53
problem probe, 300
problem swap, 300
quiz, 9
quiz the expert, 301
signups, 243
structured note taking,
    300–301
team building, in, 200
think sheets, 9
thought stimulator, 301
Tinker Toys, 8
two step, the, 301
value clarification in
    leadership, 243
ventilating feelings, 8

P

Pair. *See* Dyad.
Panel presentation, 306, 353, 362
Pareto's analysis, 153–154, 362
Past/present/future approach,
    186–187
Performance aids, 328
Personal needs analysis, 193
Personal growth enactment, 70,
    262, 323, 362
Personal incidents, 33–34, 108,
    263, 281, 300, 303
Phillips 66 method, 192–193, 362
Pictures, photos, working with,
    49–51, 64, 303
Point-of-view teams, 263, 362
Prediction
    definition, 363
    film work, in, 263–265
    small group work, in, 34
Pre-work, 8, 234–236, 263, 299,
    300, 336, 340, 363
Problem census, 9, 300, 363
Problem participants, 20–25
Problem solving, 151–196
    alternatives, choosing among,
        182–185
    defining the problem, 152–156
    generating data, 153–156
    generating solutions, 165–180
    openers for training, 152
    planning and implementing the
        solution, 185–195
    predicting success, 184–185
    principles of, 193–195

ranking procedures, 183–184
techniques for
    ABC approach, 155–156,
        347–349, 358
    analogy, 159, 162, 176–179,
        195, 358
    attribute listing, 174–175, 358
    brainstorming. *See*
        Brainstorming.
    card posting, 172–173, 185,
        359
    checklists, 155, 174, 187, 322,
        359
    checksheet, 155, 359
    client-centered approach, 173,
        359
    Delphi technique, 170–172, 359
    force field analysis, 111,
        156–157, 205, 360
    forced relationship technique,
        175
    Gordon technique, 179, 360
    idea reinforcement teams,
        191–192, 361
    idea writing, 172, 361
    imaging, 162
    journalist's six questions,
        162–163, 173, 187,
        301–302, 361
    jury technique, 191, 361
    metaphors, 159–162, 195,
        205, 362
    morphological analysis, 175,
        362
    nominal group technique, 170,
        362
    Pareto's analysis, 153–154, 362
    past/present/future approach,
        186–187
    personal needs analysis, 193
    Phillips 66 method, 192–193,
        362
    predicting success, 184–185
    problem census, 9, 300, 363
    problem description, 53
    problem swap, 300
    present vs. preferred states, 301
    purposeful creative thinking
        (PCT), 179
    quality circles, 188–189, 363
    quality control, 187–188
    rotational problem solving,
        163, 186

scatter diagram, 154, 363
slip method, 158, 169–170,
    363
small group psychological
    reinforcement, 192, 364
statistical procedures, 154–155
structured analysis, 109,
    158–159, 364
training approaches, 152
upside down approach, 173,
    365
value analysis (value
    engineering), 157–158, 365
Processing. *See* Reporting.
Profile, 143, 363
Program design, 334–336
Projective technique, 50–51, 363
Props for empathy, 252–253, 363
Purposeful Creative Thinking
    (PCT), 179
Puzzles, 121–132
examples, 5, 121–132
purposes, 121, 152, 302, 363

Q

Quality circles, 188–189, 363
Quality control, 187–188
Questions and answers, 19,
    304–308
Question sheets, 265–267, 363
Quizzes. *See* Instumentation.

R

Ranking procedures, 183–184, 330
Rating scale, 142–144, 337, 363
Recorder, 17, 25, 363
Reference material, using, 37
Responsibility/accountability chart,
    201–202, 363
Right-brain thinking, 57, 130–131,
    245–246
Risk analysis, 16–17, 109, 289,
    363. *See* Worst-case scenario.
Reinforcement, 363
Role negotiation, 27, 204, 363
Role playing, 67–93
    anxiety reduction, 70–71
    behavior modeling, 86–89,
        91–93, 358
    case study and, 293

definition, 67, 363
demonstration type, 69–70
dramatic skit, 69–70, 359
evaluation of, 84–85
evaluation of *training* via, 314
group, 76, 360
informal, 68–69, 361
lecture and, 302
multiple, 72–74, 247, 362
multiple group, 76, 91, 362
personal growth enactment, 70, 261, 262, 323, 362
spontaneous, 69
total group, 76
observers, using, 74–76
purposes, 67–68
questions and answers re, 85–86
ranking of value, 338–339
special techniques
  behind the back, 84
  double, the, 83
  empty chair technique, 83, 359
  mirror technique, 83–84
  multiple role taking, 84, 362
  role reversal, 83, 363
  soliloquy, 83, 364
spontaneous, 68, 364
spread sheet, 78, 364
structure, using, 74, 364
T-column in, 78
total group, 76–77, 364
video, using, 78–79
writing your own role play, 77
Rolestorming, 167

S

Scatter diagram, 154, 363
SEA formula, 190
Seating, 14, 24, 236–241, 247–248, 343
Seminar, 353, 363
Sensitivity training. *See* T-group.
Sentence-completion type instrument, 144–146, 301, 312, 363
7-S analysis, 158, 363
Silence, use of, 253, 255
Simulation, 95, 103–104, 364
  administration, 104
  advantages/disadvantages, 103–104

design of, 104
  examples, 103
Simulation-game, 94, 95, 364
Slip method, 158, 169–170, 363
Small group psychological reinforcement, 192, 364
Small group work, 13–66
  advanced techniques, 39–66
  advantages, 13–14, 344
  basic techniques, 26–38
  assigning tasks, 14–15, 24
  buzz group, 13–14, 158, 261, 271, 359
  case study and, 291–292
  composition, 14, 24–25
  dyads. *See* Dyads.
  guide sheets. *See* Worksheets.
  leadership and, 20, 25
  monitoring, 18–19, 25
  observers. *See* Observers.
  problem participants
    coping procedures, 25
    types, 20–24
  program design and, 335
  recorder, 17, 19, 25
  seating. *See* Seating.
  spokesperson, 17, 19, 25
  techniques for. *See specific techniques listed in index.*
  thought questions, 15
  triads. *See* Triads.
  using small groups effectively, 13–25
Smoking, handling of, 240–241, 248
Sociogram, 18, 295, 364
Soliloquy, 83, 364
Song, 58–59
Spaced learning, 327, 364
Spokesperson, 17, 19, 364
Spontaneous role playing, 69, 364
Standups, 242–245
Stop-film technique, 263–264, 364
Stress management training, 28, 32, 45, 63
Structured analysis, 109, 158–159, 364
Structured role playing, 74–75, 364
Study groups, 189–190
Support system, 29, 53
Symbolic analogy, 176–177, 364

Symposium, 353, 364
Synectics, 173, 364

T

T-column
  definition, 16, 364
  examples, 7, 9, 16, 30, 31, 78, 110, 156, 158, 185, 200, 289
  purposes, 16
Team building, 197–210
  conditions for success, 197–198
  definition, 197, 364
  evaluation of, 207
  feedback, giving, 207–208
  first day, 201–202
  first session, starting the, 199–201
  instrumentation in, 204, 206–207
  preliminary work, 198–199
  second day, 202–203
  tools for, 203–206
  vertical training and, 352
Team instruction/teaching. *See* Cotraining.
T-group, 27, 51, 94, 193, 198, 238, 255, 338–339, 346–347, 352, 364
Terminology for training activities, 352–354
Theory X and Y, 112, 203
Think sheet, 9, 364
Thought questions, 15
Toastmaster's club, 279, 299, 329, 346
Total group role playing, 76–77, 364
Trainer
  definition, 364. *See also* Facilitator.
  development, 346–347
  line manager as, 350–352
  style of, 2, 345
Transactional analysis, 63–64
Transfer of learning, 60, 320–333
Triads, 14, 28–29, 72–74, 141, 149, 261, 321–322, 364
Tri-column, 109, 111, 301, 319
Trios. *See* Triad.
Trust (blind) walk, 4, 241–242, 345, 365

U–Z

Upside-down approach to problem solving, 173, 365
Value analysis (value engineering), 157–158, 365
Vertical training, 352, 365
Video. *See* Film.

Viewing-listening teams, 15–16, 262–263, 365
Vignettes, using film, 264, 365
Visualization, 42–48, 365

Worksheets, 18, 73, 293–295, 320, 320, 336. *See the Appendix for various examples*.

Workshop, 353, 365
Wrong-way—right-way, 278–279, 365
Worst case scenario, 43, 366. *See also* Risk taking.

Yes-no instrument, 142, 365